Aquariology: The Science of Fish Health Management

AQUARIOLOGY

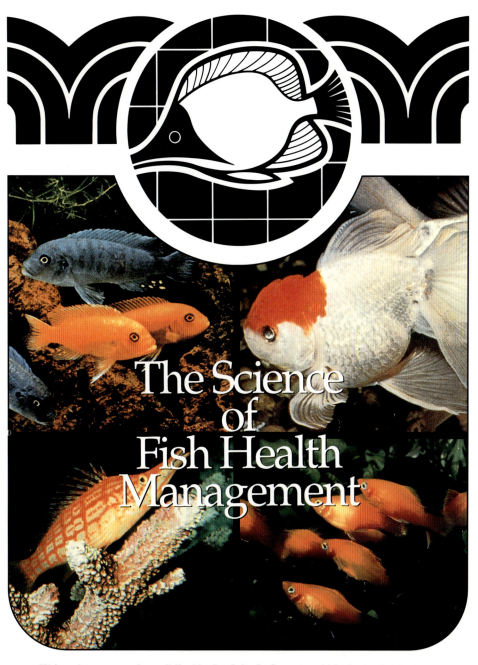

The Science
of
Fish Health
Management

Written by expert authors; Edited by Dr. John B. Gratzek and Ms. Janice R. Matthews.

Tetra Press

Tetra Press
Aquariology: The Science of Fish Health Management
A Tetra Press Publication

Gratzek, Dr. John B.,
Aquariology: the science of fish health management; edited by
Dr. John B. Gratzek with Janice R. Matthews

L.C. Catalog card number 91-067993
ISBN number 1-56465-105-3
Tetra Press item number 16855

1. Gratzek, Dr. John B.   2. Matthews, Janice R.

Tetra would like to gratefully acknowledge the following sources
of photographs and artwork:
For the chapters "Getting Started," "Maintaining Aquaria," and
"Infectious Diseases" © Dr. John B. Gratzek; for "Anatomy"
© Prof. Emer. Howard E. Evans; for "Fish Genetics" © Dr. Joanne
Norton; for "Fish Physiology" © College of Veterinary Medicine,
University of Georgia; for "Nutrition and Feeding" © Dr. Robert A.
Winfree; for "Physiological Mechanisms of Fish Disease" © Dr.
Richard E. Wolke; for "Diseases of Marine Fishes" © Dr. George
C. Blasiola. Additional illustrations were provided by Tetra Ar-
chives, except as otherwise noted.

Printed in Hong Kong.

First edition
10 9 8 7 6 5 4 3 2 1

Production services by Martin Cook Associates, Ltd., New York

Table of Contents

Anatomy, Genetics, and Breeding

Aquarium Fish Physiology and Nutrition

Diseases and Parasites of Aquarium Fish

Foreword

The keeping of ornamental fish is an enjoyable pastime for millions of people throughout the world. The origin of fish-keeping dates back to antiquity. The concept of modern aquarium-keeping had its first origins in Germany and England and quickly spread throughout the world. In Japan, the most popular form of fish-keeping is an outdoor koi (colored carp) pond. For over a century, maintaining a koi pond has been a symbol of good luck for Japanese households. In the United Kingdom, the most common form of fish-keeping is an idyllic garden pond, and in the United States, now the world's most developed market in terms of households maintaining an aquarium, the maintenance of exotic marine fish is proving increasingly popular. In Central Europe, Germany, and Holland, an emphasis on live plants — in some cases dominant over fish — makes an aquarium a truly lovely showpiece in any home.

Why do people maintain ornamental fish? In 1990 Tetra commissioned an independent market study in the United States. This study revealed that over 9 million households have an active aquarium, and surprisingly, 40 percent of these households have more than one aquarium. When asked, "Why do you have an aquarium?" the most common response was "because of the relaxa-tion and entertainment it provides." A close second was "the enjoyment of tropical fish as a hobby." "The decorative value of an aquarium" was third. The final reason for maintaining an aquarium was "the identification of tropical fish as pets." Regardless of reason, keeping an aquarium is truly rewarding and enjoyable.

Tetra Werke is the world's largest company solely devoted to the manufacture of products for ornamental fish and reptiles. Located in Germany, Tetra began as a privately owned business almost forty years ago. In 1974 it was acquired by the Warner-Lambert Company, a Fortune 500 pharmaceutical and consumer products company. This book has been largely underwritten by Tetra to allow everyone to understand the technical aspects of successfully maintaining ornamental fish in a confined environment.

We are particularly indebted to Dr. John Gratzek, Janice Matthews, and their world-renowned coauthors for their endless hours of research and documentation which have made this book possible. We hope you enjoy, appreciate, and benefit from the information in this book. Most important, we sincerely hope you will both understand and practice the procedures necessary for successful ornamental fish-keeping.

Alan R. Mintz
General Manager
Tetra Sales (U.S.A.)

Establishing a Healthy Aquarium

Getting Started with Aquaria

John B. Gratzek

The simplest definition of an aquarium is a container capable of holding water in which fish and other aquatic organisms can live over a long period of time. Aquariology is the study of keeping fish in aquaria. It explores the reasons for keeping fish and requires a knowledge of the biological characteristics of fish, as well as of such aspects of their husbandry as feeding and nutrition, reproduction, water quality management, sources and control of stress, and disease control.

This book is written with the hope that it will provide both basic knowledge for the beginning aquarist and more specific information for advanced aquarists, producers of ornamental fish, and those wishing to keep fish as laboratory research subjects.

Choosing Appropriate Equipment

Selecting the aquarium: Obvious considerations will determine the size of the aquarium. Available space in a particular room, the size and type of fish you wish to keep, and the cost are factors which will influence your decision. In general, larger aquaria for a given number of fish will result in fewer problems than smaller aquaria with the same amount of fish. Pollutants accumulate more slowly in a larger tank, increasing the interval between required water changes. A

larger aquarium also has the advantage of flexibility—providing space for several species of smaller fish or one or two very large fish. Additionally, a larger aquarium will provide the space for planting an interesting variety of living plants.

For the beginning aquarist, it is recommended that the aquarium be no smaller than 10 gallons (38 liters) and preferably larger. A 30-gallon (114-liter) aquarium would be an ideal size for the novice. If lightly stocked, a tank of this size provides sufficient volume of water to dilute out accumulated fish wastes. At the same time, it affords ample room for fish growth and addition of new residents. For breeding purposes, a larger aquarium will provide space for particularly territorial fish as well as escape room for small fish.

Wholesalers in the pet-fish trade prefer to use aquaria between 25 and 30 gallons (95 to 114 liters) in size. To facilitate netting fish, as well as cleaning, tank height is minimized. Retailers usually employ a series of 10- to 15-gallon (38- to 57-liter) aquaria to display freshwater fish; larger aquaria house saltwater fish and the larger freshwater species.

Aquaria are sold in many shapes, from rectangular to hexagonal or cylindrical. If due attention is paid to water quality, fish will do fine in any of them. Very deep aquaria may be difficult to clean; additionally, plants may not do well in very deep aquaria because of poor light penetration to the aquarium bottom.

A sturdy stand must be selected and carefully balanced to prevent the weight from shifting once the aquarium is filled with water.

It is a good idea to clean a new aquarium to remove fingerprints and to make its glass surfaces as clear as possible before filling it with water. A small amount of dishwashing detergent dissolved in lukewarm water is perfectly acceptable for cleaning aquarium glass, provided that the aquarium is *thoroughly* rinsed with warm water afterward to remove all traces of cleanser. Scale which has collected at the water line of used aquaria can be removed with commercially available preparations designed for the removal of lime deposits. Weak acid solutions such as vinegar may also be used to remove lime deposits. Some soaking time is necessary for removal of scale regardless of what preparation is used. An alternative method is to scrape scale away with a razor blade.

Supporting the aquarium: The stated capacity of an aquarium is somewhat more than the actual volume. For instance, a standard 10-gallon (38-liter) aquarium with inside measurements of 19.25 inches (38.9 centimeters) long, 10 inches (25.4 centimeters) deep, and 11 inches (27.9 centimeters) wide will hold about 9.16 gallons (34.7 liters). Addition of gravel, rocks, or inside filters will further reduce the water volume.

One gallon of water weighs 8.34 pounds; consequently the water in a "10-gallon" aquarium—about 9.16 gallons—would weigh about 76 pounds. (The water in a "38-liter" aquarium would weigh about 35 kilograms.) Gravel adds still more weight. If a filled aquarium is either moved or placed on a stand which is not level, the resulting twisting stress on the glass is likely to result in breakage and leaks.

Aquarium stands constructed from metal or wood are available in a wide range of styles. Stands which include a cabinet below the aquarium have the advantage of hiding equipment such as air pumps and canister filters, and can be used for storage. For research purposes where many tanks are used, double-tiered racks constructed of 2-by-4-inch lumber (standard construction studs) bolted together can be easily constructed. A rack need not have a complete solid surface to support the aquaria; placing either end of the aquaria on a 2-by-2 or 2-by-4-inch board is adequate. Racks can be built so that the long axes of the aquaria are side by side. This configuration allows an investigator to utilize space more efficiently.

Providing cover and lighting: Most aquaria are manufactured so that various types of covers or hoods fit them snugly. If a cover is not used, evaporation can be a problem. As water evaporates, the concentration of dissolved minerals and organics (uneaten food, plant detritus, fish wastes, etc.) will tend to rise. A cover will keep the air directly over the water closer to the temperature of the water, minimizing heat loss and maximizing the efficiency of the heater. The cover also prevents fish from jumping out of the aquarium, an otherwise very frequent occurrence.

Most aquarium hoods have spaces provided for the installation of artificial lighting. Either ex-

For research purposes, an arrangement such as this one at the University of Georgia's College of Veterinary Medicine works well.

There are many lighting, filtration, and heating systems available on the market. Fluorescent light fixtures are common and varied.

clusively incandescent or fluorescent illumination can be used. In some specially designed units, a combination of both types is provided. Incandescent fixtures are less expensive than fluorescent ones, but incandescent bulbs will use more electricity and will give off more heat than fluorescent bulbs, which burn "cooler" and will not substantially affect the water temperature. Another distinct advantage of fluorescent lights is that they can be purchased in sizes which cover the entire length of the aquarium and consequently provide an even distribution of light for plant growth.

The aquarist has a wide choice of types of fluorescent bulbs which emit various spectra of light waves, some of which will stimulate plant life, including algae. If living plants are not used in the aquarium, bulbs are available which are more suitable for highlighting the coloration of a tank's fish than for stimulating plant growth. Full-spectrum bulbs for plant growth are available under a variety of trade names. The wattage required for optimal plant growth depends on the size of the aquarium. In general, 1.5 watts per gallon of water is adequate. For example, a 30-gallon (114-liter) aquarium would require a single 40-watt tube or a pair of 20-watt tubes. The performance of fluorescent tubes will degrade over time. Their replacement as often as every six months is recommended by some experts to assure optimal conditions for plant growth.

For research purposes, individual aquarium lighting is not required unless the experimental protocol requires a definite photoperiod. Generally, outside rooms with windows will provide enough natural light to facilitate observing fish. In rooms where natural light is unavailable, establishing a photoperiod of between eight and twelve hours using normal room lighting is advisable.

Buying a heater: A desired water temperature can be easily maintained by using a thermostatically controlled immersible water heater. Without heaters, water temperature will fluctuate with room temperature.

Cold-water fish such as goldfish prosper over a wide temperature range. For example, goldfish will overwinter in iced-over backyard ponds. Most species of tropical freshwater fish as well as marine tropical fish do well at 75 degrees F (24 degrees C), but can tolerate temperatures 10 degrees F (6 degrees C) above or below that optimum at which the metabolic processes of the fish are at maximum efficiency. However, as temperatures drop lower than an acceptable range for a tropical variety, there is a depression of all body functions, including appetite, growth, and the immune system. Temperatures above the optimum range can cause stress by reducing the amount of available oxygen in the water, resulting in increased respiration. Increased respiratory rates can accelerate the development of disease problems relating to poor water quality or to the presence of parasites which affect gills. For special needs, where very cold water is necessary, refrigerated aquaria are available.

The wattage of a heater describes its power— the more wattage, the more heat will be delivered to the tank. Larger aquaria will require heaters of higher wattage, as will aquaria which are situated in cooler areas. As a general rule, use from 3 to 5 watts per gallon of water, depending on the room temperature. For example, if the room temperature is kept 8 to 10 degrees F (4 to 6 degrees C) lower than the desired aquarium temperature, as in a basement area, use a heater delivering at

Proper aeration of aquarium water will ensure the success of plant growth in the "natural aquarium."

least 3 watts per gallon. Buy an accurate thermometer to use when setting the heater's thermostats and for periodic checks of water temperature. Some brands of aquarium heaters have their thermostats set to regulate water at a specified temperature.

Both immersible and fully submersible heaters are available, as are low-wattage heating pads that are placed outside and under the tank being heated.

Buying an air pump: An air pump is a necessity for a modern aquarium and serves many functions. A simple diffuser stone positioned at the bottom of an aquarium serves to circulate water by the upward movement of air bubbles. As bubbles contact the surface of the water, the agitation increases the air–water interface, causing an increase in the rate of diffusion of atmospheric gases into the water and of dissolved carbon dioxide from the water. Air pumps can be used to move water through gravel beds, in conjunction with outside filters, and through cartridges containing water-softening or ammonia-removing resins. The "lifting" of water is accomplished by

directing a stream of air bubbles through a tube. The upward buoyancy of the bubbles acts like a piston moving water through a tube. A variety of air pumps is available, and all generate some sound which should be evaluated prior to purchasing the pump.

Filters and filtration materials: All of the many varieties of filters available for use in aquaria can be categorized functionally as mechanical, biological, or chemical. Many combine two or more of these modalities in a single unit.

A mechanical filter functions by trapping suspended particulate matters which could include uneaten food, fish wastes, or any kind of biological or inert particles, in a filter matrix. The size of particle which a mechanical filter will remove and the time required for removal depend on the density of the filter material. Filter media include gravel, floss, foam, or inert particulate materials such as diatomaceous earth. These act as a mechanical barrier to fine suspended particles when adsorbed to a filter screen. Mechanical filters will eventually clog and their media will require cleaning or replacement. The time required for clogging is related to pore size. Filters with a pore size small enough to retain bacteria, for example, if installed in an aquarium without some sort of prefilter, would last a matter of minutes prior to clogging. In aquaria, mechanical filters are expected to remove large particles. Removal of particles as small as the free-swimming stages of most protozoan parasites by filters is possible. However, the pore size of the medium must be small enough to trap the parasites and there must be no possibility for the parasites to bypass the filter as the medium clogs. Some parasites have the ability both to swim and to change shape. This enables them to pass through filter materials, much like a water-filled balloon being forced through a small opening.

Biological filters oxidize fish waste products, primarily by changing ammonia to nitrates. The bacteria involved in this process, collectively known as nitrifiers, are common in nature and

Scanning electron micrographs (3000x) show one of the major effects of conditioning. Unconditioned gravel (top) is barren of life, but after conditioning (bottom), bacteria are visible on the gravel surface.

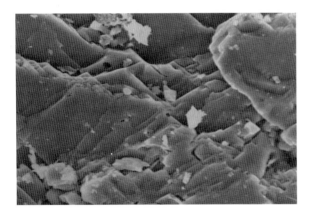

are introduced into the aquarium along with water and fish. They also are called chemo-autotrophic bacteria, because they require ammonia and nitrite ions for their growth. Bacteria of the genus *Nitrosomonas* utilize ammonia excreted by the fish as an energy source and oxidize it to nitrite ion. A second group of bacteria, belonging to the genus *Nitrobacter,* oxidizes nitrites to nitrate ion. These nitrifying bacteria initiate the conversion of nitrogenous wastes to free nitrogen. The second stage of the process, denitrification, is carried out by a different set of bacteria in the absence of oxygen. This makes it impractical to incorporate denitrification into home aquarium filter systems. Nitrifiers gradually colonize the surface of gravel, floss, foam filters, tubing, and any other solid surface, including the inner surface of the aquarium glass. (Note the scanning electron micrographs showing nitrifying bacteria on the surface of aquarium gravel.)

Chemical filtration entails passing aquarium water through some substance capable of changing the chemistry of the water. The type of change produced will depend on the substance included in the filter. Common chemically active filter media include:

1. Activated carbon. The physical structure of activated carbon includes a network of spaces responsible for adsorptive capacity. Activated carbon will adsorb a wide variety of organic substances, including color- and odor-producing substances. It effectively removes from solution dyes and chemicals used for treatment of fish disease problems, as well as dissolved heavy metals such as copper. It will remove neither ammonia nor nitrite ion from solution, nor will it soften water. Its primary use in home aquarium systems is to clarify water. Many manufacturers supply disposable inserts such as floss pads permeated with carbon particles or bags of activated carbon. Periodic replacement is necessary since temperatures required for reactivation of the carbon approach those attained in a blast furnace.

2. Ammonia-adsorbing clays. Also known as zeolites, these clays are sold in the form of chips. They require rinsing under a running tap prior to use in order to avoid clouding the aquarium's water. Many have the capacity to adsorb positively charged cations such as ammonium (NH_4^+) and can be used in filters. Since some zeolitic clays will also remove other types of cations such as calcium or magne-

sium, they also act as water softeners.

3. Ion-exchange resins. In some areas, water is "hard"; that is, it contains extremely high levels of calcium and magnesium ions. Frequently, the pH of such water is relatively high (7.8 to 9.0). Although a surprising number of fish can tolerate high levels of these minerals in water, many species will only breed under softer, more acidic water conditions. Thus many fish culturists prefer to adjust pH downward in their tanks. Doing so is difficult in the presence of calcium carbonates because the latter have a buffering effect. However, synthetic resins can be placed in a filter to soften water.

Resins which exchange sodium ions for calcium and magnesium ions are called cationic exchangers. When water is passed through this type of resin, a water test will indicate that the water has been softened. Many aquarists utilize softened water without problems for the fish. If softened water is used, the addition of a few grams of magnesium salts (Epsom salts) and calcium salts in the form of dolomitic limestone and/or oyster shell may be indicated.

The use of "mixed-bed" resins in a filter will essentially remove both cations (calcium and magnesium) and anions such as sulfates and carbonates. The resulting water is then said to be deionized. Fish cannot tolerate completely deionized water. However, partial deionization may be necessary in lowering pH in some hard-water areas.

4. Oyster shell or coral gravel. These media are usually used in a filter in areas where soft water has a tendency to become acidic abruptly. These materials contribute calcium carbonate to the

Attached to the side of the aquarium, this outside power filter has disposable inserts to facilitate the periodic cleaning that all such filters require.

water, increasing hardness and buffering capacity. In soft-water areas of the country, water in an unbuffered aquarium may decrease in pH to a point where fish are severely stressed or die.

5. Peat moss. Peat moss has been used in filters to soften water, usually for breeding purposes. It is likely that peat moss releases a hormone-stimulating substance into solution which induces spawning. Use of peat moss in a filter will impart a light brown color to water.

Choosing a filter: There is no good or bad filter. The various types available have distinct applications, depending on a variety of factors, including expense, tank size, number and/or size of fish kept in an aquarium, and whether the aquarium houses saltwater or freshwater fish. Practically every hobbyist, experienced retailer, or authority will have his or her own strong opinions on exactly what is best, but successful filtration always has both a mechanical and biological component. (Chemical filtration is required on a basis of need for special water requirements.)

These processes can be carried out using very simple or very expensive filter units—fish do not know the difference as long as the water quality is good. All filters provide for the movement of water through the filtering material, either by the air-lift principle or by electrically driven pumps. Filters may be located inside or outside of aquaria. All eventually tend to clog, resulting in reduced flow rates and inefficient filtration. All filter media, whether floss, foam pads, activated carbon, gravel, or plastic rings used for

A corner filter, which works by the air-lift principle, is appropriate for a small aquarium.

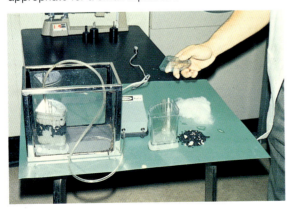

mechanical filtration, will eventually be colonized by nitrifying bacteria. The bacteria are firmly attached to the filter materials and are not removed by vigorous rinsing. Naturally, hot water, soaps, and various disinfectants will kill these bacteria and destroy the beneficial effects of biological filtration. All filters require periodic cleaning to remove debris which, although trapped within a filter matrix, is in fact still adding to the organic pollution of the aquarium water.

Since the mechanical and biological functions of filtration materials are so intertwined, it is recommended that when a filter is serviced, at least some of the media contained therein never be discarded. The easiest way to accomplish this is to include gravel, plastic, or ceramic rings in a filter along with disposable filter media such as activated carbon. Since activated carbon loses its filtering capacity after a period of time, placing it in a bag within the filter will simplify changing.

1. Corner filters. Included in many aquarium "beginner kits," an inexpensive corner box filter can be effectively utilized in smaller aquaria. Most corner filters are operated by the air-lift principle. Their filtration capacity is limited. For general filtration purposes, they function best when a small permanent sack of gravel or similar substrate is incorporated along with mechanical and chemical filter material (floss and activated carbon) to ensure that some bacteria-laden "conditioned" material remains after cleaning. Corner filters are frequently used in small aquaria for holding fish during a quarantine period or during a brief treatment period. Many aquarists interested in breeding fish use corner filters in their spawning setups.

2. Outside power filters. Most outside filters are constructed so that they can be easily hung from the rim of an aquarium. Various types of electrically driven filters are available, but most are driven by rotary impeller motors. However, an outside filter is defined only by location, and air-lift driven units are also available.

Outside power filters can be loaded with any type of filter material that meets the aquarist's needs. These generally include floss or foam pads, positioned to keep larger particulate matter from clogging activated carbon or other filter material. If gravel or other materials such as ceramic or plastic rings are included, the filter will in time develop a biological function. The waste-processing capacity of such units will be limited when

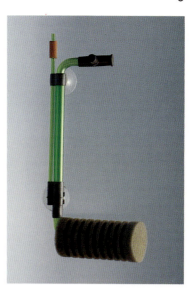

Outside power filters can be set up easily, and trapped debris rinsed periodically, with little disturbance of the enclosed environment. Foam (sponge) filters are also popular in situations where no gravel bed is to be used in the aquarium.

compared to an undergravel filter. However, aquarists wanting to avoid gravel beds for any reason will find such modified outside filters a useful alternative for use in breeding, fry rearing, or quarantine tanks.

All outside filters require periodic cleaning. Obviously, debris trapped in a filter remains in contact with the aquarium water. Depending upon the flow characteristics of the brand of outside filter being used, water may bypass the filter media as the filter clogs. This will result in less efficient filtration with little or no change in flow rate. By comparison, other filter types do not allow bypassing of water, so flow rate slows down as the filter clogs.

Cleaning outside filters is much easier if particulate media such as gravel, ceramic rings, or activated carbon are placed in separate net bags. Floss or foam pads should be cleaned whenever debris buildup is evident. Gravel bags need only

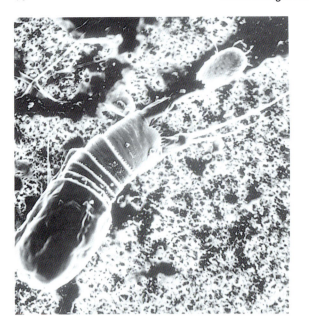

A thriving community of invertebrates will eventually develop within the filter system. This electron micrograph shows rotifers living upon a foam filter (260x).

tanks occasionally require isolation for treatment purposes, for maintaining biological filtration in quarantine tanks, and in tanks used for breeding fish.

Foam filters which have been in use for some time and which have developed a bacterial flora can be used to maintain and "seed" new aquarium systems with nitrifying bacteria. This is a simple way of avoiding the accumulation of ammonia and nitrites in freshly set-up aquaria that characterizes "new-tank syndrome."

Like all filters, foam filters will develop a thriving community of various invertebrates which provide food for fish in the aquarium. Many of these invertebrate forms are rotifers of various types. Rinsing foam filters under a stream of tepid chlorinated water will not kill the bacteria present, but may reduce the population of invertebrates temporarily. However, soaps, disinfectants, or deter-

be rinsed under tepid tap water. Activated carbon should be replaced according to the manufacturer's suggestions.

3. Foam filters. Foam pads function very efficiently as mechanical filter media. They can be used in place of floss or floss pads in any type of filter. They eventually will develop a flora of nitrifying bacteria and function well as biological filters. Foam blocks must be rinsed periodically to restore their mechanical function. The most popular types of foam filters are powered by the air-lift principle. Larger units driven by rotary-impeller power heads are also available. Foam filters certainly are less efficient than outside power filters in their mechanical action, but will ultimately develop a good biological function as well. They are useful in systems where gravel is not required or desired as a biological filter bed. They also can be used either as a tank's sole filter or as a supplement to other kinds of filters. Single pads are suitable for smaller aquaria; multiple filters can be used in larger systems. Such filters are employed with considerable success for research aquaria at the University of Georgia for a variety of experimental uses. They are especially useful as adjunct filters in recirculating systems where

Undergravel filters, the author's preference, come in many shapes and sizes. The simplest is a small flat plate (top) powered by a single air lift. For a larger aquarium, an undergravel filter with larger lift stacks powered by several air lifts (below) is ideal.

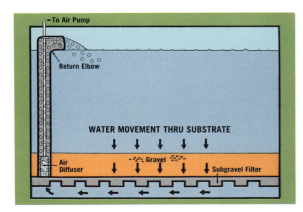

As water moves through the gravel into the undergravel filter plate, it carries oxygen to the nitrifying bacteria in the gravel. These bacteria process the fish wastes, converting ammonia to nitrites and eventually to nitrates. In this system, the entire gravel bed essentially acts as a biological filter.

gents may kill or inactivate all of the bacterial and invertebrate populations. Similarly, drying foam filters will inactivate bacteria and invertebrates. However, filters can be stored wet for several days without appreciably reducing their biological effectiveness.

4. Undergravel filters. Undergravel filters consist of a plastic plate equipped with one or more air lifts. At least 3 inches (7.6 centimeters) of washed gravel should be put over the plate. The air flow displaces water through the lift stacks, circulating water through the gravel bed. This brings both oxygen and organic wastes into contact with bacteria attached to the gravel. As long as this flow is maintained, the entire gravel bed of such a filter is biologically active. In a gravel-bottomed aquarium without water circulation, only the top centimeter or two is biologically active. Undergravel filter plates are sold in sizes adequate for the largest aquaria or for goldfish bowls. The flat plate types appear to be adequate for smaller aquaria. However, for larger aquaria, models with corrugated bottoms and larger-diameter lift stacks are likely to produce better water circulation. Undergravel units are widely employed in marine aquaria, where dolomitic limestone or coral gravel is used as the filter bed. As ammonia or nitrite poisoning is of special concern in marine tanks, the rapidity with which an undergravel filter removes these toxic substances makes it a natural choice for the marine tank.

At this writing, it appears that more and more aquarists are utilizing undergravel filtration for freshwater aquaria. Because undergravel filters act as both mechanical and biological filters, they need not be supplemented with other types of filters if (and this is an important "if"!) debris is periodically removed from the filter bed and water is changed regularly. The gravel bed is easily cleaned when water is changed by using a distended siphon tube to remove debris deep in the gravel bed. If water is changed on a regular basis, water can be kept clear without the use of activated carbon.

Of course, additional filters of any type can also be used with an undergravel filtration system. For example, an external power filter loaded with a filtering substance such as activated carbon, peat, or ammonia-adsorbing clays could be used to effect some desired change in water chemistry. Although undergravel filters are usually powered by air displacement, an alternate method is to place rotary impeller–driven units known as power heads on top of the lift stack. Placing a siphon tube from an outside power unit in a lift stack is a good way to operate an undergravel filter in conjunction with an outside power filter.

One disadvantage of undergravel filters is that some fish burrow into gravel or else actively move gravel about the bottom. This exposes the filter plate, creating breaks in the gravel which lead to a reduced water flow through the bed. This can be avoided by placing a plastic screen 3 to 4 centimeters (about 1.5 inches) below the surface of the gravel. Perhaps the chief disadvantage of undergravel filters is their immobility. There is no way to remove an undergravel filter from a tank that is being treated with therapeutic agents toxic to nitrifying bacteria, such as methylene blue, formaldehyde, or many antibiotics. Another frequently cited disadvantage is that rock formations reduce the effective surface available for water flow. From experience, I do not feel that rock formations cause sufficient blockage of the filtration surface to be of any consequence.

There is some controversy regarding the suitability of an undergravel filter for plant growth. It has been suggested that root movement which may be associated with the use of undergravel filters inhibits plant growth. However, experts in the field of hydroponics are able to grow a wide variety of plants without any root substrate and suggest that the aeration and micronutrients supplied to roots by an undergravel filter would bene-

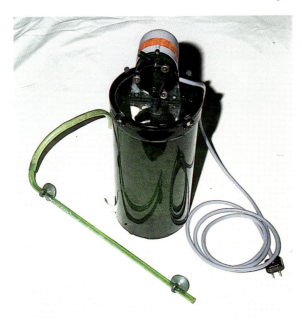

Canister filters are suitable for larger aquaria and can be loaded with a variety of filtering materials such as ceramic rings, ammonia absorbers, floss, and activated carbon.

fit the plants. Some recommend that when plants are to be used with an undergravel filter, the gravel layer should be increased to approximately 5 inches (13 centimeters). An alternative is to purchase plants which have been propagated in plant plugs containing fertilizers in a root-support growth medium. Plants can also be placed in small pots with good potting soil. It is important to place a layer of aquarium gravel over the soil in pots to stabilize it under water.

5. Canister filters. Canister filters take their name from their general shape. Their powerful motors pull water through a sealed container filled with various filter media. These filters are particularly useful in large or heavily stocked aquaria, which require a greater filtration capacity. Canister filters can be purchased in a variety of sizes. These units have two distinct advantages over other kinds of filters: they have enough volume to accommodate a series of filter substrates stacked in series, which greatly enhances their effectiveness, and they can be placed in a location remote from the aquarium. This latter feature is useful in display aquaria, for filters can be located in an adjacent work area.

Newer designs of canister filters are available in which the impeller is located at the bottom of the canister. This feature makes it very easy to prime the units and ensures that the impeller assembly never runs dry. Because of the increased size of the motor when compared to that of outside filters, some canister filters can be used in conjunction with inserts which will support a film of diatomaceous earth. These units can be used for water "polishing."

The disadvantage to canister filters is their higher cost in comparison to other types of filters. Another is that since outside canisters require tubing running to and from the aquarium, connectors must be carefully tightened and rechecked periodically lest leaks develop.

Buying gravel and ornaments: The aquaria in homes or for display purposes require a gravel base which, from an aesthetic viewpoint, mimics the bottom of a pond and provides a good base for rooting plants. For most freshwater aquaria, it is important to use quartzite or granite gravel, which will not contribute carbonate ions to water. There are advantages to using calcareous substrata in tanks housing fish that prefer hard alkaline water, such as African Rift Lake cichlids or most live-bearers.

The size range of the gravel particles should be approximately 4 to 6 millimeters (3/16th of an inch plus or minus 1/16th). The particle size is important for several reasons. If an undergravel filter plate is to be used, the spaces between gravel particles will allow free water flow and ample aeration for bacteria which will eventually colonize the surface of the gravel particles. The depth of the gravel bed will depend on whether or not an undergravel filter is used and whether live plants are desired.

Sand is not recommended as an aquarium substratum. The extremely small particle size results in packing and reduces water flow. Waste that breaks down in the resulting anaerobic conditions will generate hydrogen sulfide and other highly toxic substances. Aquatic plants also require a bed which will allow diffusion of nutrients to roots.

Marine aquaria usually are equipped with undergravel filters. Calcareous gravels, which contain carbonates, are recommended for such tanks. These include dolomitic limestone, crushed oyster shell, and coral gravel, materials containing high levels of carbonates. The slow release of carbonates in marine aquaria tends to

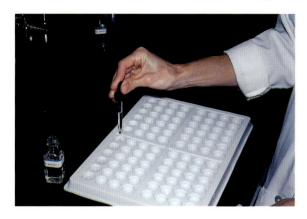

A multi-well tray allows many water samples to be tested at once.

buffer water towards the desired high (7.8 to 8.3) pH range.

Regardless of type, gravel intended for aquarium use requires removal of pulverized particles which can cloud tank water. Gravel should be rinsed under a tap while being stirred briskly, until the water runs clear.

Colored aquarium gravel is available. Although selection of color is largely a matter of human taste, white gravel reflects more light and may stress those species of fish which prefer dark areas in an aquarium.

Decorating an aquarium provides benefits both for the aquarist and for the fish. Many fish are territorial, and rock formations, plants, and a variety of other decorations will provide needed territorial landmarks and boundaries. Also, smaller fish may need to escape from larger species by taking refuge in small nooks provided by rock formations. A decorated tank also provides shade for those fish which prefer darker areas.

Not all objects are equally suitable for aquarium decoration. Coral, seashells, limestone, and marble will dissolve in fresh water and may increase the pH to an unacceptable level. Copper objects, galvanized metals, or steel can cause heavy metal poisoning, especially in areas where the water is soft and the pH is on the acid side of neutral. Rocks, driftwood, or gravel taken from streams or ponds should be soaked in a disinfectant such as chlorine bleach, then rinsed well, to avoid the introduction of snails and other unwanted invertebrates such as planarians and free-living nematodes.

The use of a background behind the aquarium serves to beautify the tank as well as to create the darker area preferred by certain shy species of fish. A variety of selections is available for outside use, including paints, paper with fresh- or saltwater motifs, and plastic materials constructed to create a three-dimensional illusion. Inside backgrounds constructed of a variety of waterproof inert materials are also available.

Buying water test kits: The serious aquarist should invest in test kits which will enable him or her to measure pH, hardness, ammonia, and nitrite levels. For saltwater aquaria, a hydrometer and copper test kit are also recommended. Most test kits sold for application in aquaculture are easy to use. They are based on color changes in the sample being tested, which is then compared to a color standard. Some kits are supplied with liquid reagents which over time may deteriorate. Others provide powdered reagents, which may be more stable over time. If it is necessary to test many aquaria, these kits can be used in conjunction with a tray containing many wells, each containing a water sample from a tank to be tested. This method provides a quick overview of water conditions in many aquaria.

Setting Up the Aquarium

Choosing a location: We will assume that you have purchased or built a stand which will support the weight of the fully set-up aquarium. If the tank is not level or appears to be unstable, it may be a good idea to shim the stand, or, alternatively, to fasten it to a wall to avoid accidental tipping. This can be done using an L-shaped piece of metal. The aquarium should be placed in an area where it is likely to be viewed, but not in an area where accessibility is limited. Regular maintenance will be much easier if it is possible to have working room above and behind the aquarium. Do not place the tank in direct sunlight. Otherwise, algae will rapidly accumulate and the aquarium may overheat. However, indirect light or even a short period of direct light in addition to the use of overhead lighting can be useful in stimulating plant growth. Placing aquaria close to air conditioning vents or over heat vents can complicate the task of regulating water temperature.

Equipping the interior: Once the aquarium is in the desired position, install the undergravel filter plate if this type of filter is going to be used.

Be careful not to displace gravel substrate while filling the tank with water. Rocks and plants can be more easily placed in tanks filled one-third to one-half capacity with water.

Then add washed gravel to a depth of 2 to 3 inches (about 5 to 8 centimeters) if an undergravel filter will not be used, to a depth of 3 inches (7.6 centimeters) if an undergravel filter will be used without live plants, and to a depth of 5 inches (12.7 centimeters) if such a unit will be used with plants. For better plant growth, mix a soil additive or a proprietary slow-release fertilizer with the gravel. These products are available at pet-supply outlets.

After the washed gravel is added, fill the aquarium with water to about one-third of capacity; rock formations and plants are easier to set in place if some water is present. If an undergravel filter is being used, direct water over a shallow pan to avoid displacing gravel under it. Some aquarists prefer to slope the gravel slightly toward the front of the aquarium, which they claim facilitates removing debris from the aquarium.

Construction of caves and recesses makes for more interesting viewing while providing more timid fish with shelter. Do not use any type of rock which has the potential for releasing minerals, such as limestone, marble, or clays. Rocks collected from streams can be used. However, they should be thoroughly cleaned by brushing with water, rinsed, and dried prior to placement in the aquarium.

Plants, be they living or plastic, should be positioned with the taller-growing varieties toward the back of the aquarium and in a position to hide lift stacks, siphon tubes, or heaters which you will be adding. Because living plants require a favorable water quality in addition to plant nutrients and good lighting, some experts suggest waiting to add plants until after the aquarium has been established for a period of time. Presumably, in an established aquarium, nitrification would be in place and nitrates would be available for plant nutrients.

Although fish in ponds can tolerate water temperature fluctuations, in an aquarium there is no advantage to allowing such fluctuations, which can easily be avoided by installation of a heater. Heater placement will depend on the type purchased. Totally immersible types can be positioned horizontally at the level of the gravel, a location which may enhance plant growth. Models which are not totally immersible are usually clipped to the aquarium side; they require that the aquarium water level be kept at or above the level of the thermostat to avoid overheating of the water. With either type, promoting water circulation by positioning airstones at gravel level or using power filters for circulation will help ensure uniformity of water temperature throughout the aquarium.

Water temperature should be set prior to addi-

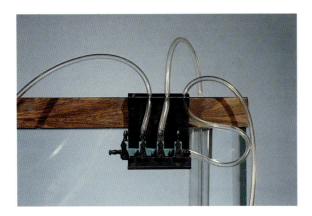

Loop the air line through notches in a tubing manifold to avoid the possibility of back-siphoning.

tion of fish to avoid any possible stress in the fish from drastic accidental changes in temperature. A good temperature for a wide variety of freshwater fish as well as plants is 75 degrees F (24 degrees C). Let the heater acclimate to the water for an hour prior to connecting the electricity. Then adjust it slowly in order to avoid possible overheating. A light will indicate whether the heating unit is on. For the first twenty-four hours, frequently check the temperature and adjust the thermostat as required to obtain the desired water temperature.

A few safety precautions should always be followed around tanks where a heater is in use. Never connect the heater unless the tube housing the heating element is immersed in water. Always disconnect the heater when changing water or lowering the tank's water level for any reason. Adjust the thermostat only when you have time to check the temperature of the water continually.

Providing aeration for the aquarium is the next matter of concern. Aquarium water is aerated by agitation of its surface by the outflow of power filters, a stream of bubbles produced by an airstone or by a stream of water splashed from the lift stacks of an undergravel filter. Gas exchange occurs at the surface of the water. Placement of an airstone toward the bottom of an aquarium will both circulate and aerate the water. Aeration of aquarium water provides oxygen required by fish, plants, and nitrifying bacteria. Aeration can always be increased by directing water flow from power filter outlets over the surface of the aquarium water. Undergravel filters have the built-in

advantage of "pulling" oxygenated water through the gravel bed.

When lines to airstones or lift stacks are attached to pumps located below the aquarium, there is a possibility of back-siphoning if the pump is accidentally disconnected or if there is a power outage. This can be avoided by positioning the air pump higher than the aquarium. If this is not possible, make sure that the air tubing to each outlet has a loop sufficiently high to avoid a siphon effect. Loops can be made by using the notches in a tubing manifold or by using plastic inserts in air tubing which prevent abrupt bending and the formation of anti-siphon loops. Check valves are also available, which can be placed in air lines to prevent back-siphoning problems.

A minimal agitation of the water surface from any type of aeration will generally result in oxygen levels of between 6 and 7 parts per million (ppm). Excessive agitation may disturb some more timid species such as discus fish. However, moderate circulation of water is tolerated by most fish and promotes plant growth.

At this point the aquarium should have gravel in place and be equipped with a filter, heater, and perhaps airstones. Fill the aquarium to the top with tap water. The air pump can be turned on immediately, but wait for a thirty- to sixty-minute period for the thermostat to adjust to ambient water temperature prior to plugging in the heater. The next step is to assure water quality that will support fish.

Dechlorinating the water: In many municipal water supplies, chlorine is added at the pumping plant to destroy bacteria pathogenic to humans. In tap water, dissolved chlorine concentrations usually measure between 0.2 ppm and 0.7 ppm, depending on the time of the year. Water for aquarium use must be chlorine-free, since even 0.2 ppm will kill fish by destroying gill tissues. Chlorine can be removed from tap water in three ways:

1. Aeration of water, resulting in diffusion of chlorine into the air. The use of a faucet-end aerator commonly found in households will aerate water and remove chlorine. Simply pouring water from one pail to another three or four times will also drive chlorine from solution. Letting tap water stand in pails for a few days also allows chlorine to dissipate gradually. This process can be speeded up by aerating the water with an air diffuser.

2. Passing water through activated carbon. Many of the faucet-end water purifiers sold to improve the taste of water are charged with activated carbon. Larger canisters available from water conditioning companies are also available for large-use situations such as would arise in a pet store.

3. Adding sodium thiosulfate to tap water immediately inactivates chlorine. Sodium thiosulfate is sold under a variety of trade names. One molecule of sodium thiosulfate will remove four molecules of chlorine. Based on this, 0.50 milliliters (10 drops) of a 1 percent solution of sodium thiosulfate would remove 0.5 ppm of chlorine from 10 gallons (38 liters) of city water. One drop per gallon of a 1 percent solution of sodium thiosulfate would provide a sufficient safety factor to avoid the consequences of fluctuations in chlorine levels.

Removing chloramines: In some municipal water plants, ammonia is added to react with chlorine to form chloramines, which then act as the disinfecting agent. The addition of sodium thiosulfate will neutralize both chlorine and chloramines. However, ammonia is released after the sodium thiosulfate combines with the chloramines, and this could be a problem to fish under conditions where there is little or no biological filtration.

In most home aquaria where biological filtration has been established, the routine use of sodium thiosulfate rids the water of chlorine; the remaining ammonia is quickly oxidized to harmless nitrates by the resident nitrifying bacteria. This assumes a very efficient biological filter and a relatively modest water change of no more than 25 percent of the tank volume at a time.

In newly established aquaria, or when most of the water has been changed at one time, sufficient nitrifying bacteria may not be present to oxidize ammonia. In these cases, sodium thiosulfate can be used in conjunction with ammonia-adsorbing media. The most readily available of these are certain clays (zeolites) sold under a variety of brand names. The ammonia-adsorbing chips should be placed in an outside or canister filter before making a water change to ensure that the ammonia released following dechloramination is quickly removed from the aquarium. An alternative method of neutralizing ammonia without using zeolites is simply to lower the pH of the water, if the tank's residents can tolerate it. At lower pH levels (6 to 7), the majority of total ammonia will be present as the nontoxic ionized form: ammonium (NH_4^+). In many areas of the country, pH can be lowered by adding buffers which are available in aquarium supply stores or by adding monobasic sodium phosphate, NaH_2PO_4.

Chloramines can also be removed from fresh water by the use of a high grade of unused activated carbon. Activated carbon which has been used may remove colors and odors, but will not remove chloramines.

In marine aquaria where pH levels are kept between 7.8 and 8.3, chloramine treatment with sodium thiosulfate would result in the generation of free ammonia. Zeolites are ineffective in removing ammonia from salt water, and lowering the pH in marine aquaria is not recommended. Before adding salt mix to tap water to make synthetic seawater, pretreat the requisite volume of tap water with sodium thiosulfate, then filter it through zeolite held in a household colander; alternatively, pass the tap water through virgin activated carbon prior to mixing it with salt.

If chloramines are present in locations where tap water is hard, with a high (7.8 to 9.0) pH, the ammonia resulting from treatment with sodium thiosulfate could injure fish if biological filtration has not been established. In such areas, pH may be difficult to adjust downward and water may have to be pretreated with sodium thiosulfate, then slowly poured through a pail containing zeolite chips before being used in the aquarium. (Holes in the bottom of the pail will facilitate this operation.) In any case, where chloramine removal is deemed necessary, treated water should be tested for total combined chlorine levels and ammonia to make sure that the treatment chosen was effective. Commercial products are also available that bind the ammonia produced by dechloramination into an organic complex that is harmless to fish. The complex is then metabolized by the biological filter.

Controlling pH: Water in various parts of the country may have different pH values, and in some cases the water may require some adjusting prior to addition of fish. Generally, fish can tolerate quite a wide pH range without problems. A pH of 6.5 to 7.8 for freshwater species is an acceptable range for maintenance of optimal health.

Purchasing and Adding Fish

Choice of fish: It has been customary to start new or unconditioned aquaria with hardy fish, supposedly more tolerant of ammonia and nitrites. There is no question that some varieties are less susceptible to nitrite intoxication than others. Our experience suggests that various species of tetras, such as the serpae tetra (*Hyphessobrycon callistus*), are less susceptible to nitrites than live-bearing fish such as swordtails, guppies, and platys. Common goldfish, zebra danios, and many barbs are also relatively hardy fish. If some form of conditioned filter—such as gravel from a conditioned aquarium or a conditioned foam filter—is added to a new aquarium, there will be less reason to fear the ammonia-nitrite problem.

A decision on what type of fish to eventually put into your aquarium is purely a matter of preference. However, you should be aware that some fish are incompatible with each other or with living plants. Different fishes also thrive in different water conditions. Some fish species may prefer brackish water. Others may do well in hard water with elevated pH, while still others may flourish in soft water with a lower pH.

A "community" tank exists when several species of fish are maintained together in an aquarium. In many cases, a few goldfish are included with species of live-bearing fish such as guppies or egg-laying species originating in South America. Such mixtures provide interesting visual variety but do not remotely reflect natural fish populations. If you are interested in goldfish, consider having an aquarium with nothing but goldfish. Alternatively, many aquarists like to create an aquarium with a few species of fish native to a particular part of the world. In many cases the schooling behavior of fish is not seen unless several fish of the same species are kept together.

How many fish in an aquarium?: In any new aquarium without an efficient biological filter system, just a few fish should be added initially. This introduction should be followed with regular water changes on a weekly basis for at least a month. As nitrifying bacteria develop in the filter material, more fish can be added.

The number of fish which an aquarium will support depends on several factors. A common rule which has been used by aquarists is that for every gallon (3.8 liters) of water, one may add 1 inch (2.5 centimeters) of length of freshwater fish or 0.5 inches (1.25 centimeters) of saltwater fish. Other aquarists suggest that the total inches or centimeters of fish which can be added should equal the number of inches or centimeters, respectively, which the aquarium measures along its long axis. A standard 10-gallon (38-liter) aquarium, for example, measures about 19 inches (48 centimeters) and thus could support nineteen 1-inch fish or twenty-four 2-centimeter fish.

It should be noted that some aquarists disregard all formulas and crowd their aquaria with fish. Their success is based on a good filtering system, a program of regular water changes, aeration, and due attention to nutrition and disease control. Nonetheless, it is generally better to have fewer fish in an aquarium to avoid deterioration of water quality and to minimize the risk of disease, which is enhanced by crowding.

Selecting healthy fish: Reputable retailers are not interested in selling an obviously sick fish, but often it is very difficult to detect fish which are carriers of a parasite and which with time will develop signs of disease. It is always prudent to select fish from aquaria where no disease has been evident over a period of time. Fish should be active, with a full underbelly. Signs of disease include clamped fins, lack of color, skin blemishes, white spots, excessive body slime, failure to eat, and inactivity. Some hobbyists will not purchase a fish (especially an expensive one) until they have observed it over a period of time in a retail shop. Particularly when evaluating marine fish, it is a good idea to ask a retailer if the animals in question have been routinely treated for parasites.

Quarantine: Quarantine refers to the isolation and observation of fish prior to introducing them into an aquarium. The objective of quarantine is to determine whether the specimen has a disease which could be transmitted to other fish. The assumption is that a serious disease is likely to develop during the isolation period. A quarantine period can vary in length, but fourteen days is common. In fish health management involving food fish, public aquaria, or fish used for research, fish may be routinely treated during the quarantine period. In cases where many fish are involved, a few fish may be killed and examined for parasites or chronic disease conditions. If disease is present, the fish are treated with a specific medication during the quarantine period. If a disease is detected which is either difficult or impossible to treat, a decision is made regarding the eventual use or disposition of the animals.

Quarantine of fish prior to their introduction into the home display aquarium is a rare, but nevertheless a recommended, practice. It is particularly advisable when adding new fish of questionable disease status to an established aquarium housing valued fish.

Adding fish to the aquarium: Although fish can live over a considerable range of water temperatures, sudden temperature changes can stress fish. It is a good practice to minimize stress by making sure that the temperature difference between the fish's transport container, usually a plastic bag, and the home aquarium is minimal (ideally less than 3 degrees F or 1.6 degrees C). In most situations, this can be done by floating the plastic transport bag in the aquarium water for ten to fifteen minutes. Keep the bag inflated during this period, since draping an uninflated bag over the side of an aquar-

Using a transport bag can allow you to introduce fish to the tank, while minimizing the shift in pH and temperature.

ium will minimize diffusion of oxygen by reducing water–air surface area.

Adding fish to the aquarium can be done in different ways, depending on the concentration of ammonia in the water of the transport container. Timely transport of a few fish in a plastic bag from a retail outlet to a home aquarium typically results in very low ammonia levels. However, on a commercial scale where hundreds of fish are transported, the ammonia levels in the transport water may be very high. Since the pH of the water in heavily packed bags is usually 6.5 to 6.8, the ammonia is in the nontoxic form. However, addition of fresh chlorinated water with a high pH (7.8 to 9.0) will serve to convert nontoxic ammonium to toxic ammonia, resulting in gill damage. This problem is particularly serious when marine fish are shipped considerable distances.

In most instances involving home aquaria, the practice of mixing aquarium water with the contents of the transport container, then adding the mixture to the aquarium, is unlikely to hurt the fish. Simply adjusting the pH of the aquarium water to approximately 6.8 to 7.0 will ensure that the ammonia levels remain low.

For wholesalers, retailers, and others who handle substantial numbers of fish crowded in bags, it is best to transfer the fish from the transport bag to the aquarium by the careful use of a net. The objective is to keep any polluted transport water and any associated disease organisms from entering the aquarium. Netted fish can be injured by contact and friction, especially if many fish are netted together. Netting injuries can be avoided by positioning a net just at the surface of a shallow container or pail filled with temperature- and pH-adjusted aquarium water. Fish in the transport bag are then "poured" into water but still contained by a net. A rapid transfer of fish into an aquarium can be effected with minimal contact of fish with the net.

Some wholesalers and brokers (trans-shippers) prefer to acclimatize fish by the slow addition of fresh water to the transport bag or to a container to which both fish and transport water have been transferred. In a matter of a few minutes, a total water change has been made and the fish can be transferred to aquaria without netting. This is an acceptable method provided that: (1) the pH of the incoming water does not differ from that of the transport water by more than 0.5 pH units in either direction and is not alkaline, (2) there is no great difference in water temperature, and (3) the water is dechlorinated.

It is always a good idea to determine the pH of the transport water, which generally will be between 6.5 and 6.8. Adjustment of aquarium water pH to between 6.8 and 7.0 prior to addition of freshwater fish is a sound and safe practice whenever the pH of the aquarium water is either much higher or much lower than the latter values.

Contrary to a widely held belief, most fish can tolerate rapid pH changes between the extremes of pH 6 and pH 9 if ammonia and other pollutants are not present. Fish in nature are often exposed to these variations without harm. Moreover, the author has experimentally shifted fish from pH 6 to pH 9 water without affecting their health. Nonetheless, overall it pays to err on the side of caution when contemplating pH changes in established aquaria. Both the direction and magnitude of pH changes must be evaluated, and this is a very complex subject. In addition, certain fish such as the neon tetra are quite intolerant of radical changes in water conditions. Thus, it is considered prudent not to alter pH by more than 0.5 units in a given twenty-four-hour period in a tank containing fish.

In the acclimation of marine fish, transport water should not be added to the aquarium, for the high pH of marine aquaria will ensure that toxic ammonia is present. After temperature equilibration, fish should be transferred to aquaria by careful netting or other appropriate methods, such as utilizing plastic containers with holes punched in the bottom as sieves. Fish can be caught easily, water allowed to drain, and the fish can be transferred quickly into the aquarium. As a rule, you can also avoid problems by refraining from adding transport water to aquaria.

Selected References

Baensch, H. 1983. *Marine Aquarists' Manual.* Tetra Press.

Hunnam, P.; Milne, A.; and Stebbing, P. 1982. *The Living Aquarium.* New York: Crescent Books.

Ladiges, W. 1983. *Coldwater Fish in the Home & Garden.* Tetra Press.

Randolph, E. 1990. *The Basic Book of Fish Keeping.* New York: Fawcett Crest.

Spotte, S. 1979. *Seawater Aquariums: The Captive Environment.* New York: Wiley-Interscience.

Vevers, G. (translator). 1973. *Dr. Sterba's Aquarium Handbook.* London: Pet Library, Ltd.

Maintaining Aquaria

John B. Gratzek

Once an aquarium has been established, successfully maintaining it becomes the aquarist's next job. This task will be simplified if one understands some important concepts about water, the "conditioning" period, and ways to circumvent or cure certain common problems in an established tank.

Understanding Water

A chemically pure molecule of water consists of two hydrogen atoms combined with one atom of oxygen with the common formula, H_2O. Such chemically pure water is found only after treatments such as distillation, reverse osmosis, or ion-exchange processing.

In its natural state, water quality varies considerably from location to location, depending upon which physical, chemical, and biological processes are predominant at a given spot. The composition of surface water from various geographical areas will vary with the acidity of rainwater. Once precipitation contacts ground, its chemical character will change depending on the composition and solubility of local geological formations and on the duration of contact. For instance, water flowing through a highly vegetated area such as a swamp would be expected to contain various organic components. As rainwater flows over soils and rocks, on the other hand, it becomes mineralized.

Groundwater from wells in a particular area may differ considerably in composition from surface water. Because of the demand for oxygen by decomposition processes, water will lose oxygen and gain carbon dioxide as it passes through surface layers of soil. Once it reaches the water table, minerals characteristic of the area will be added. For example, well water from a limestone area will be high in such dissolved solids as calcium and magnesium salts. Well water usually has low oxygen levels and frequently has a high iron content. The simple expedient of aerating well water prior to adding it to an aquarium will oxygenate it and convert the soluble ferrous form of iron to the insoluble ferric form. Consequently, iron will settle out as a rusty orange precipitate, and iron-free water will result.

Most aquarists utilize tap water for raising and propagating fish. Because regional and/or local health departments are responsible for the safety of water for human consumption, tap water routinely is treated with chlorine or chloramine to kill pathogenic microorganisms. Sodium fluoride is often added to prevent caries in humans. Alum is added occasionally to clarify water. In some municipal water plants, ammonia is added to react with chlorine to form chloramines, which then act as the disinfecting agent. This is done to prevent the direct combination of chlorine with naturally occurring organic compounds to form carcinogenic compounds.

The measurement of substances dissolved in water is usually expressed as parts per million and abbreviated as ppm. One ppm is equal to one milligram of dissolved material per liter of water (approximately 1.3 ounces in 10,000 gallons of water) and is abbreviated to mg/l. These terms are interchangeable. Some substances are best measured as parts per billion, abbreviated as ppb. One ppb is equal to one microgram per liter, abbreviated to µg/l.

Water Terminology

Many terms are used to describe the properties of water. While some of these terms are more appropriate to the description of pond, lake, or stream water, all are useful in describing changes which develop in an aquarium.

Biochemical oxygen demand: This is a measure of the amount of oxygen consumed by the biological process of respiration in a container of water at a specific temperature (20 degrees C or 68 degrees F) in the dark for a five-day period. By inference, the more oxygen used, the more organic materials (bacteria, algae, diatoms, organics) were present in the original water sample. The name of the test is often abbreviated to BOD. The BOD of fresh water is low; the BOD of water in an aquarium where the water has not been changed is high.

Chemical oxygen demand: The chemical oxygen demand (COD) is a measure of organic matter in water and provides a good estimate of the BOD. To measure COD, dichromate is added to a container of water. Results are expressed as the oxygen equivalent of the dichromate consumed during the oxidation process.

Both BOD and COD tests are used to monitor water pollution. Pollution by biological or organic substances such as the waste products of fish occurs because the decomposition of organic materials in a closed aquatic system utilizes oxygen. The end result of this waste processing by bacteria will be a decrease in pH of the water. In practical terms, a good aquarist will prevent the accumulation of organics by not overstocking aquaria, not overfeeding, and paying strict attention to proper tank cleaning procedures.

Total dissolved solids: This term describes the concentration of all dissolved mineral substances in water, such as carbonates, bicarbonates, chlorides, phosphates, and sulfates. Other elements in lesser concentrations could include nitrates, iron, copper, magnesium, and manganese. The biological significance of total dissolved solids is that fish cannot regulate their salt-to-water balance (osmoregulate) if the concentration of dissolved minerals is too high. Experience suggests that freshwater fish do well in waters which contain 400 ppm or less of total dissolved solids. However, in the case of such physiologically plastic species as desert pupfish, the upper limits for survivability may be as high as 5,000 ppm. Of practical importance to the aquarist is the possibility of osmotic shock when sensitive fish are moved abruptly from water with high dissolved solids to water with low dissolved solids.

Water hardness: The degree of water hardness is directly proportional to the concentrations of mineral ions in the water. Although other mineral ions such as iron, zinc, boron, copper, lead, and silicon may be present in trace amounts, calcium and magnesium are the dominant chemical species found in solution. Thus hardness is usually expressed in terms of the amount of calcium carbonate ($CaCO_3$) present in solution. Water hardness can be expressed as parts per million or by using one of several arbitrary scales of measurement. On the German scale, which is widely used by aquarists, the term "DH" refers to degrees hardness. One DH is equivalent to 17 ppm. A useful classification of "soft" versus "hard" water is given in the following table:

water quality	ppm
Soft:	0 to 75 ppm
Moderately hard:	75 to 150 ppm
Hard:	150 to 300 ppm
Very hard:	300+ ppm

From the aquarist's perspective, the most immediate practical aspect of water hardness is that softer water has less buffering capacity. This means that pH can drop abruptly in an aquarium filled with soft water, whereas pH tends to be stabilized in aquaria with hard water. Extremely soft water can pose other management problems for aquarists. It is erroneously believed by many hobbyists that distilled water or water passed through a reverse-osmosis filter is "pure" and therefore good for fish. This is not the case. Fish lose minerals (electrolytes) through urine and gills; minerals must be replaced for optimal health. Blood electrolyte balance is maintained by minerals in the diet and by adsorption of dissolved minerals through the gills. High mortalities associated with larval freshwater fish kept in very soft water can easily be attributed to mineral and electrolyte imbalances. As a group, fish can tolerate a wide range of water hardness levels, although each species has a preferred range of dissolved mineral concentrations. Levels of 50 ppm $CaCO_3$ sustain most freshwater fish without problems. A hardness level of 100 ppm is desirable for most Central American fishes, among them many popular live-bearers, and fish from Africa's Rift Lakes will live and prosper in water classified as very hard.

pH: In water, electrons often move from one atom to another to form charged entities called ions. The pH of water is a measure of the relative amounts of hydrogen ions (H^+) and hydroxyl ions (OH^-) present in solution. At a pH of 7.0, a solution is called neutral since there are an equal number of hydrogen and hydroxyl ions present. Various substances in the water can tip the balance between these ions. A pH value less than 7.0 signifies acidic conditions, in which hydrogen ions are more abundant than hydroxyl ions, while values greater than 7.0 signify alkaline conditions, in which hydroxyl ions predominate. Freshwater fish can live in extremes of pH from 3.8 to 9.0. However, in freshwater systems an optimum pH for the vast majority of species would be close to neutrality. In practice, pH values in closed freshwater systems should be kept between 6.8 and 7.8. Marine aquaria should be maintained between 7.8 and 8.3. While higher pH levels (7.8 to 8.5) are not intrinsically harmful to fish, such pH values will contribute to the toxicity of any ammonia present in the system.

Low pH values can develop in an aquarium through addition of acidic tap water, mistakes in adjusting pH with mineral acids, and biological degradation through bacterial respiration—especially when water is poorly buffered. Low pH values in freshwater aquaria can affect both the fish and the bacterial oxidizing system. At pH values below 5.5, the rate of oxidation of ammonia by bacteria (*Nitrosomonas*) is reduced, resulting in increased ammonium levels. pH values between 4.0 and 5.0 will in themselves have deleterious effects on the great majority of freshwater

and all marine fish. Histological studies of fish kept in low-pH water indicate that the gill epithelium is damaged, a situation which could result in reduced respiratory function and death from anoxia, and/or in dangerous blood chemistry changes.

Alkalinity and buffering capacity: Alkalinity of water refers to the concentration of basic substances such as bicarbonate (HCO_3^-), carbonate (CO_3^{-2}), and hydroxide ion (OH^-) present in solution. The amount of these bases present, as determined by titration, is referred to as total alkalinity and is expressed as ppm equivalents of carbonate. In general, total hardness measurements will be very close to measurements of total alkalinity, because calcium and magnesium generally are associated with the carbonate minerals which are the principal sources of alkalinity in water.

A buffer is a combination of an acid or base with a salt which, when in solution, tends to stabilize the pH of the solution. Water with high alkalinity is naturally more strongly buffered than water with low alkalinity. In nature and in aquaria where water is poorly buffered due to a low alkalinity, pH levels tend to decrease over time. This downward shift results from the gradual release of carbon dioxide from respiratory processes of aquatic animals, plants, and bacteria. As carbon dioxide is added to water, it reacts, forming carbonic acid (H_2CO_3). The pH drops because the carbonic acid is a source of hydrogen ions, which react with carbonate or bicarbonate. (An increase in hydrogen ions results in lower pH.) On the other hand, removal of carbon dioxide, as for instance by plants during photosynthesis, causes the pH to climb.

In practical fish-keeping terms, water becomes acidified in a closed aquatic system because respiratory processes increase hydrogen ion concentration. A pH "crash," where levels may fall as low as pH 3.8, can develop in soft waters when all the buffering capacity (bicarbonates plus carbonates) is utilized. Two simple expedients for replenishing the alkalinity (buffering capacity) of the water are to: (1) change a portion of the water and (2) add commercially available buffers. Bicarbonate buffers water against sudden changes in pH by combining with hydrogen ions to form carbon dioxide and water. (Refer to the section on buffers further on in this chapter for additional information on their use in aquaria.)

Chlorine: To destroy pathogenic microorganisms, urban water supplies are chlorinated by the addition of molecular chlorine (Cl_2) or calcium hypochlorite, $Ca(OCl)_2$. In water, dissolved (free) chlorine reacts to form hypochlorous and hydrochloric acids:

$$Cl_2 + H_2O \rightarrow HOCl + H^+ + Cl^-$$

In water with a high pH, the hypochlorous acid (HOCl) will dissociate into hydrogen and hypochlorite ions; with decreasing pH, the ions will shift back to hypochlorous acid. The hypochlorite ion is of particular importance because it in turn dissociates into a chlorine ion and atomic oxygen, which is a strong oxidizing agent and causes extensive gill damage to fish.

When molecular chlorine and hypochlorite ions react with water, they result in different proportions of chlorine, hypochlorous acid, and hypochlorite ion, depending on the pH of the water. These three chlorine-containing species are called the free chlorine residual, and all have disinfectant properties. However, all are toxic to fish. Chlorine and hypochlorite also react with nitrogenous organic compounds, including ammonia, to form chloramines, which are also toxic to fish. The term "combined chlorine residual" refers to chloramines. The term "total chlorine" is the sum of free chlorine plus chloramines. Residual chlorine levels should be 0.003 ppm or less to avoid damage to fish. Removal of chlorine compounds is discussed in the previous chapter.

Chloramines : Some city water supplies have high levels of organic compounds. These can interact with chlorine to form trihalomethanes, which have a cancer-producing potential. The solution to this problem has been to add ammonia and chlorine at the water plant to form chloramines, which have the ability to disinfect water but will not react with organic substances to form the carcinogenic trihalomethanes. While the production of chloramines is acceptable from a public health aspect, fish producers, hobbyists, and retailers in some cities where chloramines are produced have noted fish mortalities. Methods of chloramine removal are discussed in the previous chapter.

Dissolved oxygen: The amount of oxygen in water is affected by many variables. For example, warmer water will increase the metabolic rate of the fish and hence their demand for oxygen, but warm water will dissolve less oxygen than colder water. The solubility of oxygen (as well as other gases) also decreases with increasing salinity levels. The amount of surface area also affects oxygen exchange between air and water; creation of surface turbulence by aerators or by the outflow of water pumps will maximize this. In fish-production ponds, oxygen levels can fluctuate widely because of temperature variations, demand for oxygen by decomposition processes, and surface turbulence. In closed systems such as aquaria which have adequate aeration and water circulation, low oxygen levels are rare.

Oxygen levels are reported as parts per million. A dissolved oxygen level of 5 ppm would be adequate for tropical fish. Dissolved oxygen levels in a sampling of pet shops in the Athens, Georgia area ranged from 5 ppm to 8 ppm.

Elements associated with fish excretion and nitrification: While ammonia, nitrites, and nitrates are not normally associated with fresh water supplies, both are commonly found in aquaria for a finite period of time soon after the aquarium is set up. This period of high ammonia and nitrites, previously discussed, is referred to as the conditioning period or the run-in period. The basis of

Impurities in an aquarium lead to fish stress and disease. Understanding the nitrogen cycle and testing the water regularly for nitrites are important. Bi-weekly water changes by "hydro-cleaning" dirt and debris from the gravel allows nitrifying bacteria to cultivate; foam filters also are excellent for the cultivation of aerobic bacteria.

NITROGEN CYCLE

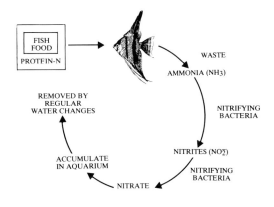

FISH FOOD
PROTEIN-N

WASTE
AMMONIA (NH_3)

REMOVED BY
REGULAR
WATER CHANGES

NITRIFYING
BACTERIA

ACCUMULATE
IN AQUARIUM

NITRITES (NO_2^-)

NITRIFYING
BACTERIA

NITRATE

the problem is that when the aquarium is initially set up, there are insufficient numbers of ammonia- and nitrite-oxidizing bacteria (nitrifying bacteria) to utilize these nitrogenous products. Both ammonia and nitrites are toxic for fish; methods to avoid these problems are covered under a later section. When chloramines present in tap water are passed through activated carbon canisters, ammonia results from the dissociation of chloramines. If the carbon canister is not changed regularly, *Nitrosomonas* bacteria can colonize in the carbon canister, resulting in nitrite production. This problem would only occur in areas where chloramines are present in water and an activated carbon filter is used to remove chlorine. Regular testing for nitrites and/or frequent changing of the activated carbon would prevent this problem from developing.

Other elements in water: Copper in water can kill fish, but most cases of copper toxicity are the result of man-made problems rather than natural copper levels in water, which are rarely over 0.05 ppm. New copper pipes, especially in soft-water areas, could leach out enough copper ions to reach toxic levels for some species. Older copper pipes which have been subjected to oxidation present no problem. Addition of copper to control algae in ponds or for the control of certain diseases can lead to fish mortalities if dosage is not regulated.

In city water supplies, other heavy metals such as zinc or lead should not cause problems; however, zinc toxicities have occurred from placing fish in galvanized vats. Iron in water is not a problem to most aquarists, since it is only toxic in the ferrous (soluble) form which occurs when water is very low in oxygen and high in carbon dioxide—conditions which are not found in well-aerated aquaria. Aeration quickly oxidizes iron to insoluble forms (rust) which are not toxic.

Chemicals used for control of diseases of plants or animals are usually toxic to fish if present in high enough concentrations. Their levels in municipal water supplies are too low to cause public health problems or problems for the aquarist. Water from contaminated wells or rivers could contain a variety of toxins. Many state public health laboratories conduct testing of water for known contaminants. However, water taken from rivers in which various industrial chemicals have been spilled may result in prob-

lems for the aquarist—especially if sensitive fish are being raised or bred.

Using Water Additives and Conditioners

Many preparations sold under a variety of trade names may be useful to the aquarist interested in varying water conditions to meet specific needs. Some of these include:

Dechlorinating solutions: Most dechlorinating solutions sold contain sodium thiosulfate. A suitable solution consists of a 1 percent solution of sodium thiosulfate in water. At this concentration, 0.5 millimeters (10 drops) of the solution per 10 gallons (38 liters) of water will remove chlorine in most city water supplies with an ample safety factor. This reaction is almost instantaneous. In practice, dechlorination can be done as fresh water is added to the aquarium or even several minutes afterwards, since at tap-water levels the harmful effects of chlorine are not immediate.

Buffers: These are useful in areas with relatively low alkalinity or natural buffering capacity. Such waters are easily adjusted to any desirable pH. In waters with high alkalinity levels (highly buffered), pH adjustment is difficult. To lower pH, the water may have to be partially softened prior to adding a buffer. Since buffers are designed to keep the pH at a desired level, the amount of buffer added to water will not significantly change the pH but will only serve to keep the pH stable for a longer period of time or until the next water change.

pH adjusters: These consist of chemicals or solutions of chemicals which, when added to water, will either raise or lower the pH. There is some danger of lowering or elevating pH to dangerous extremes. pH adjusters may not hold pH levels as long as buffers will and may have to be added more frequently to maintain a desired pH level. Baking soda (sodium bicarbonate, $NaHCO_3$) will elevate pH. Normally, a solution is made and small amounts are added to the aquarium, with frequent pH testing to avoid excessively high pH levels.

Dilute solutions of phosphoric acid or hydrochloric acid have been used to reduce pH. In many areas of the country, the addition of monobasic sodium phosphate (NaH_2PO_4) to water will decrease pH. As opposed to acids, monobasic sodium phosphate is not dangerous to handle and can be purchased in aquarium retail outlets or chemical supply companies. In some areas of

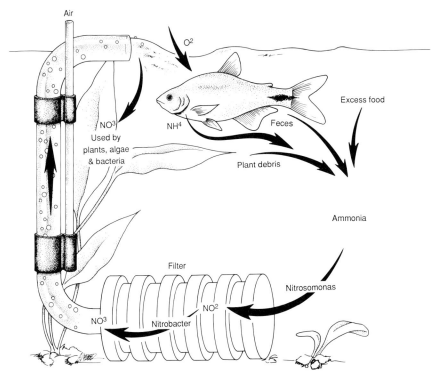

The nitrogen cycle in a freshwater aquarium. Ammonia from fish waste and from bacterial decomposition of protein-containing foods is converted to nitrites by *Nitrosomonas* bacteria. These nitrites are then converted to nitrates by other bacteria (*Nitrobacter*). Living organisms, including algae and a variety of bacteria, utilize nitrates as nutrients. Plants, in turn, provide oxygen to the environment and a supply of food to plant-eating fish. The conversion of ammonia to nitrites and then to nitrates is called nitrification.

the country, it may form a precipitate (which will result in cloudy water); this is harmless to fish and will settle out within a few days.

Water softeners: As mentioned earlier, the difference between hard and soft water lies in the amount of calcium and magnesium salts. Harder water almost always has higher alkalinity (a higher pH), more carbonates, bicarbonates, and hydroxides, and a good buffering capacity. Since this type of water is naturally buffered at a higher pH, lowering the pH will be difficult unless the water is softened using ion-exchange resins. Ion-exchange resins are available which will remove calcium and magnesium ions as well as carbonates.

The placement of peat in a filter also will soften water, as well as reduce pH levels, presumably by the release of humic acids. Ammonia adsorbers which have ion-exchange capabilities will not only adsorb ammonia but will soften water and stabilize pH at approximately 7.5.

The aquarist is always advised to measure hardness levels carefully and to monitor pH levels when using softeners, buffers, or pH adjusters. Overuse of softeners could deplete essential minerals required by the fish and could cause radical lowering of pH by reducing alkalinity.

Ammonia removers: Ammonia adsorbers sold in aquarium supply stores are naturally occurring clays (zeolites) which have ion-exchange properties. They are efficient in reducing ammonia during the run-in period, but nitrite production is not significantly reduced. Zeolites incorporated into a filtering system will tend to stabilize pH and soften water. They can be easily regenerated by immersion in a 1 percent salt solution. Liquid ammonia removers are also commercially available.

Nitrification starters: A variety of products are sold to reduce the elevations of ammonia and nitrites during the initial conditioning period of a new aquarium system. Some of these products consist of freeze-dried bacteria—presumably species of *Nitrosomonas* and *Nitrobacter,* which oxidize ammonia to nitrite and nitrites to nitrates, respectively. Laboratory tests using a wide variety of such products

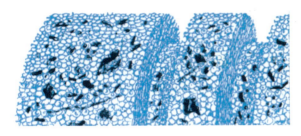

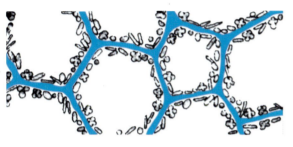

Filtration based on a continuous nitrogen cycle is referred to as biological filtration. Waste products are broken down biologically into a relatively harmless substance, nitrate. Mechanical filtration is based on the removal of impurities from the water through filters (above). Proper filters, containing activated carbon or charcoal, allow an equal flow of oxygen through the filter cartridge (below); this ensures colonization of nitrifying bacteria and a continually functioning cycle.
Source: Tetra Archives.

have failed to demonstrate that they significantly lessen the conditioning period.

Problems During the First Weeks After Setup

Understanding nitrification: After fish are added to a new aquarium, the water chemistry of the aquarium gradually changes as a result of the excretion of fish wastes and the presence of uneaten food scraps. Unless initially seeded with a source of nitrifying bacteria, any new closed aquatic system will pass through a period characterized by elevated levels of ammonia and nitrites. This run-in or conditioning period ends when nitrites disappear from the aquarium. This period is variable and can only be determined by periodic water testing.

At different times during the conditioning period, water testing for ammonia, nitrites, and nitrates will give varying results. A test done a few days after the fish are introduced into the aquarium may result in a positive ammonia test only. After a few more days, a test of the water may be positive for both ammonia and nitrites. Toward the end of the conditioning period, nitrites will gradually disappear. Subsequent testing will reveal the presence of nitrates only, which signals the completion of the conditioning period, and additional fish may be introduced. The entire conditioning period may last from four to twelve weeks.

How to minimize the run-in or conditioning period: Although some run-in period is inevitable, whether this initial period of elevated ammonia and nitrates is seriously stressful or relatively mild depends upon the aquarist's actions.

Prior to the addition of fish, condition the aquarium by seeding it with bacteria and a suitable nutrient for the bacteria. Salts of ammonia can be used, as can urea (10 ppm). This system can be accelerated by seeding the tank with some gravel from a conditioned tank, or if such is not available, adding a cup of organic soil (such as from a compost pile) to provide nitrifying bacteria. If organic soil is used, it is a good idea to mix the soil with a quart (about 1 liter) of water, shake briskly for a minute or two, and then filter the mixture through a few layers of cheesecloth prior to adding it to the aquarium.

With any of these methods, water should be checked for ammonia and nitrites periodically. In the event that water test kits are not available, frequent (twice a week) water changes of 50 percent or more will solve many problems. Massive daily water changes for five or six days may be needed to keep nitrite levels below a toxic level.

For immediate conditioning, add 20 percent of used or biologically active gravel from a conditioned aquarium, or place a conditioned foam filter in the new aquarium. In some cases, addition of conditioned gravel or foam filters may greatly reduce the levels of ammonia and nitrites as well as shorten the conditioning period. Failure to eliminate the conditioning period completely most likely results from not adding enough gravel or gravel with active bacteria.

Start by adding a very few hardy fish for the first month or two. Then add additional fish over time until the capacity of the aquarium is reached.

Toxicities associated with the conditioning period: Ammonia can be present in two forms, as ammonia (NH_3) which is toxic to fish and as an

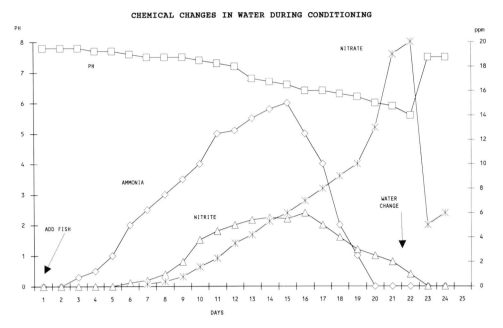

Ammonia, nitrate, and nitrite levels during conditioning when the water is not given the recommended changes. Conditioning ends when nitrites and ammonia are absent. This requires variable lengths of time. In the example shown above, it occurred after about twenty-three days. In an established conditioned aquarium, ammonia and nitrites ordinarily should be undetectable. Nitrates, on the other hand, are normal and indicate that the biological filtration system is operating properly. When water was finally changed, nitrate levels were reduced and pH was readjusted.

ammonium ion (NH_4^+) which is nontoxic. The percentage of these forms depends on the pH. The higher the pH, the more ammonia will be present. For this reason, the pH values of freshwater aquaria are best kept close to neutral (pH 7).

Ammonia toxicity is more of a problem with saltwater fish than with freshwater fish for two reasons. One is that saltwater aquaria are kept at a pH between 7.8 and 8.3, so any ammonia present has a higher proportion in the toxic form. The other is that saltwater fish swallow water continuously, a behavior which results in the absorption of more ammonia than freshwater fish, which do not drink. Consequently, a positive ammonia test is more serious in saltwater aquaria than in freshwater aquaria.

Ammonia can result from lack of biological filtration, which may occur during the conditioning period, from overloading the capacity of the biological filter by the addition of too many fish, or from overfeeding, which overwhelms the capacity of the filter to oxidize the excess ammonia resulting from degradation of protein.

The toxic effects of ammonia can be acute or chronic. Very high levels of ammonia may kill fish in a short period of time by decreasing the oxygen-carrying capacity of blood and interfering with neural function and with osmoregulation.

The chronic effects of ammonia poisoning are related to hyperplasia and hypertrophy, or thickening, of gill epithelium. These result in decreased gas exchange and decreased excretion of ammonia, which in turn lead to increases in blood pH and osmoregulation problems, including the inhibition of the transport of monovalent cations. The toxicity of ammonia is intensified with increasing temperature and low oxygen levels.

How to solve ammonia problems: When ammonia appears in the conditioning period, it may be present alone or in combination with nitrite. If the ammonia accumulation is not accompanied by nitrite elevations, the problem can be approached in one of three ways.

1. Water changes are the best way to immediately solve ammonia problems. Water changes, along with the introduction of a conditioned foam filter or conditioned gravel, are a good idea if the aquarium has not passed through the condition-

ing period. The more conditioned gravel added, the faster the response will be.

2. If the pH of the water is in the 7.5 to 8.4 range, decreasing the pH to neutrality will decrease the toxicity by converting ammonia to nontoxic ammonium.

3. Ammonia adsorbers (zeolites) can be used to remove ammonia. However, if they are used during the conditioning period, the development of nitrites will not be inhibited and may still cause problems.

4. Zeolites will not absorb ammonia from salt water. Ammonia problems in saltwater aquaria must be solved by increasing biofiltration, avoiding overstocking and overfeeding, and instituting a program of water changes.

After taking remedial action by any of the above methods, ammonia levels should be monitored frequently to determine whether the problem has been solved. Additionally, fish should be observed closely. They should eat better and be more active in response to correction of ammonia problems.

How to solve nitrite problems: Nitrite is generally toxic in both freshwater and marine aquaria. When nitrites are absorbed by fish, nitrite ions combine with hemoglobin to form methemoglobin, which cannot transport oxygen, resulting in oxygen deprivation and death of the fish. Nitrite toxicity is diagnosed by positive nitrite tests of water and by detection of brown blood on postmortem examination of fish.

Nitrites are usually present during the run-in period or whenever the biological activity of the filter is destroyed. However, some freshwater and saltwater fish are resistant to the effects of nitrites, probably because these fish do not adsorb nitrites or because they have the ability to metabolize or excrete nitrites quickly. For example, channel catfish are very susceptible to nitrites and will concentrate nitrite ions far beyond those levels found in water. Goldfish are much less susceptible to nitrite toxicity than are channel catfish, and various species of tetras appear to be completely resistant. Consequently, in a mixed community tank during the conditioning period, some species will die while others will survive the effects of nitrites.

Nitrite problems can be solved in a number of ways.

1. The quickest way to rid an aquarium of nitrites is to change the water. In a home aquarium or even a large central system, nitrites will accumulate during the conditioning period until *Nitrobacter* bacteria have proliferated sufficiently on filter materials to a point where nitrites are cleared. Water may have to be changed daily for four to seven days before the nitrite levels drop to safe (0.1 ppm) levels. Massive amounts of water need to be changed to dilute nitrites to safe levels. In some cases the gravel also may have to be flushed to remove nitrite ions from it.

2. Moving fish to a "hospital" or holding aquarium will stop the adsorption of nitrites immediately. Fish can be returned to the main aquarium after water tests are negative for nitrites. Water quality in the hospital aquarium need not be a problem, since the fish should stay in it no longer than four to seven days. The hospital aquarium can be as simple as a large plastic pail. Water quality can be maintained by water changes, but aeration and mechanical filtration are required. A small corner-box filter is suitable for such uses, especially if loaded with ammonia adsorbers.

3. If you had added gravel or a foam filter from a conditioned aquarium when the new aquarium was initially set up, it would have either eliminated ammonia and nitrite problems or greatly reduced the length of the run-in period and the amounts of offending toxins produced therein. When a nitrite problem is encountered after the aquarium is established, the addition of a small amount of conditioned gravel will not reduce nitrite levels as appreciably or quickly as a conditioned foam filter will. There is more water movement through the sponge, which has more surface area with nitrifying bacteria.

Various products are available which claim either to shorten or to eliminate the conditioning period. Some of the products are advertised as containing nitrifying bacteria. However, in the face of a nitrite problem, the addition of a relatively few active bacteria would not appreciably reduce nitrite levels quickly enough to avoid severe stress or death of fish.

4. Raising the concentration of table salt (NaCl) in aquarium water to 100 ppm will prevent the uptake of nitrites by some fish. Approximately 38 grams (1.16 ounces), or about 7 teaspoonful, of salt added to 10 gallons (38 liters) of water will attain this level. Many characins and cyprinids, as well as some types of ornamental catfish (*Corydoras* species), will not tolerate such salt concentrations, however.

5. Methylene blue has been used to treat methemoglobinemia in humans and domestic animals. However, its addition to aquarium water containing nitrites does not effect a cure, probably because it is not readily absorbed by fish. Furthermore, methylene blue has been shown to kill nitrifying bacteria in aquaria. Its use is not indicated to treat nitrite toxicities in the aquarium.

The Established Aquarium

When an aquarium has an efficient nitrification system, regular water changes with simultaneous cleaning of the gravel should keep water conditions optimal. A conditioned aquarium will have no detectable levels of ammonia or nitrites, and will have a pH between approximately 6.5 and 7.8 if freshwater or 7.6 to 8.4 if saltwater.

If water changes are not done on a regular basis, a conditioned aquarium may undergo chemical changes as a direct result of the process of nitrification and accumulation of waste products, collectively referred to as dissolved organics.

Trouble-Shooting Problems

In aquaria where water is low in alkalinity and unbuffered, hydrogen ions accumulate and pH drops. Severe drops, usually to pH lower than 5.5,

An example of typical chemical changes in an unbuffered established aquarium in which water is low in alkalinity. Nitrification and accumulation of waste organics can cause a sudden severe acidity, called a pH crash.

THE ESTABLISHED AQUARIUM

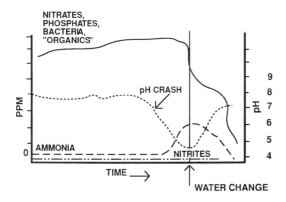

can lead to an inhibition of nitrification and the accumulation of ammonia related to the inhibition of *Nitrosomonas*. The accompanying figures illustrate changes in an established aquarium which has gone through such a pH crash.

Ammonia/ammonium problems: Ammonia levels should remain undetectable in an established aquarium unless the system is overloaded with fish, or decomposing excess food results in ammonia levels which surpass the capacity of the biological filtration system. A positive ammonia test after overfeeding is common. The ammonia spikes from one overfeeding incident will disappear within twenty-four hours. A dead fish will also add to the ammonia load in the aquarium. Occasionally, a cadaver will remain hidden by plants and go unremoved, leading to such a problem.

Transitory pulses of ammonia can also result from the use of medications such as antibiotics and some parasiticides. Removal of the medicant by a water change will usually restore nitrification and eliminate ammonia. Note also that the presence of some medications, such as formaldehyde, in the water will give a false test for ammonia.

Nitrite problems: In an established aquarium, nitrites should be undetectable. While ammonia levels may increase due to pH drops, nitrites usually are not observed. Nitrites can appear after adding some medications to an aquarium, but as in the case of ammonia, nitrite levels will drop after the bacteria-inhibiting medication is removed by a water change. Some parasiticides such as methylene blue have been shown to destroy nitrifying bacteria, resulting in nitrite elevations.

pH problems: Fluctuations of pH in an aquarium will depend on several factors, including the amount of fish, level of organics, nitrification, and the buffering capacity (alkalinity) of the water.

The relative acidity or alkalinity of water is measured by pH. During the process of nitrification, hydrogen ions are given off by the oxidation of ammonia to nitrites by *Nitrosomonas*. The greater the amount of biological activity (nitrification), the more hydrogen ions are released. Organic materials in the aquarium also release hydrogen ions as they are decomposed by nitrification. Overstocking and overfeeding of fish thus can lead to pH problems, especially if the water is soft and poorly buffered. Finally, the natural alkalinity of the water (i.e., the levels of carbonates, bicarbonates, and hydroxides) determines the extent to which the water is buffered against pH drops. In some areas of the country where alkalinity levels in the water are very low, the pH of an aquarium must be watched carefully and buffers may need to be added.

Correcting low pH: The following methods may be used to correct low pH.

1. A water change will replenish the natural buffers in the water supply, but if these are low, pH may revert to low levels within a matter of days.

2. If low pH is a recurring problem, the water can be buffered using commercially available buffers preset to various pH values, usually between pH 6.5 and 7.5. If such buffers are used, they must be used in sufficient amounts to hold the pH at the desired level until the next water change. The amount of buffer to add can be determined by trial and error. Adding more buffer does not significantly change the pH, but only extends the time that the pH of the water will be held at the desired level. Generally, in soft-water areas where acid rain is a problem, buffers should be added with every water change.

3. Dolomitic limestone, coral gravel, or oyster shell can be incorporated into an outside filter or an inside corner filter. Ammonia adsorbers also buffer freshwater aquaria to approximately pH 7.5. The amount to use must be established by trial and error. For each 10 gallons (38 liters) of water, 100 grams (about 3 ounces) of any of the above substrates should be adequate for pH adjustment. With time, the natural carbonates elaborated from these natural elements will become exhausted, and fresh materials may be required. Another disadvantage is that dolomitic limestone may result in a pH which is too high, unlike commercially available buffers which are set to adjust the pH to a specific level.

4. Sodium bicarbonate is a pH adjuster rather than a buffer. If added in excess to an aquarium, the pH can be elevated to unacceptably high levels. A 10 percent solution of baking soda can be safely used to raise the pH of an aquarium. Gradually add small amounts, with frequent testing of the pH. Unless extreme care is taken during this process, the pH can quickly jump to very high levels. Also, since sodium bicarbonate by itself is not a buffer, the desired pH may not hold for very long.

Correcting high pH: High-pH water is usually hard, high in alkalinity, and well buffered. Consequently, lowering the pH of this water often requires removing some of the natural hardness and alkalinity. Mixing softened with unsoftened water may result in water with a desirable pH. Determining the proper proportions must be done by trial and error.

1. By softening the water with a mixed resin (anionic and cationic exchanger), the natural buffering capacity of the water will be reduced and the pH in the aquarium will most likely be lowered. One may use softeners sold for residential use, large canisters, or small units sold exclusively for aquarium use. All contain ion-exchange resins. Distilled water (or water treated by reverse-osmosis processes which remove all minerals) can be used if some unsoftened water is added to the softened water. Consider 1 parts of reverse-osmosis water to 1 part of tap water; some experimentation with proportions may be required. Commercial water softeners remove calcium and magnesium ions by an exchange process with sodium ions.

In addition to commercially available ion-exchange resins, water can be softened by ammonia-adsorbing clays which are in fact natural ion exchangers. The softening ability of ammonia adsorbers can be renewed by soaking the chips in a strong salt solution (3 percent salt) for a few hours.

2. Monobasic sodium phosphate (NaH_2PO_4) may be added slowly, with frequent pH testing. In very hard water, a precipitate may develop, causing cloudy water. This causes no harm to the fish and will settle out in time.

3. Dilute solutions of acids such as phosphoric or hydrochloric acids have been used to reduce pH. In addition to the obvious dangers of handling strong acids, acids are adjusters and unless added slowly with frequent monitoring, they could cause pH levels to drop below optimal levels. Frequently, such acids are used to adjust pH in commercial establishments with central filtration systems.

4. Commercially available buffers are highly effective in soft-water areas, but are not effective for decreasing pH in very hard water. However, after the water is softened, buffers can be added to adjust pH.

5. Placement of some types of peat moss in the filter will soften water and lower pH, but water will take on a brown color from the tannins present. This is not harmful to fish and can be removed by filtering water through activated carbon.

A distended-end siphon tube allows easy removal of accumulated wastes from the aquarium's gravel bed.

Nitrate problems: Nitrates are the end product of nitrification and are essentially nontoxic for freshwater fish. In the aquarium, the appearance of nitrates suggests that the biological filtration system is operating. Generally, nitrates will increase in an aquarium, but levels will be reduced by the plants, including algae, and by certain nitrate-utilizing bacteria such as *Pseudomonas* and *Aeromonas,* which may be pathogenic for fish.

Plants should not be introduced into an aquarium until the conditioning period is complete and nitrates are present. Normally, regular water changes will keep nitrate levels between 5 and 25 ppm, depending on the frequency of change.

Phosphates, which also stimulate plant and algal growth, also increase in an aquarium over time. Under normal aquarium conditions, where

Water plants don't always receive the attention they deserve. Regular water changes, fertilizer, elimination of old or brown leaves, and proper illumination help maintain a healthy aquarium as seen at right. *Source:* Tetra Archives.

water is partially replaced every two to three weeks, phosphorous compounds pose no problem to the health of fish. Some city water supplies may have high concentrations of phosphates.

Organics: The term "organics" covers a wide variety of substances and can include products from any living creature within an aquarium system. In addition to the obvious fish and plants, aquarium water contains a variety of bacteria and organic molecules resulting from the metaboic processes of plants, fish, bacteria, and all of the phytoplanktonic and zooplanktonic forms found in an aquarium.

Pheromones may accumulate in aquaria and act as growth inhibitors or even inhibitors of the immune system of fish. Despite a paucity of knowledge in this area, such putative inhibitors are removed by regular water changes and, possibly, through the regular use of activated carbon in the filter system.

Maintaining a Healthy Aquarium

Avoiding problems is always preferable to solving them. Simple preventative measures will increase your chances of maintaining a trouble-free aquarium.

The importance of water changes: Fresh water

dilutes accumulated waste products, including ammonia, nitrites, and nitrates; corrects pH problems; and reduces the numbers of pathogenic bacteria and parasites which may be present during a disease.

The amount of water to change should be proportional to the number, size, and type of fish in the aquarium. As a rule of thumb, many aquarists change 20 to 30 percent of the water every seven to fourteen days. In special cases where an aquarium may be overloaded with fish, changes of up to 80 to 90 percent may be required. In such cases, it is important to avoid sudden temperature and pH shifts.

Planted aquaria require some periodic water changes, but because of the plants' ability to use nitrates, excessive water changes may reduce the vitality of the plants. On the other hand, some plants do not prosper under autotrophic water conditions and actually relish the reduction of nitrates that follows partial water changes. In the author's experience, changes of 10 to 20 percent of the water every two weeks did not alter the vitality of plant life.

Water changes should be done so that accumulated wastes are removed from the gravel bed by use of a distended-end siphon tube. Gravel should be cleaned with every water change. By inserting the end of the siphon tube deep into the gravel, detritus is removed which otherwise would clog the gravel bed, depriving nitrifying bacteria of oxygen and ammonia and/or nitrites. Such clogged areas would develop into anaerobic pockets where nitrates and sulfates could convert to nitrites and hydrogen sulfide, both of which are toxic to fish. The cleaning of gravel in this manner will not dislodge nitrifying bacteria from the surface of the gravel particles.

The benefit of plants in the aquarium: Plants in the aquarium provide cover, hiding places, territorial limits, and protection for very young fish. More important, plants utilize nitrates and phosphates, and consequently assist in maintaining water quality in the aquarium. Planted aquaria have been referred to as "natural" or "balanced" aquaria. Strictly speaking, a balanced aquarium is one in which the production of fish wastes is utilized completely by plants. Plants provide oxygen for the fish while consuming carbon dioxide, nitrates, and phosphates.

Keeping fish healthy: For a healthy, thriving aquarium, remember these points.

1. Initially add only a few fish to avoid rapid buildup of ammonia and nitrites. Only add additional fish after thirty to forty-five days, when a good biological system has been established.
2. During the initial conditioning period, test the water every day for ammonia, nitrites, and pH. If ammonia and/or nitrites are present, make a water change.
3. For tropical fish, maintain the water at a temperature no lower than 70 degrees F (21 degrees C) and preferably at 75 degrees F (24 degrees C). Goldfish and other cold-water fish tolerate lower temperatures.
4. Feed fish a high-quality food in amounts which they will consume in three to five minutes. Although most aquarists feed their fish once or twice a day, several feedings of smaller amounts of food are desirable if time permits. Avoid overfeeding, for this can lead to water-quality problems. Remove excess uneaten food in case of accidental overfeeding.
5. Periodically change the water and clean the gravel. A distended-end siphon tube will remove fine silt from the gravel without removing gravel. The amount of water to change depends on the number of fish. Many aquarists change 20 to 30 percent of the water every seven to fourteen days.
6. Quarantine new fish prior to adding them to your aquarium.
7. At the first sign of a problem, check water for pH, ammonia, and nitrites.

Selected References

Baensch, U., and Baensch, H. A. 1975. *Beginners Aquarium Digest.* Tetra Press.

Moe, M. A., Jr. 1982. *The Marine Aquarium Handbook: Beginner to Breeder.* Marathon, Fla.: Norns Publ. Co.

Hawkins, A. D., ed. 1981. *Aquarium Systems.* New York: Academic Press.

Spotte, S. 1979. *Fish and Invertebrate Culture: Water Management in Closed Systems.* 2nd ed. New York: Wiley-Interscience.

———. 1979. *Seawater Aquariums: The Captive Environment.* New York: Wiley-Interscience.

Ward, B. 1985. *The Aquarium Fish Survival Manual.* New York: Barrons.

Aquatic Plants and the Natural Aquarium

Janice R. Matthews

A well-planted fish tank is undeniably a thing of beauty. It is also a contributor to fish health. Most fish behave more normally, display better coloration and finnage, and reproduce more successfully in well-planted surroundings. Many aquarists feel that tanks stocked solely with fish are akin to old-style zoos in which animals languish in barren, barred cages. Just as zoos around the world are now seeking better ways to replicate natural environments, so tropical fish hobbyists are becoming increasingly interested in replicating natural environments for their finned companions.

Most aquarists landscape their tanks with plants, either living or artificial. Both types of landscaping have advantages and disadvantages, and for this reason, some people combine them both in the tank. Artificial plants provide instant greenery of an admittedly decorative and often amazingly realistic appearance. They do not die, turn thin, or become eaten (but will eventually fade and become brittle after long immersion). They are easy to maintain, for they require no special lighting and no attention to differing needs. They can be cleaned and sterilized if the need should arise. Some types provide good shelter for fry or timid fish species. However, quite obviously, artificial plants cannot function biologically like living plants—a critical point in the closed, interdependent world of the aquarium.

The Concept of the Natural Aquarium

The natural environment for most tropical fish includes live plants, and in the aquarium living plants serve many of the same functions that they do in the wild. Plants provide shelter, shade, and for some fish, food. Leafy plants compete with their tiny relatives, the algae, for nutrients and thus help reduce or eliminate the "green water" that results from algae disbursed throughout the aquarium water. They increase the browsing surface for fish that eat tiny water animals such as rotifers. Finally, they "balance" the aquarium, a concept which comes up frequently enough to require some explanation.

The balanced aquarium: Fish and plants complement each other in two important ways. First, well-lit plants release oxygen, which fish need, and in return require carbon dioxide, which fish release. Second, plants use nitrogenous fish wastes as nutrients for their own growth, thus helping prevent a buildup of toxic nitrogen products in the aquarium.

This natural recycling of nitrogen, called the nitrogen cycle, involves bacteria as well. Ammonia, a decomposition product of fish waste, is oxidized to nitrites by one group of bacteria. A second group uses nitrites and produces nitrates. Both the ammonia and the nitrates can be utilized directly by algae and leafy plants. (For a complete nitrogen cycle, fish would then eat the plants, in which the nitrogen of the nitrates is combined with carbohydrates to form amino acids, the basic units from which proteins are synthesized.) In an aquarium, where one is continually adding nitrogenous compounds via fish waste and extra food, an abundant supply of healthy plants can provide an important margin of safety against the excessive accumulation of nitrates.

The natural aquarium: The term "natural aquarium" can mean different things to different people. For some, it simply means any aquarium with both fish and living plants. To others, it may mean a balanced aquarium, in which an attempt has been made to make the complementary relationship of fish and plants as self-sufficient as possible. To still others, it can refer to an attempt to simulate specific natural habitats such as the Amazon basin or a Southeast Asian stream.

In Europe, where home aquaria have been part of the scene for much longer than in the United States, nearly every aquarium includes living plants. Gaining favor is the "Leiden" style aquarium, in which plants, not fish, are the major focus of the tank. Whichever definition one espouses, live plants are a critical component of the natural aquarium.

Growing Healthy Aquarium Plants

Aquatic plants are not difficult to keep healthy and attractive, as long as their basic requirements are met. As is the case for terrestrial plants, these include adequate light and fertilization, a suitable growing medium, and the right temperature. Preventing problems always takes less time and ef-

Below is an aquarium that simulates an Amazon basin habitat, with a layout of the plant population.

1. 30 *Vallisneria spiralis*
2. 2 *Hygrophila difformis*
3. 1 *Samolus floribundus*
4. 1 *Echinodorus horizontalis*
5. 6 *Ammania gracilis*
6. 12 *Egeria densa*
7. 2 *Hygrophila difformis*
8. 3 *Hygrophila stricta*
9. 2-3 *Anubias barteri*
10. 12 *Cryptocoryne wendtii*
11. 5-7 *Heteranthera zosteraefolia*

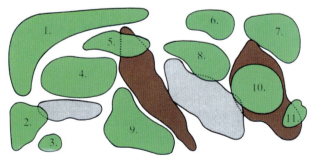

fort than attempting correction once things have gone awry. Short-cutting these requirements will only lead to trouble.

Lighting for the natural aquarium: In an aquarium with artificial plants, lighting is a fairly flexible affair. However, when living plants are kept, lighting requirements become crucial. Plants must have light of the proper sort for photosynthesis, the crucial process by which they combine carbon dioxide and water in the presence of light energy to form the carbohydrates upon which nearly all living things depend for energy.

Light is made up of a number of light waves of different lengths. Some of these our eye interprets as different colors. Others lie outside our visual range. In a somewhat similar way, the light-sensitive plant pigment chlorophyll is sensitive to certain lengths of light waves, namely the longer red-to-yellow waves and the shorter blue-to-violet waves. These waves are absorbed by chlorophyll, providing the energy input which photosynthesis requires.

The light required by aquarium plants is best provided artificially, for if the aquarium is placed where it will receive direct sunlight, excessive algal growth will be a continual problem. Light fixtures with incandescent bulbs are cheaper to purchase, and fish with orange or red colors look brighter under them. However, they are more expensive to operate, give off heat, and fail to provide optimum light for plants. Aquatic plants kept under incandescent light will soon show thin stalks, and their leaves will turn pale.

The type of fluorescent light called full spectrum best simulates sunlight in a home aquarium. Fluorescent tubes labeled as "wide spectrum" or "broad spectrum" are roughly equivalent. Any of these should be satisfactory if used at the appropriate wattage for the tank and type of plants. A knowledgeable retailer can recommend good

The aquarium pictured below exemplifies a Southeast Asian habitat, the typical plants mapped out at bottom.

1. 6 *Microsorium pteropus*
2. 15 *Microsorium pteropus*
3. 5 *Microsorium pteropus*
4. 25 *Cryptocoryne affinis*
5. 12 *Rotala rotundifolia*
6. 15 *Cryptocoryne walkeri*
7. 7 *Vallisneria spiralis*
8. 5 *Cryptocoryne balanese*
9. 6 *Limnophila sessiflora*
10. 4 *Hygrophila difformis*

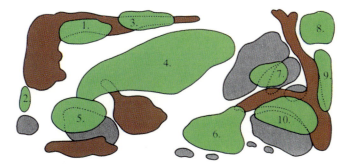

brands of plant-stimulating fluorescent lights.

As a rule of thumb, aquaria should receive an average of twelve hours of light a day. An automatic timer is relatively inexpensive and can be helpful. A second rule of thumb is to use 1.5 watts of lighting per gallon of water. Thus, a 15-watt tube would be sufficient for a 10-gallon (38-liter) tank, but a 40-gallon (142-liter) tank would require two 30-watt tubes. Very deep aquaria (over 18 inches or about 45 centimeters) may require additional wattage and/or a longer duration of lighting each day. Use of very dark gravel may also increase lighting requirements.

Fluorescent lighting becomes dimmer as the tubes age, so they should be replaced when they have reached about half their advertised life expectancy rather than being used until they quit. As a general guideline, when used an average of twelve hours per day, fluorescent tubes should be replaced every two years. (A sticker mounted on the inside or back of the lighting fixture can be annotated when bulbs are changed, much in the manner that a service record is kept on an automobile.)

Temperature and water quality: Some aquarium plants, being aquatic species which grow wild in North American lakes, streams, and marshes, grow well in an unheated aquarium. However, the tropical aquarium plant species do best at an average temperature of 75 degrees F (24 degrees C). They also do best when heat originates from the bottom of the aquarium and flows upward, a condition which can be met by using a submersible heater and a thermometer which is placed at the point where the gravel and water meet.

Plants grow best if their roots are not continually disturbed. Thus, a canister filter, outside power filter, or foam filter is a good choice for the natural aquarium. If an undergravel filter is preferred, one can use deep gravel (approximately 5 inches or 13 centimeters) to provide ample undisturbed root space and/or place the plants in pots with good potting soil covered with aquarium gravel to prevent soil from coming out of the pot. The latter system works surprisingly well.

Strong water circulation appears to be beneficial for the leaves of most aquatic plants. For this reason, experts recommend positioning a filter's water return in such a way as to provide a current through the leaves of the plants. However, unnecessary aeration should be avoided. An airstone drives out carbon dioxide, which plants consume, and increases oxygen, which plants are already releasing. Thus, it may disturb the very balance one is trying to create in the aquarium.

Like fish, aquatic plants also are sensitive to water quality and require frequent water changes to maintain proper pH and prevent the accumulation of excessive nitrogenous compounds. The schedules recommended for optimum fish health will keep aquarium plants thriving as well.

The planting medium and use of additives: Some aquarium plants have a floating habit and require no planting medium. Most, however, need a substrate in which to nourish themselves via healthy roots. A variety of gravels, sands, and rocks is available in pet stores. However, most experts recommend the time-honored standard #2 or #3 gravel for the aquarium with living plants. The gravel should be thoroughly washed in warm water in a separate container before it is placed in the aquarium.

In nature, aquatic plants would receive a continual influx of nutrients from their surroundings. To encourage better plant growth in the closed world of the aquarium, nutrients and fertilizers can be added to the gravel, the water, or both. A knowledgeable pet-store operator can guide you to appropriate commercially available products and their use. Other products are sold which coat plant leaves (and fish bodies) with a light colloid layer to protect them from injury. Such formulations also help plants absorb natural trace elements from the water, condition the tap water, and neutralize heavy metals.

Selecting Aquarium Plants

Although there are at least 3,500 aquatic and swamp plant species, in approximately a century of organized aquarium study, a mere dozen (and their variations) have come into such widespread use that they form the bulk of live plant sales today. Another forty or so additional species are found with varying frequency. Of the others which have been tried (and many, obviously, have not), most are unsuited for the aquarium for reasons of size, growth habit, or lack of adaptability to aquarium conditions.

The intent of this chapter is to provide concrete and helpful advice to help the fish-oriented aquarist maintain aquarium plants in a relatively

The "old faithful" aquarium plants with running stems (as pictured here and on the next two pages) do best with bright light and cool water. They grow rapidly and will require periodic trimming. This page, *Cabomba* and its flower.

trouble-free manner. For this reason, no attempt has been made to catalog the available array of plants. Rather, a handful of popular species are presented for your consideration. All are relatively tolerant of varying water conditions. Most do best under moderate to strong light, and propagate fairly freely on their own. They have stood the test of time and have much to recommend them.

Plants That Tolerate a Range of Water Temperatures

Most aquarium plants require a heated tank. A welcome exception is provided by five old faithful aquarium plant species that many of us knew as children. All of the latter require bright light but cool water, making them ideal candidates for the goldfish bowl or backyard fish pond. They will also survive in a moderately heated tank.

Three of these favorites—*Cabomba, Egeria (Anacharis),* and *Myriophyllum*—have running stems to which leaves are attached. They are usually bought in bunches and are sometimes sold under the false name of seaweed. The other two—*Vallisneria* and *Sagittaria*—are grasslike in form. Enormous quantities of each of these are marketed each year, and each is easily obtained and propagated. They also grow wild in North America.

Cabomba (Washington plant, fanwort, water-shield)

Perhaps the most widely sold aquarium plant, *Cabomba* is recognized by its frondlike, fan-shaped, light-green leaves that grow paired on opposite sides along a running stem. A member of the water-lily family Nymphaeaceae, it grows wild throughout all of North America except the extreme north.

In good condition, *Cabomba* is extremely attractive as a group planting, but it actually grows better when planted singly. It prefers cool, lime-free, soft water, and is tolerant of temperatures of 68 to 80 degrees F (20 to 27 degrees C). Unless kept in a strong light, *Cabomba* is apt to become long and stringy. Overly warm water will produce the same undesirable result. It is also brittle, and in a goldfish aquarium will soon be picked to pieces. Although *Cabomba* foliage forms a good refuge for young fish, it is not sufficiently dense to make a satisfactory spawning plant.

Egeria (Anacharis, Elodea, ditch-moss, Canadian pond weed)

Of the three common cool-water aquarium plants with leaves attached to a running stem, *Egeria* is the one with flattened, straplike leaves rather than feathery ones. Species are found growing wild from Canada to the midwestern United States, but apparently not in the Deep South.

This is perhaps the most rapidly growing of all the common aquarium plants. Long strands may grow an inch a day, especially in poor light. (However, the resulting plants are usually stringy and pale; if kept very long under poor illumination, the leaves turn brown and the plant rots.) Given enough light, it is very adaptable.

Egeria does best at temperatures of 48 to 70 degrees F (9 to 22 degrees C). It is lime-tolerant and capable of thriving in hard water. Because it can grow tall, it should be planted in bunches in the middle or back of the tank.

Tradition has it that this is the best oxygenator of the common aquarium plants, and some aquarists claim that a good supply of it clears green water. However, growth and oxygenating power actually bear little relationship to each other.

Myriophyllum (water milfoil, foxtail)

This plant's fine, hairlike leaves attached along a gracefully bending stem make a perfect bushy maze to catch spawn from egg-laying species and to hide young fry from hungry older fish. Several species of *Myriophyllum* are available.

Pictured here are *Egeria* and its surface-reaching flower (inset).

Myriophyllum.

best oxygenators and is quite hardy. Take care to match the species to your tank size. The leaves of larger varieties may grow longer than the water depth, bend at the surface, and shade out other plants.

Vallisneria is a good group plant and tolerates more extremes of temperature than many aquarium plants. For decades, it has been a mainstay of both heated and unheated aquaria. It prefers medium-hard water. Like any plant with a definite crown, *Vallisneria* should be planted carefully to keep the crown just at the surface of the gravel.

Individual *Vallisneria* plants are either male or female; nearly all are the latter and may bear little floating, white, cuplike flowers on the ends of long thin spirals rising from the plant's crown. However, few seeds ever germinate, and the plants propagate principally by runners.

Sagittaria (arrowhead)

This well-known aquarium plant has straplike

The long-leaved ones are better spawning plants, but the short-leaved ones are more durable. Both red and green varieties are available. Different species have various ranges throughout North America, and a South American form is also common in the aquarium trade.

Myriophyllum varies in form and color according to growing conditions. It requires good light, or it will become pale and the leaves will break off. A cold-water plant, it grows best below 68 degrees F (20 degrees C) and generally should not be planted in tanks with a water temperature above 75 degrees F (24 degrees C).

Myriophyllum naturally floats just below the surface, but can be easily fastened into clumps in the gravel so it will appear to be rooted. It is most often planted in bunches. Its tendency to break off and float suits the needs of fishes such as dwarf gouramis and sticklebacks which like to introduce plant material into their nests, but may offend a hobbyist's sense of neatness.

Vallisneria (eel grass, tape grass, corkscrew)

As its common names indicate, this aquatic plant has narrow leaves which each rise vertically in undulating lines from a common base. It grows wild from Nova Scotia to South Dakota, south to the Gulf of Mexico.

In strong light, *Vallisneria* multiplies rapidly to form a dense screen useful for covering the sides and back of the tank. It is considered one of the

Vallisneria are grasslike plants that thrive in cool water and bright light, both in the aquarium and in North American ponds and streams. Most forms have straight leaves.

Vallisneria spiralis, also known as corkscrew.

Sagittaria platyphylla, one of a large group of bog plants with variously shaped emergent leaves as well as straplike, underwater leaves.

leaves under water and arrow-shaped leaves above the water surface. These latter leaves of wild species are common along watery borders almost everywhere in North America, and form the basis for naming the plant after the mythological Sagittarius the Archer.

Sagittaria comes in a great many species, most of them bog plants rather than true aquatics. The leaf shape varies so greatly within a given species that classification within the group is based almost entirely on flowers and mature fruits. About half a dozen species are being used successfully as aquarium plants.

Under full illumination in a flat tank, *Sagittaria* occasionally will develop long lance-shaped leaves above the surface of aquarium water and attractive cuplike white flowers with a yellow ball in the center.

Another useful background plant, *Sagittaria* has many advantages in the aquarium. It is comparatively slow-growing, does not tangle easily, and is relatively hardy. It is very tolerant of temperature extremes, but thrives best between 50 and 72 degrees F (10 to 22 degrees C). Interest-

ingly, *Sagittaria* and *Vallisneria* are said to seldom prosper in the same tank.

Hardy Warm-Water, Bright-Light Plants

Four adaptable species that do particularly well in heated aquaria deserve brief mention for their popularity. All are relatively easy to care for, require moderate to high lighting, and do best in waters of 70 to 80 degrees F (22 to 27 degrees C).

Ceratopteris (water sprite, Indian fern)

This popular plant comes in two different forms, floating and rooted. For this reason, for many years it was thought to be more than one species, and it has two common names. It is a true fern with light-green, deeply cut fronds. The floating form, which grows best under strong light, makes good cover for fry or timid fish. It is a favorite among those who breed fancy guppies. This form teams well with plant species, such as *Cryptoco-*

Ceratopteris thalictroides (water sprite).

The common, hardy plants pictured on this page and the next all thrive in water temperatures suitable for tropical fish species, and require bright light. Left is *Ludwigia* and its flower.

Java fern *(Microsorium pteropus)*.

ryne, which need reduced light. It prefers slightly acid water, but will adapt to somewhat alkaline conditions.

At its best as a single plant in small and medium-sized aquaria, *Ceratopteris* is a rather soft plant, upon which fish and snails often feed readily. Luckily, it grows rapidly and self-propagates easily from buds that develop on its leaves. As old plants become too large or worn-looking, they can be replaced with young offshoots.

Ludwigia

This favorite leafy-stemmed plant includes many aquarium species. One popular species has a

Hygrophila corymbosa, which will grow to a large size under favorable conditions.

reddish cast, particularly on the undersides of leaves. To keep this color, the plant needs significantly more intense illumination than other leafy-stemmed plants. For this reason, one should not attempt to keep this species in a deep tank.

Like other aquarium plants that are actually bog species rather than true aquatics, *Ludwigia* will often rise above the water and out of the top of the tank when given the very strong top-lighting that it prefers. On the other hand, if it is given inadequate light, the leaves will turn brown and fall off.

Hygrophila (or Nomaphila)

This adaptable Southeast Asian native is a good choice for groups in larger aquaria. Many aquarists consider this to be the best of all the leafy-stemmed plants. It grows faster than *Ludwigia* and requires less light. The plant requires moderately intense illumination during the day, and each evening it closes its upper leaves. Sometimes *Hygrophila* will suddenly lose its upper leaves if tank water is not changed often.

Microsorium (Java fern)

This true fern is an enduring plant which should be anchored to rocks or driftwood rather than planted directly in the gravel. It is quite accommodating as to light, but thrives best with regular water changes and peat filtration.

Popular Warm-Water Plants That Tolerate Low Light

Without a doubt, one group of plants dominates this section: *Cryptocoryne* (crypts).

A few of the many varieties of *Cryptocoryne.* Leaves of these popular tropical forms grow from a crown, which should be planted above the gravel surface. Pictured on this page are: top left, *Cryptocoryne cordata;* top right, *C. crispulata;* bottom left, *C. purpurea.*; below, *C. willisi;*

Cryptocoryne (crypts)

Members of the genus *Cryptocoryne* are said to be the world's most popular tropical aquarium plants. To the aquarist's delight, they come in a remarkable variety of shapes and growth forms, a few of which are shown here. Most have heart-shaped, lanceolate, or oval leaves.

Because *Cryptocoryne* is a genus of tropical Southeast Asian origin, many species thrive in the warmer (70 to 80 degrees F, 22 to 27 degrees C) waters of the tropical fish tank. Crypts grow rapidly, and most species require less light than most of the other common aquarium plants. However, a few species have quite different light requirements, so the aquarist would be well advised to research the species he or she intends to cultivate.

Cryptocoryne thrive best if their roots remain undisturbed in a well-balanced tank. Frequent replanting tends to set back their growth. Rosette-forming plants that propagate by runners, they should be planted with the crown visible. In general, they are very sensitive to environmental changes such as temperature fluctuations, waste buildup, and sudden changes in lighting.

Centerpiece Plants

Included here are the great variety of bog and true aquatic species whose main contribution to the tank lies in their perceived beauty. Most of these have rather broad, often arrow-shaped leaves arising on stems from a common crown, and

The large Amazon swordplant (*Echinodorus bleheri*) is suitable only for big tanks.

The Madagascar lace plant is the most difficult type of *Aponogeton* to grow, yet the most popular because of its peculiar leaves.

many eventually grow fairly large. Centerpiece plants often have special needs beyond those of the standard aquarium milieu and thus grow best as solo performers rather than in combination with other centerpiece species.

Echinodorus (swordplants, Amazons)

The best known of the centerpiece plants are probably the Amazons and other swordplants of the family Alismataceae. These are marsh plants that thrive best when only partly submerged. Many have a tendency to grow out of the water and produce aerial leaves, and a few also become extremely large, sometimes in as little as one or two years. One of the "dwarf" species would be more suitable for most tanks.

Research is in order if you plan to keep a swordplant in your tank, for habits and needs vary widely within this group. Some are good group plants; others are suitable only as single plants in large aquaria. Some species require intense illumination; others die with it. Some *Echinodorus* species reproduce rapidly by runners. Others produce flowering stalks with shrunken flowers and tiny adventitious plants. (To help these new plants grow roots more rapidly, weight the stalk down.)

Aponogeton (Madagascar lace plant)

Recognizable by its skeletonlike pierced leaves, which appear fragile but are actually quite tough, this plant is somewhat difficult to grow but nonetheless extremely popular for its unusual appearance. Some related species have large leaves with crinkled edges and no piercing, and thus superficially appear quite different.

A native of regions with extreme seasonal changes, most *Aponogeton* species undergo dormant periods which alternate with rapid growth and bloom. They produce strange stalked flowers and large, bright-green, naked seeds that sprout immediately into robust seedlings. *Aponogeton* are sometimes purchased as dormant bulbs and should be planted in a separate pot to facilitate removing them from the aquarium during subsequent dormant periods.

Plants of Special Use in Fish Breeding

Aquarists who are interested in breeding tropical fish should consider researching and including one of the aquarium plant species which grow in large clusters or mats that float just below the water surface. Common examples include *Riccia* (crystalwort), *Lemna* (duckweed), or *Nitella* (stonewort, musk grass). If you plan to breed bubble-nesting species, you may want to add floating plants such as water sprite (*Ceratopteris*), under which those fish will construct their nests. Remember, however, that if allowed to cover the water surface, any floating plants will block light to rooted plants below.

When properly planted, *Eleocharis* (hair grass) will form a regular carpet on the bottom of the

Riccia fluitans (crystalwort) is a true floating species and a favorite of fish breeders, but will shade out plants beneath it.

tank, making perfect thickets to protect baby fishes. Along the edges of ponds and streams throughout the eastern and southern parts of the United States, many species of hair grass grow wild. Most propagate from runners, and many are suited to aquarium culture.

Propagating Aquarium Plants

One of the advantages that living plants have over plastic replicates is that the former will multiply the return on your investment. Many reproduce freely in the home aquarium with relatively little attention or effort on the aquarist's part.

Both terrestrial and aquatic plants reproduce by two methods: sexual and asexual. The latter, also called vegetative propagation, is most common among aquatic plants. Very few true aquatics depend upon flowers and seed formation. In home tanks, even those aquarium plants which flower readily rarely produce viable seeds.

The means by which vegetative propagation occurs are varied. Many of those aquatic plant species that have small leaves on long running stems are easily propagated by cuttings pruned off their long shoots. The remaining plant will sprout new shoots from the stubs, becoming fuller and more attractive as a result. Common examples include *Cabomba* and *Myriophyllum*. *Egeria* is similar, but forms roots and branches only at intervals of every eighth or ninth joint.

Plants such as *Cryptocoryne* that produce a rosette of leaves from a central crown at first may look as though they have no branches. However, careful examination will reveal that the leaves grow in small clumps on very short stems. Once a rosette has formed several leaves and some roots on its own, it can be carefully separated from the parent plant.

Grasslike plants such as *Sagittaria* and *Vallisneria* send out a series of horizontal runners that end in young plants. *Cryptocoryne* and some swordplants do the same. These should not be separated from the parent until they have several large leaves and good root development.

Another common method of vegetative propagation is the production of young plants upon mature leaves or bloom-stalks of the parent plant. Swordplants and water sprites are examples. When the leaves and roots are well developed, these offspring may be carefully

The presence of excessive algae can suppress plant growth and good health.

separated from the parent for planting in relatively bright light.

Setting Up a Planted Aquarium

Whether an aquarium should be planted first or stocked with fish first is a matter of some disagreement. Whichever is done, it is worth emphasizing that, like fishes, plants do best when attention is paid to water quality. In general, plants do better in neutral or only slightly acid or alkaline water.

Buying plants: If you have a choice, it is best to select young or half-grown plants, for they adapt better and last longer. Avoid plants covered with algae, as it will soon spread throughout the aquarium. A balanced aquarium can be planted two-thirds full of plants, so buy according to its size.

The numbers of snails present must be kept down for plants to thrive, as they will browse on leaves. The trumpet snail pictured here does not eat plants.

Beginning fish hobbyists are often fascinated with the idea of decorating aquaria with a wide variety of plants. However, a more successful scheme is to use only a very few kinds in a tank, concentrating on relatively trouble-free generalists. When an aquarium is stocked with a wide variety of plant species, it becomes difficult to give all of them the conditions best suited to their nature. One attractive compromise is to use one or two kinds of live plants, but to supplement with plastic plants for visual variety.

Planting the aquarium: First, look the plants over. Remove any old yellowish leaves. Now and throughout the planting process, make sure the plants are kept moist. An easy method is to lay them in water in a temporary container and cover them with a wet newspaper to keep them submerged. Allowing plants to half-dry may set their growth back markedly.

Fill the aquarium only about 5 or 6 inches (13 to 15 centimeters) deep with water before planting, and set any rockwork in place first. This shallow depth will make it easier to plant spreading roots properly.

Remove the larger rooted plants from the temporary container first. If they have been fastened into wired bundles, remove the wire. No matter how attractive they may look in the bundle, they never grow that way naturally and should not be planted like that. If a large plant is buoyant, place a small stone or two over the gravel covering the roots to anchor it. Spread the roots as widely as possible, and cover them well. Allow each sufficient space so that there will be room for the new runners that the plant will eventually send out.

Small plants and those with long strands like *Egeria* should be placed last. Separate stemmed plants like *Egeria, Cabomba,* and *Myriophyllum* slightly so that water and light may pass between the stems at the base.

Filling the aquarium: First, double-check that the aquarium is well supported. If you are able to produce the slightest bit of rocking by raising or lowering any corner, stabilize this before going any further. Water is heavy, and any uneven strain will sooner or later crack the glass or cause a leak.

While filling the aquarium, divert the stream of water with your hand, a pan, or a large sheet of paper to prevent the plants from being disturbed. If any plants do float up, they can easily be replaced after the aquarium is filled without your getting wet up to the elbows. Use a pair of slender

sticks such as chopsticks, fondue forks, rulers, or pencils. Push the plant into the gravel with both sticks, then withdraw one and use it to heap gravel about the plant roots. Then pull out the other stick. Usually the plant will stay down.

Maintaining a Planted Aquarium

With adequate light and filtration, ongoing care of aquatic plants is largely a matter of maintaining water quality, fertilizing at intervals, and protecting plants from damage.

Frequent water changes: Most aquatic plants are quite sensitive to pH, doing best with a range of 7.0 to 7.2. A 20 percent to 50 percent water change every two weeks will keep the tank from developing a low pH over time, and will stimulate plant and fish growth.

Fertilization: In their natural environment, plants draw nourishment from the earth in which they grow. In an aquarium, where plants are being kept in a closed system on a gravel substrate, fish cannot be expected to supply all the fertilizer elements that aquatic plants need for best growth. Thus, it is usually necessary to use an aquarium fertilizer, especially in a newly established tank.

A great many types and forms of aquarium fertilizer are available commercially. Some are liquids designed to be added to the tank water. Others are tablets to be pushed into the gravel near plant roots. Used with care, houseplant formulations have also been employed successfully by some aquarists. Fertilizers should be added after periodic water changes, so that the plants can benefit from their full recommended concentration for the longest possible time.

Controlling excessive algal growth: Algae should not be a problem in a well-maintained, plant-filled tank kept out of direct sunlight. If they are, one should first look to one's management practices and vow to make whatever corrections are needed.

Some hobbyists mistakenly minimize light and fertilization in an attempt to limit algal growth. Healthily growing leafy plants in an aquarium actually compete with algal growth, thereby reducing algae numbers, whereas excessive algal growth often occurs in a tank with deteriorating leafy plants.

If older leaves have a thick carpet of algae or if

plants are covered by a loose coat of filthy-looking, dark, blue-green algae, check the water's pH and your water-change schedule. Algae are most apt to thrive in water that has not been changed frequently enough.

Chemical treatments in the form of commercially available products will help clear a tank of runaway algae. The glass tank walls will probably need to be scraped clean, and any ornaments may need to be removed and scrubbed. A major water change is probably long overdue. To keep the tank clear after all this work, increase the intensity and duration of light provided, fertilize the plants well, and practice frequent water changes.

Minimizing fish and snail damage: Some fish (such as characins of the tetra family) are eager vegetarians. Others, such as angelfish, use their mouths to clean off leaves as spawning sites, and in their vigor, they may suck holes right through the leaves.

Other fish that appear to be "pecking" at leaves may or may not actually be feeding upon the plant. Algae and tiny animals such as rotifers, protozoa, and minute worms live and reproduce in a well-balanced aquarium. Largely invisible to human eyes, these cover plant leaves as well as gravel, glass walls, and other surfaces, providing cafeteria feeding for a variety of fish. Unfortunately, in their eagerness, some fish such as mollies may wear off the surface of the leaves.

When fish are kept with living plants, a certain amount of damage is probably inevitable. Avoiding the most avid vegetarians and including hardy, rapidly growing plants will minimize the problem. Providing large numbers of plants relative to the numbers of fish will make individual damage less apparent, as will regular removal of damaged leaves. Supplementing the diet of these fish species with a commercial conditioning food may help to satisfy their appetite for living plant food.

Snails are another matter. Snails often browse on plants when supplies of prepared food, dead fish, or algae are low. Their numbers must be kept under control if plants are to thrive. Distinct roundish holes in leaf surfaces are a dead giveaway to snail damage. Chemicals for snail control are commercially available. However, many aquarists prefer more natural methods. The efficiency of hand-picking can be increased by floating a partially wilted lettuce leaf on the water surface, where it will act as attractive bait. Gold barbs and blue gouramis are said to relish snails.

Minimizing damage to plant roots and crowns: Most plants grow best with minimal root disturbance. Certain large cichlids and large plecostomus catfishes dig about vigorously in gravel. To counteract this, one can place boulders about the plants as barriers or place the plants in separate pots within the aquarium.

Although modern filtration systems remove the cloudiness caused by overfeeding, they cannot remove decaying food that settles to the tank bottom to lodge itself in among plant stems and roots. As a result, gravel blackens, plant roots turn black and slimy, and leaves (or entire crowns) break loose and float. In extreme cases, gravel must be replaced to correct the problem. Obviously, prevention is the better course.

Guidelines for Success

Live plants are both beneficial and attractive, and should not be difficult to keep if the following guidelines are heeded.

1. Select plants carefully. Choose kinds which can be expected to do well, concentrating on familiar, popular varieties which have proven themselves. Young plants in good condition will prove most rewarding. Avoid plants with yellowed leaves, spindly stems, or excessive algae.

2. Plant carefully. Groom plants before putting them into the aquarium, and pay careful attention to proper planting depth and spacing. Fertilize the gravel and/or the water, following manufacturers' instructions.

3. Maintain adequate light. Both intensity and amount of light are important for proper plant growth. For twelve hours of each day, provide 1.5 watts of wide-, broad-, or full-spectrum light per gallon (3.8 liters) of tank water.

4. Maintain good water quality. This includes maintaining proper temperature for the plants you've chosen, proper pH and chemistry through frequent water changes, and enough water circulation to promote plant growth.

5. Groom plants occasionally. Pinch back rapidly growing stems and remove old, dying leaves. Replace older plants with younger offspring.

6. Protect the leaves from excessive damage. Limit or avoid snails and plant-eating fish species.

7. Fertilize at regular intervals. Follow the recommendations for the formulation you have chosen.

Selected References

Bruenner, G. [no publ. date]. *The Hobbyist Guide to the Natural Aquarium.* Tetra Press.

Fassett, N. C. 1957. *A Manual of Aquatic Plants*. 2nd ed. Madison: University of Wisconsin Press.

Reid, G. K. 1967. *Pond Life.* Racine, Wis.: Western Publishing Co.

Popular Freshwater Aquarium Fish: Description, Behavior, and Care

John B. Gratzek and Janice R. Matthews

Although estimates vary, apparently about 500 species of tropical freshwater fish appear from time to time in local aquarium stores, and about 180 of these account for some 95 percent of the fish in home aquaria. Even this may seem like an overwhelming variety. However, knowing the characteristics that allow one to recognize natural groupings lends organization to this otherwise bewildering array. Most of the species which appear fairly regularly in the local aquarium market occur in the seven easily recognizable groupings which form the basis for this chapter.

To successfully keep any type of freshwater fish, one should have some knowledge of the fundamentals of its food and temperature requirements and of its pattern of behavior in a community tank. Does it dig? What are its environmental and social preferences? How aggressive is it? One needs information, too, on its compatibility with any other species being considered for a community tank. One also must know the size of aquarium which the species requires, its preferred water temperature, and its pH and water hardness preferences.

To help aquarists make a sensible, planned selection of fish for their tanks, this chapter briefly presents information on some common types of aquarium fishes. Readers wishing more detailed information may consult the references listed at the end of the chapter.

All scientific classification is based on similarity of form. Biologists construct sets of groups based on degree of structural similarity between organisms. The animal kingdom includes about eleven major groups called phyla, each embracing a diverse assemblage of animals which share some major commonalities. Fish belong to the phylum Chordata, which also includes all the other backboned organisms, such as birds and mammals.

Each phylum, in turn, is divided into classes. True bony fish belong to the class Osteichthyes (sometimes called Pisces). The Chondrichthyes encompasses the sharks, rays, skates, and other fishlike forms which lack a swim bladder and have a cartilaginous skeleton. A third class, the Agnatha, contains the primitive jawless fishes.

A class, in turn, is divided into orders, and an order is divided into families. A family contains a single genus or a group of related genera. Each genus, in turn, is composed of one or more related species.

The species is usually considered to be the basic breeding unit. In some cases, groups of individuals of a single species vary enough in appearance to seem worthy of a separate name, even though they still, at least theoretically, are capable of breeding with one another. Scientists refer to these subgroups as varieties, forms, or breeds.

The genus and species, which are usually in Latin, make up what we commonly call the "scientific name" of a particular kind of animal. In most tropical fish stores, fish are known only by their common name, which is usually in the native tongue. However, common names can vary from country to country, or even from region to region. In scientific circles, only the Latin names have validity. These are included after the common name of the fish in the examples which follow each group discussed below.

Rosy barb (*Barbus conchonius*).

Barbs and Carplike Fish (Suborder Cyprinoidei)

Native to Asia, Africa, Europe, and North America, this suborder comprises a great variety of popular and beautiful aquarium fish. Practically all are peaceful, have no special requirements, and thus are well suited for the mixed community tank. Hardy and undemanding, they are highly suitable for the small tank of the beginner. Most are not unduly sensitive to temperature changes. They eat almost any food offered to them, but prefer plant protein. Nearly all of these species spawn readily, and the young fish are easily reared.

Some cyprinoid species eat detritus such as uneaten food, decaying plant leaves, and fish waste products, rummaging around in tank gravel in their search and stirring up the aquarium bottom, to the detriment of fine-leaved aquatic plants. For this reason, plants such as *Cryptocoryne* which have large plain leaves are recommended for an aquarium with these scavengers. Alternatively, an efficient filtering system which removes suspended detritus can allow the aquarist to keep some of these useful bottom feeders in a community tank with fine-leaved plants.

Other cyprinoid species are vividly colored shoaling fish, preferring the upper and middle water regions and taking their food from the water surface or as it slowly sinks down to the bottom. These species require space for free swimming, and the foreground of their tank should therefore be without plants.

A selection of barbs, danios, loaches, and other carplike fish of the suborder Cyprinoidei, which are suited for a community tank, are discussed on the following pages.

Rosy barb (*Barbus conchonius*)

Native to northern India, rosy barbs can be kept in an unheated aquarium. They are one of the few fish species which do well with goldfish. Peaceful, active fish, they should not be kept together with shy species. Because they are scavengers, rosy barbs will dig in a soft sandy tank bottom and nibble at delicate plants. They are easily bred, spawning in fine-leaved plants.

Sumatra barb, tiger barb (*Barbus tetrazona*)

Native to Borneo, Thailand, and Sumatra, tiger barbs are often kept in small schools of four or more. They should not be kept with angelfish,

Sumatra barb or tiger barb (*Barbus tetrazona*).

Pearl or gold danio (*Brachydanio albolineatus*).

Clown loach (*Botia macracantha*).

since tiger barbs are fin nippers. Old fish tend to become lazy. They benefit from frequent partial water changes. Tiger barbs breed readily and the young are easily reared.

Pearl danio (*Brachydanio albolineatus*)

Native to running water in Sumatra, Burma, and Thailand, the pearl danio is one of the hardiest aquarium fish and one of the easiest to breed. A very active swimmer and jumper, the pearl danio is best kept in a good-sized aquarium with a cover.

This species lays nonadhesive eggs in plant thickets. To raise young successfully, the aquarist must devise some way to keep adult fish from getting at the eggs after they fall to the bottom. (One suggestion is a small rearing tank, from which parents are removed immediately after eggs are laid.) Professional breeders separate the sexes and feed them well until the females are loaded with eggs. They then place a number of breeders in a box with a screen bottom floating in

a trough. As spawning takes place, eggs rain through the screen bottom.

Zebra danio (*Brachydanio rerio*)

Native to eastern India, zebra danios are active but peaceful and easily maintained schooling fish suitable for beginners. They are easily bred by the same procedure as used with pearl danios and will crossbreed with them, but the resultant hybrids are sterile and have a washed-out appearance.

Clown loach, tiger botia (*Botia macracantha*)

Native to Sumatra and Borneo, these peaceful schooling fish need hiding places among stones or roots. They rarely spawn in aquaria, but probably breed among plant thickets.

Goldfish (*Carassius auratus*)

Native to China, goldfish were undoubtedly the first pet fish of all, for there are records of them being kept as early as 500 A.D., having been bred from native wild carp.

The various goldfish varieties, especially veiltails, should not be mixed with warm-water species. However, zebras, zebra barbs, and white cloud mountain fish can be kept together with goldfish. They all exist well in an unheated aquarium at a temperature of between 64 and 72 degrees F (18 to 22 degrees C). Goldfish are hardy to much lower temperatures and can even survive winter in a garden pond under a thin layer of ice.

Because goldfish dig, the aquarium bottom should be covered with large gravel or pebbles. Fine-leaved, delicate plants will be promptly eaten. Feed goldfish sparingly, or the water will rapidly become dirty.

Goldfish come in many forms, from black moors with protuberant eyes to fantails, redcaps, pearl-scale, and others. The more bizarre forms

Zebra danio (*Brachydanio rerio*).

White cloud fish (*Tanichthys albonubes*).

Goldfish (*Carassius auratus*): above, black
moor form; top, Chinese veiltail form.

young. As they mature, they become aggressive
and may attack larger fish by attaching their sucking mouth to them. For this reason, a closely
related but peaceful species, the Siamese flying
fox, *Epalzeorhynchus siamensis,* is a better
choice.

White cloud mountain fish (*Tanichthys albonubes*)

Native to China and Hong Kong, these are active,
peaceful schooling fish recommended for beginners. Since they are undemanding, they are suitable for almost any aquarium, including an
unheated one. A tank with a fair amount of swimming space, bright lighting, and a dark bottom is
best.

Three-lined rasbora, scissortail (*Rasbora trilineata*)

This is one of several species of rasboras, all of
which are native to Malaysia. All are peaceful
schooling fish with no special demands and vari-

are generally more delicate, and tend to need
efficient filtration and frequent partial water
changes. Breeding goldfish usually is possible
only in large tanks.

Chinese algae eater (*Gyrinocheilus aymonieri*)

Native to Thailand, these fish eat algae only when

Chinese algae eater (*Gyrinocheilus aymonieri*).

Three-lined rasbora (*Rasbora trilineata*).

Siamese flying fox (*Epalzeorhynchus siamensis*).

able breeding ease. Rasboras do well with soft water, low pH, and a dark-bottomed tank.

Siamese flying fox (*Epalzeorhynchus siamensis*)

Less brightly colored than the Chinese algae eater, this species is probably the single most effective algae eater available for the home aquarium. A single specimen could keep several aquaria algae-free. Its nonaggressive behavior in aquaria containing multiple species makes it ideal for home fish-keeping.

Live-Bearers (Family Poeciliidae, Live-Bearing Toothcarps)

In the wild, the species of this family are limited to South and Central America. Most of these fish have absolutely no special demands and breed easily in captivity, making them very suitable for the beginner. Popular members of the family Poeciliidae include guppies, swordtails, platys, and other fish called "live-bearing toothcarps."

Males are easily recognized by the gonopodium, a rodlike copulatory organ which is a modification of the anal fin. The females of many poeciliid species have a dark-colored mark on the belly in front of the anal fin, the so-called "gravid spot" or "pregnancy mark." Among poeciliid fish, sperm is introduced into the female through the male's gonopodium and, in many cases, is stored by the female so that fertilization can occur over a long period of time. Thus, sperm stock from a single mating fertilizes several successive batches of eggs.

Depending on water temperature and poeciliid

species, development of the young can take from four to six weeks. The offspring (5 to 12 millimeters, or 0.2 to 0.5 inches in length) are fully developed young fish when born. They immediately accept finely powdered dried food, which can be supplemented with brine shrimp (*Artemia*).

Even within the community tank, the young of these species are easily raised, particularly if the aquarium has a dense layer of floating plants to prevent larger fish from finding and eating the fry in the first days after birth. However, a methodical breeder will separate pregnant females into small separate rearing tanks with bushy plants, and remove the mother immediately after she has given birth, for nearly all females eat their young if given a chance. (Alternatively, commercially available breeding traps can be used to separate newborn fry automatically.)

For advanced aquarists, an attractive advantage of this group is that some species are so closely related that they will readily hybridize—a

Males of two of the many live-bearing forms of guppies (*Poecilia reticulata*): below, fantail guppy; bottom, triangle guppy.

Black molly (*Poecilia sphenops*).

Red wagtail platy (*Xiphophorus maculatus*).

situation which can lead to interesting experiments. By crossbreeding and pairing different varieties, an endless number of combinations of coloration and form can be achieved. Examples of this include the popular forms of swordtails and platys and the breeding forms of guppies.

Males of two of the many livebearing swordtails (*Xiphophorus helleri*): below, Simpson's swordtail; bottom, red tuxedo swordtail.

Guppy, millions fish (*Poecilia* [formerly *Lebistes*] *reticulata*)
Native to South America, Trinidad, and Barbados, these prolific breeders are active and peaceful. The guppy was one of the earliest aquarium fish, and these essentially "wild form" fish were undemanding and sturdy. Many breeding varieties have been developed, which are more colorful but require a bit more care and reproduce less prolifically.

Black molly (*Poecilia* [formerly *Mollienesia*] *sphenops*)
Native from Mexico to Venezuela, these active, peaceful fish eat algae. Black mollies do best in hard water with a lot of light and warmth, but are otherwise a suitable fish for beginners. They reproduce easily in a community tank with hiding places for the young fry.

Swordtail (*Xiphophorus helleri*)
Native to Mexico and Guatemala, swordtails prosper best with a varied diet. Only the males possess the swordlike extension of the caudal fin. All members of the genus *Xiphophorus* can be crossbred to produce fertile offspring, making them ideal subjects for genetic study.

Platy (*Xiphophorus maculatus*)
Native to Mexico and Guatemala, platys are highly recommended as lively, colorful fish for beginners. Basically a swordless swordtail, their breeding requirements are the same.

Killifish, Egg-Laying Toothcarps (Family Cyprinodontidae)

This is a family containing a large number of species which are distributed in many American and African

Lyretail killifish (*Aphyosemion australe*).

Striped panchax (*Aplocheilus lineatus*).

countries, in Asia, and in parts of southern Europe. In nature, most live short lives in shallow waters which often completely dry up each year, killing the fish. However, under aquarium conditions, sturdy specimens may live for several years.

Killifish are not really suitable for the beginner. Some experience and a lot of careful attention to water quality, feeding, and general husbandry are essential for success. Many killifish have such special requirements with regard to water quality and feeding that they are difficult to keep in a community tank. Many are so aggressive, too, that even certain species within this family should not be kept together. However, some of the most magnificently colored aquarium fish are to be found in this family, and fond aquarists have formed specialist killifish associations in many countries.

For most killifish, peat filtration or appropriate buffers and/or ion exchangers should be used to keep water in the slightly acid range. Water should

be soft, and peat should be used as a bottom material.

In nature, adult fish lay their fertilized eggs in mud, where they survive the dry period in dormancy. With the onset of the rainy season, the eggs hatch and the young mature in the temporary ponds. The regular addition of commercially available peat extracts to aquarium water optimizes conditions for killifish reproduction. Most killifish should be fed small portions several (at least four to five) times a day.

Lyretail killifish (*Aphyosemion australe*)
Native to coastal waters of West Africa, this relatively undemanding lyretail thrives in a shallow, heavily planted tank with a dark peat bottom. Relatively nonaggressive, it can be kept in a community tank if other inhabitants are of a similar size and disposition.

Firemouth epiplatys (*Epiplatys dageti*)
Native to tropical West Africa and surrounding areas, this hardy surface-dwelling fish does well in a community tank with fine-leaved plants, upon which eggs are deposited after spawning.

Striped panchax (*Aplocheilus lineatus*)
Native to northern India and Sri Lanka, this surface-dwelling fish is an example of a species unsuited for a community tank. Its preferred food is small fish, and it is vicious toward smaller specimens. Light-sensitive, the striped panchax does best in a large tank with the water surface covered with floating plants.

Catfish (Suborder Siluroidei)

Only a few species among the many catfish families have become commonplace in aquaria—un-

Firemouth epiplatys (*Epiplatys dageti*).

Peppered catfish (*Corydoras paleatus*).

Glass catfish (*Kryptopterus bicirrhis*).

derstandably, the many predatory species are not particularly popular with the average hobbyist.

Catfish include many bizarre, even comical or grotesque, forms. Bottom dwellers, they utilize leftover food, but due to competition in a community tank they usually require supplementary feedings several times a day. Sinkable food pellets or compressed tablets are well suited for feeding catfish. Sliced pieces of frozen or parboiled zucchini squash appear to be relished by many species and provide a good source of vitamin C.

The scaleless bodies of catfish are covered by overlapping bony plates in some species. In addition, all catfish have barbels, which serve as taste and touch sense organs. These delicate "whiskers" may be worn away through constant digging in coarse gravel or by sharp objects in the aquarium. Most catfish prefer well-washed sand or small gravel of roughly 1/16 inch (1.6 millimeters) in diameter. With armored catfish, feeding within an area of fine sand is recommended to

Suckermouth catfish (*Plecostomus punctatus*).

prevent food from falling into crevices formed by coarser gravel. (This area can be provided by filling a shallow dish with sand and burying it in the gravel substrate.)

Peppered catfish (*Corydoras paleatus*)
Native to the middle Amazon in southern Brazil, these scavengers are peaceful bottom dwellers suitable for a community aquarium. They are the hardiest and sturdiest of the several kinds of armored catfish and can be bred in the aquarium. Having sensitive barbels, they should be kept in an aquarium with a bottom of fine, dark sand rather than coarse gravel.

Plecostomus, suckermouth (*Plecostomus punctatus*)
These natives of the Amazon are also peaceful, bottom-dwelling scavengers. They feed mostly at night, hiding among dark plants, roots, or stones during the day. Because the suckermouth does not damage plants and digs very little, this species is a desirable one, but no details about its breeding are available.

Glass catfish (*Kryptopterus bicirrhis*)
Native to Indonesia, Borneo, and Sumatra, these delicate and transparent shoaling fish are active during the day. They are best kept in groups in large, not overly bright community tanks with other delicate species and a few bushy aquatic plants. Both sex determination and breeding habits are unknown.

Tetras, Characins (Suborder Characoidei)

Members of this group are native to the tropical and subtropical areas of America and Africa. This

Cardinal tetra (*Paracheirodon axelrodi*).

Head-and-tail-light or beaconfish
(*Hemigrammus ocellifer*).

vast suborder with many varieties includes approximately fourteen families. The family Characi-
dae in turn includes fourteen subfamilies, with
many fish suitable for aquarium life.

Most fish in the characin family can be recognized easily by the so-called adipose fin, a little
fin without fin rays found on the back between the
dorsal and caudal fins.

The popular aquarium species of characins are
schooling fish, shown off to their best advantage
in a community aquarium with other members of
this family. Schools of smaller species (up to 1.5
inches, or 4 centimeters, in length) should have at
least five specimens. With larger fish, three would
be sufficient. Schooling fish require a good deal
of swimming space. Therefore, an aquarium under 24 inches (61 centimeters) in length is not
recommended. A related recommendation is that
one should keep the number of different species
to a minimum, but the number of fish within each
species large.

Tetras prefer slightly amber-colored soft water
which is clear, clean, and well-oxygenated. Efficient filtration and aeration are necessary to maintain optimal conditions for growth and
reproduction. Tetras thrive in brightly lit tanks with
enough vegetation for hiding places and ample
room for free swimming. The coloration of these
fish is usually considerably more intense when the
tank has a dark bottom.

The characins coexist well with labyrinth fish,
small barbs, and dwarf cichlids. Live-bearers are
less suitable as tankmates, because they prefer
somewhat different water conditions.

Generally, tetras are easy to keep, even for a
beginner. They prefer foods of animal origin, although a few varieties are vegetarians. They are

not bottom feeders, and obtain their food from the
surface of the water or as it sinks toward the
bottom.

With few exceptions, breeding tetras is a challenge usually reserved for experienced aquarists.
These fish spawn in pairs or schools between
plants, in the typical fashion of egg scatterers.
After an active chase of the female by the male,
tetras lay numerous eggs above or on delicate
plants. Obviously, aquaria planted with bunches
of clean, fine-leaved plants will increase the reproductive success of the fish. The development
of their eggs is left to chance; very few tetra
species care for the eggs and young.

Cardinal tetra (*Paracheirodon axelrodi*)
Native to the Rio Negro in Brazil, this peaceful
species is considered by many to be one of the
most beautiful ornamental fish. Cardinal tetras are
best kept in schools in a community aquarium.
Colors are most brilliant in soft water which has

Flame tetra (*Hyphessobrycon flammeus*).

Plain metynnis (*Metynnis hypsauchen*).

X-ray fish or pristella (*Pristella maxillaris*).

been filtered through peat and which has a pH value below 7. Inducing cardinal tetras to spawn is extremely difficult, so most of these fish are caught in the wild and shipped to market.

Head-and-tail-light, beaconfish (*Hemigrammus ocellifer*)
Native to the Amazon River basin, these fish are well suited for the community tank. Dim light and a dark tank bottom highlight the fluorescent gold spots for which the fish are named.

Neon tetra (*Patacheirodon innesi*).

Flame tetra (*Hyphessobrycon flammeus*)
Native to Brazil in the region of Rio de Janiero, the flame tetra was one of the earliest imported members of its genus. It shows its colors best when fed a special color-enriching diet.

Plain metynnis (*Metynnis hypsauchen*)
Native to the Amazon region, this species looks like a small piranha but in actuality is a shy, peaceful vegetarian. It will eat most aquarium plants. A schooling fish, it shows to best advantage in groups of six or more in a tank without other species.

Neon tetra (*Patacheirodon innesi*)
Native to the upper tributaries of the Amazon River, this is probably the most popular aquarium fish in the world. Neon tetras are peaceful schooling fish with a long life span. They require relatively warm water and prefer small feedings several times a day. Neons are easily bred in very soft, slightly acid water kept at 75 degrees F (24 degrees C).

X-ray fish, pristella (*Pristella maxillaris*, [formerly *P. riddelei*])
Another native of the Amazon tributaries, these peaceful schooling fish need a great deal of swimming area. The pristella's delicate colors show best with a dark aquarium bottom.

Cichlids (Family Cichlidae)

This large family contains several hundred species. Most originate in South and Central America and Africa; only two species are found in Asia. Larger specimens of this family are often aggressive and predatory, and they have a tendency to dig and uproot the tank bottom, a behavior which renders them unsuitable for planted tanks. However, among the smaller or dwarf species are a number of appealing varieties well suited for a planted community aquarium.

Most cichlids have a lengthy life span and are not very sensitive to water temperature. However, since these fish require larger amounts of food than do smaller fish, their water will be polluted faster. A regular change of one-third of the water every three to four weeks is generally recommended.

An aquarium containing cichlids must include several points of refuge (such as roots, rocks, submerged flowerpots, or coconut shells) for hiding and spawning. For dwarf cichlids, the tank must also be densely planted.

Their extremely interesting reproductive behavior accounts for the popularity of many species of cichlids, so most aquarists will want to keep both sexes. Sometimes it is not easy to pair prospective breeders. Buying four to six young fish and waiting until some pair off naturally is the recommended procedure.

Most cichlids attach their eggs to a firm surface such as stones, slate, wood, or leaves, where the male fertilizes them. Some spawn in the open, others in shelters such as caves. The open-breeding species are true partners, with both parents protecting the eggs. Among the shelter breeders, the female alone is usually responsible for brood protection.

Some cichlids are mouthbrooders. After the eggs have been laid, they are immediately taken up into the female's mouth, where they are fertilized. The eggs develop there. After they hatch, the young may leave their mother's mouth tem-

Firemouth cichlid (*Cichlasoma meeki*).

porarily but invariably return at night or if danger threatens.

Most cichlids are strongly territorial. In the confines of a tank, a rival can only hide to escape. Consequently, adequate tank size with ample escape room and hiding places such as rock formations are very important.

Generally, cichlids have no special food requirements. Many varieties can do without live foods altogether. Live foods should, of course, be included in the diet of the predatory species. Interestingly, cichlids will readily learn to accept flaked foods from their owner's hand. The care and maintenance of cichlids is interesting and rewarding. References for further reading are provided at the end of this chapter.

Zebra cichlid, orange-blue mouthbrooder (*Pseudotropheus zebra*)

One of the many brightly colored cichlids from the African Rift Valley lakes, this very aggressive

Male zebra cichlid or orange-blue mouthbrooder (*Pseudotropheus zebra*).

Oscar (*Astronotus ocellatus*).

Dwarf rainbow cichlid or kribensis (*Pelviachromis pulcher*).

species should be kept in a large tank (30 gallons, or 114 liters, of water or more) with plenty of hiding spaces. A single striking blue male may be kept with several of the orange-red females, but only with the same species. Zebra cichlids are not community fish.

Firemouth cichlid (*Cichlasoma meeki*)

Native to Guatemala and southern Mexico, these sometimes quarrelsome fish can be kept in a community aquarium only if the other fish are at least 5 centimeters (2 inches) long. Firemouth cichlids are easily bred, but are aggressive and prone to dig holes when breeding. The tank should include caves, pots, or pieces of piping in which fish can hide.

Oscar (*Astronotus ocellatus*)

Native to the southern Amazon River basin and Paraguay, oscars grow quickly. Only the young fish are considered suitable for the beginner. Oscars also dig, so they should be kept in an aquarium with driftwood or rocks. When large, they become aggressive. Large oscars are kept by themselves in aquaria holding 30 to 50 gallons (about 114 to 190 liters) of water. A favorite food is live goldfish, commonly called "feeder goldfish."

Dwarf rainbow cichlid, kribensis (*Pelviachromis pulcher* [formerly *Pelmatochromis kribensis*])

Native to the Niger River in tropical West Africa, these are peaceful, active, long-lasting fish that are suitable for any community aquarium with other peaceful fish. Because they are sensitive to water cleanliness, regular partial water changes are recommended. The aquarium should include suitable hiding places, for in the wild this species spawns in a cave. Parents share in caring for the eggs and young for several weeks.

Angelfish (*Pterophyllum scalare*)

Native to the middle Amazon (Guyana), this peaceful fish is suitable for community aquaria with other quiet species. It does not disturb plants. Angelfish are available in a great many varieties which differ in color and size. They need clean water, for excess nitrates may result in fin rot. Angelfish often spawn in the aquarium, depositing eggs on a broad, rigid plant leaf, stand

Two of the many forms of angelfish (*Pterophylum scalare*): left, marbled angelfish; right, gold angelfish.

Convict cichlid (*Cichlasoma nigrofasciatum*).

Kissing gourami (*Helostoma temmincki*).

pipe, or slate. Since parents sometimes eat their young, experts advise moving the eggs to a separate tank before they hatch (which occurs in about thirty hours).

Convict cichlid (*Cichlasoma nigrofasciatum*)

Native from Mexico south through Central America, this is a beginner's cichlid, hardy and easy to breed. In a community tank, convict cichlids may be aggressive during spawning and with young, especially if the aquarium is small.

Discus (*Symphysodon* species)

Native to parts of the Amazon River, these costly but elegant fish are regarded as kings among freshwater aquarium fish. They are not easily kept, being very sensitive to water quality and needing a large tank and a varied diet. The young are unusual in that they feed directly upon a secretion which both parents produce on the sides of their heads and bodies.

Gouramis and Other Labyrinth Fish (Suborder Anabantoidei)

The anabantoids, originating from poorly aerated waters in Asia and Africa, are characterized by an additional breathing apparatus, the labyrinth organs, situated adjacent to the gill cavities behind the eyes. With the help of this organ, anabantoids obtain additional oxygen by breathing air from above the water surface. If denied access to the surface, they will die.

Anabantoids are sensitive to low temperatures, especially when young. Therefore, the aquarium should be provided with an adequate heater and a hood to retain the heat. If the tank is covered, however, a provision for air circulation must be made.

The pectoral fins of anabantoids are often long and filamentous and can be extended in front of the fish, where they serve as sensory organs in

Discus (*Symphysodon* species).

Siamese fighting fish (*Betta splendens*).

Dwarf gourami (*Colisa lalia*).

Pearl or mosaic gourami (*Trichogaster leeri*).

the search for food. Most labyrinth fish require plants in their environment to provide hiding places and shade in case the light is too intense. A well-lit tank with enough plants and rock arrangements to result in a dark bottom is optimal.

Most species have no special requirements regarding water quality and food. They are well suited for the community tank and are recommended to the beginner.

Breeding labyrinth fish is interesting and not difficult. They are best kept in pairs. Several pairs can be kept together in a single tank (except in the case of *Betta splendens,* the Siamese fighting fish). Do not allow a tank to become dominated by an excess of male fish.

Most species build nests of small air bubbles, incorporating some plant material, and anchor the nest to floating plants. Once in the nest, only the male—generally recognizable by more intense coloration than females—cares for the eggs and young until they are able to swim freely and

begin to accept food.

Labyrinth fish are peaceful, hardy fish ideal for community aquaria. All find temperatures between 76 and 84 degrees F (24 to 29 degrees C) to be suitable. Those mentioned below are all bubble-nest builders, laying their eggs within clumps of air bubbles blown between floating plants.

Kissing gourami (*Helostoma temmincki*)
Native to India and Malaya, these fish take their name from the habit of males "kissing" each other—actually a challenge behavior between rivals rather than an expression of affection. The wild form is greenish gray, but a domestically developed pink strain is often seen in pet shops. Young kissing gourami are suitable for the community aquarium, but adults may eventually become too large. Their nests contain few or no bubbles. The eggs simply float near the surface.

Siamese fighting fish (*Betta splendens*)
Native to India and Thailand, these are peaceful

Paradise fish (*Macropodus opercularis*).

Blue gourami (*Trichogaster trichopterus sumatranus*).

Bumblebee fish (*Brachygobius xanthozona*).

Dwarf sunfish (*Elassoma evergladei*).

toward other fish. However, males of their own species must be kept separate, since they will fight until one of them dies. Specially bred varieties occur in vivid red, blue, green, purple, and combinations. Because of their air-breathing habit, single fish can be kept in very small bowls or jars. If in sight of one another, males will display toward each other through the glass.

Dwarf gourami (*Colisa lalia*)
Native to India, these are recommended for a community aquarium with other small fish. They are less shy with floating plants present, and diffused lighting will show the colors of the males better. During breeding, males become aggressive toward other fish in the tank. Dwarf gouramis use soft plant material to build a high, wide bubble nest.

Paradise fish (*Macropodus opercularis*)
Native to Korea, Taiwan, and South China, where they live in rice fields, paradise fish are the oldest ornamental fish after the goldfish. They can be kept in an unheated aquarium, but should not be

Puffer fish (*Carinotetraodon somphongsi*).

kept with smaller fish, for they are somewhat aggressive. They require regular feeding.

Pearl or Mosaic gourami (*Trichogaster leeri*)
Native to Malaya, Thailand, Sumatra, and Borneo, adult males of these peaceful fish are considered to be among the most beautiful ornamental fish. They need hiding places in floating plants, or they act shy and look pale. When raising young, the male develops a red-colored belly.

Blue gourami (*Trichogaster trichopterus sumatranus*)
Native to Sumatra, this is one of the easiest kept ornamental fish for any aquarium. Blue gouramis are peaceful fish, easily bred and very productive. Thousands of young fish may result from a single mating.

Miscellaneous Other Fish

Approximately 350 million pet fish are kept in aquaria all over the world, but only a few of the commonly kept fish species belong to groups other than those mentioned so far. Most of the fish included in this last catch-all group are unusual in the aquarium. However, there are some extremely interesting forms among them with which the aquarist might like to become familiar. Many of these are native to brackish waters and require the addition of some salt to the aquarium. Only a sampling follows. For a fuller appreciation of the variety of fishes available, the reader is referred to books mentioned at the end of this chapter.

Bumblebee fish (*Brachygobius xanthozona*)
Native to Borneo and Indonesia, this striking yel-

low-and-black striped fish is so shy that it is best kept in a separate tank with numerous hiding places. The female deposits eggs in caves, and the male guards them. Bumblebee fish require hard water with salt added (20 to 60 grams in 20 liters of water, or about 1 to 2 ounces in 5 gallons), a condition which some aquarium plants will not tolerate.

Puffer fish (*Carinotetraodon somphongsi*)
Native to Thailand, this fish will quickly clear a tank of snails, but if not fed properly, it will also bite holes in the leaves of plants. Not a fish for the beginner, it can be kept in a community tank only under certain conditions, and even then, not with smaller fish.

Dwarf sunfish (*Elassoma evergladei*)
Native to Florida and nearby states in North America, this attractive, peaceful little fish is extremely hardy and especially suited for the unheated tank or garden pond. Dwarf sunfish are best kept in a tank with many hiding places, bushy plants, and free-swimming space. They breed easily, but the young require the finest live foods at first.

Selected References

Anonymous. 1977. *Simon and Schuster's Complete Guide to Freshwater and Marine Aquarium Fishes.* New York: Simon and Schuster.

Axelrod, H. R., and Vorderwinkler, W. 1983. *Encyclopedia of Tropical Fishes with Special Emphasis on Techniques of Breeding.* 27th ed. Neptune City, N.J.: T.F.H. Publications.

Baensch, U. 1983. *Marine Aquarists Guide.* Tetra Press.

——. 1983. *Tropical Aquarium Fish.* Tetra Press.

Hunnam, P.; Milne, A.; and Stebbing, P. 1982. *The Living Aquarium.* New York: Crescent Books.

Ladiges, W. 1983. *Coldwater Fish in the Home and Garden.* Tetra Press.

Contributors

JOHN B. GRATZEK received a bachelor of science degree in biology and chemistry at St. Mary's College in Minnesota, where he studied the parasites of muskrats. Pursuing his interests in animal disease, he was awarded the Doctor of Veterinary Medicine degree from the University of Minnesota in 1956 and a Ph.D. in the study of animal virology from the University of Wisconsin in 1961. Dr. Gratzek presently heads the Department of Medical Microbiology in the College of Veterinary Medicine at the University of Georgia. He is past president of the American College of Veterinary Microbiologists and the International Association for Aquatic Animal Medicine, and serves on the aquaculture committee of the American Association of Animal Health.

JANICE R. MATTHEWS received a bachelor of science degree in botany from Michigan State University, a master's degree in science education from Harvard University, and an education specialist degree in science education from the University of Georgia. Her interests center on the communication of scientific information between professional scientists and the general public. Mrs. Matthews has coauthored two textbooks, edited a number of others, and written numerous scientific and popular articles. She has been a nature center director, serves as science curriculum coordinator for a private school, and currently is biomedical editor for the University of Georgia's College of Veterinary Medicine.

Anatomy, Genetics, and Breeding

Anatomy of Tropical Fishes

Howard E. Evans

There are many shapes and sizes of tropical fishes, from the tiny mosquito fish (*Gambusia affinis*) of Texas, less than one inch (2.5 centimeters) long, to the large pirarucu (*Arapaima gigas*) of South America which reaches a length of 8 feet (2.4 meters). The smallest fish in the world is probably *Pandaka pygmaea* of the Philippines, which is mature at 0.4 inches (10 millimeters), and the largest is the whale shark, *Rhincodon typus,* measured at 45 feet (13.7 meters). For a comprehensive summary of the fishes of the world, see Nelson (1984).

The shape of the body usually is indicative of the habitat or behavior of the fish. Bottom-living fishes and fishes that cling to rocks in swift streams usually are flattened dorsoventrally, as are rays (*Dasyatis*) and many catfish (*Plecostomus*). Bottom-living fish that burrow or enter the substrate are usually serpentine or elongate, as is the kuhli loach (*Acanthophthalmus*). Mid-level fish are either "compressed" (flattened from side to side) as are tetras, or they are "fusiform" (torpedo-shaped) as are pencilfish and killifish. Extreme examples of compressed fish are the angelfish (*Pterophyllum*) and the sole (*Achirus*). The latter case is atypical, since all soles and flounders begin life as normally shaped fish but adapt to life on one side as they grow older. Although the eyes migrate to one side (which we call the dorsal surface instead of the right or left side), the fins, mouth, and oper-cular flaps retain their original positions. There are thus both right-sided and left-sided flatfish, the side being determined by the position of the eyes. The flounders and the dabs have their eyes and color on the right side.

In addition to these common shapes, there are the truncate cowfish, globiform puffer, filiform pipefish, and bizarre seahorse (*Hippocampus*), not to mention the froglike mudskipper (*Periophthalmus*) with its bulging eyes, which spends so much time hopping around out of water.

Fins and Locomotion

The shape and construction of the body determine the locomotor ability of the fish to a great extent. Stiff, boxlike fishes encased in plates or covered by spines, such as the *Corydoras* catfish or the seahorse, rely entirely upon their fins for locomotion and are therefore rather slow. Not all fishes have multiple fins. In several, the fins on the median plane fuse so that the dorsal fin is continuous with the caudal and anal fins. Standard fishes have dorsal, caudal, and anal fins, and paired pectoral and pelvic fins. A small adipose fin lacking fin rays is present behind the dorsal fin on catfish, salmonids, and some tetras. Barbels, or whiskers, are named according to their site of origin.

Caudal fin: Rapid propulsion usually is a func-

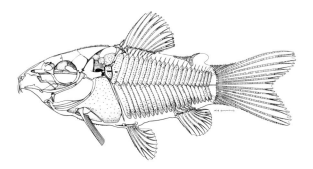

The skeleton of an armored catfish (*Corydoras*). Note the bony plates with spines covering the body and making it quite rigid.

tion of the caudal fin, or tail, aided by the pectorals in leaping. Serpentine or elongate fishes rely on an undulatory motion of the entire body for rapid movement. Fast-moving fishes usually have a forked tail and a narrow caudal peduncle with stabilizing finlets or lateral ridges, as are seen on mackerel. The tails of small fishes may be evenly or unevenly forked or may bear a ventral extension, as in the swordtail, or a median extension, as in the emperor tetra. There are round tails, square tails, triple tails, and veiltails, most of which can be modified by selective breeding.

Directional terms, names of fins and barbels, and planes of the body in a channel catfish (*Ictalurus punctatus*).

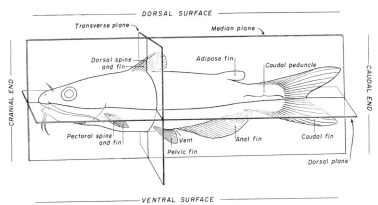

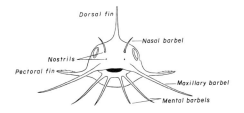

Pectoral fin: In addition to locomotor functions, the pectoral fins are used to counteract the forward movement of the body caused by the jet effect of water being forced out of the opercular opening. Enlarged pectoral fins are seen in fishes that leap out of the water, as do hatchetfish (*Gastropelecus*) and *Carnegiella.*

Pelvic fin: The pelvic fins stabilize the body against pitch and are used to counterbalance lift. They also produce roll when required. Pelvic fins may be located under the throat, at mid-body, or even further back. In gobies, the pelvic fins form a suction cup or a pedestal upon which they rest. The mudskipper "stands" upon the pelvic fin pedestal and uses the pectoral fins to hop when on land. The pelvic fins of the gourami and angelfish consist of a few elongated rays and function as tactile feelers.

Dorsal fin: The dorsal fin is usually prominent and serves as a stabilizer during forward motion. It can be used as a brake when the fish curls its caudal end. In many fishes the dorsal fin is erected for threat or courtship display and may be quite large or colorful, as in the Siamese fighting fish or sailfin mollies. In some marine fishes, such as the triggerfish (*Balistes*) and seahorse (*Hippocampus*), the dorsal fin is the primary locomotor fin. One or more spines may be associated with the dorsal fin. Some of these may be isolated from one another, as in the marine and freshwater sticklebacks (family Gasterosteidae), which may have three to sixteen isolated spines. These spines serve a defensive function and can inflict a painful wound. The spines of catfish are often accompanied by a poison gland.

Anal fin: The anal fin always is located behind the vent or anal opening, whichever is present. Like the dorsal fin, it serves as a stabilizer, and in some tetras it is very large.

In the live-bearing family Poeciliidae, which includes guppies, platys, and swordtails, the male has a rodlike anal fin called a gonopodium that serves as a copulatory organ. The presence of this spe-

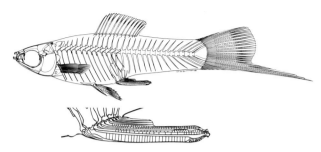

Skeleton of a male swordtail (*Xiphophorus helleri*). Inset shows structure of the anal fin, which is modified as a gonopodium for insemination.

cialized fin in guppies and platys enables one to recognize the male easily. (See also under "The Reproductive System.")

The Integument

Skin: The skin of fishes, as in all vertebrates, consists of an epidermis and a dermis. The epi-

Skin and scales of the swordtail (*Xiphophorus helleri*). A: Surface view with one scale removed; note that epidermis remains attached to the scale. B: Section to indicate a rupture of the scale pocket with the loss of a scale. Inset shows the underside of the scale with pigment-bearing melanophores in the dermis. C: Section to show a regenerating scale. Note that the epidermis has healed, closing the scale pocket. Growth and ossification of the new scale in the dermis has begun.

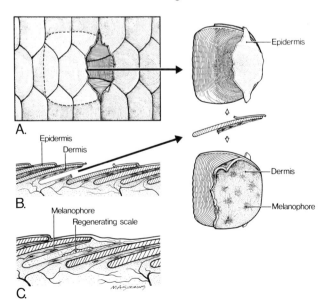

dermis is very thin (six to eight cell layers) and has unicellular mucous glands with a network of fine capillaries. The mucous glands of both the male and female discus (*Symphysodon*) produce a whitish secretion upon which the young fry feed for about three days before they start to take live food. The lungfish (*Protopterus*) uses skin mucus to enclose itself in a thin cocoon for aestivation in the mud during the dry season. Some parrotfishes (*Scarus*) enclose themselves in a cocoon of mucus every night while resting.

In addition to mucous glands, taste buds are widely distributed in the epidermis of many fishes. These taste buds transmit impulses over branches of the facial nerve to the hindbrain. There also may be pigment cells and alarm cells that produce pheromones. In silvery fishes, there are few if any pigment cells in the epidermis, whereas in others such as the red oscar (*Astronotus*), the pigment is primarily in the epidermis. The epidermis is easily broken when a fish is handled or is bitten by another fish, rendering the dermis vulnerable to infection.

The dermis usually contains many melanophores and a rich plexus of blood vessels and nerves. Scales develop in the dermis and lie within pockets close to the surface. When a scale is lost, that portion of the epidermis attached to its free surface is lost with it. As the epidermis grows and the wound heals, osteogenic cells remaining in the ventral wall of the scale pocket initiate the formation of a new scale.

Scales: The scale of a teleost fish is usually thin and flexible. Since it is a dermal scale, rather than an epidermal scale as in reptiles, it is not shed regularly, although it can be replaced if lost. It is composed of a type of bone tissue and is constructed in a manner that resembles plywood. A typical scale has two primary layers: a bony or hyalodentine surface layer that may bear spines, ridges, or grooves; and a deeper basal plate of woven lamellar composition.

The bony layer is usually acellular, although typical osteocytes may be seen in several families of fishes (Mormyridae, Gymnarchidae, Osteoglossidae). The lamellar layer of the basal plate consists of directionally alternating strata (as many as twenty-five layers) of parallel collagen fibers mineralized to vary-

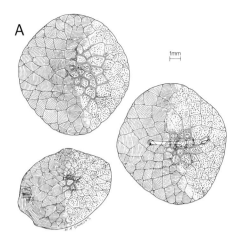

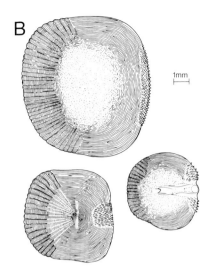

A: Scales of an arowana (*Osteoglossum bicirrhosum*), one of five living species of ancient bony-tongued fishes. These large scales lack radii and circuli. B: Scales of an oscar (*Astronotus ocellatus*), showing radii, circuli, and cteni. The exposed surfaces of all scales are on the right.

ing degrees and incorporating occasional or numerous calcified concentrations called Mandl's bodies. Although the basal plate of the scale is formed primarily by horizontal layers, several fishes (barbs, minnows, and carps) show transverse fibrils which divide the horizontal bundles into more or less regular segments. Such transverse fibrils may serve to spread mineralization through the basal plate and to bind the stratified layers together.

Most scales have concentric ridges, or circuli, in the bony layer that are deposited throughout life around the margins of the scale. When several circuli are close together, a ring, or annulus, is

formed. These annuli vary in width or density due to metabolic growth stimulation or inhibition, and thus can be used to determine the age of a fish if there is some environmental periodicity in the annual cycle. The annuli are crossed by grooves, or radii, on most scales.

The radii, which appear as spokes from the center of the scale, are usually more numerous on the cranial or covered portion of the scale. There is a peculiar lack of mineralization in the lamellar layer beneath the radii of the scale, giving the appearance of clefts. Some species have many more radii on their scales than do others, and some lack radii entirely.

The cranial portion of each scale is overlapped by scales ahead and to the sides of it. On their exposed surface, scales may be smooth (cycloid) or spiny (ctenoid). Usually only the caudal margin of the scale bears spines or appears comblike. In

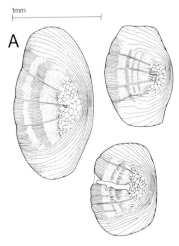

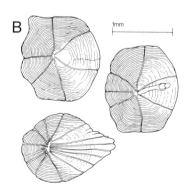

A: Scales of the black tetra (*Gymnocorymbus ternetzi*), have a cellular center and lack complete circuli. B: Scales of a Sumatra barb (*Barbus tetrazona*), have complete circuli and prominent radii in all quadrants.

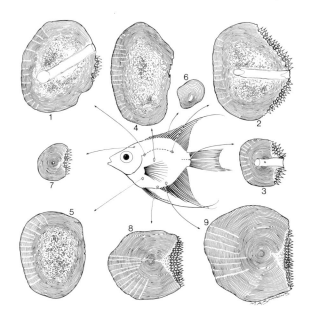

Types of scales seen on an angelfish
(*Pterophyllum*). All of the scales show growth rings
or circuli. 1, 2, 3: Ctenoid lateral line scales
enclosing a canal. 4, 5: Cycloid scales with a large
central focus. 6: Cycloid scale with a small focus
and no radii. 7: Ctenoid scale with a small focus
and no radii. 8, 9: Ctenoid scales with a small
focus and long radii.

angelfish, the spines seen on the caudal edge of
the scale form in such a manner that the terminal
spine of each radial row is the youngest. As each
new spine forms, its base (which lies beneath the

Scales of a swordtail (*Xiphophorus helleri*), at the
middle of its body, show pattern of overlap. In the
central shaded area, five scales overlap.

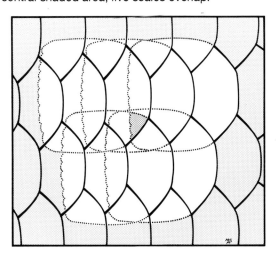

tip of the older spine) is indented and cradles the
older spine. When observed by transmitted light,
the apex of each spine appears to be capped by
the successive spine, but that is only an illusion.

A single fish may bear several kinds of scales.
The size and shape of the scales may vary on
different parts of the body, and sometimes there
are scaleless areas, particularly on the head.
Scales on particular parts of the head and body
may have sensory canals passing through them.
Each species of fish has its typical pattern of
sensory canals, which begin as surface structures
in the embryo and are gradually enclosed by
scales or bone. Most commonly there is a lateral
line canal on each side of the body that begins on
the head and extends to the caudal peduncle.
Many fishes have only a portion of this canal
present, and in some it is discontinuous or absent.
The lateral line canal opens to the surface by one
or more pores through the scale. This allows
water to enter the canal and transmit pressure
changes or vibrations via neuromasts that lie
within the canal.

Not all fishes have scales. Most catfish (family
Siluridae) and many species of eels lack scales.
Genetic variants of the carp (*Cyprinus carpio*) that
are incompletely scaled are called "mirror carp,"
and those without scales are referred to as
"leather carp." Various percentages of spawn
from a carp hatch will exhibit such abnormal
scalation.

Scale replacement: When a scale is lost, the
scale pocket fills with gelatinous material and the
epidermis heals rapidly. In the center of the floor
of the scale pocket, one or more scale papillae
develop as an aggregation surrounded by uncal-
cified bone matrix called osteoid. Osteoblastic
activity is seen on both surfaces of the developing
scale as it enlarges to fill the scale pocket.

Regenerated scales can sometimes be recognized by a difference in size, conformation, or
spacing between the annuli or radii. There may be
multiple growth centers in the new scale or uneven ossification. In some minnows, such as the
common shiner (*Notropis cornutus*), regenerated scales are easily recognizable because they
lack the silvery appearance of an original scale.
When melanocytes are numerous beneath a layer
of reflecting guanin crystals, a silvery appearance
results. Since the melanophores are most numerous on the underside of the scale and are lost with
it, there is often a change in the color pattern of

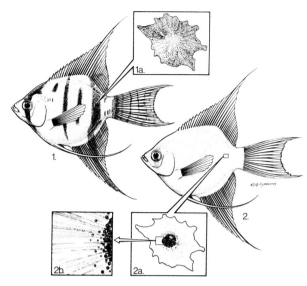

Angelfish (*Pteryophyllum*) have dark bars (1) when pigment is diffused in the melanocyte (1a), which is the usual condition when the fish is calm. When the fish is excited or in bright light, the color fades (2) because the pigment granules concentrate in the center of the melanocyte (2a). Pigment granules appear to move along microtubules (2b) under the influence of sympathetic nervous innervation. Note that the shape and size of the melanocyte remains the same regardless of the coloration.

the regenerated scale due to a difference in the number or distribution of new pigment cells that migrate into the area.

Color and pattern: The colors of fishes are produced by pigment cells in various combinations with the properties of refraction and reflection of light as it passes through these cells and scale structures. The various kinds of pigment cells, or chromatophores, differ in their chemical composition and appearance, although they have a common origin as endoplasmic reticulum. The most common chromatophores are the melanophores, with black or brown melanins contained in organelles called melanosomes. Xanthophores (yellow pigment cells) utilize pteridines synthesized in the cell and deposited as pterinosomes, whereas erythrophores (red pigment cells) concentrate carotenoids of dietary origin in vesicles of various sizes. Several types of pigment organelles may occur in a single cell.

Iridophores (guanophores) are not pigment cells. They utilize crystalline deposits of purines to produce structural colors by reflection, scattering,

diffraction, or interference of light. They have also been called refractosomes.

Changes in color or pattern can be gradual or rapid. A developmental or morphological change in color is a slow process that depends upon the accumulation of pigment from food or water, an increase in the number of pigment cells (melanophores), or a change in the scale pattern. Physiological color change mediated by neural mechanisms can be slow or almost instantaneous. It results from the intracellular redistribution of pigment-containing organelles, or chromatosomes, within a pigment cell. When chromatosomes contract (aggregate) to the center of the cell, color fades. Normally this is a response to fright or to bright light. When pigment granules are dispersed in the pigment cell, the entire cell darkens and the overall effect is that the color pattern appears more intense. Pigment granules are transported along radial microtubules within the chromatophore. The cell maintains its shape

A female platy-swordtail hybrid, showing a band of concentrated melanocytes in the dermis beneath the scales. Where pigment cells are scarce or lacking, the scale outline is not visible. Excessive growth of macromelanophores on various sites of the head, fins, or body can result in melanomas or erythroblastomas (pigment-cell tumors) and the death of the fish. There is a genetic basis for this development.

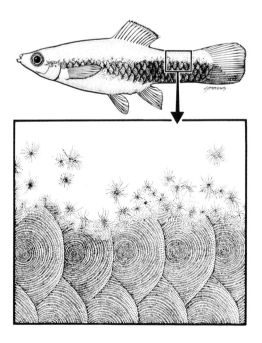

regardless of the aggregation or dispersion of the pigment granules.

Pigment-cell tumors: In 1932, Myron Gordon of the New York Aquarium was one of the first investigators to utilize hybrids of the Mexican swordtail (*Xiphophorus helleri*) and the platy (*X. maculatus*) to study melanosis, a neoplastic condition characterized by large spreading tumors in the skin. He showed (Gordon 1927) that the tumors had a hereditary basis and could be produced by crossing a normal female swordtail with a stippled and spotted male platy to produce a mottled platy-swordtail hybrid which frequently developed melanosis. Several varieties of hybrids in the aquarium trade have been named for their red or black benign or malignant color patterns.

There is the likelihood that one or more genes (oncogenes) are the causative agents of tumor formation in fishes. Several benign and several very malignant melanomas have been produced. The nature of these tumors suggests that they arise from cells of neural-crest origin. (For a review of normal and neoplastic melanophores in the skin of the swordtail, see Vielkind and Vielkind 1982.)

The Skeletal System

Structure of the head: The head consists of the skull, opercular bones, gill arches, and jaws, with

Bones of the jaw and opercular flap. The maxilla in most fishes is toothless and does not form a margin of the mouth opening. The premaxilla and mandible are usually toothed, except in cyprinid fish. The branchiostegal membrane and its rays serve as a gasket for closing the gill opening.

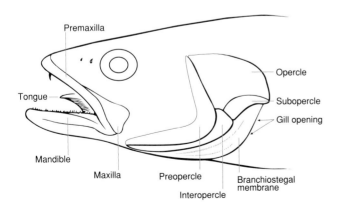

the associated teeth, soft parts, and sensory organs such as the eye, ear, and brain.

The operculum is a muscle-controlled flap on each side of the head that covers the gill chamber and acts as a valve to open and close the pharynx for water and food intake or water and debris outflow. The flap is stiffened by several bones, the largest being the opercular bone, which articulates with others whose outlines are sometimes visible on the skin surface. Muscles associated with the opercular flaps can close the gill chamber (adductors) or open it (abductors). Abduction will also flare the "cheeks," as in threat displays or when allowing fry to enter for protection, as do some cichlids.

The branchiostegal rays are a series of flat bony bars that stiffen the branchiostegal membrane, which stretches from the lower margin of the opercular flap to the isthmus or midline of the throat. This structure functions as a gasket for better closure when the operculum is adducted and the pharynx is expanded for water intake. The right and left branchiostegal membranes may be fused along most of their length on the midline, thus restricting the exit from the gill chamber. The eel, seahorse, and *Plecostomus* provide extreme examples of this narrowing of the opercular exit. In fishes that must attach to the substrate in order to hold their position, water enters and leaves the gill chamber through openings on the opercular margin of the isthmus rather than through the mouth.

The skull: The skull of a fish has more bones (approximately 185) than are found in the skull of any other vertebrate. To understand the skull, it is best to consider the component parts as units.

The skull includes an inner, brain-containing neurocranium, and the branchiocranium, which consists of outer groups of articulating bones such as the jaws, the hyoid apparatus, and gill-bearing arches. Other less easily categorized bones include groups such as the two bones in the sclera of each eyeball and the circumorbital series around the eye that enclose a sensory canal. Not all fishes have the same number of individual bones; some bones fuse with one another, and others are lost in development or evolution.

1. The neurocranium, or braincase, of a fish, when viewed by itself, does not sug-

gest the appearance of a fish's head. It is rather triangular in lateral view. The base or horizontal axis is formed by the parasphenoid and basioccipital bones. The dorsum is formed by the ethmoid bone rostrally, followed by the frontal, parietal, and supraoccipital bones. If a fish has a high crest on the skull, this is formed by the supraoccipital bone. The caudal portion of the neurocranium is formed largely by the exoccipital, basioccipital, and otic bones that enclose the inner ear.

The otic capsule contains the membranous labyrinth of the inner ear. This labyrinth consists of three semicircular ducts: a utriculus, a sacculus, and a lagena. Each of the chambers has an ear stone, or otolith, which functions for sound reception (see also "Balance and hearing").

The basicranial region is formed primarily by the basioccipital bone, which articulates with the vertebral column. Rather than a freely articulating joint, there is an opisthocoelous facet on the basioccipital bone that resembles one end of a vertebral centrum. In minnows and carps (the family Cyprinidae), the basioccipital bone has a ventral median plate that bears a cartilaginous pad against which the "pharyngeal teeth" (see later in this section) bite. When this pad dries, it becomes very hard and is spoken of as a "carp stone," "Karpfenstein," or *la meule.*" The basioccipital bone has a caudal extension that forms a ventral arch through which the dorsal aorta passes.

2. The branchiocranium consists of the jaws, the hyoid apparatus, and the gill basket.

The upper jaw, palatine arch, and lower jaw on each side of the branchiocranium comprise the oromandibular region. In the cyprinid fishes (barbs, carps, and minnows), the upper jaw consists of a toothless premaxilla and maxilla. The premaxilla in most fishes excludes the maxilla from the mouth opening. The upper jaw of many fishes is protrusible, as in the goldfish.

The hyoid apparatus consists of the hyomandibular bone, symplectic bone, the opercular series, the tongue elements, and the branchiostegal rays.

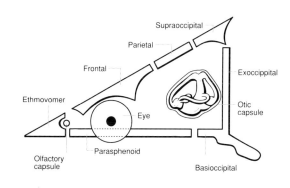

Schematic view of the fish neurocranium or braincase. This fusion of skull bones houses the brain and membranous labyrinth of the ear. The remaining bones of the head cover or articulate with the neurocranium.

Sense organs and brain of a spotted sea-trout (*Cynoscion nebulosus*) in dorsal view. The dashed outline below the semicircular ducts indicates the position of the sacculus and lagena of the inner ear.

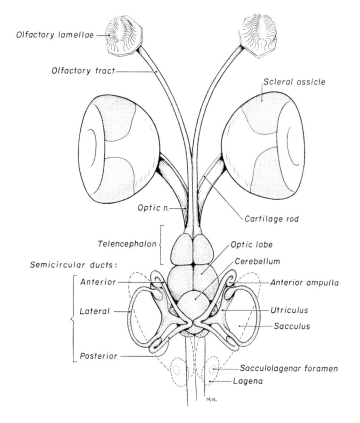

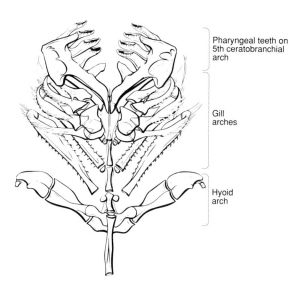

The pharyngeal skeleton of a golden shiner (*Notemigonus chrysoleucas*) in dorsal view. A median element of the hyoid arch supports the tongue. Four gill arches bear rakers and filaments. The modified fifth gill arch bears the pharyngeal teeth.

The hyomandibular bone is an elongated bone which functions as the suspensory element between the skull and the jaws, hyoid apparatus, and opercular bones. The upper end of the hyomandibular bone articulates in a socket on the skull. The lower portion of the hyomandibular bone is tightly bound to the preopercular bone, and its ventral end gives rise to a stout tendon which passes to the symplectic bone. It is upon

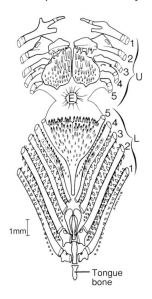

Upper and lower pharyngeal teeth of an angelfish (*Pterophyllum*) as seen through the open mouth. E: esophagus; L 1-4: gill arches; L 5: lower pharyngeal teeth on fused right and left ceratobranchials; U 1-5: upper ends of gill arches. Note the paired, tooth-bearing upper pharyngeal plates.

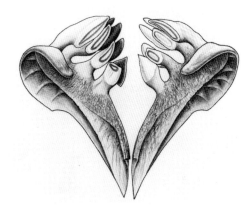

Pharyngeal teeth on the fifth ceratobranchials of a goldfish (*Carassius auratus*) in dorsal view with the rostral end at the bottom. There are four functional teeth on each side, and the tooth replacement sequence appears to alternate left and right sides. The median (first) tooth is always slightly ahead of the other three. In this illustration, the replacement teeth, on the right side of the fish, are young and stain darkly. On the left side, the replacement teeth are older and covered by nonstaining enamel. The pointed first tooth on the left arch has already moved into functional position, and the remaining three functional teeth will soon be shed and replaced by those behind them. This cycle continues throughout the fish's life.

the medial side of this tendon that the interhyal bone, which suspends the tongue apparatus, is attached. The symplectic is a splintlike bone which is wedged into the posterior notch of the quadrate bone. On the posterior margin of the hyomandibular there is a hemispherical opercular condyle that fits into a socket on the opercular bone. This joint permits movement of the opercular flaps. Other bones within the opercular flap are the subopercular and interopercular bones.

The hyal elements, or tongue apparatus, support the floor of the mouth and pharynx. A small nodular interhyal bone represents an ossification in the tendon connecting the hyoid arch to the cartilaginous union between the hyomandibular and symplectic bones. The next bone medially is the epihyal, which in turn attaches to the angular. The ceratohyal is the longest bone of the series, followed by the dorsal and ventral hypohyals, and, on the midline, by the basihyal within the tongue and urohyal behind it.

The branchial region consists of the gill-bearing arches and their associated gill rakers and pharyngeal teeth. A typical arch is composed of

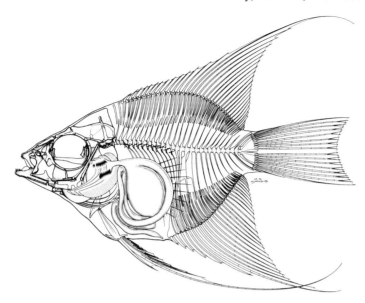

The skeleton and digestive tract of an angelfish (*Pterophyllum*). Left gill arches have been removed to show the position of pharyngeal teeth at the entrance to the esophagus. The stomach is saclike, and there are three loops of intestine.

a series of bones on each side: the basibranchial, hypobranchial, ceratobranchial, epibranchial, and pharyngobranchial bones. Frequently the fifth arch consists of a large tooth-bearing ceratobranchial bone (as in minnows and carps) or a combination of tooth-bearing ceratobranchials and pharyngobranchials that oppose each other (as in cichlids). These latter structures are spoken of as the "pharyngeal teeth" or the "pharyngeal mill."

Sound-transmitting bones (Weberian ossicles) of the horned dace (*Semotilus atromaculatus*). Several families of fishes have one or more movable elements that pivot on the vertebrae and serve to conduct sound from the gas bladder to the inner ear via pressure on a perilymphatic sac.

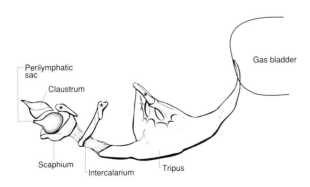

The gill rakers are arranged in two rows on the medial side of the gill arch, and the gill filaments are attached to the lateral side of the arch. The entire gill basket is tightly bound to the roof of the pharynx dorsally and to the hyoid apparatus ventrally.

The vertebral column: The length of the vertebral column and the number of vertebrae are not always related. Length is dependent upon the shape of the fish, but the number of vertebrae may be affected by the temperature of the water in which the fish develop. Eels have the most vertebrae, whereas discus, angelfish, and other short fishes have the fewest. When comparing two fishes of the same species from different habitats, the fish which developed in colder water will be the most likely to have more vertebrae.

Fish vertebrae are amphicoelous, having a spindle-shaped centrum with a central canal through which the notochord passes. Between vertebrae, the notochord expands to fill the space. Vertebrae are attached to each other by a fibrous ring at the margin of the centrum which allows only limited movement. Above the centrum are the neural arch and spine, which enclose the spinal cord. The dorsal fin has anchoring interneural bones intercalated between the neural spines. Below the centrum are ribs on each side in the abdominal region and hemal arches in the caudal region. The hemal arch encloses the caudal artery, which is a continuation of the dorsal aorta and the caudal vein, which returns blood to the heart. A ventral continuation of the hemal arch is the hemal spine. Anchoring the anal fin in the body musculature are interhemal bones intercalated between the hemal spines.

Vertebrae at the cranial end of the vertebral column may be modified to cradle the gas bladder or to serve as sound-transmitting ossicles. All carps, characins, catfish, and loaches (ostariophysid fishes) have some type of linkage between the gas bladder and the inner ear, which has been derived from parts of the first three vertebrae. These small bones are called the Weberian ossicles. On each side, there is a fixed claustrum and a movable scaphium formed by the first vertebra, an intercalarium formed by the second, and a tripus formed by the third, all interconnected by ligaments. The caudal end of the tripus is attached to the gas bladder. These ossicles have been given several different names. Some of these names suggest homologies with mammalian ear ossicles, but they are not the same. Vibrations received by the bladder cause the tripus to rock and pull on the ligament, which is attached to the scaphium via the intercalarium. The scaphium pivots on the first vertebra, and as it is pulled caudally, it releases pressure on an enclosed perilymphatic sac. This sac in turn is connected to a perilymphatic duct which abuts on the sacculus of the inner ear and transmits pressure changes to the membranous labyrinth, rocking the otoliths and thereby stimulating the "hair" cells of the sensory maculae.

The girdles: The pectoral girdle anchors the pectoral fin to the skull. It consists of a posttemporal bone, a supracleithrum, and a cleithrum. Fin articulation is between the cleithrum and the basal elements of the pectoral fin.

The pelvic girdle consists of a triangular plate embedded in the ventral body musculature. Typically, it is located immediately ahead of the vent, but in many fishes the pelvic girdle is at the level of the throat beneath the pectoral fins. The girdle elements of each side are united anteriorly on the midline.

The Musculature System

The muscles of the body wall are striated and arranged as segmental myomeres along the trunk. The myosepta are attached to the vertebrae. When the muscle fibers between two myosepta contract and shorten, the body bends laterally. A wave of contractions passing down the body results in lateral undulations and forward movement.

Muscles of the fins are slips of myotomic musculature. When the fin elements are specially developed, such as to form a gonopodium for insemination, the fin muscles are hypertrophied.

In some fishes, parts of the body musculature have been modified to serve as electroplaxes to generate and store electric charges. The electric eel (*Electrophorus*) of South America can generate in excess of 350 volts; the electric catfish (*Malapterurus*) of the Nile has a lower voltage. The electric ray (*Torpedo*) of the Atlantic and Pacific coasts of North America utilizes its pectoral disc musculature to generate potent discharges that stun its prey. Lesser electric fishes include the African mormyrids and the South American gymnotids or knifefishes that communicate with each other electrically.

The striated muscles of the head serve to activate the jaws, gill arches, and opercular flaps. Six muscles (two oblique and four rectus) serve to move each eye. In addition, fish have a small muscle attached to the lens, the retractor lentis, which serves to focus an image on the retina.

The Nervous System

The brain: The brain of a fish does not fill the cranial cavity. It is surrounded by fat and can easily be exposed without damage. As the head grows, the brain increases in length. The increase may involve all regions to some extent, but the greatest lengthening is that of the olfactory tract.

Grossly recognizable parts of the brain include the olfactory bulbs, olfactory tract, and forebrain lobes of the telencephalon; the pineal body and pituitary gland of the diencephalon; the optic lobes of the mesencephalon; the cerebellum or the metencephalon; and the acoustic, vagal, and facial lobes of the myelencephalon.

The olfactory bulb of the brain remains closely attached to the base of the olfactory sac, which contains the olfactory lamellae. There is no ventricle in the olfactory bulb, nor is there a ventricle in the telencephalon. During development, the telencephalon in fishes is everted and covered by a thin, closely applied roof plate. The dorsomedial portion is considered the hippocampus; the lateral portion represents the pyriform area and amygdala. A rostral commissure connects the basal areas, while a hippocampal commissure above connects the hippocampi. The telencephalon has a central striatal area and a medial or ventromedial septal area.

The diencephalon is small in fishes. An epithalamus is represented by the pineal body, a light-receptive organ which may be accompanied by a pineal "window" of the skull for light transmission.

The thalamus proper has a very small dorsal region and a larger ventral region. Optic projections from the retina go to the ventral thalamus as well as to the optic lobe of the mesencephalon. The hypothalamus is the largest portion of the diencephalon in fishes and can be seen readily on the ventral surface of the brain. The hypothalamus receives gustatory and olfactory impulses as well as optic connections from the tectum.

The mesencephalon is proportionately large in fishes and forms prominent optic lobes. The superficial layer of the optic tectum receives most of the projecting fibers from the retina, and in a fish lacking eyes, the optic lobe would be noticeably reduced. However, deeper portions of the optic tectum, even in blind fishes, are still represented because of

The brain of a goldfish (*Carassius auratus*). The large vagal lobes of the medulla indicate the presence of many taste buds in the mouth. Goldfish reject food that does not taste good to them.

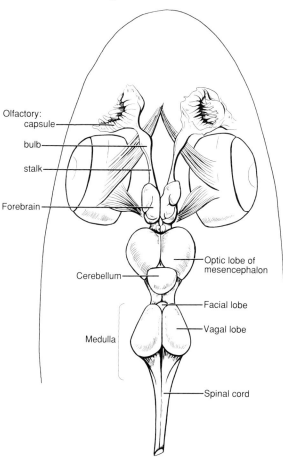

somatic sensory projections from the brain stem and visceral projections from the hypothalamus. Thus, the optic tectum is essentially a correlation center that discharges to lower centers and to the cerebellum through relays in the tegmentum or reticular formation.

The cerebellum (metencephalon) is large in most fishes and particularly so in electric fishes. It often has an enlarged medial portion, called the valvula cerebelli, projecting beneath the optic tectum. Impulses from lateral line nerves in cranial nerves V, VII, IX, and X pass to the cerebellum. Auricular lobes, associated with the vestibular apparatus for balance, may be visible externally in some fishes.

The medulla or hindbrain (myelencephalon) indicates most noticeably which gustatory sensory modalities are utilized by a fish when feeding. On the dorsal surface, the central nuclei of cranial nerves carrying afferent impulses from taste buds are enlarged and visible grossly. The visceral afferent column at the level of the facial nerve, which receives impulses from taste buds on the skin and barbels as well as communis fibers from the lower body surface, is seen as a median facial lobe in minnows or as paired median facial lobes in catfish. The enlargement of the medulla at the level of the afferent glossopharyngeal and vagal nerves forms the vagal lobes of the brain and represents the input of taste buds on the palatal organ and pharynx. Thus a fish that recognizes its food on the skin or barbels will have a large facial lobe, whereas one that samples its food in the mouth will have large vagal lobes. Some fishes (such as shiners) do neither and have very small facial and vagal lobes, whereas others do both and show enlargements of both.

Cranial nerves: There are ten cranial nerves in fishes, designated by Roman numerals. Olfactory nerves (I) are very short and pass from nasal sac mucosa to the olfactory bulb. Optic nerves (II) are large and stiffened by a cartilage rod; at the level of the telencephalon they cross completely. Oculomotor nerves (III) innervate the dorsal, ventral, and medial rectus and the ventral oblique muscles. Trochlear nerves (IV) supply the dorsal oblique muscles. Trigeminal nerves (V) innervate the jaw muscles and are sensory to the pelvic fin "feelers."

Abducent nerves (VI) supply the lateral rectus muscles of the eye. Facial nerves (VII) are sensory to taste buds on the skin of the head, body, and fins. Vestibulocochlear nerves (VIII) receive impulses from the ampullae of the semicircular ducts, utriculus, sacculus, and lagena. They are joined by fibers from the acousticolateralis system. Glossopharyngeal nerves (IX) are sensory to the pharynx. Vagal nerves (X) innervate taste buds of the palatal organ, pharynx, and the musculature of the gut.

The spinal cord: The spinal cord of fishes usually extends through the entire length of the vertebral canal. In a fish with over 200 vertebrae, such as an eel, the spinal cord is of considerable length and the spinal nerves exit segmentally along its length. On the other hand, in short fishes with fewer than twenty-five vertebrae, such as the puffer, the spinal cord is extremely short and only a cauda equina of spinal nerves continues down the vertebral canal. The ocean sunfish (*Mola mola*) is an extreme case where the length of the brain almost equals the length of the cord.

Dorsal and ventral nerve roots join outside of the vertebral canal, and the dorsal ganglion also lies at this point. The dorsal ganglion is often very large in fishes and is supplied by a capillary plexus. The ganglion has bipolar and unipolar neurons as well as intermediate types. The dorsal and ventral roots do not always leave the cord at exactly the same level. Visceral efferent fibers course in both dorsal and ventral roots.

Some fishes have a few pairs of nerves between the branchial nerves and the first spinal nerves. These are referred to as occipital or occipitospinal nerves, and they emerge from the skull or from behind the skull. In most instances these occipital nerves join the first two to four spinal nerves and form plexuses which supply hyoid and pectoral girdle musculature.

At the caudal end of the spinal cord in fishes, there is a caudal neurosecretory system consisting of vessels (urophysis) and glandular cells interrelated in some manner and of undetermined function.

Sensory Activitites

The nervous system of fishes operates on a reflex level, wherein the inputs of olfaction, taste, vision, touch, balance, and hearing interact without much cerebration. Since a fish's major activity is feeding, and its major concern is being eaten, its sensory system is perfected to maximize the former and minimize the latter. Sense organs are numerous and range from very simple free nerve endings for chemical reception to very specialized electroreceptors capable of low-voltage recognition.

Touch: General tactile (trigeminal) sensation is well developed in fishes and is often associated with modified pelvic fin rays such as those seen in gourami, angelfish, and sea robins. These fishes utilize their filamentous fins as "feelers" along the bottom or as "early warning" devices when extended from a hiding place. The barbels of a catfish serve for both touch and taste. The sensation of touch is carried by the trigeminal or fifth cranial nerve, and taste by the facial or seventh cranial nerve on the barbel. There are

The brain and cranial nerves of a spotted sea-trout (*Cynoscion*), a drum that feeds by sight.

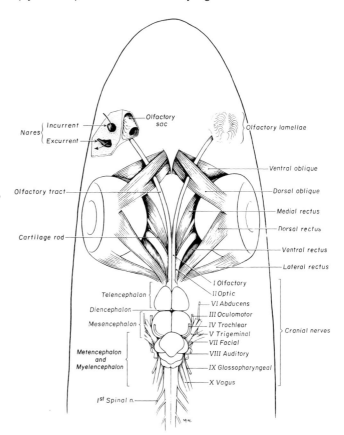

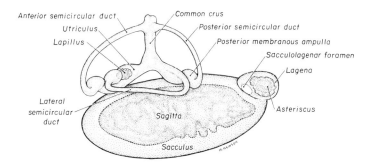

Membranous labyrinth of the inner ear of a spotted sea-trout, showing the three ear stones or otoliths in their respective chambers.

also numerous pressure receptors in the lips and pharynx.

Taste: Gustatory sensations are received by taste buds which look very similar to those of other vertebrates (Kapoor, Evans, and Pevzner 1975). However, they may be located anywhere on the fish body or fins as well as within the oral cavity. Taste buds are particularly numerous on the barbels; there may be in excess of 1,600 buds per square centimeter (over 10,000 buds per square inch) in the brown bullhead (*Ictalurus nebulosus*). When the barbels of a catfish are extended to each side, they act as triangulating devices to home in on a source of food molecules that are being disseminated in the water. If the food source is directly ahead of the fish, the sensations being received are equally strong from both barbels, and the fish swims ahead. If the stimulus is stronger in one barbel than the other, it indicates to the fish that a turn is being made away from the stimulus, and a compensatory movement is made to head for the target. If a barbel is lost, it will regenerate. While this is taking place, the fish circles toward the side of the lost barbel since it does not perceive any reduced stimulus from that side.

There is a difference in the innervation of taste buds on the surface of the skin versus those within the oral cavity that is reflected by the size of the receptor nuclei in the brain. Taste buds of the skin and barbels are innervated by the facial nerve (VII) and transmit to the facial lobe of the medulla, whereas those within the oral cavity and pharynx are innervated by the vagal nerve (X) and transmit to the vagal lobes on each side of the medulla (see also under "Cranial nerves"). A fish

that characteristically mouths its food and rejects items it has engulfed, such as a goldfish, will be found to be utilizing vagally innervated taste buds. Such a fish will have greatly enlarged vagal lobes of the brain. Fishes that utilize taste buds on the barbels and skin, such as catfishes, have enlarged facial lobes.

Smell: Olfaction serves a social function in fishes for recognition of status within the group or it serves to warn of the presence of a predator requiring fight or flight reactions. The olfactory sac has an incurrent and excurrent opening separated by a baffle that projects above the surface and directs the water current. In teleost fishes there is no connection between the olfactory sac and the pharynx. Within the olfactory sac there is an olfactory rosette consisting of many lamellae covered by receptor mucosa. Below the mucosa there is an olfactory bulb of the brain which receives the short primary olfactory neurons of cranial nerve I.

Sight: The visual system is very important for most fishes, but some are able to get along quite well without eyes, as is shown by the blind cave characin (*Astyanax*), which lives and breeds well in captivity as well as in the wild. Fishes active at night are characterized by large eyes, a common feature of nocturnal reef fishes. Fishes of caves, muddy rivers, or abyssal depths often have very reduced eyes.

All fishes are nearsighted, as can be surmised from the spherical lens and the weak accommodation mechanism of the retractor lentis muscle. The sclera of all fishes has a pair of bony plates or ossicles to stiffen it. There are a few modifications of the eye in fishes whose behavior requires vision both in air and water, such as the four-eyed fish (*Anableps*), which has a constriction between the dorsal and ventral portions of the cornea, and the mudskipper (*Periophthalmus*), with its bulging, froglike eyes.

Balance and hearing: It is difficult to separate the sense of balance from that of hearing, because several parts of the ear serve both functions. The inner ear within the otic bones of the skull is relatively large. It consists of three semicircular ducts with ampulae: a utriculus, a sacculus, and a lagena. Most often, all of these

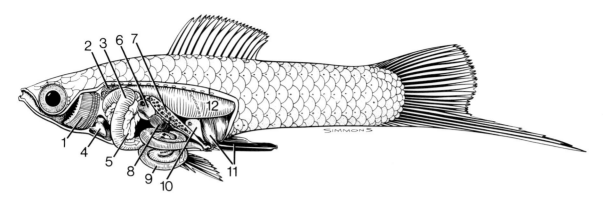

Viscera of a male swordtail (*Xiphophorus helleri*). 1: gill lamellae; 2: head kidney; 3: stomach; 4: heart; 5: liver; 6: spleen; 7: testis; 8: gallbladder; 9: intestine; 10: urinary bladder; 11: gonopodium and its muscles; 12: gas bladder.

chambers, which are filled with endolymphatic fluid, communicate with each other. Within the utriculus, sacculus, and lagena, there are sensory cells with sterocilia upon which rests an otolith. The otoliths are free to move and respond to vibration or to changes in position and acceleration. Any movement of the otolith is transduced as an auditory impulse via the eighth cranial nerve. The sacculus is the largest chamber in drum fish and the saccular otolith, called the sagitta, is likewise large. It is the ear stone most frequently used for determining the age of a fish and can be seen clearly on a radiograph or within a cleared skull. As would be expected, those fishes that produce sounds as part of their courtship behavior, such as drums, have the largest otoliths.

The lateral line sensory canals with their enclosed neuromasts also transmit the reception of vibrations and water movement to the acoustico-lateral system. Present on the head and along the body, these water-filled canals have pores that open to the surface through the skin or scales. They are particularly well developed in cave fishes.

Other important sensory organs include the electroreceptors of mormyrids, gymnotids, and sharks, which appear as jelly-filled pit organs, rosettes, or ampullae of Lorenzinni.

The Digestive System

The mouth: The mouth is the limiting factor determining the size and type of food eaten. Toothless fishes such as cyprinids (barbs, danios, goldfish) gulp their food and lacerate it in the pharynx by means of pharyngeal teeth before swallowing. Fishes with teeth on their jaws, such as cyprinodontids, cichlids, and characins, use their teeth to nibble and tear bits of food from larger pieces. They may also have upper and/or lower pharyngeal teeth in the pharynx for further maceration. Some fishes have a very wide mouth opening, as do catfish and cichlids, whereas most tetras and cyprinids have small mouths. In general, bottom feeders have protrusible jaws on the underside of the head, midlevel feeders have terminal nonprotrusible jaws, and surface feeders have transversely oriented jaws that may or may not be protrusible. One of the most restrictive mouth openings is seen in the seahorse, which has small toothless jaws fused into a tube that is capable of suction but little else.

The lips: The lips may be thick, thin, or expanded into a suction pad, as in *Plecostomus*. In some fishes the lips are so thick that they hide the teeth (cichlids); in others, such as the piranha or bucktooth tetra (*Exodon*), the teeth are clearly visible externally even when the mouth is closed. The lips usually have several ridges or papillae on their inner surface and may have papillae along their free margins. When the papillae are numerous, the lips appear thick. There is a distinct labial groove between the lip and the jaw. On the labial margin of the jaws the teeth are arranged in rows that are partially or completely hidden by papillae.

The barbels: Extending from the lips may be a pair or more of barbels. Barbs, carps, and danios

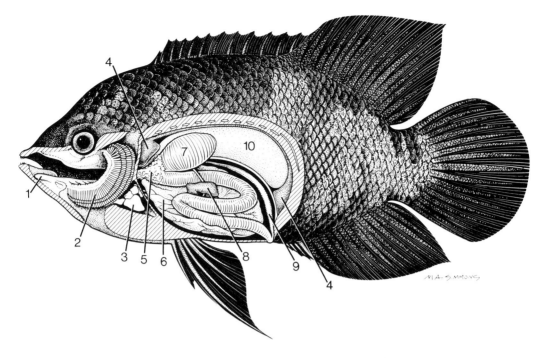

Viscera of a male oscar (*Astronotus*). 1: tongue; 2: gill lamellae; 3: ventricle of heart; 4: kidney; 5: pancreas; 6: liver; 7: stomach; 8: spleen; 9: testis; 10: gas bladder.

have small barbels without an internal stiffening rod. Goldfish (*Carassius*) have no barbels, whereas carp and koi (*Cyprinus*) have two pairs of small barbels. It is interesting that hybrids of carp and goldfish usually have only one pair. Barbels are gustatory and tactile sensory structures by virtue of the taste buds and the free nerve endings that they bear. In catfishes the long barbels are moved by muscles and they are used as long-distance directional sensors, in contrast to the trailing or protruding barbels which serve as close-range sensors for the majority of fishes.

The oral cavity and valves: The upper and lower oral valves separate the papillate labial cavity from the smooth oral cavity. Oral valves are thin flaps which extend from one angle of the jaw to the other. They are in apposition when the jaws are closed and thus serve to occlude the oral cavity when water is being forced out of the opercular openings.

The oral cavity is the region between the oral valves and the gill chamber. Its lining is smooth, and on the ventral surface lies the tongue, which may be fleshy or covered with teeth. There is often a frenulum extending from the tongue to the level of the oral valve.

The pharynx: The pharynx is the chamber be-

tween the oral cavity and the esophagus through which water and food pass. The water passes between the branchial bars, over the gill lamellae, and out the opercular flaps, whereas the food is trapped by the gill rakers, lacerated or crushed by the pharyngeal teeth, if present, and swallowed by entering the esophagus. The smaller the food items eaten, the more numerous the gill rakers. Filter feeders have long, slender gill rakers.

Pharynx construction reflects the diet of the fish to a fair degree because it is the site of food retention prior to swallowing. Carnivorous fishes have an array of sharp gill rakers as well as teeth on the tongue, palatine bones, and vomers which aid in retaining the prey and forcing it into the esophagus. Several fishes, including the cyprinids which lack teeth on their jaws, have pharyngeal teeth on the fifth ceratobranchials that bite against a pharyngeal pad on the roof of the pharynx. Many other fishes, such as cichlids and wrasses, have both upper and lower pharyngeal teeth that serve as either retention or crushing devices. The teeth on these bones which line the pharynx are replaced frequently, in the same manner as are the teeth on the jaws (Evans and Deubler 1955). Pharyngeal teeth are charac-

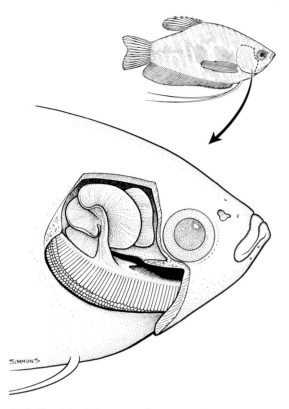

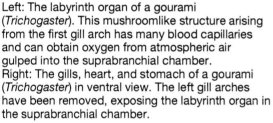

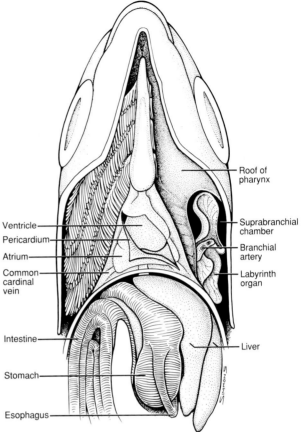

Left: The labyrinth organ of a gourami (*Trichogaster*). This mushroomlike structure arising from the first gill arch has many blood capillaries and can obtain oxygen from atmospheric air gulped into the suprabranchial chamber.
Right: The gills, heart, and stomach of a gourami (*Trichogaster*) in ventral view. The left gill arches have been removed, exposing the labyrinth organ in the suprabranchial chamber.

teristic for each species and are frequently used in keys or descriptions.

The digestive tract: In general, carnivorous fishes have a short gut and herbivorous fishes have a very long one. In the stone-roller minnow (*Campostomer*), an algae feeder, the intestine is six to nine times the length of the body and has loops that encircle the gas bladder.

The esophagus is short, and in many fishes it has a duct leaving its dorsal surface that can pass air into the gas bladder. Such fishes that gulp air are called physostomous, in contrast to those with no connection from esophagus to gas bladder, called physoclistous. Often the stomach is simply a widening of the gut tube with no discernible chamber, as in the swordtail, but it can be pouchlike and distensible, as in cichlids such as

the oscar. The spleen, which may be triangular or oval, is usually attached along the stomach or at the fundus.

At the junction of the stomach and the duodenum in some species there are pyloric cecae of variable number and size. There may be only one or two, or they may number in the hundreds. Pyloric cecae serve a digestive function and are capable of reflux emptying.

The small intestine is indistinguishable externally from the large intestine in teleost fishes. If the intestine opens to the outside, as in the swordtail, an anus is formed. If it opens into a cloacal chamber that also receives urinary and genital products, then the external opening is called the vent.

The liver is relatively large in fishes and frequently incorporates the pancreas in whole or in part. A gallbladder is usually present, and the bile may be green, brown, or yellow.

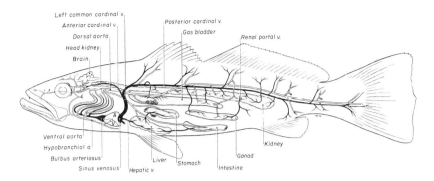

Above: A schematic representation of the circulatory system. Only venous blood (in black vessels) enters and passes through the heart to be aerated in the gills. The atrium of the heart (A) receives blood from the sinus venosus and passes it into the ventricle (V). Below: The heart and gills of a spotted sea-trout (*Cynoscion nebulosus*) in left lateral view. A: First branchial arch connecting ventral to dorsal aorta. B: Cross-section of a gill arch. Note shunt connections between afferent and efferent branchial arteries which allow oxygenated blood to bypass the capillary bed in the gill and continue to the dorsal aorta. C: A schematic gill filament, with several lamellae indicated as cross-connections. Each lamella consists of a platelike capillary plexus between the afferent and efferent filament artery.

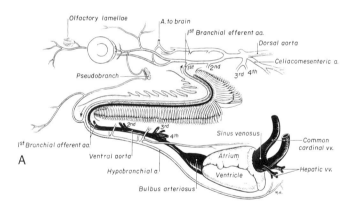

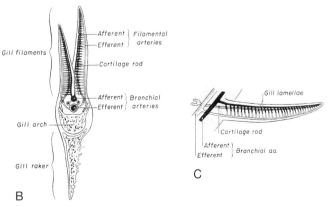

The Respiratory System

Oxygen is carried to the gills in the water current that enters the mouth and leaves through the opercular flaps. The rate at which water is passed through is dependent upon the muscles of the pharynx and operculum or upon the speed of swimming. There is also some oxygen exchange through the skin, pharynx, and gut. Loaches gulp air and pass it through their gut for respiratory purposes. Ganoid fishes have a saccular gas bladder, and lungfish have paired saccular bladders which enable them to cope with adverse environmental conditions.

Several fishes, such as the anabantids (gourami, *Betta*), can utilize atmospheric oxygen by virtue of a labyrinth organ in the pharynx. The labyrinth is an expansion of the first gill arch, with an extensive vascular plexus that projects dorsally into an air-filled chamber of the pharynx. Blood diverted from the gill filaments is passed through this plexus to be oxygenated and then flows into the dorsal aorta.

The Circulatory System

Blood cells are formed in the kidney, liver, and spleen. The erythrocytes are oval and nucleated. Some arctic fishes with low oxygen requirements lack hemoglobin and thus have clear blood. Leukocytes may constitute 10 percent of the blood. Lymphatic vessels are present in teleosts, but there are no lymph nodes. Capillary networks or retia are present in the gas bladder for the introduction or removal of gas (oxygen, nitrogen). Within the red muscle strip of the lateral body wall, the capillary network functions for heat exchange; fishes such as tuna are capable of raising their body temperature 4 to 6 degrees F (approximately 2 to 3 degrees C) above ambient temperatures. In the oviduct and ovarian wall of live-bearing fishes, there are networks for nutrient exchange which can be considered placentae.

Fishes have a one-way circulatory pathway through the heart. All venous blood from the organs, body wall, and fins returns to the heart via superficial and deep veins. It is passed through the four chambers of the heart, without aeration, into the ventral aorta located in the throat. (For a discussion of circulation in fishes, see Satchell 1991.)

Aeration: Aeration is a function of the gills that requires mechanical activity to pass a stream of water over the gill surfaces and out of the opercular opening. Most fishes accomplish this by the use of numerous muscles which open and close the mouth, dilate and constrict the pharynx, and open and close the opercular flaps. The structure of the gill, with its well-vascularized and numerous lamellae, has secondary pathways via shunts that allow the blood to pass from the venous side (afferent branchial artery) to the arterial side (efferent branchial artery) without going through the capillary bed. Such shunts would be used when the oxygen tension is high in an oxygen-rich environment and the demand in the tissues is low due to inactivity. The efferent branchial arteries converge to form a dorsal aorta which courses caudally beneath the vertebral column, giving branches to the kidney, viscera, and body wall along the way.

The heart: The heart lies in a pericardial cavity that is completely separated from the body cavity. Its position is in the throat, ventral to the gills. The heart wall is supplied by hypobranchial vessels from the gill rather than from the dorsal aorta. Likewise, the pseudobranch also receives a special blood supply from the efferent branchial artery.

The heart has four chambers: the sinus venosus, atrium, ventricle, and bulbus arteriosus. The sinus venosus is a thin-walled transverse chamber extending across the dorsal aspect of the pericardial cavity. It receives the common cardinal veins (ducts of Cuvier), which drain the head and body wall from each side, and the hepatic veins, which drain the liver. Backflow of blood is prevented by the sinoatrial valve, which is a fold of the sinus wall extending into the atrium.

The atrium is the largest and most expansible

chamber of the heart. Because of its thin wall and venous blood within, it appears dark. It extends across the pericardial cavity dorsal to the ventricle and balloons around the other chambers.

The ventricle is the thickest walled chamber of the heart and therefore appears white even when filled with blood. It is pyramidal or cone-shaped, with its apex directed anteriorly. It exits into the bulbus of the heart.

The bulbus arteriosus is almost spherical and smaller than the ventricle. It is an intrapericardial portion of the ventral aorta and is rich in elastic fibers. It serves as an elastic relief chamber for the emptying of the ventricle, but is capable of contraction. In sharks, gars, and some other fishes, this chamber is elongated, has a series of three or more valves, and is called a conus arteriosus. It is said that in primitive bony fishes such as shad and bonefish, elements of both the conus and the bulbus are present.

The ventral aorta is the outflow path to the gills. Bony fishes usually have four gill units on each side, and each receives a large branch from the ventral aorta called an afferent branchial artery. This vessel forms capillary nets in the gill lamellae, which then drain into an efferent branchial artery.

The dorsal aorta is formed by the joining of right and left efferent branchial arteries above the gills. It passes caudally beneath the vertebral column, giving rise along the way to paired segmental intercostal, renal, and spinal arteries as well as to unpaired arteries to the gas bladder and viscera. Posteriorly, where the paired ribs fuse to form hemal arches, the dorsal aorta enters the hemal arch and passes into the tail. The caudal vein also lies within the hemal arches beneath the aorta.

The Gas Bladder

The gas bladder, also called the air bladder or swim bladder, is composed of one or two chambers in tandem connected by a short duct. A single-chambered gas bladder may have paired lobes at the cranial end, or the entire bladder may be partially divided longitudinally. In some members of the herring family, the gas bladder may have many diverticulae at the cranial end. Cyprinid fishes have a two-lobed tandem bladder with a sphincter in between. The caudal chamber

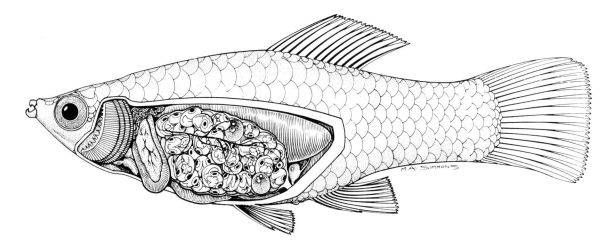

A female swordtail (*Xiphophorus helleri*) with sixty-eight young in late gestation. The ovaries are enclosed in a transparent, vascularized mesovarium. Note that only two mature eggs failed to develop. Fish that give birth to living young, as do most species in the family Poeciliidae, are called viviparous.

is connected with the esophagus via a pneumatic duct, enabling the fish to gulp air and pass it into the bladder. Such fishes with an open connection are spoken of as physostomous fishes; without such a connection, they are called physoclistous. The gas bladder functions primarily as a hydrostatic organ adjusted for neutral buoyancy. A vascular rete, referred to as the "gas gland," secretes oxygen or nitrogen into the bladder (or removes it) so as to allow the fish to remain at a given level. The gas bladder also serves in phonation, audition, and in some fishes such as gars, for accessory respiration.

The Reproductive System

Reproductive specializations in fishes are numerous and often uniquely suited for maintaining maximum survival under adverse environmental conditions. In general, those fishes that congregate in large numbers to spawn (like the cod, eel, and herring) have few if any structural modifications and little if any sexual dimorphism. Fishes that court and pair or raise their young in high-risk habitats have evolved various mechanisms for ensuring fertilization and protecting their eggs. Males and females can differ in size, shape, and color. Sex reversal is common in some (wrasses), and dramatic changes can take place in color, pattern, and size. If a fish is first a functional male, it is said to be protandrous; if first a female, protogynous. There are hermaphroditic, or self-

fertilizing, fishes that have functional ovaries and testes, such as *Rivulus marmoratus* in Florida. The sailfin molly (*Poecilia latipinna*) is gynogenetic: Although there is male courtship and insemination, the sperm only activates the egg, and no fusion of pronuclei takes place.

The ovaries and oviducts are usually paired, although in several species there are examples (such as the swordtail) of fused ovaries with single oviducts. The testes of the male may be paired or partially fused, and sperm are produced in tremendous numbers. Sperm can be released as a cloud over the spawning grounds, or, as in live-bearing fishes, small unencapsulated packets (spermatophores or sperm balls) are inserted into the cloaca of a female via a copulatory organ, the gonopodium.

The gonopodium of poeciliids consists of elongated fin rays 3, 4, and 5, which begin to look different at about fourteen weeks of age in the guppy or eighteen weeks in the swordtail. Accompanying the modifications of the anal fin rays are enlargements of the fin supports and their associated muscles. The fan of muscles on the interhemal spines provides great mobility for the gonopodium, which bends forward and to the side to transfer a sperm mass into the oviduct of the female. Several of the genera in this family crossbreed, and all of them are quite polymorphic, so that many hybrids and varieties of poeciliids have been produced. A variety of terminal hooks and claws on the gonopodium have been shown to be essential for the proper functioning of the mechanism (Rosen and Gordon 1953).

Eggs may be large and few, as in the tilapia and sea catfish, or small and numerous (several million), as in the sturgeon. There are eggs that float (pelagic) and eggs that sink (demersal), eggs that stick (adhesive), and eggs that are carried around in the mouth or on the body of the parent. Some fish eggs hatch in twenty-four hours (*Amphiprion,* the clown anemone fish), three days (*Danio,* the zebrafish), thirty days (*Fundulus,* the killifish), or longer. Eggs may be retained and hatched internally so that live young are produced; these are the viviparous fishes (see Tavolga 1949; Wourms 1981).

About thirteen families (122 genera, 510 species) of teleosts are viviparous (Breeder and Rosen 1966). They may be lecithotropic, in which the young are dependent upon yolk, or matrotrophic, in which the female provides a continuous supply of nutrients, or a combination of both. The eggs in live-bearing fishes either remain within an ovarian cavity (ovisac) or remain within the ovarian follicles of the ovary. In the swordtail (*Xipho-*

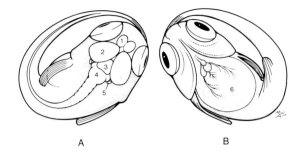

Dorsal (A) and ventral (B) views of a prenatal swordtail (*Xiphophorus helleri*) removed from an ovarian follicle (see previous figure).
1: forebrain; 2: optic lobe of midbrain; 3: cerebellum; 4: hindbrain; 5: otolith; 6: pericardial sac. Note the large brain and the heart with its pericardial sac vasculature that serves as a placenta.

phorus), the paired ovaries fuse into one which has a central lumen continuous with the oviduct. The young develop within ovarian follicles on the inner surface of the fused ovaries, and they derive part of their nutrition from a placenta formed by their pericardial sac.

Reproductive tract of a pregnant swordtail (*Xiphophorus helleri*) in left lateral view. The mesovarium (1) has been reflected and a portion of the left ovary removed to show the cavity between the ovaries and the young within ovarian follicles. (2) Eggs are fertilized within the ovary by sperm deposited in the oviduct (4) via the gonopodium. The young develop within the ovary and utilize their egg yolk and a pericardial placenta (3) for nutrition. When the fish are ready to be born, they emerge into the central lumen and pass through the oviduct and genital pore. There is no cloaca in this species, since the intestine (5) opens separately.

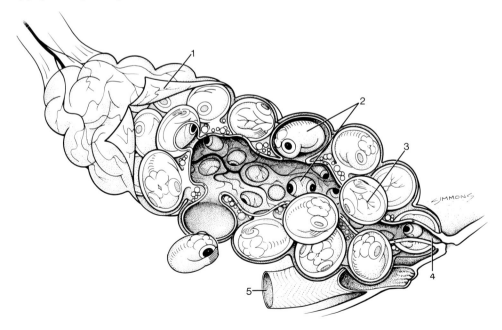

The most common live-bearing aquarium fishes are in the family Poeciliidae, which includes about 136 species fishes in twenty genera now found throughout the world, although all were originally from Mexico and Central and South America. An interesting exception to the live-bearing mode is seen in *Tomeurus,* a monotypic genus with two species from South America. Although this fish normally lays eggs, it has internal fertilization (fin rays 6 to 9 of the anal fin are greatly modified to form a distensible sac when brought forward), and on occasion the eggs are retained and the young are born alive. This latter case is called facultative viviparity.

When two or more broods of embryos of different ontogenetic stages develop simultaneously within the ovisac, it is called superfetation. Thus there may be oocytes maturing and being fertilized within the follicles of the ovary while others are partially developed or even being born. Most poeciliids can store sperm for several months, so the presence of the male is not necessary for all broods. Gestation usually lasts about a month. Eggs within the ovarian follicles of the swordtail are about 2 millimeters (0.08 inches) in diameter and appear to have almost enough yolk for their needs. The dry-weight increase of the swordtail embryo is only about 30 percent during gestation, which is a low level of maternal–fetal transport. The swordtail is considered to be an unspecialized matrotrophe.

At the other extreme, the dry-weight increase of the embryo in *Poeciliopsis turneri* is reported to be 1,840 percent and that of *Heterandria formosa,* 3,900 percent. The latter two fishes are considered to be specialized matrotrophes with a follicular placenta and superfetation. In the four-eyed fish (*Anableps*), the postfertilization weight has been reported (Knight et al. 1985) to increase 298,000 percent. Placental transfer in this fish is accomplished by apposition of the maternal follicular epithelium (within follicular pits) to absorptive surface cells (vascular bulbs) of the pericardial trophoderm. The pericardial trophoderm is an extension of the somatopleure, which replaces the yolk sac during early gestation. The follicular placenta of *Anableps* is probably the most efficient maternal–embryonic nutrient transfer system in teleost fishes.

The Urinary System

The kidneys are elongate structures that lie below the vertebral column and may extend from the head to the end of the abdominal cavity. They are sometimes expanded cranially and/or caudally, as in the oscar, or at midbody, as in the goldfish. The kidneys in adult fishes are mesonephric in structure and function for excretion as well as blood formation. Gobies retain a functional pronephric kidney, but in most fishes there is only a remnant on each side of the embryonic pronephric kidney at the level of the first five vertebrae. This head kidney functions as a lymphoid organ. The remainder of the kidney is mesonephric and drains via a mesonephric duct into a bladder or into a cloaca. Several fishes, including the swordtail, have urinary bladders.

For more information on the biology and anatomy of fishes see Bond (1979), Harder (1975), Love (1970, 1980), and Moyle and Cech (1982).

Selected References

Bond, C. E. 1979. *Biology of Fishes*. Philadelphia: W.B. Saunders.

Breder, C. M., Jr., and Rosen, D.E. 1966. *Modes of Reproduction in Fishes*. New York: Garden City Press.

Evans, H. E., and Deubler, E. 1955. Pharyngeal tooth replacement in *Semotilus atromaculatus* and *Clinostomus elongatus,* two species of cyprinid fishes. *Copeia* 1: 31–41.

Gordon, M. 1927. The genetics of a viviparous top minnow *Platypoecilus:* the inheritance of two kinds of melanophores. *Genetics* 12: 253–83.

———. 1932. The scientific value of small aquarium fishes. *New York Zool. Soc. Bull*.: 1–8.

Harder, W. 1975. *Anatomy of Fishes.* Part I. Text. Part II. Figures. Stuttgart: E. Schweizerbart'sche Verlag.

Kapoor, F. M.; Evans, H. E.; and Pevzner, R. 1975. The gustatory system in fish. *Adv. Marine Biol*. 13: 53–108.

Knight, F. M.; Lombardi, J.; Wourms, J.P.; et al. 1985. Follicular placenta and embryonic growth of the viviparous four-eyed fish (*Anableps*). *J. Morphol.* 185: 131–42.

Love, R. M. 1970. *The Chemical Biology of Fishes*. New York: Academic Press.

————. 1980. *The Chemical Biology of Fishes.* Vol. 2. *Advances, 1968–1977.* New York: Academic Press.

Moyle, P. B., and Cech, J., Jr. 1982. *Fishes: An Introduction to Ichthyology.* New York: Prentice Hall.

Nelson, J. S. 1984. *Fishes of the World.* 2nd ed. New York: John Wiley & Sons.

Rosen, D. E., and Gordon, M. 1953. Functional anatomy and evolution of male genitalia in poeciliid fishes. *Sci. Contrib. N.Y. Zool. Soc.* 38(1): 1–47.

Satchell, G. H. 1991. *Physiology and Form of Fish Circulation.* Cambridge: Cambridge University Press.

Tavolga, W. N. 1949. Embrynoic development of the platyfish (*Platypoecillus*), the swordtail (*Xiphophorus*), and their hybrids. *Bull. Amer. Mus. Nat. Hist.* 94(4): 161–230.

Vielkind, J., and Vielkind, U. 1982. Melanoma formation in fish of the genus *Xiphophorus:* a genetically-based disorder in the determination and differentiation of a specific pigment cell. *Can. J. Genet. Cytol.* 24: 133–49.

Wourms, J. P. 1981. Viviparity: the maternal–fetal relationship in fishes. *Amer. Zool.* 21: 473–515.

Fish Genetics

Joanne Norton

Knowledge of genetics can help the fish breeder to develop new or improved strains and to avoid some of the errors that cause inefficiency or undesirable results.

This chapter is neither a general introduction nor a review; it is intended to be somewhere in between. I have tried to present a broad overview of fish genetics to make readers aware of knowledge in many areas, some of which have not been mentioned in aquarium literature. I touch on many aspects of fish genetics, even though some of them are of no practical use to most aquarists, because anyone who is generally informed about fish genetics should be cognizant of topics such as gynogenesis and polyploidy. Many references are given to provide a good start for the reader who wants to locate literature on fish genetics.

Great advances in fish genetics have been made since Mendelian laws were found to apply to a fish, the medaka (*Oryzias latipes*), in the early 1900s. This chapter deals mainly with ornamental tropical fishes. Wohlfarth (1983), Yamazaki (1983), Purdom (1983), and Allendorf and Thorgaard (1984) reviewed the genetics of food and game fishes.

Genetics means the study of inherited variation (called polymorphism). Highly polymorphic fishes include the guppy, *Xiphophorus* species (see summary by Borowsky 1984), goldfish, betta, and some species of African cichlids. In the guppy, there are many color pattern factors, most of which are expressed only in the male (see review by Yamamoto 1975). There are numerous species of mollies (*Poecilia*), most of which can produce fertile hybrids. Most species of *Xiphophorus* will hybridize with most of the other species in the genus, and fertile hybrids often are produced. Pigment-pattern genes occur in most species of *Xiphophorus* (Kallman and Atz 1966; Kallman 1975).

Biochemical polymorphism in fishes, which will not be included in this chapter, is discussed in Section 7 (pp. 223–339) of Schröder (1973), in Smith, Smith and Chesser (1983), and in Echelle, Wildrick and Echelle (1989).

The Genetic Material

Genetic factors, called genes, are composed of DNA (deoxyribonucleic acid), which exists in the cell in the form of a long double strand, comparable to a twisted ladder (called a double helix). Each gene has a certain sequence of the two pairs of chemical bases that connect the two strands of the ladder. Each gene makes possible the production of a certain protein, and thus genes are the carriers of genetic codes that make an organism develop and behave in specific ways. A chromosome is a long strand of DNA that consists of many genes. At certain stages of cell division, the chromosomes shorten into rods, which can be counted. Chromosome numbers vary among species of fishes. Since the reviews by Park (1974) and Ojima, Uyeno and Hayashi (1976), chromosome counts of about 1,000 teleost species (bony fishes) have been made (Yamazaki 1983).

When a cell outside the gonads divides, producing two replicas of itself, each chromosome is duplicated. Thus the chromosomes of the daughter cells are the same as the chromosomes of the cell that divided. This type of cell division is called mitosis.

Another kind of cell division occurs in the formation of the germ cells, called gametes (ova and sperm). In this division, called meiosis, the chromosome number is halved. The number of chromosomes in a gamete is called haploid, or n. When an ovum (n) and sperm (n) unite, forming a fertilized egg (zygote), the 2n, or diploid, chromosome number results. Thus in a diploid cell there are pairs of chromosomes, one chromosome of each pair having come from each parent.

A gene occurs at a certain place, called locus (plural, loci), in a chromosome. Only chromosomes with matching loci will pair and then segregate during meiosis. Such chromosomes are called homologous chromosomes.

Basics of Inheritance

Simple Mendelian inheritance: Genetic variation can result when there is a mutation, a permanent change in a gene. Genotype refers to the genetic makeup of an individual, while phenotype refers to the observable traits. The genotype of an albino molly, in which *a* is the symbol for the gene for albinism, is *aa*. The phenotype of this fish is white with pink eyes.

In the simplest example of Mendelian inheritance, a gene is expressed even when present in only a single dose. Such a gene, called a dominant gene, is denoted by a capital letter or more than one letter beginning with a capital. An example is the plumetail character in the platy, in which the central rays of the caudal fin are elongated. The gene for plumetail, *Pl,* is dominant to wild-type (Entlinger 1974). Using + (plus) for wild-type, we can write the three possible kinds of genotypes as *Pl Pl, Pl* +, and ++. A fish with a double dose of the gene for plumetail, *Pl Pl,* is homozygous for plumetail, whereas a *Pl* + fish, which has a single dose of the gene for plumetail, is

In platys, plumetail is due to a dominant gene.

heterozygous for plumetail. Wild-type is ++. When a homozygous plumetail female is crossed with a wild-type male, all of the ova will have the *Pl* gene, but none of the sperm will have this gene. All of the offspring (the F_1, or first filial generation) will have the genotype *Pl* +, and all will be plumetails. The second filial generation, or F_2, is obtained by mating F_1 individuals, brother to sister. The F_2 can be predicted by finding all of the combinations of every possible kind of ovum with every possible kind of sperm of the female and male parents, respectively. This can be done on a checkerboard, called a Punnet square. Remember that each gamete receives only one of each pair of chromosomes, and therefore only one of each pair of genes. A ratio of 3 plumetail:1 wild-type occurs in the F_2.

An F_1 cross with typical dominant and recessive alleles in platys.

		kinds of sperm	
		Pl	+
	Pl	*Pl Pl* (plumetail)	*Pl* + (plumetail)
kinds of ova			
	+	*Pl* + (plumetail)	+ + (wild-type)

An incomplete dominant gene is expressed differently when present in single and double dose. An example is the gene for dark (*D*) that is heterozygous in black lace angelfish (like a wild-

Wild-type angelfish, called silver by hobbyists, have vertical black stripes on a silver body. *Source:* Tetra Archives.

type or silver but with more black pigment) and homozygous in black angelfish (those that are black all over) (Seligmann 1958). When a black (*DD*) female is mated to a wild-type ("silver," ++) male, the ova all carry *D*, whereas the sperm are all +. This cross produces all *D*+ offspring, which are black lace. Crossing these F₁ black lace, brother to sister, is expected to produce a 1:2:1 ratio in the F₂, as follows:

An F₁ cross involving an incompletely dominant allele (*D*) in angelfish.

		kinds of sperm	
		D	+
	D	*D D* ("true" black)	*D* + (black lace)
kinds of ova	+	*D* + (black lace)	+ + (wild-type)

The ratio can vary from 1:2:1 because "true" blacks (*DD*) can have a high mortality rate. Therefore many spawns from black lace parents yield fewer than 25 percent blacks.

A recessive gene is expressed only when pres-

The black lace angelfish, top, is heterozygous for dark, while the black angelfish pictured above is homozygous for dark. *Source:* Tetra Archives.

ent in a double dose. A rare exception occurs when a chromosome carries a recessive gene and the other chromosome of the pair breaks and loses some genes; this deletion will be discussed in the section on chromosome aberrations. An individual that is homozygous for a recessive factor not only exhibits the trait but breeds true for that character when mated to another individual that is homozygous for the same gene. For example, albino guppies (*aa*) produce 100 percent albino offspring.

Three kinds of gold angelfish have been discovered: Naja gold, Hong Kong gold, and "new gold"

(Norton 1982b). Because "new gold," the most recent gold, is the only gold angelfish still widely available, it will be referred to as "gold" in the rest of this chapter. The gold angelfish has a recessive gene, D^g (Norton 1982b). When a gold is mated to a wild-type, ++, all of the F1 offspring have wild-type phenotype but are heterozygous for gold (+D^g). Mating F1 individuals, brother to sister, produces an F2 in the ratio of 3 wild-type : 1 gold.

An F₁ cross of phenotypically black (wild-type) angelfish carrying a recessive gold allele (D^g).

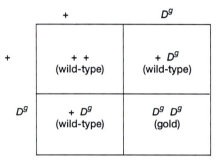

	+	D^g
+	+ + (wild-type)	+ D^g (wild-type)
D^g	+ D^g (wild-type)	D^g D^g (gold)

A backcross involves mating an F1 fish to the parent that is homozygous for the recessive gene. In this instance, the backcross would be F1 (+D^g) mated to gold ($D^g D^g$):

A backcross of an F₁ to the parent homozygous for the recessive gene, hence $D^g D^g$, in gold angelfish.

	+	D^g
Dg	+ D^g (wild-type)	D^g D^g (gold)

The advantage of a backcross, which produces offspring in a 1:1 ratio, is that it supplies a greater proportion of the homozygous recessive genotype than is obtained by mating F1 with F1.

Four recessive genes affect background body color in guppies. The gold guppy, described by Haskins and Druzba (1938), has about half as many black pigment cells (called melanophores) as the wild-type; this allows its yellow pigment to show. Goodrich *et al.* (1944) explained the colors as due to the recessive gene for gold; they also

The angelfish in the foreground is a new gold that is heterozygous for veiltail.

explained the color for blond, in which the melanophores are smaller than in wild-type. "Cream" is homozygous for both gold and blond. Albinism in guppies is due to another recessive gene (Haskins and Haskins 1948). Yet another recessive gene results in "blue," in which there is no yellow pigment (Dzwillo 1959).

Albinism, which occurs in many fishes, is due to a recessive gene in most species, such as the albino paradise fish (*Macropodus opercularis*) (Kosswig 1935; Goodrich and Smith 1937). An exception in which albinism is not due to a recessive gene occurs in the common krib (*Pelviachromis pulcher*). Langhammer (1982) reported that albinism in this fish is due to an incomplete dominant. He stated that heterozygous fry have melanophores in the upper half of the orbit of each eye, while homozygotes lack melanophores at any age. He also noted dark spots in some fins of

This female krib (*Pelviachromis pulcher*) is heterozygous for a dominant gene for albino.

heterozygous adults. I made all of the possible kinds of crosses involving homozygotes, heterozygotes, and wild-type kribs, and concur that the gene for albino is an incomplete dominant. The homozygotes grow more slowly than wild-type or heterozygotes. Using 10x magnification, I observed a small cluster of melanophores in the upper part of the orbits of the eyes of homozygous fry. I additionally found some melanophores not only in the eye orbits and fins but also on the body of heterozygous fry. Adult heterozygotes have some melanophores on the body, resulting in a faint gray pattern on a nearly white fish. The presence of melanophores in albino kribs is similar to the situation in albino guppies, in which a few melanophores are present in the embryos (Haskins and Haskins 1948).

The gold platy has fewer black pigment cells than a wild platy. *Source:* Tetra Archives.

Two-factor inheritance: The result of a cross involving two pairs of factors, sometimes called a dihybrid cross, can be predicted in essentially the same way as for monohybrid crosses.

Taking an example in guppies, we can use the symbols *g* for gold and *b* for blond. Fish homozygous for *g* are gold, fish homozygous for *b* are blond, and fish homozygous for both *g* and *b* are cream. All others are wild-type. A 9:3:3:1 ratio occurs in the F_2 when there are two pairs of factors and four phenotypes.

The scales and dermis of a wild platy (*Xiphophorus maculatus*) contain small black pigment cells, called micromelanophores, and yellow pigment cells, called xanthophores, producing an olive-brown color. Gordon (1927) referred to the micromelanophore pigmentation as "stippled." The gold platy, which was discovered in domesticated stocks, has very few micromelanophores in the scales and dermis, so yellow pigment is not masked by black pigment cells. In addition, the gold platy has a greatly increased number of xanthophores compared with wild-type (Kallman and Brunetti 1983). Gordon (1931) found that gold is due to a single recessive gene (*st*).

In guppies, a double recessive homozygote for blue (*rr*, lacking xanthophores) and blond (*bb*, having very small micromelanophores) is called "white" (Dzwillo 1962). Crossing a blond (*bb++*) with a blue (*++rr*) guppy produces all wild-type

An F₁ dihybrid cross showing independent inheritance of two traits in guppies.

sperm of F1 male (+ *g* + *b*)

		+ +	+ *b*	*g* +	*g b*
		+ + + + (wild-type)	+ + + *b* (wild-type)	+ *g* + + (wild-type)	+ *g* + *b* (wild-type)
	+ *b*	+ + + *b* (wild-type)	+ + *b b* (blond)	+ *g* + *b* (wild-type)	+ *g b b* (blond)
ova of F1 female (+ *g* + b)	*g* +	+ *g* + + (wild-type)	+ *g* + *b* (wild-type)	*g g* + + (gold)	*g g* + *b* (gold)
	g b	+ *g* + *b* (wild-type)	+ *g b b* (blond)	*g g* + *b* (gold)	*g g b b* (cream)

Young zebra angelfish. The small ones are homozygous for zebra. The larger ones, heterozygous for zebra, grow faster.

(+b+r) F$_1$. The 9:3:3:1 F$_2$ ratio can be figured out by using a checkerboard.

In the molly (*Poecilia sphenops*), black and various degrees of black spotting are due to two pairs of dominant factors with additive effect; in *P. latipinna,* only one pair of dominant genes is involved (Schröder 1964). In *P. sphenops,* each dose of the genes for *M* or *N* increases the amount of black pigmentation. *MMNN* individuals are solid black with a black iris at birth. Fish with any three of the dominant factors are black, with a light iris and belly at birth; at maturity, these are solid black, with a black iris. *MM++* and *++NN* fish are unspotted at birth, but strongly mottled at maturity. *M+N+* individuals are slightly mottled at birth and strongly mottled when mature. *M+++* and *++N+* fish are unspotted at birth and slightly mottled at maturity. There is no spotting in *++++* fish. Many strains of black mollies are not true breeding; some of the offspring are not solid black. If these black mollies are *P. sphenops,* perhaps they could be used to obtain true-breeding blacks by selecting breeders only from black fry that have a black iris.

There are a number of modified two-factor ratios, which occur when there are either more or fewer than the four phenotypes that make up the typical 9:3:3:1 F$_2$ ratio. If one of the two pairs of factors is not completely dominant, six phenotypes occur in the F$_2$. Angelfish with the dominant zebra pattern (Norton 1982a) have three black vertical stripes on the body. There are only two black stripes on the body of the wild-type (silver) angelfish. Veil angelfish have an incomplete dominant gene that causes elongation of the caudal fin (Sterba 1959). A double dose of the gene for veiltail results in a very long tail, whereas a single dose of this gene results in a shorter veiltail. When a homozygous zebra angelfish is mated to a long-veil (homozygous for veil) silver, the F1 are all zebra short-tail veiltails. There are six phenotypes in this modified two-factor ratio:

3 zebra, long-veil
6 zebra, short-veil
3 zebra, without veil
1 silver, long-veil
2 silver, short-veil
1 silver, without veil

The numbers in this theoretical ratio add up to 16, just as they do in the typical 9:3:3:1 ratio. In practice, the number of fish with long veiltails usually is fewer than the predicted number due to the low viability of long-veils.

When both pairs of factors are incomplete dominants, even more phenotypes occur in the F$_2$. Then each genotype produces a different phenotype, and the F$_2$ ratio is 1:2:2:4:1:2:1:2:1. A black angelfish without veiltail (*DD++*) crossed

An F$_2$ cross involving three color patterns in convict cichlids showing the effects of masking the expression of one pair of genes to yield a modified ratio of offspring.

	+ +	+ s	p +	p s
+ +	+ + + + (striped)	+ + + s (striped)	+ p + + (striped)	+ p + s (striped)
+ s	+ + + s (striped)	+ + s s (spotted)	+ p + s (striped)	+ p s s (spotted)
p +	+ p + + (striped)	+ p + s (striped)	p p + + (pink)	p p + s (pink)
p s	+ p + s (striped)	+ p s s (spotted)	p p + s (pink)	p p s s (pink)

with a silver with long-veil (++*VV*) would produce this ratio in the F₂ were it not for the fact that homozygous *D* and homozygous *V* can be deleterious. Therefore it is common to get fewer than the expected percentages of the genotypes that are homozygous for one or both of these genes.

A modified two-factor ratio also occurs when there are fewer than four phenotypes in the F₂. In the convict cichlid, there are three known color patterns: wild-type (with black vertical bars on the body), spotted (with black splotches on the body), and pink (with black pigment in the eye but not on the body). These patterns are produced by two pairs of factors in which both the spotted pattern and pink are recessive to wild-type (Norton 1970b). The symbol *p* is used for pink, *s* for spotted pattern, and + for wild-type. A pink female (*pp*++), crossed with a spotted male (++*ss*), produces striped (+*p*+*s*) F₁. The F₂ are in the ratio predicted by the checkerboard.

There are only three phenotypes because all pink individuals look alike whether they have the genotype for striped or spotted pattern. Thus two classes, (genetically striped) pink and (genetically spotted) pink, are lumped into one. The ratio is 9 striped : 3 spotted : 4 pink. When the genes of one pair mask the expression of the genes of another pair, the genes causing the masking are said to be epistatic to the genes of the other pair. Because the epistatic factor in this instance is recessive to wild-type, this is an example of recessive epistasis.

Another type of modified two-factor ratio occurs when an epistatic factor is dominant to wild-type. In angelfish, marble pattern (an irregular black pig-

This marble angelfish is homozygous for marble.

ment pattern) is dominant to wild-type (Norton 1982a). Zebra also is dominant to wild-type (Norton 1982c). Crossing a homozygous marble angelfish with a homozygous zebra produces F₁ offspring with the marble pattern and only slight zebra influence in the form of blue spangles in the unpaired fins and green on the head of the adult (Norton 1982d). These F₁ fish produce an F₂ of 12 marble : 3 zebra : 1 silver. This is an example of dominant epistasis, in which marble almost completely masks the effect of zebra.

Polyfactorial inheritance: When a characteristic is affected by a number of pairs of genes, these genes are called multiple factors, and this type of inheritance is termed polyfactorial or polygenic. Polyfactorial inheritance is suspected when the F₁ is intermediate between the parents, and the F₂ covers a range of one extreme to the other, with a high percentage of individuals being intermediate and comparatively few at the extremes. It is possible, from some crosses, to get individuals that are more extreme than either parent. Sailfin mollies (*Poecilia velifera, P. latipinna,* and *P. petenensis*) have more dorsal fin rays than short-fin molly species. Crossing a sailfin with a short-fin molly produces F₁ offspring in which the number of dorsal fin rays is intermediate between the parents. A range of dorsal fin ray numbers appears in the F₂, with a high proportion of intermediates and few at the extremes.

Linkage: Two genes that are at different loci on

The spotted convict cichlid shown here is less common than the striped morph.

The blushing angelfish is homozygous for stripeless.

Lyretail mollies have extensions of the upper and lower caudal fin rays. *Source:* Tetra Archives.

the same chromosome are linked. During formation of the gametes, these factors do not assort at random, but tend to stay together. If the genes are close to each other, they usually stay together and are inherited as a unit. But, during meiosis, linked genes that are farther apart can be separated by a process called crossing over. This results in an exchange of homologous (sections having matching loci) parts of a pair of chromosomes. If crossing over occurs in the formation of some of the gametes, then two kinds of gametes are produced: noncrossover gametes (in which no crossover occurred) and crossover gametes (in which an exchange of genes by crossover happened). The rate of crossover between two genes is predictable once the crossover rate of the two loci is known. By finding crossover percentages of more than two loci on a chromosome, it is possible to discover the location of genes on a chromosome, a process called chromosome mapping.

In *Xiphophorus,* a number of loci involving pigment patterns are known (Kallman and Atz 1966; Kallman 1975). Anders, Anders and Klinke (1973) discussed the maps of the sex chromosomes of *X. maculatus* and *X. variatus.* More recently, starch gel electrophoretic methods were used to locate enzyme loci (Morizot, Wright and Siciliano 1977; Morizot and Siciliano 1979, 1982a, b). At least sixty polymorphic loci in *Xiphophorus* are known (Morizot and Siciliano 1982b). Chromosome mapping can be useful in studying the location of genes such as those influencing inherited development of tumors in *Xiphophorus.* Biochemical linkage studies also have been done with the guppy (Shami and Beardmore 1978) and four species of

Poeciliopsis (Leslie 1982). For a review of gene mapping in these fishes, as well as in trout, salmon, and sunfishes, see Morizot and Siciliano (1984).

Chromosome aberrations: There are several kinds of chromosome aberrations which occur during meiosis and which affect the expression of genes.

A translocation results when a segment of a chromosome breaks off and becomes attached to another chromosome, often of another pair. This changes the location of linkage groups and therefore usually is detected by genetic methods before being observed cytologically. In a reciprocal translocation, chromosomes that are not of the same pairs exchange parts.

In nondisjunction, both chromosomes of a pair go to the same cell at the reduction division of meiosis instead of separating and going to different cells.

A deletion occurs when a piece of a chromosome breaks off and is lost. When a dominant gene is lost and only its recessive allele is inherited, the individual may exhibit the recessive trait. An individual receiving both chromosomes of a pair having the same deletion usually does not live.

When a broken segment of a chromosome reattaches with its ends reversed in direction, this is an inversion, which results in a reversal of the gene locations for that segment of the chromosome. This results in a change in crossover rates of the genes on the inverted section of chromosome.

Pleiotropy: A pleiotropic gene affects more than one character. An example of pleiotropy occurs in the blushing angelfish, which not only lacks the black vertical body stripes of the wild-type angelfish but also has large body areas, including the gill covers of juvenile fish, that are dull rather than shiny because these areas have decreased numbers of iridophores, cells that reflect light (Norton 1982a). The adult blushing angelfish, like the gold angelfish, lacks red color in the iris of the eye.

Multiple alleles: There are many instances in which more than one mutation has occurred at a single locus, resulting in multiple alleles. In angelfish, the dominant genes for stripeless and zebra behave as alleles (Norton 1982c). Diagrammatically we can show the chromosomes in the three possible kinds of gametes.

The zygote and somatic (nonreproductive) cells ordinarily carry only two of these chromosomes, one from each parent. The possible kinds of angelfish have the chromosome combinations as shown in the chart below.

Because the genes for zebra and stripeless are alleles, a fish homozygous for zebra cannot have stripeless, and a fish homozygous for stripeless cannot have zebra. Only two of a set of alleles occur in an individual. The phenotypes of the six possible genotypes are: #1, silver; #2, stripeless; #3, zebra; #4, blushing; #5, zebra; #6, stripeless, with a few black splotches on the body. Different results of crosses are obtained when multiple alleles are involved instead of genes at different loci on the same chromosome or on different pairs of chromosomes. If stripeless and zebra were on

Above, female calico veiltail molly; below, black veiltail molly.

different pairs of chromosomes, then crossing a homozygous zebra with a blushing (homozygous stripeless) would produce offspring heterozygous for each of these factors. Crossing one of these offspring with silver (wild-type) would produce four kinds of offspring, including silver, in a 1:1:1:1 ratio. But this does not happen. When one of the offspring of a homozygous zebra and blushing is mated to a silver, the offspring are zebra and stripeless, in equal numbers, and no silver, because each of the offspring receives either zebra or stripeless from its heterozygous parent. In some instances, genes that behave as multiple alleles are discovered later, after a crossover between them occurs, to be closely linked instead. No crossover between zebra and stripeless has been reported.

In the platy (*Xiphophorus maculatus*), a series of codominant multiple alleles produce tail-spot patterns composed of micromelanophores (Gordon 1931). Eight such alleles occur in natural populations (Kallman and Atz 1966). This locus is on an autosome, not on a sex chromosome (Gordon and Fraser 1931). Later it was found that the tailspot locus consists of at least two closely linked genes instead of one (Kallman 1975).

Penetrance: A dominant gene has complete penetrance if it is expressed in every

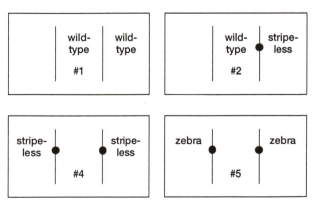

Some veiltail mollies have very wide tails, like this female from a veiltail crossed with *Poecilia mexicana*.

A *maculatus*-type platy with the twin-spot pattern at the base of the tail.

individual having that gene. If a recessive gene in the homozygous state is always expressed, then that gene has complete penetrance. When a dominant gene, or a recessive gene in double dose, is not expressed in all individuals carrying those genes, then such genes have reduced penetrance. In some instances, penetrance is higher in one sex than the other. In *Xiphophorus maculatus,* strain Jp 163, there is a gene producing spots in the dorsal fin (spotted dorsal, *Sd*); this *Sd* gene shows zero penetrance in many progenies when the Jp 163 stock is hybridized with other populations of the species (Kallman 1970b).

Expressivity: Variable expressivity occurs when a characteristic due to a particular gene differs among individuals. For example, variable expression of the plumetail character in the platy results

in variations in the length, width, and shape of the plumetail platy's caudal fin extension. The plume may be wide, long and narrow, or short and pointed.

In the molly, the lyretail mutation was discovered in a female raised by a fish breeder in Singapore (Ong 1960). Lyretail is due to a single autosomal dominant factor (Schröder 1964). Schröder, who never got 100 percent lyretails from lyretail parents, suggested that either the gene for lyretail is closely linked to a sterility factor or else homozygous lyretails are lacking in vigor and do not reach reproductive age. However, 100 percent lyretail broods have been reported (Knepper and Knepper 1963). Modifiers, genes that affect the expression of another gene, cause variation in the size and shape of the tails of lyretail

The dorsal and caudal fins of this female veiltail molly are very large.

Some platys from Lake Peten in Guatemala, as well as some swordtails, have a gene that, when coupled with the gene for twin spot, results in Guatemala crescent at the base of the tail.

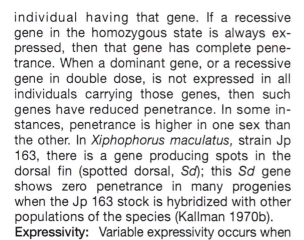

mollies (Schröder 1964). Thus there is variable expression of lyretail.

The veiltail molly has a large caudal fin and all of its other fins are also enlarged. A single female veiltail was discovered in a fish pool (Wolfsheimer 1965; Wood 1968). Veiltail is due to a single dominant gene (Norton 1974) with variable expressivity, the tail varying in size and shape. Many veiltail molly males are unable to breed because of their deformed gonopodia. Crossing a veiltail female with a lyretail male produces four kinds of offspring: veiltail, lyretail, lyreveil (having both veiltail and lyretail), and common (Norton 1974). Variable expression occurs not only in veiltails but also in lyreveils, which have genes for veiltail and lyretail. A lyreveil with a large tail has an enlarged tail with short extensions at the upper and lower edges of the tail. A lyreveil with a small tail looks very much like a lyretail, having a somewhat larger tail than in a lyretail. Genetic testing by crossing with a common is necessary to accurately differentiate between a lyretail and a small-tail lyreveil. The genes for lyretail and veiltail are nonallelic (Norton 1974).

Variable expressivity of pigment-pattern genes in *Xiphophorus* is responsible for numerous variations in domesticated platys and swordtails. For example, color intensity of red platys and swordtails is influenced by modifiers of the platy gene for red body. The red dorsal fin color of the platy (*X. maculatus*) spreads over most of the body due to modifiers of red dorsal that are added by crossing a red-dorsal platy with a wild swordtail (*X. helleri*).

The expression of two of the tail-spot alleles, comet and twin-spot, in the platy (*Xiphophorus maculatus*) is changed by a different modifier of each (Gordon 1956). A dominant modifier (*Cg*) changes twin-spot (two black spots at the base of the tail) to Guatemala crescent, a broad crescent at the base of the tail. Guatemala crescent has been found in platy populations only of the Lake Peten region in Guatemala. However, the same modifier also occurs in the swordtail (*X. helleri*) (Gordon 1956; Atz 1962). Guatemala crescent did not appear in hybrids of twin-spot *X. maculatus* crossed with *X. milleri, X. couchianus,* and *X. nigrensis* (Kallman 1975). The *Cg* modifier has no effect on the other tail-spot patterns. Also, in *Xiphophorus,* a dominant factor (*E*) changes the comet pattern to wagtail, but has no effect on any other tail-spot patterns tested. In comet, the upper and lower edges of the tail are black, called "twin bar" in the trade. All of the fins are black in a wagtail. The *E* gene occurs in *X. helleri,* not in *X. maculatus* (Gordon 1946), and natural populations of *X. helleri* are homozygous for *E*. Another modifier affects a tail-spot pattern of *X. variatus* (Borowsky 1984).

Yellow and red pigment patterns of *Xiphophorus* also may vary in their expression when they are incorporated into the genetic makeup of other species of *Xiphophorus*. Yellow patterns of *X. pygmaeus* become red patterns when introduced into *X. maculatus* (Zander 1969), but the red dorsal (*Dr*) gene of a Jamapa strain of *X. maculatus* produces yellow dorsal fins in *X. montezumae* (Zander 1969), now known as X. *nezahualcoyotl* (Rauchenberger, Kallman and Morizot 1990).

Lethal or deleterious genes: In guppies, the recessive gene for albinism is deleterious when homozygous (Haskins and Haskins 1948). Insemination of a female by an albino male usually results in only one small brood instead of the multiple broods common in poeciliids. Albino guppies are more sensitive to poor environmental conditions than are non-albino guppies, and their life-span is shorter than that of wild-type guppies. The F2 from an albino crossed with a wild-type would theoretically be in the ratio of 3 wild-type :1 albino. The actual ratio obtained by Haskins and Haskins (1948) was 51.1 wild-type :1 albino. However, females varied in the percentage of albino offspring they produced.

Albinism also is harmful in swordtails. Albino and wild-type embryos were present in the expected ratio in dissected females that previously had produced broods having fewer than the expected percentage of albino fry (Gordon 1942). Albino embryo mortality occurs shortly before or after birth. Some swordtail females produce close to the expected percentage of albino offspring, whereas other females produce fewer than the expected percentage of albinos.

In guppies, recessive lethals linked to color-pattern genes on the Y chromosome (a sex chromosome) prevent the production of offspring homozygous for these genes (Winge and Ditlevsen 1938; Haskins et al. 1970).

Inheritance and Sex

Sex-limited factors: Factors that can occur in both sexes, but are expressed in only one sex, are called sex-limited.

In the guppy, the zebrinus (Ze) pattern consists of two to five vertical stripes on the rear part of the body. This pattern is due to a dominant autosomal (not on a sex chromosome) gene that is expressed only in males (Winge 1927). A female can carry Ze and pass it on to her daughters (which will not show the pattern) and sons (which will exhibit zebrinus).

Most guppy factors are not expressed in the female, even when present, because most of the factors are expressed only under the influence of male hormones (Hildemann 1954).

Sex determination: Autosomes are chromosomes that do not carry primary sex-determining genes. Some fish, as well as some other animals (including humans), have a pair of sex chromosomes (called gonosomes), which play a major part in determining the sex of an individual. In a number of animal species, including some fishes, the sex chromosomes of a pair differ in size. However, there are some fish species in which there is genetic evidence that sex chromosomes exist but these sex chromosomes have not been observed for one of several possible reasons: (1) cytological studies have not been made, (2) interpretation of the very small fish chromosomes is difficult, or (3) there is no difference in size of the sex chromosomes of that species. Angus (1989) reviewed sex determination in poeciliid fishes. Although fish chromosomes are small and numerous, a number of karyotypes (cytological observations of chromosome complements) have been done. Yamazaki (1983) listed fish species in which sex chromosomes have been observed. Rishi (1979), who reported sex chromosomes in the giant gourami (Colisa fasciata), also discussed other instances in which sex chromosomes have been reported in fishes, including multiple sex chromosomes, in which an individual has more than two sex chromosomes. Multiple sex chromosomes were reported first by Uyeno and Miller (1971). Ewulonu, Haas and Turner (1985) found multiple sex chromosomes in a killifish (Nothobranchius guentheri) and listed the ten addi-

tional teleost species (bony fishes) in which multiple sex chromosomes occur.

In mammals and some fishes, the female has two sex chromosomes of the same kind (XX). The female is said to be homogametic. The male is called heterogametic because his sex chromosomes are different (XY). In birds and some fishes, the female is heterogametic (WY) and the male is homogametic (YY).

It was discovered many years ago that guppies have heterogametic males (Schmidt 1920; Winge 1922). However, atypical sex determination, resulting in XX males and XY females, sometimes occurs in guppies (Winge 1930, 1934; Winge and Ditlevsen 1947). Nayudu (1979) reported a brood of guppies in which a fourth were XX males. Some very old laboratory stocks of guppies, the oldest being from 1920 and 1927, produce a high percentage of females (Farr 1981). Kallman (1984) reviewed the literature on XX males and XY females as well as the literature on sex inheritance and unbalanced sex ratios in Poeciliopsis, limias, mollies, and Xiphophorus helleri.

More than two kinds of sex chromosomes occur in the genus Xiphophorus, in which a number of species are known to have sex chromosomes. In the 1920s and 1930s it was reported that, in domesticated stocks of X. maculatus, females were heterogametic and males were homogametic (Bellamy 1924, 1928; Gordon 1927; Kosswig 1934). Then Bellamy (1936) discovered homogametic females and heterogametic males in X. variatus. Later, Gordon (1947, 1951) found that some populations of X. maculatus had XX females and XY males, while other populations had WY females and YY males. Kallman (1965,

Crosses and Resulting Sex Ratios in Wild Platy (*Xiphophorus maculatus*) Populations					
Parents		*Sex Ratio of Offspring*		*Genotypes of Offspring*	
♀	♂	♀	♂	♀	♂
WY	XY	1	1	WX, WY	XY, YY
WY	YY	1	1	WY	YY
WX	XY	3	1	WX, WY, XX	XY
WX	YY	1	1	WY	XY
XX	XY	1	1	XX	XY
XX	YY	0	1	(none)	XY

1970a) found that both the X and W chromosomes occur in the same populations in 90 percent of the *X. maculatus* range. The W chromosome has not been found in *X. maculatus* from two river systems in Vera Cruz, Mexico (Kallman 1973). There are two kinds of males (XY or YY); in all except two of the natural populations investigated, there are three kinds of females: WY, WX, and XX (Kallman 1973). In the laboratory, WW females were obtained by appropriate crosses (Kallman 1968). Males and females with different sex chromosome genotypes look alike and breed at random. Gordon (1952) found that the sex ratio of the offspring depends upon the sex chromosome genotypes of the parents. For wild populations of *X. maculatus,* Kallman (1965, 1973, 1975, 1984) discussed the six possible kinds of crosses and resulting sex ratios in the offspring (using the symbols ♀ for the female and ♂ for male, see table, previous page).

Sex chromosomes were identified by the pigment-pattern genes on them (called markers) and by the sex ratios (Kallman 1965, 1970a). Atypical sex, in which the phenotype is not what is expected from the genotype, has been found for all genotypes (Kallman 1968, 1984). There are two kinds of Y chromosomes in *X. maculatus, X. milleri,* and *X. montezumae* (see discussion by Kallman 1984): Y (more common, always resulting in a male when combined with an X chromosome) and Y'(which can result in either male or female when combined with an X chromosome). Whereas Kosswig (1964) follows an old theory that sex in fishes is determined by many genes on numerous chromosomes, Kallman (1984) provided evidence that most instances of *Xiphophorus* atypical sex determination (such as an XX male) are due to the effect of a single autosomal gene on the sex-influencing gene on a sex chromosome. Avtalion and Hammerman (1978) suggested a similar mechanism of sex determination in *Serotherodon* (*Tilapia*).

Kallman (1983) listed the *Xiphophorus* species that, unlike *X. maculatus,* do not have the W chromosome. The XX female, XY male sex-determining mechanism occurs in *X. variatus, X. milleri, X. xiphidium, X. pygmaeus,* and *X. nigrensis.* The sex chromosomes of these species, and also of *X. maculatus,* are homologous (Kallman and Atz 1966). Kallman (1983) concluded that the sex chromosomes of *X. montezumae* also are homologous to the sex chromosomes of the above six species.

Sex linkage: A gene on a sex chromosome is called sex-linked when it is linked to the primary sex-determining gene on that chromosome. Schmidt (1920) first found Y-linked inheritance, which was in the guppy. The factor Maculatus, *Ma,* which produces a black spot in the dorsal fin, was found to be inherited only by sons from their fathers. There are many color patterns in wild guppies (Haskins et al. 1961), and many of these genes have been utilized in guppy domestication (Dzwillo 1959). Yamamoto (1975) listed thirty-seven genes that are sex-linked in guppies. Some of these genes are X-linked, some are Y-linked, and all are dominant in the male. Although most are not expressed in the female, a female carrying an X-linked gene will pass this gene on to her sons and daughters. The Y chromosome in the guppy has a segment that is not homologous (does not have matching loci) with any part of the X chromosome. A gene on this nonhomologous segment of the Y is absolutely linked, as its segment does not exchange with the X chromosome by crossing over. One of these absolutely linked genes always occurs on the Y chromosome: *Ma* (Maculatus), *Pa* (Pauper), *Ir* (Iridescens), or *Ar* (Armatus).

Three genes (*Fla, Cp,* and *Nill*), each at a different locus, appeared in domesticated guppy stocks. These sex-linked genes are expressed in both sexes and may be on either the X or Y chromosome; the patterns are expressed in juveniles as well as in adults and are due mostly to melanophores. Winge and Ditlevsen (1947) stated that Flavus (*Fla*) was X-linked, and they observed no crossovers. However, Nayudu (1979) found *Fla* on both the X and Y chromosomes. Nayudu also discovered that males heterozygous for *Cp* and homozygous for *Fla* had smaller tails than males heterozygous for both genes. Dzwillo (1959) found that the factor Pigmentierte Caudalis (Cp) is X-linked, dominant in both sexes, and produces veiltail in males when present along with the Y-linked gene called Double Sword (Ds). Schröder (1969) confirmed that *Cp* is X-linked and reported a crossover rate of 8.5 percent. Nayudu's (1979) observations were the same as those of Dzwillo and Schröder except that the crossover rate was lower and the *Cp* gene was on both sex chromosomes in the same fish in some stocks.

A number of incompletely sex-linked genes (genes that can move from one sex chromosome to the other by crossover) occur in *Xiphophorus* (Gordon 1937, 1947). These genes, which produce pigment patterns, can occur on the X and Y chromosomes (Gordon 1947; Kallman 1965), but no pigment-pattern factors occur on the W chromosome in females from natural populations (Kallman 1970a). Crossover rate (less than 1 percent) between the W and Y is about the same as between the X and Y (Gordon 1937; MacIntyre 1961; Kallman 1965, 1970a). There are sex-linked genes that produce macromelanophore (large black pigment cell) patterns in *X. maculatus, X. xiphidium, X. variatus, X. milleri, X. pygmaeus,* and *X. nigrensis* (see Kallman 1983). In addition, there are sex-linked xantho-erythrophore (yellow and red) patterns in *X. maculatus* and *X. pygmaeus* (see Kallman 1983). The genes for xantho-erythrophore patterns are closely linked to the macromelanophore loci in *X. maculatus* (Kallman 1975). There are three unlinked macromelanophore loci in *X. cortezi* (Kallman 1971). A sex-linked gene that controls the age of maturation and adult size is present in *X. maculatus, X. milleri,* and *X. nigrensis* (see Kallman 1983).

Kallman (1975) reviewed the genetics of pigment-pattern genes in *X. maculatus* and discussed their enhancement or suppression when they are introduced into the genomes (gene complements) of other species of *Xiphophorus* through crosses and subsequent backcrosses. Melanomas (black cancers), which can occur when there is increased expression of a macromelanophore pattern, can result both from certain interspecific crosses, often involving macromelanophore patterns of *X. maculatus,* and

from crosses of one population with another. Pigment-cell abnormalities in *Xiphophorus* were reviewed by Atz (1962) and Zander (1969).

In *X. maculatus,* some pigment patterns look alike but are due to different genes in different populations (Kallman 1970b). Three sex-linked patterns (spotted dorsal fin, red dorsal fin, and red anal fin) occur in populations of *X. maculatus* in the Rio Jamapa, Mexico, as well as in the Belize River, Belize. Each one of these genes is different in platys of the two river systems, and also the set of modifiers is different for each population.

Kallman (1970c) summarized the inherited patterns in *X. maculatus,* which include these sex-linked pigment genes:

1. Macromelanophore patterns. Although there are more than two dozen alleles, there are six basic patterns in addition to the wild-type (without a macromelanophore pattern): spotted dorsal fin, stripe-sided, spot-sided posteriorly only, spot-sided anteriorly only, heavily spotted all over, and black-banded.
2. A large, complex pigmentary system that includes: red dorsal fin, red anal (and pelvic) fins, red body, ruby throat, orange caudal peduncle, yellow caudal fin, and red caudal fin.
3. Deep yellow anal spot.
4. Red mouth, pigmentation of the lower jaw, expressed only in males.
5. Red iris, which is more intense in males than in females, and yellow iris.
6. Shoulder spot, a black mark with iridescent areas on both sides. This, unlike the other sex-linked genes, is recessive.

The eye of this wild platy (*Xiphophorus maculatus*) has a red iris, due to a dominant sex-linked gene.

There are known at least nineteen red or yellow sex-linked patterns in *X. maculatus* (Kallman 1965, 1970a; Borowsky and Kallman 1976). Their penetrance is 100 percent in their own population, but may be as low as 30 percent when introduced into the gene pool of another population; expressivity also varies (Kallman 1975). The Jamapa population is distinct in that it tends to enhance the expression of pigment genes.

Adult size in *Xiphophorus*: Although the size of many animals is controlled by multiple factors, the adult size in some species of *Xiphophorus* is controlled by modifier genes acting along with sex-linked genes that affect the age of onset of sexual maturity. In general, early-maturing male platys (*X. maculatus*) do not grow as large as late-maturing males. The discovery that sex-

This wild swordtail (*Xiphophorus nezahualcoyotl*) was known formerly as *X. montezumae.*

linked genes control time of onset of gonad maturation in *X. maculatus* was possible because these maturation-determining genes are linked to pigment-pattern genes, which are used as markers by the geneticist. Kallman, Schreibman and Borkoski (1973), working with a Belize stock in which males are YY and females are WY, found that the Y chromosome is marked by either *Ir* (red iris) or *Br* (red body). Females are heterozygous, having either red iris or red body. Males homozygous for red body take twice as long to reach sexual maturity as males homozygous for red iris. These late-maturing males are larger than the early-maturing ones. Heterozygous males, having both red body and red iris, are intermediate in both age of maturation and adult size.

Kallman and Borkoski (1978) reported that at least five alleles of *P* control the time of onset of gonad maturation in *X. maculatus*. Range in the age of initiation of maturity in males and females was from eight to seventy-three weeks; some fish of one genotype never matured sexually. Males and females grew at the same rate until the male's growth rate decreased at the onset of sexual maturity. Males with fully developed gonopodia continued to grow, but the amount of additional growth varied with the *P* genotype. Now nine *P* alleles are known in *X. maculatus* (Kallman 1989).

The *P* locus on the Y chromosome also is present in other species of *Xiphophorus*. Adult size and the age of onset of sexual maturity in males is controlled by multiple alleles at the *P* locus on the Y chromosome in *X. milleri* (Kallman and Borowsky 1972), *X. montezumae* (Kallman 1983), and *X. nigrensis* (Kallman 1984). Kallman (1984)

discussed evidence that *X. helleri,* in which there are early- and late-maturing males, may also have sex chromosomes, even though no sex-linked trait has been found in this species.

Kallman (1983) found that, in the population of *X. montezumae* that he investigated, females are XX and males are XY. There are two kinds of Y chromosomes, one (Y-M) with a macromelanophore locus, and the other (Y-+) without a macromelanophore locus. Autosomal genes caused 9.5 percent of the XY-+ individuals to become females. The X chromosome and also the Y-+ chromosome carry a *P* allele, *a,* that causes maturation at a small size. The Y-M chromosome has an allele, *b,* which causes maturation at a larger size.

The variation in adult size of males in other species of *Xiphophorus,* as well as other poeciliids, may also be due to *P* gene polymorphism (Schreibman and Kallman 1977; Kallman 1989). In two populations of *X. nigrensis,* the slender body shape of small males differs from the deeper bodies of large males (Kallman 1983).

Hormone treatments: In some species of fish it is possible to obtain functional males by treating genetic females with a male hormone (androgen). Also, functional females have been produced by treating genetic males with a female hormone (estrogen). For example, Grobstein (1948) converted genetic female platys (*X. maculatus*) to males by treating the females with methyltestosterone (an androgen). The first hormone-induced sex reversal in both directions, male to female, and also female to male, was done in the medaka (Yamamoto 1953, 1955, 1958).

For reversal of sex differentiation in fish, it is necessary to treat them before their gonads have differentiated (Yamamoto 1953, 1962). In guppies the gonads have already differentiated in fry when they are born (Goodrich et al. 1934; Dildine 1936). By treating female guppies with methyltestosterone twenty-two days after they were mated, Dzwillo (1962) obtained some XX male offspring. These XX males, bred to untreated XX females, produced all female offspring. Takahashi (1975) also reversed the sex of guppies from female to male by treating embryos before birth.

Sex reversal from genetic female to phenotypic male has been accomplished not only in *Xiphophorus,* the medaka, and the guppy, but also in tilapia, goldfish, coho salmon, Atlantic salmon, chinook salmon, and rainbow trout. Reviews of sex control in fishes can be found in Yamamoto (1969), Schreck (1974), Donaldson and Hunter (1982), and Yamazaki (1983).

In some fishes, certain color patterns that are sex-limited to the male can be brought out in females by treating them with male hormone. Gordon (1955) gives instructions for making a solution of methyltestosterone for treating female guppies to discover their genetic makeup. Half-grown females are treated for two to four weeks by adding the hormone to the aquarium water every other day. Adult females are treated for six weeks. I tested females of the killifish, *Nothobranchius neumani,* in which there are red-tail and blue-tail males, but no such color in the females. By adding methyltestosterone to their water, I obtained females that developed either red or blue tails. However, in mangrove mollies (*Poecilia orri*), in which males have either red or yellow dorsal fin and tail color and females have colorless fins, adding methyltestosterone to their water did not cause females to develop fin color by the time their anal fins were starting to become masculinized.

Hormone treatments have been used by commercial ornamental fish producers to enhance the color of fish. Treating juveniles with methyltestosterone for three weeks changes a brown discus to a colorful "rainbow" or "blue-face" discus, and a black lace angelfish to a green angelfish (Norton 1971b). These treated fishes, imported from the Far East, were being sold at very high prices in the early 1970s. Their color fades a few months after hormone treatment is discontinued.

Another commercial use of male hormone is to change the secondary sex characters of swordtails from female to male. By treating large female swordtails with male hormone, the producer not only obtains large "males" (looking like males but not fertile) but he can also obtain equal numbers of "males" and females. It is common to see large swordtails that look like females but in which the anal fin is beginning to develop into a gonopodium. Hormone treatment of swordtails has become widely used by tropical fish producers having strains that produce small males. Female hormones also are used by some producers to increase the size of swordtails before they are treated subsequently with male hormone.

Guppy males also can be treated with female hormone to increase their size. Larr (1977) gives these instructions for treating male guppies with female hormone:

At maturity, this blushing smokey angelfish developed gold, pink, and turquoise colors.

"Dissolve one 250 mg capsule of Stilbestrol in 12 oz. of 70 percent ethyl alcohol. This in turn is diluted with distilled water to make one quart of stock solution. Add one drop of stock solution per two gallons of tank water every third day. Treatment should be started on young males at two weeks of age and be continued for about twenty to twenty-five days."

A person buying guppy breeding stock should realize that a large male may have been treated instead of having inherited large size.

There are disadvantages in using hormones to improve the appearance of fish. First, the product is misleading, not a reflection of its genotype. Second, because the true phenotype is masked, selection and culling are impaired; therefore, strain deterioration instead of improvement is likely to occur, and sex ratios may deviate greatly from 1:1. Third, there is a possibility of causing sterility in hormone-treated fish; this was reported in rainbow trout (Billard and Richard 1982).

Genetics and Breeding

Inbreeding: In a wild population of fish, deleterious recessive genes are eliminated in homozygous individuals but can be maintained for generations in heterozygous individuals. Inbreeding of domesticated fishes tends to increase the

The female lyretail sword (center) has all fins enlarged, including long extensions of the upper and lower caudal fin rays.

proportion of homozygotes, which can result in decreased vigor or viability. However, inbreeding accompanied by careful selection can result in desirable strains with no decrease in vigor and productivity. Sometimes a strain will decline in the early generations, but then improve with continued inbreeding, if selection is rigorous.

Laboratory stocks of some fish species have been maintained for many years. By the mid-1970s, stocks of *Xiphophorus* had been kept for many generations at the New York Zoological Society (Kallman 1975). *X. maculatus* had been inbred 31, 48, and 57 generations; *X. helleri*, 29 and 33 generations. Thus there are exceptions to the widely held belief that inbreeding invariably causes deterioration of fish stocks.

Mrakovcic and Haley (1979) reported inbreeding depression in the zebra danio (*Brachydanio rerio*). Kincaid (1983) reviewed the work on inbreeding of food fishes (rainbow trout, brook trout, Atlantic salmon, carp), in which inbreeding depression may result from one generation of brother–sister mating.

Selection: Some strains of fish can be improved by selecting for desirable genes and eliminating undesirable genes. Improvement may stop after one or two generations or after many generations, depending on the number of genes involved.

A gold angelfish strain can be obtained in two generations, starting with one gold individual, because gold is due to a recessive gene. Crossing a gold with a wild-type (silver) angelfish produces all wild-type offspring. Some golds, all of which are true breeding, will appear in the F2. On the other hand, the red cap (an orange area) of the

gold blushing angelfish varies from a small dot to an area reaching from the mouth to the dorsal fin. Because there are a number of intermediates in the size of this orange area, the number of genes involved must be more than two. If many genes are involved, selection for maximum red cap area would take more generations than it would if fewer genes were involved. However, once the available genes that increase the size of the red cap have been accumulated by selection, further selection cannot increase red cap size. Selection can sort out and accumulate genes, but no more. It is a common fallacy that selection, continued for enough generations, can produce unlimited increased expression of a character, in this case an all-red angelfish. Incidentally, the red cap character may not be limited to the gold blushing angelfish. Some silver angelfish, for example, have a dusky amber area at the same location, and this may be the red cap masked by black pigment. The blushing smokey male in the figure (p. 104) also has an amber area on his head.

Progeny testing: A dominant gene having 100 percent penetrance can be eliminated easily by discarding all individuals that have the character. A recessive gene, however, is not eliminated by selection, and can be carried for generations by heterozygous individuals. A recessive gene can be eliminated by progeny testing prospective breeder fish to find out whether or not they carry that gene. For example, to obtain an angelfish strain that is free of the gene for gold, nongolds can be tested by crossing them with a gold. Those nongolds that produce no gold offspring from this cross are the ones that do not carry the gene for gold, and these are the fish to save for breeders

Probably a guppy–molly hybrid, this male was infertile.

that will not produce golds.

Progeny testing also is useful in breeding fish in which the desirable modifiers are unknown in one of the parents. In the lyretail sword, modifiers affect the quality of the tail. A well-shaped tail has long extensions of equal length and is clean (without fin ray extensions) in the center part of the tail. The lyretail sword male, which has a long, malformed gonopodium, is unable to inseminate the female. Therefore, a lyretail female, which has a dominant gene for lyretail (Norton 1967b), is crossed with a nonlyretail male, either a common-fin or hi-fin. The nonlyretail male can be tested for dominant lyretail modifiers by mating him with a lyretail female having a good tail. This male should be discarded if his offspring have poor tails. Besides being influenced by modifiers of the gene for lyretail, the lyretail sword's caudal fin is affected by injury; an injured tail grows back ragged or even as a veiltail.

Sperm competition: Live-bearing females of many species store sperm and produce a number of broods from just one insemination. For example, sperm may remain viable in *Xiphophorus* females for up to ten months, resulting in successive broods (Van Oordt 1928; Kallman 1975).

Winge (1937) put a bred female guppy with a different male after she had a brood, and he found that all of the next brood were fathered by the second male. Also, in the platy (*X. maculatus*), females mated to two males on different dates produced second broods in which the sperm of the second male fertilized most of the ova (Vallowe 1953). Platy (*X. maculatus*) and swordtail (*X. helleri*) females that were artificially inseminated with mixed sperm of both species produced offspring mainly fathered by males of their own species (Clark 1950). Most species of *Xiphophorus* will cross, but *X. signum* is an exception (Rosen 1979). Kallman (personal communication to Rosen 1979) artificially inseminated *X. helleri* and *X. signum* females with mixed sperm from males of both species. No hybrids resulted; ova were fertilized only by sperm of their own species.

Sperm competition can occur not only between species but even between sperm carrying and not carrying a particular gene. In guppies, vertebral fusion produces a shortened body (palla), due to a single gene. When females were inseminated by heterozygous palla males, each succeeding brood contained a lower percentage of palla offspring (Lodi 1981); it was concluded that sperm without the palla gene were more viable than sperm having the palla gene.

Hybrids: Many fish hybrids have been recorded, both in natural populations and in cultivated fishes. Wohlfarth (1983) reviewed the literature on interspecific hybrids in Chinese carp, sunfish, catfish, and tilapia. Fish hybrids were reviewed by Schwartz (1972) and Dangel, Macy and Withler (1973). Chevassus (1983) reviewed the effects of hybridization in fish.

Hybridization has been important in the development of many aquarium strains of live-bearers. Most of the many colorful types of platys and swordtails in the trade have both platy and swordtail ancestry. Many interspecific molly crosses produce fertile hybrids.

Crossing fish of different populations, different species, or different inbred lines sometimes results in progeny that are larger and more vigorous than either parent. This effect is called hybrid vigor or heterosis. Some interspecific and intergeneric crosses produce hybrids with a growth rate intermediate between the parents. This occurs in salmonids (Suzuki and Fukuda 1972) and acipenserids (Burtzev and Serebryakova 1973).

Sterility: Many interspecific crosses of fishes produce infertile hybrids, but fertile hybrids are obtained from some crosses. From my experience, a guppy-molly hybrid is an example of an interspecific hybrid that is likely to be sterile. Kosswig (1973) discussed various causes of sterility in fishes.

In *Xiphophorus,* one type of sterility is due to lack of mobility of the sperm (Karbe 1961). In other hybrids, F1 females may be fertile, but males may be sterile because spermatogenesis (formation of sperm) is not complete (Karbe 1961). If these females are backcrossed with males of either of their parent species, some fertile males can be obtained. Repeated backcrosses can result in a greater proportion of fertile males in the progeny.

When a hybrid of *Xiphophorus maculatus* and *X. helleri* is backcrossed to *X. helleri,* some of the offspring have a sex chromosome of *X. maculatus* and some do not; those that have the *X. maculatus* chromosome can be discerned because of a pigment-pattern factor (a marker) on that chromosome. Many of those individuals having an *X. maculatus* sex chromosome are sterile. Some of these sterile fish have no germ cells in their gonads (Berg and Gordon 1953). Some of those that do have germ cells were made fertile with hormone treatment (Oztan 1963).

Chevassus (1983) reviewed the various types of sterility in food fishes.

Unisexual fishes: In some species of fish, usually all of the individuals are females. In the Amazon molly (*Poecilia formosa*), gynogenesis occurs, a situation in which the ova are activated by sperm of males of another molly species, such as *P. sphenops,* but no genetic material of the sperm is added to the ovum (Hubbs and Hubbs 1932; Turner 1982). The offspring are all females and genetically like their mother. Unisexual fishes also occur in some species of *Poeciliopsis* (Schultz 1969, 1977, 1980), goldfish (*Carassius auratus gibelio*) (reviews by Schultz 1980; Kirpichnikov 1981), and the atherinid *Mendina clarkhubbsi* (Echelle, Echelle and Crozier 1983). Chevassus (1983) discussed artificially induced gynogenesis in food fishes.

Single-sex populations: All-male populations, in which stunting of fish due to crowding is reduced, have been produced in sunfish (Childers 1967) and tilapia (Mires 1977). Many tilapia crosses have been made (Hickling 1960; Balarin and Hatton 1979; Wohlfarth and Hulata 1981). There have been attempts to find which crosses will produce all-male tilapia broods (Pruginin et al. 1975; Hulata, Wohlfarth and Rothbard 1983).

All-female and mostly-female groups of chinook salmon (*Oncorhynchus tshawytscha*) were produced by using sperm of genetic females that had been treated with male hormone to produce phenotypic males (Hunter et al. 1983). Also, when coho salmon (*O. kisutch*) ova were fertilized with sperm from sex-reversed chinook females, they produced one group of 100 percent female offspring and four groups that had over 92 percent females (Hunter et al. 1983).

Polyploidy: When a haploid (n) ovum, which contains a single complement (one of each pair) of chromosomes, unites with a haploid (n) sperm, which also contains a single complement of chromosomes, the resulting fertilized egg, and the ensuing individual, has two sets of chromosomes and is a diploid (2n). A polyploid has additional chromosomes. The role of polyploidy in fish evolution has been reviewed (Schultz 1980; Allendorf and Thorgaard 1984; Ferris 1984). A triploid (3n) has three sets of chromosomes, and a tetraploid (4n) has four sets.

Triploid hybrids of the all-female *Poecilia formosa* were produced by using males of either domesticated black mollies or *Poecilia vittata* (Rasch et al. 1965; Schultz and Kallman 1968). Triploids result when a diploid (2n) ovum unites with a haploid (n) sperm. About 1 percent of laboratory broods of *P. formosa* have one or more triploids (Schultz and Kallman 1968).

Triploid Amazon mollies also occur in the wild (Prehn and Rasch 1969). In some populations, over 90 percent of these female mollies are triploids (Rasch and Balsano 1974). Although most laboratory-produced triploids of *P. formosa* are sterile, natural triploids are fertile; they produce triploid progeny that are all females (Rasch and Balsano 1974; Strommen, Rasch and Balsano 1975).

Certain species of fishes, including salmonids and freshwater suckers, are thought to have become tetraploids during their evolution (see review by Schultz 1980). There are advantages in the artificial production of certain triploid and tetraploid fishes. For example, triploid channel catfish grow to a larger size and utilize food more efficiently compared with their diploid siblings (Wolters, Libey and Chrisman 1981). The grass carp is useful for control of aquatic vegetation, which it eats, but this fish reproduces excessively. However, triploid grass carp are sterile and their population can be limited in waters where they are introduced. Tetraploids can be useful when they can be crossed with diploids, producing triploids. Polyploids have been obtained in a number of species of fishes by physical or chemical treatment (see review by Purdom 1983). Cold-shock treatment of fertilized eggs produced triploids in channel catfish (Wolters et al. 1981, 1982), common carp (Gervai et al. 1980), and *Tilapia aurea* (Valenti 1975). Heat shock of eggs induced tetraploidy in *Tilapia aurea* (Valenti 1975) and rainbow trout (Thorgaard, Jazwin and Stier 1981; Chourrout 1982). By heat-shock treatment of channel catfish eggs, Bidwell, Chrisman and Libey (1985) obtained tetraploids, triploids, diploids, and mosaics (having tissues with mixed ploidy); the authors stated that their tetraploids may be sterile. Hydrostatic pressure is another method that has induced polyploidy in salmonids (Onozato 1983; Benfey and Sutterlin 1984; Chourrout 1984), rainbow trout (Chourrout 1984), and grass carp (Cassani and Caton 1986).

Environmental influences on phenotype: A fish's rate of growth, adult size, and color are affected not only by its genotype but also by many environmental factors, including temperature, water

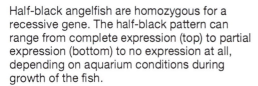

Half-black angelfish are homozygous for a recessive gene. The half-black pattern can range from complete expression (top) to partial expression (bottom) to no expression at all, depending on aquarium conditions during growth of the fish.

quality, kind of food, and frequency of feeding.

Substrate color can affect the color of some fishes. For example, red swordtails raised in a tank with a light-colored bottom are a lighter shade of red than their siblings raised in a tank with a dark bottom. Fish farmers produce the deepest red swordtails and platys in pools with dark substrate. Deep-red swordtails and platys retain their color for months after they are moved from dark- to light-colored pools or tank bottoms.

Carotenoids in the food affect red and yellow colors of many fishes. For example, the gold blushing angelfish has golden body color if it is fed newly hatched brine shrimp or frozen krill. This fish fades to near white after its diet is changed to frozen adult brine shrimp.

Breider (1935) reported that the sex ratio of the swordtail (*X. helleri*) was not affected by age of stored spermatozoa in the female, age of parents,

Raised in continuous light, both this silver angelfish (top) and this black lace angelfish (bottom) failed to develop stripes on their bodies.

or a number of environmental factors, including temperature. However, there are more recent reports of environmental influence on sex ratios in fish. Temperature affects the sex ratio in *Rivulus*

When raised with fourteen hours of light each day, the zebra lace angelfish has three vertical body stripes.

The cobra angelfish is heterozygous for dark and homozygous for zebra. If raised in continuous light, it develops spots, like this, instead of the vertical stripes it develops if raised with fourteen hours of light each day.

marmoratus (Harrington 1967, 1971) and *Mendina mendina* (Conover and Kynard 1981). Sullivan and Schultz (1986) studied the effect of temperature variation on sex ratios in two strains of *Poeciliopsis lucida*. Pregnant females were kept in water varying from 24 to 30 degrees C (75 to 86 degrees F). In one strain, the sex ratio of the offspring was 1:1 in the entire temperature range.

If a zebra lace angelfish has only one dose of the gene for zebra, instead of two as in the cobra angelfish, it develops spots and partial vertical stripes when raised in continuous light.

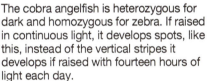

A silver angelfish raised with four hours of light each day (top) does not develop the two prominent body stripes of an individual raised in a fourteen-hour day; some of these short-day individuals (bottom) develop only a black spot on the body.

The other strain produced mostly males when the female parent was kept at 30 degrees C (86 degrees F) and more females than males when the female parent was held at 24 degrees C (75 degrees F). Sex ratios of some species of fish are affected by pH. In a dwarf cichlid (*Pelviachromis*), over 90 percent males develop in acid water, whereas over 90 percent females develop in neutral water, according to Heiligenberg (1965), who gave no data, however.

The fish hobby literature contains undocumented reports of poorly devised experiments on the effect of pH on the sex of fish (Ostrow 1978, 1979). Rubin (1985) tested the effect of pH on five species of dwarf cichlids (*Pelviachromis pulcher, P. subocellatus, P. taeniatus, Apistogramma borelli, A. caucatoides*) and one species of swordtail (*Xiphophorus helleri*). At low pH, a high percentage of males was produced in all six species. The low pH values ranged from 5.05 to 6.20, depending on the species. The high pH values ranged from 6.90 (*P. pulcher*) to 7.80 (*X. helleri*). At an intermediate pH (6.10), *P. pulcher* produced about equal numbers of males and females. Because similar results have not been reported for a poeciliid, repeated experiments using *Xiphophorus* (such as *X. maculatus*) of known sex chromosome genotype are needed to check Rubin's results.

Insufficient feeding can affect gene expression in some instances. An example is the half-black angelfish, which is black on the rear part of the body. Individuals that are stunted by inadequate feeding fail to develop the half-black pattern (Norton 1985b, 1989). After starting the fry on inadequate feedings, I began heavy feeding of some of these stunted fish and observed the half-black pattern beginning to develop in some of them ten days after the heavy feedings were started. No half-blacks developed in any of the stunted siblings that were kept on low rations. The half-black pattern disappeared in fry that were switched to low rations. This resulted in fish that were genetically half-blacks but looked like silvers.

Even though they appear healthy, angelfish that are genetic half-blacks will develop only a partial pattern or no half-black pattern at all if water changes are insufficient.

When the angelfish half-black pattern is either developing or decreasing in size, a smaller black area (compared with full half-black pattern) covers the tail and a rounded spot at the base of the tail. Because the half-black pattern is labile in young angelfish, a genetic half-black can have a full pattern, partial

This marble angelfish is heterozygous for marble.

pattern, or no pattern. Adult half-blacks have set patterns that are not altered by environment. Adults that exhibit the half-black pattern will keep it, whereas genetic half-blacks that never developed the half-black pattern will not develop it even if their environment improves.

Some angelfish pigment patterns are affected by the length of day, called photoperiod (Norton 1982f). The marble and smokey patterns appear the same in fish raised in a fourteen-hour day or in continuous light. However, a silver angelfish raised in continuous light has no stripes. A black lace (heterozygous for dark) has black vertical body stripes if the lights are turned off at night (fourteen hours of light); raised in continuous light, the black lace is a uniform gray color, without stripes. A zebra angelfish has three black vertical body stripes if raised in a fourteen-hour day; raised in continuous light, it has only a few black

This leopard angelfish, heterozygous for smokey, homozygous for zebra, was raised in a short day of four hours of light.

This marble angelfish resulted from a marble x gold cross. It has the gene for marble on one and the gene for gold on the other of a pair of chromosomes.

This black velvet angelfish is heterozygous for dark and gold; a pair of chromosomes has the gene for dark on one and the gene for gold on the other. This angelfish also is blushing (homozygous for stripeless).

This smokey angelfish is heterozygous for smokey and also heterozygous for veiltail.

dots or splotches. A black (homozygous for dark) raised in continuous light does not have the faint vertical bars on the body that are present if the lights are off at night. A zebra lace, which is heterozygous for dark and either heterozygous or homozygous for zebra, has three black vertical stripes if raised in a fourteen-hour day. If raised in continuous light, this fish develops as a "cobra," gray with black dots, if it is homozygous for zebra

This white (gold blushing) angelfish is homozygous for both gold and stripeless. With adequate carotenoid content in its diet, the fish would be golden rather than white.

and heterozygous for dark; if it is heterozygous for zebra and also heterozygous for dark, the pattern consists of two irregular black vertical bars on a gray body (Norton 1982g).

A short day also can affect some angelfish patterns (Norton 1985a). A silver angelfish raised in a four-hour day (four hours of light, twenty hours of darkness) has only a single black stripe or spot on the body. The "leopard" angelfish, a black-dotted fish that I obtained from a pet shop, later changed to a smokey. This male, when tested by crossing him with a silver, was found to be homozygous zebra and heterozygous smokey. Crossing a homozygous zebra female with this male produced offspring that were 50 percent homozygous zebra and 50 percent genetically like the leopard parent (homozygous zebra and heterozygous smokey). Raised in a fourteen-hour day, these developed as zebras and smokeys. A

The true-breeding chocolate angelfish is homozygous for smokey.

A gold marble angelfish that is homozygous for marble (above) has a more extensive black pattern than one that is heterozygous for marble (top).

second spawn, raised in continuous light, produced smokeys and fish with some black spots but no stripes (as is known to occur in zebras raised in continuous light). A third spawn, raised in a four-hour day, developed as 50 percent zebra and 50 percent leopard. A fourth spawn, raised in an eight-hour day, also consisted of 50 percent zebra and 50 percent leopard. Thus the leopard angelfish is a heterozygous smokey, homozygous zebra that is raised in a short day (Norton 1985a).

Some angelfish pigment patterns that have been influenced by either short day or continuous light remained unchanged a year after the fish were transferred to a fourteen-hour day. The time

needed to set the patterns at a certain photoperiod varies with the genotype of the angelfish (Norton 1982f).

Angelfish Breeding—Practical Application of Genetics

Angelfish usually are bred inefficiently, by making crosses that produce two or more types of offspring even though it is possible in many instances to produce 100 percent of the desired type. It takes much time to sort angelfish in mixed spawns. An additional disadvantage of sorting is that some angelfish patterns, such as black lace and smokey (mottled on rear part of body), fade when the fish are disturbed, making accurate sorting difficult. Therefore, it is desirable to make crosses that decrease or eliminate the necessity to sort the offspring.

The inheritance of the major angelfish pigment patterns is known (Norton 1971a, 1982a–1982g, 1983, 1985a, b, 1989). Genes responsible for angelfish pigment patterns are:

    smokey, dominant to silver (wild-type)
    stripeless, dominant to silver
    zebra, dominant to silver
    dark, dominant to silver
    marble, dominant to silver
    gold, recessive to silver
    half-black, recessive to silver

In angelfish, the half-black pattern is due to a recessive gene (Norton 1985b, 1989), which is expressed only when these fish are fed and maintained for rapid growth rate (see "Environmental influences on phenotype"). Because I have seen blushing half-black (homozygous for both stripeless and half-black), zebra half-black (heterozygous for zebra and homozygous for half-black), zebra lace half-black (homozygous for half-black, heterozygous for both zebra and dark), black lace half-black (heterozygous for dark and homozygous for half-black), marble half-black (heterozygous for marble, homozygous for half-black), and smokey half-black (heterozygous for smokey, homozygous for half-black), I deduced that the gene for half-black is not an allele of the genes for stripeless, zebra, dark, marble, or smokey (because only two of a set of alleles occur in an individual).

The genes for zebra and stripeless, which be-

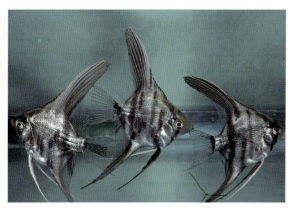

Crossing a silver angelfish with a gold marble produces some marbles with vertical stripes, called "barred marble." Above: a juvenile; top left: three half-grown individuals; left: an adult.

have as alleles, were discussed in the section "Multiple alleles." The genes for dark, marble, and gold act as another set of alleles (Norton 1982c). It may be discovered in the future that the genes for dark, marble, and gold are not all alleles, but that instead there exists a close linkage. It will be realized that they are not all alleles if a crossover is detected or if a fish is found to have all three of these genes.

Gold, when homozygous, prevents the expression of zebra and smokey (Norton 1982c). I do not know of any published report on the phenotype of a fish that is homozygous for both gold and half-black, although Bill Lutz (personal communication) obtained no gold half-blacks in the F_2 from a cross of gold and half-black.

Of the angelfish dominant genes, only zebra produces the same phenotype whether heterozy-gous or homozygous. However, homozygous zebras are slower growing than heterozygous zebras (Norton 1982d). At eight weeks of age, homozygous zebras are about half as large as their heterozygous siblings. Homozygous zebras become good-sized adults and are prolific breeders

Presence of the gene for gold results in increased expression of the genes for dark and marble. A fish heterozygous for marble is not as intensely pigmented as a fish that is heterozygous for both marble and gold. An angelfish heterozygous for both dark and gold is black when adult and darker than a black lace as a juvenile (up to about quarter body size).

The true black angelfish (homozygous for dark) was the only kind of black angelfish available until the mutations to marble and gold occurred. Because some true blacks are low in vigor and not prolific breeders, they should be replaced by blacks that are heterozygous for dark. These are angelfish having the following genotypes:

1. heterozygous for both dark and marble
2. heterozygous for both dark and gold
3. heterozygous for both dark and gold, homozygous for stripeless (black velvet)

Only one strain is needed to produce black velvet angelfish, because black velvet crossed with gold blushing (white) produces 50 percent black velvet and 50 percent white offspring (Norton 1984a). The reason for this ratio is that the genes for dark and gold behave as alleles, so the offspring receive either a gene for dark or a gene for gold from the black velvet parent.

The genotypes and phenotypes of the common angelfish are shown in the table that follows.

Genotypes and phenotypes of the common angelfish.		
	Genotype	Phenotype
Number of doses	Gene	
1	smokey	smokey
2	smokey	chocolate
1	stripeless	lacks stripes (may have one or a few black splotches)
2	stripeless	blushing
1	zebra	zebra
2	zebra	slow-growing zebra
1	dark	black lace
2	dark	black
1	marble	marble
2	marble	extensively pigmented marble
1 1	dark marble	black, with faint marble pattern
2	gold	gold
1 1	smokey dark	smokey pattern on dusky background
1 2	smokey stripeless	blushing smokey
1 2	marble stripeless	blushing marble
1 1	zebra stripeless	unstriped, with some black splotches, more markings than in stripeless without zebra
1 1	dark stripeless	butterfly (gray, may have one to several black splotches on body)
1 2	dark stripeless	"blue" (blushing, gray body)
2 2	gold stripeless	white (blushing gold)

Genotypes and phenotypes of the common angelfish.		
	Genotype	Phenotype
Number of doses	Gene	
1 1 2	gold dark stripeless	black velvet
1 1	gold marble (onseparate chromosomes)	deeply pigmented marble
1 1	gold gold marble	black marbling on gold
2	gold marble	black marbling on gold, more extensive than in heterozygous gold marble
1 1 or 2	dark zebra	zebra lace
2	half-black	half-black

Below: A male red albino sailfin molly. Bottom: A wild red platy is not as intensely colored as this domestic red platy.

The situation in marble angelfish is confusing because not every genotype produces a different phenotype. Presence of the gene for gold in some marbles causes this complication. When the gene for marble is the only mutant pigment-pattern gene present, there are only two types of marble angelfish: (1) heterozygous marble, having a gray and black marbled pattern, and (2) homozygous marble, a much darker-colored fish having very little white. Crossing a marble with a gold produces a third marble phenotype in which there is about the same percentage of white as in heterozygous marble (without gold), but the marble pattern is jet black instead of gray and black (Norton 1982c); in this genotype, the genes for marble and gold are on separate chromosomes of the same pair of chromosomes. Another kind of marble, called "gold marble" in the trade, looks like the jet black–patterned marble (which is always heterozygous for marble) that is obtained from a gold and marble cross, but the gold marble angelfish can be either homozygous for marble or heterozygous for marble (with the gene for gold on the other chromosome of the pair). In general, heterozygous gold marbles have a somewhat less extensive black pattern than the homozygous ones, based on ten gold marble angelfish that I tested (Norton 1988). There are now seven kinds of marble angelfish (Norton 1990a).

Crossing a gold marble with a silver (wild-type) angelfish produces another type of marble, which I call "barred marble." Juvenile (nickel-sized body) barred marbles resemble silvers but have some additional dark gray marks, most of which are vertical. Half-grown (silver dollar–sized body) barred marbles have irregular, black, mostly vertical markings in addition to a vertically striped

Crosses producing selected angelfish color patterns.		
Desired color pattern	Conventional cross	Improved cross
black lace	black lace X black lace. Offspring: 50% black lace, 25% true black, 25% silver	silver female X true black (homozygous for dark) male. Offspring:100% black lace
marble	heterozygous marbles. Offspring: 50% heterozygous marble (fast-growing), 25% homozygous marble (slow-growing), 25% silver	silver X homozygous marble. Offspring: 100% heterozygous marble (fast-growing)
smokey	smokey X smokey. Offspring: 50% smokey, 25% chocolate, 25% silver	silver X chocolate. Offspring: 100% smokey
zebra	heterozygous zebra parents. Offspring: 50% heterozygous zebra, 25% homozygous zebra (slow-growing), 25% silver	silver X homozygous zebra. Offspring: 100% heterozygous zebra
black (heterozygous for both dark and marble)	black parents (heterozygous for dark and marble). Offspring: 50% black (heterozygous for dark and marble), 25% true black (slow-growing), 25% homozygous marble (slow-growing)	homozygous marble female X true black male. Offspring: 100% black (heterozygous for dark and marble)
black (heterozygous for both dark and gold)	black parents (heterozygous for dark and gold). Offspring: 50% black (heterozygous for dark and gold), 25% true black (homozygous for dark, low vigor), 25% gold	gold female X true black (homozygous for dark) male. Offspring: 100% black (heterozygous for dark and gold)

The molly in the foreground is the offspring of a female sailfin molly (*Poecilia velifera*) and a 4-inch-long orange-finned *P. mexicana* male; it is over 4 inches (12 centimeters) in length. *Collected by:* Ross Socolof.

Calico mollies are orange and black. Top: a female; middle: a male calico sailfin; bottom: a male large-dorsal veiltail calico.

The red molly pictured (top) has a red body and red eyes. Chocolate mollies have red eyes and varying amounts of black pigment on the fins and body. Some, like this female (middle), have orange pigment; in contrast, the male (bottom) is almost solid black.

pattern like that of a silver angelfish. The adult barred marble has a faint wild-type (striped) pattern, which can fade in or out in a second, in addition to a marbled pattern that consists mostly of irregular, vertical black markings that never fade.

Conventional, inefficient crosses and more efficient methods for producing some of the types of angelfish are compared in the table.

Introgressive Hybridization

Introgressive hybridization has played an important role in the development of aquarium fishes. By this method, one or more genes from one species are added to the genetic makeup of an-

The best hi-fin swordtails are very colorful and have wide, full dorsal fins, as in this male (top) and this excellent-quality female red hi-fin lyretail (above).

other species. For example, a large dorsal fin (called sailfin) is possible to obtain in almost any color of molly that has a small dorsal fin. By introgressive hybridization, the desired one or more genes for color are added to the sailfin molly genome by first crossing the sailfin molly with the shortfin molly having the desired color. This cross is followed by several generations of backcrossing the colorful hybrids with the sailfin. The sailfin molly (*Poecilia velifera*) does not have black spots, whereas black-spotted mollies with small dorsal fins are common in pet stores. Crossing *P. velifera* with a black-spotted shortfin molly produces offspring with intermediate-sized dorsal fins, and some of these fish have black spots. Subsequent crosses of black-spotted hybrids with *P. velifera* will increase the number of *P. velifera* genes each generation. Also, each generation will include some black-spotted individuals with larger dorsal fins than that of their black-spotted parent. The eventual result is a black-spotted fish that otherwise looks like *P. velifera*.

Gordon (1946) discussed the production of the wagtail (black-finned) pattern in swordtails by incorporation of the platy dominant gene for comet into the swordtail genetic complement. This was done by first crossing a swordtail with a comet (also called twin-bar) platy, in which the upper and lower edges of the tail are black. The addition of the swordtail gene, E, which is a modifier of comet, resulted in the wagtail pattern in the F1, but in general appearance these fish were intermediate between a platy and swordtail. A series of backcrosses to swordtails produced fish that looked like swordtails, but were wagtails because they had the comet gene from the platy and the swordtail modifier, E. Red swordtails were produced by adding a platy gene for red body to the swordtail genome by introgressive hybridization (Hubbs 1940; Gor-

The dorsal fin of this male brick-red hi-fin swordtail is wide and has an excellent shape.

This female red-velvet hi-fin swordtail has an excellent, large dorsal fin.

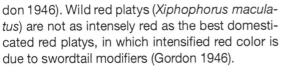

Many hi-fin platys have dorsal fins that are too small (top) or too narrow (above).

Branching of the dorsal fin rays results in a broad, excellent dorsal fin in this male sunset hi-fin platy (top) and this male red wag hi-fin platy (above).

don 1946). Wild red platys (*Xiphophorus maculatus*) are not as intensely red as the best domesticated red platys, in which intensified red color is due to swordtail modifiers (Gordon 1946).

Many possibilities exist for the development of new strains of mollies by introgressive hybridization. I made the first step to develop an orange–dorsal fin sailfin molly by crossing a sailfin female (*Poecilia velifera*) with a male shortfin molly (*Poecilia mexicana*) that had orange dorsal and caudal fins. The F1 had orange fins and the dorsal fin size was intermediate between the dorsal fin sizes of the parents. I obtained red mollies with medium-sized sailfin dorsals by crossing an albino sailfin molly and a red molly having a small dorsal fin. Dorsal fin size in red mollies can be increased further by additional generations of crossing those red males with the largest dorsal fins with albino females of a sailfin strain.

Developing and Improving Aquarium Fishes

New and improved strains of aquarium fishes have been produced by numerous fish breeders. The betta and fancy guppy are examples of fishes that have been improved tremendously in recent years.

I developed the orange-and-black calico molly (Norton 1981). Starting with a small male (1.5 inches or about 3.8 centimeters) that was black with some gold on the front part of the body, I made crosses with large wild mollies (*Poecilia gracilis* and *P. mexicana*); individuals with the most orange color and largest body size were saved, resulting in some 3- to 3.5-inch (7.6- to 8.9-centimeter) fish. Next, dorsal fin size was increased by crossing one of these calico females with an albino sailfin male. The second generation from this cross included some red mollies, which

This "ghost" angelfish is heterozygous for stripeless. Some individuals have one, or sometimes several, black blotches on the body.

are albino with orange or red pigment either as spots or almost solid red (Norton 1984b). Veiltail also has been added to calico mollies.

In live-bearers, it sometimes is possible to derive a strain from a single male even if he is unable to breed. A few hobbyists have used male lyretail swords, which are unable to breed, by artificial insemination, using methods similar to that of Clark (1950). In 1980, albino red mollies were imported from Singapore. No females were supplied, and all of the males had their gonopodia amputated. I squeezed sperm from one of these males and artificially inseminated an albino sailfin female. The resulting albino offspring included

some individuals with red spots. Subsequent crosses and selection led to red mollies which were larger and had improved color and dorsal fin size, compared with the imported males.

The chocolate molly is an albino (having pink eyes) with orange or red pigment in addition to varying amounts of black pigment; some individuals are entirely black, with pink eyes. I developed a strain of red mollies by first crossing a calico female, which carried albino, with a chocolate male. In later generations, albino individuals with much red and little or no black were obtained by selecting breeders with the least black pigment. Opinion varies as to whether a fish having any black pigment should be considered as an albino. For our purposes, I shall call an albino any fish having pink eyes, even though there may be black pigment on the fish. Breider (1938) reported *Xiphophorus* hybrids in which pink-eyed albino individuals were black or had black patches at birth. The black pigment later faded, then reappeared in older fish. Gordon (1950) also reported albino platy-swordtail hybrids that were pink-eyed but had black pigment at birth. The chocolate molly and the black-pigmented platy-swordtail hybrids of Breider and Gordon are examples of fish in which one or more certain genes override the effect of the gene for albino. The red coral swordtail is similar. This swordtail is a red albino with the same dominant factor that causes the black band on the body of a tuxedo swordtail. In the red coral swordtail, the red body has a wide white lateral band which develops some black pigment in many

Two sides of an unusual male angelfish discovered by Scottie Shroff in a spawn of golds. The fish was a genetic mosaic, having mixed tissue areas (some gold, others gold–dark), subsequent to a mutation early in its development. Half of its offspring inherited the gene for gold and the other half the gene for dark.

A female pearlscale angelfish.

older individuals (Norton 1969).

A mutation in an aquarium stock of swordtails resulted in a male with an enlarged dorsal fin, called "hi-fin" (Wolfsheimer 1960). Hi-fin is due to an autosomal dominant factor (Schröder 1966). The hi-fin character was transferred to platys by introgressive hybridization (Hearin 1963). Homozygous hi-fins ordinarily do not occur (Schröder 1966; Norton 1967a). A cross of a hi-fin ($H+$) with a common ($++$) produces 50 percent hi-fin ($H+$) and 50 percent common offspring. Two hi-fin parents produce a ratio of 2 hi-fin ($H+$):1 common ($++$), because HH offspring usually do not survive. I have found only one instance in which all of the offspring were hi-fins. This was a brood of about fifty platys, some of which grew slowly and did not reach reproductive age.

Good quality hi-fin swordtails are rare, and there is great variation between a poor quality hi-fin with a small, narrow, or poorly shaped dorsal fin and a good quality hi-fin. Hi-fin platys also are extremely variable. A narrow dorsal fin has unbranched anterior dorsal fin rays. A wide hi-fin dorsal fin has rays with repeated dichotomous branching. A fault that occurs in some hi-fin swordtails and platys, even if their parents do not manifest the fault, is "pinched dorsal," in which a few anterior dorsal fin rays are bent backward near the base of the fin. Evidence that pinched dorsal

fin is caused by a recessive modifier of hi-fin came from three broods produced by hi-fins that did not have pinched dorsal fins: two of thirteen hi-fin platys, three of fifteen hi-fin platys, and four of fifteen hi-fin swordtails had pinched dorsal fins. Because the hi-fin dorsal fin size and shape are affected by numerous genes, it is unwise to outcross a good hi-fin strain unless the purpose is to add other characteristics. I obtained only fish with poor dorsal fins in the offspring of a good hi-fin swordtail and a low-fin swordtail.

All of the fins are enlarged in a lyretail sword. The lyretail male's gonopodium is very long, an inch (2.5 centimeters) or more, and he is unable to inseminate the female. Some aquarists have suggested cutting off most of the gonopodium to enable the male to breed. This is not effective because a male swordtail is not able to copulate without the structure, called the holdfast mechanism, at the tip of the gonopodium. Clark, Aronson and Gordon (1954) found that swordtail males were not able to inseminate females after the tips of their gonopodia were amputated. Because lyretail sword males are not able to breed, lyretail females are mated to nonlyretail males, producing 50 percent lyretail offspring. The hi-fin and lyretail characters can be combined, producing a hi-fin lyretail.

The clown angelfish is a zebra lace that develops an irregular pattern instead of the three vertical body stripes of the more common type of zebra lace.

The size and shape of the caudal fin of the veiltail molly is variable, and veiltails with large, wide tails are scarce. The objective in breeding veiltail mollies is to incorporate the veiltail modifiers that result in large tails. It is not known how many or in which wild mollies such modifiers exist. One method to try to improve veiltail mollies is to use introgressive hybridization to introduce the dominant gene for veiltail into the genomes of various species of mollies. This amounts to combing the species for the desirable modifiers of veiltail. The initial cross of a veiltail female (most veiltail males are not able to breed) with a male of a certain species should be followed by at least one backcross of an F1 veiltail female to a male of the same species as her father.

Recognizing useful genetic variations: Mutations that occur in domesticated stocks may be lost unless someone recognizes their value and works with them. In many instances it is impossible to know by the appearance of a variation whether or not it is genetic. For example, a silver angelfish raised in continuous light looks like an angelfish heterozygous for stripeless that was raised in a fourteen-hour day.

Veiltail swordtails were reported in 1970 (Norton 1970a). In swordtails, veiltail is not entirely genetic, although a veiltail is a modified lyretail. After a lyretail sword's caudal fin is cut off or injured, the tail grows back as a veiltail instead of a lyretail. The commonly encountered ragged tails of lyretail swords commercially produced in pools could be due to inherited variation of lyretail or it could be the result of injury, perhaps by trapping, netting, and sorting of these fish. I had a veiltail swordtail in which veiltails resulted from tail injury due to an infection of the caudal fins of lyretails. A veiltail swordtail female mated to a common male produced three lyretail, four veiltail, and eight common. An infection on the edge of the caudal fin was observed in a few of the fry when they were five days old; these developed veiltails. There was no tail infection in any fish that were not lyretails. One of the fry with a tail infection was found by microscopic examination to have a protozoan infection on the tail. In these swordtails, the veiltail is due to the gene for lyretail along with an inherited predisposition to tail infection.

A gold angelfish with striking black markings was found by Scottie Shroff, who gave this male to me. The parents, grandparents, and great-grandparents of this fish were golds. Crossing this unusual male with a gold female produced no

The golden color of this molly, collected by Ross Socolof in a cave in Mexico, is due to a recessive gene.

offspring like him; instead, he produced offspring like that of a black male, the type of black that is heterozygous for gold and dark. The offspring were 50 percent blacks and 50 percent golds. Backcrosses of the Shroff male to his gold daughters produced blacks and golds, but none of the golds had black markings. The Shroff male is a mosaic, which results when a mutation occurs in a cell of the embryo. In this instance, cells arising from that cell have the gene for dark along with the gene for gold; the rest of the tissues are homozygous for gold. If the gene for dark is in the reproductive tissues of the Shroff angelfish, then this male would produce two kinds of sperm, one kind with the gene for gold and the other kind with the gene for dark.

The pearlscale angelfish has raised scales in wavy rows, causing the body to glitter. This trait is

The orange color of this "peach" molly was the result of adding the genes for golden, from the golden form of the Mexican cave molly, to an albino molly.

due to a recessive gene (Norton 1990b) that has been added to other colors of angelfish besides gold.

"Clown" is an inherited variation of zebra lace in angelfish (Norton 1983). The zebra lace has three vertical black stripes on the body, while clown is a zebra lace with irregular black markings. At least some clown parents produce offspring in which all of the zebra lace are the clown variation.

The utilization of desirable gene modifiers was discussed earlier in the chapter. There are genes in wild fish populations which could be useful in ornamental fish breeding. In addition, wild populations may exhibit useful genetic variations that might be added to domesticated fishes. The golden cave molly is an example of a wild fish that has a useful gene for molly breeding. Ross Socolof collected some mollies from a cave in Mexico. He sent four of these, three gray and one golden, to me; I found that the golden color in these mollies is due to a single recessive gene. Combining golden with albino resulted in an attractive pastel orange color (Norton 1986) called peach.

Mutations are important in adding to the variety of aquarium fishes. If a fish with a desirable new character is discovered, it should be saved, and an attempt should be made to increase the stock and find out whether the variation is inherited. One of the most exciting aspects of fish-keeping is the discovery and propagation of a valuable new fish.

References

Allendorf, F. W., and Thorgaard, G. H. 1984. Tetraploidy and the evolution of salmonid fishes. In *Evolutionary Genetics of Fishes,* ed. B. J. Turner, 1–53. New York: Plenum Press.

Anders, A.; Anders, F.; and Klinke, K. 1973. Regulation of gene expression in the Gordon-Kosswig melanoma system. II. The arrangement of chromatophore determining loci and regulating elements in the sex chromosomes of Xiphophorin fish, *Platypoecilus maculatus* and *Platypoecilus variatus.* In *Genetics and Mutagenesis of Fish,* ed. J. H. Schröder, 53–63. New York: Springer-Verlag.

Angus, R. A. 1989. A genetic overview of poeciliid fishes. In *Ecology and Evolution of Livebearing Fishes (Poeciliidae),* eds. G. H. Meffe and F. F. Snelson, Jr., 51–68. Englewood Cliffs, N.J.: Prentice-Hall.

Atz, J. W. 1962. Effects of hybridization on pigmentation in fishes of the genus *Xiphophorus. Zoologica* (N.Y.) 47:153–81.

Avtalion, R. R., and Hammerman, I. S. 1978. Sex determination in *Sarotherodon* (Tilapia). I. Introduction to a theory of autosomal influence. *Bamidgeh* 30:110–15.

Balarin, J. D., and Hatton, J. P. 1979. *Tilapia—A Guide to Their Biology and Culture in Africa.* Stirling, U.K.: University of Stirling.

Bellamy, A. W. 1924. Bionomic studies on certain teleosts (Poeciliinae). I. Statement of problems, description of material, and general notes on life histories and breeding behavior under laboratory conditions. *Genetics* 9:513–29.

———. 1928. Bionomic studies on certain teleosts (Poeciliinae). II. Color pattern inheritance and sex in *Platypoecilus maculatus* (Gunth.). *Genetics* 13:226–32.

———. 1936. Inter-specific hybrids in *Platypoecilus:* one species ZZ-WZ; the other XY-XX. *Proc. Nat. Acad. Sci.* 22:531–35.

Benfey, T. J., and Sutterlin, A. M. 1984. Triploidy induced by heat shock and hydrostatic pressure in landlocked Atlantic salmon (*Salmo salar* L.). *Aquaculture* 36:359–67.

Berg, O., and Gordon, M. 1953. Relationship of atypical pigment cell growth to gonadal development in hybrid fishes. In *Pigment Cell Growth,* ed. M. Gordon, 43–71. New York: Academic Press.

Bidwell, C. A.; Chrisman, C. L.; and Libey, G. S. 1985. Polyploidy induced by heat shock in channel catfish. *Aquaculture* 51:25–32.

Billard, R., and Richard, M. 1982. Inhibition of spermatogenesis and vitellogenesis in rainbow trout by hormonal additives in the diet. *Prog. Fish-Culturist* 44(1):15–18.

Borowsky, R. 1984. The evolutionary genetics of *Xiphophorus.* In *Evolutionary Genetics of Fishes,* 235–310. See Allendorf and Thorgaard, 1984.

Borowsky, R. L., and Kallman, K. D. 1976. Patterns of mating in natural populations of *Xiphophorus* (Pisces: Poeciliidae), I. *X. maculatus* from Belize and Mexico. *Evolution* 30:693–706.

Breider, H. 1935. Über Außenfaktoren, die das Geschlechtsverhältnis bei *Xiphophorus helleri* Heckel kontrollieren sollen. *Zeit. Wiss. Zool.* 146:383–416.

————. 1938. Die genetischen, histologischen und zytologischen Grundlagen der Geschwulstbildung nach Kreuzung verschiedener Rassen und Arten lebendgebärender Zahnkarpfen. *Zeit. Zellforsch.* 28:784–828.

Burtzev, I. A., and Serebryakova, E. V. 1973. A hybrid beluga X sterlet (*Husa huso* [L.] X *Acipenser ruthenus* [L.], Pisces): Karyology, gametogenesis and potential status. *Abstr. Proc. 13th Int. Congr. Genet. Genetics* 74:s35.

Cassani, J. R., and Caton, W. E. 1986. Efficient production of triploid grass carp (*Ctenopharyngodon idella*) utilizing hydrostatic pressure. *Aquaculture* 55:43–50.

Chevassus, B. 1983. Hybridization in fish. *Aquaculture* 33:245–62.

Childers, W. F. 1967. Hybridization of four species of sunfishes (Centrarchidae). III. *Nat. Hist. Surv. Bull.* 29:159–214.

Chourrout, D. 1982. Tetraploidy induced by heat shocks in rainbow trout *Salmo gairdneri* R. *Reprod. Nutr. Develop.* 22:569–74.

————. 1984. Pressure-induced retention of second polar body and suppression of first cleavage in rainbow trout: production of all-triploids, all-tetraploids and heterozygous and homozygous diploid gynogenetics. *Aquaculture* 36:111–26.

Clark, E. 1950. A method for artificial insemination in viviparous fishes. *Science* 112:722–23.

Clark, E.; Aronson, L. R.; and Gordon, M. 1954. Mating behavior patterns in two sympatric species of Xiphophorin fishes; their inheritance and significance in sexual isolation. *Bull. Am. Mus. Nat. Hist.* 103:135–226.

Conover, D. O., and Kynard, B. E. 1981. Environmental sex determination: Interaction of temperature and genotype in a fish. *Science* 213:577-79.

Dangel, J. R.; Macy, P. T.; and Withler, F. C. 1973. Annotated bibliography of interspecific hybridization of fishes of the subfamily Salmoninae. *National Oceanic and Atmospheric Administration Tech. Mem.*, NMFS NWFC 1. 48 pages.

Dildine, G. C. 1936. Studies on teleostean reproduction. I. Embryonic hermaphroditism in *Lebistes reticulatus. J. Morphol.* 60:261–77.

Donaldson, E. M., and Hunter, G. A. 1982. Sex control in fish with particular reference to salmonids. *Can. J. Fish. Aquat. Sci.* 39:99–110.

Dzwillo, M. 1959. Genetische Untersuchungen an domestizierten Stämmen von *Lebistes reticulatus* (Peters). *Mitt. Hamburgh. Zool. Mus. Inst.* 57:143–86.

————. 1962. Über künstliche Erzeugung funktioneller Männchen weiblichen Genotyps bei *Lebistes reticulatus. Bio. Zbl.* 81:575–84.

Echelle, A. A.; Echelle, A. F.; and Crozier, C. D. 1983. Evolution of an all-female fish, *Mendina clarkhubbsi* (Atherinidae). *Evolution* 37:772–84.

Echelle, A. A.; Wildrick, D. M.; and Echelle, A. F. 1989. Allozyme studies of genetic variation in poeciliid fishes. In *Ecology and Evolution of Livebearing Fishes (Poeciliidae)*, 217–34. See Angus 1989.

Entlinger, G. 1974. The brush-tail platy. *Trop. Fish Hobbyist* 22(1):95–98.

Ewulonu, J. K.; Haas, R.; and Turner, B. J. 1985. A multiple sex chromosome system in the annual killifish, *Nothobranchius guentheri. Copeia* 1985:503–508.

Farr, J. A. 1981. Biased sex ratios in laboratory strains of guppies, *Poecilia reticulata. Heredity* 47(2):237–48.

Ferris, S. D. 1984. Tetraploidy and the evolution of catostomid fishes. In *Evolutionary Genetics of Fishes*, 55-93. See Allendorf and Thorgaard 1984.

Gervai, J.; Peter, S.; Nagy, A.; et al. 1980. Induced triploidy in carp, *Cyprinus carpio* L. *J. Fish Biol.* 17:667–71.

Goodrich, H. B.; Dee, J. E.; Flynn, B. M.; et al. 1934. Germ cells and sex differentiation in *Lebistes reticulatus. Biol. Bull.* 67:83–96.

Goodrich, H. B.; Josephson, N. D.; Trinkaus, J. P.; et al. 1944. The cellular expression of two new genes in *Lebistes reticulatus. Genetics* 29:584–92.

Goodrich, H. B., and Smith, M. A. 1937. Genetics and histology of the colour pattern in the normal and albino paradise fish, *Macropodus opercularis* L. *Biol. Bull.* 73:527–34.

Gordon, M. 1927. The genetics of a viviparous top-minnow Platypoecilus: the inheritance of two kinds of melanophores. *Genetics* 12:253–83.

————. 1931. Morphology of the heritable color patterns in the Mexican killifish, *Platypoecilus. Am. J. Cancer* 15:732–87.

————. 1937. Genetics of *Platypoecilus*. 3. Inheritance of sex and crossing over of the sex chromosomes in the platyfish. *Genetics* 22:376–92.

————. 1942. Mortality of albino embryos and aberrant Mendelian ratios in certain broods of

Xiphophorus helleri. Zoologica (N.Y.) 27:73–74.

———. 1946. Introgressive hybridization in domesticated fishes. 1. The behavior of comet, a *Platypoecilus maculatus* gene in *Xiphophorus helleri. Zoologica* (N.Y.) 31:77–88.

———. 1947. Genetics of *Platypoecilus maculatus*. IV. The sex-determining mechanism in two wild populations of the Mexican platyfish. *Genetics* 32:8–17.

———. 1950. Heredity of pigmented tumours in fish. *Endeavour* 9:26–34.

———. 1951. Genetics of *Platypoecilus maculatus*. V. Heterogametic sex-determining mechanism in females of domesticated stocks originally from British Honduras. *Zoologica* (N.Y.) 36:127–53.

———. 1952. Sex determination in *Xiphophorus (Platypoecilus) maculatus*. III. Differentiation of gonads in platyfish from broods having a sex ratio of three females to one male. *Zoologica* (N.Y.) 37:91–100.

———. 1955. *Guppies as Pets*. Neptune City, N.J.: T.F.H. Publications. 32 pages.

———. 1956. An intricate genetic system that controls nine pigment cell patterns in the platyfish. *Zoologica* (N.Y.) 41:153–62.

Gordon, M., and Fraser, A. 1931. Pattern genes in the platyfish. *J. Hered.* 22:169–85.

Grobstein, C. 1948. Optimal gonopodial morphogenesis in *Platypoecilus maculatus* with constant dosage of methyl testosterone. *J. Exp. Zool.* 109:215–33.

Harrington, R. W., Jr. 1967. Environmentally controlled induction of primary male gonochorists from eggs of the self-fertilizing hermaphrodite fish, *Rivulus marmoratus* Poey. *Biol. Bull.* 131:174–99.

———. 1971. How ecological and genetic factors interact to determine when self-fertilizing hermaphrodites of *Rivulus marmoratus* change into functional secondary males, with a reappraisal of the modes of intersexuality among fishes. *Copeia* 1971:389–432.

Haskins, C. P., and Druzba, J. P. 1938. Note on anomalous inheritance of sex-linked color factors in the guppy. *Am. Naturalist* 72:571–74.

Haskins, C. P., and Haskins, E. F. 1948. Albinism, a semilethal autosomal mutation in *Lebistes reticulatus. Heredity* 2(2):251–62.

Haskins, C. P.; Haskins, E. F.; McLaughlin, J. J. A.; et al. 1961. Polymorphism and population structure in *Lebistes reticulatus*. In *Vertebrate*

Speciation, ed. W. Frank Blair, 320–95. Austin: University of Texas Press.

Haskins, C. P.; Young, P.; Hewitt, R. E.; et al. 1970. Stabilised heterozygosis of supergenes mediating certain Y-linked colour patterns in populations of *Lebistes reticulatus. Heredity* 25(4): 575–89.

Hearin, B. 1963. New introductions from the Delta Aquarium. *Trop. Fish Hobbyist* 12(1):5–14.

Heiligenberg, W. 1965. Color polymorphism in the males of an African cichlid fish. *J. Zool.* 146:95–97.

Hickling, C. F. 1960. The Malacca *Tilapia* hybrids. *J. Genet.* 57:1–10.

Hildemann, W. H. 1954. Effects of sex hormones on secondary sex characters of *Lebistes reticulatus. J. Exp. Zool.* 126:1–15.

Hubbs, C. L. 1940. Speciation of fishes. *Am. Naturalist* 74:198–211.

Hubbs, C. L., and Hubbs, L. C. 1932. Apparent parthenogenesis in nature, in a form of fish of hybrid origin. *Science* 76:628–30.

Hulata, G.; Wohlfarth, G. W.; and Rothbard, S. 1983. Progeny-testing selection of tilapia broodstocks producing all-male hybrid progenies—preliminary results. *Aquaculture* 33:263–68.

Hunter, G. A.; Donaldson, E. M.; Stoss, J.; et al. 1983. Production of monosex female groups of chinook salmon (*Oncorhynchus tshawytscha*) by the fertilization of normal ova with sperm from sex-reversed females. *Aquaculture* 33:355–64.

Kallman, K. D. 1965. Genetics and geography of sex determination in the poeciliid fish, *Xiphophorus maculatus. Zoologica* (N.Y.) 50:151–90.

———. 1968. Evidence for the existence of transformer genes for sex in the teleost *Xiphophorus maculatus. Genetics* 60:811–28.

———. 1970a. Sex determination and the restriction of pigment patterns to the X and Y chromosomes in populations of a poeciliid fish, *Xiphophorus maculatus,* from the Belize and Sibun rivers of British Honduras. *Zoologica* (N.Y.) 55:1–16.

———. 1970b. Different genetic basis of identical pigment patterns in two populations of platyfish, *Xiphophorus maculatus. Copeia* 1970: 472–87.

———. 1970c. Moon of a million faces. *Trop. Fish World* 1(5):4–7, 26, 36–37.

———. 1971. Inheritance of melanophore patterns and sex determination in the Montezuma swordtail, *Xiphophorus montezumae cortezi* Rosen. *Zoologica* (N.Y.) 56:77–94.

———. 1973. The sex-determining mechanism of the platyfish, *Xiphophorus maculatus.* In *Genetics and Mutagenesis of Fish,* 19–28. *See* Anders et al. 1973.

———. 1975. The platyfish, *Xiphophorus maculatus.* In *Handbook of Genetics.* 4, ed. R. C. King, 81–132. New York: Plenum Press.

———. 1983. The sex-determining mechanism of the poeciliid fish, *Xiphophorus montezumae,* and the genetic control of the sexual maturation process and adult size. *Copeia* 1983(3): 755–69.

———. 1984. A new look at sex determination in poeciliid fishes. In *Evolutionary Genetics of Fishes,* 95–171. *See* Allendorf and Thorgaard 1984.

———. 1989. Genetic control of size at maturity in *Xiphophorus.* In *Ecology and Evolution of Livebearing Fishes (Poeciliidae),* 163–84. *See* Angus 1989.

Kallman, K. D., and Atz, J. W. 1966. Gene and chromosome homology in fishes of the genus *Xiphophorus. Zoologica* (N. Y.) 51:107–35.

Kallman, K. D., and Borkoski, V. 1978. A sex-linked gene controlling the onset of sexual maturity in female and male platyfish (*Xiphophorus maculatus*), fecundity in females and adult size in males. *Genetics* 89:79–119.

Kallman, K. D., and Borowsky, R. 1972. The genetics of gonopodial polymorphism in two species of poeciliid fish. *Heredity* 28:297–310.

Kallman, K. D., and Brunetti, V. 1983. Genetic basis of three mutant color varieties of *Xiphophorus maculatus:* the gray, gold and ghost platyfish. *Copeia* 1983(1):170–81.

Kallman, K. D.; Schreibman, M. P.; and Borkoski, V. 1973. Genetic control of gonadotrop differentiation in the platyfish, *Xiphophorus maculatus* (Poeciliidae). *Science* (Wash., D.C.) 181: 678–80.

Karbe, L. 1961. Cytologische Untersuchung der Sterilitätserscheinungen bei anatolischen Zahnkarpfen, ein Beitrag zum Speziationsproblem. *Mitt. Hamburg. Zool. Mus. Inst.* 59:73–104.

Kincaid, H. L. 1983. Inbreeding in fish populations used for aquaculture. *Aquaculture* 33:215–27.

Kirpichnikov, V. S. 1981. *Genetic Bases of Fish Selection.* Berlin, Heidelberg: Springer-Verlag.

410 pages.

Knepper, M., and Knepper, N. 1963. Our marble lyretail mollies. *Trop. Fish Hobbyist* 12(3):5.

Kosswig, C. 1934. Farbfaktoren und Geschlechtsbestimmung (nach Untersuchungen an Zahnkarpfen). *Der Züchter* 6:40–47.

———. 1935. Über Albinismus bei Fischen. *Zool. Anzeig.* 110:41–47.

———. 1964. Polygenic sex determination. *Experientia* 20:190–99.

———. 1973. The role of fish in research on genetics and evolution. In *Genetics and Mutagenesis of Fish,* 3–16. *See* Anders et al. 1973.

Langhammer, J. K. 1982. Albinism in *Pelviachromis pulcher. Buntbarsche Bull.* 93:8.

Larr, E. C. 1977. So you want big male guppies! *Livebearers* 33:11.

Leslie, J. F. 1982. Linkage analysis of seventeen loci in poeciliid fish (genus *Poeciliopsis*). *J. Hered.* 73:19–23.

Lodi, E. 1981. Competition between palla and normal bearing spermatozoa of *Poecilia reticulata. Copeia* 1981(3):624–29.

MacIntyre, P. A. 1961. Crossing over within the macromelanophore gene in the platyfish, *Xiphophorus maculatus. Am. Naturalist* 95: 323–24.

Mires, D. 1977. Theoretical and practical aspects of the production of all male *Tilapia* hybrids. *Bamidgeh* 29:94–101.

Morizot, D. C., and Siciliano, M. J. 1979. Polymorphism, linkage and mapping of four enzyme loci in the fish genus *Xiphophorus. Genetics* 93:947–60.

———. 1982a. Protein polymorphisms, segregation in genetic crosses and genetic distances among fishes of the genus *Xiphophorus* (Poeciliidae). *Genetics* 102:539-56.

———. 1982b. Linkage of two enzyme loci in fishes of the genus *Xiphophorus* (Poeciliidae). *J. Hered.* 73:163–67.

———. 1984. Gene mapping in fishes and other vertebrates. In *Evolutionary Genetics of Fishes,* 173–234. See Allendorf and Thorgaard 1984.

Morizot, D. C.; Wright, D. A.; and Siciliano, M. J. 1977. Three linked enzyme loci in fishes: implications in the evolution of vertebrate chromosomes. *Genetics* 86:645–56.

Mrakovcic, M., and Haley, L. E. 1979. Inbreeding depression in the zebra fish *Brachydanio rerio* (Hamilton Buchana). *J. Fish. Biol.* 15:323–27.

Nayudu, P. L. 1979. Genetic studies of melanic

color patterns and atypical sex determination in the guppy, *Poecilia reticulata*. *Copeia* 1979(2):225–31.

Norton, J. 1967a. Inheritance of the hi-fin dorsal in swordtails and platies. *Trop. Fish Hobbyist* 15(5):45–49.

———. 1967b. True hi-fin lyretail sword. *Trop. Fish Hobbyist* 16(1):4–9.

———. 1969. Genetics of red coral swordtails. *The Aquarium* 2(10):73–78.

———. 1970a. The veil swordtail. *The Aquarium* 3(3):32–33, 56–58.

———. 1970b. Three colors of convict cichlids. *The Aquarium* 3(11):8–9, 52–53.

———. 1971a. Angelfish—breeding and genetics. *The Aquarium* 6(10):34–41.

———. 1971b. Green angelfish and colorful discus. *The Aquarium* 5(1):8–13.

———. 1974. Genetics of fancy mollies. *Today's Aquarist* 1(2):28–36.

———. 1981. Calico molly. *Freshwater and Marine Aquarium* 4(7):22–24, 78–79.

———. 1982a. Angelfish genetics: part one. *Freshwater and Marine Aquarium* 5(4):15–18, 90–91.

———. 1982b. Angelfish genetics: part two. *Freshwater and Marine Aquarium* 5(5):22–23.

———. 1982c. Angelfish genetics: part three. *Freshwater and Marine Aquarium* 5(7):8–10, 91–92.

———. 1982d. Angelfish genetics: part four. *Freshwater and Marine Aquarium* 5(8):15–17.

———. 1982e. Angelfish genetics: part five. *Freshwater and Marine Aquarium* 5(9):8–10.

———. 1982f. Angelfish genetics: part six. *Freshwater and Marine Aquarium* 5(10):38–40.

———. 1982g. Angelfish genetics: part seven. *Freshwater and Marine Aquarium* 5(11):40–41.

———. 1983. Clown angelfish. *Freshwater and Marine Aquarium* 6(5):15–17, 89, 91.

———. 1984a. Black velvet angelfish. *Freshwater and Marine Aquarium* 7(7):10–11.

———. 1984b. Red mollies. *Freshwater and Marine Aquarium* 7(10):86–87.

———. 1985a. Leopard angelfish. *Freshwater and Marine Aquarium* 8(2):10–14.

———. 1985b. Half-black angelfish. *Freshwater and Marine Aquarium* 8(8):18–23.

———. 1986. Peach molly and other new mollies. *Freshwater and Marine Aquarium* 9(9):12–17.

———. 1988. Gold marble angelfish. *Freshwater and Marine Aquarium* 11(9):88–90.

———. 1989. Half-black combinations in angelfish. *Freshwater and Marine Aquarium* 12(5):26–28, 134.

———. 1990a. Seven kinds of marble angelfish. *Freshwater and Marine Aquarium* 13(5):127–29, 134–35.

———. 1990b. Pearly—a new angelfish mutation. *Freshwater and Marine Aquarium* 13(12):90–92.

Ojima, Y.; Uyeno, K.; and Hayashi, M. 1976. A review of the chromosome number in fishes. *Kromosome* II-1:19–47.

Ong, Y. W. 1960. The lyretail black molly, a new strain. *Trop. Fish Hobbyist* 8(12):24–34.

Onozato, H. 1983. Artificial polyploidization in fishes and its application in aquaculture. *Fish Genet. Breed. Sci.* (Suisan Ikushu) 8:17–29 (in Japanese).

Ostrow, M. E. 1978. Data on sex ratios. *Trop. Fish Hobbyist* 27:39–40.

———. 1979. Sex ratios and pH in platies. *Trop. Fish Hobbyist* 27:44–46.

Oztan, N. 1963. The effects of gonadotropic and steroid hormones on the gonads of sterile hybrid fishes. *Rev. Fac. Sci.* (Istanbul) B25:27–47.

Park, E. H. 1974. A list of the chromosome number of fishes. *Coll. Rev. Coll. Lab. Art Sci., Seoul Nat. Univ.* 20:346–72.

Prehn, L. M., and Rasch, E. M. 1969. Cytogenetic studies of *Poecilia* (Pisces): I. Chromosome numbers of naturally occurring poeciliid species and their hybrids from eastern Mexico. *Can. J. Genet. Cytol.* 11:888–95.

Pruginin, Y.; Rothbard, S.; Wohlfarth, G.; et al. 1975. All male broods of *Tilapia nilotica* X *T. aurea* hybrids. *Aquaculture* 6:11–21.

Purdom, C. E. 1983. Genetic engineering by the manipulation of chromosomes. *Aquaculture* 33:287–300.

Rasch, E. M., and Balsano, J. S. 1974. Biochemical and cytogenetic studies of *Poecilia* from eastern Mexico. II. Frequency, perpetuation, and probable origin of triploid genomes in females associated with *Poecilia formosa*. *Rev. Biol. Trop.* 21:351–81.

Rasch, E. M.; Darnell, R. M.; Kallman, K. D.; et al. 1965. Cytophotometric evidence for triploidy in hybrids of the gynogenetic fish, *Poecilia formosa*. *J. Exp. Zool.* 160:155–70.

Rauchenberger, M.; Kallman, K. D.; and Morizot, D. C. 1990. Monophyly and geography of the Río Pánuco basin swordtails (genus *Xiphophorus*) with descriptions of four new species.

Amer. Mus. Novitates No. 2975. 41 pages.

Rishi, K. K. 1979. Somatic G-banded chromosomes of Colisa fasciatus (Perciformes: Belontidae) and confirmation of female heterogamety. Copeia 1979(1):146–49.

Rosen, D. E. 1979. Fishes from the uplands and intermontane basins of Guatemala: revisionary studies and comparative geography. Bull. Am. Mus. Nat. Hist. 162(5):267–376.

Rubin, D. A. 1985. Effect of pH on sex ratio in cichlids and a poecilliid [sic] (Teleostei). Copeia 1985:233–35.

Schmidt, J. 1920. Racial investigations. IV. The genetic behavior of a secondary sexual character. C. R. Trav. Lab. (Carlsberg) 14(8):1–12.

Schreck, C. B., ed. 1974. Control of Sex in Fishes. Blacksburg: Virginia Polytechnic Institute and State University.

Schreibman, M. P., and Kallman, K. D. 1977. The genetic control of the pituitary-gonadal axis in the platyfish, Xiphophorus maculatus. J. Exp. Zool. 200:277–94.

Schröder, J. H. 1964. Genetische Untersuchungen an domestizierten Stämmen der Gattung Mollienesia (Poeciliidae). Zool. Beiträge 10(3): 369–463.

———. 1966. Über Besonderheiten der Vererbung des Simpsonfaktors bei Xiphophorus helleri Heckel (Poeciliidae, Pisces). Zool. Beiträge (NF) 12:27–42.

———. 1969. Radiation-induced spermatogonial exchange between the X and Y chromosomes in the guppy. Can. J. Genet. Cytol. 11:948–54.

———, ed. 1973. Genetics and Mutagenesis of Fish. New York: Springer-Verlag. 356 pages.

Schultz, R. J. 1969. Hybridization, unisexuality and polyploidy in the teleost Poeciliopsis (Poeciliidae) and other vertebrates. Am. Naturalist 103:605–19.

———. 1977. Evolution and ecology of unisexual fishes. In Evolutionary Biology, ed. M. K. Hecht, W. C. Steere, and B. Wallace, Vol. 10, 277–331. New York: Plenum Press.

———. 1980. Role of polyploidy in the evolution of fishes. In Polyploidy—Biological Relevance, ed. W. H. Lewis, 313–40. New York: Plenum Press.

Schultz, R. J., and Kallman, K. D. 1968. Triploid hybrids between the all-female teleost Poecilia formosa and Poecilia sphenops. Nature 219: 280–82.

Schwartz, F. J. 1972. World Literature to Fish Hybrids with an Analysis by Family, Species, and Hybrid. Ocean Springs, Miss: Gulf Coast Res. Lab. Publ. Gulf Coast Res. Lab. Mus. No. 3. 328 pages.

Seligmann, E. B., Jr. 1958. Factors governing color variations in angelfish. The Aquarium 27: 176–79, 189.

Shami, S. A., and Beardmore, J. A. 1978. Genetic studies of enzyme variation in the guppy, Poecilia reticulata (Peters). Genetica 48:67–73.

Smith, M. W.; Smith, M. H.; and Chesser, R. K. 1983. Biochemical genetics of mosquitofish. I. Environmental heterogeneity of allele frequencies within a river drainage. Copeia 1983(1): 182–93.

Sterba, G. 1959. Über eine Mutation bei Pterophyllum eimekei. I. Anamnese und Beschreibung. Biol. Zentralbl. 78:323–33.

Strommen, C. A.; Rasch, E. M.; and Balsano, J. S. 1975. Cytogenetic studies of Poecilia. V. Cytophotometric evidence for the production of fertile offspring by triploids related to Poecilia formosa. J. Fish. Biol. 7:1–10.

Sullivan, J. A., and Schultz, R. J. 1986. Genetic and environmental basis of variable sex ratios in laboratory strains of Poeciliopsis lucida. Evolution 40(1):152–58.

Suzuki, R., and Fukuda, Y. 1972. Growth and survival of F_1 hybrids among salmonid fishes. Bull. Freshwater Fish. Res. Lab. 21:117–38.

Takahashi, H. 1975. Functional masculinization of female guppies, Poecilia reticulata, influenced by methyltestosterone before birth. Bull. Jpn. Soc. Sci. Fish. 41:499–506.

Thorgaard, G. H.; Jazwin, M. E.; and Stier, A. R. 1981. Polyploidy induced by heat shock in rainbow trout. Trans. Am. Fish. Soc. 110:546–50.

Turner, B. J. 1982. The evolutionary genetics of a unisexual fish, Poecilia formosa. In Mechanisms of Speciation, 265–305. New York: Alan R. Liss.

Uyeno, T., and Miller, R. R. 1971. Multiple sex chromosomes in a Mexican cyprinodontid fish. Nature 231:452–53.

Valenti, R. J. 1975. Induced polyploidy in Tilapia aurea (Steindachner) by means of temperature shock treatment. J. Fish Biol. 7:519–28.

Vallowe, H. H. 1953. Some physiological aspects of reproduction in Xiphophorus maculatus. Biol. Bull. 104:240–49.

Van Oordt, G. J. 1928. The duration of life of the

spermatozoa in the fertilized female of *Xiphophorus helleri* Regan. *Tijds. Ned. Deerk. Vereen, Ser.* 3:77–80.

Winge, Ø. 1922. One-sided masculine and sex-linked inheritance in *Lebistes reticulatus. J. Genet.* 12:145–62.

———. 1927. The location of eighteen genes in *Lebistes reticulatus. J. Genet.* 18:1–42.

———. 1930. On the occurrence of XX males in *Lebistes,* with some remarks on Aida's so-called "nondisjunction" males in *Aplocheilus. J. Genet.* 23:69–76.

———. 1934. The experimental alteration of sex chromosomes and vice versa, as illustrated in *Lebistes. C. R. Trav. Lab. Carlsberg Ser. Physiol.* 21:1–49.

———. 1937. Succession of broods in *Lebistes. Nature* 140:467.

Winge, Ø., and Ditlevsen, E. 1938. A lethal gene in the Y-chromosome of *Lebistes. C. R. Trav. Lab. Carlsberg Ser. Physiol.* 22:203–10.

———. 1947. Colour inheritance and sex determination in *Lebistes. Heredity* 1:65–83.

Wohlfarth, G. W. 1983. Genetics of fish: applications to warm water fishes. *Aquaculture* 33:373–81.

Wohlfarth, G. W., and Hulata, G. I. 1981. *Applied genetics of tilapia.* International Center for Living Aquatic Resources Management, Studies and Reviews 6. 26 pages.

Wolfsheimer, G. 1960. The Simpson swordtail. *Aquar. J.* 31(11):544–45.

———. 1965. Latest in mollies. *Aquar. J.* 36(6):274–76.

Wolters, W. R.; Libey, G. S.; and Chrisman, C. L. 1981. Induction of triploidy in channel catfish. *Trans. Am. Fish. Soc.* 110:310–12.

———. 1982. Effect of triploidy on growth and gonad development of channel catfish. *Trans. Am. Fish. Soc.* 111:102–105.

Wood, J. A. 1968. A new molly. *The Aquarium* 1(5):6.

Yamamoto, T. 1953. Artificially induced sex-reversal in genotypic males of the medaka (*Oryzias latipes*). *J. Exp. Zool.* 123:571–94.

———. 1955. Progeny of artificially induced sex reversals of male genotype (XY) in the medaka (*Oryzias latipes*) with special reference to YY-male. *Genetics* 40:406–19.

———. 1958. Artificial induction of functional sex-reversal in genotypic females of the medaka (*Oryzias latipes*). *J. Exp. Zool.* 137:227–62.

———. 1962. Hormonic factors affecting gonadal sex differentiation in fish. *Gen. Comp. Endocrinol. Suppl.* 1:341–45.

———. 1969. Sex differentiation. In *Fish Physiology,* ed. W. S. Hoar and D. J. Randall, Vol. III, 117–75. New York: Academic Press.

———. 1975. The medaka, *Oryzias latipes,* and the guppy, *Lebistes reticularis* [sic]. In *Handbook of Genetics,* 133–49. See Kallman 1975.

Yamazaki, F. 1983. Sex control and manipulation in fish. *Aquaculture* 33:329–54.

Zander, C. D. 1969. Über die Entstehung und Veränderung von Farbmustern in der Gattung *Xiphophorus* (Pisces). I. Qualitative Veränderungen nach Artkreuzung. *Mitt. Hamb. Zool. Mus. Inst.* 66:241–71.

Breeding Aquarium Fish

Paul V. Loiselle

It is widely believed that much expert knowledge is required to induce most tropical fish species to spawn successfully in captivity. This simply is not true. Certain easily mastered fundamentals are common to nearly all cases. In addition, fish can be divided into several operational groups based upon common features of their reproductive biology. Within these reproductive guilds, members can be handled in much the same manner in captivity. In the pages that follow, both general guidelines and more specific pointers are presented. Anyone willing to read them carefully and to follow the procedures outlined therein can expect to spawn and rear an enormous variety of aquarium fish successfully.

These are not the only approaches that will work under home aquarium conditions, nor do I make any pretense of having covered the topic of this chapter exhaustively. Due to space limitations, fascinating details of the basic reproductive biology of these groups have been omitted. Readers are urged to consult the references at the chapter's end, and the often extensive bibliographies contained therein, as a useful starting point to increase their knowledge and enhance their mastery of aquarium fish breeding, the most interesting and challenging aspect of the aquarium hobby.

Basic Reproductive Patterns of Aquarium Fishes		
Category	Characteristics	Selected Examples
Live-Bearers		
	Females deliver live young.	poeciliids (guppies, mollies, platys, swordtails), goodeids, halfbeaks
Egg Layers With No Parental Care		
Type 1 egg scatterers	Young pass through yolk-sac developmental stage between egg and fully mobile fry.	danios, rasboras, kissing gourami, monos, barbs, tetras, Corydoras, loaches, glassfish
Type 2 egg scatterers	Young fully mobile upon hatching; no diapause (period of arrested development).	silversides and allied atherinids, rainbowfishes, cyprinodontid killifish
Annual fishes	Eggs go through diapause; adults with rapid growth and short life-span.	killifish adapted for ephemeral habitats

Basic Reproductive Patterns of Aquarium Fishes		
Category	Characteristics	Selected Examples
Egg Layers That Practice Parental Care		
Paternal custodial species	Males care for eggs and zygotes; usually polygamous. Well-developed spawning site preferences.	
Aphrophils	Bubble nest builders; usually able to breathe atmospheric oxygen.	many Belontiidae and Anabantidae, including *Betta, Colisa, Cetenopoma*
Speleophils	Spawn in cavities, either naturally occurring or ones they have constructed. Typically inhabit well-oxygenated habitats.	gobies, sticklebacks, armored suckermouth catfishes, darter perch, sculpins
Agoraphils, Phytophils	Spawn in the open upon plants, solid surfaces, or in nest in sand or gravel.	*Copella, Polycentrus, Gymnarchus, Bagrus,* sunfishes
Paternal brooders	Males cary zygotes until eggs hatch or fry are free-swimming.	*Osteoglossum, Glossamia, Betta, Loricaria, Luciocephalus,* some cichlids
Biparental custodial species	Both parents care for eggs; parents are monogamous. May be agoraphils, speleophils, or mouthbrooders.	Monogamous substratum-spawning cichlids; some piranhas and snakeheads; *Arapaima*
Maternal custodial species	female cares for eggs; polygamous or polygynous. Speleophils or mouthbrooders.	*Scleropages;* polygamous cichlids, e.g. *Apistogramma, Nanochromis, Haplochromis, Oreochromis*

General Guidelines for Breeding Aquarium Fish

Use of fairly large aquaria with tight covers, careful monitoring of the breeding pair, and attention to the nutritional requirements of the newly mobile offspring, called fry, do much to assure reproductive success for any aquarium species. Other commonalities are outlined below. Supplement the information given here with more specific guidelines in the later sections of this chapter.

Pairing and aggression: The mating system of a great many fish is based upon territoriality and aggression. Fighting can have serious consequences if the defeated contender cannot move beyond the reach of the victor. In most cases, to avoid loss of prized fish, one simply must house species in tanks large enough to allow each sex to keep out of each other's way and with plentiful hiding places. Determination of minimum tank size often can be made only on a species-by-species basis and requires a certain amount of research. Err on the side of caution.

Tank management: In addition to the regular aquarium, one or more separate tanks usually must be established for various aspects of the breeding procedure, such as conditioning the breeders, spawning, or rearing the fry. Each of these must be provided with a mature sponge filter, properly treated water, and a sealed thermostatic heater. The nitrogen cycle in each must also be managed carefully through a system of regular partial water changes.

To maximize the likelihood of very young fry encountering prey, water level in a rearing tank is often lowered to one-quarter or one-third of its maximum capacity at first. As the young grow larger, the water level is slowly raised until the tank is completely full. Lowering the water level in this manner will not adversely affect sponge filter operation, but the heater should be tilted at an angle as necessary to keep it properly submerged.

Conditioning: In many cases, it is desirable to move potential breeders into separate tanks for special attention aimed at getting them into top reproductive condition. The two sexes should be housed separately and fed two or three times a day with a diet high in live or frozen high-protein foods, such as wingless fruit flies, frozen bloodworms, white or Grindal worms, glassworms, adult brine shrimp, or where appropriate, small fish. Tubificid worms pose some risk of systemic bacterial infection in aquarium fish and should not be used as food.

Use of a delivery tank: Because of the widespread occurrence of cannibalism, a delivery tank is often necessary when breeding live-bearing fishes. Its size must reflect both that of the female and her expected fecundity, for in most cases it will serve as the initial rearing tank for the fry born therein. In general, its water should be of the same chemical makeup and temperature as the female's former quarters. A tight cover for the tank is an excellent investment, for many of these fish are excellent jumpers, particularly when skittish from being moved.

In most cases, a sponge filter poses minimal risk to fry, and its associated microfauna often provide an important dietary supplement. An established sponge filter should be allowed to operate for a day or so before the gravid female is introduced, to spare her the necessity of experiencing the fluctuations in nitrite concentration typical of a new tank. The delivery aquarium should experience the same daily light/dark cycle as the female's previous residence.

Feeding fry: The fry of many species initially require infusoria. Culturing these microorganisms requires a certain amount of practice. There is always an element of chance with regard to which infusorians will predominate in a given culture, and not all are equally satisfactory as fry food. Microworms are a more easily cultured alternative and more nutritionally consistent. When feeding either infusoria or microworms, introduce as little of the culture medium as possible into the rearing tank. Even small quantities can fuel a potentially dangerous bacterial bloom.

Artemia (brine shrimp) nauplii are the largest of the living foods commonly used for fry. They are easily hatched in quantity on relatively short notice, are both nutritious and highly palatable to fry, and pose minimal risk of introducing potentially dangerous microorganisms into the rearing tank. Successful fish breeders rely upon them as fry food whenever possible.

Several feedings a day ensure maximum growth, but each feeding must be small. Microworms and nauplii both die within a few hours of being added to the water and once dead, decay rapidly. The short-term danger is that this organic matter will generate a bacterial bloom; the long-term hazard is the potential for the buildup of toxic nitrites produced by the organic matter's breakdown.

Managing the rearing tank: Frequent partial water changes are the easiest way to maintain a suitable growing environment in a closed system. Begin with changes of 10 percent of the tank's volume, with an increase to up to 80 percent every other day to encourage maximal growth once the fry have been moved to larger rearing tanks. The interval between changes can be extended through the use of chemically active media such as Poly-Filter™ or ChemiPure™.

Cannibalism: In general, if a breeder desires optimal survival of fry, one must be prepared to sort growing fry by size, as larger ones will eat smaller siblings. Some recommend that only the largest individuals in a tankful of fry be reared to maturity. However, because of a widespread phenomenon known as male growth superiority, the fastest growing and largest individuals in a spawn usually prove to be males. Thus, culling usually is better limited to the elimination of individuals that show obvious physical or colorational abnormalities.

Selective breeding: One often hears complaints that the current aquarium strains of some fish are not the equals of wild stock or even of the aquarium strains of a few decades past. Few populations of ornamental fish have been maintained in captivity long enough for true inbreeding depression to have occurred. Rather, such deterioration stems from a lack of selective breeding. The only way to maintain a quality strain of any fish is to select the most colorful and vigorous individuals for future breeding stock, rather than relying upon chance sexual encounters.

Live-Bearing Fishes

Species that deliver live young are a distinct minority, but include many of the most popular and

The distinctive tail spike of this male red swordtail (*Xiphophorus helleri*) is a unique feature of this popular live-bearer. However, the distinction between the male's rodlike gonopodium and the female's unmodified anal fin is a feature common to all poeciliids.

generally available ornamental fishes.

Basic biology relevant to the breeding of live-bearing fishes: All live-bearing fishes are characterized by internal fertilization. In some families (Anablepidae, Jeneysiidae, Poeciliidae), the male's anal fin has been modified into a specialized, phalluslike structure, the gonopodium. In the freshwater stingrays, the male's ventral fins have been modified to perform this function. Sperm transfer in the Goodeidae and the Hemiramphidae occurs through direct contact between the cloacal openings of the male and female. In the pipefish, the female deposits her eggs in the male's brood pouch, where fertilization occurs.

Live-bearing fishes span the continuum from ovoviviparity, in which the female produces heavily yolked eggs that contain all the stored food the developing embryo will require, through true viviparity, in which the young are directly connected to and nourished by the female's circulatory system. Such distinctions have considerable bearing on the care of gravid individuals. Ovoviviparous live-bearers seem more prone to miscarriage, while the nutritional demands of gravid viviparous females are greater.

The usual developmental interval in live-bearing fishes ranges from twenty-eight to thirty-two days, with an extreme of almost a year in freshwater sting rays and the surfperches of the family Embrotocidae. The length of this interval is influenced by ambient temperature, photoperiod, the female's nutritional state, and age. The interval between broods is shorter when females are well nourished and housed at the upper end of their preferred temperature range. In a number of poeciliid species, females deliver small broods of fry every few days because eggs are fertilized as they mature rather than being fertilized only after a batch has accumulated.

Once the female has dropped her young, she becomes receptive to male courtship. The apparently continuous interest most male live-bearers display in the cloacal region of accessible females represents an effort to monitor their reproductive status. The interval of female receptivity is brief, and in nature, competition for access to such females is intense.

In species in which the sexes differ little in size or males are the larger sex, especially those characterized by sharp sexual dimorphism, the female may suffer injury unless the fish are housed in a tank large enough to allow her to escape male attentions. Alternatively, such species can be housed in multi-female groups, which forces a male to divide his attentions among all the females present.

Among those species in which the female is larger, the female has a greater say in the selection of her consort. For the male, merely approaching the female may pose a risk ranging from predation to emasculation. These species should be housed only in tanks large enough to allow each sex to keep out of the other's way and should be provided with plenty of cover. Determination of suitable tank size can be made only on a species-by-species basis and requires a certain amount of research.

Determinate male growth: In many poeciliid species, further linear growth ceases once a male's anal fin undergoes its metamorphosis to become the gonopodium. The mature male may become deeper-bodied, but he does not grow any longer. Thus, late-maturing males grow larger than early-maturing ones. The factors that determine the onset of gonopodial metamorphosis are complex. Genetic factors largely determine the onset of male reproductive maturity, and many wild populations have both early-maturing and late-maturing males. Where living conditions fluctuate markedly and in an unpredictable fashion, early-maturing males predominate. Where the environment is more predictable and living conditions more stable, the late-maturing males are more common.

Aquarium conditions seem to favor the smaller early-maturing male, perhaps because limited swimming space tends to make the hit-and-run approach to courtship of early-maturing males disproportionately effective. The buildup of metabolites that typically occurs when fry are reared in aquaria also appears to trigger early gonopodial metamorphosis and consequent male stunting. When members of a species not known to manifest this genetic polymorphism are raised in an environment where metabolic wastes are not allowed to accumulate, males mature later and average larger than counterparts reared under closed conditions. The implications of this phenomenon on the aquarium husbandry of these fishes are obvious.

Sex reversal: In some *Xiphophorus* and *Poecilia* species, old females develop the full array of secondary male sex characteristics, including metamorphosis of the anal fin into a gonopodium.

However, while they look like males, documented evidence of functional sex changes in these fish is lacking. Like many lower vertebrates, poeciliids have gonads that are comprised of both testicular and ovarian elements. As long as it remains functional, the dominant element suppresses the activity of the subordinate. Female poeciliids have only a finite number of follicles in their ovaries capable of maturing into eggs. Once a female has exhausted these, the dominant ovarian element of her gonads no longer produces the hormones that suppress the activity of their testicular analog. Secondary development of female characteristics in older males appears not to occur because there is no such built-in limitation on testicular activity.

Management of gravid females: Representatives of seven families of live-bearing fishes are more or less frequently kept as freshwater residents. Most of these fish breed regularly without any encouragement from their keeper. The central problem facing the prospective breeder is that of saving as many fry as possible from being devoured. Cannibalism varies in intensity from one species to the next. In some instances, newly dropped fry are ignored by conspecifics unless the latter are themselves poorly fed. One need only set a pair or trio up alone in a well-planted 80- to 120-liter (20- to 30-gallon) tank and feed the adults generously to breed these species sucessfully. Once fry appear, offer appropriate food on a regular schedule. Remove older fry to a separate rearing tank to make room for younger siblings and to provide an environment that promotes optimal growth.

Other live-bearers are so predatory that such an approach will not give satisfactory results under aquarium conditions. In these cases, a special delivery tank is needed (see previous section, "General Guidelines"). A 40- to 60-liter (10- to 15-gallon) aquarium suffices for most commonly raised species. Provide a dense layer of floating vegetation to shelter the newly delivered fry and a tight cover to keep the skittish female from jumping out.

In general, it is unwise to move a gravid female later than a week prior to the anticipated delivery date. The closer her projected delivery date, the more vulnerable she is to stress-induced miscarriage. With larger species such as the sailfin mollies, swordtails, and more robust goodeids, avoid any serious trauma later than ten days prior to

The dark gravid spot visible over the vent of the female of this pair of variatus platys (*Xiphophorus variatus*) occurs in many poeciliid and goodeid species.

delivery. These fish tend to struggle more actively when netted, and thus run a greater risk of injuring themselves and their brood.

If a female's prior reproductive history is unknown, err on the side of caution and isolate the female as soon as her flanks show signs of swelling when seen from above. Once a female has dropped her fry, the next delivery date can be easily projected.

With most live-bearing species, developing fry will cause the female to fill out noticeably. In many cases, the eyes of the young become clearly visible through the body wall a few days before delivery. Some poeciliids and goodeids have a conspicuous dark area over the vent, known as the gravid spot, which tends to become darker as the female's pregnancy advances.

Feed the female generously with a combination of commercially available conditioning foods and live and frozen foods. As soon as the condition of the female's abdomen indicates that birth is imminent, keep live food such as *Daphnia* constantly present in the delivery tank. Postpartum adults have a ravenous appetite, and the availability of alternative foods may reduce the incidence of maternal cannibalism. If this is not possible, the female should be checked as frequently as possible and removed immediately after dropping her fry. Females usually begin delivering at first light and are done by noon.

Use of breeding traps: A breeding trap is often recommended to allow newly delivered fry to drop out of the female's reach, either into a delivery tank or into a separate compartment of a plastic box suspended from the tank rim. Regrettably, commercially available breeding traps are far too small to accommodate most gravid female live-bearers for any length of time. The detainee typically struggles frantically to escape, and in so doing, she is likely to miscarry. The longer she is restrained, the more likely a gravid female is to injure herself, but delaying the gravid female's transfer into the trap risks premature delivery.

As a rule of thumb, never attempt to use a breeding trap with any female live-bearer whose total length is equal to or greater than the minimum depth of the compartment into which she would be placed. Even so, one has no guarantee that a female will accept such limitations on her movements. Many of the smaller goodeids simply do not tolerate confinement in a breeding trap.

As a safer alternative, a day or two before the female's expected delivery, reduce the water level in the tank to a depth of 15 to 20 centimeters (6 to 8 inches), then cover the bottom with Java moss and the surface with floating plants such as foxtail and floating fern. This will severely limit the female's mobility without triggering self-destructive behavior. The fry, on the other hand, can slip easily between the stems and leaves.

A delay in delivery of a few days usually stems from an excessively optimistic projection of the female's due date rather than from the operation of any complicating factors. Be patient. Intervention is apt to provoke premature birth, and the prognosis for premature fry is not favorable.

It is sometimes recommended that the female be given the opportunity to recuperate for a few days before being returned to a community tank or reintroduced to the presence of males. Assuming her original home is well planted and other females are present to distract the attention of amorous males, such sequestration is not necessary.

Rearing live-bearer fry: Once the fry are born and the female removed, bring the water level in the tank back up to normal again. Most live-bearer fry can take finely powdered prepared foods for their first meal, but also greatly relish live foods such as *Artemia* nauplii and microworms. Give several small feedings daily to ensure maximum growth. Fry reared in a long-established, well-lit, planted aquarium, with its associated community of microscopic organisms, typically grow faster and more uniformly than those reared in bare aquaria. Fry can remain in the delivery tank for their first month, then should be transferred to

more spacious quarters. Breeder flats of 120 to 160 liters (30 to 40 gallons) can provide excellent housing for up to fifty fry.

Change part of the water frequently (see "General Guidelines"). Inattention to proper tank maintenance can quickly lead to mass mortality and/or a tank of stunted individuals.

Promptly segregate the sexes as soon as they can be reliably distinguished. The ability of many poeciliids to store sperm means that a single chance sexual encounter can eliminate a female for life from a planned breeding program. Males of most live-bearers become functional well before secondary sexual color or finnage distinctions develop fully, but with practice it is possible to recognize males before they attain reproductive competence.

Egg Layers That Do Not Practice Parental Care

Some egg layers practice parental care; others do not. The former modify the environment in a manner that favors the survival of their otherwise vulnerable zygotes. The latter seek out the microhabitat that affords their zygotes the best chance for successful development. Prospective breeders must carefully recreate such an environment in the spawning tank. To facilitate this task, the great many species of fish in this category are divided into subgroups (see the table at the beginning of this chapter).

Most egg-scattering fishes can be readily classified, but a few species defy facile classification. The zygotes of the pygmy sunfish (*Elassoma evergladei*) develop in the type 1 manner, but the adults display a type 2 spawning pattern.

Breeding Techniques for Type 1 Egg Scatterers

Egg scatterers include a large number of species with highly idiosyncratic reproductive behavior and management requirements. Thorough research is thus needed to set up an appropriate breeding tank. Seek the advice of other aquarists who have successfully bred the species in question under local conditions. Their experience will often supplement published accounts in a useful manner.

Rearing, selecting, and conditioning breeding stock: It is better to purchase ten to twelve juvenile fish and rear them to sexual maturity rather than buy a "proven" breeding pair or trio. Young adults are typically more vigorous and fertile than older individuals. Many type 1 egg scatterers display secondary sex differences less obvious than those of live-bearing fishes. In general, female type 1 egg scatterers (those whose young pass through a yolk-sac developmental stage) are heavier bodied than males and typically look much fuller in the flanks when seen from above. Depending upon their mating system, the females may be either larger or smaller than the males. Males generally are more brightly colored than females and often have longer or more elaborate finnage. The anal fins of male characins and some allied fishes are covered with minute hooks that will catch briefly in a fine-meshed net.

Fish large enough to be sexed are old enough to be spawned successfully, and should be moved into separate conditioning tanks for seven to ten days and fed with high-protein foods (see "General Guidelines").

Males are typically ready to breed sooner than females. Ripe females of most species appear visibly full, especially when examined from above. In "translucent" species, the ovaries of ripe females will appear notably more granular than do the testes of males when the fish are viewed against strong backlighting.

Setting up the spawning tank: A covered all-glass aquarium is recommended. For the smaller characoids, barbs, and rasboras, 20 liters (5 gallons) will suffice; for robust and prolific species, tank capacity should be 80 liters (20 gallons) to 140 liters (35 gallons).

Because of the zygotes' sensitivity to bacterial attack, the spawning tank must be carefully sterilized before being used. Fill the tank half full of tap water as hot as is briefly bearable, then add 1/2 cup (120 milliliters) of liquid laundry bleach (5.25 percent sodium hypochlorite) per liter or quart of water. Wearing kitchen gloves, use the resulting solution to wash both its interior and the glass cover thoroughly with a previously unused kitchen sponge. Drain the bleach solution, rinse the tank thoroughly with very hot tap water, then cover it tightly and allow it to cool to room temperature. That portion of the heater to be submerged in the spawning tank and any gravel, rockwork, or plastic appliances should be treated likewise. This may seem a very dangerous means of preventing the entry of bacteria into the spawning tank. However, under elevated water temperatures, chlorine bleach breaks down to yield chlorine, which leaves the water as a gas, and common table salt, which is quite harmless to fish.

Filling the spawning tank: If the species to be bred will spawn readily in tap water, it is a simple matter to fill the tank with extremely hot water, put the heater and other appliances in place, cover the tank tightly, and allow it to cool overnight. Then plug in the heater, connect a mature sponge filter, add an appropriate spawning substratum, and the tank is ready for use. If water in the

Scrupulous attention to both water chemistry and tank cleanliness is essential when working with type 1 egg scatterers from "blackwater" habitats, such as the cardinal tetra (*Paracheirodon axelrodi*).

breeding tank must be made harder and more alkaline, appropriate additives should be dissolved in hot water and added to the tank immediately after it has been filled. Salts go into solution more readily in hot water.

Species from "blackwater" habitats will breed successfully only in nearly sterile acid water with no detectable hardness. Blackwater is characterized as being soft, highly acidic, and in nature stained a dark reddish color from decayed plant matter. The simplest method is to begin with deionized water, available at most supermarkets by the gallon. Add Tetra's Blackwater Extract™ according to manufacturer's instructions. Once the desired pH value has been reached, add a level teaspoon (5 milliliters) of table salt (sodium chloride) per liter or quart of treated water to provide the small quantities of dissolved salts which are present in naturally occurring blackwater but are absent from deionized water. Finally, sterilize this solution by boiling it for several minutes in a glass vessel which is then covered, immediately removed from the heat, and allowed to cool to room temperature. Blackwater so treated can be stored in sealed vessels until needed or added directly to the spawning tank.

Selecting a spawning substrate: Live plants should be employed only for those species with zygotes which can tolerate substantial numbers of bacteria in their environment. Java moss is well accepted by most of these species, can be rinsed under a vigorous stream of water without damage, and prospers under the dim illumination characteristic of most breeding setups.

Alternative spawning substrata include bunches of washed willow roots and Spanish moss, both of which have been used for decades by commercial fish breeders. More readily available to the home aquarist are the finer grades of reusable plastic filter floss (well accepted by the smaller species) and "mops" of nylon yarn (see under "BreedingTechniques for Type 2 Egg Scatterers"). As a rule, fish prefer to place their eggs on dark-colored substrata.

Some type 1 egg scatterers produce nonadhesive eggs. These fish spawn over coarse gravel bottoms in nature. One can easily construct a spawning grid from two pieces of plastic egg crate diffuser grating, one cut to the exact internal dimension of the spawning tank, the other cut one cell row shorter in both length and width. Offset the smaller piece half a cell row inward from their common edges and bond the two together with cyanoacrylate glue. Such a grid is easily sterilized. Placed so the shorter of the two pieces rests on the aquarium bottom, the grid affords eggs excellent protection from cannibalism while assuring adequate water circulation around them. Remove the grid immediately after spawning once the adults have left the tank.

Induction of spawning: In nature, many type 1 egg scatterers spawn in the wake of the moderate spates produced by a rainstorm. Such localized precipitation briefly lowers water temperature 1 or 2 degrees C (2 or 4 degrees F). To duplicate this important environmental stimulus, the water in the breeding tank should initially be somewhat cooler than that of the conditioning aquaria.

Introduce the plumpest female and most brightly colored male into the breeding tank in the evening, taking care to acclimate them to its slightly cooler water. (Do not feed them! To do so is to encourage the sort of bacterial growth you have been at pains to prevent.) Slightly adjust the thermostat setting of the heater to allow the water temperature to rise overnight to that of the conditioning aquaria. Left together overnight, most species will spawn at first light.

Check the fish in the morning. If spawning has occurred, the female will have a distinctly deflated appearance. Eggs will appear as tiny glass beads scattered through the spawning material or over the tank bottom. Remove the breeders at once. If spawning has not occurred, allow the fish the remainder of the day together.

If by the end of this time, no eggs are present,

Some type 1 egg scatterers, such as *Rasbora heteromorpha*, are more readily induced to spawn in captivity if set up as groups rather than as single pairs.

remove the original pair. Siphon off any fecal matter from the bottom of the spawning tank and discard it along with its accompanying water. Remove half of the remaining water, and replace it with cooler sterile water of the same chemical makeup. (The water that has been drawn off can be rendered usable again by boiling.) Introduce another pair from the pool of breeding stock, or, if only a single pair is available, feed them heavily for several days and try them again.

Some references recommend that type 1 egg scatterers be spawned in trios of two males to a single female. The possible advantages must be balanced against the certain disadvantage of a third hungry mouth once spawning is completed. The same holds true for the group breeding recommended for some hard-to-breed species. A larger aquarium will be necessary when using more than a single pair of fish.

Care of developing zygotes: Not uncommonly, a small percentage of the eggs fail to develop normally, usually because they were never fertilized. Dead eggs become opaque due to bacterial activity and may rapidly develop a fluffy appearance due to a saprophytic fungus, *Saprolegnia.* Left untreated, the dead organic material in the water can fuel a substantial bacterial bloom under some conditions. Resistance to bacterial and fungal attack varies greatly; as a rule, the zygotes of blackwater species are most vulnerable. It may be necessary to experiment a bit with available antibacterial agents before finding a suitable treatment. Used according to the manufacturer's instructions, MarOxy™, a commercial medication featuring stabilized chlorine oxides as active ingredients, appears effective.

Zygotes typically hatch from twelve to forty-eight hours after spawning. The yolk-sac fry look like tiny glass slivers or commas with conspicuous dark eyes. Sometime between four and seven days after hatching, they become free-swimming fry which must be fed.

Rearing the fry: Type 1 egg-scatterer fry must be offered live food of a suitable size (see under "General Guidelines"). *Artemia* and many infusorians are attracted to light, whereas most blackwater fry are photophobic. Lowering the water level in the tank by one-half to two-thirds will increase the probability that the fry and their intended food will encounter one another. As a rule, the frys' light aversion disappears in about three weeks as they develop their species-typical color pattern. Once they have reached this point, the tank should be refilled to its full volume, and the fry are also large enough to take finely powdered prepared foods.

Excess organic matter from overfeeding causes the biggest danger in this early period. To minimize the risk of overfeeding, provide many small feedings daily. As additional insurance, one may add a dozen or so ramshorn or Malaysian live-bearing snails to the rearing tank as soon as the fry become mobile.

Newly mobile fry are weak swimmers and cope poorly with strong currents. Initially, allow only enough air to flow through the sponge filter unit to gently agitate the water surface. During this time, rinse the sponge cartridge regularly under lukewarm running water to keep its surface free of blockage. As the fry grow, increase the rate of water flow through the cartridge, which will correspondingly reduce the risk of surface blockage.

Daily siphoning of the tank bottom and replacement of 5 to 10 percent of its total volume with thoroughly dechlorinated fresh water of the same temperature and chemical makeup is recommended for all type 1 egg-scatterer fry, and is absolutely essential for particularly delicate species. As the fry grow older, increase the amount of water replaced and extend the interval between water changes to every four to seven days. When rearing species that require chemical modification of replacement water, a chemically active medium such as Polyfilter™ placed in a supplemental inside box filter or an air-driven outside filter will allow less frequent water changes without endangering growing fry.

Begin reducing the population density of fish per volume of water once they have developed their species-typical pattern of dark pigment. If the largest individuals present are more than twice again the size of the smallest, sort by size in order to avoid sibling cannibalism.

Breeding Techniques for Type 2 Egg Scatterers Without Diapause

Type 2 egg scatterers (those whose young hatch fully mobile) represent a smaller and considerably more homogeneous assemblage of fishes than type 1, but one still must research the biological idiosyncrasies of a given species to maximize the chances of a successful spawning effort. Popular representatives of this group are the killifishes

(Family: Cyprinodontidae), Australasian rainbow-fishes (Family: Melanotaeniidae), sailfin rainbow-fishes (Family: Telmatherinidae), Madagascar rainbowfishes (Family: Bedotiidae), and ricefishes (Family: Oryzatiidae). In much of the older aquarium literature, killifish and other type 2 egg scatterers are characterized as being difficult to breed successfully in captivity. In reality, they are more easily induced to spawn than most type 1 egg scatterers.

The zygotes of some type 2 species (those in this section) develop without interruption from fertilization through hatching. Those of others (the annual fishes) are characterized by the normal occurrence of a diapause, or period of arrested developmental activity. The breeding requirements of annual fishes will be discussed in a later section.

Selection of breeding stock: Many type 2 egg scatterers have rather short life-spans and display a pronounced drop-off in fecundity and male sexual capacity with increasing age. This trend is most pronounced among killifishes. Large individuals with impressive finnage usually make poor breeding stock. At an early age, type 2 egg scatterers become strongly sexually dimorphic in both color and fin development, so one is easily assured of having both sexes. However, there are advantages to having several individuals of each sex available. Females spawn a restricted number of eggs at a time, and in species in which males drive vigorously, setting up trios of one male and two females spares the females physical abuse.

To prevent uncontrolled spawning and to keep inter-male aggression within bounds, maintain males and females in separate tightly covered conditioning aquaria. Most species can be maintained on prepared food, but feeding females heavily with live and high-protein frozen foods will maximize egg production. If feeding white worms, alternate them with other high-roughage foods (such as crustaceans and insects) to avoid fatty degeneration of the gonads.

Preparation of the spawning tank: There are two approaches to breeding these fishes in captivity. In the continuous setup, the breeders are maintained in a heavily planted tank and allowed to breed *ad libitum.* The fry are reared together with the adults and require only the regular and generous provision of small food such as *Artemia* nauplii. Adults of most type 2 egg scatterers will disregard their progeny if heavily fed, but fry can also be removed to a separate rearing tank as soon as they are noticed. Do not keep snails in the tank, as they will efficiently seek out and devour fish eggs. This method does not produce large numbers of fry, but demands minimal effort from the breeder.

The hunt-and-pick approach requires the aquarist to harvest eggs from an artificial spawning substratum on a regular basis and incubate them separately. The tank size, furnishings, and water condition should be appropriate for the species being bred, but scrupulous attention to cleanliness is less important than for type 1 egg scatterers, as the eggs will not remain therein for any length of time after spawning.

Spawning mop construction: Manufactured spawning substrates are well accepted by these fish, but are not well designed for easy removal of eggs. Hence most serious breeders construct "spawning mops" out of nontoxic synthetic yarns.

Spawning mops can be constructed in several ways. Deep green or brown, 100 percent synthetic, guaranteed colorfast materials must be used. Their construction is relatively time-consuming, but one should produce a mop whose strands will not become tangled and which can be placed on the tank bottom for those type 2 egg scatterers which display a strong aversion to spawning near the water's surface. Make several mops to offer a male a choice of spawning sites and females a choice of hiding places.

Newly constructed mops should be soaked overnight in a 10 percent chlorine bleach solution, then rinsed thoroughly under hot running water for

Melanotaenia maccullochi, a type 2 egg scatterer, prefers spawning sites in the middle or near the bottom of the spawning tank. This preference is shared by other Australasian rainbowfishes.

several minutes before being used. Sterilize mops in this same way before moving them from one tank to another to avoid the risk of undetected eggs being moved from one tank to another.

Inducing spawning and caring for zygotes: To induce spawning, merely introduce a male and one or two previously conditioned females into the tank in the evening; fish will begin spawning with first light the following morning and will typically be finished by noon. Wait until evening to remove the day's egg production from the spawning mops, as the eggs require a period of contact with water before their shells toughen to the point where they can be safely manipulated.

If a pool of females has been conditioned for the spawning effort, remove the spent female(s) to a separate tank for a few days of reconditioning, and replace with an equivalent number of fresh individuals. If only a single pair or trio is available, retain the adults in the breeding tank and feed them generously with live food. Prepared or frozen foods may not be entirely consumed, and might trigger a bacterial bloom that would considerably depress the number of fertile eggs harvested daily.

When using only a pair or trio of fish, daily egg input will lessen after the first day but should then remain fairly constant as long as individuals are well fed. If the number of viable eggs drops abruptly a week to ten days after the pair is placed in the tank, it may signal excessive bacterial buildup. Change 60 to 75 percent of the water, and replace or resterilize the spawning mops.

Spawn-laden mops should be patted or allowed to drip nearly dry. Individual eggs or clusters will stand out like tiny glass beads against the nearly dry, dark-colored strands of the mop. Needle-nosed forceps of the type employed to handle postage stamps are ideal for picking eggs off the mop. Slip the tips of the forceps under the individual egg or cluster, then carefully bring them together and lift upwards to push the egg free from the substratum without exerting lateral pressure. If the egg were to be gripped directly, it might be ruptured in the attempt to pull it free from the mop.

Transfer eggs into a clean plastic or glass 50- to 250-milliliter (about 1 to 8 fluid ounces) hatching container filled with water from the breeding tank. Allow 2.0 milliliters of water per zygote (15 zygotes per fluid ounce) for a safe, conservative stocking rate. The hatching container must have a tight-fitting cover to prevent evaporative water loss and consequent alteration of hardness and pH during development. Adding a bacteriostatic agent to the water is advisable. Dilute a single drop of commercially available acriflavine in ten drops of water, then add just enough of the resulting stock solution to the hatching container to impart a pale yellow color to the water. One treatment is usually all that is necessary.

Do not consolidate more than three days' worth of zygotes in a single container, as there is a tendency towards increased mortality among younger zygotes when the age span is greater than this. Check the containers daily, and remove any opaque or fungus-covered eggs with an eyedropper. Such losses should not exceed 10 percent of the total number of eggs over the entire length of the incubation period. Very high mortali-

A typical annual fish habitat in southeastern Brazil, home to several *Cynolebias* species. Below: As it appears during the rainy season.

The same habitat during the dry season.

ties within the first day or two after spawning typically indicate a high proportion of infertile eggs. This may be due to unfavorable conditions within the spawning tank or to male infertility. A sudden upsurge in losses later on usually signals deteriorating conditions in the hatching container, probably as the cumulative result of overstocking.

Rearing fry: Most type 2 fry can take *Artemia* nauplii immediately upon hatching. To maximize the likelihood that they will encounter these prey, move the newly mobile young by eyedropper from the hatching container to a rearing tank with its water level one-quarter to one-third of its maximum capacity. As the young grow larger, slowly raise the water level until the tank is completely full.

Type 2 egg-scatterer fry are voracious feeders and typically grow rapidly. They are quite vulnerable to nitrogen-cycle mismanagement. Velvet disease, the malady that wreaks the most havoc among type 2 fry, seems invariably to follow episodes of overfeeding or deviation from the regular pattern of partial water changes in the rearing tank. Prevention is much simpler than cure. If serious losses begin to occur, before beginning treatment, transfer all surviving fry to new quarters with fresh water and a mature sponge filter from an unaffected tank to reduce both the number of pathogens present and a major source of environmental stress.

As fry grow older, afford them more growing room. Killifish in particular should not be crowded if male finnage is to attain its maximum development. Because they hatch over an extended period of time, a batch of type 2 egg-scatterer fry is heterogeneous in size. This invites sibling canni-balism. This problem, most pronounced among killifishes, can be minimized by reducing the disparity between the oldest and youngest fry in the rearing tank by placing similarly sized fry in different tanks. Due to precocious male growth superiority, the smaller individuals in any given batch are likely to be females. Other secondary sexual differences usually begin to develop between eight and twelve weeks after hatching. These fish usually begin spawning between six months and one year after hatching.

Breeding Techniques for Annual Fishes

The reproductive pattern of most annual killifishes is markedly seasonal in nature because the temporary pools in which they live are capable of supporting fishes for a very brief time. These fish, usually thought to pose the ultimate challenge to the amateur fish breeder, are in reality no more difficult to breed than other type 2 egg scatterers, given a little research into their maintenance requirements. A number of approaches are detailed in publications of the American and British killifish associations. The method outlined below mimics the natural cycle of these fishes and requires the least effort to implement.

Choosing and conditioning breeding stock:
In view of the short life-span of annual fishes, young individuals must be chosen. Obtain trios rather than pairs, as males should be obliged to divide their attentions to minimize the risk of injury to females.

Annual fishes do best in rather soft, neutral to slightly acidic water, and demand careful attention to environmental cleanliness and proper nitrogen-cycle management. Most live longer and remain reproductively active longer at temperatures under 25 degrees C (77 degrees F). Proficient jumpers, they must be kept in a tightly covered tank.

Sexes must be conditioned separately. Most males fight ferociously in the presence of females, and the females' pattern of ripening a relatively small number of eggs daily leads to uncontrolled spawning if the sexes are housed together.

The fecundity of annual fish is directly influenced by the quantity and quality of their food. Feed at least twice, and preferably three times, each day. A high-protein diet is essential (see under "General Guidelines"). Tubificid worms can safely be included in their diet.

A vigorous young pair of *Cynolebias nigripinnis,* a South American diver. Like all annual fishes, this species displays extreme sexual dimorphism.

Preparation of the spawning tank: In a securely covered tank of appropriate scale (20 to 60 liters or 5 to 15 gallons), place a mature sponge filter, several floating yarn mops (see under "Breeding Techniques for Type 2 Egg Scatterers Without Diapause") to serve as hiding places for spent females, and a heater if needed.

Furnish the tank with a container filled with loose, waterlogged peat. The net-wrapped peat pellets sold in garden shops for horticultural use can be safely added to the breeding tank without further treatment. A less desirable alternative is to use one of the several brands of fibrous peat marketed for the purpose of acidifying aquarium water. To prevent lowering the pH in the breeding tank to toxic levels, these must be boiled in several gallons of demineralized water in a glass or enameled vessel for at least an hour before being added—a practice that leaves the entire house smelling like a peat bog after a heavy rain! Never use either the peat moss sold in bulk as a soil amendment or whole sphagnum moss as a spawning substratum for these fishes. To do so may have disastrous results.

Empty 1- or 2-liter (1- or 2-quart) plastic ice cream containers make excellent peat containers if weighted down with two or three small rocks. Fill a container no more than half full with the soaked peat pellets or conditioned fibrous peat. The depth is determined by whether the species to be bred is a plower (all of the African annual killifishes; South American *Cynolebias*) or a diver (all other Neotropical annual killifishes). Plowers need only enough depth to bury their eggs in a furrow as they move over the bottom. Divers require peat slightly deeper than the total length of the male in order to bury themselves completely when spawning. Partially cover the container, either by cutting a hole in the plastic lid just large enough to allow the breeding pair to move freely in and out or by covering the top with two strips of glass set far enough apart to provide an access slit.

Spawning and incubation: Once they are placed together in the breeding tank, it rarely takes more than a few minutes for fish to discover the peat container. Annual killifish begin spawning at first light and have usually concluded by noon. Spawning typically is so vigorous that peat is tossed several inches into the water column with each bout.

With smaller species, one can hold a single pair or trio in the breeding tank and feed normally, with partial water changes every two or three days for seven to ten days before the eggs are harvested. The heartier appetites and greater fecundity of the most robust annual species justify removing the fish for heavy reconditioning after two or three days of access to the spawning medium without feeding.

Transfer the peat-filled container from the breeding tank to a kitchen strainer. Gently hand-squeeze or allow peat to drain until, when a handful is gently compressed, the resulting bolus will adhere together for a few moments before beginning to crumble and/or the outer surface is dry to the touch. Do not worry about damaging any eggs present in the peat. The eggs have extraordinarily hard shells and can resist far more pressure than a single human hand can exert unaided upon the medium in which they are embedded.

Place the barely moist peat in a plastic bag and seal it tightly. On the outer face of a second bag, use a quick-drying indelible marker to indicate both the species whose eggs are contained therein and the date when the peat was harvested. Insert the first bag inside the second, and seal it in the same manner. The package can now be stored at ordinary room temperature. Alternatively, the egg-laden peat can be stored in plastic refrigerator containers with tight-fitting lids.

Hatching may be from six weeks to nine months away, depending upon the species, the moisture content of the peat, and the temperature at which it is stored. Examine the stored peat every few weeks; if it appears perceptibly drier, repackage it. Plastic containers with tight-fitting lids can be stacked easily, but their contents are more inclined to lose water, so they must be inspected more frequently.

Hatching eggs and rearing fry: To attempt a hatching, empty the egg-laden peat into a shallow glass container and cover it with water from an established aquarium to a depth of no more than 2.5 centimeters (1 inch). Within an hour's time, the first fry will make their appearance. Whatever fry can be expected from this rehydration will have hatched within six hours. Transfer these fry to a rearing tank, as for other type 2 egg-scatterer fry. A single batch of peat may yield several hundred fry. Make certain that adequate tank space to rear them is available before beginning to hatch them out.

Drain the peat again as described above, and

The bubble nest of the dwarf gourami (*Colisa lalia*) protrudes above the surface and is anchored to the plants beneath: seen from the side (top left) and from below (left). The male diligently holds station beneath the nest (above), alert to the approach of both potential mates and possible egg predators.

replace it in storage for another two to three weeks, then wet it again to provoke further development and ultimate hatching of any resting eggs present. In species with very long incubation periods, the number of such eggs is often quite high and one may need to repeat the wetting process several times.

A package's initial wetting often does not yield a very impressive muster of fry. Failure to obtain a hatch even after two or three rewettings may mean that: 1) few eggs were deposited in the peat; 2) few zygotes survived the developmental interval; or 3) the young fish require additional help in breaking free of their shells. Poke through the moist peat; if few fertile eggs are encountered or most of the eggs are covered with fungus, little can be done. However, if the peat contains substantial numbers of "eyed" eggs, increasing the amount of free carbon dioxide in solution will pop the stubborn eggshells. Sprinkle a few pinches of finely powdered dry food over the surface of the hatching tray, and the collective respiration of the resultant bacterial bloom will provide this. As a quicker alternative, add about 1/2 cup (120 milli-

liters) of room-temperature club soda to the water in the tray.

Annual fry can take *Artemia* nauplii immediately upon hatching. Fed generously and often, they display phenomenally rapid growth rates. Care for them like other type 2 egg scatterers, but stock at a lower density than other egg layer fry.

All of these species exhibit both early male growth superiority and sibling cannibalism. Sort by size as soon as possible. Secondary sex characteristics usually begin to appear by the third week after hatching, and some species make tentative spawning attempts a week later. At this point, separation of the sexes is essential to prevent lethal fighting among young males and to allow proper conditioning of females.

Egg Layers That Practice Parental Care

Many people are surprised to discover that such "primitive" animals as fish are capable of complex

While many male anabantoids grow intolerant of one another with the onset of reproductive activity, few species take this tendency to the extreme evinced by these two male Siamese fighting fish (*Betta splendens*).

parental behavior. In actuality, such behavior is both widespread and long-standing. Among the aquarium fishes, some thirty families out of sixty-eight have at least some parental representatives. Luckily, this impressive assemblage can be easily subdivided into manageable units.

Breeding Techniques for Bubble-Nest Builders and Other Paternally Custodial Egg Layers

Though not rich in aquarium residents, these reproductive guilds include fish that rank among the most easily bred of all egg layers. The popular aphrophils, or bubble-nest builders, are discussed as a paradigm for this group, followed by a brief supplementary treatment of idiosyncrasies of those species with different spawning site preferences.

Selecting and conditioning breeding stock: Select several vigorous, young, well-colored individuals of each sex as breeding stock, for courtship in these species is variably expressed and one cannot automatically assume that any male and female randomly placed together will prove compatible.

Although many of these species will spawn in a community tank, such spontaneous reproductive efforts rarely produce fry. To increase chances for successful spawning, a more controlled environment must be provided. Begin by conditioning the sexes in separate tanks within sight of one another. Such deliberate arousal tends to make

The distinctive anabantoid spawning embrace is exemplified by this pair of dwarf gouramis (*Colisa lalia*).

females more receptive to male advances once the sexes are placed together and almost always triggers the onset of nesting behavior in males. Males of the more aggressive belontiids, such as *Belontia signata* and *Betta splendens,* must each be provided with separate quarters to prevent damaging or even lethal fights.

Feed the intended breeders heavily during the conditioning period, which typically lasts two to three weeks. At least two, and preferably three, feedings a day are essential, of which half should be of live food or high-quality frozen foods such as bloodworms, glassworms, adult brine shrimp, or, where appropriate, small fish. Females will become quite heavy-bodied as their eggs mature.

Preparing the spawning tank: These fish do not require a spotless environment, for the placement of zygotes at the water's surface, combined with the males' hygienic behavior, minimizes the risk of bacterial or fungal attack. A well-established aquarium with a blanket of green algae on its back and sides makes an ideal breeding tank.

It is essential that the tank be large enough to allow the female adequate room to maneuver and that it afford her some possibility of concealment. The two sexes may not be in full reproductive synchrony when first placed together, and males of many of these species will attack sexually unreceptive females vigorously. A layer of floating plants, clumps of bunch plants such as *Anacharis* or *Hygrophila,* inverted flower pots with enlarged drainage holes, or nylon yarn mops (see under "Breeding Techniques for Type 2 Egg Scatterers Without Diapause") increase the female's margin of safety.

The breeding tank also must be large enough to provide adequate growing room for the resulting young. Aphrophil fry are extremely fragile until they fully develop aerial respiration. Attempts to transfer them prior to this point typically result in massive losses. Smaller belontiids require a 60-liter (15-gallon) aquarium; for a spawn of larger fish such as kissing gourami, a 100-liter (25-gallon) breeder flat is barely sufficient.

None of these fish prosper in extremely hard alkaline water, but most are otherwise indifferent to its chemical composition. Fill the tank no deeper than 20 cm (about 8 inches), and insert the thermostatic heater at an angle. A mature sponge filter is the fibration system of choice, but whatever type of filter is employed, regulate its operation to minimize disturbance of the water surface. Air-driven units should pass no more than a single bubble through the return stem each minute. Provide a tightly fitting tank cover; failure to do so invites large-scale fry mortality during the period of transition to aerial respiration. The tank may be brightly lit. These species are either indifferent to the level of illumination or positively stimulated by bright light.

Induction of spawning and management of zygotes: These fish are polygamous under natural conditions, but if fish are set up in multiple female groups in the aquarium, males will usually court one female and attack the others. Females also may squabble seriously with one another. Set these fish up as single pairs. To moderate the tempo of behavioral interaction and reduce the risk that the female will be attacked, move a single pair into the spawning tank just before turning the tank lights off for the night.

Aphrophils typically spawn with the arrival of the rainy season in nature. Spawning appears to follow most swiftly if breeders are introduced to the tank immediately before the arrival of a low-pressure front. It also is sometimes helpful to replace part of the water in the breeding tank with fresh, slightly cooler water of the same chemical makeup.

Monitor the interaction between the male and female carefully. A certain amount of chasing and nipping is not unusual, but persistent harassment, evinced by badly torn fins and missing scales, can lead to the female's death. If such behavior is observed, immediately remove the female. If only a single pair is available, one can separate initially incompatible fish with a glass partition and condition them further until their demeanor suggests readiness to spawn. The main disadvantage of this approach lies in the male's tendency to build his nest immediately adjacent to the partition, which causes the nest to break apart when the barrier is lifted. If one floats the lid from a cup- or pint-sized (250- to 500-milliliter) plastic container near the partition, the male will usually construct his nest beneath it instead.

After a period of reciprocal circling, the couple will move immediately below the nest. The male then arches his body around that of the female, who releases a number of eggs which are immediately fertilized. In those species with buoyant eggs, the zygotes float up into the nest. Otherwise the male will pick them up in his mouth and spit them between the nest's bubbles. Such behavior is repeated until the female is spent, at which point the male will immediately drive her away from the nest so that she cannot devour the eggs. If she cannot hide, she may be killed. Remove her from the tank immediately.

In nature, males drive off egg predators, maintain the integrity of the bubble mass, retrieve eggs that may fall from the nest, and remove (and/or eat) infertile eggs. In the more benign environment of captivity, a male's presence is rarely essential to the survival of the zygotes. Many breeders remove the male almost as soon as spawning is completed. Retaining the male with the bubble nest allows one to witness a suite of complex and fascinating behavior patterns. However, once the fry are fully mobile, the male is apt to eat them if they cannot disperse. Remove him prior to this point.

Rearing of fry: The technique for rearing aphrophil fry is in most respects identical to that used for type 1 egg scatterers. Most require infusoria for their first three to seven days of active existence, followed by microworms or the smallest of *Artemia* nauplii. Their appetites are hearty, making the culturing of microscopic food in sufficient quantity a major project in itself. Anabantoid fry are initially lethargic about actively seeking out food; a low water level reduces the volume within which the infusoria can disperse. Once the fry have grown large enough to take nauplii, the water level can be gradually raised.

Fry are extremely susceptible to velvet disease if exposed to the stress of elevated nitrite levels. Partial water changes are essential, but anabantoid fry are very sensitive to both abrupt temperature drops and dissolved chlorine. The transition period between purely branchial respiration and development of the ability to utilize atmospheric oxygen is particularly dangerous. Mortalities can be minimized if the rearing tank is tightly covered and water changes are stopped until all the fry are regularly rising to the surface to gulp air. Chemically active filter media are a useful tool for maintaining water quality during this interval.

The sort of biparental custodial behavior exemplified by this pair of *Heros sajica* is extremely unusual among fishes.

Sort the fry by size as soon as they are capable of atmospheric respiration. If reducing the total number of fry being reared, remember precocious male growth superiority. For maximal growth, stock the fry at the densities recommended for type 2 egg scatterers.

Once secondary sexual characteristics become evident, segregate the young fish by sex. Males of pugnacious species will scrap incessantly and must be reared in isolation for their finnage to develop its full potential.

Modifications for other paternally custodial fishes: The spawning requirements and behavior of the remaining paternally custodial guilds share many similarities with the bubble-nest builders. However, one must carefully research the reproductive idiosyncrasies of a particular species before attempting breeding.

Most of these species are fairly small and require only a 60-liter (15-gallon) tank. In nature they occupy habitats that range from blackwater streams and marshes to brackish lagoons and river estuaries, and most are relatively intolerant of deviations from the conditions that prevail in their native habitat. Replicate such conditions closely when setting up the breeding tank. A combination of extra caves and abundant bunch plants should be added to provide plentiful shelter for the female.

The species to be bred must be furnished with a choice of spawning sites compatible with its reproductive pattern. Cavity spawners respond to clay flower pots cut in half lengthwise or pieces of chlorinated polyvinylchloride (CPVC) pipe of an appropriate diameter. For those species which excavate their own spawning site, bury such structures in the substratum.

For species that utilize a single plant leaf as a spawning site, the various swordplants of the genus *Echinodorus* are particularly convenient because they respond well to potting and thus can be easily moved from one tank to another as needed. Furthermore, their leaves are quite tough, which allows them to stand up to the site-cleaning that is an integral part of the prespawning behavior of these species. Plastic replicas are also well accepted.

Other species that spawn in the open and mouthbrooders require minimal attention with regard to spawning sites. For species that dig a pit, the particle size of tank gravel should be fine enough to be easily manipulated. If the fish spawns upon a solid surface, provide a number of rocks of various shapes, pieces of waterlogged driftwood, or plastic replicas of the foregoing.

Such paternally custodial egg layers as sunfish and darters are cool-water species that require a low-temperature resting period to mature their gonads. The proximate trigger to spawning is usually a simultaneous increase in day length and water temperature. Tropical species, on the other hand, usually respond positively to a tropical rainstorm, simulated by replacement of part of the breeding tank's volume with fresh water a few degrees cooler.

Removing the female immediately after spawning is prudent, although males of most of these species are more tolerant than are male anabantoids. Only when the normal sequence of parental behavior breaks down need the aquarist concern himself with the developing zygotes. In this case, it may be necessary to resort to artificial incubation (see under "Breeding Techniques for Monogamous Cichlids"). Males should be removed as soon as the fry become free-swimming.

Breeding Techniques for Monogamous Cichlids

Monogamy, absolutely correlated with biparental care of the zygotes, is extremely unusual among fishes. The treatment in this section concentrates exclusively upon the family Cichlidae, but the aquarist wishing to spawn other monogamous fishes should find the methods equally relevant.

Most authors divide cichlids into substratum-spawning versus mouthbrooding species. However, the aspect of cichlid reproductive biology most relevant to the aquarist is their mating system, for the presence or absence of a long-term bond between the sexes determines how the fish will be handled before and after spawning.

Monogamous cichlids have an undeserved reputation for being difficult to breed in captivity. They are less flexible in their space requirements than are many other egg-laying fishes, and the complexity of their reproductive behavior demands more concern with the preliminaries to spawning than with subsequent management of the zygotes. The key to breeding them successfully lies in obtaining a compatible pair.

Preparing the spawning tank: Cichlid conditioning and breeding typically take place in the aquarium where the adults are normally maintained. With few exceptions, monogamous cichlids are among the larger ornamental fishes. Sexually active individuals are intensely territorial and extremely fecund. Cichlids in the 8 to 15 centimeter (about 3 to 6 inches) standard length (SL) size range routinely produce spawns of up to 500 fry. Those of larger species can number in the thousands. For all these reasons, adequate living space is of critical importance. I can state categorically that 95 percent of the aquaristically undesirable activity attributed to cichlids results from attempts to keep and breed them in tanks too small to allow the normal expression of their behavior. Only the so-called dwarf cichlids can be successfully bred in 40- to 60-liter (10- to 15-gallon) tanks. Ideally, most species in the 10 to 15 centimeter (about 4 to 6 inches) SL range should be given a 160-liter (40-gallon) breeder flat. A 200-liter (50-gallon) aquarium represents the bare minimum for larger species, which should really be provided with tanks in the 300-liter to 400-liter (75- to 100-gallon) range.

Cichlids combine hearty appetites with considerable sensitivity to dissolved metabolic wastes. Their tendency to dig vigorously makes undergravel filters impractical. Sponge or canister filters can be successfully employed with dwarf cichlids and most medium-sized species. Large cichlids require a high-capacity outside power filter. Adherence to a routine of frequent partial water changes is essential. Outfit the tank with a sealed-unit thermostatic heater and a close-fitting cover.

Cichlids are very sensitive to overhead motion. They do best in tanks positioned at roughly chest level or higher. They appear more at ease under a cover of floating plants and with a gravel layer to eliminate light reflection from the tank bottom. The tank must be well furnished with both cover and potential breeding sites.

Determine the spawning site preference of a given species before setting up its quarters. Some, such as angelfish and discus, do well in densely vegetated habitats. Many of the family's medium-sized or larger members will destroy plants and require alternate furnishings such as rockwork, driftwood, clay flower pots, or sections of CPVC pipe. The foundations of any rockwork must be placed solidly on the tank bottom rather than on the gravel surface, where the fish will undermine them.

Management of pair formation: Four methods are commonly used. The first requires a much larger tank than the other three methods.

1. The Naturalistic Method. In nature, a cichlid pair has many suitable targets against which to redirect their aggressive behavior. As long as these intruders can move beyond the boundaries of a defended area, they run minimal risk of injury. Kept as a single pair in captivity, cichlids often turn upon one another.

If six to eight young conspecifics are raised to maturity together in a large enough tank, the first pair to form will exclude the remaining fish from a portion of it and settle down to breeding. A single male and female will also pair readily and spawn freely if kept in a community of behaviorally compatible heterospecifics.

2. The Target Fish Method. A potential spawn predator need not be physically accessible to a cichlid pair to discharge its stabilizing function. Isolated by a clear partition, it will be attacked with the same fury as if it were physically accessible. Thus, one can partition off a portion of the breeding tank and place a solitary specimen of any comparably sized cichlid in it, out of reach of the breeding pair. A more efficient approach, however, is to place a breeding pair on either side of the partition. A piece of plastic egg crate diffuser grating works well. If glass is used instead, a filter must operate in each compartment and the glass must be kept clean. If the target fish cannot be clearly seen by the pair, the spawning effort may fail and the female may be killed by the males.

3. The Privileged Sanctuary Method. Males of most monogamous cichlids grow a good deal larger than do females. Divide the breeding tank with a barrier with several openings which allow the female free movement from one side to the other while confining the male to a single larger compartment that includes the future spawning site, which should be placed as close to the barrier as possible. This approach allows the pair to interact directly with minimal risk, for the female can move out of the male's reach should his attentions become overbearing or dangerous.

4. The Incomplete Divider Method. In sight of one another, a male and female often will perform their respective parts of the spawning act even when physically separated. Either plastic diffuser grating or a glass barrier raised slightly from the tank bottom near the spawning site will allow enough of the male's sperm to diffuse through to fertilize some fraction of the egg plaque. This method protects the female, yet because it allows fry to move freely between the two compartments it allows both sexes to assume a parental role. Its disadvantages are that it totally eliminates normal behavioral interactions between the adults and that many of the female's eggs will not be fertilized. Breeders often use this method for single pairs of very large cichlids that are so aggressive and fecund that it seems desirable to trade off a percentage of the spawn to guarantee the safety of hard-to-replace breeding stock.

Postspawning management: Pairs will usually

The exclusively female brood care shown by this female *Apistogramma agassizi* is a prerequisite for the evolution of both harem polygyny and open polygamy in cichlids.

signal their intent to spawn by a sudden increase in the frequency of pit digging and nipping off of the future spawning site. Spawning can be expected within twenty-four hours of the appearance of the female's ovipositor, a conspicuous blunt-tipped tube that protrudes from her vent.

Postspawning behavior normally includes well-developed and highly efficient custodial and hygienic elements. Occasionally, this care breaks down, resulting in parental cannibalism. Faced with this situation, one should remove the zygotes from the breeding tank and hatch them artificially. Such episodes are typical of young pairs and usually cease once the fish have grown older.

Artificial rearing: Artificial hatching of cichlid eggs must be regarded as a method of last resort, for no matter how carefully the spawn is handled, a significant percentage of the resulting fry will be congenitally deformed. Remove the egg plaque to a 2- to 5-gallon (about 8- to 20-liter) aquarium with fresh water of the same temperature and chemical makeup as that in the breeding tank. Place an airstone next to the plaque and bleed a gentle stream of air into the tank to create a gentle current that mimics the fanning behavior of the female. Zygotes of cave-spawning cichlids are markedly light-sensitive. Cover their tank with brown wrapping paper until the fry are fully mobile.

Add a bacteriostatic agent to the hatching tank. Neutral acriflavine used at half the recommended medicinal dosage or MarOxy used at the manufacturer's recommended dosage are more effective than methylene blue, the traditional choice.

After hatching, fry should be housed in such a hatching tank for no more than a few days. During this period, slowly replace the original medicated water with fresh water from the tank to which they will ultimately be transferred. To move the fry, carefully siphon off all but 1 or 2 liters or quarts of the hatching tank's volume, then pour the remaining water and fry into the rearing tank. This is far safer than netting them.

Most fry (and their parents!) will take *Artemia* nauplii and finely powdered prepared foods; the few very small species can manage microworms. Cichlid fry should be fed at least two or preferably three or four times daily. The schedule of partial water changes in the breeding tank should reflect their voracious feeding habits.

In nature, custodial care persists until the fry no longer respond to parental efforts to control their movements (six to eight weeks in most species). Brood protection effectively precludes normal foraging behavior, so the female does not yolk up a second batch of eggs during this time. In captivity, a female may mature another clutch of eggs and attempt another spawning well before the fry are fully independent. Separate parents and offspring as soon as the pair shows persistent signs of respawning. Their behavior toward their older progeny at this point varies from indifference to active hostility.

Cichlid fry grow rapidly but unevenly. If not sorted by size, they will usually cull one another quite efficiently. Because they are characterized by precocious male growth superiority, the end result will be a strongly male-biased sex ratio among the hardy survivors. It is rarely in one's best interest to try rearing an entire brood of one of these more prolific species. The optimal course of action is to randomly net out a few hundred fry for future rearing when separating them from their parents, and use the remainder as a source of live food for other large fish. This course of action duplicates the eventual fate of nine out of every ten cichlid fry in nature.

Breeding Techniques for Polygamous Cichlids (Harem Holders and Maternal Mouthbrooders)

For many decades, virtually the only cichilds available to aquarists were characterized by a monogamous mating system. However, many cichlids with maternal care have a mating system in which one or both sexes interact with multiple spawning partners during the duration of a single reproductive period. In harem polygyny, a single male controls access to and spawns with the same group of females over an extended period. In open polygamy, the association between the sexes is restricted to the sexual act itself and both male and female may have multiple partners during a single spawning effort; these latter cichlids all practice maternal mouthbrooding. This group includes the popular mbuna and peacock cichlids from Lake Malawi.

Management of polygynous harem holders: Most of these cichlids are dwarf species, but females expand their territories after spawning has occurred. If the tank is too small, the male, even if bigger than the female, runs risk of serious injury or even death after spawning is complete. Aquaria in the 60- to 80-liter (15- to 20-gallon) range will comfortably and safely house a single male and two or three females of most of these species. More than a single male may be housed in the same tank only if each has sufficient space to stake out his own domain. The non-dwarf species, of course, require considerably larger quarters.

Dwarf representatives of this group are given to hiding for extensive periods when housed alone. To help eliminate this shyness and elicit a more reliable manifestation of female parental behavior, add six to twelve smaller schooling fish. The behavior of such "dither fish" serves to reassure the cichlids that their immediate environment is danger-free. Choose a species that will neither outcompete the cichlids at feeding time nor pose a significant threat to mobile cichlid fry. Do not use catfish or loaches, as they pose a threat to cichlid fry and are often attacked or killed by the adults before spawning.

Except for the robust *Acarichthys* and *Guianacara* species, these fish are tolerant of aquatic plants and appear to do better in heavily planted aquaria. Overall, their maintenance requirements are identical to those of their monogamous relatives. Females are usually reliable and efficient parents, but young mothers may devour their first few clutches. Eggs can be artificially incubated following the procedure outlined for monogamous cichlids.

Parental care usually persists for three to four weeks in captivity. As she begins to ripen a new batch of eggs, the female loses interest in, then drives away, her older progeny. Remove them for rearing elsewhere. Fry can be fed and managed in the same way as monogamous cichlid fry. All are extremely sensitive to dissolved metabolic wastes, so regular partial water changes are essential. Sibling cannibalism is not prevalent among most of these cichlids.

Prespawning management of openly polygamous cichlids: No openly polygamous mating system is characterized by the long-term association of a male and female. Virtually all failures with these fish stem from the mistaken belief that they can be maintained as isolated single pairs. The inevitable consequence of such efforts is a badly battered or dead female.

The smallest tanks within which most of these fish can be safely housed is 200 liters (50 gallons); tanks in the 300- to 360-liter (75- to 95-gallon) range are far better. Larger species require even more room.

Two approaches are equally effective in protecting individual females from continuous male harassment. The simplest maintains the fish as single pairs in a rather crowded community tank of behaviorally and environmentally compatible cichlids. Most amateur breeders are partial to this approach because it allows them to maintain a wider variety of species in the space at their disposal. The second is to maintain openly polygamous cichlids by themselves in single male–multiple female groups so that the sheer number of potential spawning partners keeps a male from concentrating on one female long enough to injure or kill her. A ratio of three females to one male seems to be the lower limit. Commercial breeders are partial to this approach because it maximizes output of fry while eliminating all possibility of accidental hybridization.

The maintenance requirements of openly polygamous cichlids are otherwise similar to those of their monogamous counterparts. All have hearty appetites and fortunately are not fussy eaters.

Postspawning management of openly polygamous cichlids: These cichlids spawn freely in either a mixed-species community or when housed in single-species "harems." Among most of these species, the female picks up her eggs immediately after depositing them and fertilization subsequently takes place inside her buccal cavity. In nature, after spawning, the female seeks out a sheltered spot well away from the breeding site. When essentially herbivorous species, such as the mbuna, are maintained as single-species breeding groups in reasonably well-furnished tanks and fed well, a purely naturalistic approach is quite feasible, for fry run little risk of predation. In most cases, however, survival in a mixed-species community is a chancy proposition, and a parental female comes in for a good deal more harassment than she would be likely to encounter either in nature or in a single-species breeding group.

For at least the first three and preferably seven days, keep the ovigerous female in the breeding tank with ample cover. Attempts to move her any earlier may cause her to prematurely spit out the progeny permanently. Then move her to a nursery tank of 20 liters (5 gallons) or more, depending upon her size. Never house more than one female per tank. If using several compartments, separate the fish with an opaque partition. If ovigerous females can see one another, they may become so disturbed that they will expel or devour their broods.

Many females maintain a light intake of food during the incubation period, but it is not essential to offer food. Replace part of the water in the tank every three to five days until the young become mobile. Metabolic functions do not cease simply because a fish is not eating, and developing zygotes also generate a significant amount of metabolic waste.

If faced with the need to artificially rear the zygotes of these advanced mouthbrooding cichlids as an emergency measure, one can find many published workable designs for an "artificial mouth." All have some arrangement for gently circulating water in a small container to imitate the tumbling which developing young are given in their mother's buccal cavity. Bacteriostatic preparations should be used as suggested for artificial hatching of other cichlid eggs, but at a lower concentration. Partially change the water every other day, adding sufficient medication to replace the amount lost in this process. Mortalities are inevitable, even with the best of care. Check the vessel frequently and remove any dead young before their decomposition fouls the water, leading in turn to further losses.

The duration of buccal incubation varies between species and is also influenced by ambient temperature. In nature, the female seeks out a secluded area to release her fry. In captivity, females are often reluctant to release their offspring in the bare surroundings of a nursery tank, or may be so ill at ease that they will pick them up again at the slightest disturbance. Once the fry have become free-swimming, it is a relatively simple matter to remove them from the buccal cavity of females 7.5 to 10.0 centimeters (about 3 to 4 inches) SL and larger. Hold the female within the folds of a net, head down over a container filled with water from the nursery tank. Gently pull open her lower jaw and immerse her head in the container. The young will usually swim out. Gentle shaking may be required to dislodge the last few.

Smaller species should be handled somewhat differently. Insert the female head down in an ordinary kitchen baster from which the squeeze bulb has been removed. Replace the bulb, then insert the tip of the baster into a container filled with water from the nursery tank. Squeezing the bulb gently several times will force water back and forth through the female's buccal cavity and flush the fry into the receiving container. If several minutes of squeezing produce no effect, remove the baster from the water. Hold it, opening down, over the container for a few moments, then reimmerse it and repeat the cycle of flushing. Fry should begin to emerge from the opening of the baster after a few squeezes.

Some breeders advocate a period of reconditioning for the female prior to her reintroduction to the society of other fishes. This is not essential provided the dominance in her tank of origin is disrupted somewhat by a partial water change coupled with a rearrangement of the tank furnishings.

Fry of these cichlids are robust and may be handled in the same manner as substratum-spawning cichlids. Stock at the same densities recommended for live-bearers. Most grow rapidly, even by cichlid standards.

Selected References

Balon, E. K. 1975. Ecological guilds of fishes: a short summary of the concept and its applications. *Verh. Internat. Verien. Limnol.* 19: 2430–39. (The grouping of aquarium fish by reproductive pattern employed in this chapter was based upon Balon's concept of spawning guilds. Recommended reading for all serious fish culturists.)

Emmens, C. W. 1953. *Keeping and Breeding Aquarium Fishes.* New York: Academic Press.

(Many useful suggestions on setting up a large-scale breeding effort, choosing and conditioning brood stock, and rearing fry. No longer in print, but copies often can be found in second-hand book shops specializing in scientific and technical titles.)

Goldstein, R. J. 1973. *Cichlids of the World.* Neptune City, N.J.: T.F.H. Publications. (Helpful suggestions on the artificial hatching of cichlid eggs and the management of cichlid fry.)

Innes, W. T. 1959. *Exotic Aquarium Fishes.* Philadelphia: Innes Publications. (The most useful manual of aquarium husbandry to date published in English. Suggests approaches to spawning most of the major groups of ornamental fishes. The section dealing with live foods and their culture is particularly helpful.)

Jocher, W. 1972. *Spawning Problem Fishes.* Books I and II. Neptune City, N.J.: T.F.H. Publications. (An excellent English translation of a two-part German work. "Recipes" for spawning a selection of the more challenging aquarium fishes. Heavy emphasis upon type 1 egg scatterers native to blackwater habitats.)

Loiselle, P. V. 1985. *The Cichlid Aquarium.* Tetra Press. (The most current and comprehensive English language reference on the husbandry of the major biparentally custodial and maternally parental aquarium fishes.)

Mayland, H. J. 1978. *Cichliden und Fischzucht.* Hannover, Ger.: Landbuch-Verlag. (Text is in German. Superb color photographs of the reproductive behavior of a wide variety of aquarium fishes.)

Pinter, H. 1986. *Labyrinth Fish.* New York: Barron's Educational Series. (The most current general reference on the aquarium husbandry of the major aphrophil aquarium fishes.)

Socolof, R. B. 1980. Tropicals. In *Fish Farming Handbook,* ed. E. A. Brown and J. B. Gratzek, 163–205. Westport, Conn.: Avi Publishing Co. (Detailed account of methods employed to produce tropical fish on a commercial scale.)

Wickler, W. 1973. *Breeding Behavior of Aquarium Fishes.* Revised English language edition. Neptune City, N.J.: T.F.H. Publications. (Valuable overview of the reproductive biology of aquarium fishes from the perspective of an internationally recognized authority on fish behavior.)

Contributors

HOWARD E. EVANS received his Ph.D. degree in Zoology from Cornell University in 1950 and joined the faculty of the New York State Veterinary College. In 1986, Dr. Evans retired as professor and chairman of the Department of Anatomy and professor-at-large of Biological Sciences to become professor emeritus of veterinary and comparative anatomy. His publications include studies of tooth replacement and taste in fishes; reptile and bird anatomy; and anatomy of the dog. He is an associate editor of the *Journal of Morphology*. From 1960 to 1983, Dr. Evans served as Secretary, Vice-President, and President of the World Association of Veterinary Anatomists.

JOANNE NORTON received bachelor of science, master of science, and Ph.D. degrees in botany from Ohio State University. She began raising tropical fish in 1958. Working in her home, she has investigated the genetics of live-bearers and has developed and introduced to the hobby a number of new fish. In freshwater angelfish, she discovered the inheritance of pigment-pattern genes and pearlscale. After finding that photoperiod influences the expression of several angelfish pigment-pattern genes, Dr. Norton determined the genotypes and day lengths required to produce certain color patterns. She has published two booklets, one on platys and the other on platys and swordtails, written 70 articles, and edited *Livebearers* for its first eight years. She is continuing to work on angelfish genetics and on attempts to improve and develop new mollies.

PAUL V. LOISELLE received his master of science degree from Occidental College in Los Angeles and Ph.D. from the University of California at Berkeley. An accomplished aquarist with over twenty years of experience, Dr. Loiselle has served as a consultant for the ornamental fish farming industry in Florida and is currently curator of freshwater fish at the New York Aquarium. He is the author of *The Cichlid Aquarium,* coauthor of the *Marine Aquarist Manual*, and coeditor of *Aquarium Digest International*. His experience in the pond culture of fishes began during five years of Peace Corps service in West Africa.

Aquarium Fish Physiology and Nutrition

Fish Physiology

Robert E. Reinert

In the broadest sense, an understanding of fish physiology includes an understanding, in chemical and physical terms, of all the mechanisms that operate in fish. Since there are more species of fishes than of all the other species of vertebrates put together, and because of the extremely wide variety of habitats fishes occupy, there are often large differences in the physiological strategies they use to live in particular environments. Even if we only consider the physiology of one species, the task of trying to explain all the factors involved in how that species functioned would not only be beyond the scope of this chapter, but beyond that of any reasonably sized textbook. Therefore, this chapter is only an introduction to a few of the basic physiological functions of fishes. Included will be the senses, respiration, osmoregulation, and the stress response. It is our hope that this introduction to fish physiology will provide some initial insight into how fishes function in their environment and encourage the reader to learn more about these intriguing animals.

The Sensory Systems

In fishes, the sense organs provide the only input from the outside world to the nervous system. Thus, the reactions of fishes are largely the results of responses to external stimuli that have been transduced to electrical impulses by the various sensory receptors and relayed to the brain. Most fishes possess traditional vertebrate sense organs that provide for sight, hearing, touch, taste, and smell. They also possess the lateral line system, which is unique to fishes and the aquatic stages of amphibians. In the following pages, we will discuss some of the basic principles involved in the operation of these senses and their importance to the overall well-being of fishes.

Vision

Morphology: In many ways the fish eye is structurally similar to the eye of terrestrial vertebrates. For example, both have a cornea, an iris, a lens, and a retina that contains rods or rods and cones. However, because air and water have different effects on the properties of light, a number of features of the fish eye have been modified so it can function at a high level of efficiency in water. One principal difference between the eye of most terrestrial vertebrates and most fishes is the shape of the lens. Anyone who has ever looked at an underwater object while swimming knows that it is impossible to see the object clearly unless you are wearing a face mask. This is because the greater the density difference between two mediums, the greater will be the angle of refraction as the light passes from one to the other. When light strikes our eye in air, the majority of the refraction occurs at the air–cornea inter-

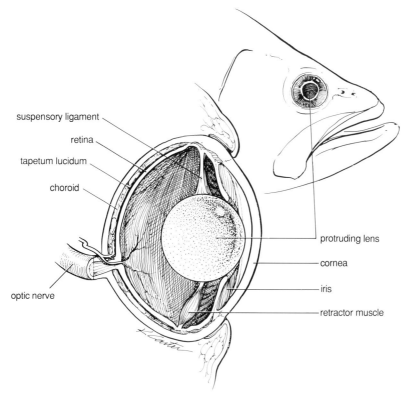

suspensory ligament

retina

tapetum lucidum

choroid

optic nerve

protruding lens

cornea

iris

retractor muscle

The spherical lens of most fish eyes focuses by moving within the eyeball.

they focus by changing the position of the lens in much the same manner as a camera is focused. The relaxed position in most teleost (bony) fishes is when the lens is in the forward position. In this position, near objects in front of the fish are in focus. Accommodation to more distant objects in front of the fish is accomplished by moving the lens back toward the retina with the retractor lentis muscle. In many sharks the lens is closer to the retina in the relaxed position. These fishes accommodate to close objects by moving the lens forward with the protractor lentis muscle.

Another difference between the teleost eye and that of most terrestrial vertebrates is that the lens of most teleost fishes protrudes through the pupil. Along with the ellipsoid shape of the retina, this gives most fishes an extremely wide angle of vision that includes the area in front and continues laterally to almost directly behind them. Also, when fish swim, the side-to-side head movement coordinated with eye movements tends to eliminate any blind spots behind them.

The structure of the eye in some elasmobranchs (sharks, skates, and rays) differs in several ways from that of the teleost eye. The elasmobranch lens is often more flattened and does not extend through the pupil. Also, unlike the fixed pupil of most teleosts, many elasmobranchs can control the amount of light entering their eye by constricting or dilating their pupil in a manner similar to that of terrestrial vertebrates. The light-adapted pupil has been shown to take many shapes, from that of a pinhole in the blacktip shark (*Carcharhinus limatus*) to a horizonal slit in the bonnet-head shark (*Sphyrna tiburo*). Also, although most teleosts lack any type of protective covering over the cornea, many sharks have a nictitating membrane. This membrane probably protects the eye when a shark is feeding, because

face. The primary purpose of our lens is to fine-tune this refraction and focus the light on the retina. In water, however, the density of water and our eye are about the same. Consequently, there is little refraction as the light passes into our eye, and because our lens is somewhat flattened, it is not capable of refracting the light enough to focus it on the retina. The layer of air in a face mask bends the light enough so our lens can focus it. To compensate for the lack of refraction by the cornea, the lens in most fish eyes is spherical. This shape and the high density of the lens result in a refractive index of about 1.67. This is the highest refractive index of any vertebrate lens and is sufficient to bend the light so it can be focused on the retina.

The shape and relative rigidity of most fishes' lenses also necessitates that fish have a method of focusing (accommodation) that is different than that of most terrestrial vertebrates. For example, humans focus light on the retina by changing the shape of the lens. Most fishes, however, do not change the shape of their lens because they must maintain the optimal refractive index. Instead,

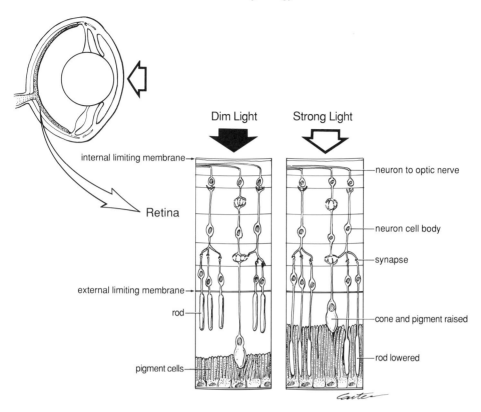

Movement of rods, cones, and pigment in the retina of a teleost fish. In light adaptation, the rods are moved away from the light and are protected by forward movement of pigment.

it closes over the eye just before the shark strikes its prey.

The retina of a fish is organized in a manner similar to those of other vertebrates. Closest to the light is a clear layer of nerve cells and nerve fibers. Just behind this layer are the photosensitive rods and cones. The outermost layer of the retina is the pigmented epithelium. In many teleosts, there is a reflective mirrorlike area, the tapetum lucidum, interspersed among the cells of the pigmented epithelium. Guanine crystals are the reflective substance in the tapetum lucidum of most fishes. Some teleosts, however, have other reflective materials. A yellow "melanoid" substance has been reported to occur in gars (Lepisosteidae) and catfishes (Ictaluridae), and a pteridine appears to be the reflecting substance in gizzard shad (*Dorosoma cepedianum*). The tapetum increases the sensitivity of the eye in low light by reflecting light back over the rods. Similar materials found in the eyes of other animals, such as cats and

deer, are the cause of the so-called "glassy-eyed" look when light shines into their eyes.

In fishes, as in other vertebrates, rods appear to be primarily for vision in dim light and cones primarily for color vision in more brightly lit situations. Rods show a higher degree of convergence in their neural connections (a number of rods may be connected to a single nerve fiber) than cones and consequently respond to lower levels of light.

The number of rods and cones and their distribution in the retina vary with different species of fishes. Generally, those that are active at twilight (crepuscular) or live in low-light environments have a higher ratio of rods to cones than those that live in more brightly lit environments. For example, the crepuscular eel-pout (*Lota lota*), has a rod:cone ratio of about 238:1, whereas fishes such as the mackerel sharks (Lamnidae), which are active in a more highly lit environment, have a rod:cone ratio of 6:1. Because most deep-sea fishes live in an environment with very little light, their retinae contain either only rods or rods with a very sparse number of cones.

The fovea is a depression in the retina containing closely packed cone cells for increased visual acuity. Although it is common in higher vertebrates, it is rare in fishes but has been reported for some species. For example, three species of serranid basses have been shown to have well-developed depressions containing high concentrations of cones. The exact position of these areas on the retina seems to be related to the horizontal or vertical feeding habits of the fish.

Light/dark adaptation: An interesting feature of the teleost eye is the manner in which these fishes control the amount of light striking their rods and cones. Humans and many other higher vertebrates control the amount of light entering their eye by contracting or dilating their pupil. However, because their lens extends through the pupil, most teleosts have adapted another method, which involves synchronized movements of the rods, cones, and pigment granules in the pigmented epithelium. Under conditions of bright light, the pigment granules migrate toward the outer segments of the rods and cones. At the same time, the rods move back into the pigment and the cones move toward the light. This arrangement protects the rods from the effects of bright light by enclosing them in the pigments and at the same time exposes the cones to the light. In low light, the pigment granules move away from the rods and cones. At the same time, the rods move toward the light and the cones move away from it. The time required for light and dark adaptation in fishes is considerably longer than the contraction or dilation of the pupil in higher vertebrates. For instance, in young salmon, light and dark adaptation take about twenty-five minutes and one hour, respectively.

Visual pigments: The light environment of fishes is much more varied than that of most terrestrial vertebrates. This is due to the light-scattering and absorption properties of water and the materials in water. Because of these large differences in both quality and quantity of light in their environment, fishes have evolved the widest range of visual pigments of any of the vertebrates. The two basic groups of visual pigments in fishes are rhodopsins and porphyropsins. Classically, rhodopsins are found in marine fishes and porphyropsins in freshwater fishes. However, many freshwater fishes, such as some species of

charcids and cyprinids, have mixtures of both pigments. Some migratory fishes, such as lampreys (Petromyzontidae) and coho salmon (*Oncorhynchus kisutch*), also have both pigments and undergo seasonal changes in their rhodopsin-porphyropsin ratios.

All of the visual pigments studied in fishes have two major components: a lipoprotein moiety called an opsin, and a chromophore consisting of retinene$_1$ (an aldehyde of vitamin A$_1$) or retinene$_2$ (an aldehyde of vitamin A$_2$). The rhodopsins, which are similar to the visual pigments found in humans, contain retinene$_1$ and the porphyropsins, retinene$_2$. Within each of these two major groups of visual pigments, differences in the opsins determine which wavelengths of light are maximally absorbed by the pigment. When light is absorbed, the pigment undergoes conformational changes that result in the generation of an electrical impulse. This impulse is transmitted to the brain, where its integration results in the sensation of sight.

There have been a number of attempts to relate the maximum spectral absorption qualities of visual pigments to the different spectra found in various aquatic environments. In many marine teleosts, the visual pigments appear to be those that are most sensitive to the wavelengths that predominate in the environment in which the fishes live. For example, many fishes living in the deeper waters of the ocean, where all but blue light (shorter wavelengths of about 470 to 480 nanometers, or nm) is filtered out, have pigments that maximally absorb these shorter wavelengths. Conversely, many fishes that inhabit shallower, more turbid waters have pigments that are shifted toward the longer yellow-green wavelengths that penetrate these waters. Other fishes have pigments that appear to maximize the contrast between prey and the background light. In some predatory reef fishes, the visual pigments are most sensitive to the wavelengths that predominate at dawn and dusk, when these fishes are most active.

Color vision: One of the best indications that some fishes have color vision is that they have cones, which are the color receptors in higher vertebrates. In order to distinguish differences in wavelength (i.e., color) from differences in brightness, an organism must have receptors that respond to different wavelengths. In 1801 Thomas Young correctly suggested that three basic types of color receptors could account for the sensation of color vision. For example, in humans there are three basic types of cones that have pigments that have their maximal sensitivities at 440 nm (blue), 535 nm (green), and 575 nm (yellow), respectively. In most fishes that have color vision, there are also different types of cones. Goldfish (*Carassius auratus*) have three types of cones that have maximal sensitivities at 455 nm (blue), 535 nm (green), and 620 nm (red). Basically, the theory for color vision is that blue, green, or red light will cause the particular cone that is sensitive to it to respond. The result will be the sensation for that particular color. However, if the color is some combination of these, the cones will respond more or less in proportion to the amount of blue, green, or red in that color, and the sensation will be for that color.

The most conclusive evidence of color vision in fishes comes from conditioned-response tests. These tests involve conditioning a fish to a particular event and then measuring the response. For example, a goldfish can be shown a number of cards that are different hues but the same brightness. Several seconds after being shown a particular hue, the fish is shocked. By monitoring the heartbeat, it can be shown that, often after only a few trials, the fish learns to associate that particular hue with the impending shock. The heart rate declines in anticipation of the shock. This and other types of conditioned-response tests have demonstrated that many fishes do respond to color and often over much the same range as humans. The primary biological advantage suggested for color vision over non-color vision is that it enhances the perception of various targets against a variety of backgrounds.

Hearing and Equilibrium — The Inner Ear

Underwater sound: Although sound obeys the same physical laws in air and water, many quantitative differences result from differences in the compressibility and density of the two media. For example, in both water and air, a sound wave results from the compression of particles that rebound after compression and impart their directional energy to neighboring particles. However, because molecules in water are closer together than in air, the motional energy is transferred from molecule to molecule faster. Therefore, sound travels about 4.8 times faster in water than in air.

The near-field and far-field effects are another factor that plays an important part in underwater acoustics. These terms refer to the ratio of the pressure of the sound waves to particle displacement (movement of the water). In the near-field, the pressure of the sound wave and the particle displacement are out of phase. Particle displacement increases more rapidly than pressure as one moves closer to the sound source. Therefore, in the near-field, small pressure changes result in relatively large changes in particle displacement. In the far-field, particle displacement and pressure have a constant ratio. The point at which the ratio between the two becomes constant is termed the near-field/far-field boundary. Because water is much denser and therefore less compressible than air, the extent of the near-field effect in water is about five times greater than in air. Also, the lower the frequency of the sound source, the greater will be the extent of the particle displacement.

A general rule for determining the extent of the near-field effect is that the near-field/far-field boundary will be about one-sixth the wavelength from the sound source. For example, at a frequency of 20 cycles per second, the near-field will extend about 12.5 meters (41.0 feet) from the sound source. At a frequency of 1,000 cycles per second, it will only extend for about 0.25 meters (0.82 feet). Because of differences in the acoustical characteristics of air and water, terrestrial vertebrates almost always are exposed to sound in the acoustical far-field. Fishes, however, are exposed to both and have evolved the lateral line system, which is especially sensitive to particle displacement caused by low-frequency vibrations.

Most of the sound generated in either air or water is reflected back into that medium at the air–water interface. This means that fishermen in a boat can talk without being detected by the fish, but any sounds such as the banging of a tackle box or the scraping of feet will be transmitted into the water and possibly be detected by the fish. In the aquatic environment, along with compression waves, any movement of water such as fin movement, water currents, the movement of a fishing lure through the water, the bow wave generated when a fish swims, or the scraping of a tackle box on the bottom of a boat is considered an acoustical phenomenon. The two sound-detection systems in fishes are the inner ear and the lateral line system.

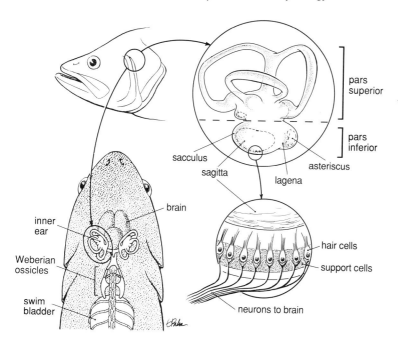

Fish have no outer or middle ear, but do possess an inner ear (above, right) composed of interconnected ducts and chambers with otoliths inside. A cross-sectional magnified view (below, right) shows a portion of an otolith resting on sensory hair cells.

Morphology of the inner ear: Fishes do not have an outer or middle ear; however, they do have an inner ear that is similar in many ways to the inner ear of higher vertebrates. In both groups of animals, the inner ear consists of a membranous system of connecting ducts and chambers. In most teleost fishes, the lower portion (the pars inferior) has two chambers, the sacculus and the lagena. Each of these chambers contains a calcarious ear stone called an otolith. The upper portion (the pars superior) consists of three semicircular canals that extend through the horizontal, vertical, and longitudinal planes and one chamber, the utriculus, which also contains an otolith. Each of the semicircular canals has an ampulla (chamber) that responds to changes in the inertia of the fluid in the semicircular canals. In most of the fishes studied, the primary function of the pars superior seems to be as an equilibrium and gravity detector, and the main function of the pars inferior is sound detection.

Hearing: Because a fish is about the same density as water, sound waves move through its body at about the same amplitude and frequency as they move through the water. If the sound waves moved through all of the fish's body at the same amplitude and frequency as they move through the water, the fish would not be able to detect sound. The otoliths, however, are about three times as dense as most of the other tissues. Therefore, when a sound field strikes an otolith, it is not as easily set in motion as the rest of the tissues. Consequently, the phase and amplitude of the otolith movement are different from that of the rest of the body. In each chamber, the otolith is suspended in fluid and rests on a sensory epithelium (macula) composed of hair cells. From each hair cell an apical bundle of cilia (minute, short hairlike processes) projects into the chamber. The out-of-phase movement of the otolith with regard to the cilia stimulates (bends) the cilia. This causes the hair-cell membrane to change shape. Depending on the direction in which the cilia bend, there is an increase or decrease in the rate of impulses from the sensory axon with which the hair cell makes contact. These changes in firing rate travel to the auditory center of the brain and result in the sensation of hearing.

The swim bladder is important to the hearing of fishes because it contains a different medium than that through which the sound is traveling. The swim bladder is a saclike structure containing gases that is located in the abdominal cavity above the viscera. Because gas in the swim bladder is more compressible than water, sound waves cause the walls of the swim bladder to vibrate. This in turn causes surrounding tissues in the fish to vibrate, which stimulate the otolith organs. It has been shown that deflating the swim bladder decreases hearing sensitivity.

A wide variety of sizes and shapes of swim bladders are found in different species of fishes. For example, in herrings (Clupeidae) and anchovies (Engraulidae), projections of the swim bladder enter the skull and press against the wall of the inner ear. In adult mormyrid fishes (a group of

African freshwater fishes), portions of the swim bladder are separate from the main swim bladder and are enclosed within the skull in contact with the inner ear. There have been few studies concerning the relationship between hearing and the shape, size, proximity to the inner ear, and complexity of the swim bladder in fishes. Until there are more studies concerning these factors, it will be impossible to assess the overall role of this organ in the hearing of fishes.

The Weberian ossicles are a series of three or four small bones derived from the vertebrae and are very important in the hearing of some fishes. These bones couple the swim bladder to the inner ear and are attached to the vertebrae by elastic cartilage that allows them some freedom of movement. The Weberian ossicles are found only in minnows, catfishes, and other fishes belonging to the superorder Ostariophysi. Their primary function appears to be to mechanically transmit vibrations from the swim bladder to the inner ear. It has been shown that removal of one of these bones will decrease the range of hearing.

There is no doubt that there are substantial differences in hearing abilities between different species of fishes. It is difficult, however, to determine what the true hearing abilities of fishes are in natural surroundings. This is primarily due to the acoustical problems associated with most testing procedures. For example, most hearing studies with fishes have been done in small aquaria where it is difficult to separate the effects of the near- and far-field. Also, reflections and alterations of sounds at the air–water interface and by the sides and bottom of the aquarium make it very difficult to generate "pure" sounds. One way to alleviate these problems is to work in a more natural open environment. This approach, however, presents other difficulties, such as the presence of ambient noise and the problems associated with trying to observe fishes from considerable distances.

Fishes with the broadest range and the lowest threshold of hearing are those with Weberian ossicles. In order of decreasing range and increasing threshold, they are followed by fishes with swim bladders. Fishes with the poorest hearing are those without swim bladders, such as the sharks. For example, the upper limit of hearing for most ostariophysian fishes with Weberian ossicles is 6,000 to 13,000 cycles per second (Hertz, or Hz). By comparison, the upper hearing range of young

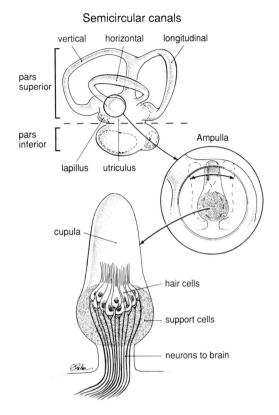

Increasingly enlarged views of one of the three ampullae of the inner ear, which serve as sensory receptors for equilibrium.

adult humans is about 20,000 Hz. The upper limit for fishes with swim bladders but without Weberian ossicles is about 800 to 3,000 Hz. Sharks respond to frequencies of 55 to about 500 Hz. It should be noted, however, that while there does seem to be a general trend in the hearing abilities of fishes within these groups, there are extremely large variations from species to species within and between the groups.

Equilibrium: Anyone who has ever been scuba diving quickly realizes that in an aquatic environment there is a sensation of being weightless in a three-dimensional world. When there is a lack of visual clues, it is very easy to become disoriented and lose all sense of direction. Fishes, however, have a very sensitive system of gravity and directional equilibrium receptors that allow them to sense their position at all times. The otoliths are generally associated with gravity detection in fishes. When the fish changes position relative to gravity, the otolith moves on the macula. This causes the sensory cilia to bend and results in a change in the rate at which impulses from the otolith organ are sent to the brain. In theory, by maintaining the same impulse rate in the otolith organs from both inner ears, a fish would be in balance relative to gravity.

The semicircular canals (one in hagfish, two in lamprey, and three in all other fishes) are the organs of dynamic or spatial equilibrium in fishes. As is the case with higher vertebrates, each of the three canals is aligned in a different plane. The horizontal plane responds to side-to-side motion of the head, the vertical plane to up or down motion of the head, and the longitudinal plane to rotation about a head-to-tail axis. Perhaps a better way to visualize these motions is to think of the yaw, pitch, and roll of a ship. These motions are sensed in the ampullae of the semicircular canals, each of which contains hair cells similar to those on which the otoliths rest. Cilia from a number of hair cells (generally twenty to seventy) are covered with a gelatinous matrix called a cupula, which extends up into the canal. When a fish moves in any direction, there is a corresponding movement of the endolymph fluid in the canal. The movement of the fluid causes the cupula and its associated cilia to bend. This in turn changes the firing rate of the neurons associated with the hair cells. These changes in the spontaneous firing rate are transmitted to the equilibrium centers in the medulla, and the fish makes the appropriate body and eye movements to maintain its position in the water. A fish is constantly reacting to changes in impulses from its gravity and dynamic equilibrium systems. Even at rest, many fishes must continually make adjustments with their fins to maintain their equilibrium because their center of gravity is slightly above the midline through their body. If this type of fish loses the ability to react to changes in these impulses, it will roll over on its back. This phenomenon is often observed by fishermen when they try to return fishes such as largemouth bass (*Micropterus salmoides*) or northern pike (*Esox lucius*) to the water.

The Lateral Line System

The sensory systems discussed thus far—vision, hearing, and equilibrium—are all senses that are familiar to us because of our own experience with them. The lateral line system, however, is found

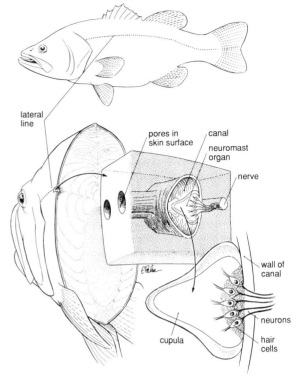

Increasingly enlarged views of the lateral line system, which senses water movement.

only in fishes and the aquatic stages of amphibians, and therefore is harder for us to conceptualize. Perhaps the most descriptive term for this system is the German word *Ferntastsinn,* which means "distant touch." This system responds to any type of water movement, including currents, reflections of the fish's bow wave, and movements of other fishes.

Morphology: The sensory receptors of the lateral line are called neuromast organs and are similar to those of the ampullae organs of the inner ear. Each neuromast organ consists of a number of hair cells enclosed in a cupula. In a manner similar to the auditory and equilibrium hair cells, movement of the cupula and the associated movement of the enclosed cilia cause an increase or decrease in the frequency of the impulses sent to the brain. There are two basic types of lateral line receptors: epidermal organs, which are found in the skin with the cupulae extending into the surrounding water; and canal organs, which are located in a system of canals beneath the skin. All fishes have one or both of these types of receptors. Some of the more primitive species, such as the hagfishes and the lamprey, only have epidermal organs. Most of the more advanced fishes, however, also have well-developed lateral line canals. In many fishes, not only do the lateral line canals extend along the sides of the fishes, but they often branch and extend out along the head. Neuromast organs in these canals are usually arranged in series along the sides of the fish, with their cupulae projecting well up into the canal. Water movement in any direction striking the sides of the fish causes the mucus in the lateral line canal to vibrate, which stimulates the neuromast organs.

Function: There is no doubt that the lateral line system is extremely important to fishes. The main function of this system is the detection of particle displacement that results from low-frequency vibrations or the movement of water. For instance, even without the use of their inner ear, most fishes still respond to low-frequency vibrations below 200 Hz. However, when the nerves innervating the lateral line are cut, these responses are lost. The lateral line is very important in the detection of prey and predators. In water where the visual field is poor, it is probably the lateral line system that first detects the presence of a fishing lure moving through the water. Also, a blinded fish can avoid solid objects due to the sensitivity of the neuromast organs to changes in the bow waves reflected back to the fish. Fish in an aquarium probably use their lateral line system to sense the location of the aquarium walls. Along with vision, the lateral line also appears to play an important part in the schooling behavior of some fishes. For instance, pollock (*Pollachius virens*) with their eyes covered maintained their position in a school with nonblinded fish. This schooling ability was lost when the lateral line nerves were cut.

An interesting generality concerning fish behavior and the lateral line is that the more active the species, the greater is the percentage of canal organs compared to epidermal organs. The explanation is that the skin between the canal and the water acts as a buffer between the water continuously passing over the fish and the neuromast organs, and thereby lessens the problem of "environmental noise."

Chemoreception — Olfaction and Taste

The sensory systems discussed thus far use two types of sensory receptors. Photoreceptors transduce energy from the electromagnetic spectrum into nervous impulses responsible for sight, and mechanoreceptors transduce the movements of water into electrical impulses responsible for the "distance touch" sense of the lateral line and the hearing and balance functions of the inner ear. The sensory receptor organs for the next two senses, olfaction and taste, are categorized as chemoreceptors. They transduce chemical phenomena into nervous impulses responsible for the sensations of olfaction and taste.

Because chemoreception in fish takes place in a medium where the molecules are frequently dissolved in water, it is often difficult to distinguish whether olfaction or taste is responsible for a particular reaction. We do know, however, that fishes do have distinct olfactory and taste organs that are similar in morphology to those of terrestrial vertebrates. Olfaction in fishes is primarily important for detecting substances at a distance, and taste, in most fishes, is considered a contact sense for testing the palatability of substances. If one considers that the molecules responsible for the sensations of olfaction and taste in terrestrial vertebrates must enter a mucous layer before they contact the sensory organs, chemoreception in both fishes and terrestrial vertebrates can be considered an aquatic phenomenon.

Olfactory organ morphology and function: In most fishes, olfactory organs are more sensitive than organs for taste. Thus, they are more important for sensing dilute quantities of substances at a distance. The olfactory organs of fishes are similar to those of humans and other higher vertebrates in that they are located in the same general area and have the same innervation. However, unlike humans, only rarely in fishes does the olfactory organ open into the mouth.

Among fishes there are a number of variations in the morphology of the olfactory organ. The simplest form is a single median nostril with just one opening, as found in the primitive lampreys and hagfishes. Sharks and rays have paired olfactory organs located on the ventral side of the snout. The opening of each organ is divided into two parts by a fold of skin. Most teleosts have paired olfactory organs located on the snout above the mouth. In most instances, each olfactory organ has a separate inlet and outlet for water, which is passed through the olfactory organ in three ways: 1) breathing movements compress an olfactory pouch and force water in and out of a single opening in rhythm with the respi-

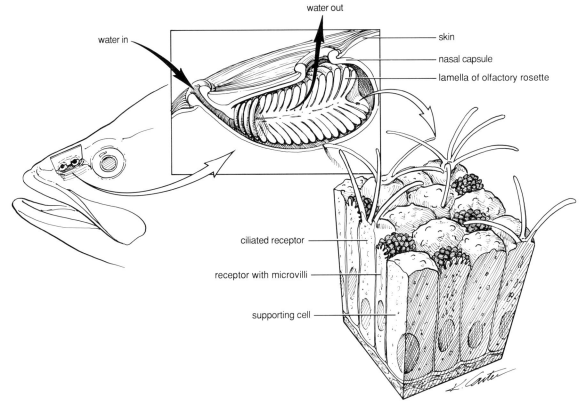

Increasingly enlarged views of the olfactory organ of a fish. As water passes through the organ, odorants contact the surface of sensory cells.

ratory movements (as in the three-spine stickleback, *Gasterosteus aculeatus*); 2) cilia, or breathing movements, or both, of the fish cause water to circulate through the anterior opening and out the posterior opening (as in the yellow perch, *Perca flavescens*); 3) water is deflected in and out of the olfactory organ by the fish's movement through the water (as in the northern pike).

The shape of the olfactory sac in fishes varies considerably from species to species. The three basic shapes are: round, which is generally associated with fishes that are primarily sight feeders; oblong, which is generally associated with fishes that use both vision and olfaction to locate food; and elongate, which is generally associated with fishes that have poor vision and a highly developed sense of smell. There is also considerable variation in the arrangement of the sensory epithelium that lines the olfactory sac. In most fishes, the epithelium is raised from the floor of the sac and forms a series of rosettelike folds, which greatly increase the surface area. The number and arrangement of these folds also varies a great

deal among species, and together with the size and shape of the olfactory sac generally correlates with the importance of olfaction to the fish. For example, species of puffers (Tetraodontidae), which are highly visual reef fishes that live in very clear water, have no olfactory sacs; rainbow trout (*Oncorhynchus mykiss*), which rely on both vision and olfaction, have an oblong-shaped olfactory sac with about eighteen folds; and channel catfish (*Ictalurus punctatus*), which have a highly developed sense of smell, have an elongate-shaped olfactory sac with about 142 folds. Because the number of lamellae in the olfactory sacs of some fishes has been shown to increase with growth, it has been suggested, but not proven, that as fishes grow older, their sense of smell becomes more acute.

The olfactory sensory receptor cells in fishes are bipolar neurons with cylindrical dendrites that terminate at the surface of the epithelium. Olfaction is the only sense in which the receptor cell is a direct extension of its respective cranial nerve and not connected to it by one or more synapses.

There appear to be two general categories of receptor cells, which are distinguished by the form of the distal free end of the dendrite: cells having cilia and cells having microscopic projections (microvilli) on their surface. Although it has not been conclusively proven, it is generally assumed that olfactory receptor sites are located on cilia or microvilli that extend above the surface of the epithelium. There appear to be several basic types of arrangements of the sensory cells on the olfactory epithelium. These range from sensory cells that cover the entire epithelium, except for the dorsal part of the folds, to small isolated islands of sensory cells arranged somewhat like taste buds.

We do not know how a fish or any other animal transduces information about an organic molecule into the sensation of smell. The most accepted theory is that the cilia or microvilli of the receptor cell have different receptor sites that respond to the steric fit of certain shaped molecules. Odors appear to be correlated with the steric conformation of the molecules. For example, in humans seven basic odors have been postulated: camphoraceous, musky, ethereal, floral, pungent, putrid, and pepperminty. It has been observed that substances with similar molecular configurations have similar odors. According to the theory, molecules with intermediate shapes produce intermediate odor sensations by fitting, and thereby stimulating, several different receptor sites. This would explain how a relatively few different types of receptor sites could be responsible for many different odor sensations.

Sensitivity to pure compounds: Both electrophysiological and behavioral techniques have been used to measure the sensitivity of olfactory organs of many different fishes to a wide variety of materials. These tests have shown there is a wide range of sensitivities among fishes and between different organic materials. Fishes with highly sensitive olfactory organs are termed "macrosmatic," and those with less highly developed systems are termed "microsmatic." Good examples of microsmatic fishes are the minnow (*Phoxinus phoxinus*) and rainbow trout. Both can detect β-phenylethyl alcohol at concentrations in the low parts per trillion. This range of sensitivities is about the same as that of humans. Compared to many other terrestrial animals, humans are not considered to have a highly developed sense of smell. However, if one considers that 2 1/2 ounces

(about 75 grams) of a material dissolved in 1 million 20,000-gallon railroad tank cars of water is equivalent to about 1 part per trillion, it is easy to see that olfaction is a highly sensitive detection system in these fishes and in humans. The American eel (*Anguilla rostrata*) can truly be classified macrosmatic. Its lowest threshold for the above-mentioned chemical is about 80 to 100 times lower than that of the minnow or rainbow trout. This degree of olfactory sensitivity is about the same as that of macrosmatic terrestrial animals such as dogs.

Amino acids are a class of compounds that have been studied a great deal in relation to their effect on the olfactory system of fishes. Because they are the building blocks for protein, it is not surprising that a number of researchers have tried to find which ones or what combination might prove to be an attractant to fishes. For instance, in field tests where amino acids were pumped into water and their attractiveness to winter flounder (*Pseudopleuronectes americanus*), mummichog (*Fundulus heteroclitus*), and Atlantic silversides (*Menidia menidia*) was measured, a number of amino acids were found to be effective attractants. Although there was a good deal of overlap in preferences among species, different species did prefer different amino acids. In laboratory tests in which different amino acids were introduced into large tanks containing carp (*Cyprinus carpio*), the most positive responses were to the amino acids valine and lysine. In general, electrophysiological and behavioral tests with a variety of fishes suggest that of the classes of compounds tested, amino acids appear to have the greatest stimulatory effect. Other pure substances that evoked the feeding response were ammonia, lactic acid, creatinine, and glutamic acid.

Repellents: An interesting finding concerning amino acids was that the odor from biologists' hands rinsed in water running down a fish ladder acted as a repellent to coho salmon. The most active ingredient from the hand rinsings was found to be the amino acid L-serine, which is a common amino acid in mammalian skin. It has been suggested that the avoidance response to L-serine has evolved as a method for alerting migrating salmon to the presence of mammalian predators such as sea lions and bears. Based on this information, a number of products have been developed that are supposed to mask the human scent when sprayed on a fishing lure. In addition, some are advertised to contain compounds that act as fish attractants.

It is interesting to note that the electrical response of the olfactory epithelium is about the same for L-serine as it is for a number of other amino acids. Yet, many of these other amino acids attract certain species of fishes, whereas L-serine, at least to migrating salmon, is a repellent. This suggests that although electrophysiological studies can be useful in estimating the threshold levels of sensory systems to different compounds, they do not indicate how the animal will integrate or react to these stimuli.

Food extracts: Natural food extracts such as the slime excreted from earthworms, and tissue fluid extracts from clams, shrimp, and fish elicit feeding responses in various species of fishes. It is probably the specific combination of amino acids in foods, perhaps with certain other chemicals, that forms a particular "odor profile" recognized by fishes. For example, seven amino acids (glycine, alanine, valine, threonine, glutamic acid, leucine, and serine) were found to be the main constituents of an extract from a marine worm (*Arenicola marina*) that attracted Atlantic cod (*Gadus morhua*) and whiting (*Merluccius bilinearis*). Glycine alone was the most attractive of the amino acids in the mixture. When glycine and alanine were excluded, the mixture was no longer attractive to the fishes. Differences in the attractiveness of certain amino acids to fishes is probably one of the reasons why fish raised on a particular food often resist changing to a new diet.

Because of their relatively poor eyesight, sharks appear to rely heavily on olfaction. They have been shown to respond to the odor of food at concentrations as low as 100 parts per billion, the equivalent to about 250 ounces (about 7.0 kilograms) of food extract in 1,000 railroad tank cars of water. The right- and left-handed turns that result in the typical figure-eight search pattern of sharks are probably the result of the animal moving in the direction of the nostril that receives the greatest stimulus from the odorant. It has been reported that water flowing over a stressed fish elicits a greater response from a shark than water flowing over one that is not stressed.

Body odor and social behavior: A large number of behavioral studies both in the laboratory and in the field have shown that olfaction is very important to fishes in many ways in addition to feeding. For instance, blinded bluntnose minnows (*Pimephales notatus*) have been taught to distinguish between the odors of aquatic plants and invertebrates. When their olfactory epithelium was destroyed, the fish no longer responded to these odors. The ability to discriminate between different body odors has been demonstrated for fishes such as yellow bullhead (*Ictalurus natalis*), which are able to discriminate between members of their own species and between two species of frogs. Also, minnows have been trained to react to body odors of fifteen different species of fishes from eight different families.

Recognition of body odors may be very important in many aspects of the social behavior of fishes. Along with vision and the lateral line system, olfaction may play a part in the schooling behavior of some fishes. A number of studies have shown that olfaction is very important in many phases of sexual behavior and parent–offspring relations. For example, male gobiids (Gobiidae) show courtship behavior when they are exposed to a small amount of water in which gravid females had been placed for only a few minutes. The ovarian fluid was the only body fluid that elicited the courtship response. Male goldfish are also strongly attracted to water from containers holding ovarian fluids and eggs from the same species. The majority of studies concerning the relation between olfaction and sexual behavior in fishes have been done with tropical aquarium fishes because of the ease with which they can be bred in aquaria. There is no doubt, however, that similar relationships exist for common species of fishes.

Crowding factor: A factor or factors that are species-specific and that retard growth, reproduction, and depress heart rate have been extracted from tank water in which fishes have been kept under crowded conditions. This crowding factor has been reported for zebra fish (*Brachydanio rerio*), goldfish, carp, and blue gourami (*Trichogaster trichopterus*). The majority of the heart-rate-inhibiting factor for goldfish and carp was extracted from water with chloroform and was in the neutral lipid fraction. It has been suggested that the factors inhibiting growth, heart rate, and reproduction are either very closely related or the same substance. An interesting aspect of this work that has not been investigated is the significance of the crowding factor in wild populations or in the crowded conditions that often exist in commercial pond culture operations.

Fright substance: The fright reaction—in which fishes stop feeding, concentrate, then seek cover or flee when a member of their species has been injured—was first reported in 1938. Since then it has been reported for many species of ostariophysian fishes and has been associated with olfaction. The fright reaction is initiated by a fright substance, called *Schreckstoff* in German, given off by the injured skin of fishes. The chemical makeup of the compound or compounds is not known; however, histological observations suggest the substance is produced by specialized epidermal cells that do not open to the surface and only release the fright substance when the skin is injured. Fishes killed without injuring the skin do not elicit the response. Also, the fright reaction can be induced by skin extracts of different species. The intensity of the response is generally greater the more closely related the species.

Although the fright reaction is mediated by the olfactory system, fishes with inoperable olfactory systems in the same water or intact fishes in other tanks also display the reaction if they are in visual contact with the fish displaying the initial reaction. Although latency periods of up to five minutes have been reported, dye studies have shown that response to the fright substance generally occurs thirty to sixty seconds after it reaches the fish. Some differences in reaction times may be due to differences in the substance's concentration in the water. Repeated exposure and season also have been reported to affect the degree of response. Fishes that show the fright response can react to very low concentrations of skin extracts. Species of European Cyprinidae reacted to concentrations that were estimated to be in the parts per trillion.

Migration and imprinting: Sockeye salmon (*Oncorhynchus nerka*), coho salmon, chinook salmon (*O. tshawytscha*), and chum salmon (*O. keta*), captured on their spawning runs, were tagged, had their nostrils plugged, and were released with intact conspecifics. The majority of the intact fishes selected their home streams, while those with their nostrils plugged were random in their selection. Although it has been suggested that operations such as plugging the nostrils affect other behavioral traits that may be responsible for the homing behavior, the majority of the evidence suggests that olfaction is very important in the spawning migration of these fishes.

It has been determined that salmon imprint on some odor or combination of odors in their home streams during their fry stage. The imprinting appears to occur when these fishes are undergoing the physiological changes (smolting) that take place prior to their migration to the ocean. Critical periods for imprinting have been reported to take anywhere between thirty-six hours to two months.

A number of questions remain unanswered concerning the role of olfaction in migration. For example, in some streams where fishes make long spawning runs, the chemical stimuli are mixed and diluted by other streams that flow into the home stream. How do these fishes recognize the odor when they return on their spawning run? The answer may be that they imprint on a series of odors as they move downstream instead of just the odor of their natal area. What is the chemical makeup of the odor or odors to which they respond? Although it is known they respond to the organic fraction of the water, the makeup of this fraction is unknown. For species in which there are always some fish in the streams, such as Arctic char (*Salvelinus alpinus*) and Atlantic salmon (*Salmo salar*), it has been suggested that home stream waters are scented by pheromones from nonmigrating members of the population. However, in tests with coho salmon, the odor of juvenile fish was a less powerful attractant than home stream water without the odor of juvenile fish. These and other studies of behavior of migratory fishes suggest there are still a number of unanswered questions concerning the overall imprinting process. They leave no doubt, however, that olfaction is a very important part of this process.

Artificial imprinting: An interesting aspect of the imprinting process has been the use of artificial odorants such as morpholine to imprint salmon in hatcheries. Morpholine (C_4H_9NO) is a colorless, acrid-smelling heterocyclic amine that does not occur naturally in the environment. It can be detected by unconditioned salmon at concentrations of about 1 part per trillion. In Wisconsin, coho salmon were imprinted on this compound for several weeks prior to and after smolting. They were then tagged and released directly into Lake Michigan. When the spawning run began about

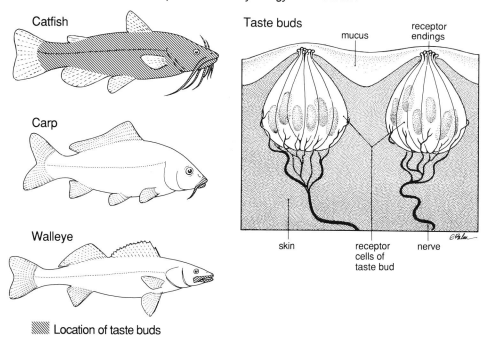

Catfish

Carp

Walleye

Taste buds

mucus

receptor endings

skin

receptor cells of taste bud

nerve

▨ Location of taste buds

Typical vertebrate taste buds occur in fishes, to varying extents and often in widely varying locations.

eighteen months later, morpholine was metered into a stream about 0.5 kilometers (0.3 miles) south of the original release site at a concentration of about 50 parts per trillion. Of the study fish captured in the stream, 218 had been exposed to morpholine and only 28 were control fish. The number of morpholine-treated fish recovered in the stream represented about 2.7 percent of those stocked. This percent return is similar to the percent return for normal homing Great Lakes salmon. Versions of this study were repeated over several years. In each instance, the majority of the morpholine-treated fish returned to the stream scented with morpholine. In one study in which an additional group of fish was treated with phenethyl alcohol (PEA), the majority of the morpholine-treated fish returned to the stream scented with morpholine, and the PEA-treated fish returned to the stream scented with PEA. Brown trout (*Salmo trutta*) and rainbow trout have also been successfully imprinted with morpholine and PEA.

Although the process of imprinting on compounds in water has primarily been studied in salmonids, studies of this process in other fishes could prove to be very rewarding and provide a great deal of information about the relation between olfaction and behavior of fishes. For exam-

ple, in New York a study of walleye (*Stizostedion vitreum vitreum*) in Lake Chautauqua showed that over 90 percent returned to their home stream during their spawning run. Other fishes such as white bass (*Morone chrysops*), striped bass (*Morone saxatilis*), and certain stream-run populations of lake trout (*Salvelinus namaycush*) also return to their home streams. Also, within a lake many species appear to return to the same spawning areas each year. Are these fishes imprinting on certain odor profiles in the water, or are they using other senses to return to their spawning areas?

Morphology and function of taste receptors: In addition to their location in the mouth, taste receptors in fishes are often located in the pharynx, on gill rakers, and on gill arches, and in some fishes they are widely scattered over the outer surface of the body. For example, freshwater fishes such as catfishes have thousands of external taste buds on their bodies, with especially dense concentrations on their barbels. It has been estimated that for a yellow bullhead that is 25 centimeters (about 10 inches) long, there are about 175,000 taste buds on the external body surface and about 20,000 in the mouth and throat. By comparison, there are about 10,000 taste buds on the human tongue. Species such as carp and sturgeons (Acipenseridae) also have large numbers of external taste buds. In some marine fishes, such as the sea robins (Triglidae) and hakes (Gadidae), taste buds are located on specialized pectoral fins that have been modified into feelers. If one considers the poorly lit surroundings in which many of these fishes live, it is reasonable to assume that their ability to literally taste the environment as they move through it is a definite asset in finding food.

Fishes appear to have at least three types of taste receptors: taste buds that are similar to those of higher vertebrates, spindle cells, and free nerve endings. Taste receptors located in the mouth, pharynx, and on gill arches and rakers are similar to the taste buds of higher vertebrates. Dense concentrations of taste buds are also located on the palatal organ, a raised area on the roof of the mouth of cyprinid fishes such as carp, minnows, and suckers. Taste buds consist of three different types of cells: elongate receptor cells arranged somewhat like the segments of an orange, supporting cells, and basal cells. In teleosts, the receptor cells of the taste bud are reported to have one or two microvilli that extend above the surface of the cell. Elasmobranch taste buds have from three to twelve microvilli. Receptor sites for the taste substances are believed to be located on the microvilli, and the mode of action is probably similar to that described for olfaction. Free nerve endings, which are the terminal structures of the taste bud nerve, surround the taste buds and form a plexus in the space between the nuclei of the receptor cells and the basal cells. Specialized epidermal spindle cells, which resemble the receptor cells of the taste bud, are found around the head and body of some minnows. There are many free nerve endings in fishes, and some of these are also believed to act as taste receptors. For example, although the free fin rays of sea robins do not have any specialized taste cells, they do contain a large number of spinal nerve endings. These fishes show positive reactions when the fin rays touch certain chemicals.

The size of specific areas of a fish's brain can often be used as a measure of the importance of a particular sense to the fish. In fishes that rely on taste to find food, the facial and vagal lobes of the medulla are often enlarged. For example, the vagal lobes are larger than the remainder of the brain in suckers, a fish that has a large number of taste buds.

Sensitivity of taste receptors: Gustatory sensitivities of a number of different fishes have been tested for a variety of substances using both electrophysiological- and behavioral-response techniques. These tests suggest that many fishes respond to a wide variety of tastes. For example, taste buds of the palatal organ of carp respond to acetic acid, sucrose, dextrose, levulose, glycine, quinine, NaCl, human saliva, carbon dioxide, and the extract of silkworm papae. For many substances, the sense of taste in fishes is more sensitive than it is in humans. The thresholds for sucrose and salt in minnows are reported to be 2×10^{-5} M and 4×10^{-5} M, respectively, where M stands for molar. These values are about 512 and 184 times lower than those reported for humans. The threshold value for minnows for fructose is about 2,500 times lower than that of humans. Actual threshold values for many substances may be even lower because they are calculated from baselines determined from the fish's response to solutions that theoretically contain zero concentrations of the substances being tested. Sensitive gas chromatographic techniques, however, have shown that in many instances the so-called zero-concentration control substances contain contaminants to which the fishes may respond.

In most fishes, taste is considered a close-range or contact sense used primarily as the final screening process to accept or reject food. However, in some, such as the catfishes, taste is so sensitive that it is also used to detect substances at a distance. As was the case with olfaction, taste receptors in catfishes and other fishes are very sensitive to certain amino acids and combinations of amino acids. Action-potential responses from the maxillary barbel nerve of channel catfish were obtained from concentrations of L-alanine of about 10^{-12} M. Threshold values for glycine, L-arginine, L-serine, L-glutamine, and L-cysteine ranged between 10^{-9} and 10^{-10} M. Behavioral tests with brown bullhead (*Ictalurus nebulosus*) and yellow bullhead suggest that these fishes have a gustatory acuity that is similar to the olfactory acuity of many other fishes. For example, they can use their sense of taste to locate food at a distance of at least twenty-five body lengths. In one study, yellow bullheads rapidly located a food source (liver juice or 0.01 M cysteine hydrochloride) that was dripped into a tank containing 600 liters (about 160 gallons) of water. By means of taste alone the fish exhibited a true gradient searching pattern in the absence of a current. When taste receptors on one side of the body were impaired, the fish would circle to orient the side with intact taste receptors toward the food source. The search patterns suggest these fish were using taste receptors on different parts of their bodies to locate food sources in much the same manner that olfaction is used. Thus, the taste sensation actually begins when these fish are some distance from their food, intensifies as they get closer, and is strongest when the food is ingested.

Respiration

Oxygen is as important to the survival of fishes as it is to the survival of terrestrial organisms. One major difference, however, is that fishes live in an environment that is oxygen-poor relative to terrestrial habitats. Two characteristics of water make it a relatively poor medium for respiration: 1) even under the most ideal conditions, water only contains about 3 percent of the oxygen found in air; 2) water is about 800 times denser than air, so more energy is required to move it across the gills than to move air across the lungs. The fish gill is very efficient at removing oxygen from water. To understand how this efficiency is achieved, it is necessary to examine some of the basic morphological and physiological characteristics of this very impressive organ.

The Respiratory Pump

To get an adequate supply of oxygen, fishes must keep a constant supply of water flowing across their gills. In the relatively primitive lampreys and hagfishes, the gills are basically a series of pouches. With the exception of one species of hagfish, each pouch has an opening that leads from the pharynx to the exterior. Gill filaments and their associated secondary lamellae are attached to the walls of the pouches. In lampreys, contractions of muscles in the outer walls of the pouches pump water out over the gill filaments. When the muscles relax and the pouches expand, water is drawn in. Because adult lamprey use their mouth to attach to prey, it is important that they do not have to use their suckerlike mouths to take in water for respiration. In hagfish, muscle contractions in the velum (part of the foregut), in the gullet, gill pouches, and gill ducts force water through the external openings of the gill pouches. When these muscles relax, fresh water enters the system through a single nostril on the snout and flows through the nasal passage to the velum.

In most jawed fishes, water is taken in through the mouth during the respiratory cycle. In some sharks, rays, and dogfish, however, there are a pair of reduced gill slits or spiracles located between the first gill slit and the ear capsule. Along with the mouth, these serve as inlets for water during the intake portion of the respiratory cycle. Sharks and rays have separate valvelike openings for each gill slit. In most bony fishes, the gills are covered with an operculum that has a single opening at the rear.

Among teleosts, the volume of the buccal and opercular chambers is increased through a series of muscular actions, and water flows in through the open mouth. Then, through another series of sequential muscular actions, the volume of the two chambers is decreased. By timing this with the closing of the mouth and the closing and opening of the opercular valve, water is pumped over the gill and out through the opercular valve. The pumping action is similar in elasmobranchs, except that some water is taken in through the spiracles, and parabranchial chambers take the place of the opercular chamber.

Certain active fishes, such as tuna, trout, mackerel, and some sharks, pass water over their gills by keeping their mouths and gill chambers open as they swim (ram gill ventilation). This is very efficient, and many species are able to suspend active breathing and rely on ram gill ventilation when they swim at speeds greater than 1.5 kilometers (0.93 miles) per hour. Some fishes, such as adult tuna, mackerel, and the mackerel sharks, have lost the ability to pump water over their gills and suffocate if they are prevented from swimming.

The Gill

Efficient passage of oxygen from water to the blood and passage of carbon dioxide from the blood to water requires that a relatively large surface area of the fish containing a rich blood supply be brought in close contact with the water. The design of the fish gill fulfills these requirements very well. The two main components of the gill that form the sieve through which the water passes are gill filaments and their associated

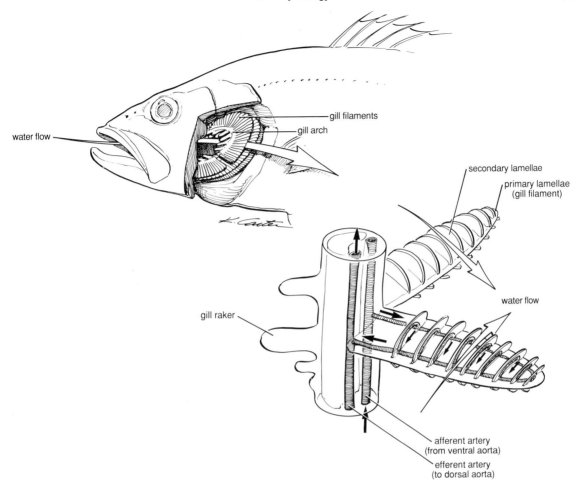

Extreme close-up of one gill arch, showing two gill filaments and their associated secondary lamellae. A unique feature contributing to fish gill efficiency is the countercurrent flow of blood and water.

secondary lamellae. In teleost fishes, two rows of feather-shaped gill filaments extend from each of four gill arches on both sides of the fish. Along both sides of each filament are very small, thin, plate-shaped secondary lamellae. These are the actual sites of respiratory exchange. Each of the secondary lamellae is covered by a thin layer of epithelial cells that are supported internally by pillar cells. Blood in the secondary lamellae flows through capillarylike channels created by the pillar cells. These channels are so narrow that only one red blood cell at a time can literally squeeze through them. In most fishes, the cell wall of the secondary lamellae is only about 1 to 6 microns thick (about 1/68 to 1/11 the thickness of a human hair). Tips of the filaments from one gill arch touch those of the adjacent arch and form the horizontal portion of the sieve. The associated secondary

lamellae form the vertical portion. The channels created by this sieve are about 0.02 to 0.05 millimeters wide and about 0.2 to 1.6 millimeters long. This sievelike design brings almost all the water flowing past the gill in contact with the secondary lamellae and their rich blood supply.

The fact that blood flowing through each gill lamella moves in a direction opposite to that of the water greatly increases the effectiveness of the gill as a respiratory organ. This "countercurrent" exchange system is much more efficient than a co-current system in which blood flows in the same direction as the water. In a co-current system, the diffusion gradient between two fluids is very large when they first come together, but rapidly decreases as the two fluids move in the same direction and approach equilibrium. In such a system, there can never be more than a 50 percent transfer from one fluid to the other. In contrast, by reversing the flow of one of the fluids, there is always a diffusion gradient. Consequently, diffusion from one fluid to the other can exceed 50 percent. The countercurrent system in the gill creates a diffusion gradient that allows oxygen to enter and carbon dioxide to leave the blood the entire time that water is in contact with the secondary lamellae. The value of countercurrent flow was demonstrated in a study in which the flow of water over a fish's gill was reversed. When water and blood flowed in the same direction, the efficiency of oxygen uptake decreased from 51 percent to 9 percent.

The number of gill filaments and secondary lamellae varies considerably among species. Fishes that are more active generally have a greater number of both filaments and lamellae and consequently, a larger total gill area. For example, the total gill area of an active species such as mackerel is about 1,040 square millimeters per gram (45.7 square inches per ounce) of body weight while that of a sluggish fish such as toadfish (Batrachoididae) is about 151 square millimeters per gram (6.6 square inches per ounce) of body weight. The total area of the gill can be ten to sixty times greater than the rest of the surface area of the fish. As impressive as this seems, the total area of the lung of most terrestrial mammals is greater. It would seem to be an advantage for fishes to have an even larger gill surface area. Respiration, however, is not the only function of the gill. It also is an important site of ion and water exchange, and further increases in the surface area of the gill would result in excessive ion and water imbalances that could be fatal to the fish (see the osmoregulation section of this chapter).

Under ideal conditions, fish can extract over 80 percent of the oxygen from water that passes over their gills. The highest figure for the lung in humans is about 25 percent. Unfortunately, the gill also is very efficient at filtering other materials from water, many of which are harmful to fish. The highly solvent nature of water also adds to this problem. Most substances that enter water are dissolved and therefore are subject to being passed over the gill during respiration. Various pesticides, heavy metals, and many other materials can be concentrated in fish tissues through direct uptake from water by the gills (bioconcentration). When these concentrations are added to those accumulated from eating contaminated food (bioaccumulation), it has been shown that fish can accumulate concentrations of these materials that are often thousands, and in some instances millions, of times higher than concentrations in the water. Because the gill is such an efficient all-around filter, it is important for anyone working with fish to maintain good water quality and take every precaution to keep pollutants out of the water.

Fish Blood

Circulation: The bright red color of the fish gill is indicative of the rich blood supply flowing through it. Blood from the heart reaches the gills via the ventral aorta, and then flows to the afferent (inward–flowing) brachial arteries in each gill arch. Branches of the brachial artery form small arterioles that supply blood to the secondary lamellae. As blood flows through the lamellae, individual red blood cells are forced through the narrow channels. At this point, when the red blood cells are closest to the water, oxygen is picked up by hemoglobin in the red blood cells and carbon dioxide is released. After blood passes through the lamellae, it flows via branches of the efferent (outward–flowing) brachial arteries to the dorsal aorta and then to the rest of the body. The blood supplies oxygen to the tissues, picks up carbon dioxide, and then is returned to the gill by the pumping action of the heart to repeat the process.

Hemoglobin and gas exchange: Blood transports oxygen to fish tissues in essentially the same way that it does in terrestrial animals. The principal oxygen–carrying component of the blood is hemoglobin in the red blood cell. Fish blood can carry about fifteen to twenty-five times the amount of oxygen carried in the same volume of water. Of that amount, about 99 percent is carried by hemoglobin. An important characteristic of hemoglobin is that its affinity for oxygen is very sensitive to changes in the concentration of carbon dioxide and pH (hydrogen ions). This affinity decreases as the concentrations of carbon dioxide and hydrogen ions increase. Conversely, as the concentration of oxygen increases, the affinity of hemoglobin for carbon dioxide and hydrogen ions decreases. Because of their effects on the affinity of hemoglobin for oxygen, the concentration of carbon dioxide and hydrogen ions are controlled within very narrow limits by the buffering system of the blood.

Transport of gases from the gills to tissues and

from the tissues to gills is a very complex process that involves a number of intricate biochemical reactions. The brief discussion that follows is only meant as a summary of this process. At the gill, as the red blood cell passes through the secondary lamellae, the number of free oxygen molecules in the water is greater than the number in the red blood cell, so oxygen diffuses into the red blood cell, where it is bound by hemoglobin. Blood leaving the gill is normally about 85 to 95 percent saturated with oxygen, whereas venous blood returning to the gill is about 30 percent to 60 percent saturated. As oxygen is bound by hemoglobin at the gill, the affinity of the hemoglobin for carbon dioxide decreases, and carbon dioxide is released. Because the number of free carbon dioxide molecules in the red blood cell is now greater than the number in the water, carbon dioxide diffuses from the blood through the lamellar membrane into the water.

Blood flows from the gill to the various tissues. In the tissues, the blood enters an environment that contains more free carbon dioxide molecules than the red blood cell due to the metabolic activities of the tissues. Because of their increased concentration, carbon dioxide molecules diffuse into the red blood cell. The increased concentration of carbon dioxide molecules and their reaction with water also cause an increase in the number of hydrogen ions. The increase in carbon dioxide and hydrogen ions decreases the affinity of hemoglobin for oxygen. This results in an increase in the number of free oxygen molecules in the red blood cell. Because this number is greater than that in the tissues, oxygen diffuses into the tissues. When the red blood cell returns to the gill, the cycle is repeated.

The tendency for carbon dioxide and hydrogen ions to decrease the affinity of hemoglobin for oxygen is called the Bohr effect. This is a very important reaction because it increases the efficiency of oxygen exchange at the tissues. Although it is physiologically advantageous for fish under normal conditions, there are circumstances when the Bohr effect can cause serious problems. For example, anything that causes prolonged vigorous activity, such as capture by hook and line or by a net, can cause a buildup of carbon dioxide and lactic acid in the blood. If these levels increase until they exceed the buffering capacity of the blood, there will be a decrease in the pH of the blood and a corresponding decrease in the affinity of hemoglobin for oxygen at the gill. This can cause fish to die from lack of oxygen and generally occurs when fish are stressed. Active fishes such as trout and salmon have a very strong Bohr effect and therefore are especially sensitive to low pH in their blood. For this reason, when it is necessary to keep fish under crowded conditions, keep their water well aerated.

Strategies for Increasing Oxygen Uptake

Fish can increase oxygen uptake through several short-term responses. One is to increase the pumping or ventilation rate of the gills so more water is passed over the gills. Another is to increase the flow of blood through the gills by increasing the rate or stroke volume of the heart. Efficiency of gas exchange can also be increased by dilating the filamental arterioles, which increases the flow of blood through the secondary lamellae.

These short-term strategies, however, are too demanding energetically to be continued for prolonged periods, and they also can lead to osmotic problems. Fortunately, there are other ways fish can increase their respiratory efficiency for prolonged periods. The most common of these is to increase the number of red blood cells and the concentration of hemoglobin in them. The efficiency with which hemoglobin combines with oxygen at the gill and releases it at the tissues can also be changed. For example, it has been shown that increases in temperature lower the affinity of hemoglobin for oxygen. However, if fish are allowed time to acclimate to the higher temperature, the efficiency of their hemoglobin exceeds that of the nonacclimated fish. The key to long-term adjustment to changes in water quality is that fish need time (generally days or even weeks) to adjust to their changed environment. Most fish normally are not subjected to rapid changes in water quality in their natural environment and therefore cannot make rapid physiological adjustments to such changes. For this reason, rapid changes in water quality of captive fish should be avoided.

Osmoregulation

Osmoregulation involves a number of physiological processes that together maintain the proper internal salt–water balance in fishes. In a manner of speaking, the gill membrane of freshwater and marine fishes is suspended between the blood and the water, media of very different ionic concentrations. To understand the osmotic problems this creates for fish, it is necessary to review the principles of diffusion and osmosis.

Diffusion is the movement of molecules from an area of higher concentration to one of lower concentration. For example, when a bottle of perfume is opened, molecules diffuse from the high concentration in the bottle out into the room. Given enough time, the system will reach equilibrium, with equal numbers of perfume molecules inside and outside the bottle. Osmosis is the diffusion of water through a semipermeable membrane. If a solution of sugar in water is separated from pure water by a membrane permeable only to water, the water will diffuse through the membrane into the sugar solution. The pressure it would take to stop the movement of water into the sugar solution is called the osmotic pressure of the solution. The more concentrated the solution, the greater will be the osmotic pressure. Water will always pass from the solution having the weaker osmotic pressure through a semipermeable membrane to the solution with the higher pressure until the two solutions reach the same pressure. If, as is the case with most living tissues, the membrane is also permeable to certain dissolved substances, water will move from the weaker solution to the stronger one while the dissolved substances will move more slowly in the opposite direction. Again, movement will continue until the two solutions reach the same osmotic pressure.

Because of differences in the salt content of their environments, freshwater and marine fishes face different osmotic problems. In freshwater fishes, the concentration of dissolved salts (ions) in the blood is greater than the concentration in the water (i.e., the fish's body fluids are hypertonic to the water). Therefore, the osmotic pressure of the blood is greater; water diffuses through the gill membrane into the blood, and ions such as sodium (Na^+) and chloride (Cl^-) diffuse into the water. In marine bony fishes, the situation is reversed. The concentration of ions in the seawater is greater than that of the blood (i.e., the fish's body fluids are hypotonic to the water). Water diffuses out of marine bony fishes and ions diffuse in. Elasmobranch fishes maintain an osmotic pressure in their blood that is higher than that of the seawater. Because the osmotic pressure of their blood is greater than the seawater, these fish

behave osmotically like freshwater fishes. This specialized physiological strategy is discussed later in this section. If the osmotic process in each of these groups of fish were not regulated in some way, it would be impossible for them to maintain the salt–water balance of their body fluids at the concentrations necessary for life.

At first glance it would seem that a simple solution to the osmotic problem would be for all fish to have membranes that are impermeable to water and salts. If this were the case, however, the membranes would also be impermeable to respiratory gases and to excretory products such as ammonia. Neither the respiratory nor excretory functions of the gill would be possible. Therefore, as is most often the rule with biological systems, instead of complete optimization of one system at the expense of another, there is a compromise. In this instance, the compromise is that the gill is permeable to water and salts.

In both freshwater and marine fishes, osmoregulation requires the use of energy in the form of adenosine triphosphate (ATP). A large amount of the standard metabolic energy (the energy required for basic metabolic chores such as respiration and digestion) of fish is used for osmoregulation. Consequently, even when a fish is motionless and apparently resting, it still must use considerable energy to maintain its internal salt and water balance. Any factors that increase the osmoregulatory demand above the normal level for more than a short period can be very harmful.

Freshwater Fishes

The kidney: Two basic osmotic problems faced by freshwater fishes are getting rid of excess water and maintaining the proper salt concentration in their body fluids. Excess water is eliminated by an efficient kidney system that produces a very copious, dilute urine. The kidneys of most fish are reddish, paired longitudinal structures found just below the vertebral column. The basic structure of the kidney is the nephron, which consists of a renal corpuscle and a convoluted tubule. The renal corpuscle consists of an open-ended, double-walled capsule (Bowman's capsule) and a mass of capillaries called the glomerulus, which are tightly coiled inside the capsule. The tubule from each nephron drains into the main collecting duct for that kidney and

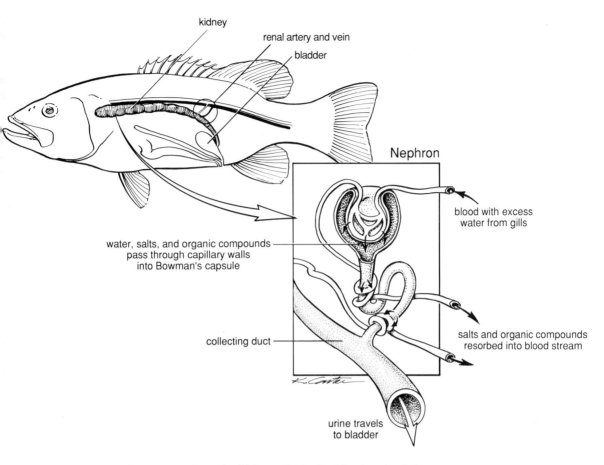

kidney

renal artery and vein

bladder

Nephron

blood with excess water from gills

water, salts, and organic compounds pass through capillary walls into Bowman's capsule

salts and organic compounds resorbed into blood stream

collecting duct

urine travels to bladder

Functional elements of a nephron from the kidney of a typical freshwater fish.

then to the exterior.

The most important function of the kidney of freshwater fishes is to eliminate excess water. One might think of a freshwater fish as a leaky boat, with the major leak at the gills, and the kidneys as the pumping system used to control the leak. Relatively speaking, the leak is quite extensive. Terrestrial vertebrates only produce up to 1.5 percent of their body weight per day as urine. Freshwater bony fishes, however, may produce more than 20 percent. Along with water, ions and organic materials such as glucose and amino acids are also filtered out of the blood as it flows through the glomerulus. However, as the filtrate passes through the convoluted tubule of the kidney, most of the ions and organic materials are reabsorbed back into the blood, while the majority of the water is passed out of the fish as a very dilute urine. For example, almost all of the Na^+ in the filtrate is reab-

sorbed; however, usually less than 50 percent and sometimes as little as 5 percent of the water passes back into the blood.

The gill: Although the reabsorption of ions in the kidney is very efficient and produces a very dilute urine, there is still a substantial loss of ions because so much urine is produced. To counter this loss and the loss of ions through diffusion at the gill, ions are absorbed from the water by the gills. Principal sites of this uptake appear to be the membranes of the secondary lamellae and specialized "chloride cells" located on the gill filaments, primarily at the base of the secondary lamellae. Although there still are many unanswered questions concerning the details of this very complex process, the most prevalent theories suggest that uptake of Na^+ and Cl^- ions against a concentration gradient is mediated by a class of enzymes called ATP-ases. These enzymes are located within the cell membrane and are often referred to as "ion pumps." They require energy in the form of ATP for the active transport of ions through the cell membrane against the concentration gradient. They also require the presence of counter-ions. For example, the inward movement of Na^+ seems to be coupled with the outward movement of hydrogen ions (H^+) and ammonium ions (NH_4^+), and the inward movement of Cl^- is apparently coupled with the outward movement of the bicarbonate ion, HCO_3^-. These reactions are essential not only in the osmoregulatory process but also are an important part of the acid-base and excretory function of the gill, because they serve as a mechanism for the elimination of excess H^+, HCO_3^-, and NH_4^+ ions.

The transepithelial potential, an electrochemical gradient across the gill membrane, is another aspect of gill physiology that plays an important part in osmoregulation. The charge of the electrical gradient is such that the inside of the gills of freshwater fishes is generally negative relative to the outside. It has been suggested that this difference in charge between the inside and the outside of the gill membrane decreases the tendency for positively charged ions to diffuse out through the gill membrane. It also decreases the amount of energy needed for the active transport of positively charged ions from water into the blood.

Marine Fishes

Because the blood of marine bony fishes has a lower osmotic pressure than the seawater (i.e., is hypotonic), their osmotic problem is the reverse of that of freshwater fishes; water diffuses out through their gills and salts diffuse in. Solving the water part of their osmotic problem is relatively simple. Marine bony fishes replace water lost through their gills by drinking 7 to 35 percent of their body weight in seawater per day. As the salinity of the water increases, they compensate by drinking more seawater. Unfortunately, although this replenishes the lost water, it also increases the salt concentration of their blood. The salt content of the blood is increased further by salts that diffuse in through the gills. Because the osmotic problems of freshwater and marine fishes differ, the roles of the kidney and gills as osmoregulators also differ. In marine bony fishes, the kidney functions to conserve water and excrete salts, and the gills also excrete salts.

The kidney: Although the basic structure of the kidney of marine bony fishes is similar to that of freshwater fishes, it is generally less developed. The glomeruli, the principal sites where water is filtered from the blood, are generally smaller and fewer in number than those in freshwater fishes. In fact, a number of marine fishes have no glomeruli. Also, the distal segment of the kidney tubule is missing. The distal segment is the principal site for the reabsorption of monovalent ions such as Na^+ and Cl^- in freshwater fishes. Because their glomeruli are generally less developed and their kidney tubules are more permeable to water, marine bony fishes produce a urine flow that is only about 1/10 to 1/20 that of freshwater fishes.

While the principal function of the freshwater bony fish kidney is to get rid of water, it appears the main function of the marine bony fish kidney is to excrete magnesium sulfate. The majority of the divalent magnesium and sulfate ions taken in during the drinking process are excreted in the feces. However, about 20 percent of these ions do enter the blood. Available evidence suggests that almost all the magnesium and sulfate ions that are absorbed into the blood are excreted by the kidney. Although other ions such as sodium and chloride, are found in the urine, it is the gill that serves as their major excretory pathway.

The gill: The principal osmotic function of the gills of marine bony fishes is active transport of excess Na^+ and Cl^- from the blood to the water. Chloride cells appear to be the major site for transport, and ATP-ases appear to play a major part in the sequence of biochemical events involved in the actual transport process. There are, however, major differences in the transport process between freshwater and marine bony fishes. For one, in marine bony fishes, the ATP-ases are polarized in the opposite direction (they transport salts outward), and the counter-ion for the ATP-ase responsible for the transport of Na^+ appears to be potassium instead of the H^+ or NH_4^+ ions. For another, the transepithelial potential of marine bony fishes is such that the inside of the gill membrane is positive relative to the outside. Energetically this may make it easier for these fish to excrete positively charged ions against the inward diffusion of ions from the seawater. For fishes such as salmon that migrate between fresh and salt water, the direction of ion transport at the gills reverses when they move from one environment to the other. Changes in the osmoregulatory functions of the kidney in such fishes are more a matter of quantity than direction. For example, urine output of salmon that move from salt to fresh water will generally increase from 8- to 12-fold as a result of the increased influx of water and the resulting increase in the glomerular filtrate.

Elasmobranch Fishes — A Special Strategy

Elasmobranchs have evolved an osmotic strategy that is somewhat different than that of either freshwater or marine bony fishes. Basically they maintain a very high concentration of urea and other nitrogenous waste products in their blood. This is made possible, at least in part, because the gills of these fish are relatively impermeable to urea. Also, most of the urea and other nitrogenous waste products in the glomerular filtrate are reabsorbed from the kidney tubules. The result is that the urea concentration in the blood of most elasmobranchs is about 2 percent to 2.5 percent, while that of most other vertebrates is only about 0.01 percent to 0.03 percent. In most animals, a blood urea concentration above 0.5 percent is lethal. The combination of salts at concentrations similar to those in bony fishes and nitrogenous waste products increases the osmotic concentration of the blood so that it is slightly hypertonic to the seawater. As a result, these fish have a glomerular filtrate and a urine flow that is higher than that of marine bony fishes. Energetically this is probably a more efficient osmoregulatory strategy than that of marine bony fishes because the osmotic gradient between seawater and the blood is less for elasmobranchs than for marine bony fishes.

The Stress Response

Although most people intuitively understand what stress and the stress response mean, both of these terms have been given a number of definitions. For this discussion, we will consider a stress or stressor to be the stimulus acting on a fish and the stress response to be the physiological response of the fish to the stimulus. Defining the point at which a stimulus acting on a fish actually becomes a stress is difficult because, even under the best of conditions, fish are subjected to a wide variety of chemical and physiological changes. At what point does any one or any combination of these changes become severe enough to become a stress? Although there really is no accurate way of defining this point, we will consider a stimulus to be a stress if it requires a physiological response from the fish to adapt to the stimulus.

Some familiar examples of the alarm phase of the stress response are the sudden jolt of energy you feel when you realize you have almost fallen asleep while driving, the superhuman feats of strength performed by people in emergency situations, and the "pumped up" feeling an athlete gets before the game. These responses to stress situations are part of a series of physiological reactions called the general adaptation syndrome. This syndrome is divided into three phases: the alarm reaction, when stress hormones are released; a stage of resistance, during which adaptation occurs; and, if the animal cannot adapt, a stage of exhaustion followed by death. These reactions were initially observed in terrestrial vertebrates. However, similar, but not identical, reactions have been observed in fish.

The Stress Hormones

Organs of stress hormone production: The stress response is mediated by two groups of hormones: catecholamines, which are associated with the more immediate reactions to stress; and corticosteroids, which are more related to the adaptive phase. The catecholamines, adrenalin (epinephrine) and noradrenalin (norepinephrine), are produced by chromaffin tissue and nervous tissue. Chromaffin tissue, which is analogous to the medullary (inner) portion of the adrenal gland of higher vertebrates, is located in the anterior dorsal part of most fishes, embedded in the head kidney. Nerve tissues associated with the production of catecholamines are the nerve endings (adrenergic nerve endings) that innervate organs such as gill, and the heart. Catecholamines produced by chromaffin tissue are carried by the blood to various target organs. Catecholamines produced by adrenergic nerve endings affect the organs innervated by the nerves and apparently have little effect on concentrations in the blood. Corticosteroids (mainly cortisol) are produced by interrenal tissue, which in most fish is also found in the area of the head kidney. Interrenal tissue is analogous to the cortical (outer) portion of the adrenal gland.

Method of release: Release of the stress hormones is controlled in two ways: by direct nervous stimulation; and by releaser substances and adrenocorticotrophic hormone (ACTH) produced by the brain and the pituitary gland, respectively. Catecholamines are released by direct stimulation of nerve tissue. Therefore, the effect of these hormones on organs innervated by adrenergic nerve endings is very rapid and generally represents the first phase of the stress response. Release of catecholamines from chromaffin tissue is also controlled by the nervous system. Increased levels of these hormones can be detected in the blood of fish within several minutes of the initial stress. Release of the corticosteroids is controlled by a releaser substance produced by the hypothalamus in the brain and by ACTH produced by the pituitary gland, which is located directly beneath the brain. When the presence of a stress is sensed by the brain, a releaser substance produced by the hypothalamus stimulates the release of ACTH by the pituitary. The ACTH is carried by the blood to the interrenal tissue, where it stimulates the secretion of corticosteroids, which are carried by the blood to the various organs they affect.

Principal effects: Some of the most obvious effects of catecholamines are on the circulatory system—increased cardiac output and constriction or dilation of blood vessels. In some instances, epinephrine causes dilation of a particular set of blood vessels and norepinephrine causes constriction; in others, both hormones cause the same effect. The effect of these hormones on heart rate is not completely understood. In some studies, stress or the injection of catecholamines caused a decrease in heart rate, while in others it caused an increase. The most consistent response reported has been an increase in stroke volume, which results in an overall increase in blood pressure. During periods of stress, one of the main effects of catecholamines is to increase the flow of blood to specific organs. For example, at rest only about 65 percent of the secondary lamellae on gill filaments are perfused by blood. However, because of the increased stroke volume of the heart and the catecholamine-caused dilation of filamental arterioles, about 95 percent of the secondary lamellae can be perfused by blood in a stress situation. This results in a greater efficiency of oxygen uptake. Therefore, more oxygen is available for the in-

creased metabolic demands associated with the stress.

Catecholamines also appear to affect osmoregulation and metabolism. There is good evidence that increases in the concentration of catecholamines in blood affect osmoregulation by increasing the permeability of the gill to water and ions. In freshwater fishes, this results in an increase in the influx of water and an increase in the loss of ions from the body fluids to the water. For marine bony fishes, it means a loss of water and an increase in the influx of ions. The major metabolic effect associated with elevated levels of catecholamines in the blood is the breakdown of glycogen to glucose in the muscle and the liver. The breakdown of glycogen in muscle occurs very rapidly and provides an almost instant energy source. This, together with the increased oxygen supply, provides the fish with more energy.

The principal effects of the corticosteroids appear to be on osmoregulation and metabolism. In teleosts, these hormones appear to affect osmoregulatory processes acting on the gills, kidney, and intestinal tract. For example, increases in the concentration of cortisol in blood appear to affect active transport of ions at the gill by facilitating uptake of certain ions in freshwater fishes and excretion of ions in marine teleost fishes. The most prominent effects on metabolism involve breakdown of glycogen to glucose and the breakdown of proteins. Amino acids that result from the breakdown of protein are used to form new proteins or glucose. An example of this type of metabolic effect occurs during the nonfeeding migratory life stages of salmonids. During migration, high levels of cortisol facilitate the breakdown of protein to glucose (gluconeogenesis), which serves as a major energy source for these fishes.

Acute and Chronic Stress

The initial response to an acute stress is called the "fight or flight" response. When a fish is pursued by a predator, the stress response results in an almost instantaneous increase in the available energy, which may allow it to escape. Other energy-requiring functions such as osmoregulation are temporarily shut down so as much energy as possible can be channeled into getting away from the predator. In some ways, the purpose of the stress response is similar to that of the supercharger in a car. It is a short-term measure to produce large amounts of energy to deal with emergency situations. Most acute stresses are short-term. The fish either escapes or is caught. If it does escape, the stress is relieved, and the fish can recover from the adverse osmotic effects. In the wild, fish can alleviate stresses caused by changes in water quality by moving to a more favorable habitat.

In captivity, however, fishes are often subjected to relatively long periods of stress. The physical act of handling, changes in water quality, and crowding are all stress factors associated with captivity that have been shown to elicit the stress response. The trauma or "fright" associated with being pursued and captured and then held in a foreign environment can result in fishes being stressed for prolonged periods. A common cause of death in stressed captive fish is osmotic imbalance (osmotic shock). This occurs as a result of the increased blood flow through the secondary lamellae and the increased permeability of the lamellae to water and ions. A fish can correct the osmotic problems caused by a short-term stress, but if the stress is prolonged, death often occurs from several hours to several days after the initial stress. Stress also suppresses aspects of the immune response, such as phagocytoses and intracellular killing by macrophage cells. A frequent result is the outbreak of a disease from several days to about two weeks after fish have been moved from one environment to another.

Studies with salmon suggest fish can become conditioned to the stresses associated with capture. In one study, blood cortisol levels in coho and chinook salmon that had been netted and released twice daily for periods of ten, fifteen, and twenty days were lower than those of unhandled controls. In our work, we have found that when wild bluegill are acclimated to capture, there is little mortality associated with moving them. It has been suggested that hatchery fish generally have lower resting levels of stress hormones than wild fish. Although this makes them easier to handle, they may be less alert and therefore at a disadvantage when they are released and forced to compete with wild fish.

A fish exposed to a chronic stress can either compensate and adapt to the stress, or fail to compensate and die. Even if a fish does compensate, its performance capacity will be reduced during the period of compensation. In many instances, even after compensation, the performance capacity will be lower under the new set of conditions. For example, fish can adapt to rather wide changes in water temperature, but within this broad temperature range there is a preferred range in which the fish generally grows and performs best. The further the temperature is above or below this range, the poorer will be the overall performance. Changes in the allocation of energy to the various systems within the fish are one of the principal reasons for the changes in performance. The systems responsible for the basic metabolic functions necessary for life, such as the nervous system, the respiratory system, and the systems that control osmoregulation, have a higher priority for energy than growth or reproduction. Under conditions of little or no stress, there is an energy surplus that can be put into growth and reproduction. However, the further conditions are from the preferred range, the greater the stress and therefore the greater the amounts of energy the fish must use to make the proper physiological adjustments. Thus, the energetic cost needed by the fish to maintain itself under the new set of conditions may be such that growth and reproduction are adversely affected. Examples of the adverse effects of chronic stress on captive fishes are common and are often caused by poor water quality. If the water quality or other factors causing the problem are corrected, growth generally improves, and in many instances the fish begin to reproduce.

Alleviation of the Stress Response in Captive Fish

There are several ways to decrease the stress response in captive fishes. One is to decrease the overall "awareness" of the fish. The less aware a fish is of external conditions and factors such as discomfort and pain, the lower will be the stress response. One way to accomplish this is with anesthetics such as Tricain Methane Sulfonate (MS-222). This technique is widely used when fishes are moved in hatchery operations. Elimination of a fish's visual awareness of the surroundings also appears to have a calming effect. For example, cortisol levels in stressed juvenile steelhead trout began to decrease within seven hours in fish held in the dark, but remained high in those held in the light.

Adding salts such as sodium chloride to the water in which freshwater fishes are transported and cooling the water are techniques widely used in hatcheries to increase survival. Salt reduces the effects of the stress response by lowering the osmotic gradient between the water and the blood. This, in turn, reduces the influx of water and the loss of salts and therefore reduces osmotic shock. This technique has proven to be very successful in diminishing the stress response for both warm- and cold-water fishes. We have found that the addition of about 1 percent sodium chloride to water used to transport bluegill from local ponds to our laboratory increased survival from less than 50 percent to over 90 percent. Cooling the water that fishes are transported in slows their metabolic rate, which tends to reduce the stress response. Also, in most instances the stress response will be lower in fishes captured from colder water. Consequently, the best time to capture most fishes in the wild is in the spring, fall, or winter when the water is cool.

Selected References

Ali, M. A., ed. 1979. *Vision in Fishes*. New York: Plenum Press.

Bond, C. E. 1979. *Biology of Fishes*. Philadelphia: Saunders College Publishing.

Brown, M. E. 1957. *Fish Physiology*. Vol. 1. *Metabolism*. Vol. 2. *Behavior*. New York: Academic Press.

Health, A. G. 1987. *Water Pollution and Fish Physiology*. Boca Raton, Fla.: CRC Press.

Hoar, W. S., and Randell, D. J., eds. 1969. *Fish Physiology*. Vol. 1. *Excretion, Ionic Regulation, and Metabolism*. Vol. 2. *The Endocrine System*. Vol. 3. *Reproduction and Growth, Bioluminescence, Pigments, and Poisons*. 1970. Vol. 4. *The Nervous System, Circulation, and Respiration*.1971. Vol. 5. *Sensory Systems and Electric Organs*. Vol. 6. *Environmental Relations and Behavior*.1978. Vol. 7. *Locomotion*. 1979. Vol. 8. Energetics and Growth. 1983. Vol. 9. *Reproduction*. Part A. *Endocrine Tissues and Hormones*. Part B. *Behavior and Fertility Control*. 1984. Vol. 10. *Gills*. Part A. *Anatomy, Gas Transfer, and Acid-Base Regulation*. Part B. *Ion and Water Transfer*. New York: Academic Press.

Kleerekoper, H. 1969. *Olfaction in Fishes*. Bloomington: University of Indiana Press.

Love, M.S., and Cailliet, G. M., eds. 1979. *Readings in Ichthyology*. Santa Monica, Calif.: Goodyear Publishing.

Marshall, N. B. 1966. *The Life of Fishes*. Cleveland: World Publishing Co.

Northcutt, R. G., and Davis, R. E., eds. 1983. *Fish Neurobiology*. Vol. 1. *Brain Stem and Sense Organs*. Vol. 2. *Higher Brain Areas and Functions*. Ann Arbor: University of Michigan Press.

Pickering, A. D., ed. 1982. *Stress and Fish*. New York: Academic Press.

Smith, L. S. 1982. *Introduction to Fish Physiology*. Neptune City, N.J.: T.F.H. Publications.

Tavolga, W. N., Popper, A. N., and Fay, R. R., eds. 1981. *Hearing and Sound Communication in Fishes*. New York: Springer-Verlag.

Toshiaki, J. K., ed. 1982. *Chemoreception in Fishes*. New York: Elsevier Scientific.

Nutrition and Feeding of Tropical Fish

Robert A. Winfree

Fish are an extremely diverse group. It is therefore not surprising that this diversity is reflected in their food habits. No single food will meet the needs of all species of ornamental tropical fish at every stage of their life cycle. The more common aquarium fish have been selected for fish-keeping, at least in part, for their flexible food habits. Yet many beautiful species kept only rarely in aquaria require special foods that are available in the wild but which often are not easily provided in aquaria. A basic understanding of the food habits of fish in the wild can aid in the selection of foods appropriate for a wide variety of fish in aquaria.

Few species of fish can be neatly categorized as strict carnivores (meat eaters) or herbivores (plant eaters). Furthermore, the type of food selected in the wild may vary seasonally with its availability. Most species kept in aquaria are more or less omnivorous, seeming to require, or at least to prefer, a variety of animal and vegetable matter.

The blue tilapia (*Tilapia aurea*) is an example of a species with highly flexible food habits. When they are young, these fish commonly feed on zooplankton, but may also prey upon smaller fish. As tilapia grow larger, they usually filter food from the water or grub through bottom sediments for food. Still, all sizes of tilapia readily accept a wide variety of prepared foods. Flexible food habits

such as these are a real asset when several species are reared in the same aquarium.

Many highly specific terms, not used in this chapter, have been coined to describe particular food habits. However, to apply such terminology broadly can give false impressions about the food habits of a given species. Few species of fish have precisely the same food habits as any other species, and few retain the same food preferences as they age. Feeding habits often are reflected in morphology as well. A more generalized classification, based largely on the method of feeding rather than on the items consumed, follows.

Fish that nibble at plants or that pick at small plankton or benthic animals can be called grazers. Many common aquarium species fit in this group. The young of most species feed on zooplankton. Generalized grazers such as guppies and mollies feed on a wide variety of plant and animal foods. Other species can be very selective. For example, the blue tang (*Acanthurus coeruleus*) and some loricariid catfish (such as *Farlowella*) eat almost nothing except for algae in the wild. Adults of some marine angelfish and butterfly fish graze primarily on sponges and coral polyps, respectively. The bluehead wrasse (*Thalassoma bifasciatum*) and several other marine species commonly remove

Many fish are morphologically adapted for particular modes of feeding. A knowledge of their food habits in nature will enable the aquarist to select appropriate foods for captive fish. Top: the suckermouth catfish (*Plecostomus*) is a vegetarian scavenger; middle: the tiretrack eel is a predator; bottom: a scat (*Scatophagus*) feeds on both plant and animal matter.

and consume crustacean parasites from other species of fish, but these "cleaner fish" also feed on zooplankton or benthic organisms.

Fish that concentrate planktonic plants or animals by straining the water are called filter feeders. Finely spaced gill rakers enable them to separate food from the water efficiently. Some species use brushlike pharyngeal teeth to further concentrate or select foods. Many African cichlids are filter feeders, as is the paddlefish (*Polydon spatula*).

Bottom feeders or scavengers include some carps, loaches, sturgeon, and catfish, which are able to obtain nourishment from plant and animal debris (detritus) and from the invertebrate animals that live in the sediment. Bottom feeders often have sensitive fleshy lips and ventrally positioned sucking mouthparts. Barbels are a type of sensory appendage common to bottom feeders. Some species even have taste buds in their abdominal skin. The type of sediment influences feeding success. Soft sand and mud are easily processed, but coarse bottom gravels can interfere with feeding. Sediment makes up 10 to 20 percent of the stomach contents of some bottom-feeding fish. The sediment may carry nutrients in the form of fine particles or surface films and may also aid in the digestion of algae or other foods.

Only a small percentage of fish are totally predatory, but some of these are adapted for preying on a specific type of organism. A consistent source of small fish, worms, or live plankton may be required to keep such species well fed. However, some predatory species can also be trained to accept frozen foods or even dry diets.

Several species, from more than a dozen freshwater or marine families, have evolved into highly specialized parasites which feed on the fins, scales, or body fluids of other fish. Some species have even evolved to mimic the appearance and behavior of harmless fish. Such behavior allows a parasite to approach its host with less likelihood of being recognized as a threat.

Feeding Stimuli

Most species of fish can eventually be trained to eat prepared diets, but not all diets are equally acceptable to all fish. Even the most nutritious diet cannot maintain a fish that fails to recognize the food. Recognition is affected by instinct and by training. The interaction of feeding stimuli is complex. Hunger, security, and state of health are important motivational factors that are easily overlooked. Temperature, water quality, and illumination (duration, direction, and intensity of light) are especially important. Cyclical rhythms—including seasonal, reproductive, tidal, and solar cycles—control feeding activity in the wild and may persist in tank-reared fish.

Many fish will not feed after being moved to a new tank, whereas others will approach food within minutes of capture from the wild. A new fish that fails to feed for a day or two is not cause for concern, but longer fasts may require changing the diet or the conditions under which the fish is held.

If the tank is arranged to mimic a natural environment, the fish may be calmed and therefore may feed better. For some, this can mean as little as including a piece of plastic pipe or a clay flower pot for shade, but providing a well-landscaped tank for timid fish is never a mistake. Aquaria can be so brightly lit that some fish refuse to feed. The intensity of illumination should be reduced if fish stay in hiding or cluster in the corners.

Fish locate food by various visual, chemical, or mechanical clues. After locating a potential food item, fish frequently examine and even taste it before deciding to swallow. Many predatory species swallow prey quickly and regurgitate unsuitable foods later. Because of differences among species, broad generalizations about the most important sensory characteristics are inappropriate. Fish can often be trained to accept unique foods. Recognition of these new foods may not involve previously important clues.

Flavors: Olfaction and taste are important for most species and may be especially significant for bottom feeders and others in turbid water. Although there are specific anatomical receptors for taste and smell, flavors must dissolve in the water to be detected. Fish do not necessarily respond to the same chemical stimulants as humans. Although some food ingredients stimulate fish to feed, a number of others are actually repellent. Certain amino acids, nucleotides, and carboxylic acids have attractant properties. Sweets and fats are less effective. Mixtures of synthetic amino acids approximating the composition of natural foods are more powerful as feeding stimulants than are single compounds. Combinations of organic chemicals may soon be developed to augment or extend the flavor of natural ingredients in prepared foods. However, synthetic chemicals alone do not yet elicit activity equivalent to that of fresh foods. Seafoods are especially strong attractants. Experimentation re-

Many predacious fish are not easily trained to accept nonliving food. A consistent supply of live foods may be required to keep such fish healthy. The large South American tiger shovelnose catfish (*Pseudoplatystoma fasciatum*) is among these species.

mains the best method to determine acceptable flavors for fish foods.

Sound: Sound is important in the feeding behavior of some fish, such as channel catfish (*Ictalurus punctatus*). Scattering food over a small part of a catfish pond can cause a frenzied search for food by fish throughout the pond. Fish commonly congregate in the feeding area even before the fish farmer arrives, possibly because they have detected the sound of his footsteps or his truck.

Buoyancy and color: Buoyancy is also important for some species. Fish adapted to feeding at the surface may not pursue food which has settled to the bottom. Some bottom dwellers may not surface to take floating food either, but the majority of aquarium fish are less picky. Shallow-water species have good color vision, and color may be an important feeding stimulus. Lighter-colored foods seem to be more acceptable during initial training. Some species seem to prefer red or green foods.

Feeding of predatory fish: Many predacious fish are not easily trained to accept nonliving foods. Predators commonly utilize scent or touch to locate food or are triggered to feed by visual stimuli. For some species, the peculiar characteristics of live food are especially important to trigger feeding. Detection of prey can involve visual clues, vibrations, and even changes in electrical fields.

The food preferences of a predator newly introduced to the aquarium can be inferred by offering a variety of potential live foods. A method for training a predator to accept prepared foods is as follows. Provide a preferred live food until the fish is eating regularly, then gradually reduce the amount offered. Substitute freshly killed food organisms on subsequent days. Some manner of simulating movement, such as dropping the food into water currents at the tank surface, may be necessary to attract the attention of the fish. Introduce soft meaty foods for a portion of the killed organisms in later feedings. If prepared foods are still refused, try coating foods with a puree of organisms to which the fish is already accustomed. Training is more easily accomplished with small individuals before they have developed inflexible habits. Sometimes the training process can be accelerated by introducing other individuals of the same or similar species that are already trained to take nonliving foods.

There are undoubtedly many unique fish with such highly specialized food habits that they are impractical for the hobbyist to keep. For example, some marine fish feed on sponges, coral polyps, marine algae, or live zooplankton. It can tax an aquarist's ingenuity to supply the authentic article or to find substitutes. Fish recently collected from the wild can be especially difficult to train. As technology advances, appropriate prepared foods will no doubt be developed for species now thought to require living food.

Functional Anatomy of Feeding and Digestion

The digestive system of a fish is relatively simple when compared to that of higher vertebrates such as humans. However, there is great variation between species. Mouthparts of fish frequently are specially modified for unique food habits. Some species, such as seahorses and mormyrids that feed on zooplankton or small bottom invertebrates, have tubular sucking mouthparts. Such fish may be incapable of eating larger foods. In contrast, some predators capture and swallow prey much larger than would at first seem possible. Special joints enable them to open their mouths to enormous proportions while their esophagus expands to allow large prey to be swallowed whole. Some predators, such as the sea-trout (*Cynoscion nebulosus*) and the sargassum fish (*Histrio histrio*), cannot distinguish their own kind from other prey. Hatchery production of such cannibalistic species is particularly difficult.

Not all species have teeth, but when they are present they are often adapted for special functions. For example, predators such as gar and pike have needlelike teeth designed to incapacitate and restrain prey. On the other hand, predatory catfish generally have small teeth. These catfish, like many other predators, do not bite small prey but rather inhale them with suction created by the mouth and gill flaps. The teeth of piranha are used to slash or cut flesh from prey rapidly, whereas the pacu, a closely related group, have teeth adapted for crushing nuts and fruits. The front teeth of parrotfish are fused into a powerful clipper, used for feeding on coral and coarse algae. Parrotfish also have a set of pharyngeal teeth at the rear of the mouth cavity to grind the food before swallowing. The pharyngeal teeth of tilapia are almost like a brush and help to separate minute foods from debris or water.

Anatomists define the stomach as the part of the gut that secretes acid. Hydrochloric acid secreted from stomach glands activates enzymes that digest protein. Tilapia are able to digest algae because stomach acids rupture the algal cells and release nutrients. The stomach of predators is often sac-shaped and can accommodate enormous amounts of food. Another stomach adaptation is found in puffer or blowfish, which can rapidly inflate their stomach with air or water. This adaptation protects the puffer against predation by increasing its size. A heavily muscularized portion of the stomach functions like a gizzard in some herbivorous and detritivorous species, including *Prochilodus, Citharinus,* mullet, and some surgeonfish. Digestion may be impaired in *Labeo* and other cyprinid fish, as they have no true stomach.

Partially digested food passes from the stomach into the intestine, where it is digested further and nutrients are absorbed into the body. Bile salts produced by the liver and stored by the gallbladder neutralize stomach acids and emulsify dietary fat. The pancreas secretes enzymes that digest carbohydrates into the intestine. The intestine of herbivorous species is often elongated and is more complicated than that of carnivorous fish. The inner surface of the intestine may be folded or have fingerlike projections that extend into the intestinal cavity. Such structures increase surface area for absorption. Small sacs, called caecae, open into the intestine of many species and also serve digestive or absorptive functions. Foods not completely digested during passage through the intestine leave the body through the anal opening.

Food Nutrients and Their Functions

Protein and energy: Protein is the major nutrient required for growth of fish and, on a dry-weight basis, makes up most of the body structure. The importance of proper protein nutrition cannot be overemphasized. The essential components of proteins are amino acids, which are used by fish to synthesize new body tissues and enzymes. In addition, proteins are a significant source of dietary energy. Proteins vary in their ability to support growth, depending upon their source and processing. Nutritionists often use purified casein (milk protein) or a blend of casein and gelatin to provide the protein in research diets. Although limited amounts of casein or gelatin are sometimes included in formulated feeds, seafoods and fish meals provide the best combination of digestible amino acids. Feed dried at very high temperatures loses nutritional value, because essential amino acids bind to other components and become unavailable.

Fish are especially efficient at converting food to body tissues, so they need less food to grow than do many other animals. However, since the diet of fish contains relatively little carbohydrate matter, the amount of protein is high as a percentage of the diet. Because protein is the most expensive part of the diet, it is important to feed just the right amount and type for best growth. Excessive dietary protein is ultimately excreted as ammonia by the fish.

The amount of protein required in the diet depends upon several variables, including the species of fish, the growth rate, and the amount of natural food available. In a typical production scheme for trout, five or more foods are fed in sequence as the fish grow. These dry foods vary in particle size and level of protein to match the specific requirements of each size of fish. A similar phase-feeding regimen has also been developed for catfish. Tropical fish hatcheries are not usually so large as to make phase feeding necessary for cost control. However, by selecting ap-

Newborn fish such as these channel catfish (*Ictalurus punctatus*) grow rapidly and require a very rich food for maximum growth and survival.

propriate foods for each stage of production, producers and hobbyists can benefit from accelerated growth rates and improved fish health and survival.

Fish fry and larvae grow rapidly and require a very rich diet for maximum growth and survival. In the wild, protein makes up 50 percent or more of their diets on a dry-weight basis. High-protein foods are important in the hatchery, too. The protein requirement of fish gradually decreases as they gain in size. Young adults of many species can be reared on foods containing 35 to 40 percent protein. Less protein may be appropriate for some older fish but not usually for breeders. Foods produced for pond use usually contain only 25 to 35 percent protein, because pond fish are expected to forage for much of their food. Protein requirements are dramatically affected by water temperature. When fish are held at cool temperatures, their growth rate falls, so lower dietary protein levels may be appropriate.

Fats and essential fatty acids: Food components that can be separated in the laboratory with solvents such as ether or chloroform but not with water are called lipids or crude-fat. Several different classes of chemicals can be isolated from lipids, including triglycerides (true fat), fatty acids, steroids (precursors to hormones), phospholipids, and several important vitamins and pigments. We commonly refer to crude-fat or lipid simply as fat for convenience.

Fats can supply energy for normal body needs, sparing proteins for growth. Carbohydrates can also serve this function. If a feed is well designed, it will supply just enough energy for maximum growth without producing fatty fish. Tank-reared fish are especially prone to fattiness because they expend little energy searching for food. Thus, the ratio of dietary fat to other food nutrients is important. Most production feeds contain only 5 to 8 percent fat on a dry-matter basis. Even so, greater amounts of fat are appropriate for very young fish, for carnivorous species offered foods low in carbohydrates, and for egg development. Additional processing steps are sometimes used to raise the fat content of hatchery diets to 12 percent or more.

Nutritionists caution against using too much saturated fat, such as beef tallow, in fish feeds. Hard fats are not digested easily and can interfere with metabolism at temperatures below their melting point. Dry commercial feeds are usually balanced for level and type of fat, but the amount of fats in fresh meats can be deceiving. Beef heart can vary from about 15 percent to more than 50 percent on a dry-matter basis. Only the leanest cuts of meat should be used as fish food, and these should be carefully trimmed to remove all visible fat, or a nutritional imbalance is likely to result. Reproductive success of some fish species is reduced when nonessential saturated animal fats or vegetable oils make up too much of the diet.

Several carnivorous species require a source of fish oil in their diet to supply essential polyunsaturated fatty acids of the linolenic group. Recent evidence indicates that specific dietary fatty acids may also be important to reproductive success (survival of fertilized eggs). Fats commonly make up 20 to 50 percent of the moisture-free fraction of fish eggs. Commercial fish breeders and hobbyists have reported for many years that certain foods are especially valuable for conditioning fish to breed. However, the specific nutritional basis of fish reproduction has remained largely undetermined. Diets containing polyunsaturated fats derived from marine fish or invertebrates (krill, brine shrimp, clams, squid, or annelid worms) are increasingly being recommended for conditioning freshwater and marine fin-fish and shrimp to breed. The specific lipid composition of the fish and invertebrates used as fish food varies with the site of harvest, probably reflecting local differences in algae and their other foods. Lipid composition is at least one factor responsible for differences in quality among strains of brine shrimp (*Artemia salina*) used as food for larval fish.

Feed mills may use fish meals that include fish oils, or they may add oil to the diet. Several suitable oils, including cod-liver oil, are available to feed manufacturers. All the fish oils tend to turn rancid through oxidation, and they eventually can become toxic. Rancid fish oil has an especially disagreeable odor, although it can be hard to distinguish from that of the fresh oil. Feed manufacturers add chemical preservatives to the oil as protection.

Lecithin is a substance commonly separated from soybean oil. It contains phospholipids that are valuable nutrients and it facilitates the dispersion of dietary fat during digestion. A specific requirement for a lecithin supplement has not been proven for fishes, but it is sometimes added to foods at a level of 1 to 2 percent for the reasons mentioned above.

Carotenoid pigments: Fat-soluble carotenoid pigments (carotenes and xanthophylls) are responsible for the yellow, orange, red, and green colors of the skin, flesh, or eggs of many fish and crustaceans. The brilliant blue and violet colors of crustaceans also result from carotenoids, although the blue colors of fish have other origins.

There is mounting evidence that some of these pigments are important nutrients. Survival of fertilized eggs to hatching has been correlated to the concentration of pigments in the embryonic yolk and in the prespawning diet of the female fish. Carotenoid pigments may serve a protective function for delicate membranes and other sensitive tissues in the developing embryo. Astaxanthin, a red carotenoid pigment, is also reported to have reproductive functions in male fish. The amount of vitamin E (and other antioxidants) needed in the diet is higher when oil supplements or carotenoid pigments are included.

Some foods that are rich in pigments include brine shrimp, krill, and other species of zooplankton. Bright-red, orange, or yellow roe from fish and crustaceans is sometimes sold in fish markets. Roe is also rich in essential oils. Commercial sources for xanthophyll pigments include red fish oil, meals or extracts of fish roe and crustaceans (shrimp, krill, or crawfish), marigold petals, algae, alfalfa, corn gluten, annatto, paprika, and others. Purified or synthetic carotenoid pigments are also available. These are not the same as the food colors commonly sold in food markets.

Analytical determination of the carotenoid pigment content of an ingredient will not necessarily indicate the value of the ingredient in fish food. The various carotenoid pigments have different physiological properties that can even change during processing and storage. Furthermore, species of fish differ in their ability to metabolize specific pigments. Controlled feeding trials, using several species of fish, remain the best method to compare ingredients for color enhancement.

A catfish with ocular cataracts. Cataracts can cause blindness in fish given foods containing inappropriate levels of certain minerals, vitamins, or amino acids.

Carbohydrates: Carbohydrates such as starch and sugars make up 20 to 40 percent of most commercial foods. They apparently are not essential for growth, but they are inexpensive sources of energy. In fact, carbohydrates are so commonly distributed in feedstuffs that it would be difficult to exclude them completely from a practical food. Most fish tolerate 30 to 40 percent carbohydrate in their diet, but a condition similar to diabetes results when unbalanced foods are fed. Trout are normally given foods containing less than 20 percent digestible carbohydrate. Too much carbohydrate in the diet of very young fish can prevent them from obtaining enough of other essential nutrients.

Raw starch, the principal nutrient contained in cereal grains, is digested incompletely by fish. High levels of raw starch in the diet can even interfere with the digestion or assimilation of other nutrients. However, starch that is gelatinized by cooking is more digestible and often is used as an economical binder to stabilize foods against disintegration in water. Floating foods usually contain high levels of carbohydrate to facilitate processing.

Vitamins: Vitamins are organic compounds that serve as catalysts for many biochemical reactions in body tissues. Deficiency of almost any vitamin can result in retarded growth and increased susceptibility to disease. Some vitamins may be present in adequate amounts in common feedstuffs, but the cost of supplementing vitamins in a prepared food is low compared to the consequences of a vitamin deficiency. Current practice is to supplement the food with a prepackaged blend of vitamins, called a premix, when fish are reared in confinement or in high-density pond cultures. Purified research diets are commonly supplemented with fourteen vitamins: A, D_3, E, K, thiamine (B_1), riboflavin (B_2), niacin, pyridoxine (B_6), pantothenic acid, folacin, B_{12}, ascorbic acid (C), biotin, and inositol. Choline (a non-vitamin micronutrient) is also added. Ingredients that are naturally rich in conjugated B-vitamins, such as yeast and whey, are also commonly included in hatchery diets (even though newly developed vitamin premixes may make these unnecessary for most applications). This is because the conjugated forms of these vitamins tend to be more resistant to the leaching effect of water than are manufactured supplements.

Changes in culture practices or diet can change vitamin requirements. Fish stocked at low densities in ponds may obtain enough vitamins from the wild plants and animals that supplement their diet. This is one reason why simple foods that are unsuitable for aquarium use may be adequate for use in ponds. The requirements for several B-vitamins increase when fish are treated with antibiotics, because microbes that can synthesize vitamins in the gut are killed by antibiotic treatments. The requirement for vitamin A may increase when fish are exposed to stress. Certain dietary ingredients (including fish or vegetable oils, raw seafoods, and raw egg white) also in-

The mouthparts of the sheepshead (*Archosargus probatocephalus*) are functionally adapted for scraping and crushing. In this species and others, indigestible shell or sand in the diet may be important for the digestion of coarse foods such as algae. *Photo by:* Tom Smoyer, Harbor Branch Oceanographic Institute.

crease requirements for specific vitamins (including vitamins E and K, thiamine, and biotin). Vitamin E is another lipid component that has been correlated to hatching success. Choline chloride can react to reduce the potency of water-soluble or fat-soluble vitamins in a vitamin premix. Consequently, it is commonly added to manufactured foods separately from the vitamins. Several mineral nutrients can also catalyze vitamin breakdown; therefore, mineral supplements normally are not combined with the vitamins in a premix.

Feed mills generally oversupplement vitamins to compensate for losses anticipated during processing, storage, and feeding. Nevertheless, certain vitamins are among the most perishable components in the food. Vitamin C, for example, can be depleted from a dry food within a few months after manufacture. The feed industry is working to improve the shelf life of foods by developing stabilized forms of vitamins and by modifying processing and packaging methods. However, the best protection against vitamin deficiencies is probably to vary the diet regularly and to buy foods in small quantities that can be used up within a couple of months. The vitamin content will be prolonged by storing extra food and vitamin supplements in a freezer. Feeding fresh or frozen vegetables and live foods can serve to supplement the diet of aquarium fish.

Minerals: Minerals are required in the body for bones, teeth, scales, and tissue fluids. They also serve a variety of supporting functions in body chemistry. For example, iron in the hemoglobin molecule enables blood to carry oxygen to the cells. Calcium and phosphorus are the major minerals most likely to be lacking in fish diets. Fish extract some calcium from hard waters, but fish kept in soft water need calcium in their food. Natural forms of phosphorus found in plants are not available to fish in unplanted aquaria. Bone from fish or meat meal is an excellent source of both calcium and phosphorus, as are several manufactured supplements. Several other minerals, collectively called the minor minerals (because they are required in minute amounts), may also need to be supplemented in the food. Among these are manganese, iodine, copper, zinc, iron, cobalt, selenium, and possibly chromium. The minerals magnesium, sodium, potassium, and chloride are also essential in the diet, but usually are present in adequate amounts. Many minerals are poisonous if present in excess, so mineral supplements should not be added to the food indiscriminately.

It was mentioned earlier that silt and sand commonly make up 10 to 20 percent of the diet of bottom-feeding fish. These are probably ingested inadvertently with food, but nonetheless sand is important to certain fish. Species with a functional gizzard or pharyngeal mill can use grit to abrade algae and other foods for digestion. A hard surface on which to gnaw may also be important for marine parrotfish, triggerfish, and porgies, which commonly graze on coral rock or barnacles. Such fish may fail to prosper in an aquarium environment when denied their regular foods. A novel solution to this problem, incorporating food in a plaster matrix, is sometimes used in public aquaria. (For further information, see under "Plaster blocks.")

Fiber: Most research into fish nutrition has been

Sample formulas for tropical fish foods[1]						
	Gel	Pellet	Pellet	Paste	Paste	Granule
Protein content (%)[2]	40	45	35	45	35	50
Ingredients (%)						
Meat, fish, or shrimp	42	50	50	72	72	—
Fish meal	—	27	14	10	—	80
Rolled oats	11	18	31	9	20	—
Whole-wheat flour	—	—	—	—	—	11.5
Frozen spinach	10	—	—	—	—	—
Unflavored gelatin	5	—	—	—	—	—
Cod-liver oil	2.5	—	—	2	1	3.0
Bone meal	2	—	—	2.5	2.5	—
Vitamin mixture[3]	2.5	2.5	2.5	2.5	2.5	2.5
Guar or cellulose gum[4]	—	2.5	2.5	2.0	2.0	2.5
Sodium propionate	—	—	—	—	—	0.5
Vitamin E (IU)[5]	150	250	250	150	150	400
Water	25	—	—	—	—	—

[1] Directions for preparation are included in the text.

[2] The protein content given is for a food reduced to 10 percent moisture (air dry). Protein content is listed so that these formulas may be compared to dry commercial foods. Variations in ingredients can cause the finished foods to vary from the protein content shown.

[3] The amount of vitamins required depends on the composition of the particular supplement to be used. Follow the manufacturer's recommendations. Review the information presented under "Shelf life and vitamin refortification" in the text.

[4] Added as a preservative to inhibit growth of mold during drying.

[5] Added as an antioxidant to inhibit fat spoilage.

conducted with predatory fish, especially trout and catfish. These species have little, if any, ability to digest ingredients that are high in fiber content. Alfalfa meal, for example, is almost completely indigestible by channel catfish. When low levels of dietary fiber were added to the diet of fish fed purified research diets, growth rate and food conversion efficiency improved. However, higher levels of fiber reduced feeding vigor and growth rate. Dietary fiber facilitates the passage of food through the gut of higher animals, and it may serve such a function for fish as well. Young fish are less able to tolerate foods of low nutrient density and high fiber content, apparently because they are not able to obtain adequate amounts of nutrients.

Unidentified nutritional factors: Throughout the history of fish culture, there have always been certain food ingredients which apparently contained nutrients for which no requirement was yet proven, but which seemed to improve growth or reproductive success when added to a balanced diet, even in relatively small amounts. The active components of many such feedstuffs already have been identified. Consequently, nutritionists are able to select ingredients on the basis of known nutritional content rather than be bound by inflexible traditional-formula feeds. Premixed supplements can be added to guarantee that a feed formula will meet known requirements for vitamins, minerals, and fatty acids. Development of a suitable vitamin premix has made it possible to replace ingredients such as fermentation products (whey, yeast, and distillery by-products), wheat germ, and liver, previously essential for

Vitamins are essential for normal growth. The food offered to the four fish on the right had been stored for too long before use. The larger fish on the left was fed the same food after it had been refortified with vitamin C.

feeding trout. Suitable feeds have also been designed without fish meal using improved methods for processing soybeans and for synthe- sizing amino acids, along with new information about fatty acid requirements. Recent discoveries about the significance of fish oils and carotenoid pigments in reproduction have already been discussed.

Not all nutritional factors have yet been identified, however. Sometimes particular fish will refuse their food and only a change of diet will entice them to feed again. For example, some fish, including scats, surgeonfish, marine angelfish, and some loricariids, that feed heavily on algae or other plants, languish in captivity if vegetable matter is deleted from their diet. Leafy vegetables, such as spinach or lettuce, are suitable for some fish but not for all.

Biochemists recently have documented pharmacologic properties in literally thousands of extracts taken from marine plants and invertebrates. Many of these compounds have never been isolated and studied before. It is tempting to speculate that the special nutritional needs of some fish could stem from a requirement for previously unknown nutrients or from the protective action of certain foods against disease. A better understanding of the nature of unidentified factors should result from more complete knowledge of nutritional biochemistry and of the differing requirements among species. However, for the foreseeable future, prudent fish culturists and

feed manufacturers will continue to include certain ingredients in the diet as sources of unidentified nutritional factors. Specific recommendations for ingredients are discussed throughout this chapter.

Choices in Fish Foods

The development of scientifically prepared foods was spurred by a combination of economic factors and scientific accomplishments early in the twentieth century. The foods used in fish hatcheries of that time were made up mostly of fresh meat by-products, especially liver. Raw fishery products and dried feedstuff such as cereal grains and oilseed meals were not utilized effectively until the scientific bases of nutrition and the composition of potential feedstuffs were better understood.

It is now possible to prepare completely nutritious foods from a variety of common and inexpensive ingredients. Vitamins and other nutrients contained in fresh or live foods can be incorporated into prepared foods as well. Live foods and fresh meats or seafood are no longer essential for rearing most fish, although they remain of use for some species.

The natural foods of fish are highly perishable. The actions of degradative enzymes, microbes, and atmospheric oxygen rapidly change food composition unless it is stabilized by preservation. Fresh foods can lose nutrients and become unpalatable or even poisonous within a few hours of harvest, so preservation is essential unless a continuous supply of fresh food is available. Freezing and dehydration are the most common methods of preservation today, but moist shelf-stable foods are under development. Quick deep-freezing remains the best method of preservation, retaining most of the original nutritional content. However, frozen foods can spoil if allowed to thaw, and open packages must be carefully sealed to prevent freezer burn (uncontrolled dehydration and resultant rancidity).

Dried foods have the advantages of greater convenience and lower cost. Several of these have been developed, including dried natural foods such as plankton and several prepared foods. Most large-scale commercial fish farms use dried foods of one kind or another. Dried natural foods are not the equal of their live or quick-frozen counterparts. Essential nutrients, especially vitamins, can be lost during preparation. Essential fatty acids can turn rancid after drying if they are not stabilized by antioxidants. Such dried "treats" can still be palatable to fish, and they are popular with aquarists for this reason. However, they should not be used exclusively. Feeding a variety of dry prepared foods, perhaps supplemented with fresh meats and live plant and animal foods, is a practical solution (for further information, see under "Making Your Own Fish Foods" and "Live Foods and Their Culture"). Freeze-dried foods are superior to those dried by any other method and are generally worth their higher cost. However, these are also subject to oxidative rancidity if not stabilized by antioxidants, as are all dry foods that contain any unsaturated fats.

Prepared foods (flakes, meals, pellets, and granules) are made up of a variety of ingredients that are ground into a fine powder and sometimes processed further. Fine grinding blends minute amounts of essential ingredients, such as vitamins, evenly throughout the food. The simplest dry foods are ground meals. Meals are comparatively inexpensive to produce and are widely used for feeding small fish in ponds. A simple formula used on some Florida tropical fish farms combines one or two parts of oats and wheat by-products to one part of fish meal. Even after fine grinding, the ingredients in these foods can separate during feeding. Simple meal foods generally are not suitable for extended use in confined tanks and aquaria.

Pelleted foods are prepared by subjecting a meal to moisture, heat, and pressure to bind the ingredients together. With special processing and careful selection of ingredients, pellets can be made to resist disintegration in water for several hours. Several additives developed for the food processing industry can be used to bind ingredients that normally do not stick together. Among the most effective binders are gelatinized starch, alginate, and guar. Lignin, cellulose gums, and a number of other binders can be used where extended stability is not required. Water-stable foods are especially valuable for fish that eat slowly. Different formulas and processing techniques are used to produce floating or sinking pellets. Pelleted foods can be crumbled to make smaller granules, which then can be separated into several sizes for feeding to different-sized fish. Frequently, however, different formulas are prepared for fish of different sizes.

Flakes can be prepared solely from the same ingredients used in pelleted foods or fresh foods can be included. The ingredients are combined with water and blended into a thick slurry. The mixture is pressed onto a hot rotating drum, where it dries quickly and is flaked off by a knife blade.

Selecting Prepared Fish Foods

With the myriad of fish foods available, it may seem difficult to determine which are appropriate for your fish. Cost should not be the major consideration when selecting fish foods. Inappropriate or inferior foods do not save money in the long run.

Most popular species of aquarium fish will eat flake foods. Because flakes soften quickly without disintegrating in the water and do not sink rapidly, they are especially suitable for aquarium use. As the flakes gradually pass through the water column, they are progressively fed upon by top-feeding species (such as guppies), mid-water species (such as tetras), and bottom-dwelling species (many catfish). Granules are also fine for many fish. However, granules have the disadvantage of sinking rapidly and becoming lost in tanks with gravel bottoms. The excess food will spoil unless cleaned up by catfish, loaches, or other scavengers. Sinking pellets are a good choice for some bottom-feeding fish, because the pellets are relatively dense and permit a large fish to eat

Foods made at home can be varied to suit many difficult species, but must be carefully formulated to be well balanced.

its fill more easily than with flakes. Floating pellets are good for cichlids, catfish, goldfish, and other large fish that feed at the surface. Floating pellets are especially useful in garden pools or ponds, because the fish can be watched as they surface to eat, reducing the likelihood of overfeeding. Floating pellets do not disintegrate as quickly in the water as do most sinking pellets.

Foods for fish reared in aquaria, tanks, or cages must be formulated to supply all their nutritional requirements. These foods are called "complete." Some are referred to as "hatchery foods" or "cage foods." They tend to be more costly than incomplete foods intended for pond use, because they contain higher quality ingredients and are supplemented with extra vitamins. Foods recommended for feeding to pond fish such as minnows or catfish are not, as a rule, appropriate for tank use. Serious deformities related to nutritional deficiencies can result when they are fed to fish in aquaria, but more often the fish just waste away or succumb to disease.

Larger farm-supply stores frequently carry economical feeds that are suitable for pond culture. Commercial minnow foods are appropriate for small live-bearers. Catfish foods are accepted by many larger fish, including exotic catfish, cichlids, and goldfish. Trout foods are made in as many as ten sizes. Several different formulas are available as granules of different sizes. The smallest granules are designed for feeding to newly

hatched fish. They are also suitable for the young of many other species, but are too rich for most adult fish. Larger pellets can be crushed for feeding to adults of smaller species.

Good dry foods contain fish meal, grain, vitamins, minerals, and preservatives. Fishery products, such as fish or crustacean meals, are prominent in the list of ingredients. Soybean meal and meat and poultry by-product meals can make up part of the formula, but should not totally replace fish meal. Vitamins, minerals, binders, and preservatives are included to ensure complete nutritional content or to protect nutrients against deterioration during storage. Many of the substantial improvements in the quality of recent fish foods result directly from the use of these additives. Special ingredients sometimes are added as a source of unidentified nutritional factors. These include meats (liver and glandular meals), seafoods (fish roe, liver, and solubles), fermentation by-products (yeast, whey, and brewer's or distiller's products), wheat germ, algae, and others.

Fish may be attracted by colored foods, and therefore some manufacturers color foods which are naturally tan or brown. Only a few ingredients, however, contain the specific carotenoid pigments that can intensify skin colors of fish. Crustacean meals (shrimp, crab, lobster, brine shrimp, copepods, and krill), salmon skin or roe, red oil extracts of fish or crustaceans, marigold petals, alfalfa, paprika, certain algae, and the concentrated pigments astaxanthin and canthaxanthin are among these.

A few commercial foods contain androgenic steroid hormones, such as testosterone, which enhance skin color by accelerating development of breeding colors. Testosterone accelerates the growth rate of some fish, but can interfere with reproduction. Steroids added to the diet will sometimes result in reproductive sterility or can even reverse genetically female fish to functional males or vice versa. The specific effect of these steroid hormones depends on several factors including, but not necessarily limited to, the specific

When raw seafoods are used as feed regularly, fish can develop thiamine deficiency, resulting in failure to feed, clamped fins, and nervous incoordination. These are signals to change the diet. Here, a snook shows wasting symptomatic of hypothiaminosis.

chemical used, dose, duration of treatment, and age at start of treatment. Steroids can also be absorbed from the water by fish.

Even among complete foods there can be significant differences, so it is best to experiment and to alternate foods regularly. Fresh or frozen foods make a welcome change for most fish and are essential for a few species.

Shelf life and vitamin refortification: Sunlight and heat accelerate nutrient breakdown in dry foods, as does moisture. To prolong the potency of nutrients, supplies should not be stored in the culture room but rather in an air-conditioned room or in a freezer (below 0 degrees C or 32 degrees F). Dry fish foods that have accidentally become wetted should be discarded immediately. Bacteria and fungus can grow rapidly on the nutrients in wet fish food, creating risk of food poisoning.

Producers of bulk feeds for fish farming recommend using a product within two or three months of manufacture. The same time frame is probably appropriate for aquarium foods once the container has been opened. The main reason for this is because certain vitamins and oils in the feed gradually break down on contact with oxygen, a change that cannot be detected easily. Manufacturers can extend the shelf life of their dry fish foods through special processing and packaging. One technique is to top-dress the food with vita-

mins, fats, and preservatives just before packaging. Another is to seal the food in airtight containers with a controlled atmosphere such as nitrogen to exclude air. Of course, bulk commercial foods repackaged for sale under a new label are less likely to receive the same care.

When dry foods are sealed in airtight containers and stored in a freezer, they will remain fresh for much longer than those stored at room temperature. Refrigerators are less suitable for storage of dry foods because the food can become damp from condensation. Dry food stored for too long can still be used if it is alternated with fresh supplies. It is also possible to resupplement the food with vitamins, although it is not always practical to do so. Vitamin C is the least stable ingredient in complete foods. Refortification of this vitamin alone can improve growth rate and survival of fish fed an otherwise complete food.

To refortify small quantities of food, vitamins are blended into the food with a liquid carrier (20 to 50 milliliters of carrier to every kilogram of food [0.32 to 0.80 fluid ounces per pound]). The carriers most often used are oils, especially cod-liver oil. Tallow (beef fat) and soybean oil work well in many cases. Aquarists should review the information on fats presented earlier in this chapter. Liquified gelatin is also used as a carrier, although vitamins dissolved in water tend to be less stable than those mixed into oils.

Bulk vitamins can be obtained by mail from pharmaceutical or chemical companies. Vitamin pills, bought at a pharmacy and reduced to a fine powder with a mortar and pestle, are equally suitable as fish food additives, only less convenient. The purity of manufactured vitamins is equal to, or better than, natural supplements available from "health food" outlets. For 1 kilogram (2.2 pounds) of dry food, 50 to 500 milligrams of vitamin C should be used. The higher level provides a safe margin for vitamin loss in the water. Although fish may receive some benefit from multivitamin supplements designed for others (1 to 2 doses per kilogram or 2.2 pounds of food), the

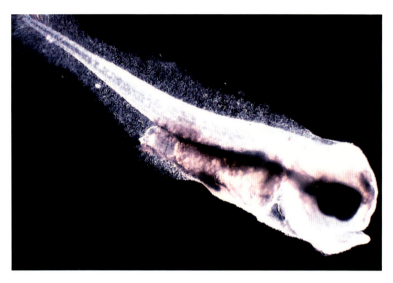

The young of many oviparous species, including *Scatophagus argus,* are so small that dried foods or *Artemia* nauplii are too large as a first diet. Smaller live foods such as rotifers, nematodes, mollusk larvae, ciliates, or even phytoplankton are essential to rear such species.

cies, but are not always well balanced. A good practice to follow is to vary the formula occasionally and also to feed complete, prepared foods. Several adaptable formulas are outlined in the accompanying table. Moist gels, pastes, and pellets can be prepared in a typical kitchen. Dry foods are more difficult to prepare properly. The hobbyist should take advantage of the excellent selection of commercial foods available rather than try to make all of his or her own food.

Gelatin diets: Among the simplest and most acceptable of home-prepared foods are gels. Formulas vary widely and are generally imprecise. A typical formula that uses gelatin as the binder is shown in the table. To prepare this food, mince raw meats or seafoods in a meat grinder or blender with a little water to facilitate blending. Blend in the gelatin, oats, and bonemeal and simmer the mixture in a saucepan until just about to boil (about 90 degrees C or 194 degrees F). Do not add vitamins until the mixture has cooled to 60 degrees C (140 degrees F). If the temperature is too high, vitamin potency will be reduced. If too low, the gel may not set properly. Dry fish foods can be added before the gel sets if a little more water is used in the formula. Minced vegetables can also be used if the amount of water is reduced. Pour the mixture into trays or freezer bags, and refrigerate it until hard, then store it in the freezer. Freezer bags with zipperlike closures are especially convenient; they can be filled to a depth of about 2 centimeters (about 1 inch) and laid on a flat surface to cool. Such bags are easily stacked to maximize freezer space. Gel foods can be chopped or shredded after they have set. If the formula is modified, the amount of binder should be limited to only as much as is needed to make a firm gel (usually 1 to 5 percent by weight). Excessive amounts of gelatin in the diet are not good for fish, because although it is pure protein, it is also poorly balanced. When a gel fails to harden, the cause is likely to be either insufficient cooking or too much handling during cooling.

vitamin requirements of fish are not really comparable to those of humans or other animals. Vitamin supplements designed specifically for fish have recently appeared on the market.

To prepare for resupplementing a dry food, oil carriers should be warmed, if not already liquid. Gelatin must be dissolved in water for use (2.5 grams of unflavored gelatin in 50 milliliters of boiling water, or 0.1 ounce to 1.8 fluid ounces). The gelatin solution or oil should be cooled to 60 degrees C (140 degrees F) before adding vitamins. The vitamins should be blended into the carrier. Then the mixture should be blended evenly throughout the food. A kitchen mixer works well for small quantities. A clean cement mixer is suitable for larger batches. To prevent spoilage, extra vitamins, fish oils, and refortified foods should be frozen in airtight freezer bags until used. These same procedures can be used to incorporate measured doses of medicine into a dry food. Medicated foods are especially useful for treating sick fish in ponds.

Making Your Own Fish Foods

Aquarists rearing large numbers of fish may prefer to prepare some of their own foods. Foods made at home can be varied to suit many difficult spe-

Paste foods and moist pellets: An early method for preparing traditional paste foods was to combine minced meat, oatmeal, and cool water in a saucepan and to bring this mixture to boiling while stirring constantly. After the mixture cooled to 60 degrees C (140 degrees F), other dry ingredients or vitamins were added and the food was refrigerated or frozen until feeding. The oatmeal and other cereals used as binders in early formulas required cooking, but heat is not essential now that there are binders capable of setting in cold water. Such food binders facilitate processing and can delay disintegration of the food in water, but they may also impair

Clear glass or plastic bottles are usually chosen for small working cultures of microalgae, ciliates, rotifers, and *Artemia*.

the flavor and digestibility of the food if used to excess. With a little experimentation, paste foods suitable for many species can be prepared in meat grinders, food processors, or blenders. Review the information provided in the table and elsewhere in this chapter for selection of ingredients. Even with binders, paste foods tend to dissipate and to foul the water more quickly than other types of food, so they should be used carefully in aquaria. Among the better choices of binders are alginates, pregelatinized starches, guar, and cellulose gum. These are used at a 1 to 5 percent level in the food, except for starch, which may make up 10 percent or more of the diet. Instant potato flakes and instant cereals for infants can be used as feed binders, but they require some heat to achieve maximum binding. Pastes can be frozen in thin layers and chopped into small pieces for later feeding.

Moist pellets are especially suitable for larger fish. The formulas shown in the table are prepared by passing the ingredients through an electric meat grinder several times. Most grinders come with an assortment of chopper plates having holes of varying diameter through which the food is extruded. Several sizes of pellets can be made by using different plates.

Plaster blocks: Dry foods are sometimes embedded in a plaster of paris matrix for feeding parrotfish and other coral grazers. A common application of this for the home aquarium is the

so-called "weekend feeder" block. A typical formula calls for about 250 milliliters (8 fluid ounces) of high-purity dental plaster (100 percent calcined gypsum or calcium sulfate hemihydrate), 125 milliliters (4 fluid ounces) of tap water, and 125 milliliters of dry feed. The plaster and water are blended until smooth (like cookie dough), and the dry feed is folded in. Expanded (floating) feed is recommended, because compressed (sinking) pellets can expand in water and cause the plaster to crumble. The soft mixture is pressed into a plastic ice cube tray or a lightly coated (with cooking oil) muffin pan. After hardening (from fifteen to sixty minutes), the blocks can be removed from the mold and stored in a refrigerator. Feed blocks are wet and therefore perishable. Plaster can increase water hardness in aquaria and thus may affect pH.

Dry starter foods: A formula for a granulated dry starter food (the first food given to fish) is given in the table, since these foods often are not available in the small quantities needed by aquarists. The dry ingredients used in a starter food should be ground to a fine powder. A food blender will work. Use a fine kitchen strainer to separate large particles for regrinding. Blend water into the dry mixture with a food mixer, about 250 to 400 milliliters per kilogram of dry food (4 to 6 fluid ounces per pound). Then spread the moist mixture in a thin layer (about 3 millimeters or 1/4 inch deep or less) to dry at room temperature in

An inexpensive plastic box with a thin layer of appropriate medium works well for culturing terrestrial species such as microworms and white worms.

front of a fan. If an oven is used to dry fish food, the nutrient content of the food is likely to be severely reduced. Redistribute the food from time to time so that it will dry evenly. Dry food can be crushed with a rolling pin and sieved through screen strainers for particles of appropriate size. Sodium propionate (a digestible food preservative) is included in the formula to inhibit decay while the food is drying.

Ingredients: Fresh fish are a source of high-quality protein and are widely accepted among fish. The best source is frozen fillets sold for human consumption. Roe (fish eggs) is a good supplement, although it tends to fall apart unless it is cooked or is combined with a binder. This tendency may be an advantage when very small fish are fed. Fatty species of fish, such as carp, herring, mullet, and mackerel, should be avoided for use in feedstuffs, as should spoiled fish and offal. Because fish fillets are deficient in vitamins and minerals, they should not be fed as the only food item. Caution should be employed with raw fish, as they frequently contain an enzyme that can destroy the vitamin thiamine, and because they can be contaminated by disease organisms. Feed mills precook fresh fish to reduce these risks.

Some fish will readily accept squid, clams, and scallops when they seem to ignore everything else. The precautions for shellfish are the same as for raw fish. Fresh shrimp or krill are very well accepted by fish. The shell should be removed to feed shrimp to small fish, or the whole body can be ground into prepared foods. Whole shrimp or krill can be fed to larger fish.

Meat is a valuable addition to the diet, but only lean cuts are acceptable and these must be trimmed of all visible fat. Aquarists like to use beef heart because it resists deterioration in water and is easily chopped to size. Beef heart can vary from about 15 percent to more than 50 percent fat on a dry-matter basis, depending on how carefully it is trimmed. Liver, spleen, or other pulpy meats should be blanched in boiling water to coagulate fluids that could otherwise foul the tank water. Poultry may be acceptable to fish that refuse the strong flavor of beef heart or liver.

Hard-boiled egg yolk, which is easily broken into fine particles, often is fed to fry as a first food. If whole eggs (fresh or dried) are included in a food, they should be precooked. Many dairy products dissipate quickly in tank water and spoil, making them unsuitable for direct aquarium use. However, whey, casein, skim milk, cheese rind, and other by-products can be included in compounded diets for flavor and nutrients.

Live aquatic plants will meet the special needs of herbivorous fishes, but the most desirable plant species often are not available. Vegetables are an acceptable substitute for many fishes, are commonly available, and are generally of good quality. They can be offered raw, although many species prefer softer blanched or prefrozen vegetables. Bright-green or yellow varieties are among the most nutritious. Blanched spinach and crumbled frozen lettuce are common favorites.

Quality control: There is more to food manufacture than picking the right ingredients to blend together. Changes that occur during processing and storage can destroy certain nutrients. Excessive heat during processing can inactivate vitamins (especially vitamin C) and can reduce protein quality by inactivating certain amino acids (especially lysine).

Fish and vegetable oils may spoil unless excluded from oxygen by careful packaging and protected by antioxidant additives. Certain mineral nutrients and some foods, including blood meal, can catalyze and accelerate spoilage by oxidative rancidity. Antioxidants protect dietary fat from rancid spoilage. Ethoxyquin is commonly used (at a 0.0125 percent level) to stabilize dry commercial foods. Vitamin E can be substituted in homemade foods, at a level of 400 to 500 International Units (IU) per kilogram (2.2 pounds) of dry food. Use 150 to 200 IU of vitamin E for moist foods. The acetate derivative of vitamin E is chemically stabilized. It retains its vitamin potency longer than unstabilized forms, but it is ineffective as a feed antioxidant.

Several common feedstuffs can contain chemicals that are toxic or that can reduce the value of other ingredients when they are combined. Toxins in oilseeds, including soybean, cottonseed, and rapeseed, can reduce the growth rate of fish if they are not inactivated fully during processing. Manufacturers must be especially diligent in selecting supplies when these ingredients are used. Fresh or dried eggs should never be fed raw, because a component in the egg white will inactivate the biotin (a vitamin). Many raw seafoods contain an enzyme which has been implicated in paralysis and death of fish from thiamine (another vitamin) deficiency. This enzyme is frequently found in fatty fish and mollusk species used for bait. It is less common in fillets prepared for human consumption, but even these are not without risk. A suspect ingredient can be fed for as long as several months before a problem shows up. By that time it may be difficult to trace the cause.

Live Foods and Their Culture

Early attempts to feed fish in captivity depended largely on live foods. Many species of smaller fish, invertebrate animals, and aquatic plants were evaluated repeatedly by trial-and-error methods to see which best supported captive fish. The live foods that eventually became most popular were those that could be collected easily and that were relatively nutritious.

Despite advances in fish nutrition, there remains a need for fresh foods, including live organisms. The least costly way to rear some fish is still to stock the fry, or even the adult broodfish, directly into ponds that have been fertilized to encourage growth of food organisms. Although many species of fish can take dry foods as fry, others require foods too small for conventional manufacturing methods, such as the minute, floating aquatic plants and animals collectively termed plankton.

Plankton can be netted or trapped from ponds for feeding to fish in tanks. A simple but effective plankton trap is made of a small submersible pump, about 1 meter or yard of flexible hose, a small reflector lamp, and a fine-meshed plankton net. The lamp is suspended just over the surface of the water, often clipped to a small raft, and when turned on at night it serves to attract plankton to the pump suspended below. The plankton is caught when water is pumped into the partially submerged net, which is also suspended from the raft or in a nearby bucket. To keep the animals alive until harvest, the water in the net should be aerated during warm weather.

Some types of live foods, including copepods and *Tubifex* worms, are known to carry fish diseases. The risk is greater for live foods collected from the wild than for those reared in captivity. Some of the animals collected as food also may compete with or prey upon aquarium fish. Marine plankton collected for food should be rinsed with fresh water before feeding, so as to limit disease introductions to a marine aquarium. However, rinses cannot be expected to remove internal parasites from an organism.

In marine fish hatcheries, a rotifer, *Branchionus,* is commonly offered as food for very small larvae. If they are gradually adjusted to reduced salinities, marine *Branchionus* can be used in freshwater aquaria as well. Rotifers need to be replaced more often in freshwater tanks because they perish more quickly than in a marine tank. There are freshwater rotifers, including species of *Branchionus,* but they are cultured less commonly for hatchery use. As the fish grow in size (or for hatchlings of larger size), copepods, small crustaceans or worms, and larvae of certain insects are useful.

Rotifers are stocked at a rate of about twenty organisms per milliliter (0.061 cubic inch) of tank water. When even smaller dinoflagellates, mollusk larvae, or ciliates are used for food, higher concentrations are appropriate. Lower concentrations can be used with larger fry fed larger zooplankton. The concentration can be calculated by drawing a sample of tank water into a calibrated pipette. Count the number of planktonic animals in a one-unit area (for example 0.1 milliliter) in the pipette. Multiply that count by the number of units in one milliliter (0.061 cubic inch) to determine the count per milliliter. Add more food as the count declines due to larval feeding or live-food mortality.

Controlled rearing of many aquatic food organisms is technically complex. Nevertheless, advanced aquarists may want to experiment with rearing microalgae and rotifers or other live foods. Seed cultures can be collected from the wild or purchased from scientific supply companies. Suppliers can be located through advertisements in aquarium magazines or a biology teacher may be able to recommend a source. Instructions for culture can usually be obtained from the same suppliers. Methods for hatching or culturing some of the more common live-food organisms follow.

Infusoria: Infusoria (ciliated protozoans, including *Paramecium*) are among the smallest live foods commonly cultivated for fish larvae. Freshwater and marine ciliates can be isolated and cultivated using the same techniques, with appropriate salinity. Ciliates commonly appear as a result of overfeeding. They reproduce rapidly, causing the water to turn cloudy, and eventually reach concentrations of hundreds or thousands of organisms per milliliter of water. Ciliate cultures can be started from pond or aquarium water and sediment, or they can be bought by mail. Larger organisms can be separated from ciliate cultures by pouring the culture through a fine sieve such as a brine-shrimp net. The choice of tank is not critical; a 1- or 2-liter (or quart) beverage bottle is convenient for experimentation. Suitable foods for culturing ciliates include boiled grain, lettuce, hay, and even dry fish food or dried milk. Commercial "infusoria pellets" also are available. It is important to limit the amount of food, however, or the culture will spoil quickly. When dry foods are used, 0.1 to 0.2 grams of food per liter of water per day is enough. Aerate the culture and keep it away from bright lights to keep out filamentous algae. Transfer about 5 percent of the volume to new media after about a week to start a new culture. Ciliates are very small, so a magnifying glass or microscope is useful to check the cultures. If you remove the airstone from a ciliate (or rotifer) tank, the ciliates will rise to the surface, where they can be dipped out for transfer to fish tanks. Ciliates can also be concentrated with a very fine sieve or a plankton net (20-micrometer mesh).

Microworms: One of the simplest live foods to culture for larval fish is the nematode *Panagrellus.* Also known as microworms, these are suitable as a first or second food for many fish too small to feed on brine shrimp. An excellent growth medium is made from 50 grams (1.5 ounces) of finely ground corn flour and 100 milliliters (0.42 cups) of water. If you add 0.5 milliliters of liquid propionic acid to the medium as a preservative, the culture will not spoil as quickly. Spread the medium evenly on the bottom of the culture vessel to a depth of about 5 millimeters (3/8 inch). Inexpensive clear plastic boxes (sold as shoe boxes) work well. Then sprinkle 0.5 grams (0.015 ounces) or more of live dry bakers' yeast on the surface. Transfer and distribute 5 to 10 percent of an established culture as an inoculum. Place a lid on the box and set it aside in a shaded area at room temperature. After about a week, the worms will begin to swarm up the walls of the box. A new culture should be started when the box is first opened, since the culture is likely to be contaminated during harvest. Worms can be scraped or swabbed from the walls for a week or more. Another method for harvest is to place upright pieces of plastic pipe or small plastic balls (about 5 centimeters or 2 inches in diameter) in the medium. After a few days, when these are covered by worms, they can be removed and the worms rinsed into the fish tank. Microworms are not easily separated from their media by sieves, washing, or sedimentation, since they are nearly the same size and density as their food.

Brine shrimp: Brine shrimp (*Artemia salina*) are minute crustaceans collected from saltwater ponds around the world. They are essential for operating hatcheries for several species. Their unique cysts remain viable when dried, so they can be stored on the shelf to be hatched months later when they are needed. One gram (0.03 ounces) of brine shrimp contains about 250,000 cysts. Each cyst contains a single animal, but not all will hatch. The different strains of *Artemia* vary in size and in nutrient content. Generally, strains from coastal waters are preferred for marine fish hatcheries. Freshwater culturists commonly use less costly strains from inland salt lakes.

Cysts are hatched in more dilute brine (1 to 3 percent noniodized table salt) or in seawater. Some strains hatch best in water of a particular salinity or pH; one should follow the recommendations of the supplier in this regard. One liter

(1.06 quarts) of brine is enough to hatch up to about 10 grams (0.3 ounces) of cysts. An excellent hatching tank can be rigged from an inverted plastic bottle with a conical neck, such as a soft-drink bottle. The bottom should be cut off and the top capped. Keep the tank warm (about 30 degrees C or 86 degrees F) and aerate it to prevent the cysts from settling out. Hatching begins in about twenty-four hours and continues over the next day or so. If the airstone is removed, the cysts will float or will settle to the bottom while the tiny crustacean larvae called nauplii will swim toward a light. Nauplii can be collected by siphoning them into another container. Pour the water through a very fine net to separate the nauplii for feeding to fish. The water can be returned to the hatching tank until the remaining shrimp have hatched. A variety of commercially available hatching devices facilitate separation of the newly hatched shrimp from their empty capsules. Unhatched cysts and empty capsules are said to cause intestinal blockage if they are eaten, and they should not be given to fish with the hatched nauplii. Nauplii hatched from regular (capsulated) cysts should be rinsed in fresh water before feeding them to marine fish in order to destroy diseases and competing organisms that might be transferred to the tank with the food.

Another approach is to decapsulate or remove the capsule from the cysts before hatching. Decapsulation makes separation of nauplii and unhatched cysts unnecessary and also disinfects the cysts. Since it involves the use of strong chlorine bleach, it should be done in a well-ventilated area and where a spill will not cause damage. The procedure is as follows. Add 5 grams (0.15 ounces) of cysts (or less) to 100 milliliters (0.42 cups) of cool tap water in a glass or plastic jar. Use fewer cysts per milliliter of water when larger batches are being decapsulated. Allow them to absorb water for a full hour and then add 75 to 100 milliliters (about 1/3 cup) of liquid bleach (5.25 percent sodium hypochlorite) to the jar. Cool the water with ice to keep the temperature below a lethal 40 degrees C (104 degrees F) when larger batches are treated. Aerate the solution or stir continuously to keep the cysts suspended until they turn from a brown color to orange (about five to ten minutes). Drain through a fine-meshed net and rinse with tap water. Rinse the cysts a second time with a 10 percent vinegar solution (equal to 0.5 percent acetic acid), and follow this with an-

other tap-water rinse. Decapsulated cysts can be hatched immediately or they can be stored in saturated brine (about 30 percent plain table salt) until needed. Cysts stored in brine will remain viable for months at room temperatures, even longer in the freezer.

Artemia begin to lose nutritional value soon after hatching, and they will perish within a few days unless they are fed microscopic foods such as unicellular algae or live yeasts. For these reasons, new batches should be started at daily intervals rather than hatching larger batches less frequently. They will not survive for long in fresh water either, so *Artemia* should be kept in salt water until ready to feed.

Earthworms and white worms: Common red earthworms can be cultured as food for larger fish. Earthworm beds should be located in a cool shaded area protected from freezing or flooding. If confined to a poorly drained or poorly ventilated box, they may suffocate if they don't escape first. Worms rarely leave a healthy bed, but when they do nothing will stop them, so indoor production beds are not recommended. A fenced and covered garden bed, or the corner of a garage or shed is better. Worm beds can be separated from walkways with upright 2-by-10-inch (5-by-25-centimeter) wooden boards. Start the bed fairly small and expand the boundaries as the population grows. Ten thousand or more worms can be grown in the space of a square meter or square yard. An excellent medium for earthworms can be blended from two parts of worm or cricket food (available from larger feed stores) and one part each of coarse wheat bran and dry sphagnum peat moss. Finely ground chicken food may substitute for worm food if the latter is not available. Propionic acid can be added to the medium at a 0.5 percent level to control molds that can grow in spoiling feed. Dry storage and good feeding practices will accomplish the same end.

Start the first bed with a 2- to 3-centimeter (about 1 inch) layer of loose crumbly soil or compost. Sprinkle a thin layer of medium over the surface and spray with water. Then add the worms to the bed. Feed them daily, giving only enough medium to last until the next day and spreading food evenly over the entire bed. The bed should be watered gently every day, taking care to saturate the new food, or the worms will be unable to feed. If the bed is kept too dry, mites eventually will take it over. Flies become a problem only when you overfeed or feed table scraps. Ants or rodents should be controlled by traps or poison baits placed outside of the bed. Adult worms congregate near the soil surface as long as they are fed daily. Tan or brown egg capsules about the size of a typed "o," called worm spawn, will also be found once the worms are breeding. It takes another three months, more or less, for the first hatchlings to reach maturity. Commercial worm farmers usually pick all the worms from a bed after a few weeks of breeding and use the top layer to start a new bed, but the bed will support good populations indefinitely if it is regularly harvested and if good medium is used.

The white worm (*Enchytraeus albidus*) is another popular oligochaete, about 1 centimeter (3/8 inch) long. It is often found in association with red earthworms and can be reared under similar conditions in a separate bed.

Feeding Practices

Proper feeding of aquarium fish requires patience and consideration. It is important to understand the fish and to appreciate differences among different species and at different stages in their life cycles. The amount of food required depends upon the type of food, culture conditions, and individual fish. In the wild, large fish may go for days at a time without feeding, whereas newly hatched larvae may feed almost continuously. Fish generally will not overeat, unless they are fed too infrequently. Two feedings a day are best for most fish, more often for newly hatched fry and perhaps less often for very large individuals.

Before feeding, frozen plankton and chopped meats are usually thawed and rinsed in a fine-meshed net to remove dissolved nutrients that might foul the water. However, some aquarists prefer to offer such foods while still frozen, because frozen foods tend to float and to disintegrate slowly as they thaw. Dry foods and minced moist foods should be fed a little at a time over a period of five to ten minutes or until the fish lose interest. Automatic feeding devices are convenient, but they must be checked frequently to be sure that they are still functional and properly adjusted. Blocks of gels or pastes dropped into the tank for feeding should be removed if not finished after ten to fifteen minutes. Fish may fail to feed for reasons other than satiety, and failure to feed may point to serious disease or water quality problems. Sometimes, a change of diet can increase feeding activity markedly.

Most problems with overfeeding result when wasted food spoils in the fish tank. Ammonia and other products of decay degrade water quality and stimulate disease organisms. Overfeeding can cause severe problems even in the large outdoor fish ponds of commercial fish farms. In an aquarium, it is not unusual for undergravel filters to clog from accumulated debris, including uneaten food. Problems associated with an occasional excess can be minimized by regular aquarium care, including cleaning the external filters, redistributing the bottom gravel, and exchanging water. Bottom-feeding scavengers, such as loaches and the common *Plecostomus,* help to clean up freshwater tanks. Several species of fish and invertebrates can be used in saltwater tanks for the same function.

Selected References

Anonymous. 1963. *Composition of Foods, Raw, Processed, Prepared.* Agricultural Handbook No. 8. Washington, D.C., U.S. Department of Agriculture. (A useful guide to compare the nutrient content of human foods that might be fed to fish.)

Anonymous. No date given. *Culturing Algae* and *Carolina Protozoa and Invertebrates Manual.* Carolina Biological Supply Co., 2700 York Road, Burlington, N.C. (Two pamphlets written by a commercial breeder of live foods.)

Anonymous. 1981. *Nutrient Requirements of Coldwater Fishes.* Washington, D.C.: National Academy Press.

Anonymous. 1983. *Nutrient Requirements of Warmwater Fishes and Shellfishes.* Washington, D.C.: National Academy Press. (The preceding two books, part of a continuously updated series of nutrition handbooks published by the U.S. National Academy of Sciences, are intended for use by professional nutritionists. They summarize information needed for formulation of commercial fish foods.)

Moe, M. A. 1982. *The Marine Aquarium Handbook: Beginner to Breeder.* Marathon, Fla.: Norns Publishing Co.

SeaScope, Vol. 1. Summer 1984. Aquarium Systems, Inc., 8141 Tyler Blvd., Menton, Ohio 44060. (A newsletter written by a commercial breeder of live foods and aquarium fish.)

Contributors

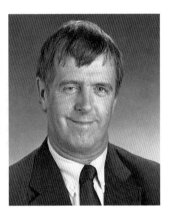 ROBERT E. REINERT did his undergraduate work at Ripon College in Wisconsin, and received his Ph.D. from the University of Michigan. He began his career with the U.S. Fish and Wildlife Service at the Great Lakes Fishery Laboratory in Ann Arbor, Michigan, before becoming Cooperative Unit Leader at the University of Georgia's Cooperative Fish and Wildlife Unit. From 1980 to the present, he has been on the faculty of the School of Forest Resources at the University of Georgia, teaching courses on fish physiology, fish biology, and computer applications. He has written numerous scientific articles, book chapters, and popular articles on fish physiology and aquatic toxicology.

 ROBERT A. WINFREE is a research physiologist with the Tunison Laboratory of Fish Nutrition, a branch of the U.S. Fish and Wildlife Service. At his Hagerman, Idaho, laboratory in the Snake River Canyon, he is leading research to improve the health and viability of hatchery-produced fish through applied nutrition. Dr. Winfree lived for several years in Florida, during which time he traveled throughout the Caribbean region working with freshwater and marine aquarium fish, both in research and in commercial production. He has also served as a technical and exhibit consultant for the world's largest totally recirculating marine aquarium system, at Walt Disney's EPCOT Center.

Diseases and Parasites of
Aquarium Fish

Physiological Mechanisms of Fish Disease

Richard E. Wolke

Pathological physiology appears a contradiction in terms—the abnormal normal. However, it is a well-recognized field of study in which the scientist seeks to understand the development and mechanisms of disease processes. It concerns itself with upsets in the dynamic biophysical and biochemical pathways which are necessary for life rather than with the static gross and histopathological findings reported in all autopsy protocols. For this reason, pathophysiology allows one to explain and to understand why an animal dies. It is the kind of information needed to bridge the gap between a prosecutor's report, which might read "chronic hepatitis" or "granulomatous hepatitis," and an appreciation of what killed the animal. This knowledge, coupled with clinical diagnostic skills and the principles of treatment, can help a breeder or culturist to prevent further losses and to recognize signs of illness should they arise again.

That is not to say that the term "chronic hepatitis" is without information. Rather, these terms presuppose that the reader has a pathophysiological knowledge of the liver and knows what will go awry under these circumstances and how this might be incompatible with life. To have such an understanding, one must know the functions of the major organs and how disease may alter those functions. In addition, one should be aware that some groups of animals have different organs than other groups of animals and that these organs may solve the same problem in a different fashion. Fish are such a group.

Fish are basically the same physiologically as higher vertebrates, but there are some surprising differences. For instance, fish are cold-blooded (poikilothermic), that is, they reflect the temperature of their environment. Most possess an air bladder for buoyancy and gills for respiration. They lack bone marrow and parathyroid glands. They possess baroceptors such as the lateral line and they have a corpuscle of Stannius, which functions in calcium metabolism. These kinds of differences cause the pathophysiology of fish to be unique and require its understanding to explain how piscine diseases result in death.

In order to determine the cause of death, the pathologist conducts a postmortem examination. This examination observes and records deviations from the normal using both the unaided eye and the microscope. The morphological deviations are referred to as lesions.

Lesions occur before death, and may reflect degeneration or cell death (necrosis), inflammation, healing, increases in cell number (hyperplasia) and increases in cell size (hypertrophy).

New growth (neoplasia), that is outside the body's regulatory controls (autonomous) is part of the cancer complex. All of these lesions occur in fish, and in this respect, fish differ little from homeothermic (warm-blooded) vertebrates. All of these changes are morphological, are seen as static, and represent an instant in time. Their development, however, reflects changes at the molecular level brought about and often maintained by disease-causing agents. Disease is an ongoing process, which, if allowed to continue unabated, results first in cell injury at the biochemical level, then loss of function which may progress from the cell to the organ and then to the organism, and finally, cell death. Cell death and advanced degeneration are the lesions apparent microscopically. The disease agents, therefore, affect cellular function and result in morphologic changes. If sufficient cells are altered, then the tissue or organ function is altered. Altered organ function may result in the organism's death or may cause malfunctioning of other organs, with the same outcome. It cannot be overemphasized that the body is highly integrated and organs are interdependent, so that separation of functions is an academic exercise which allows isolation for ease of understanding and classification. *In vivo,* this concept is absurd.

Disease agents responsible for cell and organ injury in fish are the same as those in higher vertebrates. They include microbiological agents (viruses, bacteria, fungi, protozoa, and helminths), chemical agents (heavy metals, pesticides, drugs, etc.), physical agents (mechanical trauma, heat, cold, electromagnetic radiation, etc.), nutritional imbalances, and possibly hypersensitivity reactions (allergy).

In order for the cell to live and reproduce, certain conditions must be maintained. These conditions are interrelated, and variations in one may cause variations in another. The organism will attempt to maintain the status quo (homeostasis) through autoregulation. If it is unsuccessful, the cell will be unsuccessful in living and reproducing.

The environmental conditions necessary for cell life include: maintenance of the cell membrane (wall integrity); availability of oxygen at suitable arterial partial pressure; availability of carbohydrates, proteins, and lipids for energy, structural purposes, and enzyme production; maintenance of blood pH between 7.23 and 7.5; maintenance of an appropriate blood osmotic concentration; and removal of waste products (urea and ammonia). In addition, the ultrastructural organelles of the cell must function so that energy may be produced (in the mitochondria), electrolyte and water exchange may occur with the intercellular compartment (the plasmalemma), enzymes may be produced (in the endoplasmic reticulum), cellular products packaged (in the Golgi apparatus), foreign substances and effete cellular products destroyed (by the lysosomes), and reproduction allowed (in the nucleus). If any of these environmental conditions are upset or if the organelles are injured, it is probable that the cell will begin to degenerate and eventually die.

To understand how a disease causes death, it is necessary to understand the major functions of the affected organs and how alterations of these functions may destroy the environmental conditions necessary for cell life. Of course, it is not the loss of the organ per se which is of major import, but rather the effect of that loss on the whole organism which causes somatic death.

Respiratory System

The gill of all fishes is a highly vascular organ which is in direct contact with the aqueous environment. It presents the blood to that environment, separating the two by a single or at best double epithelial cell layer, basement membrane, and an endothelium. By its very nature, it is subject to environmental abuse. Its only immediate responses for protection are to produce excessive mucus, for which it has specialized cells, or to increase its epithelial layer.

The functions of the gill are fourfold and are absolutely essential to maintain life: 1) respiration (exchange of oxygen and carbon dioxide); 2) excretion of ammonia; 3) acid-base balance; and 4) monovalent ion exchanges. Note that all are included in the list of environmental conditions necessary for cell life.

Respiration occurs because the red blood cell (RBC) carries the pigment/protein hemoglobin (Hb), which has an affinity for the oxygen molecule. The anatomical arrangement of the gill is lamellar, so that many vessels are exposed to the oxygen in the water. The partial pressure of oxygen in water is higher than in the RBC, which has given up its oxygen to body cells, and an exchange occurs by simple diffusion. The exchange works

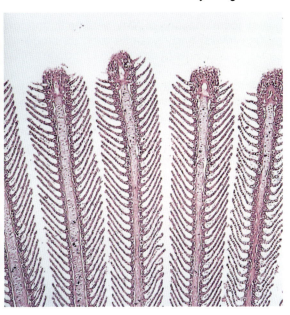

Normal gill with 5 primary lamellae and many secondary lamellae at right angles to them. 25x, hemotoxylin and eosin (H&E) stain.

because the flows of water and blood are opposite to one another, that is, countercurrent. This allows the most oxygenated water to oppose the least oxygenated blood. The exchanges are further dependent upon the partial pressure of CO_2 in the blood. That in water is less than that of oxygen, and this may be a limiting factor in the respiratory exchange. The pH may alter CO_2 concentration— the more basic the pH, the less available is the CO_2.

The ability to oxygenate tissue cells may vary from fish to fish, which explains the ease with which catfish or goldfish withstand poorly oxygenated situations, for instance, warm, stagnant aquaria or ponds. This ability is dependent on the affinity for, and capacity of, the Hb molecule for oxygen. If the percentage of Hb oxygen saturation is plotted against the partial pressure of oxygen, a typical sigmoid curve results. Fish with a high affinity for oxygen at a low partial pressure of this gas will have a curve to the left (catfish, goldfish, carp). Moving the curve to the right indicates a lesser affinity but a quicker release to tissue. This phenomenon would be present in highly active animals (mackerel, trout, salmon). Such a shift to the right will also occur if the partial pressure of arterial CO_2 or pH is increased (Bohr effect). These observations are important in regard to gill dis-

ease, in that fish with a higher affinity for oxygen may better adapt to and cope with chronic gill injury.

The second function of the gill is ammonia excretion. (Unlike higher vertebrates, the primary site for ammonia excretion in the fish is not the kidney.) Ammonia is excreted by both active and passive transport mechanisms. Active transport is dependent upon the exchange of Na^+/H^+ (sodium/hydrogen ions) for NH_4^+ (ammonium ion) and a transport enzyme. Ammonia (NH_3) buildup in the environment can be toxic because the fish is unable to pump enough of the product out of its body. The exact mechanism by which the ammonia is toxic is uncertain, but if water levels of the un-ionized form (NH_3) exceed 0.02 parts per million (ppm), death may occur.

Acid-base balance of the blood is also controlled by the gill. An increase in blood CO_2 will lead to an increase in blood carbonic acid and a drop in blood pH. This in turn is offset (buffered) by bicarbonate ions, which can be exchanged for water, Cl^- (chloride) ions, via specialized cells known as chloride cells. Hence, the two substances (carbonic acid and bicarbonate) playing a large role in maintenance of blood pH are in turn dependent upon the partial pressure of CO_2 and the activity of chloride cells.

A fourth gill function, monovalent ion (Na^+, K^+, and Cl^-) balance, varies with the fish's environment (salt or fresh water) and works in conjunction with the gut and kidney. In fact, of the three organs, the gill plays the smallest role but is responsible for Cl^- excretion via chloride cells and Na^+ via Na^+/K^+ ATPase in fresh and salt water. Since saltwater fish swallow seawater and since over 70 percent of the water is absorbed by the gut, marine fish must excrete these excess monovalent ions to maintain proper osmotic balance. Examination of gills from marine teleosts reveals more chloride cells and a different distribution of these cells than those present in freshwater animals.

It can now be understood how lesions of the gill may alter environmental conditions compatible with life. Gill lesions may be of two types: necrosis of the epithelial cells lining the lamellae, or hyperplasia (increase in number) of these same cells. In the first instance, the cells no longer present a semipermeable membrane, the integrity of the cell membrane is compromised, fluids flow back and forth, and bacteria, water, and

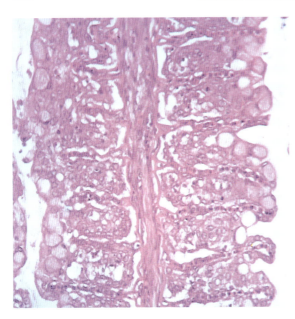

Gill with secondary lamellar epithelial and mucous cell hypertrophy and hyperplasia. 63x H&E.

debris are made available to the blood vessels. Similarly, in saltwater environments, fluid may rush outward from the vessels. Massive upsets in osmotic forces take place and infection occurs. These phenomena would be associated with a diagnosis of "acute necrotic branchitis."

If the causative agent is an irritant that does not immediately result in necrosis, the inflammatory response may be a protective overgrowth of cells (hyperplasia and hypertrophy). In this case, the problem is not that of breaching a cell membrane but rather that of having too many cell membranes. These present an essentially impermeable barrier to normal respiratory exchange, ion exchange, and NH_4^+ excretion. A histopathological diagnosis of "chronic hyperplastic branchitis with lamellar fusion" would be made in this instance.

Organisms and toxicants responsible for the necrosis of gills include myxobacteria (*Flexibacter columnaris* and *F. psychrophilia*), fungi such as *Saprolegnia,* protozoa (*Ichthyobodo*), and heavy metals (copper, zinc, and chromium). Organisms responsible for the proliferation of epithelial or inflammatory cells include *Cytophaga* (bacterial gill disease), *Mycobacterium* (tuberculosis), *Ichthyophthirius* (white spot disease or ich) and its marine counterpart, *Cryptocaryon,* as well as *Exophiala* and *Dermocystidium* (fungi). Poor water quality (combinations of NH_3, sediment, and low oxygen levels) and toxicants such as crude oil, benzene, and other hydrocarbons produce similar lesions.

A third lesion of the gill is infarction. This is a localized area of necrosis secondary to a slowed or absent blood flow (ischemia) resulting in a lack of oxygen (anoxia). While relatively uncommon, it may be the result of the fungus *Branchiomyces* growing within a lamellar blood vessel.

It can now be appreciated that destruction or overproduction of functioning gill cells may lead to oxygen deprivation, upset osmotic forces, upset acid-base balance, and retention of toxic waste products, all of which are incompatible with life.

The pseudobranch (false gill) is a structure arising embryologically from the first visceral arch. It lies on the under surface of the operculum and is easily seen as a reddish structure resembling gill tissue. Histologically, it also resembles the gill but it does not function in gas exchange; in fact, it receives oxygenated blood and shunts this blood directly to the choroid gland, which in turn oxygenates the retina. It is hypothesized that the pseudobranch may also function in controlling gases within the air bladder. The organ is seldom involved in pathological processes, but bacterial infections such as furunculosis, *Renibacterium,* and exposure to the constituents of oil spills may result in swelling, degeneration, and necrosis of its cells.

Circulatory System

The circulatory system of fishes is similar to that of higher vertebrates, although some genera contain auxiliary hearts in the caudal peduncle that assist with the pumping of blood. Arteries and veins are also similar in structure to those of higher vertebrates, with the exception that some arteries may contain valves. Both are lined by an endothelium which, on the surface of the atrium and ventricle, is multifunctional. That is to say, when stimulated by particulate foreign material in the blood and probable chemical mediators, these cells may become phagocytic. Stimulated cells are seen to swell, ingest foreign material, and eventually "bud off" to become free within the atrial lumen, hence they are called atrial macrophages.

The heart has been variously described as two-

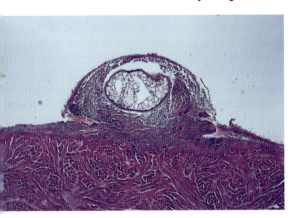

Heart with normal myocardial fibers overlaid by thickened pericardium, within which lies a parasite surrounded by inflammatory cells. 25x, H&E.

and four-chambered. There is an atrium and a ventricle. Just before the atrium is a sinus venosus and just after the ventricle, a bulbus (conus) arteriosus. The latter is composed almost solely of elastic fibers and helps maintain arterial blood pressure.

After leaving the heart, the blood passes via the ventral aorta to the gill and from the gill posteriorly by way of the dorsal aorta. Blood is returned through the caudal vein, cardinal veins, and sinus venosus.

Histologically, the myocardium is quite loose or spongiform in its architecture. One notes a compact outer cortical area and a spongy inner area. This loose arrangement allows blood to bathe the myocardial fibers, and blood cells are freely intermixed in the cardiac musculature. The ventricle and atrium are covered by a pericardial sac which appears closely adherent.

Diseases specific to the circulatory system are few. Arteriosclerosis has been reported in isolated populations of trout. Sanguinocoliasis, caused by an intravascular digenetic trematode and the piscine counterpart to schistosomiasis in humans, is not uncommon in salmonids. Most lesions present in the circulatory system are, however, secondary to other infections. Parasitic pericarditis due to metacercariae is common, as is bacterial myocarditis due to *Aeromonas*. Protozoa (micro- and myxosporidia) may also be found in the heart. Fungi such as *Exophiala* and *Branchiomyces* may infect arteries and veins. The latter is specific to blood vessels, apparently only able to grow in areas of high oxygen tension.

The effects of circulatory diseases are profound and cause damage because they result in anoxia. If the major pump is affected even slightly, anoxia of the brain may result, synapse or permanent neuronal damage ensue, and the animal may die. Vasculitis usually has more localized effects (infarction), with blockage of blood flow causing death of tissues that lie beyond the point of damage. Myocardial infarction (heart attack) is as yet unknown.

Alimentary Glands

Liver: The liver is the largest organ of the body. Commensurate with its size, it has multiple functions which cover a broad range of metabolic activities. The organ has, in addition, two capabilities which allow it to withstand extensive damage before the host shows serious signs of illness. These capabilities are regeneration and a large reserve of tissue that can be called upon when disease strikes.

Because of the liver's many functions, the signs of disease in affected animals are also multiple. They can be far more easily evaluated in warm-blooded terrestrial animals than in fish, both by physical examination and by clinical chemistry. However, liver destruction in the fish is no less incompatible with life than it is in mammals.

The basic structural unit of the mammalian liver is the lobule, which is composed of radially arranged cords (plates) of liver cells, the hepatocytes. They are arranged about a centrally located

Liver of this killifish (*Fundulus*) shows normal hepatocyte arrangement, but vacuolated areas contain spores of the coccidian parasite, *Emeria*. 100x, H&E.

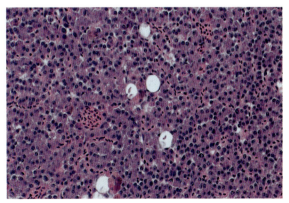

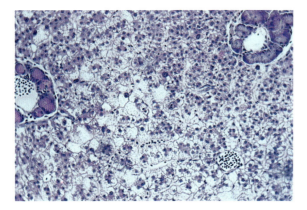

Hepatocytes of this killifish (*Fundulus*) liver are filled with fat. Vessels are surrounded by exocrine pancreas. 100x, H&E.

blood vessel known as the central vein. Blood enters the lobule from peripherally located portal triads. The triads are composed of the hepatic artery, portal vein, and the bile duct. Hence, the liver has two sources of blood: oxygenated blood from the hepatic artery, and blood carrying nutrients from the intestine via the portal system. This blood courses about the cords and empties via the central vein. The bile ductules carry bile from the hepatocytes through an ever-enlarging series of ducts to the gallbladder and eventually to the anterior intestine. The fish liver, however, is not so highly organized as that of the mammal. It lacks lobules and portal triads, and its hepatocytes are conical and arranged radially in double rows. The liver can be envisioned as a highly active organ metabolizing and detoxifying substances presented to it by the blood. Because of its anatomical arrangement, it can come in contact with disease agents or toxins by at least three routes: through the portal system, with source of origin the intestine; similarly through the bile system; and from hepatic blood in cases of bacteremias and toxemias. It is therefore evident that this organ frequently is involved when fish are exposed to aqueous toxins or suffer from generalized bacterial and viral infections.

A better appreciation of the tendency for the liver to be involved in disease processes can be acquired when one understands its physiological functions. The organ functions in three primary areas: 1) the metabolism of nutrients; 2) the detoxification of endogenous and exogenous toxicants; and 3) vitamin storage and the formation of plasma proteins and clotting factors.

The liver is responsible for the metabolism of lipids (from fats), carbohydrates (from sugars and starches), and proteins (from amino acids). In the first instance, it is bile which emulsifies fats in the gut, allowing their absorption. They are then carried via the portal system to the liver for breakdown and use. Fats are necessary for the production of cell membranes and as a source of energy. If the bile system is blocked or if bile cannot be formed properly, the lipids will not be absorbed for utilization. In instances in which aqueous toxicants are present, the ability of the hepatocyte to process fat may fail and the cells will fill with fats, leading to so-called fatty change or fatty metamorphosis. This is a nonspecific change which alerts the pathologist to the fact that something is amiss. Similarly, fatty change may occur in high-fat diets or with other upsets in nutrition, which are reflected by an increased hepatocyte lipid content. This is not an unusual finding in captive fish and reflects our rather primitive knowledge regarding fish nutrition. A deficiency of utilizable lipids, for whatever reason, is not compatible with cell life, especially as regards membrane integrity. Death of the organism may result, following a prolonged illness.

Carbohydrates are also metabolized within the liver. These sources of energy are used in the Krebs cycle and are stored as glycogen within the liver, which may store them as lipids when they are in excess. The liver plays a major role in maintaining blood sugars by manufacturing glucose from glycogen and from other sources (gluconeogenesis) such as amino acids. In cases of liver damage, these functions cannot occur. This results in a nonavailability of carbohydrates for energy sources, a condition inimical for cell life.

It is in the metabolism of proteins that fish differ most remarkably from homeotherms. Fish are ammonotelic rather than ureotelic. That is to say, they excrete ammonium ions (NH_4^+) as ammonia rather than as urea, which they also produce in smaller amounts. Higher vertebrates are ureotelic and uricotelic. Nonetheless, the source of NH_4^+ in each instance is the deamination of amino acids, and in the case of carnivorous fish, primarily the deamination of arginine. This deamination produces ATP from ADP and thereby energy. In other respects, however, the fish liver appears similar to homeotherms in its nitrogen metabolism. It is responsible for formation of new amino acids and for the synthesis of protein.

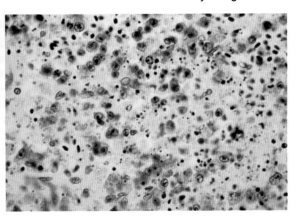

Exposure to high levels of dimethylnitrosamine resulted in necrotic, nonfunctional hepatocytes in this fish liver. 100x, H&E.

Labile proteins in carnivorous fish frequently are used for energy, even before lipid utilization. Hence, destruction of liver tissue prevents transamination and synthesis of proteins, and in carnivorous fish, results in loss of an important energy source. If amino acids are not available to viable cells, then reproduction and production of structural elements and enzymes cannot occur.

The liver is also responsible for detoxification of endogenous and exogenous toxicants. Endogenous means substances produced by the body which, in excess or in the wrong place, may be toxic. An example is bilirubin, an important constituent of bile. Bilirubin is a breakdown product of hemoglobin, the oxygen-carrying pigment of the red blood cell. In its initial stages of formation (hemobilirubin), it is toxic in excessive amounts. It is detoxified by conjugation with glucuronic acid. The conjugation takes place in the liver and results in cholebilirubin, a water-soluble, relatively innocuous substance. Similarly, exogenous toxicants such as benzo[a] pyrene also may be detoxified, in some instances also with glucuronic acid. It is important to note that the liver may produce toxicants inadvertently. When metabolized by the liver, some substances such as polycyclic aromatic hydrocarbons (PAH) are changed to a form which is highly toxic or carcinogenic. The organ does not always function in the best interest of the host. It can be appreciated, however, that because of its high metabolic activity, its wide range of biochemical reactions, and its ability to break down substances, the liver is of great interest to the pathologist and toxicologist studying aquatic pollution.

A third area of liver function is the metabolism and storage of vitamins and the production of plasma proteins and clotting factors. Of primary interest are vitamin A, which is stored in the liver and supplied to other organs on demand, and vitamin K, needed for the intrahepatic production of the clotting factor, prothrombin. Both are fat-soluble vitamins and cannot be absorbed from the gut if the liver is not producing or supplying a sufficiency of bile.

The liver also functions in the production of fibrinogen, a blood protein. This protein is the precursor of fibrin, which forms the meshwork of blood clots. Liver destruction may lead to generalized hemorrhaging, with decreases of blood oxygen at the necessary partial pressure, and cell death.

Another plasma protein, albumin, is also produced within hepatocytes. This protein is the major substance responsible for the maintenance of a normal blood osmotic concentration. In its absence, fluid tends to run into the interstitial spaces, resulting in the condition known as edema, the collection of a normal fluid in an abnormal place. The most common example of this in fish is the swollen abdomen or "water belly" which is technically known as ascites. It is a condition which is seen in a number of piscine diseases and may be due to liver destruction.

Massive destruction of piscine liver tissue may occur due to such diseases as mycobacteriosis (fish tuberculosis), systemic fungal infections such as that caused by *Exophiala,* water-borne toxicants (dimethylnitrosamines), and coccidiosis. Many helminth parasites also spend some portion of their life cycles within the liver. Most cause only local lesions as space-occupying organisms, but when their encapsulating cysts break down, severe inflammation (granulomata) may ensue and in heavy infestations, considerable tissue may be destroyed. Vitamin E deficiency may lead to excessive lipid peroxidation and fatty metamorphosis, indicated by hepatocyte lipid overloading. Such degenerations may be precursors of more serious cellular problems and eventually lead to necrosis.

Pancreas: The fish's exocrine pancreas, unlike that of warm-blooded animals, is diffusely distributed throughout the interpyloric mesenteric fat. In some species (*Morone saxatilis, Fundulus*), the exocrine pancreas is found in the anterior liver surrounding bile ducts.

The function of the exocrine pancreas is to supply digestive enzymes to the foregut. The enzymes are produced within the acinar cells (zymogen granules) and dumped into a series of pancreatic ducts which culminate at the anterior intestine close to the bile duct. The enzymes responsible for the breakdown of fats are lipases, for starches are amylases, and for proteins are proteases. Digestion is therefore dependent on the proper functioning of the pancreas, with protein and energy sources seriously depleted in its malfunctioning.

Enzymes contained in the pancreatic cells are potentially toxic to the surrounding tissue. If the pancreatic cell membranes are destroyed and the various enzymes are freed, they may digest this tissue. The mesentery contains large amounts of fat which is broken down by the freed lipases. This condition results in steatitis, or the inflammation of fat, and is referred to as acute pancreatitis.

The agent most commonly responsible for pancreatic destruction is the virus of infectious pancreatic necrosis (IPN). It is responsible for mass mortalities of young cultured salmonids and is known to affect warm-water species experimentally. A similar virus has been reported in marine fish. It is not unusual to find pancreatic necrosis microscopically in aquarium fish. The cause of this necrosis is uncertain but may be viral in origin.

Pancreatitis is also secondary to systemic bacterial diseases such as those caused by *Mycobacterium, Nocardia,* and *Renibacterium,* as well as protozoan infections (such as those caused by microsporidia) and helminths (resulting in sanguinicoliasis and metacercariae). There appear to be no specific clinical signs associated with pancreatitis, though "corkscrewing" (spinning about the longitudinal axis) has been reported as a diagnostic sign of IPN in trout.

Gas bladder: The gas bladder does not function in respiration and is embryologically an outpocketing of the alimentary tract (esophagus). It is an elongate, distensible organ which lies in the upper peritoneal cavity just below the dorsal aorta and kidney. The organ is variable in shape, according to species. The carp bladder is constricted in its middle, resulting in two compartments, while some members of the fish family Gadidae have bladders which appear corrugated about their lateral edges.

The bladder may connect with the outside

Salmonid pyloric caecae (arrow) superficially resemble worms.

through a duct to the dorsal esophagus. Fish with this arrangement are known as physostomous and include the salmonids. They can empty their gas bladders rapidly and therefore can move vertically in the water column with ease. In most instances, however, the duct is absent (physoclistous) and gases are secreted and resorbed by a gas gland and a resorptive oval, respectively.

The function of the gas bladder is to aid the fish in maintaining neutral buoyancy so that muscular energy need not be expended to keep the animal at any level in the water column. Malfunctions of the gaseous exchange within the bladder may lead to an inability of the fish to dive or to excessive energy expenditure in attempting to reach the surface. In either instance, the animal would feed inefficiently and be subject to predation. Fish with gas bladder problems are often seen floating on or near the surface with distended abdomens. When disturbed, even major efforts will not allow the animal to dive. Similarly, a gas bladder unable to be filled may cause the fish to struggle to maintain a position in midwater or near the top. When fin movement is stopped, the fish will sink. While not immediately life-threatening, such malfunctions can lead to starvation and an inability to reproduce.

A number of organisms have been found to affect the gas bladder. Among carp, *Rhabdovirus carpio* and the secondary bacterial invader *Aeromonas hydrophila* result in a thickening of the bladder wall and a filling of its lumen with a tenacious material. Myxosporidia, trematodes, and the nematode *Philometra* have also been found within the gas bladder, often resulting in an inflammation. Two fungi have been incriminated in gas bladder disease, *Phoma* and *Philaphora*.

Digestive system: The piscine digestive system includes the oral cavity, esophagus, stomach, and intestine. However, some groups of fish (Poeciliidae, Cyprinidae) lack a stomach. All have a far less complex intestinal tract than homeotherms—that of fish may be designated simply as fore- and hindgut. Since the gastrointestinal portion may be rather short, special blind-ended outpocketings may be present to increase the absorptive surface. These structures often arise near the pylorus and are referred to as pyloric caecae. To the uninitiated eye, the caecae may be mistaken for small white parasitic worms (nematodes).

The function of the digestive tract is absorption of the three major classes of nutrients and water. The food is masticated to a small extent by the teeth, although in fish it would appear that the teeth help primarily to hold prey while swallowing. Like higher vertebrates, fish have stomachs which produce hydrochloric acid and digestive enzymes. In the foregut near the pylorus, bile and pancreatic enzymes (lipases, amylases, trypsin) are released which emulsify and reduce fats to smaller fatty acids, polysaccharides to simple sugars, and proteins to amino acids, all of which can then be absorbed across the intestinal mucosa. In addition, the pyloric caecae and the intestine also produce digestive enzymes.

The gut is composed of five layers; from within outward, these are the columnar epithelium and its basement membrane (mucosa), the submucosa, the muscularis interna (longitudinal smooth muscle), the muscularis externa (circular smooth muscle), and the serosa. Of primary interest is the mucosa, which gives rise to villi and may be further thrown into folds that increase the absorptive surface. The mucosa is a semipermeable barrier necessary for life. Since the lumen of the gut is essentially outside the animal, the barrier prevents lumenal bacteria from entering the bloodstream to cause disease. Further, it prevents a loss of fluid from within the body which would cause dehydration and death and manifests itself clinically as diarrhea. Damage to the gastrointestinal tract will therefore upset two of the environmental conditions necessary for cell life — availability of nutrients and blood osmotic balance. Compromise of the mucosal barrier allowing penetration of potentially pathogenic bacteria and production of toxins may cause death of exposed cells elsewhere in the body. Signs of gastrointestinal upsets in fish are difficult to observe. One cannot evaluate fecal changes as in higher animals; at best, chronic conditions manifest themselves in weight loss. At necropsy, gastrointestinal changes are similar to those observed in homeotherms.

Diseases affecting the digestive system are numerous. They include viral and bacterial infections such as infectious pancreatic necrosis, *Aeromonas hydrophila,* and *A. salmonicida.* In these cases the problem is usually acute and vascular. The submucosa may become congested, edematous, and even hemorrhagic. In severe infections, necrosis of the epithelium may lead to sloughing, dehydration, and death. At the necropsy table, early infections may be diagnosed by an empty gut with a catarrhal exudate. Later the gut will appear red, wet, and thickened in cross section.

Protozoa cause lesions of the gastrointestinal tract. Coccidiosis (*Eimeria*) may be an important problem in goldfish and carp. Nodular thickening of the gut may be followed by ulcerations. Scrapings of affected areas will yield oocysts. Similarly, tropical aquarium fish may be infected with the flagellates *Spironucleus* and *Hexamita* (formerly called *Octomitus*), which are generally included as the disease agents of hexamitiasis. Affected animals lose weight and have a tucked-up abdomen. The gastrointestinal tract is often empty, and small (1- to 2-millimeter or about 0.06-inch) ulcerations are present. Chronic intestinal infections also may occur, such as that caused by the

Gut of goldfish (central tubular structure). Gut wall is greatly thickened in response to a coccidian, preventing proper absorption of nutrients. 25x, H&E.

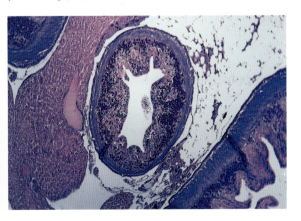

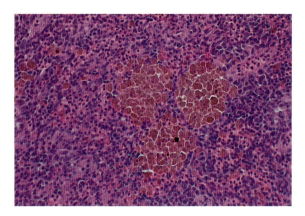

Normal clownfish head kidney with lymphoid
and hematopoietic elements. The triad of
brown circles is 3 macrophage aggregates.
100x, H&E.

microsporidian *Glugea,* which appears as raised
nodular white masses randomly involving the intestine. Impression smears of the cut surface
allow rapid identification of the organism.

Fungal infections occur as well but are less
frequent. Of interest to the aquarist are helminth
(worm) infections. Most adult helminths occupy
the gastrointestinal tract, and it is rare that a wild
fish has no parasite burden. In most instances
these parasites live in balance with their host; it
certainly is not to their advantage to be highly
pathogenic. Nonetheless, heavy infestations with
cestodes (tapeworms) or acanthocephalans
(thorny-headed worms) may result in weight loss
and even death. Diagnosis is difficult unless fecal
material can be observed and eggs identified.

Hematopoietic System

The piscine hematopoietic system includes
those organs producing blood cells, both the
red (erythrocytes) and white (leukocytes). These
organs are the spleen, the kidney interstitium,
the anterior (head) kidney, and the thymus. The
red blood cells (RBC) function to transport oxygen, while the white blood cells (WBC) function
to protect the organism against disease. Piscine white blood cells are similar to those of
other vertebrates in that they may be subdivided into two major groups: those which have
granules in their cytoplasm (granulocytes) and
those which do not (agranulocytes). The latter
group includes monocytes and lymphocytes,
cells of the lymphoid system.

The fish lacks bone marrow and produces its
red blood cells and granulocytes primarily in the
interstitium (surrounding tissue) of the tubular kidney, head kidney, and the spleen. The RBC are
oval, nucleated, and approximately 12 micrometers in length. They carry the pigment heme,
which, in conjunction with the protein globin,
forms the oxygen transport mechanism. The
number of red blood cells varies as to fish type,
an approximate mean number for bony fishes
being 2×10^6 per cubic millimeter (3.3×10^{10} per
cubic inch). It is of interest that the RBC count and
hematocrit may be quite variable, necessitating
larger experimental groups for controllable standard error. However, RBC counts in individual animals have clinical and diagnostic significance.

Diseases leading to RBC destruction or lack of
production cause death due to failure to oxygenate tissue. This anoxia (nonavailability of oxygen
at a sufficient arterial partial pressure) leads to cell
death, especially of the brain and heart.

Diseases decrease numbers of circulating
RBC, resulting in a decrease of hemoglobin and
the clinical condition known as anemia. Anemia
is a common problem in fish. It may result from
destruction of circulating cells (primary anemia) or
from a failure to produce RBC (secondary anemia). In secondary anemia, diseases which destroy the hematopoietic tissue prevent RBC
production. Examples of such conditions include
viral infections such as infectious pancreatic necrosis and infectious hematopoietic necrosis.
Renibacterium salmoninarum and mycobacteriosis may also destroy kidney and splenic tissue,
resulting in poor RBC production. *Aeromonas* and
especially *Vibrio* cause severe hemolysis and
acute (72-hour) anemia. Clinically, the infected
animals are lethargic, mortality is high, and at
immediate postmortem examination one observes very pale pink to white gill tissue.

These same diseases may be responsible for
a decrease in granulocytic cells, a condition
called leukopenia. The granulocytic cells of some
fish include cells which correspond to the neu-
trophils, eosinophils, and basophils of higher
vertebrates. The first of these cells in many fish
is not morphologically a true neutrophil, for its
cytoplasmic granules are gray with Romi-
noswsky stains and it is often mononuclear. It
functions in much the same way, however, being weakly phagocytic and found in early infec-

tions. Its job is to engulf and kill invading organisms. *Aeromonas salmonicida* (which causes furunculosis and ulcer disease of goldfish) is known to produce a toxin which destroys white blood cells, thus paving the way for the invading bacteria. Total counts of WBC are approximately 15 to 17 x 103 per cubic millimeter (2.5 to 2.8 x 10^8 per cubic inch) but may range greatly, depending on species. Of these cells, about 30 percent are granulocytic, 70 percent agranulocytic.

Seen with great frequency in most fish is the coarse eosinophilic granulocytic cell (EGC). This cell has bright red, large granules and is produced and found in the submucosa of the stomach. It is seldom seen in the peripheral blood but is commonly seen in inflammations caused by helminths. Its function is uncertain, but it may be related to the mammalian eosinophil.

Fish lack a true lymphatic system and lymph nodes. However, they do have lymphocytes, both large and small. There is mounting evidence that these cells may be divided into T and B subsets. The cells are responsible for antibody production and are produced in the thymus, spleen, and kidney. Their destruction results in immune repression, allowing disease to occur. In addition to lymphocytes, large (12 to 15 micrometers) monocytes are also produced. Monocytes are present in the circulation and migrate to sites of inflammation. There is debate as to whether some phagocytic (ingesting organisms and debris) cells arise from endothelium (blood vessel lining) and are fixed in position or migrate there from hematopoietic sites. In the first instance, one would have a functional reticuloendothelial system (RES) and in the second, the more modern concept of a mononuclear phagocyte system. It is academic, but there is argument for the RES when one considers the atrial macrophages of fish and the pleuripotential epithelial cells of the gill. All these cells have a phagocytic function and are present in more chronic infections such as mycoses, mycobacteriosis, *Renibacterium,* and verminous infestations. Again, destruction of such cells allows bacteria and fungi to gain the upper hand and eventually to kill the host. Diseases affecting hematopoietic tissue affect these cells as well.

An interesting structure in all fish is the macrophage aggregate (MA). It has been variously named, most recently being termed "melanomacrophage center." This name, however, is a

A heavily infected fish with gross dermal and opercular ulcerations.

misnomer since not all aggregates contain melanin. The MA is thought to be a precursor of the germinal centers of higher vertebrates, and it functions in the collection and breakdown of organisms and foreign substances. Increases in number and size of the MA indicate disease, starvation, and/or stress, suggesting that the structures may be of value in monitoring fish health. These groups of macrophages contain three pigments: hemosiderin, lipofuchsin, and melanin. The aggregates are commonly found in the spleen, kidney, and liver.

Integumentary System

Fish skin, well adapted to its environment, differs structurally in a number of ways from that of

Epidermis covering a scale highlights an encysted metacercaria (central bluish structure). The black pigment on either side gives rise to name "black spot disease." 25x, H&E.

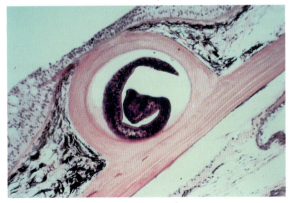

warm-blooded terrestrial vertebrates. The epidermis (outer skin) is composed, from within going outward, of a basal layer of germinal cells (stratum germantivum), a layer of squamous cells (stratum lucidum), and an outer circle. The cells formed in the basal layer move upward and outward until they are lost (exfoliated). Mitotic activity (cell division) is present in all layers. In addition, a number of special cells and structures may be present which are not present in homeotherms. These include: mucous cells which produce the thin mucous covering found on the surface of all fish; alarm cells, also known as club cells, which free a water-soluble substance that will alert other fish of danger; neuromast cells, which are multicellular organs of sense (tactile, odor, taste); chloride cells, which function in blood electrolyte exchange; pigment cells; white blood cells which serve a protective function; and scales.

The epidermis lies on a basement membrane which is above the dermis. The dermis is composed of a loose layer and a compact layer of connective tissue which also contain pigment cells (chromatophores).

The skin covers all surfaces, protects the fish from the outside environment, including microorganisms, and prevents upsets in fluid balance. It is, therefore, essentially impermeable and, in addition, its mucous covering contains antibodies (14S IgM) and lysozymes, which are antibacterial and/or antiprotozoal.

Because of its intimate relationship with the environment, the skin reflects many insults and is of clinical and diagnostic importance. For instance, when a fish becomes ill, one of the first signs is a change in color. Most frequently the fish becomes darker dorsally, and the diagnostician can see this change easily by looking down through the surface of the water. The darkening reflects changes mediated through the nervous system which cause the melanin-bearing cells to expand. (Lack of color may occur as well, but less frequently and later.) Similarly, increases in mucus production may occur in protozoal infections and in instances in which an irritant is present in the water. Commonly one may observe ulcerations of the skin. These ulcerations are often red in the center, white on their edge, and black on the periphery. The red center indicates hemorrhage; the white edge, dying (sometimes regenerating) epithelium; and the black periphery, an influx of melanophores. These ulcers may become cov-

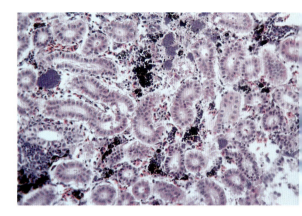

Salmonid kidney. Blue homogeneous areas to right and upper center are masses of *Aeromonas salmonicida* (furunculosis) bacteria. Black pigment is normal melanin accumulation. 100x, H&E.

ered with a white to brown cottonlike growth in fresh water which reflects secondary fungal involvement (saprolegniasis). These fungi, in the vast majority of cases, are saprophytes. The skin may reflect proliferative changes also. Reports of papillomas among saltwater fish are not unusual. Hyperplasia and hypertrophy secondary to protozoan infections are not unusual and appear as small to large white areas. Other neoplasms have been reported.

A common lesion of the skin in wild fish appears as small white or black spots (1 to 5 millimeters, or 0.04 to 0.2 inches) which are randomly distributed. These spots are the metacercariae, or encysted larvae, of various digenetic trematodes which may or may not attract melanophores to their outer cyst walls. Except in very heavy infestations, or infections of internal organs, they cause little damage.

The underlying cause of death in fish with extensive lesions of the skin is undoubtedly upsets in the electrolyte and osmotic balances of the blood. Hemorrhage also plays a role if ulcerations are extensive and acute, such as occurs in vibriosis.

Urogenital System

The urogenital system of the fish arises developmentally from a pronephros and the coelomic epithelium (gonads). The nephron (the functional excretory portion of the kidney) is not as specialized as is that of higher vertebrates but has a glomerulus, proximal and distal convoluted tubules, and in some instances, a collecting tubule, all of which dump into an archinephric duct. The latter carries waste products to the noncloacal bladder and, eventually, to a urogenital papilla. Products of the gonads (sperm and ova) also travel to the outside via the archinephric duct.

Although the fish is capable of producing urea, the primary function of the kidney is not the excretion of ammonia but rather the excretion or preservation of divalent cations (such as the ionic forms of calcium and magnesium). These cations are used to maintain proper electrolyte balance and therefore function in maintaining proper fluid distribution. Calcium is also needed for neuromuscular excitability and blood coagulation.

Fish regularly migrating from salt to fresh water (anadromous) or vice versa (catadromous) must have properly functioning kidneys to deal with the changes of the salts in the external environment. Destruction of the kidney will lead to upsets in interstitial and blood osmotic concentration, cellular hydration or dehydration, and upsets in blood pH.

The functions of the reproductive organs are self-evident. Destruction of these organs is not life threatening; in fact, sterile fish may grow more rapidly and result in a greater economic return to the culturist.

The urogenital system, especially the tubular kidney, is frequently involved in disease problems. A number of pathogenic bacteria may take up residence within the kidney and, in the process of reproduction, cause severe necrosis. Of interest to the hobbyist is *Mycobacterium,* which causes fish tuberculosis, and to the culturist, *Renibacterium salmoninarum,* which causes bacterial kidney disease. Both are chronic infections which result in slow, constant mortalities preceded by weight loss and/or poor growth. The latter is related to water hardness and the presence of divalent cations in the diet. It is reported that the harder the water, the lower the incidence and severity of the infection. *Aeromonas* may also strike the kidney, but it is more acute in its manifestation.

Mycotic diseases such as those caused by species of *Exophiala, Onchocronis,* and *Ichthyophonus* may be found in kidney tissue. Of the three, exophialosis is most prevalent and of greatest importance to the culturist.

Protozoa are also kidney pathogens, especially the coccidians and the micro- and myxosporidians. As these organisms reproduce and sporulate, they cause necrosis by expansion and pressure and may result in a severe granulomatous reaction. On occasion, external protozoa (*Trichodina* complex) may be found in the bladder and archinephric ducts. A disease of protozoan (myxozoan) cause, known as proliferative kidney disease (PKD), has become a major problem of the salmonid industry in recent years.

Diseases of the gonads are primarily of parasitic origin. Coccidiosis affects the testicles of both salt- and freshwater fish. Microsporidians cause necrosis of the ovary, and cestode larvae frequently cause marked inflammation of the ovary in many species of fish. All may be responsible for sterility.

Central Nervous System and Organs of Special Sense

The specialized and well-organized piscine nervous system uniquely suits the fish in its environment. The piscine brain lacks a cerebrum and is composed of sensory lobes, a cerebellum, and a medulla oblongata. The sensory lobes are the optic, which are located in the mesencephalon or midbrain, and the olfactory, which are preceded by the olfactory bulbs of the telencephalon or forebrain. Their functions are coordination of movement (cerebellum), sensory and motor control (medulla), sight (optic), and smell (olfactory). The degree of development of each part is often dependent on the habits of the fish. For example, bottom-feeding fish in murky water will have a more highly developed olfactory area than those depending upon sight.

The brain is surrounded by a rather simple meninx; clear differentiation into layers is not possible. The brain is further surrounded by a cushioning layer of liquid fat. Unlike higher vertebrates, fish have eleven rather than ten cranial nerves. The extra nerve functions in spinal sensation. In other respects, the cranial nerves are similar.

The organs of special sense include the eye, ear, olfactory system, taste buds, and lateralis system. The eye is highly developed, resembling all vertebrate eyes. It has a specialized retina with rod and cone visual cells and a lens which is capable of changing shape.

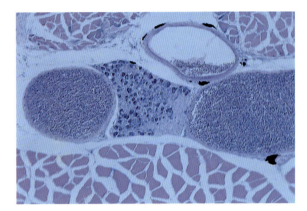

Section of a cranial nerve (center, dark and light blue) bounded on either side by spores (violet) of reproducing myxosporidia. 25x, H&E.

The ear is also highly developed, but lacks an external and middle division. Its inner portion contains semicircular canals and three chambers with otoliths. The organ functions in balance, with reception of sound waves. It is innervated by the eighth cranial (statoacoustic) nerve. The ear's innervation also includes the seventh cranial (facial) nerve, which in turn innervates the lateralis system of the head. This has led to conjecture about the function of the lateral line system, which may have some ability to sense sound waves.

The lateralis system or lateral line system is a baroceptor; that is, it is capable of sensing changes in water pressure. This allows the fish to sense prey or predators to the side or rear which it might not see. The system is composed of two canals which run the length of the body midlaterally and give rise to the so-called lateral line. In addition, there are cranial bifurcations of this system. The canals have pores to the outside and groups of sensory cells regularly spaced along their medial aspects. These cell groups are known as neuromast cells. The primary innervation to this system is the vagus (tenth cranial) nerve, but the facial nerve also plays a role.

The olfactory system is highly developed. Anteriorly the fish has two nasal openings on each side of its maxilla. These openings are in line, water passing through anterioposteriorly. Often the anterior nares have a flap of skin which may be extended to capture water or used to close the opening. The nasal chamber often contains folds lined by sensory epithelium. The anatomic arrangement of the sensory area varies greatly among families of fish. The sensory messages pass from the epithelium to the olfactory bulbs via the first cranial nerve and then are processed in the olfactory lobes.

Fish also have a highly developed sense of taste. Taste buds are plentiful on the tongue and throughout the oral mucosa. In addition, such sensory cells may be found in the skin of some species.

The consequences of a damaged central nervous system or sense organ are obvious. If the most primitive areas are involved, respiration or cardiac function will cease immediately and anoxia will result in cell death. Higher center damage will conflict with ability to feed or reproduce. In most instances, affected animals will become easy prey.

Few diseases of the brain have been reported in fish, and histopathological examination of brain sections rarely uncovers lesions. Vibriosis has been observed in association with severe granulocytic meningitis, as has an infectious pancreatic necrosislike virus. Recently, *Edwardsiella tarda* has been found in the brain of young catfish, resulting in marked encephalitis. Occasionally microsporidia may be present in brain tissue and cranial ganglia, as are metacercariae.

Lesions of the eye are more numerous. The most common clinical problem is exophthalmus, or protrusion of the eye from the orbit. This is a lesion often associated with viral and bacterial diseases. The protrusion may be due to postorbital granulomata or edema. Bacterial infections of the eye also occur, often due to corneal ulceration. The cornea may become damaged when captive fish in circular tanks touch the tank sides. Cataracts are a common problem and appear to be related to zinc or methionine deficiency. Similarly, vitamin E and vitamin A deficiencies have been associated with retinal degeneration and blindness in captive clownfish (*Amphiprion ocellaris*). A major parasite problem is *Diplostomum spathaceum* (eye fluke), a digenetic trematode which lives in the eye and causes blindness in salmonids.

Myxosoma cerebralis is a myxosporidian parasite of salmonids that occupies cartilage of the developing skull. It frequently affects the tissue surrounding the inner ear and damages the statoacoustic apparatus. Such damage is seen clinically as an inability to swim straight ahead. Affected animals appear to "chase their tails" or circle, similar to higher vertebrates with otitis. The disease is known as whirling disease and is a very serious condition which often requires slaughter of all fish in the affected hatchery.

Infections and necrosis of the lateralis system are diagnosed histopathologically. Few infectious processes have been reported. *Ichthyobodo necatrix* (causing costiasis) has been found in the head canal system. Heavy metals (cadmium, silver, zinc, copper) are known to cause a mononuclear inflammation of the supporting epithelial cells, but neuromast necrosis is rare.

It would appear that a sensory epithelium constantly exposed to the environment, such as that of the lateralis system and olfactory region, would serve to reflect water-borne toxicants quickly and perhaps diagnostically. However, this does not appear to be the case. The nasal epithelium, like the lateral line, undergoes inflammatory changes when exposed to heavy metals. It is interesting to note that salmon are capable of sensing and showing an aversion reaction to copper levels as low as 0.05 ppm. Seldom, however, are the sensory cells damaged in a fashion that can be diagnosed by the light microscope. A lesion of unknown origin sometimes present in the nares is the influx of tissue eosinophilic granulocytic cells coupled with vacuolar degeneration and necrosis of the sensory epithelium.

Endocrine System

Endocrine glands are ductless glands which vary greatly in their functions and control a wide range of activities. Among these are growth, metabolic rate, electrolyte levels, and immune response.

The piscine endocrine system is unique because it contains organs not found in the homeotherms and lacks a parathyroid gland. Endocrine glands present in the fish include the pituitary, thyroid, interrenal (adrenal cortex), chromaffin tissue (adrenal medulla), pancreatic islet cell, ultimobranchial, corpuscle of Stannius, and the urophysis spinalis or caudal neurosecretory system. The functions of the pituitary, thyroid, ultimobranchial, pancreatic islet cells, interrenal, and chromaffin tissue are similar to those in higher vertebrates.

The corpuscle of Stannius is found in the tubular kidney and grossly is present as random round white areas just below the ventral capsule. The gland may be mistaken for a lesion. It functions in calcium metabolism, causing hypocalcemia, and perhaps regulates sodium and potassium balance. The urophysis is a ventral extension of the caudal spinal cord. Its functions are multiple, including blood pressure regulation and osmoregulation.

Glands capable of such widespread effects may be subject to diseases that result in metabolic malfunctions and death in numerous ways. Examination of the literature regarding the pathophysiology of endocrine organs will reveal a dearth of information. This reflects the very few clinicopathological studies which have been done on metabolic diseases of the fish. Diabetes has been reported in Japanese carp secondary to the feeding of silkworm pupae (Sekoke disease).

Inflammatory reactions having multiple causes (for instance, IPN virus, furunculosis, mycobacteriosis, and exophialosis) may incidentally involve any of the endocrine organs. In addition, neoplastic processes have been found to affect the thyroid gland with some frequency, and goiter of uncertain cause is reported in many species of fish.

Selected References

Groman, D. B. 1982. Histology of the striped bass. *Amer. Fish. Soc.* Monograph no. 3.

Hoar, W. S., and Randall, D. J. 1969. *Fish Physiology,* Vol. 1. New York: Academic Press.

Hoffman, G. L. 1967. *Parasites of North American Freshwater Fishes.* Los Angeles: University of California Press.

Neish, G. A., and Hughes, G. C. 1980. Fungal diseases of fishes. In *Diseases of Fishes,* Vol. 6, eds. S. F. Snieszko and H. R. Axelrod, 1–159. Neptune City, N.J.: T.F.H. Publications.

Roberts, R. J. 1989. *Fish Pathology,* 2nd ed. London: Bailliere Tindal.

———. 1982. *Microbial Diseases of Fish.* New York: Academic Press.

Infectious Diseases and Parasites of Freshwater Ornamental Fish

John B. Gratzek, Emmett B. Shotts, Jr., and Donald L. Dawe

As do all animals, fish live in an environment that is full of disease-causing organisms and parasites. Parasites are organisms that derive their living from another organism, the host, and provide no benefit to the host. They are a diverse group ranging in complexity from viruses to arthropods.

In the interaction between host and parasite, the objective of a parasite is to invade the host, develop, and reproduce. The objective of the host, however, is to prevent the parasite from invading and reproducing. Thus, in this interaction parasites have evolved various structures and activities (virulence factors) which allow them to invade and survive in the host. Hosts have developed various structures and activities (defense factors) which act to prevent the invasion and development of the parasite. Several conclusions are possible in the interaction between virulence and host factors. The parasite may invade and be very active, leading to disease and possibly death of the host, an undesirable result for both host and parasite. The parasite may invade the host but be very mild in its activity, so that the host reacts mildly and both the host and parasite survive for a long time; this is desirable for the parasite and

acceptable for the host. A third possible outcome is that when the parasite invades, the host's defense reaction overwhelms the parasite and eliminates it. This is the optimal result from the host's point of view.

Fish possess a highly developed and efficient system of external and internal defenses against disease, which allows them to survive and prosper in an environment that contains large numbers of disease-causing organisms. With time and continued better understanding of the nature of this system, it should become increasingly possible to manipulate these defenses and responses to prevent infection. Prevention is much more effective and cost-efficient than treatment of disease.

Fish Immunology and Defense Factors

For convenience, the defense factors of a fish can be divided into two systems, innate and acquired. Innate factors are constant no matter what parasite the host encounters or how many times the fish has previously encountered the parasite. The innate system is composed of physical barriers such as skin and scales, secretions such as mucus, phagocytic cells such as macrophages, and proteins in the blood such as the complement system. The acquired factors are the components of the immune system of the fish that have the ability to react specifically with parasites, develop, and "remember" the interaction. Thus, in the fish immune system, the reaction to a parasite increases after an initial encounter with it. The components of the immune system are certain white blood cells, lymphocytes, serum proteins, and globulins. A great many specialized terms are involved in descriptions of this system and its workings (see accompanying glossary).

Before a parasite can develop and reproduce, it must enter the fish. The first host defense is, therefore, an epithelial membrane, either the epithelium of gills and digestive tract, or the skin or scales. In addition to being physical barriers that are difficult to penetrate, epithelial membranes are also covered with a moving layer of mucus which the parasite must penetrate before it can attach to the membrane. In the digestive tract, peristaltic actions move the mucus along. On the surface of the fish, mucus moves from the head to the tail, where it is shed into the water. Often, parasites become trapped in the mucus and are moved out of or off of the fish before they have a chance to attach to epithelial cells. In response to a surface irritant such as the attachment of a number of parasites, fish often increase their production of mucus. In some cases of heavy parasite invasion, one can observe strands of mucus stringing out from the fins and tail of the fish.

If a parasite manages to attach to a surface membrane and penetrates into the tissues of the fish, it encounters another component of the host's innate defenses, the phagocytic cells (from the Greek *phagos,* "to eat"). These cells are found in the circulatory system, wan-

---

Terms Commonly Used in Fish Immunology

Anamnestic immune response: Specific immune response to a second or later encounter with the same antigen. Also called secondary immune response. Based on the presence of memory cells and generally more rapid and intense than the primary immune response.

Antibody: A specific serum protein called an immunoglobulin (Ig) which is produced by an animal in response to the presence of an antigen and which reacts specifically with the antigen *in vivo* and *in vitro.*

Antigen: A substance which can evoke a specific humoral or cell-mediated immune response when present in an animal and which reacts specifically with the induced antibody or activated cell.

B-Cells: Lymphocytes whose development is not directly influenced by the thymus. Develop into antibody-producing plasma cells after contact with an antigen.

Cellular or Cell-mediated immunity: Immunity mediated by specifically activated cells (T-cells).

Host: A plant or animal that harbors parasites.

Humoral immunity: Immunity mediated by the presence of specific antibody.

Immunity (immune): State of being protected from infection or injury by virtue of being able to resist and/or overcome harmful agents. May either be acquired during life (generally as a result of lymphoid cell action) or be innate (native or constitutive for a species and requiring no previous experience with external agents).

Lymphocyte: Mature cell of the lymphoid tissue, also found in circulation. Major functional cell of the acquired immune system. Divided into several major functional classes of cells, including B-cells, T-cells, and memory cells.

Macrophage: A phagocytic cell found in circulation, lining blood sinuses, and wandering in the tissues. These cells present antigens to the lymphocytes to initiate an antibody response.

Memory cells: Resting lymphocytes (T- or B-cells) that have been primed by exposure to an antigen. These cells react rapidly on second exposure to the antigen and are responsible for the anamnestic response.

Opsonin: A substance that coats a particle and thereby promotes its uptake by a phagocytic cell.

Phagocytic cells: Cells capable of engulfing particles.

T-cells: Lymphocytes whose development is influenced directly by the thymus. Made up of subpopulations such as T-helper cells, T-cytotoxic cells, and T-suppressor cells.

T-cytotoxic cells: T-cells that react with antigens on cell surfaces and kill antigen-bearing cells. Major effector cell in the cell-mediated immune response.

T-helper cells: T-cells that interact with the antigen and produce soluble factors that help B-cells and other T-cytotoxic cells mature.

T-suppressor cells: T-cells that react with antigen and release soluble factors that suppress the activity of B-cells and other T-cells.

dering in the tissues, and lining vessels in organs such as the spleen and liver. Phagocytic cells engulf and break down damaged host cells. These cells are the "cleanup crew" for the fish, the method by which foreign material and damaged cells are removed from tissues. Phagocytic cells engulf parasites by extending arms of protoplasm around the parasite. When the arms meet, a vesicle forms in the cytoplasm containing the parasite. This vesicle is then joined by a lysosome, which is a package of enzymes in the cytoplasm of the cell. The joining of the lysosome and the vesicle releases the enzymes, which break down the parasite. Phagocytic cells also have metabolic activities that directly kill engulfed parasites.

The fish immune system: Once a parasite gets into the tissues of the fish, it also encounters the host's immune system. The active cells of the immune system are small lymphocytes which arise from a common stem cell source in the anterior kidney, but develop into two functional populations of cells. One population of small lymphocytes, referred to as T-cells, is influenced by the thymus. This population of cells contains three subsets: T-helper cells that aid B-cells in antibody production, T-cytotoxic cells which kill parasite-infected cells, and T-suppressor cells which act to regulate the immune response. The development of the other population, referred to as B-cells, is not influenced by the thymus. After contact with antigens, these cells develop into antibody-producing cells. Antigens are substances that stimulate the immune system to produce antibodies or specifically sensitized cells and react specifically with them. Antibodies are serum proteins—immunoglobulins—which are produced by the immune system in response to the presence of an antigen and which react specifically with it. After the phagocytes break down the parasite, they display some parasite components on their cell membrane. This is antigenic material, and the T-cells and B-cells of the fish will interact with this material to produce an antibody response. In the development of T-cells and B-cells, individual cells develop specific antigen receptors. Each cell can react with only one antigen, but within the population of T-cells and B-cells are cells that can react with all possible antigens. The phagocytic cell presents the antigen to T-helper cells and B-cells. These cells react through their antigen-specific receptors. The T-helper cells then release soluble factors that stimulate the B-cells, and the B-cells develop into antibody-producing plasma cells.

Antibodies are active against parasites and parasite products that are in the circulatory system or the tissue fluids. In these cases, antibodies can react specifically with an antigen to neutralize it, to kill the parasite, or to render the invader more vulnerable to phagocytic destruction. Parasites that develop intracellularly are not affected by antibodies. In this situation the T-helper cells stimulate the development of another population of T-cells, the T-cytotoxic cells. The T-cytotoxic cells recognize antigens on the surface of infected cells and kill the infected cells. The cell debris and parasites are then taken up by phagocytic cells and processed. This is a cell-mediated immune response, in contrast to the previously described antibody-mediated response. Cell-mediated responses are the major defense against intracellular parasites such as viruses.

In both the antibody response and cell-mediated response, the specifically reactive cells multiply after contact with the antigen. Some of the multiplying cells continue in their development to become mature plasma cells or T-cytotoxic cells. Others (memory cells) persist in an intermediate developmental stage in the fish for long periods of time. When the fish encounters the parasite for the second time, these cells mature rapidly, so the secondary (anamnestic) immune response is faster and more vigorous than the first response was. Thus, fish that survive an initial encounter with a parasite are more likely to survive a second encounter with the same parasite; they are immune.

Protecting fish by immunization: The anamnestic response in the immune system is the basis for protection of animals by immunization. To immunize an animal, one exposes it to the antigen and induces an immune response. This response generates a population of T and B memory cells. When this animal encounters the parasite in the environment, it will exhibit a secondary immune response. As a result, it will be more likely to overwhelm the parasite and recover from the infection.

Fish can be immunized against various parasites, but there are two major problems in developing immunizing agents for fish diseases. First, how does one get the antigen into the fish? The simplest method is to inject the antigen, as is done with mammals and birds. While this method will induce good immune responses in fish, it is impractical for large populations. Alternatively, fish can be fed antigens, and good immune responses will develop. Because this generally requires that the fish be fed the antigen over long periods, instability of the antigen in the food can be a problem. The most efficient immunization method is to immerse fish in an antigen suspension or spray antigen on them. In both of these procedures the antigen appears to be taken up through the cells of the gills. Both methods are practical for the immunization of large groups of fish.

A second major problem in immunization of fish involves the preparation of the antigen to be used. Because fish parasites have been studied less extensively than the parasites of mammals and birds, selecting the best preparation of the parasite to use as an immunizing agent is often difficult. Furthermore, in many cases different parasite strains have different antigens, and use of one strain as an immunizing agent will not induce protection against other strains.

Factors influencing immunological responses: How well a fish responds to an antigen can be influenced by a variety of external and internal factors. Since fish are poikilothermic (cold-blooded) animals, their metabolism varies with the water temperature. Changes in water temperature also influence the immune response of fish. Different fish species have different optimum temperatures, and fish exposed to antigens when they are in water below their optimum temperature respond very slowly to antigens. Thus, trout produce good immune responses at water temperatures where catfish produce very slow and poor immune responses. It appears that temperature changes influence the activity of the T-cell population more than the B-cell population. This temperature effect on the immune response of fish is thought to be one of the reasons why disease outbreaks occur in fish during times when the water temperature in ponds is changing.

Other water quality factors also influence the immune response of fish. It has been shown that the presence of heavy metal ions such as zinc, copper, and cadmium can depress the ability of fish to respond to antigenic stimulation. Recent reports also indicate that certain antibiotics such as oxytetracycline can depress the immune response of fish.

A major internal condition that influences the immune response of fish is stress. In the stress reaction of fish, the adrenal glands are stimulated to release adrenal corticosteroids. These hormones act to depress the activity of cells of the immune system. Thus, any activity that induces a stress reaction in a fish will reduce the ability of that fish to mount an immune response. Shipping, handling, crowding, introduction of new fish, and changes in water quality all will tend to reduce the ability of fish to resist infection. This is a major factor that must be considered when developing methods to immunize fish, since the immunization process itself is likely to induce a stress reaction.

Protozoan, Metazoan, and Crustacean Parasites of Ornamental Fish

Before turning our attention to specific examples of protozoan, metazoan, and crustacean parasites, it is important to remind ourselves of some general principles that can affect the degree to which such parasites will be a problem.

First, in nature it is rare to find a fish which is parasite-free. Fish often carry a parasite (or a population of them in the case of a few classes of parasites) without apparent signs of disease. The carrier fish may, in fact, have developed a degree of immunity to a particular parasite. Many carriers are mature fish. When introduced into a group of uninfected fish, they will initiate an epizootic (a disease affecting many animals at the same time) within the aquarium without showing any signs of disease themselves. For this reason, quarantine is a valuable procedure.

Second, many parasites that infect fish can be transmitted by direct extension through the water. Crowding of fish will increase the chances of contact between parasite and potential host. Additionally, crowding of fish will lead to changes in the organic load of the water, promoting parasitism. Third, many fish parasites require an intermediate host. For example, nematode eggs passed from fish are eaten by free-living invertebrates such as *Daphnia* and *Cyclops,* which are in turn eaten by other fish. If such intermediates are not found in the aquarium, transmission is impossible. For digenetic trematodes, a variety of wild-caught or pond-raised ornamental fish serve as the secondary intermediate host. In effect, such fish are dead-end hosts when in an aquarium.

Finally, since fish will eat dead fish in an aquarium, failure to remove dead fish from an aquarium may enhance the spread of the disease, especially in the case of sporozoan parasites. Mycobacterial infections are also transmitted in this manner.

The first steps toward a diagnosis: In any fish disease situation, one must begin with the history of the fish in question. Also, before establishing a diagnosis of parasitism, one initially must exclude other problems by reviewing basic aquariology practices such as water quality management, nutrition, and the possibility of noninfectious disease problems. Determine the source of the fish and how long they have been in their current situation. Fish taken from a pond will almost certainly have some parasites, many of which will be lost when the fish is transferred to new water. Wild-caught fish and some pond-raised fish also invariably will be infected with roundworms or flatworms. Fish which have been residing in an aquarium for several months to several years would not be expected to be infected with a parasite unless it were introduced with a new fish. Specifically determine whether fish have been treated and/or quarantined prior to the onset of the problem. Lack of quarantine is a common method of introducing parasites into an otherwise well-functioning aquarium. It is helpful to establish the history of previous disease problems and their treatment. Fish which have been treated with effective drugs in correct dosages would not be expected to have parasites which are amenable to treatment.

The next step should be to observe the fish closely. Although many sick fish react similarly to a variety of parasites, close observation of the behavior and external appearance of the fish is sometimes very helpful in arriving at a tentative diagnosis. In some cases, the parasite may be large enough to be seen with the naked eye, or the signs of the disease are so characteristic that a microscopic examination may not be required. Often, protozoan, metazoan, and crustacean parasites can readily be identified. In other cases, diagnosis of a parasitic problem can be very specific, involving dissection of the fish and microscopic examination of the tissues. A diagnosis reached by a necropsy and examination of tissues will provide the most accurate information on the particular parasite and provide a basis for the treatment required.

Clinical signs of parasitic disease: Many parasites of fish induce similar lesions and/or behaviors. Skin and fin lesions can include excessive mucus (best seen with overhead incident light), ulcerations, pinpoint hemorrhages, white spots, or whitish discolored areas which may be restricted to fins or to various areas of the body.

Behavior changes in severe cases of gill parasitism generally include depression—fish lie motionless at the bottom of the aquarium. Opercula (gill covers) may be flared and opercular movements may be increased, indicating respiratory distress. In less severe cases, fish may appear to swim in twisting motions while scraping gills on solid objects. This behavior, which appears to be an attempt to rid gills of an irritant, is called "flashing." When fish are parasitized, feeding behavior is usually reduced or absent.

Submitting samples for laboratory examination: Fish, like other animals, cannot be examined over the telephone. A clinical evaluation can best be made while fish are in an aquarium, during which time routine water-quality tests can be done. If a site or home visit is not possible, the owner may need to bring fish and aquarium water to the laboratory for examination. A small pail containing aquarium water is adequate for transporting the fish. The diseased fish should be brought while it is still alive. Fish which have recently died can be submitted by wrapping them in wet paper or towels surrounded by ice. Dead fish decompose rapidly, becoming useless for diagnostic purposes. For pH, ammonia, and nitrite testing, bring a water sample from the aquarium in a separate container. Some state veterinary diagnostic laboratories also provide testing for various heavy metals.

Biopsy procedures: In the laboratory, the fish may be biopsied. A biopsy is the microscopic examination of a wet mount of tissue which has been taken from a live fish. Tissues examined usually are snips of gills, skin scrapings, or small pieces of fins. In most instances involving sick aquarium fish, a fish owner will not allow a fish to be killed, but may not realize that biopsies can be done. Although there is always a chance that any laboratory manipulation of fish might result in death, the procedure is relatively straightforward when performed by a trained individual. An experienced diagnostician trained in biopsy recovery and microscopic examination of wet mounts for parasites or other pathological conditions can provide valuable information to help one determine which medicament should be used and what could be done to avoid future problems.

During the biopsy procedure, the fish is held in a wet hand or in a wet towel. Obviously, the procedure must be done quickly. It normally takes no more than a few seconds to recover both a fin scraping and gill snip. Doing the biopsy over an aquarium ensures that the fish will fall into water in the event that it is not properly restrained.

The procedure for obtaining samples differs slightly with the sample type. Often a diagnostician finds it helpful to position the tail fin of a small fish on a glass slide to facilitate removing scrapings from the fish. Just enough material is removed to allow for examination of the specimen without undue injury to the fish. A skin biopsy is directed toward removing a sample from an obviously affected area. A routine biopsy to check for external parasites is best done by making a light scraping of the tip of the tail fin.

Wet mounts of tissues for microscopic examination are made as soon as possible after the sample is obtained. A drop of tap water is added to the specimen, and a glass coverslip is placed over it to flatten the field of observation. Wet mounts of specimens from the skin or gill of saltwater fish use salt water or a 2.5 percent salt solution.

Anesthetizing fish: The decision whether or not to anesthetize a fish prior to taking a biopsy is based on the health, size, and activity level of the fish. For example, anesthesia may be unnecessary for a fin scraping, but if a gill snip is to be taken and the fish is active, anesthesia may be necessary. To minimize the chances of additional stress, anesthetization should be done in the water in which the fish was transported or in fresh water with the pH and temperature adjusted to

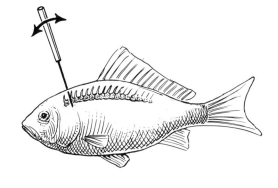

Fish can be pithed with a dissecting needle, which is inserted into the spinal canal and moved laterally, as illustrated here, or by severing the spinal cord with scissors.

that of the transport water. Water should be well aerated. Several anesthetic agents can be used (see table below), but their availability may be limited.

As a general rule, fish should be anesthetized for as short a period as possible, then removed immediately to fresh water for recovery. They should not be placed in a populated aquarium during recovery, since other fish may attack them and inflict injury.

Necropsy procedure: If enough fish are available, a microscopic examination of wet-mount preparations of gills, fins, and internal organs of a killed fish may be undertaken at the diagnostic laboratory. Select moribund fish for examination rather than dead ones; decaying fish usually teem with an array of saprophytic protozoans which were not associated with the initial problem. If there is a delay between the time of death and examination, the fish should be wrapped in a wet towel packed in ice. Even when this precaution is taken, some parasites will be impossible to observe after a period of hours. If fish happen to be preserved in formalin for histopathological evaluation, external parasites are likely to be found in the formalin. The parasites can be concentrated by centrifugation and a drop of the sediment can be examined as a wet mount.

Selected Anesthetics Which Have Been Used for Fish				
Anesthetic	Dose range per liter	Induction time (min.)	Recovery time (min.)	Source of chemical
Alka-Seltzer ®	1 tablet	1 – 2	5 – 10	Retail outlets
Quinaldine sulfate (2-Methylquinoline sulfate)	20 – 65 mg	1 – 3	5 – 20	Sigma Chemical
Benzocaine (ethyl p-amino benzoate)	25 – 100 mg	1 – 3	3 – 15	Veterinary supply outlets
Isoflurane	0.8 – 3.0 ml	3 – 8	3 – 10	Anaquest veterinary supply outlets

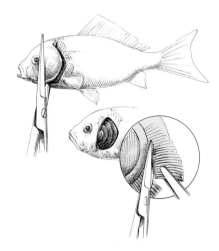

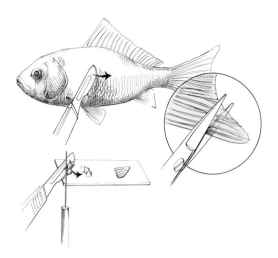

To make a gill lamellae preparation, remove the operculum. Cut out a section of the lamellae, avoiding the gill arch. Immediately place the section in water on a slide and tease the lamellae apart for microscopic examination.

Procedure for wet-mount microscopic examination of scales and fins. Use very small pieces of tissue, add plenty of water, and top with a glass coverslip. Apply gentle pressure on the coverslip to flatten the field.

Fish can be killed by pithing, that is, by severing the spinal cord with a sharp instrument. An overdose with an anesthetic agent is an alternative way of killing a fish. For this purpose, two tablets of Alka-Seltzer® in 500 to 1,000 millimeters (17 to 34 fluid ounces) of water will initially anesthetize and eventually kill the fish.

Examination of wet mounts of gills and skin should be done without delay after the fish is killed. To examine gills, remove the operculum and cut out a very small portion of the gill lamellae, avoiding the cartilaginous gill arch. Transfer the tissue to a glass slide, add a few drops of water, and use two needles to tease apart the gill lamellae. Top with a coverslip, and add enough water to fill the space beneath it completely. A slight pressure on the coverslip will serve to flatten the viewing field.

Scrapings of skin should be done from head to tail fin and should be deep enough to remove some scales. The tail fin should always be examined because parasites tend to accumulate there —perhaps from hydrodynamic effects or because these areas are devoid of scales. Take scrapings from any areas which do not look normal.

The examination of internal organs is an important part of the necropsy procedure. When the abdominal cavity is opened initially, bacterial cultures of kidneys and liver can be taken. Examination of wet-mount preparations of small pieces of

organs can reveal the presence of a variety of protozoan and metazoan parasites, granulomas, and bacteria. Staining of impression smears of internal organs such as the liver and spleen can provide a basis for the diagnosis of systemic bacterial infection. Sections of intestines of small fish can be mounted between two slides and examined for metazoan parasites by means of an inverted ocular microscope.

Factors influencing clinical illness: Young fish are more susceptible to parasites than are mature

To expose abdominal organs, three incisions are required. The first two produce a flap (A), which is then removed (B).To expose the brain, cut as shown (C) with a sharp scalpel or scissors.

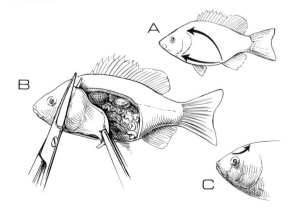

fish, partly because a smaller number of parasites is required to inflict damage to a host with a small versus a large body mass. Alternatively or additionally, mature fish may have developed specific immunity by response to previous subclinical infections or by exposure to antigens of non-pathogenic commensal organisms encountered in an aquatic system.

Environmental factors may enhance the clinical severity of parasitism, especially by those species involving the gills. Any water-quality change which can affect the efficiency of gills (pH, ammonia, nitrites, insufficient aeration) can exacerbate a parasitic infestation. Various parasites appear to be temperature-dependent. The common ciliated protozoan, *Ichthyophthirius multifiliis,* is predominantly associated with colder seasons. Coccidiosis of goldfish is a problem primarily during the winter season. Various types of monogenetic trematodes are affected by seasonal variations.

Immunity plays an important role in the relative resistance of fish to parasites. For example, fish have been shown to be resistant to *Ichthyophthirius multifiliis* after having survived an infection, and there is good evidence that fish will develop resistance to monogenetic trematodes.

Nutritional problems have long been associated with parasitism in mammals, and the same holds true for fish. For example, deficiencies in vitamin E appear to reduce macrophage activity in trout. From clinical experience it is apparent that fish fed a high-quality diet and kept in good water are less likely to develop a clinically apparent illness from parasites.

The presence of other parasites also has an effect. Mixed infestations are common and may influence the severity of the clinical disease. For example, fish debilitated with a massive infestation of metacercariae or nematodes are frequently the first to die in an epizootic caused by common external protozoans such as *Chilodonella cyprini.*

The pathogenesis of parasitic diseases: The eventual outcome of a parasitic infestation is variable. Parasites which kill fish can do so in many ways. Broadly speaking, these effects may be internal or external.

Internal parasites include those embedded in the skin as well as those which are located in specific organs of the body (muscles, intestines, liver, eyes, etc.) or within the peritoneal cavity. The types of parasites are diverse and include proto-

zoan ciliates and flagellates, sporozoans, nematodes, trematodes, and tapeworms.

Massive infestations of gills and skin can result in death due to damage to gill epithelium, which leads in turn to failure of respiration, osmoregulation, and excretion. Heavy infestations by intestinal protozoans such as *Hexamita* apparently interfere with proper nutrition, possibly due to competition for essential nutrients and/or damage to intestinal epithelium.

External parasites often provide routes of entry for pathogenic bacteria which kill the fish. Heavy infestations of migrating nematodes or metacercariae of digenetic trematodes may be tolerated if vital organs are not involved. (However, in many cases, vital organs are involved, resulting in unthrifty and disease-prone fish.) Sporozoan parasites such as *Mitraspora* in goldfish may lodge specifically in kidney tubules, causing bloat and

Ichthyophthirius, the causative organism of "white spot," is apparent on a goldfish (below). Microscopic examination (bottom) shows round to oval organisms from 30 to 1,000 microns in size which move by means of surrounding cilia. Found on gills and skin, the organisms are common in aquarium fish.

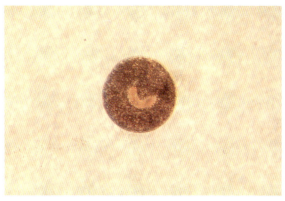

eventual kidney failure. Some parasites, such as species of *Oodinium,* may elaborate a toxin while infecting the fish.

External Protozoan Parasites

Ichthyophthirius multifiliis

This protozoan is the cause of white spot disease, commonly referred to as "ich." Distributed worldwide, it affects all freshwater fish and under aquarium conditions is very virulent. (The disease's counterpart in saltwater fish is caused by *Cryptocaryon irritans.*) These parasites are unique in that they have a complex life cycle which includes stages on the host as well as in the environment.

Ich is readily identified by most aquarists, who generally observe the disease several days after introducing new fish to the aquarium. Predominant signs include small white spots over the body. In some cases, infestation is limited to gills. Each white spot, called a theront, is the encysted feeding stage of a protozoan. Eventually, the theront enlarges, breaks through the epithelium, and drops to the bottom of the aquarium, where it attaches to objects such as gravel or tubing. At this point, the organism is referred to as a trophozoite (sometimes called trophont). The attached trophozoite then begins to undergo mitosis, producing numerous young individuals or tomites. Within the period of eighteen to twenty-one hours (at 23 to 25 degrees C or about 73 to 77 degrees F), hundreds of ciliated tomites are produced, which are released into the water. They actively penetrate skin and gill epithelium and enlarge until they are visible as white spots.

A diagnosis of ich can be confirmed by microscopic examination of skin or gills. Trophozoites may appear round or oval; occasionally a U-shaped nucleus is formed. Individual organisms vary in diameter from 30 microns to 1 millimeter. The organism moves slowly by means of cilia, which are observable with a high-power objective. *Ichthyophthirius* is one of the few fish parasites with cilia surrounding the entire organism.

Since medicaments cannot penetrate encysted theronts, all treatment is directed toward preventing reinfection of fish by free-swimming tomites. Malachite green, formalin, and malachite green–formalin mixtures have been used for treatment of freshwater fish. Copper sulfate has been used for saltwater fish.

In addition to chemotherapeutics, a few man-

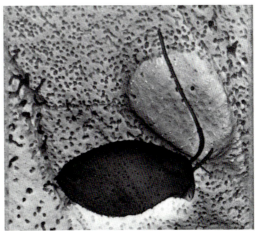

Ichthyobodo, or *Costia,* frequently affects aquarium fish. It is associated with respiratory distress and causes excess slime on the fish skin, which is noticeable as a white sheen (top). An electron micrograph (above) shows the small (less than 10 microns) flagellate that attaches to fish gills and skin.

agement procedures will serve to control infestation. Elevating the water temperatures to 26 degrees C (78.8 degrees F), several degrees over normal aquarium temperatures, for several days will tend to limit the infection by adversely affecting the heat-sensitive theronts as well as by enhancing the immune response of the host. This usually allows a cure in seven to ten days, but attention must be paid to temperature and pH regulation to avoid unduly stressing fish.

Heavy filtration with diatomaceous earth filters will tend to reduce the number of tomites. Transferring fish to a series of clean "hospital" aquaria once a day for seven days will limit the infection by keeping one step ahead of theront reinfestation. In practice, this can be done using one hospital aquarium and making daily water changes, and cleaning of the inside glass surface to remove trophozoites.

Some aquarists prefer not to medicate aquarium water because of the presence of plants and, especially in the case of marine aquaria, invertebrates. If fish are moved for treatment to a separate aquarium equipped with a heater and filter, parasites in the main aquarium will eventually die for lack of a host. To be absolutely sure that theronts are eliminated, make at least one complete water change along with removing debris from the gravel, and elevate the temperature several degrees over normal temperatures. In saltwater aquaria, it has been shown that aquaria devoid of fish for thirty days were still infective. With cleaning of gravel, water changes, and elevated temperatures, this period should be considerably reduced.

Ichthyobodo necatrix

This flagellated organism was previously named *Costia necatrix* and the name "costia" is frequently used as a common name for the parasite. A wide variety of fish can be infected, including trout, channel catfish, goldfish, and most common ornamental varieties. There is no known counterpart in saltwater aquarium fish, but similar organisms have been found on haddock off the coast of Nova Scotia.

Ichthyobodo infestations are seen more frequently in fish which have recently been shipped from a primary producer such as a goldfish producer or a tropical fish farmer. They are relatively rare in home aquaria since infestations normally affect fish at the wholesale or retail level, making them unsuitable for sale. The organism affects fish year-round, but the disease is more serious in warmer water.

Feeding directly on epithelial cells by penetration by the flagella, the parasite destroys gill and skin epithelium. Excess mucus production is frequently observed, which appears as a whitish film on the surface of the body. Respiratory distress is common, and fish appear depressed and refuse to eat. Some fish may die without visible external signs.

Diagnosis is confirmed by microscopic examination of wet mounts of skin and gills. Organisms are actively motile, small (7 microns), somewhat comma-shaped, and may be free-swimming or attached to cells by flagella. When attached,

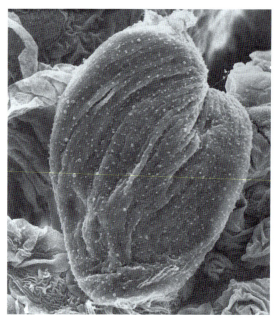

Chilodonella has slow motility, and shortly after wet-mount preparation (top), it is apt to die. An electronmicrograph (above) shows a flat organism that tends to be heart-shaped, with apical cilia and longitudinal striations.

parasites move in a circular fashion. Treatments with common antiparasite drugs are effective.

Chilodonella cyprini

There is no common name for infestations with this parasite. A saltwater counterpart, *Brooklynella horridus,* is occasionally seen. Freshwater fish infections are common in cultured food-fish species, goldfish, and a variety of freshwater tropical species. As with *Ichthyobodo necatrix* infestations, *Chilodonella* infestations are infrequent in home aquaria, since the infestation would initially be encountered by wholesalers and retailers.

Respiratory distress, clamped fins, and depression are the principal signs of infection. Excessive mucus production is commonly observed. In a few clinical cases we have observed fish with *Chilodonella* die suddenly without apparent signs of disease.

Diagnosis is confirmed by examination of wet mounts of gills and skin. Organisms appear oval and flattened with a suggestion of being heart-shaped. Cilia appear in rows. Size is approximately 50 to 70 microns. Organisms move slowly, oftentimes in a characteristically slow circular fashion. In a matter of minutes after wet mounts are made, the organisms begin to die. Dead organisms appear round, with a granular interior. The parasite is susceptible to common parasiticides. Salt at 0.3 percent (3 grams/liter) is an effective treatment.

Oodinium

Infections with *Oodinium* are commonly called "velvet," "gold dust disease," "rust disease," and "coral fish disease." Three or four species have been associated with freshwater, brackish, and marine fish. In pet shops where the organism has been established and perpetuated by contaminated nets, many species of fish can become infected. Some, such as the danios and their relatives, may show more severe clinical disease than others.

A dinoflagellate, *Oodinium* can vary in size from

40 to 100 microns. It is found on the skin and gills of fish and contains chlorophyll, which imparts color to the organism. The principal sign of the infestation is the presence of the organism on the fish skin, which gives the skin a fine dusty appearance. Observation can be enhanced by directing the beam of a flashlight on the dorsal aspect of the fish in a darkened room. On microscopic examination of wet mounts of skin and gills, pear-shaped cysts attached to the underlying tissues can be observed.

Contained within the cysts are the maturing

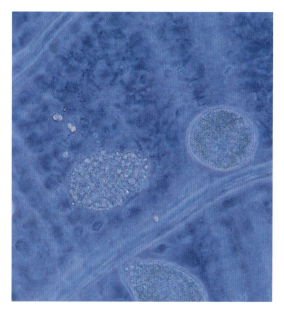

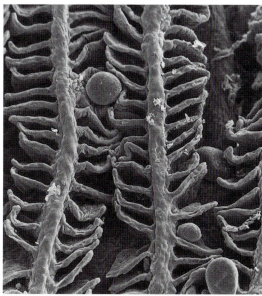

Oodinium is common in marine and freshwater aquaria. On the gills and skin of fish (below), it causes a yellow color. As is evident in both photomicrographs (top right) and electron micrographs (below right), the individual parasites are pear-shaped, anchor to tissues, and contain developing spores.

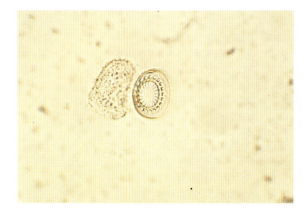

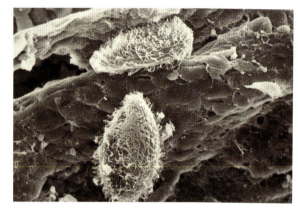

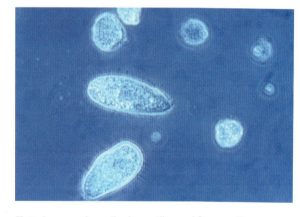

Trichodina is of questionable pathogenicity and rarely a problem in home aquaria, but the actively motile, disc-shaped organisms (top) are common in pond-raised fish. A scanning electron micrograph (above) shows the organism's prominent denticular ring and double row of cilia.

dinospores, which are released at some time after the cysts drop off the fish. The dinospores have flagella and are motile. Treatment of both fresh-water and saltwater species involves maintaining a level of 0.1 to 0.2 parts per million (ppm) of copper in the aquarium for a period of ten days. Reinfection is a common problem and may be associated with the parasite's ability to colonize the intestine.

Trichodinids

Trichodinids are ciliated, circular, and flattened, and have denticular rings. They measure approxi-

Tetrahymena is actively motile and frequently invasive on aquarium fish (top). An electronmicrograph (middle) shows organisms on the surface of a fish eye, and a stained preparation (above) outlines pear-shaped, ciliated organisms with vacuoles.

mately 40 to 60 nanometers in diameter. Three common genera include *Trichodina, Trichodinella,* and *Tripartiella.* Species of the latter two genera are smaller than *Trichodina* and have incomplete rings of cilia. They also appear to inflict more injury to gills of fish, since they attach firmly to gill tissue. A marine counterpart similar to *Trichodinella* has been associated with gills.

Parasites in this group are common on the skin and gills of pond-reared fish, especially if the water has a high organic load. All cultivated fish are susceptible, including pond-reared tropical fish, goldfish, channel catfish, and trout. Heavy infestations can cause respiratory problems in fry reared in ponds. Skin lesions have been observed, and some parasite species have been reported to infect the urinary bladder and oviducts.

Trichodinids are rarely a problem in the home aquaria, since water changes associated with shipping and transportation usually cure infected fish. It is not uncommon to observe *Trichodina* infestations on goldfish in wholesale or retail establishments; infestations are generally very light and apparently do not affect the host fish. Infected pond fish are easily treated with common antiprotozoan drugs. Removal of fish to fresh water often is also effective.

Tetrahymena

The ciliated protozoan *Tetrahymena pyriformis* is usually found as a free-living infusorian, but occasionally will become parasitic. It can be found in decaying food in any aquarium and is frequently a secondary (or tertiary) invader of lesions initiated by other parasites and/or bacteria. It is possible that various strains of *Tetrahymena* have a potential for being more virulent, especially with immunologically weakened fish in water with high organic content. Unfortunately, the term "guppy killer" has been used for the disease. Although many species of live-bearing fish can become infected, the parasite has been associated with a variety of ornamental fish, including cichlids and various tetra species.

On the body of affected fish, whitish areas surrounded by hemorrhage may occur. Foci of parasites have been found in many internal tissues, including muscles and brain, and in tissues surrounding the eye. A diagnosis is confirmed by wet-mount preparations, which will reveal hundreds of actively motile, pear-shaped, ciliated parasites approximately 60 by 100 microns.

A marine counterpart, *Uronema miamiensis,* is frequently seen on marine ornamental fish. Large areas of skin are discolored and may be hemorrhagic. Scrapings reveal many pear-shaped ciliates. The lesions appear to be complicated by

Epistylis, stalked organisms considered epiphytes, are common in aquarium fish and may mimic true fungi. Here, *Epistylis* is attached to the gill lamellae (top). Colonizing fish in highly organic water where epiphytes normally flourish, these organisms appear as white tufted areas such as these colonies (above) on the pectoral and anal fins of an ornamental catfish (*Corydoras julii*).

invasion of *Pseudomonas,* which may be responsible for the death of the fish.

Prospects for the treatment of the disease are discouraging. Improvement of water quality to reduce infusorial growth will help to avoid the problem. Baths in external parasiticides (formaldehyde, etc.) may reduce external parasites but will not affect internal parasites. Maintaining good water quality and good nutrition should assist in preventing attack by this opportunistic parasite.

Epistylis

This and related species such as *Vorticella* are stalked, ciliated protozoans which are generally found attached to vegetation or crustaceans. In aquaria or ponds high in organic matter, they proliferate and attach to fish or eggs. *Epistylis* can be found on any fish coming from any source of organically enriched water. The organism is frequently seen to affect goldfish and many species of bottom-dwelling fish such as ornamental catfish. The problem appears to be limited to freshwater fish. Frequently the parasite will be seen as a white area or white tuft on the surface of the fish body or fins. It has been found in ulcerated areas from which the bacteria *Aeromonas hydrophila* has been isolated, but which organism initiated the problem is unknown. Fish eggs may become infested, resulting in low hatchability. Diagnosis is confirmed by making wet-mount preparations of affected areas. Bell-shaped ciliated organisms on stalks are characteristic. Apical cilia are present. The body of the organism will be seen to contract periodically from an elongated form to ball-shaped. The stalk tends to coil during the contraction phase.

In aquaria, *Epistylis* problems are best avoided by regular cleaning of gravel and careful feeding to minimize the organic substrates on which the organisms multiply. Treatment can be accomplished by swabbing the affected area with tincture of iodine. Formaldehyde at 25 ppm would also be a good approach for treatment of fish. Among ornamental fish, eggs affected with the organism can be dipped (for thirty seconds) in 66 ppm of malachite green or in solutions of iodophores.

Another epistylid, *Heteropolaria colisarum,* has been associated with a variety of North American fishes, causing a problem called "red sore" disease. The same species was isolated from the skin of giant gouramis. A single treatment in a 1.5 percent salt bath for three hours or until the fish is stressed has controlled this species.

Glossatella and *Scyphidia*

Like epistylids, these organisms are considered to be free-living and problematic to fish only in water high in organic content, where they also can be found on vegetation and inanimate objects. Both of these genera are rarely found on fish in home aquaria, but may occasionally parasitize fish in production ponds. Both have a vaselike morphology with one or two rows of cilia. Heavy infestations on the body and gills of small fish can cause respiratory problems and death. These organisms are associated with pond-raised goldfish, channel catfish, and ornamental fish varieties. No marine counterpart is known. They apparently are removed from the fish when exposed to fresh water and consequently are rarely

Scyphidia is a vase-shaped organism found attached to skin and gills. It is common in pond-reared ornamental fish, goldfish, and channel catfish, but is rarely a problem in ornamental fish.

seen in commercial or domestic aquaria. Treatment in ponds can be accomplished by a variety of external parasiticides, including formaldehyde, potassium permanganate, malachite green, or copper sulfate.

Glossatella, a protozoan inhabitant of ponds high in organic matter, is characterized by a single row of cilia and a pear-shaped form. Although it can be found on the skin and gills of pond-reared fish, it is rarely a problem in home aquaria.

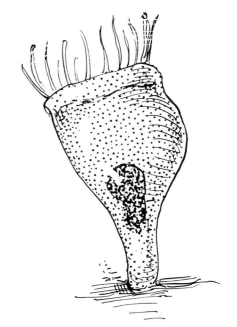

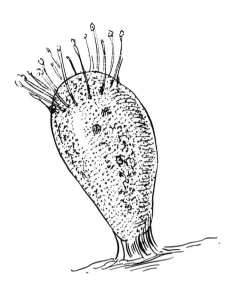

Trichophrya is a suctorian parasite common on the gills of pond-raised fish, and can be associated with respiratory distress. However, it is rare in ornamental fish in home aquaria.

Trichophrya
Suctorian parasites associated with fishes reared in ponds, *Trichophrya* frequently are found in channel catfish and may reach a level of infestation at which respiration is impaired. They have not been a problem in ornamental fishes, but it is

Cryptobia frequently affects the gills of pond-raised fish, especially goldfish.

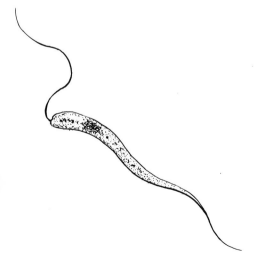

likely that infestations occasionally do occur in pond-reared tropical fish. These parasites are usually found on the gills and are identified by their characteristic pin-cushion appearance.

Cryptobia
Cryptobia are found on gills of goldfish and could be confused with *Ichthyobodo necatrix*. The parasites are flagellated and are approximately 10 microns long. By microscopic examination, the parasites appear to be attached to gill tissues by the flagella and have a wavelike movement when compared to *Ichthyobodo*. The organisms apparently are quite common but do not appear to cause disease.

External Worms

Monogenetic trematodes
Flatworms are common parasites of freshwater and marine fishes. Most species are associated with the skin and gills of fish. A few species can infect the stomach of fish, and some have been found in the urinary bladder. Monogenetic trematodes of ornamental fish can be broadly classified into two families, the Dactylogyridae and the Gyrodactylidae.

Dactylogyridae may be recognized by a four-pointed anterior end, a sucker near the anterior end, and four anterior eyespots. At the caudal end of the worm, a fixation apparatus (haptor) consists of one or two large hooks surrounded by up to sixteen smaller hooklets. Mature worms are approximately 200 microns in length. The worms have both testes and ovaries (a condition called hermaphroditism). Self-fertilization is followed by the release of eggs which develop off of the host. Eggs from some species hatch into ciliated forms in as few as sixty hours; hatching of other species may require four to five days. The ciliated larvae attack suitable hosts and lose their cilia.

Of the many genera, *Dactylogyrus* is the most important. Many species have been described. Dactylogyrids are usually associated with the gills, and for that reason are called gill flukes. If present in sufficient numbers, they can cause hyperplasia, destruction of gill epithelium, and clubbing of gill filaments, resulting in asphyxiation.

Gill flukes are common in aquarium fish and can infest species of all major groups. Pond-raised fish such as goldfish may be heavily infested. Infections often appear in imported and domestic tank-reared angelfish and discus. Clini-

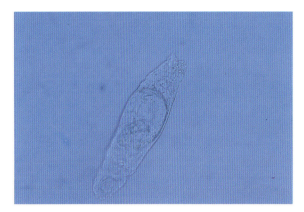

Gyrodactylus is a monogenetic trematode found on the skin and fins of fish; closely related forms are found on gills. It is common in both freshwater and marine ornamental fish. Note the embryo visible within the body of this hermaphrodite organism.

cal signs are rarely if ever associated with infestations of fish in the wild or in uncrowded ponds. However, such signs are common in aquaria and holding vats, where crowding greatly enhances the probability of transmission.

Clinical signs can include rapid respiratory movements, clamped fins, flashing or rubbing, inactive fish at the bottom of the aquarium, and death. Diagnosis can be confirmed by biopsies of gills; worms are readily apparent. Gill flukes can proliferate to numbers which can cause clinical disease in channel catfish (*Ictalurus punctatus*) held in 76-liter (20-gallon) aquaria. Under these conditions, we have determined that the parasite load per fish from a single aquarium can be quite variable—from hundreds of parasites in each of the four gill arches to none. Whether this variability is attributable to immunity or chance is not known.

A second genus of flatworms, *Gyrodactylus,* is commonly found on fish. Many species have been described. Although they occasionally may be found on the gills, these parasites are usually found on the skin.

The worms may be up to 0.8 millimeters in length, and have two points at the anterior end. An anterior sucker is present, but eyespots are absent. The worms are viviparous, and embryos with prominent hooks are commonly seen within the adult parasites. An attachment organ (haptor) with two large hooks surrounded by up to sixteen smaller hooklets is located at the caudal end.

The parasites move about the skin surface by grasping the host alternately with the anterior sucking disc and the haptor.

Inapparent *Gyrodactylus* infections are common. Parasites feed on blood and epithelium by scraping and sucking. When present, lesions can include localized hemorrhagic areas, excessive mucus, and localized ulcerations. Infected fish may have a ragged-appearing tail resulting from localized hyperplasia, necrosis of the tips of the fins, and loss of epithelial cells. Secondary infections with bacteria (*Aeromonas, Flexibacter*) are common. We have isolated *Aeromonas hydrophila* from gyrodactylids removed from goldfish, which suggests that the worms may actively transmit bacteria.

Specific treatments for monogenetic trematode infections include long-term exposure to 25 ppm of formaldehyde, short-term formaldehyde baths at concentrations from 50 to 250 ppm, 2.5 to 3 percent saltwater baths (for freshwater fish), or freshwater baths at pH 8.3 (for saltwater fish). Organophosphates have been used at 0.25 ppm for freshwater fish and 0.5 to 1.0 ppm for saltwater fish. However, it appears that with extended use of organophosphates, monogenetic trematodes have developed resistance. Experimentally, we have shown that praziquantel (Droncit™) will effectively remove monogenetic trematodes from gills and body surfaces in infected goldfish when added to aquaria at 2 ppm.

Turbellarians

Occasionally seen as free-living pests in an aquarium, these flatworms can be a source of concern for aquarists who observe small (5 to 7 millimeters, or 0.2 to 0.3 inches) white worms on the sides of the aquarium. On microscopic examination, two eyespots may be visible on some species, and living young may be seen developing within mature worms. Turbellarians may lodge on fish—especially on those which prefer the bottom of an aquarium. The worms generally have a greater effect on the aquarist than on the fish. Marine turbellarians are common.

Turbellarians develop where organic matter accumulates from overfeeding of fish and failure to clean gravel. The worms usually can be controlled by reducing feed, promptly removing excess food, and regularly cleaning gravel with a distended-end siphon hose. Formaldehyde treatments at 25 ppm for twelve to twenty-four hours followed by a water change and gravel cleaning will rid the aquarium of these pests.

Leeches

In home aquaria, leeches are occasional pests and are most frequently introduced with plants, stones, snails, and almost any other object taken from an infested pond. There are several genera, and leeches are found worldwide. They can be seen with the naked eye as small (5 millimeters to 1 centimeter, or 0.2 to 0.4 inches) wormlike organisms frequently found on the gravel or clinging to real or artificial plants. When disturbed by water motion, leeches will lengthen, and on contacting a fish (or human), immediate attachment results. Leeches will suck blood from their host, then eventually detach and drop to the bottom of the aquarium, where they multiply.

Leeches are a principal vector for *Trypanosoma,* a flagellated blood parasite. Damage to the fish during the sucking process creates an entry site for bacteria. There is a potential for leeches to transmit mycobacterial infections.

Leech contamination can be prevented by bleaching any inanimate objects (rock, gravel, pieces of wood) taken from ponds or rivers before using them for decorative purposes in the aquarium. Live plants frequently are a source of leeches and should be soaked in alum (1 tablespoon per gallon of water, or approximately 1.7 grams per liter of water) or rinsed under tepid tap water prior to addition to the aquarium. To rid an aquarium of leeches, treat it with an organophosphate at 0.25 ppm. In the authors' experience, 25 ppm of formaldehyde followed by a cleansing of the gravel twenty-four hours after treatment was successful in removal of leeches from fish and aquaria.

External Crustaceans

Parasitic copepods

Crustaceans belonging to the subclass Copepoda include the parasites *Lernaea* and *Ergasilus.* Like most other crustaceans, they lay eggs. The first larvae to hatch swim freely at first, then attach to the gills of a suitable host and enter a nonswimming phase in which they complete their maturation. After mating, the males cease being parasitic, but mated females reattach to or penetrate the fish and mature to forms which can be seen with the naked eye.

Commonly called the "anchor worm" because of the wormlike appearance of the females as

Lernaea, commonly called the "anchor worm," is a parasitic copepod. The anchor, actually its head, is embedded in the dermis of this goldfish. Eggs of *Lernaea* pass through several molts prior to parasitizing new hosts. Infected fish commonly enter commercial trade.

they cling on the fish's skin, *Lernaea* is an elongated copepod (up to 1 centimeter, or 0.2 inches). Several species have been described. A female anchors herself on the fish by burrowing into its body with her head. At its maximum length, the anchor worm takes on a characteristic V-shape from the two egg sacs protruding from the free end of the worm's body. Fish may be affected with many of these parasites, causing irritation and localized hemorrhagic reactions at the point of entry, which may become secondarily infected with bacteria.

The problem is generally seen in koi and goldfish production ponds, but any species of fish can be affected. In wholesale or retail establishments having central systems without adequate filtration or ultraviolet light sterilization, the infestation can spread throughout all aquaria. In individual aquaria within pet retail outlets, an introduced carrier fish can initiate an infection which will affect any species within the aquarium.

Since the parasite is easily recognized, continued treatment with organophosphates will control infections in large operations. Dipping freshwater fish into saltwater aquaria for five to ten minutes a day will result in death of the parasites. During this treatment, parasites will eventually turn a greenish color, wither, and be expelled from the fish. In situations where only a very few fish are affected, worms may be removed by extraction; use forceps and avoid breaking the worm. Local treatment can be done with cotton swabs perme-

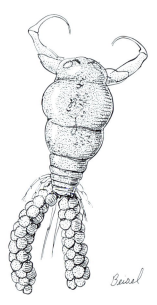

Ergasilus is a parasitic copepod found on the gills of wild-caught or pond-raised ornamental fish. It is rare in home aquaria.

ated with a suitable disinfectant (iodine, acriflavine, alcohol). Any treatment of fish should also include the removal of juvenile forms. This can be done by adding organophosphates (0.25 ppm) or by a simple successive series of water changes with gravel cleaning. Dimilin™ at 2 ppm is effective in controlling the parasite.

As a result of infection with anchor worms, many fish may not be marketable because of the external lesions. Antibiotic treatment of larger fish by intraperitoneal injection of chloramphenicol (1 milligram per 40-gram [1.4-ounce] fish) may accelerate healing of lesions. Where injection is not practical, antibiotics may be added to water to stem secondary bacterial problems. Consider using tetracyclices, kanamycin, or sulfa drugs at 12 ppm for three treatments on alternate days. Water changes between treatments are recommended. Remove activated carbon from filters and remove air stems from undergravel filters to avoid pulling medicaments through filter media. Continue aeration.

The parasitic copepod *Ergasilus* resembles the anchor worm. It is found firmly attached to the gills of fish by specialized prehensile hooks. It occasionally is found in ornamental fish production ponds, but rarely is a problem in commercial outlets or home aquaria. Under microscopic ex-

amination, the parasites appear to be multicolored. They are too small for mechanical removal. Treatment in production ponds is done with organophosphates at 0.25 to 1 ppm.

Argulus

The fish louse *Argulus* is a member of the subclass Branchiura. It is flat and has prominent eyes, sucking discs, and a stiletto. Transparent, it tends to take on the color of the fish which it parasitizes. Fish lice are easily seen with the naked eye, for they range from approximately 5 to 8 millimeters (0.2 to 0.3 inches) in length.

While sucking blood, fish lice inflict injury with the stiletto, the injection of which causes a focal hemorrhagic area. It is thought that toxic substances released by the parasite during feeding are responsible for the severe local reaction surrounding the area of the sting. Ulcerations often follow fish lice infestation; they probably are the result of secondarily invading bacteria such as *Aeromonas* and *Pseudomonas*. It has been suggested that argulids may carry these bacteria in addition to blood parasites such as trypanosomes. Wounds are frequently infected with fungi.

Fish lice can parasitize any fish but are most important in goldfish production ponds. Under pond conditions, argulids lay their eggs on plants and stones. Hatching occurs in four weeks, at which time they actively seek a host. Sexual maturity develops after lice have parasitized a fish for five to six weeks. Organophosphates at a concentration of 0.25 to 1 ppm are used to control fish lice in these situations.

Occasionally, fish lice appear on individual fish in wholesale and retail outlets. Individual para-

Argulus, the fish louse, is a parasitic branchiuran. It is common in ponds and at the wholesale level, but is rare in home aquaria.

sites can be removed with forceps. In cases involving many fish, lice can be removed by treating aquaria with organophosphates (0.25 to 1 ppm), dipping fish in potassium permanganate baths (50 to 70 ppm) for fifteen seconds, or bathing fish in formaldehyde baths (150 to 200 ppm) for fifteen to thirty minutes or until fish appear stressed.

Livoneca

Parasitic isopods (order Isopoda) are rare but spectacular when found on fish. The organisms are segmented, have several pairs of legs, and can be 1 to 2 centimeters (0.4 to 0.8 inches) in length. They generally burrow into the gill or buccal cavity, but may excavate and live in a cavity in the lateral musculature. One species, *Livoneca symmetrica,* has been described. Apparently parasites attack fish in the wild or in production ponds, and on some fish, well-concealed parasites may go unnoticed by wholesalers and retailers. *Livoneca symmetrica* can move about the fish and is readily recognized and easily removed.

Internal Protozoans

Hexamita

These flagellated protozoans are found in the gastrointestinal tracts of a variety of fish. *Octomitus* is an old term for the protozoan when the parasite was thought to have eight flagella. Similarly, the name "discus parasite" has been used because of its frequent infection of discus fish. A closely related parasite, *Spironucleus,* may be a distinct species from *Hexamita* and appears longer and possibly more sinuous. However, for practical purposes both appear to cause a similar clinical disease.

In many fishes, including trout, goldfish, and a variety of freshwater aquarium species, infections can be inapparent. However, in certain ornamental fishes such as angelfish, discus, and gouramis, the disease is characterized by poor condition, lack of appetite, unthriftiness, weight loss, and death. Clinically apparent disease most often is associated with young fish. It may be seen at the producer, wholesale, or retail level, and in home aquaria. Infestations in adult breeding angelfish can result in reduced levels of hatched eggs or in death of young fry after hatching.

The parasites are about the size of red blood cells and are very motile. Microscopic observation will show highly motile flagellates in feces, or if a fish is available for necropsy, massive

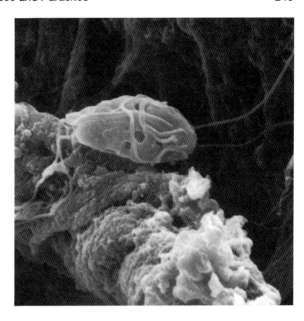

Hexamita is an important cause of mortalities in home aquaria. These actively motile flagellates are found in the intestines (and infrequently in the liver) of angelfish, goldfish, discus, and gouramis.

infestations in the intestines. In severe cases, the organisms can be found in the liver, gallbladder, and occasionally the kidney. Infections can be effectively treated by the addition of 5 ppm of metronidazole to aquarium water. Since *Hexamita* can be kept alive in laboratory media, we assume that it is an inhabitant of aquaria where organic material has been allowed to accumulate. Cleaning of gravel and filter materials will assist in treating this problem.

"Hole-in-the-head," a disease frequently seen in discus, angelfish, red oscars, and other cichlid fishes, has been associated with the presence of *Hexamita.* However, a direct causal relationship has not been established. Massive doses of metronidazole will not resolve the lesions seen along the lateral line system. In scanning electron micrographs, we have not been able to associate either bacteria or parasites with lesions. The "hole-in-the-head" condition has been variously attributed to *Hexamita,* bacterial infections, poor nutrition, dirty aquaria, and use of activated carbon. The latter observation comes from breeders of cichlids, who claim that the problem is avoided when they delete activated carbon from their filter systems. In any case, treatment should be directed toward therapy with antibiotics and metronidazole,

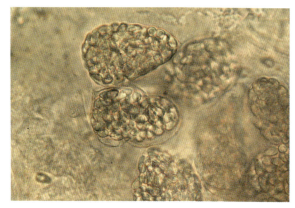

The microsporidian *Pleistophora hyphessobryconis* is the causative agent of neon tetra disease, a common affliction of aquarium fish associated with high mortalities. An affected neon tetra (top left) shows whitish area containing spores. Affected fish (below left) may have a lumpy appearance. A squash preparation (above) shows the spores typically found in wet mounts of muscles.

regular cleaning of aquarium gravel with water changes, and improved nutrition.

Sporozoans

Coccidiosis is one of the most familiar sporozoan diseases recognizable by veterinarians in mammals and birds. Coccidia are also common intestinal parasites of fish, where their life cycles are just as complicated as in mammals and birds, and the clinical signs can vary as widely.

Among ornamental fish, coccidiosis is most often observed in goldfish during the winter and spring, particularly under pond conditions when fish may not be fed and their immunological responsiveness may be decreased. *Eimeria* species are the culprits. The disease is also occasionally seen in home aquaria. Clinical signs include depression and emaciation with sunken eyes. A yellow-colored fluid can be expressed from the intestines. Diagnosis is made by identifying the oocysts in wet-mount preparations of intestinal scrapings or feces. Treatment, if required, may be attempted by inclusion of anticoccidials in food. Monensin™ at 100 ppm in food may be a good choice, or possibly Salinomycin™ at 10 ppm in food.

Other sporozoans belonging to the subphylum Cnidospora, classes Microsporidea and Myxosporidea, are frequent parasites of ornamental fish. Members of both classes have spindle-shaped polar capsules within their spores; microsporids have one, and myxosporids have two. Identification of genera of the Myxosporidea is based on position of the polar capsules.

A common microsporid is *Pleistophora hyphessobryconis*. Infection causes a disease whose signs include the appearance of whitened areas in the musculature and a resultant aberrant swimming motion. The name "neon disease" reflects the fact that this condition was originally found in neon tetras, but is misleading in that many other species of fish also are susceptible. We have diagnosed the disease in a variety of angelfish, barbs, rasboras, and tetras. In neon tetras, high mortality rates are common. In angelfish, we have noted that the parasite can cause muscle necrosis, which results in an uneven, undulating look to the body surface. In other cases involving white angelfish, a strong focalized melanophore response results in an appearance which the fish producer refers to as "black holes."

The course of the disease in groups of infected neon tetras is invariably fatal. It is not uncommon to see bloated fish, but bloating appears to be attributable to a variety of bacteria which are secondary invaders. Mycobacterial infections are also common in neon tetras, as are concomitant infections. In mature angelfish the disease has a chronic course, resulting only in deformities of the musculature.

Diagnosis of *Pleistophora* is confirmed by examining impression smears or wet mounts of muscles from the affected area in which pansporoblasts are observed, filled with spores containing one polar capsule. Treatment attempts have been discouraging. Claims of cures using either formaldehyde or naladixic acid have not been substantiated in controlled experiments. Our experience suggests that the mortality rate in a group of infected fish is initially high. The remaining fish appear healthy at first but will die off over a period of weeks, suggesting a gradual extension of the parasite within the body.

Within an aquarium system, the disease can be limited by removing dying fish before they are cannibalized. Periodic cleaning of gravel helps remove any spores which may have accumulated. In pond systems, control can be approached by draining and disinfecting ponds. In fish hatcheries in the Far East where many neon tetras are raised, the infection is probably spread by the feeding of live invertebrates such as tubifex worms, which may serve as intermediate hosts.

Many genera of Myxosporidea have been found in ornamental fish. Prominent among these are *Myxobolus, Henneguya, Myxidium,* and *Mitraspora. Myxobolus* can cause nodules on the skin and gills of various ornamental fish. Nodules may be few or numerous and from microscopic to several millimeters in size. Because of the whitish appearance of the infected areas, the

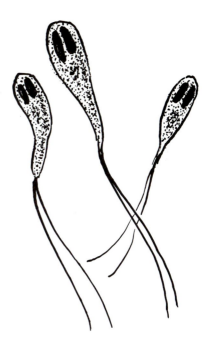

Henneguya sporoblasts appear as discrete white nodules on the fins and scales of some ornamental species. Hundreds of spores can be found in a sporoblast. The disease is not fatal.

Myxobolus produce a disfiguring disease but are not highly pathogenic. The spores produce white spots or nodules on the skin and gills of fish.

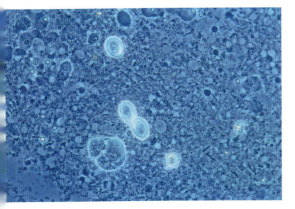

disease has been given the common name "milk-scale disease." Infections with *Myxobolus* could be confused with other parasites, such as ich. Cysts do not appear to affect the fish in any way except in appearance; they are common and largely incidental findings in routine postmortem examinations of wild-caught fish. If cysts are objectionable, they can be lanced, followed by local application of antiseptics. Isolation of fish during recovery is suggested. Prevention of the disease in ornamental fish farms would be limited to ridding ponds of carrier fish, and liming and drying ponds between production runs.

Henneguya and *Myxidium* are also found as white cysts on the body surfaces and gills of a variety of wild-caught ornamental fish. *Henneguya* is frequently found on gills of wild-caught species of *Corydoras* and on dorsal fins of *Leporinus*. Again, these parasites cause no apparent harm except in appearance. Cysts associated with *Henneguya* infestations frequently disappear in time. Presumably, spores are released into the aquarium. Whether these infections are spread from infected to noninfected fish in aquaria is unknown, although from our observations, it appears that some species of parasites may spread. On the other hand, *Henneguya* infections of *Leporinus* do not appear to spread to other fish species within an aquarium. It is possible that some species of these parasites require an intermediate host whereas others may spread directly.

In goldfish and koi, *Mitraspora cyprini,* commonly called "kidney bloater," causes massive kidney enlargement resembling a tumor. Fish become infected in ponds during the summer, but clinical signs are not seen until September or October. This disease is frequently observed in retail outlets and is common in goldfish kept in home aquaria. Apparently, asymptomatic fish are purchased in the summer and gradually bloat during the winter months. Though severely bloated, affected fish may live for months. The

Black spot disease on a silver-dollar fish is caused by larval forms of the digenetic trematode *Neascus.* The black spots may be mistaken for normal fish coloration.

Digenetic trematodes have a complex life cycle which includes both a ciliated stage that infests certain snails and a later form that attacks fish. The nodules on this live-bearer (below) contain digenetic trematodes. A histological preparation (bottom) shows trematodes in the gill cartilage of a golden barb.

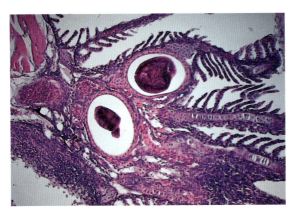

disease is transmitted when spores are shed from urine in the spring. In a few case studies, it appears that the infection has spread to uninfected goldfish within the aquarium.

Drainage of the ascitic fluid is not recommended since fluid will reaccumulate almost immediately. Experimental injections of Lasix™ have not reduced the accumulation of fluids. Addition of 0.3 percent salt to the aquarium water may assist the fish in osmoregulation. Eventually, severely bloated fish will die. Chances of the infection spreading within an aquarium could be reduced by isolation of sick fish. Any treatment with anticoccidial drugs in food would be purely experimental and unpredictable. A diagnosis can be confirmed by wetmount preparations of kidneys and identification of trophozoites or spores.

Cryptosporidia have been demonstrated in a marine ornamental fish, the naso tang (*Naso lituratus*). Signs include anorexia, regurgitation of food, and passage of feces containing undigested food. We have identified a cryptosporidia-like organism in intestinal sections of angelfish which had signs identical to those described for the naso tang. The condition appeared to be widespread in an angelfish hatchery. Fish were anorexic, lost condition, regurgitated food, and eventually died. The many unexplained deaths seen in angelfish may eventually prove to be infections with cryptosporidia or a closely related sporozoan.

Clinostomum "grubs" are actually larvae of digenetic trematodes. Here metacercariae are shown in the gill cavity of a pond-reared cichlid.

Internal Helminths

Digenetic trematodes

Digenetic trematodes in fish may occur as adult forms in the intestine of the fish or, more commonly, as intermediate stages encysted in tissues. It is rare to find tropical fish as final hosts with adult forms of the parasite within the intestine, but tropical fish frequently serve as the secondary intermediate host. In the majority of cases, the definitive host is a fish-eating bird which sheds parasite eggs into the water. These eggs eventually form ciliated miracidia which penetrate specific species of snails. After asexual development in snails, procercariae are released which penetrate fish. Here they develop into metacercariae enclosed in cysts.

Many genera of digenetic trematodes have been described, and many unidentified species exist. Since heavily infected fish are obvious to the exporter, the problem is relatively rare in retail outlets. However, some fish with inapparent signs may be shipped. Four groups of digenetic trematodes commonly seen are discussed below.

Larval forms of the genus *Neascus* are frequently seen in ornamental fish as round black spots (2 to 3 millimeters or about 0.08 to 0.12 inches) in the skin of fish. The black spots represent a melanophore reaction surrounding the encysted metacercariae. Silver-dollar fish are frequently infested. The black spots are not particularly offensive and are often mistaken for normal coloring or genetic variations!

The white to yellow larvae of species of *Clino-*

stomum are commonly called grubs. Severely infected fish are not marketed, but cysts may occasionally be seen in retail stores. In such cases, the fish should not be sold until the parasite is removed by simple excision. In many cases, grubs are within the body cavity and deeply embedded in the musculature, and thus escape detection. Heavy infection with grubs results in fish which appear to be stunted. In one instance, we removed over 100 grubs from a fish 10 centimeters (4 inches) long.

In recent years, we have noted encysted metacercariae in gills of fish raised on some fish farms in Florida. These parasites belong to the family Heterophryidae. In some cases infestations have been massive, resulting in an extensive proliferation of gill cartilage and destruction of secondary lamellae. Severely infested fish may have protruding gills. Infested fish cannot be handled and will not survive standard shipping conditions. Cysts cannot be removed by chemicals. The infestation can be controlled in fish ponds by eliminating the snails (*Pleuracerca*) which serve as intermediate hosts.

Commonly called eye flukes, *Diplostomum* larvae can be found in the lens of a fish. The resulting opacity of the lens is noted as a "white eye." Fish are frequently blinded. A wide variety of birds may serve as final hosts for the mature parasite. The problem is rarely seen in retail outlets but could be a problem in fish farms. The disease can be controlled by snail control. Fish cannot be treated.

Tapeworms

While tapeworms are common in wild-caught fish, they are rarely found in ornamental fishes. When present, they are found within the intestines of fish, attached to the intestinal wall by means of a scolex, a headlike structure with four suckers. On some species of tapeworms, hooks may be present on the scolex. A common feature of many tapeworms is that they are segmented, with each segment (proglottid) having a complete set of reproductive organs. Tapeworms are disseminated by release of proglottids and eggs. These are eaten by some invertebrate, which is in turn eaten by the fish. The parasite develops into the adult form in the fish. Ornamental fish may serve as the secondary intermediate hosts for tapeworms of fish-eating waterfowl. In such cases, encysted larvae are embedded in internal organs of the fish or on the surfaces of internal organs. Larvae can be identified by the presence of a

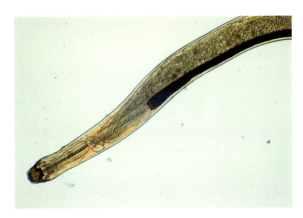

Intestinal nematodes are frequent parasites of live-bearing ornamental fish.

scolex with four suckers. Recent work suggests that praziquantel at 2 ppm in aquarium water will eliminate the parasites.

Nematodes

Often called roundworms in deference to their circular cross-section, nematodes are common in fish and can cause many problems. Worms are white to red in color, depending on species, and may range from a fraction of a centimeter to several centimeters in length. The external covering of the worm consists of a firm cuticle which maintains the circular shape of the parasite. Adult or larval nematodes can be found in ornamental fish within the lumen of the intestine, as free migratory forms in the peritoneal cavity, or encysted in internal organs or musculature. The life cycle is initiated when female worms in the intestine of infected fish shed eggs into the environment. An intermediate host such as an aquatic invertebrate (*Cyclops, Daphnia,* tubifex worms) may eat the eggs, which develop within it as larval parasites. When the invertebrate is eaten by a fish, larvae mature in the latter's intestine. At this point larvae may migrate to various organs or remain in the intestine. If this fish in turn is eaten by a larger fish, the predator also becomes infected. Details of the life cycles, required intermediate hosts, and migratory tendencies of larvae vary with the species of nematodes.

A number of nematode genera are associated with tropical fish, and it is generally believed by ornamental fish farmers that nematodes can be detrimental to fish. Larval forms of *Eustrongylides* are frequently found encysted in the muscles or peritoneum of fish. Most cause no harm and are found as red-colored worms on postmortem ex-

amination. Occasionally, cysts containing nematodes located close to the skin are confused with tumors. Nematodes found within the lumen of the intestine include *Capillaria* and *Camallanus.* *Capillaria* frequently are associated with ornamental fish, but their clinical significance is difficult to determine. They also are usually noted in routine postmortem examinations. Fish with heavy infestations should be treated (see below).

In clinical practice, infections with intestinal nematodes will initially be noticed as a red-colored worm protruding from the anus of a fish. The infestations appear to be seasonal and are frequently found in live-bearing fish such as guppies or swordtails. Treatment for *Camallanus* should be approached using common nematocides with food at the rate of 0.25 percent of food. Fenbendazol (Panacur™) would appear to be a good candidate for use with infected fish. We would suggest mixing it in commercial food enhanced with cod-liver oil and bound with gelatin. Since fish are quick to refuse food which has been medicated, withholding food for a few days prior to feeding medicated food may aid in acceptance.

Recent studies in which ivermectin has been added directly to aquarium water suggest that this drug may be useful in treating nematodes in fish. The dose used was 0.7 millimeters of a 1 percent injectable solution per 76 liters (20 gallons) of water. The dose was added over a period of four days (0.1, 0.2, 0.2, and 0.2 millimeters). At this writing, we suggest that any use of ivermectin for nematodes of fish be limited strictly to investigative purposes because of the high toxicity of the drug. Migratory forms of nematodes cannot be treated; one must avoid feeding fish with fresh-

Acanthocephalans are called "thorny-headed worms" for obvious reasons.

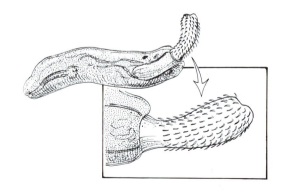

water insect larvae or free-living copepods which may carry immature forms of the roundworms.

Acanthocephalans

Found in the intestinal tract of fish, acanthocephalans receive their common name, "thorny-headed worms," from small spicules which cover their heads and serve to anchor them to the intestinal lining. Acanthocephalans can be a problem in wild marine or freshwater fishes, but are not common in ornamental freshwater fish. In the few observed cases examined at the University of Georgia, the parasite load per fish was very low—generally, one or two parasites per fish. We observed no problems under these conditions. Worm infestations were detected during routine postmortem examinations. Wild-caught ornamental fish can serve as intermediate hosts when the final host is a bird or possibly a larger fish. The presence of the intermediate forms in low numbers does not appear to affect the fish.

Bacteria and Fish Disease

Bacteria are single-celled organisms characterized by a rigid cell wall and an indefinite-shaped nucleus. Thousands of species exist, functioning in roles as varied as nitrogen fixation, decomposition, fermentation, and disease production. Bacterial nutrition is very similar to that of higher animals, though on a simpler scale. Certain amino acids are essential for growth, and while some bacteria may utilize fat or protein, the nutrients of choice are carbohydrates. Because of a rigid cell wall, bacteria excrete enzymes into their environment which break down food into a form suitable for use. Similarly, the cell wall requires that food for bacterial use be soluble. Selective mechanisms in the bacterial cell wall control the type and quantity of nutrient needed for optimal bacterial growth. Growth is also controlled by the temperature and pH of the environment, since both of these factors exert a control over enzyme breakdown of food for bacterial use.

Bacteria vary greatly in average size, and range from 0.5 to 1.0 micron in width by 8 to 10 microns in length. They occur in a number of shapes and arrangements. Most commonly they are either rodlike (bacillus) or spherical (coccus) and occur either separately or in chains. A third, less common shape is spiral. All multiply by simple cell division.

Although bacterial shape and ability to use certain types of food separate species to a certain extent, classification of bacteria is complex. The most classic separation is by cell wall structure. A Danish physician in the late 1800s noted certain staining characteristics when using dyes. Those bacteria which stained blue and had little or no fat in the cell wall were termed gram-positive. Those with more fat in the cell wall were termed gram-negative. The majority of bacteria associated with fish and aquatic environments belong to the gram-negative group.

Pathogenicity: Two facts are fundamental, relative to bacteria in aquaria: (1) not all bacteria cause disease, and (2) in any aquarium or aquatic environment, a great number of different bacteria should be considered normal flora.

In an established aquarium containing fish, one would expect to find between one million and one billion bacteria within each one-half teaspoon (5 milliliters) of water, depending on the abundance of organic nutrients and the frequency of water changes. The largest proportion of these bacteria, the normal flora (normal inhabitants), live benignly in the environment, aiding in the establishment of the dynamic equilibrium of factors necessary to assure the survival of the ecosystem. This dominant group includes bacteria responsible for decomposition of waste products (nitrifying bacteria) as well as bacteria which can utilize nitrates under conditions of low oxygen.

A second group within this bacterial population could be considered opportunistic pathogens. Under a given set of conditions, these could cause disease, usually when some other factor in the aquatic environment weakens the fish enough for the bacteria to attack successfully. It is now understood that weakening of fish results in a compromised immune system which renders the fish susceptible to bacterial attack.

Only occasionally is a third and much smaller group of bacteria present: the primary pathogens. These organisms have the ability to cause disease in normal, healthy fish. Since primary pathogens are seldom encountered in fish culture, most bacterial disease control programs center upon controlling the opportunists and maintaining the inherent immunity of fish by careful attention to nutrition and water quality. Water quality, especially avoidance and control of excessive amounts of organic materials, becomes very important and provides the basis for good aquarium management practices. Bacteria require soluble nutrients for growth and multiplication, and these foods may be provided by increased organic matter.

Site of infection: Bacterial diseases in fish may be either external or internal, but in a sense this differentiation is somewhat artificial since all pathogenic bacteria of fish release toxins, which freely diffuse throughout the body of the fish. Generally, bacterial disease of fish involves what is termed the virulence of the bacteria, that is, its ability to break down the fish tissue through the secretion of extracellular enzymes (toxins or virulence factors). This breakdown of fish tissue increases the availability of food for the bacteria, thus stimulating bacterial growth, and leads to further deterioration of the fish, and ultimately, fish death.

Many pathogenic bacteria of fish are able to initiate infections in the internal organs of fish by way of the intestines or by penetration of blood vessels in the skin or gills. In some cases, parasites may carry the bacteria and infect the fish while feeding. Parasites may provide an entry for bacteria simply by disrupting the fish's first line of defense, the mucous layer and skin. This protective layer can also be disrupted as a result of handling, crowding, or netting fish.

Regardless of the manner in which bacteria enter into a fish, essentially all of the internal organs and their critical functions can be affected. Infections which are disseminated throughout the body are called systemic infections. If the result of the infection appears very rapidly, without obvious signs of bacterial disease, the infection is said to be acute. When the course of a bacterial infection extends over a period of time and typical lesions are seen on the fish, the infection is chronic. So-called internal infections most likely arise from a combination of reduced immunity and associated stress factors. Whether or not a particular infection has an acute or chronic course depends on the type of bacteria and the virulence factors released.

Signs associated with bacterial diseases: Unfortunately, the signs and behavior of fish with bacterial diseases are common to many different kinds of bacteria, some parasites, and some noninfectious problems. The most frequent behavioral change is simple weakness, in which fish are

observed to remain motionless on the bottom of the aquarium. Generally, fish which lie on their sides are close to death. In some cases, fish will swim in circles. Others may lose their spatial orientation and continuously swim upside down. This latter problem is common in goldfish, and although a specific bacterium has not been identified, affected fish respond to antibiotic injections.

Among the physical signs of bacterial disease are hemorrhages, ulcerations, skin erosions, and ascites. Hemorrhages are particularly common. Their size may vary from pinpoint (petechial hemorrhages) to paintbrushlike reddened areas (echymotic hemorrhages). Ulcerations are distinct, often circumscribed areas of the skin where a central core of dead tissue is surrounded by a ring of reddened tissue. Pus is not associated with ulcers of fish.

Erosions of skin with scale loss are common with, but not limited to, infections with *Cytophaga columnaris.* A bacterial enzyme destroys tissues, which appear as white areas. Such areas have been termed "fin rot," "tail rot," "body rot," "mouth fungus," and "cloudy eye." Erosions can involve the loss of all tissues between fin rays or may result in total erosion of fins, including the fin rays. Frequently, muscle tissue is exposed.

Ascites, or bloat, is a fluid-filled distention of the abdomen of a fish. Frequently it is associated with exophthalmia ("popeye"), a condition in which one or both eyes protrude from the head. Ascites has been associated with chronic bacterial diseases such as those caused by species of *Mycobacterium.* The underlying cause of the fluid accumulation is destruction of kidney or possibly liver tissue.

Diagnosis of bacterial infections: In practice, the diagnosis of a bacterial infection can be done either by an educated guess or by isolation of the bacterium from the fish. The preferred term for the educated guess method is differential diagnosis, which implies that the diagnosis is certainly not definite but that a bacterial problem is a very good probability as the primary problem or as a complicating factor. (Even when the evidence points to a bacterial problem, a diagnosis is still tentative unless confirmed by isolation and identification.)

Among aquarists, retailers, and wholesalers, differential diagnosis is certainly more common than isolation and identification of the bacteria. This is largely due to the inavailability of bacteriological diagnostic services, costs, and relative worth of the fish. A tentative diagnosis of a bacterial problem can be made on the basis of observed signs and should always be preceded by attempts to identify any stress factor which may have weakened the fish. These may include extended length of transport time, poor water quality, inadequate cleaning, poor nutrition, or the presence of a concomitant parasitic infection. Such information will provide a rational basis for the avoidance of the problem, or for the simultaneous use of a parasiticide and an antimicrobial drug.

Isolation of the bacteria (etiologic diagnosis) should be left in the hands of individuals with experience in culturing fish for bacteria and interpreting results. However, for the fish producer, an etiologic diagnosis will allow records of prevalent bacteria encountered and their sensitivity or re-

sistance to antibiotics available for treatment. Fish can be submitted to appropriate private or state-supported diagnostic laboratories that may provide the service. Veterinarians have access to such laboratories, and samples may have to be submitted by them.

The selection of representative sick fish is of paramount importance in establishing a diagnosis of a bacterial infection. The fish to be cultured must be still alive, since bacteria in the water invade a dead fish within thirty minutes of death. The external site from which a sample is taken should be selected in such a position on the fish that contamination due to handling may be avoided. Where possible, restraining the fish physically to obtain the culture is preferable to the use of anesthesia, which may be toxic to some bacteria. Before obtaining internal samples, care should be taken to sterilize the external surface of the fish so as to avoid contamination by external bacteria.

To provide an etiologic diagnosis, the fish microbiologist follows very specific procedures. Material from the diseased fish is streaked onto an appropriate growth medium so as to achieve a good separation of the sample on the agar plate. This may be done by flaming (sterilizing) between streaks to reduce the bacterial population or by punching the inoculating needle into the agar plate. The growth medium to use is a matter of some dispute. Some use a growth medium which will support the growth of most bacteria (nonselective). Others use a selective medium, in which additives prevent the growth of bacteria other than those desired.

Plates are incubated next. Most bacterial organisms associated with fish diseases and aquatic environments will grow at 20 to 37 degrees C (68 to 98.6 degrees F), with an optimum at approximately 25 to 30 degrees C (77 to 86 de-

Bacteria Associated with Disease in Freshwater Ornamental Fish

Common	Infrequent	Rare
Gram-positive, aerobic to facultatively anaerobic species:		
Renibacterium salmoninarum	Lactobacillus	Nocardia
	Mycobacterium Streptococcus	
Gram-positive, anaerobic species:		
Clostridium botulinum	Eubacterium tarantellus	
Gram-negative, aerobic to facultatively anaerobic species:		
Aeromonas hydrophila complex (eggs)	Acinetobacter	Serratia liquefaciens
Aeromonas salmonicida a) typical, b) atypical	Edwardsiella tarda	Yersinia enterocolitica
Cytophaga psychrophila	Flavobacterium	Pseudomonas aeruginosa
Edwardsiella ictaluri	Pasteurella piscicida	Salmonella
Cytophaga columnaris	Pseudomonas putida	Proteus
Myxobacter	Pseudomonas fluorescens	Hafina alvei
Yersinia ruckeri	Pseudomonas	Escherichia coli
Vibrio	Plesiomonas shigelloides	Enterobacter
Pseudomonas putrifaciens		
Citrobacter freundii		

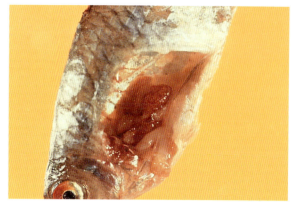

Mycobacterial infections cause a variety of gross lesions. Top left: A neon tetra shows wasting, "hollow belly," and evidence of secondary bacterial infection. Below left: An angelfish exhibits the chronic ulcers associated with systemic mycobacteriosis. Above: The white spots in the liver of this red-eyed tetra are granulomas.

grees F, or room temperature). After twenty-four hours, observation of plates begins and is continued for five days. Colonies will either be dry, shiny, or moist and greasy in appearance. With few exceptions, colonies which are definitely white or pigmented are gram-positive. Gram-negative bacteria are only rarely pigmented (orange, yellow, or purple). The Gram staining status can be ascertained by staining smears of the bacteria or by mixing colonies with a drop of 3 percent potassium hydroxide on a microscope slide. Formation of a slimy substance usually indicates that the colony consists of gram-negative bacteria.

Further identification requires characterization utilizing biochemical reactions. The next steps in the procedure are to identify the bacterium as a fish pathogen and to determine its antimicrobial drug sensitivity. Investigative studies on bacteria associated with aquarium fish suggest no differentiation between bacteria attacking ornamental fish and those attacking food fish. Rather, the main difference appears to be between cold-water and warm-water species. The descriptions which follow center upon those bacteria associated with ornamental fishes, arranged into a gen-eral classification of gram-positive rods and cocci, gram-negative nonpigmented rods (oxidase-positive and oxidase-negative), and gram-negative pigmented rods. The table on page 253 provides an overview.

Gram-Positive Rods

Most of the gram-positive rods which have been reported in fish are aerobic. Few anaerobic gram-positive rods have been linked with disease in fish, probably because they require anaerobic culture conditions for growth in the laboratory. It is clear that some gram-positive anaerobes are associated with fish problems, however, because isolates have been made from diseased fish.

Mycobacterium

Mycobacteriosis is a condition of both fresh- and saltwater fish. The disease is caused by a number of different bacterial species of the genus *Mycobacterium,* including *M. marinum, M. fortuitium, M. anabanti, M. chelonei, M. piscium, M. ranae, M. platypoecilus,* and *M. salmoniphilum.* Mycobacteriosis has been reported worldwide and has been reported in over 150 different species of fish. Mycobacteria cause a chronic progressive disease, which may be noted grossly in fish as emaciation, skin inflammation, exophthalmia, and ulceration or open lesions. On postmortem examination, gray to white nodules (granulomas) are present on internal or-

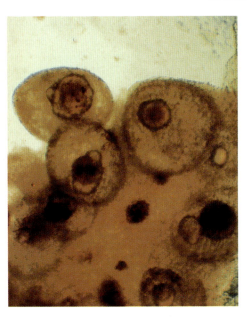

A wet-mount preparation reveals granulomas on a fish with mycobacteriosis.

gans such as the liver, kidney, and spleen. On small fish, these are best seen on wet mounts, where granulomas appear circular with a well-defined capsule.

In home aquaria, mycobacteriosis is characterized by a long course where affected fish refuse to eat, waste away, and eventually become so weak that they are unable to swim upright. Ascites (bloat) with exophthalmia is occasionally seen, indicating extensive damage to either kidneys or liver. On close observation, scales may be seen to jut out perpendicularly from the fish, indicating fluid accumulation under the scales. Older fish, long-term inhabitants of the aquarium, are frequently affected. Although many fish in an aquarium may be afflicted with mycobacteriosis, our experience suggests that only a few of these infections will be fatal.

Since it is well known that the organism is present in soil and is a normal inhabitant of the aquatic environment, the aquarist should assume that *Mycobacterium* is always present. Control by complete sterilization of the aquarium and gravel is unnecessary since reinfection is likely to occur. The disease is best controlled by a combination of strict cleaning of aquarium gravel, maintaining water quality through weekly changes, and assuring that fish are in peak nutritional condition through a balanced diet. Pay special attention to fish requirements for C, E, and B-complex vita-

mins, which may have become inactivated in dry food during storage.

Although little is known regarding how fish are initially infected, most probably the bacteria are taken in with food. It has been well substantiated that ornamental fish can become infected by eating fish food prepared from infected fish. Aquarists should be wary of feeding diets containing uncooked fish. Likewise, the feeding of sick or dying fish to large carnivorous species such as oscars is a bad practice, since fish which are doing poorly may be infected with mycobacteria.

Remove all obviously sick or dying fish prior to death since bacteria are easily spread by cannibalism. Moribund fish will die soon after removal from the aquarium or they can be humanely killed by an overdose of carbon dioxide using sodium bicarbonate or Alka-Seltzer®. Wrap fish in paper and dispose of by burial or removal in dry trash. Disposal by "flushing" always has the potential of spreading the disease to the environment.

The use of antibiotics for treatment is of questionable value since mycobacteria are surrounded by a granuloma which is relatively impervious to antibiotics. The use of antibiotics should be limited to situations where an active mycobacterial infection is suspected in a group of fish. The antibiotic should be incorporated into food and fed for at least three weeks. Compounds such as minocycline or rifampicin could be used at 0.3 percent in gelatinized diets fortified with C, E, and B-complex vitamins. The addition of antibiotics to water for treatment is controversial, since antibiotics may not be adsorbed to effective blood levels. Even when fish are fed antibiotics and seem to respond, it is a safe assumption that they are still infected.

Aquarists should be aware that mycobacterial infections can be transmitted from aquaria to humans, where the lesions appear as nodules on the fingers. Problems appear to be limited to situations where an aquarist with an open cut cleans an aquarium. Persons with cuts on fingers or hands either should avoid cleaning aquaria or should use protective gloves during cleaning.

Lactobacillus (Carnobacterium) piscicola

This is the bacterium responsible for pseudokidney or "big kidney" disease, which has been reported in salmonid fish from England, the United States, and Canada. It may be worldwide in scope and potentially could affect all freshwater and saltwater fish, since these lactobacillilike organisms are normal flora of fish. We have isolated them from ornamental species which showed no overt signs of bacterial disease.

In infected salmonid fish, the disease condition is most frequently noted in stressed fish one or more years old. Most commonly, mortality appears after spawning or as a result of handling. The disease signs vary, but usually include an ascitic abdomen and small blood-filled vesicles along the side of the fish. Internally, the liver, kidney, and spleen are involved, along with internal hemorrhaging and muscle abscesses. No control measures other than avoidance of stress have been recommended. The organism is sensitive to antibiotics, including ampicillin, tetracycline, and chloromycetin.

Nocardia

In both freshwater and saltwater fish, species of *Nocardia* (primarily *N. asteroides* and *N. kampachi*) may cause a disease that is very similar to mycobacteriosis on a clinical basis and which can be distinguished from it only by verification of staining characteristics. Signs of the disease include a long course and formation of granulomas. The organism is aerobic. Cultivated on bacteriological media, *Nocardia* organisms are longer and thinner than *Mycobacterium* and show filamentous branch formation. About 30 percent of *Nocardia* strains are acid-fast. Species of *Mycobacterium* are all acid-fast and are uniformly rod-shaped. The distribution of *Nocardia* is worldwide. From the limited data available, it appears that fish contract the disease in the natural environment. In cases of suspected nocardial infections, control measures appropriate for control of mycobacterial infections should be initiated.

Eubacterium tarantellus

This anaerobic organism has been isolated from fish in two situations in brackish water in the United States. Signs of the disease were neurological; affected fish twirled on a longitudinal axis until they died. In these outbreaks a number of estuarine species, but primarily mullet, were infected.

Clostridium

This anaerobe has been reported as a cause of a chronic disease of farmed trout in Denmark, England, and the United States. To the present time, only salmonid fish have been involved. Infected fish appear listless and have a sluggish and erratic swimming movement, alternately floating and sinking. Eventually death results. No characteristic external lesions have been noted. *Clostridium botulinum* is widespread in marine and freshwater environments, soil, and in the gastrointestinal tract of most animals, including fish. Starvation of fish has removed the organism from the gut of fish and aided in recovery. Since the organism can be part of normal gut flora, demonstration of circulating toxin aids in diagnosis. At present, this condition in salmonid fish has not been shown to present any hazards to human health.

African cichlid disease, also called "African bloat," is a disease of cichlids characterized by the development of ascites, exophthalmia, and in many cases, generalized hemorrhages. Common genera of fish involved are *Pseudotropheus zebra* and *Haplochromis moori*. Evidence points to the involvement of a *Clostridium* species as part of the African bloat problem. We have isolated a species of *Clostridium* and *Aeromonas hydrophila* from infected fish. On postmortem examination of affected fish, ascitic fluid is found and livers are yellow. Microscopic examination of liver sections or smears indicates a large amount of fat accumulation, suggesting poor nutrition.

We hypothesize that the disease onset is brought about by overfeeding, which results in the elaboration of toxins from resident *Clostridium* species. Toxins affect kidney function, resulting in bloat. Secondary bacterial invaders such as *Aeromonas hydrophila* then invade the weakened fish. Aquarists interested in African cichlids have noted that the avoidance of overfeeding (and possibly instituting a higher-fiber diet) will effectively prevent the occurrence of African bloat. This hypothesis is freely borrowed from the well-known disease in sheep which results from overeating and which is known as pulpy kidney disease. This sheep disease is induced by a toxin produced by *Clostridium perfringens* as a response to increased carbohydrates in the diet.

Control of bloat in African cichlids therefore should be directed to feeding high-quality complete diets in moderate amounts. Antibiotics are ineffective against toxins which destroy tissues. This may explain the lack of response of fish with bloat problems to common antibiotics added to aquarium water.

Large ulcers result from infection by several sorts of bacteria. Top: a gourami with ulcers. Above: a goldfish with an *Aeromonas* infection.

Gram-Positive Cocci

Staphylococcus

A species of *Staphylococcus* has been reported only in food fish from Japan and Argentina. The Japanese reports were associated with cultured yellowtail, whereas trout were affected in Argentina. The diseased fish were described as having typical signs of congestion, exophthalmia, and ulcerations of the tail. Identification of these isolates grouped them as *Staphylococcus epidermidis* and subsequent serological studies further showed these isolates to be different from human isolates of this same species. It was concluded that infection occurred from water rather than from human association, and it has been shown that this species is present in the aquatic environment. Studies in our laboratory have indicated that various species of staphylococci are common in shipping water. We have isolated staphylococci from neon tetras affected with *Pleisto-*

phora hyphessobryconis, the causative organism of neon tetra disease. We suggest that in this case, and possibly other cases, species of staphylococci may be secondary problems in fish.

Streptococcus

Species of *Streptococcus* have been shown to affect a large number of freshwater and marine fish in Japan, Norway, England, the United States, and South Africa. Fish affected include striped mullet, stingray, spot pinfish, silver trout, menhaden, sea catfish, golden shiner, Atlantic croaker, channel catfish, rainbow trout, eels, tilapia, yellowtail, danio, and ayu. External signs include exophthalmia, distended abdomen, erratic swimming, eye hemorrhage, blood-filled vesicles on the body, darkening of the skin, and vague neurological signs such as erratic twirling movements. When present, internal lesions include pale organs and accumulation of ascitic fluid. Some problems noted in Japan have been associated with Lancefield group D isolates, but the balance of disease has been attributed to a non-hemolytic Lancefield group B organism, regardless of the type of fish involved. Control of the condition rests with improved fish management.

In tropical fish farms, streptococcal infections have been a problem. A predominant sign noted by fish farmers is circling of the fish. On close examination, hemorrhages are apparent. The course of the infection is very rapid. Typically, fish still appear normal within twenty-four hours of death. Streptococci can be isolated from all organs of infected fish, including the brain. Many fish are potentially able to be infected, but most isolations have been from zebra danios and tiger barbs.

This case of fin rot resulted from infection by an atypical variant of *Aeromonas*.

We assume that stressed fish are infected by streptococcal species found in the environment. However, attempts to isolate the organisms from water, tadpoles, or fish food have been unsuccessful. A confirming diagnosis would depend on cultivation and isolation of the organism. The most effective of the antibiotics commonly used to control problems encountered on fish farms is erythromycin, which is particularly effective against gram-positive organisms.

Gram-Negative, Oxidase-Positive Rods

This group of bacteria includes some of the bacteria most frequently associated with aquarium fish. Many are found in the water and are associated with healthy fish.

Aeromonas

Since 1891, the *Aeromonas hydrophila* complex (*A. liquefaciens, A. formicans, A. punctata*) and *A.sobria* have been associated with a disease condition known as motile aeromonas septicemia (MAS), bacterial hemorrhagic septicemia (BHS), or hemorrhagic septicemia of fish. The disease has been reported worldwide in freshwater fish and from time to time from estuarine fishes. All freshwater species are susceptible.

The organism is common in the aquatic environment, and disease outbreaks usually follow a period of stress. In studies involving well-managed home aquaria, it is not uncommon to find 1,000 or more *Aeromonas hydrophila* per cubic centimeter of water. We have shown that the bacteria is associated with healthy fish. In freshwater aquarium fish, the disease strikes after some stress, such as recent shipment, lack of aeration, or poor water quality associated with nitrogenous wastes.

Aeromonas infections frequently follow infestations of parasites, which provide a route of entry for the bacteria. Monogenetic trematodes, fish lice, or a variety of external protozoan infections could be the initiating factors. All stresses, including specific vitamin deficiencies, may lead to a failure of the immune system to repel bacteria from disseminating throughout the body.

When external signs are present, they may include pinpoint or paintbrush hemorrhages in and around the gills and anal area. Large ulcers are common in advanced cases. Abdominal distention is frequently found and exophthalmia is common. On necropsy, hemorrhages may be found in all organs. Bloated fish contain ascitic fluid. Bacteria can generally be isolated from kidneys.

Control of this disease is by careful attention to minimization of stress. The disease is rare in well-managed home aquaria where fish are given a balanced diet. Unfortunately, it is most difficult to eliminate stressful conditions associated with long periods of shipping. Before shipping, attention should be given to pretreating fish with antibiotics, buffering pH, and minimizing ammonia accumulation. Importers should assume that fish are stressed and should initiate antibiotic treatments either before or at the first sign of problems. Good care of stressed fish would include water changes, a complete diet, water temperature of 75 to 80 degrees F (about 24 to 27 degrees C), shaded conditions, and antibiotic therapy. In addition to treating the aquarium water with antibiotics, larger fish with ulcerations can easily be injected with antibiotics intraperitoneally. (Antibiotics must be selected carefully and used with some care; see under "Antibiotics and Their Usage"). The effectiveness of experimental vaccines tried to date is questionable.

Aeromonas salmonicida has been reported as a disease of salmonid fish since 1894. All freshwater and marine fish are considered susceptible to this organism, which is known to exist worldwide either in the typical form or as an atypical variant. The typical disease in salmonid fish is of no particular interest to aquarists other than the fact that it is a principal disease of trout and salmon characterized by lethargy, bloodshot fins, hemorrhages of the muscles, and bloody discharges from gills and vent. Internal lesions include an enlarged spleen, kidney necrosis, and liver hemorrhage.

In nonsalmonid fish, atypical variants of *Aeromonas* can cause diseases characterized by gradually enlarging skin ulcers, with death occurring from other opportunistic bacteria. We have isolated such variants from swordtails with fin rot.

Ulcer disease in goldfish is initiated by such an atypical variant of *A. salmonicida*. A problem facing goldfish producers, it is occasionally seen at retail outlets. On goldfish farms, control measures are directed toward minimization of stress and incorporation of antibacterial drugs such as tetracycline, oxolinic acid, and potentiated sulfonamides in food. Some fish farmers claim that co-cultivation of goldfish with shiners will decrease the incidence of the disease. Others give fish bath treatments in oxolinic acid (an antibiotic) after handling. Despite active research for over forty years, no adequate and dependable vaccine is yet available.

At the retail or hobby level, ulcer disease may appear shortly after fish have been shipped. We have found that infected fish respond well to injections of antibiotics at dosages normally used for mammals. In our hands, intraperitoneal injections of chloramphenicol at levels as high as 25 milligrams per 100-gram (3.5-ounce) goldfish effected a cure. Other injected drugs such as gentamycin or tetracyclines might also be used. One injection of chloramphenicol given intraperitoneally usually gives satisfactory results; in some cases, a second injection after a week may be required. The site of injection is off-center anterior to the anal area (about 2 centimeters, or 0.8 inches). Fish can be restrained by netting. Lesions will ultimately heal. Frequent water changes, elevated water temperatures (to 75 to 80 degrees F, or about 24 to 27 degrees C), and addition of 0.2 to 0.3 percent salt to aquaria may enhance healing.

Pseudomonas

A dominant part of the aquatic bacterial population, *Pseudomonas fluorescens* for many years has been associated with a disease problem referred to as *Pseudomonas* septicemia. Isolates have been reported worldwide from diseased fish from both freshwater and marine sources. Currently, it is thought that all species of aquarium fish are potentially susceptible to this organism, which is a normal inhabitant of both freshwater and marine aquaria. Signs of the disease may be identical to those associated with a number of other bacteria. They range from fin and body ulcers and erosions to a systemic disease involving internal organs. Large ulcers on freshwater or marine fish may be caused by species of *Pseudomonas.* In all cases, infections are thought to be stress-related. Under pond conditions, they occur most commonly during cold weather.

Treatment is difficult, since several *Pseudomonas* strains are resistant to a number of antimicrobial drugs. Chemotherapeutics include tetracycline, gentamycin, or in some cases, sulfa. With larger fish we suggest intraperitoneal injections using gentamycin.

Pseudomonas anguilliseptica causes red spot disease, which has been described primarily in eels cultivated for food. It is likely that it or a related strain induces similar diseases in ornamental eels. Lesions include petechial hemorrhages in the skin of the mouth region, on the ventral aspect of the body, and on the gill opercula. Internal lesions include pale organs and generalized hemorrhages. Suggested therapy includes elevation of water temperature and antibiotic therapy using nalidixic or oxolinic acid.

Vibrio

Vibrios are commonly found in the marine environment and many species, including *V. anguillarum, V. ordelli, V. alginolyticus,* and *V. vulnificus,* are capable of causing disease. As with bacterial problems associated with freshwater species, many produce disease in fish under stress.

Red pest, caused by *V. anguillarum,* was first described in 1718 from eels in Italy. Since that time it has also been called saltwater furunculosis, boil disease, Hitra disease, and ulcer disease. Typical external disease signs are skin discolorations and red necrotic lesions of the abdomen; bloody infection at the base of fins, in the mouth, and in the vent; exophthalmia; and distention of the gut. Internally, there is a bacteremia with swelling of the kidney, liver, and spleen, and a clear viscous fluid in the gut. *V. anguillarum* has been divided into three subspecies, one of which (type B) has been given the name *V. ordelli.* The latter represents a major disease problem in the United States.

Vibrios have a worldwide distribution, and all freshwater and saltwater species are considered susceptible. Several control measures are available. An effective vaccine is used for food-producing species. Antibiotics placed in the fish food have also been used. Presently, only tetracyclines and sulfa drugs are legal for use in food-producing fish.

A number of other vibrios have been recovered from disease outbreaks from time to time. They are mentioned here because they may represent emerging fish-disease problems or may constitute a potential public health hazard. The generalized disease caused by these bacterial species is similar to that described for *V. anguillarum. V. alginolyticus* has been reported to cause disease in sea bream. However, this may represent environmental contamination rather than disease, since this species of bacteria is a very common organism in the marine environment. *V. carchariae* has been isolated with regularity from diseased sharks in the past five years and is an established pathogen for sharks. It has been noted as a disease problem in compromised rather than healthy fish. *V. damsela* has been reported to cause ulcers in a number of marine species. The organism is very cytotoxic, is common in the marine environment, and has been reported in human disease. *V. vulnificus* has been isolated from eels in Japan and England. The organism is common in the marine environment and has been isolated from humans.

In marine aquaria, *Vibrio* infections occur in fish which have experienced severe stress, such as recent shipping. Signs may include extensive hemorrhages, ulcerations, fin and body erosions, and involvement of internal organs. Fish may bloat from the accumulation of ascitic fluid. In well-managed saltwater systems where fish are kept in good nutrition and in good water, lesions attributable to these bacteria are rarely a problem. Seawater collected for routine water changes can be a source of *Vibrio*. We suggest sterilization of such water using 5 ppm of free chlorine followed by dechlorination.

It is important to stress that *Vibrio* infections may be indistinguishable from lesions resulting from *Pseudomonas* species and possibly from mycobacterial infections. The latter two types of bacterial infections are more difficult to treat due to the protective granulomas in the case of *Mycobacterium* and the high percentage of antibiotic-resistant strains in the case of *Pseudomonas* infections. Treatment of bacterial infections in marine fish can be approached either by injecting fish with antibiotics or by adding antibiotics to water. Normally, fish with ulcerations will respond better to injections. We suggest intraperitoneal injections of either chloromycetin or gentamycin. The dose for chloromycetin is 25 milligrams per kilogram of body weight; for gentamycin, 0.5 to 1 milligram per kilogram of body weight. A fish 4 to 5 inches (about 10 to 13 centimeters) long weighs approximately 70 to 100 milligrams. We have found that excessive treatment with chloromycetin does not result in toxicity, but since gentamycin is toxic for kidneys of fish, its dosages should be calculated carefully. Fish can be weighed by first weighing the aquarium with water but minus fish on a scale, then weighing it with fish, and subtracting the former weight from the latter.

Plesiomonas shigelloides

Over the past eight to ten years, this bacterium has been recovered from a variety of aquarium

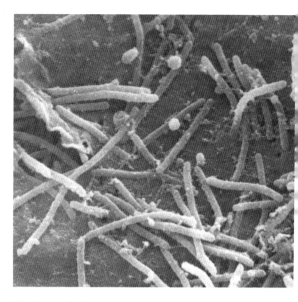

The bacteria that cause columnaris disease are evident in this electronmicrograph.

fish as well as from channel catfish. As with most bacterial infections of fish, signs of the disease include hemorrhages on the body, muscles, and internal organs, and accumulation of ascitic fluid resulting in bloat. In our laboratories we have used tetracycline, chloromycetin, and naladixic acid with success.

Gram-Negative, Oxidase-Negative Rods

Yersinia ruckeri

This member of the enteric group of bacteria was first reported from fish in the mid-1950s. Associated with a disease referred to as enteric red mouth (ERM), Hagerman red mouth, or red mouth, it has been implicated in disease problems in the United States, Denmark, Canada, Germany, England, Italy, Norway, Australia, and France. The disease characteristically affects salmonid fish, but it has been reported from various nonsalmonid fish, including goldfish, carp, lake herring, and emerald dace. External lesions include subcutaneous hemorrhaging of the mouth and throat, hemorrhage at the base of the fins, sluggishness, exophthalmia, darkening of the skin, and in some instances, erosion of the jaw and palate. Internally, there may be massive petechial hemorrhaging of the muscles, enlargement of the kidney and spleen, and a characteristic yellow fluid in the intestines.

Yersinia ruckeri is part of the common flora of

the freshwater environment and is not an obligate pathogen. Stress and water quality seem to influence the occurrence of disease. Control measures include a very effective vaccine (used in the trout industry) and an array of antibiotics and chemotherapeutics, including sulfa, tetracycline, Romet®, and oxolinic acid. Within the aquarium-fish industry, this problem appears to be limited to goldfish producers and wholesalers. The management practice of keeping water as cool as feasible will tend to limit the disease in goldfish, as will the use of antibiotics in feed.

Edwardsiella ictaluri

Another enteric bacterium, *Edwardsiella ictaluri* was first reported to infect fish in 1976, producing a disease in channel catfish which was characterized by inflammation of the intestines. A chronic version of this bacterium in channel catfish has been called "hole-in-the-head" disease, but this organism is not associated with the "hole-in-the-head" disease frequently seen in a variety of cichlids such as angelfish, oscars, and discus.

The organism also has been shown to be associated with aquarium fish. In danios, the principal sign of infection was circling of the fish; bacteria were isolated from internal organs and from the brain. The organism also has been isolated from a black ghost knife fish with neurological symptoms and from walking catfish from Thailand.

E. ictaluri should always be considered as a potential problem on fish farms and included as a possibility when neurological signs are seen in fish. When diagnosed, active infections can be treated with antibiotics given with food or in water.

Gram-Negative Pigmented Rods

Cytophaga

Since the first report of this genus in 1922, its members have appeared in the literature under a variety of names, including *Chorndococcus, Cytophaga, Flexibacter, Myxobacterium,* and at one time, *Flavobacterium.* The most common species is *columnaris,* named for the characteristic columns or stacks of organisms noted in diseased tissues.

Recent phenotypic studies of this group of yellow-pigmented bacteria, often referred to as YPB, indicate that *Cytophaga* may be separated from other YPB based upon its gliding motility, resistance to neomycin, production of the pigment flexirubin, and growth on special media. This group has been further subdivided into five sub-

groups. The first two have type species; the other three are undefined. The first subgroup, represented by *Cytophaga columnaris,* produces the enzyme chronditinase and is capable of initiating disease in healthy fish. The second subgroup usually causes disease at lower temperatures but lacks chronditinase and attacks fish which are stressed. The three remaining subgroups are associated only with stressed or compromised hosts.

Since taxonomic problems exist and the growth characteristics of *Cytophaga* are similar in disease situations, all infections are considered as a single etiology. The disease is commonly called columnaris disease. The bacterium is found worldwide, and all fish species are susceptible. All marine fish species are susceptible to the less well-defined marine counterparts of this group of bacteria.

A tentative diagnosis may be made from characteristic external lesions. These vary greatly from gill involvement to necrosis of fins and the development of large necrotic areas on the fish. These signs are often referred to as fin rot or body rot. A common form of the disease is the development of a necrotic area over the area of the dorsal fin; this particular lesion sometimes is referred to as "saddle back." Very few if any gross lesions are noted internally, but from the high percentages of isolations from blood and kidneys, it appears that bacteremias are common. Other types of bacteria, such as *Aeromonas,* may also infect fish concurrently.

Columnaris organisms are considered to be a part of the environment and have been observed growing on uneaten fish food. Most likely, the bacteria feed on organic wastes, and numbers of bacteria per volume of water increase with the amount of organic material present. These bacteria can be found on healthy fish. Development of disease is related to a stress-related decrease in disease resistance. In aquarium fish, the disease is frequently seen immediately after shipping. In well-managed home aquaria the disease condition is not common, although bacteria are present.

Columnaris may be controlled by reduction of environmental bacteria through minimization of organic substances by regular water changes with cleaning of gravel beds. When fish are showing lesions, antibacterial drugs and antibiotics must be used. Chemicals such as formaldehyde, quaternary ammonium compounds, and copper sulfate can have an antibacterial effect on *Cytophaga columnaris.* These chemicals have been used successfully in pond culture. Treatment of *Cytophaga* infections in aquarium fish should be initiated as soon as lesions are seen. In the aquarium trade, exporters attempt to reduce the incidence of this disease by pretreatment of fish with antibiotics before shipping. Wholesalers importing fish treat known problem-fish species automatically upon arrival. Antibiotics used have included sulfa drugs, tetracyclines, nitrofurans, and naladixic acid.

Flavobacterium

Another prominent member of the yellow-pigmented bacteria is the genus *Flavobacterium.* The classification of this group is in confusion at this time. For years, its primary characteristics were that its members were gram-negative, pigmented, and nonmotile. As a general rule, *Flavobacterium* may be separated from *Cytophaga* in that the former have nondiffusing pigment, are nonmotile, and do not require a special medium for growth. These organisms are found worldwide in both freshwater and marine (estuarine) environments, and all fish species are susceptible. As with *Cytophaga,* infections are more frequently associated with stressed fish. Lesions are similar to those caused by *Cytophaga,* and recommended control measures currently are the same. Under practical conditions, diseases caused by *Cytophaga* and *Flavobacterium* can be differentiated only by culture and identification of the organism.

Antibiotics and Their Usage

Antibiotics are compounds which are antagonistic to the growth of bacteria. These compounds act in a variety of ways, depending upon the type or "family" of antimicrobial drugs to which they belong. In general, their action on the bacterium is rather specific and is directed against some vital part of the bacterium.

Antibiotics in the beta lactam group, which includes penicillins and cephalosporins, interfere with formation of the bacterial cell wall. Their use in treatment of aquarium fish is limited to treatment of conditions caused by gram-positive bacteria. Polypeptides (polymyxins) interfere with the development of the cytoplasmic membrane. Aminoglycosides (gentamycin, kanamycin, tobramycin, streptomycin) interfere with protein synthesis at the 30 S ribosome level. Gentamycin and kanamycin have been used for treatment of ornamental fish, but both can be toxic to kidneys. Macrolides (erythromycin) interfere with protein synthesis at the 50 S ribosome level. Quinolines (naladixic acid, oxolinic acid) interfere with DNA metabolism. Sulfa drugs and potentiated sulfa drugs (Tribrissen®, Romet®) affect folic acid metabolism.

Mechanism of killing bacteria: Antimicrobial action upon bacteria is considered to be either "static" or "cidal." The antimicrobial drug either prevents further bacterial multiplication, allowing the host body defenses to eliminate them (static), or kills the bacteria directly (cidal).

Dosage of antibiotics: The concentration of antimicrobial drugs used to treat a bacterial disease is determined by a number of criteria. Of primary concern is the relative toxicity of the agent on the host animal. Some antibiotics tend to accumulate in a particular organ, and overdosage may kill fish. Because of species differences regarding adsorption, one should be aware of potential dangers if using antibiotics on which toxicology studies have not been done.

The effectiveness of an antibiotic will depend on the level of activity it attains, both in the water and in the fish. These effective concentrations are expressed as the minimal inhibitory concentration (MIC), which is the smallest amount of agent which will inhibit growth of the bacteria being tested, and the minimal bactericidal concentration (MBC), which is the lowest concentration which will kill the bacteria. The MBC is usually measurably higher than the MIC in the case of static agents, but will be close to the MIC in the case of cidal agents.

Since a portion of the antimicrobial drug will be broken down by body organs and/or bound to proteins in the animal tissue, only that portion which remains is available for antimicrobial drug action. For this reason, dosing must allow for some excess, usually from four to fifty times the MIC, depending upon the route, the drug, and the conditions under which the compound is being administered.

Antibiotic suitability: The suitability of an antibiotic to retard a specific bacterium may be assessed in several ways. The most common laboratory assay is a complex method referred to as the Kirby-Baur (KB) test. Results of this essay are reported as S (sensitive), I (intermediate), or R (resistant).

An alternative is the "shotgun" approach, in which treatment is empirically determined and evidence of clinical response represents success. This is the approach most used by the tropical fish industry and often by hobbyists as well. In many instances, bacterial disease strikes, and antibiotics are blindly added to the water with the hopes that they will stem the infection. In many cases, the addition of an antibiotic to aquarium water will result in a cure; in other cases, there may be no obvious amelioration of the disease. Perhaps the antibiotic was not suitable for the bacteria causing the problem. An example would be the use of penicillin for the treatment of an infection caused by a gram-negative bacterium such as *Aeromonas*. Or perhaps the bacteria were antibiotic-resistant.

Bacteria may evolve resistance to not just one, but many, antibiotics. The mechanism by which resistant strains develop is complex. Usually a basic mutation in the DNA codes for a new substance elaborated by the bacteria which makes it insensitive to the antibiotic. Another way in which bacteria become resistant is by the transfer of resistance factors. When the bacteria conjugate, a small circular fragment of DNA containing information for antibiotic resistance is passed from resistant to sensitive bacteria. The transferred fragment, or plasmid, divides along with the cell and makes subsequent generations resistant. Since the DNA associated with the plasmid is not a part of the DNA of the bacterium, this method of acquired antibiotic resistance is referred to as extrachromosomal or plasmid-mediated resistance.

In everyday practice, antibiotic-resistant strains often emerge when antibiotics are continually used in treatment. As susceptible strains are killed by the antibiotic, resistant strains come to predominate. Plasmid-mediated resistance, in particular, may present significant problems in the management of bacterial disease. Plasmids may also afford resistance to toxic ions such as copper, and may alter pathogenicity and metabolic activity of "carrier" bacteria. Plasmids are more frequently encountered in gram-negative bacteria but also occur in gram-positive bacteria. When apparent problems arise as a result of plasmids, they usually can be corrected by examining the sensitivity spectrum of the bacteria in question and making appropriate changes in therapy.

Regular (and sometimes unnecessary) use of antibiotics on fish farms or retail establishments has been documented to result in a large population of bacteria which contain plasmids for resistance to multiple antibiotics. In practical terms, the emergence of resistant bacteria can be avoided by employing antibiotics only when indicated, using a recommended dose (see further in this section), and continuing the treatment for at least three to four days.

The only certain way to determine the effectiveness of an antibiotic is to isolate the bacteria and test them for sensitivity to antibiotics, procedures which require expert laboratory assistance but may be arranged through a local veterinarian with access to a diagnostic laboratory. At the hobbyist level, the "shotgun" approach of simply trying different antibiotics may be practical. However, one should remember that antibiotics are not a cure-all. Some chronic bacterial diseases such as mycobacteriosis are not readily treated with antibacterial drugs, and antibiotics are ineffective against parasites.

Addition of antibiotics to water: Adding antibiotics to the water is the most common way aquarium fish are treated for bacterial infections. The advantages are that calculation of dosage is simple, uniform exposure of fish is assured, and any pathogens in the water or externally on the fish will be exposed to the antibiotic. Unfortunately, the adsorbability of antibiotics by tropical fish under differing water conditions has not been thoroughly investigated. Although some general guidelines can be given, the trial-and-error approach for any given water and antibiotic remains the best method of evaluation.

Water quality is a key factor in the adsorption of antibiotics by fish. Organic pollutants in water may bind antibiotics and decrease the dose available for adsorption by the fish. This suggests that water should be changed prior to the addition of an antibiotic. Water hardness also may affect antibiotic adsorption. For example, calcium ions in hard water bind to tetracyclines, resulting in failure of the antibiotic to be adsorbed. Solutions to this problem include either increasing the dosage or softening the water.

The pH of the water during therapy may also be of practical importance in antibiotic adsorption. Depending on the chemical composition of the antibiotic molecule, it will dissociate (ionize) at either high or low pH, and in this form it is less likely to be adsorbed by the fish. For example, a naturally acidic molecule such as naladixic acid

(Negram[®]) will remain non-ionized in slightly acidic water, and adsorption will be expected to be maximal if pH is adjusted to just under 7 (slightly acidic).

Previous studies suggest that selected antibiotics are adsorbed after four to five hours. Based on these studies, we would suggest a four- to five-hour exposure time followed by a complete water change. This will tend to eliminate any residual antibiotic and help to prevent the emergence of resistant bacterial strains. Short treatments followed by water changes will also tend to prevent any toxic effects on fish. Treatments should be continued on a daily basis until the fish appear cured. To prevent emergence of antibiotic-resistant strains, it is advisable to continue treatments for at least five days, even if fish appear normal three days after the initiation of the treatment.

Carbon filtration should be discontinued during treatments, since activated carbon will adsorb antibiotics. The effect on nitrifying bacteria in the filter bed also must be considered. Since many of the antibiotics used are bacteriostatic rather than bactericidal, nitrifying bacteria are inhibited only as long as the antibiotic is present. With a water change at the termination of the treatment, the bacteria should resume their normal function. Of course, foam filters or gravel could be removed from the filter bed during the treatment period. Alternatively, the treatment could be given in an aquarium without filters but with adequate aeration. If undergravel filters are used, remove air stems from the lift stack and place them in water for maximal aeration. Do not pull antibiotics through the gravel bed!

Addition of antibiotics to food: An alternative to water administration of antibiotics is to add them to the diet of sick fish. This method of administration has been used in food-fish production for many years, with some obvious advantages. Since antibiotics are mixed in with food, the dosage can be based on the average food intake of the fish. Additionally, this method affords a mechanism for gut absorption of antibiotics not suitable for water administration. Feeding also permits the use of less antibiotic than is needed for water treatment. A major shortcoming of mixing antibiotics with food is the fact that sick fish may not eat. Another serious disadvantage is that antibiotics mixed with feed may lose activity during long periods of storage. However, the practice of feeding antibiotics just prior to or after stress periods such as shipping makes good sense and can prevent bacterial infections from becoming established.

Medicated food can be purchased through commercial outlets, but the choice of antibiotics available in this form is limited. If sensitivity testing has been done or if other antibiotics are required, we suggest the incorporation of 0.75 percent of an antibiotic in a nutritionally complete gelatinized diet. Keep medicated food frozen between uses to avoid degradation of the antibiotics. Feeding should begin a few days before shipping and continue for at least five days after shipping.

Injection of antibiotics: A third means of administering antibiotics is by injecting them into fish. This method is used primarily with larger fish under conditions where

Common Antimicrobial Drugs for Treatment of Freshwater Ornamental Fish		
Compound	Dosage [1]Bath treatment	Long-term immersion
Chloramphenicol	10 – 50 ppm	12 –24 ppm (? absorption)
Tetracycline	10 – 20 ppm	12 – 24 ppm (absorbed)
Erythromycin	—	12 – 24 ppm (absorbed)
Furanace[®]	0.5 – 1 ppm, 5 to 10 min	0.01 ppm (absorbed)
Furadantoin	50 ppm, 1 hr	1.0 – 1.5 ppm (gut-absorbed)
Kanamycin	—	12 – 24 ppm (gut-absorbed)
Minocycline	—	6 – 12 (? absorption)
Metronidazole	—	5 ppm (absorbed)
Naladixic acid	—	10 – 15 ppm (gut-absorbed)
Oxolinic acid	—	12 – 20 ppm (? absorption)
Sulfamethozine	—	12 – 24 ppm (gut-absorbed)
Tribrissen[®], Romet[®]	—	6 – 12 ppm (gut-absorbed)

[1] Unless otherwise noted, treat for no longer than four hours, and less if fish show stress.

fish may have been stressed from handling, hauling, or sorting. Injection also is the method of choice with larger aquarium fish with signs (such as hemorrhages or ulcers) suggesting bacterial disease. An obvious advantage is that the fish immediately receives the dosage needed, increasing its chances of survival.

Restraint and handling of fish is best done by netting. The antibiotic is injected intraperitoneally approximately 2 centimeters (about 0.8 inches) forward of, and slightly off to one side from, the anal area. Tuberculin or microsyringes with small (26- to 28-gauge) needles work well. Dosages of injected drugs such as chloramphenicol or gentamycin should be calculated according to the estimated weight of the fish.

Antimicrobial substances commonly used in fish: A variety of drugs have been used to treat fish for bacterial disease (see accompanying table). The antibiotic most extensively used is tetracycline. Approved for food fish, this compound is bacteriostatic in nature, preventing further multiplication of bacteria. Its extensive use in aquarium fish has led to problems of bacterial resistance.

The sulfa drugs, also approved for food fish, are bacteriostatic as well. Used extensively in the aquarium trade, they probably are most effective when used in slightly acidic water. Reports of therapeutic failure may be related to their use in high-pH water. One potentiated sulfa compound which has been approved for use in food-fish operations is Romet®. Whether this compound would be adsorbed from water by aquarium fish is not known.

Aminoglycosides, which include antibiotics such as kanamycin and gentamycin, are bactericidal and have some limited use for aquarium fishes. Kanamycin has been used to treat marine fish, and its reputed effectiveness may be due to the fact that marine fish drink water and presumably absorb antibiotics from the water. Neither kanamycin nor gentamycin are likely to be adsorbed by freshwater fish, and both are potentially toxic to kidneys. However, gentamycin could be used for injection of fish.

Chloramphenicol (chloromycetin) has a bacteriostatic action. It is not adsorbed by fish due to its insolubility in water. It is the preferred antibiotic for injection of larger fish.

Another group of chemical agents, the quinoline group, contains several compounds which can be considered to fall in two groups. The first group contains the older derivatives, such as naladixic acid and oxolinic acid, all of which have relatively limited gram-positive antimicrobic spectra. Naladixic acid is better adsorbed by fish when water is slightly acidic. It has a broad spectrum against many bacterial pathogens, and to date, few resistant forms have arisen. The second group is comprised of fluorinated derivatives which have a broader antimicrobic range. Several of these currently are being examined for use in aquaculture.

Still another common group of chemical compounds are the furans, which include nitrofurantoin, furadextin, furicin, and furanase. All of these act as static compounds by blocking bacterial metabolism. Furanace® and nitrofurantoin are adsorbed by fish. Development of antibiotic-resistant strains has been minimal, but with extended usage these antibiotics can damage kidneys.

Another antibiotic used with aquarium fish is erythromycin. Its use should be limited to problems associated with gram-positive bacteria.

Diseases Caused by Fungi

The fungi are a large group of nucleated organisms which are plantlike but lack chlorophyll and are not differentiated into typical plant components such as roots, stems, and leaves. When seen on the surface of a fish, fungal infections appear as a cottonlike white mass. This mass is composed of filaments, known as hyphae, which may or may not branch. The entire mass of hyphae is called a mycelium. In the majority of fungi, the hyphae are divided into cells by cross-walls (septa).

Fungi use organic matter as a source of nourishment, and thus generally live in close association with other life-forms. Most consume dead remains and waste products of other organisms. Others live closely with other life-forms but do no harm. However, a third group of fungi are parasites, harming or injuring their host as they obtain organic nutrients from it.

Fungi typically reproduce by both sexually and asexually formed spores, but the latter are generally more important due to the greater number formed. Sexual reproduction involves the fusion of two nuclei, with the eventual formation of reproductive elements. Asexual spores are formed in special structures (sporangia) which form at the

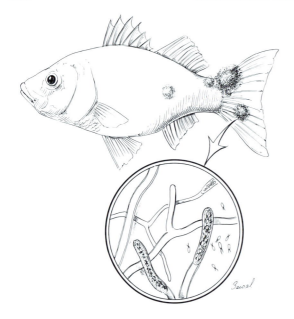

The tufts on this fish are typical of fungal infection, which is most often a secondary disease problem. Within the filamentous forms, developing spores are evident.

end of hyphae. Asexual reproduction can also occur through fragmentation of hyphae and subsequent dispersal of these fragments by wind or water. Under suitable conditions, these fragments will grow into new fungi.

Classification of fungi pathogenic for fish: The classification of fungi is complicated and exact identification as to genus and species is best left to experts. Identification of the fungi of concern to the aquarist has been confounded by a variety of problems, including failure to obtain the fungi in pure culture, failure to prove that a given isolate is truly pathogenic for fish, and failure to study the morphology of the characteristics of both asexual

and sexual reproductive organs.

Many fungi responsible for infections of fish as well as fish eggs belong to the family Saprolegniaceae, which includes a number of common freshwater molds often seen as a fuzzy, whitish growth on organisms that have died. A few genera predominate. *Saprolegnia parasitica* is the type species. Several other species of *Saprolegnia* also have been implicated in causing disease, but species cannot be differentiated by the characteristics of the disease which they induce. *Saprolegnia* infections are without doubt the most frequent fungal infections observed in ornamental fish. Other genera such as *Achlya* and *Aphanomyces* have also been implicated in infections of ornamental fish.

Predisposing factors for fungal infections: Many fish pathologists will agree that fungi of fish are rarely the primary cause of a disease episode. Spores are widespread in soil and water (especially water high in organics from uneaten food and accumulation of fish wastes), but it appears that a fish must be in a compromised state to become actively infected. The development of fungal infections in fish without obvious predisposing factors has been reported only rarely, and usually in these cases not all predisposing factors have been identified.

Temperature variation is considered to be a prime predisposing factor, with colder temperatures being most important. Florida ornamental fish farmers regularly fight fungal problems associated with water temperatures below approximately 50 degrees F (10 degrees C). (Conversely, higher-than-normal water temperatures have also been associated with outbreaks of fungal infections.) Lower water temperatures favor the growth of the fungus while at the same time lengthening wound-healing time in fish and depressing the ability of the fish immune system to resist fungal invasion.

The immune system of fish is depressed not only by temperature drops but by hormone imbalances and indeed, stress from any source. While open wounds induced by parasites, bacteria, or rough handling can serve as the initial point of invasion by a fungal spore, the immunological status of the fish plays a major role in the development of a disease. The high incidence of fungal infections in spawning salmonid fish is thought to be related to hormonal changes which reduce the effectiveness of the cellular component of the immune system to attack and kill invading organisms. Instances of fungal infection of breeding ornamental fish have been reported by commercial fish farmers.

Recognizing fungal disease: Most commonly, a fungal attack is seen as a skin or gill infection which may or may not be associated with a preexisting wound. The infection can be initiated by spores or mycelial elements. *Saprolegnia* lesions are focalized, circular, and have the appearance of cotton patches when viewed while the fish is in water. The distribution of lesions on the surface of the body may be random, but lesions often occur just forward of the dorsal fin. Frequently, the tufts of mycelia will appear brown to gray due to trapped debris. Upon removal of the fish from the water, the mycelial elements collapse, and the characteristic cottony growth pattern is not observed. Microscopic examination of the fungus will reveal a mass of elongate mycelia and sporangia containing motile spores. Although the fungus can penetrate to the muscular level, most cases involve superficial invasion of the dermis. Death is attributable to loss of body fluids and electrolyte imbalances. Superficial fungal infections can be complicated by bacterial pathogens.

A second syndrome is associated with the invasion of internal organs by both *Saprolegnia* and *Aphanomyces*. Such generalized infections have been reported in trout fry and in gouramis. In gouramis, we have found what appeared to be a species of *Aphanomyces* distributed in internal organs as well as in musculature. Histopathological analysis revealed a typical granulomatous reaction, and mycelial elements were demonstrated by special staining techniques. We suspect that with further investigation, other genera of fungi will be implicated in cases of generalized invasion. Such infections cannot be diagnosed by casual observation of the fish. In gouramis affected with *Aphanomyces,* the only signs of infection were granulomas noted on wet-mount preparations. Fungal elements were observed only after tissues were prepared for histopathological examination and stained with fungal-specific stains.

A third syndrome appears to be associated with body orifices such as the mouth, eyes, olfactory pits, and anus. Possibly tissues at these sites provide optimal conditions for spore growth in an already immunologically compromised fish.

Saprolegnia also invade fish eggs. At first, dead eggs are infected. Then the infection readily spreads to adjacent living eggs until the entire egg mass succumbs.

Control and treatment of external fungal infections: Fungal infections are closely associated with both environmental factors, which favor the propagation of the fungus (such as water temperature and organic load), and host factors (such as a predisposing disease, open wounds, or a compromised immune system). Fish producers must adjust management techniques to avoid or minimize infections and stress conditions. This "back-to-basics" approach may include water-temperature control, diet improvement, avoidance of overcrowding, more frequent water changes, improved handling procedures, quarantine to avoid parasitic diseases, and routine prophylactic treatments.

In general, established fungal infections in fish are difficult, if not impossible, to treat. Furthermore, since fungal infections generally are associated with a primary disease problem along with a management problem, therapy against other pathogens as well as the fungus must be initiated along with corrective management procedures. Additionally, the presence of an observed fungus on the surface of a fish implies that the skin has a break and is liable to bacterial infection.

Choice of drugs: At this writing, malachite green is used in aquaculture throughout the world as a fungicide that is highly effective, easy to use, and low in cost. Although allowable in ornamental-fish culture, its use in food-fish culture is not approved by the U.S. Food and Drug Administration, because it is known to be teratogenic in laboratory animals and can cause developmental anomalies when administered to eggs of rainbow trout.

Malachite green can be used as a short-term, high-dosage bath or as a longer, lower-dosage treatment. Short-term bath treatments are done in separate aquaria for individually affected fish or as a preventative for fungus development on fish eggs. Malachite green has been used in bath treatments for fish at 2 ppm for thirty minutes and for fish eggs at 5 ppm for sixty minutes. Since various ornamental fish vary in their susceptibility to malachite green, dosages and treatment times must be followed strictly.

For long-term treatments in home aquaria or in special-treatment aquaria, malachite green is added to give a final dosage of 0.1 ppm. Discontinue carbon filtration but maintain aeration during treatment. Remove air stems from lift stacks of undergravel filters to avoid dilution of malachite green by organics in the gravel bed. The treatment should be continued until signs of the infection are gone. Water changes (with care not to stress fish) at two- to three-day intervals will serve to maintain an effective dose. Antibiotics at 6 to 12 ppm can be given in conjunction with the malachite green if bacterial complications are suspected.

Commercially available formulations of malachite green should be used if available. If not, mix 10 grams (0.3 ounces) of zinc-free malachite green oxalate with 500 milliliters (about 2 cups) of distilled water. Adding the indicated amounts of this stock solution to 10 gallons (38 liters) of water will result in the following dosages:

0.2 milliliter to 10 gallons = 0.1 ppm (0.2 milliliter is equal to 4 drops)

3.0 milliliters to 10 gallons = 2.0 ppm

8.0 milliliters to 10 gallons = 5.0 ppm

It should be noted that formalin (37 percent formaldehyde) at a dosage of 250 ppm has been shown to be as effective in controlling fungus on fish eggs as malachite green at 5 ppm for sixty minutes.

Systemic fungal infections: Internal generalized mycotic infections in fish occasionally have been attributed to *Saprolegnia* and more frequently *to Aphanomyces*. Our experience suggests that systemic fungal infections in tropical fish are rarely seen.

Ichthyosporidium (*Ichthyophonus hoferi*) is frequently mentioned in the aquarium-fish-disease literature as a systemic fungus. Currently, the parasite has been grouped within the Microsporidea; consequently, the organism should be considered as a protozoan. Principally a problem with marine fish, it has been readily transmitted to freshwater species when fish meal contaminated with the organism has been used as a dietary component. Signs of the disease include invasion of the internal organs of the body, resulting in granulomas (whitish-appearing nodules) in the heart, liver, kidneys, spleen, and gonads. Skin infections result in roughened or "sandpaper" skin. Microscopic examination of wet-mount preparations reveals cystlike growths with buds. This disease can mimic systemic mycobacterial infections and can be differentiated by staining smears with acid-fast stains.

Ichthyosporidium should be suspected if fish have been fed diets containing uncooked marine "trash" fish. Incorporation of uncooked fish into diets can also spread a variety of other disease organisms, including *Mycobacterium* species. Obviously the best control of such infections is by avoidance through feeding fish uncontaminated diets.

Fungal infections of gills: Fungal infections of the gills are common and in most cases appear to be associated with *Saprolegnia* species. In freshwater fish, fungi of the genus *Branchiomyces* have been described growing within the blood vessels of the gill. Fungal spores are thought to enter the fish either by direct infection of the gill or by way of the intestine and bloodstream. While the causative agent of this disease has not been officially confirmed, within the gills of ornamental fish we have observed mycotic infections which closely mimic the condition described in carp. Infection with *Branchiomyces* species has been reported to be associated with high temperatures and water high in organic fertilizers with heavy algal blooms. The cause of death in fish is asphyxiation.

Viral Diseases of Aquarium Fish

Of all the pathogenic organisms associated with ornamental fish, the viruses are the least understood and the least studied. This is in large part related to cost restraints. The cost of establishing laboratories which have adequate equipment and personnel trained in virology is relatively high, and while the technology for virus isolation from fish has been available for thirty years, the funds required for isolation and study of potential virus-related problems in ornamental fish have not been forthcoming.

In his recent book, *Fish Viruses and Fish Viral Diseases,* Dr. Ken Wolf includes fifty-six viruses— eighteen viruses which have been isolated and have been associated with disease, five viruses of low virulence, ten viruses of unknown pathogenicity, sixteen viruses which have been observed by electron microscopy but not yet isolated, and seven instances where viruslike particles have been observed in fish. Not unexpected is the observation that the majority of the better-characterized viruses that have been isolated are associated with food fish.

What is a virus?: The definition of a virus is best approached by comparing its principal characteristics with those of other known groups of organisms, for these extremely small particles have some of the properties of living things but lack others.

A virus has no independent metabolism. It cannot live outside of a living cell, because it does not have the necessary components to generate energy or to produce basic components of cells such as amino acids, proteins, carbohydrates, or fats. A virus is composed solely of genetic material (either DNA or RNA) surrounded by a protective protein covering referred to as a capsid. The capsid consists of protein subunits called capsomeres. The organization of the capsomeres and of the capsid as an entity is useful in the classification of viruses.

Once the genetic material of a virus enters the cell of its host, it redirects the host's cellular machinery to produce copies of the viral nucleic acid and the protective proteins which are assembled into capsids. Viruses are released either from cells that burst open or from living cells that remain viable as they continue to shed viruses.

So small that they only became visible upon invention of the electron microscope, viruses are measured in nanometers. There are 25 million nanometers in an inch, and most virus groups range from 30 to 200 nanometers. (In contrast, bacteria usually measure 1 to 4 microns; 1 micron is equal to 1,000 nanometers.) The extremely small size of viruses led to the term "filterable virus," since filters which easily retained bacteria allowed viruses to pass.

Since viruses depend on a living cell for growth, they must contact a susceptible host before the viruses are inactivated by environmental factors. The host-to-host transfer of viruses has been well studied in mammals. Classical methods of spreading mammalian viruses have been via aerosol transfer, direct contact with infected body fluids, insects, or by infected food or water sources. In fish, transfer to a susceptible host is by direct exposure through the water. Gills are probably the initial organs of exposure.

Viral specificity and classification: Viruses show a very marked specificity for classes of animal life. Viruses are found to parasitize bacteria, fungi, plants, insects, amphibians, reptiles, and mammals. The term "species specificity" refers to the fact that viruses generally have a narrow host range. For example, the virus causing the disease hog cholera is found to infect only porcine species. One exception is the rabies virus, which can affect any mammal.

Fish viruses appear to have relatively narrow species specificities, although this has yet to be tested for many of the viruses that have been definitely associated with fish diseases. It is well known that viruses of salmonid fish have a range which is limited to other salmonids. Similarly, channel catfish virus will not affect trout or salmon. This type of specificity underlies the concept of "natural resistance" and has as its basis whether or not a virus can successfully be taken in by a cell, avoid the cell's enzyme systems, use the cell to reproduce itself, and finally assemble its component parts into what we know as a virus.

Viruses are classified into groups based on the presence of either DNA or RNA as their genetic material, presence of an envelope, structure of the proteinaceous capsid, number of capsomeres, site of intercellular development, and size. Presently there are fourteen main classes of viruses, but many viruses are still unclassified. Readers interested in the further study of viruses should consult other texts, such as Braude (1982). The classification of a virus is not based on which animals are infected.

Pathogenicity of viruses: Viruses can cause serious disease problems, moderately severe problems, or can infect a fish without obvious signs of disease. In many cases, the virulence of a virus is associated with other factors, such as age of the fish, and predisposing stressors, such as shipping, concomitant parasitic infections, water temperature, or nutritional status. In many cases, isolates of the same class of virus from an animal will differ markedly in virulence. Such virulence differences form the basis for the development of virus vaccines called "modified live viruses." Differences in virulence have been attributed to the manner in which a virus interacts (both quantitatively and qualitatively) with the various tissues of the infected animal. For instance, vaccine strains of poliovirus will not affect nervous tissue, yet will propagate and eventually stimulate the production of antibodies, which confer protection from further attack by the virus.

Some viruses are virulent. They can infect every organ of the body, resulting in death due to failure of vital life systems, or can cause a general depression of the immune system, resulting in secondary bacterial infections. Viral hemorrhagic septicemia of trout is a good example of a very virulent virus. Infectious pancreatic virus of trout is moderately virulent for fry but essentially avirulent for mature trout. Other viruses may not kill fish but are disfiguring. Lymphocystis virus produces massive enlargements of individual cells, which may resemble tumors. If such masses interfere with feeding, fish die of starvation.

Many fish viruses which have been observed by electron microscopy have not been isolated. The mere presence of a virus in tissues of a fish does not mean that it is causing a disease. In fact, several viruses isolated from a variety of fish produce no apparent disease condition. The isolation of viruses from apparently normal animals and fish has spawned the term "inapparent infection." The term "carrier" refers to an animal with an inapparent infection from which a virus can be isolated.

In many cases with well-studied animal viruses, animals can indeed be carriers of virulent viruses to which they have developed an immunity. In fish, the carrier state is also common in several well-studied viral diseases. This carrier state is one of the principal obstacles to viral disease control, especially when new stock are introduced into a breeding establishment.

Detection and isolation of viruses: Virological studies are complicated by the fact that a virus is a very sophisticated microorganism which can only live and grow in living cells, whether in the animal or in flask-grown cultures of cells from the animal.

Cell cultures can be established directly from fish as required, and some cell cultures can be developed into cell lines perpetuated indefinitely by subculturing. Many cell lines are used in the isolation of fish viruses. Some of these will not support the growth of any known fish virus; others will support a broader selection of known fish viruses. Because of potential specificity, it is generally considered important to use cell cultures which originate from a species closely related to the animal from which a virus recovery is attempted.

Inoculation of cell cultures with bacteria-free preparations of fish tissues is the standard technique for virus isolation. If a virus is present, the cells will begin to die. It is important to show that uninfected control cells remain healthy and that the changes in the cell cultures are not caused by contaminating bacteria. Virologists refer to the cellular changes as a cytopathogenic effect. Once a virus is isolated in cell cultures, it can easily be classified and used for further disease characterization. The isolation of a virus implies that a diagnostic system is available. This is of particular practical importance for detection of potential stock of uninfected breeding fish.

Fish viruses have been detected by direct examination of tissues with an electron microscope. However, while demonstrating the presence of a virus, this method does not establish whether the observed virus is actually causing the disease. To establish that, one must associate the virus with the disease on a regular basis. In addition, when given to unexposed fish, the virus isolated in cultures of fish cells must produce a disease similar to that seen in the field. The entire process of isolating a virus and proving that it is associated with a disease is complex, time-consuming, and expensive.

Diagnosis of viral diseases: Most fish viruses can only be definitely diagnosed by isolation and identification of the virus itself. (An exception is the lymphocystis virus of fish, which produces very characteristic lesions.) Laboratories specializing in fish pathology may be able to identify a virus isolate by the ability of specific antibodies to inactivate the isolate. Other tests include staining suspected infected cell cultures with a battery of fluorescein-tagged antibodies which will react with virus material, then detecting fluorescing cells by microscopy. Both of these tests assume that the virus has been isolated previously, has been well studied, and is one to which specific antibodies have been produced in laboratory animals.

Other techniques exist for detecting viruses directly in tissues. These rather sophisticated methods depend on the availability of specific antisera and/or molecular genetic techniques.

In practice, in most instances involving ornamental fish, a viral disease is suspected when all other possible causes of disease have been eliminated. Reaching this decision involves a detailed study of the fish as well as water quality.

Prevention, control, and treatment of viral diseases: The association between a virus and its host cell is an intimate one. A successful antiviral treatment must spare the life of the cell and inactivate the virus. The difficulty in reaching this goal is attested to by the fact that there are no antiviral drugs available to treat viral diseases of pets and domestic animals. In human medicine, drugs for cold sores and influenza are available and give some relief. Specific drugs for acquired immuno-deficiency syndrome (AIDS) apparently will pro-long life in affected patients. At this writing, the potential of developing antiviral drugs for use in fish is poor due to low demand, high costs, and lack of suitable delivery systems.

Vaccines to prevent viral diseases of humans and animals are common. Most consist of strains of live viruses which have been modified so that they no longer produce a disease but will stimulate the production of antibodies against the virus. The presence of antibodies in the vaccinated host confers protection to inva-sion by the virulent wild-type virus. Vaccines using killed strains are also used, but their abil-ity to confer immunity does not compare favor-ably with that of modified live vaccines.

In veterinary medicine, there is always a concern that some modified live-virus vaccines might revert to the native virulence. In fish medi-cine, the experimental use of modified live-virus vaccines suggests that trout can be immunized by exposure to modified infectious he-matopoietic necrosis virus and to killed-virus preparations of infectious pancreatic necrosis virus. Although vaccines based on other meth-ods might be developed, some serious ques-tions remain unanswered. The age of the fish when it is most susceptible to the virus is a most important factor. If only very young fish are susceptible to the virus, administration of a vaccine may not confer protection because the very young fish may not have a sufficiently ma-ture immune system to respond to the vaccine. A very serious consideration is the possibility of a modified live virus being virulent to nontarget species in the watershed where the vaccine is produced. Governmental approval of any vac-cine would have to include tests showing that nontarget fish are not affected and that the vaccine cannot revert to virulence for the target fish. Another serious limitation is the route of vaccination. To be acceptable, any modified live vaccine would have to be given by adding it to the water. Killed-virus vaccines certainly would circumvent the problem of reversion of the vi-rus, but they must be injected into each animal, which in present-day fish-culture practices is not practical. And last, the development and

testing of a vaccine by a commercial vaccine producer would be done only after the market potential was considered.

Avoidance of viral disease is the most practical approach available to primary fish producers and to hobbyists. The first ground rule is that any fish is a potential carrier of a virus and that the virus may be virulent to similar (or possibly even other nonsimilar) species.

For hobbyists, an extensive quarantine period is the best available method for reducing the possibility that a newly introduced fish will spread a virus. The simple holding of a fish for a period of at least twenty-one days will provide an ample period for the fish to sicken and die, if a disease is present, or to develop an immunity to a possible virus. Naturally, routine treatments for other dis-eases can be initiated during this period.

As mentioned, fish may become virus carriers and may shed viruses without developing signs of disease. If this is a problem, test fish should be introduced into the quarantine tank for two weeks. If the test fish sicken, the quarantined fish should be suspected of carrying some type of pathogenic organism, including a virus. Quaran-tine procedures should be taken seriously. Aquaria holding quarantined fish should be in a separate room or preferably in an entirely different location. Pails, nets, and siphon tubes can easily carry enough virus to initiate an infection and should only be used for quarantine tanks.

Another way to avoid viruses is to purchase fish from hatcheries that are known to have healthy fish. The virus-free status of their fish may have been established by laboratory examination of fish or by a long history of having problem-free fish. Viral diseases in trout are avoided by pur-chasing eggs from certified virus-free hatcheries.

Known Viral Diseases of Ornamental Fish

Lymphocystis disease: Lymphocystis disease is a common malady in both freshwater and ma-rine tropical fish. The DNA-containing iridovirus affects cells of fish, resulting in an increase in the size of individual cells up to 50,000 times their normal volume. Signs of the disease vary with the intensity of the infection. Initially, patches of fins may develop a slight opalescence where cells are beginning to enlarge. On the surface of the skin, small, whitish blebs give the skin a sandpaperlike appearance. In advanced cases, large tumorous growths can be found on any surface of the body. Close inspection of affected areas with a hand-held lens will reveal that the wartlike growths consist of enlarged cells. Involvement of eyes is not uncommon. Growths of cells on or immediately adjacent to mouthparts can lead to starvation. The virus can affect internal organs, but this is usually not a concern in ornamental fish.

A diagnosis of lymphocystis disease can be made by wet-mount preparations of affected tissues removed from the fish. Microscopic examination will reveal massive cells (0.5 to 1.0 millimeter across) with a thick capsule. It is generally thought that the virus is spread from fish to fish by contact of the virus with small openings in the skin caused by rough netting, fighting, or parasites. Once the virus becomes established, adjacent cells are infected.

The course of the disease in ornamental fish is variable, probably because of differences in individual immune responses. In some cases, the cells appear to be rejected by the fish. In other instances, the cells disappear, only to reappear at some later time.

Large tumorous masses which interfere with feeding can lead to starvation. We have successfully removed such masses surgically, then cauterized the exposed cut areas. Marine fish with lymphocystis disease have been observed to clear themselves of infected cells when placed in an aquarium with Pacific anemones. This suggests a possibility that anemones secrete a substance which stimulates the immune system of fish.

Goldfish iridovirus: In a routine survey of goldfish for the presence of viruses, researchers at Northeastern University isolated an iridovirus on two occasions from swim-bladder tissue of healthy goldfish (*Carassius auratus*). When fifteen goldfish were injected intraperitoneally with virus, eight fish died seven to twenty days later and showed hemorrhages within the peritoneal cavity. Attempts to reisolate the virus were unsuccessful. In a second trial, virus which had been passed for five and seven times in cell cultures caused no mortalities in test fish after fifty days of observation.

The presence of a virus in native goldfish is interesting. The apparent lack of pathogenicity under experimental conditions does not negate the possibility that the organism may be pathogenic for goldfish under natural conditions. The primary isolation of these agents from air-bladder tissues suggests a possible involvement with the common air-bladder problems in goldfish.

Spring viremia of carp: This acute disease is characterized by hemorrhages which affect carp during the spring months. The causal agent, *Rhabdovirus carpio,* is capable of killing carp of all ages. Common names of the disease (infectious dropsy of carp, acute infectious dropsy) reflect the common sign of ascites (bloat). The virus has never been isolated from North America, and research suggests that the common goldfish is not susceptible to the virus. Goldfish farmers rarely report massive spring die-offs of goldfish with hemorrhagic lesions, an observation which suggests that either the virus is not present or that these fish are not susceptible.

Ramirez dwarf cichlid virus: This virus was first observed when, between one and three days after importation from South America, all the fish in five different shipments of *Apistogramma ramirez* became ill, showing inactivity, inappetence, respiratory distress, and weakness as suggested by uncoordinated swimming. Fish appeared pale, with generalized hemorrhages in the skin and eyes. Notable internal signs included pale shrunken organs and an enlarged spleen.

Mortality ranged from 40 to 80 percent. The Ramirez dwarf cichlid virus was found in spleen cells of diseased fish, and examination of the fish failed to uncover other disease agents which could have caused the mortalities. Although virus isolation attempts were not made in this study nor were infectivity studies done, the complete pathological picture was highly suggestive that the virus particles observed by electron microscopy were associated with the disease.

In examining disease problems with dwarf cichlids, University of Georgia investigators have diagnosed systemic *Tetrahymena pyriformis* infections which resulted in 100 percent mortalities. We did not examine these fish for virus infections. However, it is possible that the virus described here depresses the natural defense mechanisms of the fish, rendering it susceptible to the parasite.

Rio Grande cichlid rhabdovirus: This virus was isolated from specimens of *Cichlasoma cyanoguttatum,* which died of an acute disease that killed all the fish in the shipment within a week. The disease has been experimentally transmitted to *Tilapia zillii, Cichlasoma cyanoguttatum,* and *Cichlasoma nigrofasciatum.* (The latter species is commonly known as the convict cichlid.) Rhabdoviruses are bullet-shaped viruses which have been associated with many species of fish. Recent studies by University of Georgia investigators suggest that rhabdoviruses are also associated with freshwater angelfish (*Pterophyllum scalare*). Whether cichlid viruses will infect any other fish species is an interesting but unanswered question.

Viruses associated with freshwater angelfish: During the period from 1987 to 1989, the tropical fish industry encountered an apparently new disease syndrome in angelfish (*Pterophyllum scalare*). Its principal signs appeared to be behavioral changes. Fish crowded together in either a head-up or a head-down posture and refused to eat. Thus they rapidly lost weight and died. Excessive slime seemed to be another prime characteristic of the disease. Some fish developed "injected" fins, which give a red or bloody appearance to finnage.

Reports from the field suggested that seemingly healthy fish developed the disease after shipping or following transfer to a different aquarium. Reports from fish producers indicated that breeding fish could transmit the disease to fry, but that fry might recover if unstressed. In some cases, exposed fry matured without finnage. It appeared that many fish are healthy carriers of the disease agent, and that the mixing of apparently healthy carriers with naive fish resulted in an increased death rate as unexposed fish became infected.

Research teams in the veterinary colleges at the University of Georgia and at the University of Florida began investigating what some producers were calling "angelfish plague" or "angelfish AIDS." (These names were based on the observation that the problem was both infectious and apparently incurable.) During the initial phase of our studies of sick angelfish sent to us from both domestic and foreign sources, we identified many problems that clearly were not viral in origin and could be contained by routine treatment and control measures. In some cases, for instance, very poor water quality was the problem. In other cases, poor nutrition or parasites were causing deaths. Sometimes the disease signs were quite similar to those of the so-called angelfish plague. In one case submitted by a producer, examination of intestinal tissues revealed a sporozoan closely related to the *Chloromyxum* group.

The virus hypothesis was strengthened by the observations of angelfish producers that the disease spread easily, that it weakened fish, making them susceptible to other diseases, and that adult fish could carry the disease without visible signs of infection. We had seen similar cases in the late 1970s and early 1980s where an obvious diagnosis could not be made but the possibility of virus involvement had been considered. The possibility that viruses were associated with angelfish also had been suggested by a finding of herpesviruslike particles in the spleens of dying fish (Mellergaard and Bloch 1988), but the virus had not been isolated.

As cases were presented (usually by air freight), we placed fish from each bag in a separate aquarium so that fish could be observed over a period of time. Living fish were examined for internal and external parasites as well as for bacterial infections, and whole fish were preserved in 10 percent buffered formalin for histopathological studies.

In studying suspect angelfish, we decided to look directly for viruses in tissues of sick fish with an electron microscope, in addition to using cell-culture techniques. Healthy fish were examined as experimental controls. This was a prudent step, for direct electron microscopic examination of internal tissues revealed the presence of parvoviruses, paramyxoviruses, and herpesviruses in both the healthy and the sick groups of fish. In addition, when using cell cultures derived from *Tilapia mossambica,* we successfully isolated both paramyxoviruses and parvoviruses.

While these results are proof that angelfish do carry viruses, proof that a particular virus is the actual cause of a disease lies in associating the virus with the disease on a regular basis. In addition, as stated earlier, a virus isolated in cultures of fish cells must produce the disease when given to unexposed fish, and the disease produced must be similar to that seen in the field. At this writing, infectivity tests are being conducted with viruses isolated from cell cultures.

Control measures for viral angelfish infections: Research will eventually provide means by which fish can be easily tested for suspected viruses. This will provide the basis for selection of healthy breeding stock and monitoring hatcheries for suspected disease agents. However, because antiviral therapy and vaccines are not a viable option at this time, standard approaches to avoid viruses should be employed. In particular, breeders of angelfish or discus should not purchase new breeding stock from outside sources where problems have developed.

If it is absolutely necessary to acquire new breeding stock, new fish should be placed under strict quarantine until at least one spawning has taken place and fry have been reared successfully to one-quarter of their adult size. Another way to determine whether adult fish are carriers of a virulent virus is to add fry to the quarantine tanks. Death of the added fry should serve as a potential "virus alert" in the absence of other well-known disease agents. While such methods may seem time-consuming and troublesome, they are the safest way to introduce new fish into a hatchery.

Diagnosis and treatment of angelfish problems: Since many diseases of angelfish elicit identical signs in the fish, one either must diagnose and treat accordingly, or medicate in a broad manner for external and internal parasites. During the quarantine period, treat fish with 3 to 5 ppm of metronidazole in water or 0.25 percent in a gelatinized diet to rid fish of *Hexamita*. Gill flukes (and tapeworms in the intestine), if present, will be eliminated by using one of the following treatments: 3 to 6 ppm of praziquantel (Droncit™) in water, 25 ppm of formaldehyde in water, or 0.25 ppm organophosphates in water.

Bacterial fin-rot problems, associated with parasites or more commonly with bacteria, may be an important sequel to the so-called angelfish plague. Consequently, addition of antibiotics to water or food may reduce mortalities.

While these recommendations for treatment during quarantine will help solve many problems, a true viral infection is not treatable. From case history studies, it appears that fish which have recovered from the infection will become carriers and may infect their own young as well as other fish. The wise breeder or hobbyist will be very wary of mixing new fish, even after quarantine and treatment. In addition, it is easy to spread viruses from tank to tank by nets, sponge filters, or even wet hands.

Where did the angelfish plague agent come from, will it go away, and can it return? Reports suggest that healthy angelfish are being produced, a situation which may indicate that the causative agent has somehow mysteriously disappeared. From experiences with other diseases such as rabies in wildlife, however, scientists know that disease cycles are common. These often peak every three to seven years, depending on the virus. During the low periods of such cycles, the disease agent has not disappeared but is present in an inapparent form in some animals. As young susceptible fish appear, the virus may have ample time to mutate and cause a new episode of disease. Thus, the chances are that if the suspected viral agent does wane, it will return in the future. However, by that time, research groups may be able to better understand the biology of the disease and be in a better position to suggest effective control measures.

Selected References

Andrews, C.; Excell, A.; and Carrington, N. 1988. *The Manual of Fish Health*. Tetra Press.

Anne, W., ed. 1980. *Fish Diseases. Third COPRAQ Session*. New York: Springer-Verlag.

Berry E. S.; Shea, T. B.; and Gabliks, J. 1983. Two iridovirus isolates from *Carassius auratus* (L.) *J. Fish Dis*. 6: 501–10.

Braude, A. 1982. *Microbiology: Basic Science and Medical Applications*. Philadelphia: Saunders.

Hoffman, G. L., and Meyer, F. P. 1974. *Parasites of Freshwater Fishes*. Neptune City, N.J.: T.F.H. Publications.

Mellergaard, S., and Bloch, B. 1988. Herpesvirus-like particles in angelfish, *Pterophyllum altum*. *Dis. Aquat. Organisms* 5:151–55.

Reichenbach-Klinke, H., and Elkan, E. 1965. *The Principal Diseases of Lower Vertebrates. Disease of Fishes*. Neptune City, N.J.: T.F.H. Publications.

Roberts, Ronald J., ed. 1978. *Fish Pathology*. London: Bailliere Tindall.

Wolf, K. 1988. *Fish Viruses and Fish Viral Diseases*. Ithaca, N.Y.: Cornell University Press.

Zabata, Z. 1985. *Parasites and Diseases of Fish Cultured in the Tropics*. London: Taylor & Francis.

Diseases of Ornamental Marine Fishes

George C. Blasiola

Less is known about the diseases of ornamental marine fishes than about those of economically important marine and freshwater species. Parasites clearly are of major importance, and nearly all marine fish sold in the aquarium trade harbor them. Bacteria and fungal infections often accompany infestations by parasites. The successful control of fish diseases requires an enhanced ability to recognize the problem, pinpoint the cause, and implement appropriate corrective measures. Though not all disease outbreaks can be averted, the use of preventative measures can minimize infectious disease outbreaks.

Quarantine

Preventative measures are essential to avoid the development and transmission of diseases in marine aquaria. One of the most important of these is the procedure of quarantine. Newly captured fish invariably harbor disease agents which may be introduced to established aquatic systems. In the natural environment, mildly parasitized fish generally are able to maintain their defense system against invaders very successfully. Insofar as microbial diseases are concerned, fish can be actively infectious or the fish can be a carrier,

harboring the disease in a latent stage in equilibrium with its own physiological state without the overt clinical signs often associated with the disease. Either way, the host is still capable of spreading the disease agent.

Quarantine measures are defined as the isolation of new animals that are suspected of harboring infectious disease for specific time intervals required for the completion of life cycles by various parasitic agents, in an effort to prevent introduction of pathogens to disease-free aquatic systems. In the case of marine ornamental species, one should assume that all newly acquired fish may harbor disease agents and should be quarantined accordingly.

Quarantine facilities (also known as hospital tanks) are essential for averting the transmission of marine fish diseases to established aquaria. All new fish must be placed into quarantine facilities for specific periods of time to ascertain whether they are carrying a transmissible disease. During the quarantine process, preventative treatments can be administered to eradicate any developing infestations and/or infections.

The quarantine facility in its simplest form is an isolated container, either an aquarium, bowl, or vat not connected to the main aquatic system. The capacity of the quarantine facility can range from 10 to 20 gallons (38 to 76 liters) to hundreds of gallons or liters, depending on the number of fish involved. The tank should be equipped with a standard filtration system, including heater, airstone, and other required items. The bottom of the tank should have an adequate layer of aquarium sand or gravel and enough coral or rock to provide ample hiding places.

Water conditions in the quarantine tanks should be adjusted to approximate those of the aquatic system to which the fish will be transferred after the isolation period. This will require a regular system of water tests and record keeping.

As they are placed in the quarantine facility, all fish must be examined for frayed fins, open lesions, and ulcers, which could be indicative of an infection. Any signs of abnormal behavior which would be indicative of parasitic infestations should also be noted. The examination should be repeated the next day, after the fish have begun to adjust to their new environment. At this time, watch particularly for signs of increased respiration, abnormal presence of white spots, excess mucus secretion, or scratching, all of which could indicate the presence of various external parasites.

Before introducing new specimens to the quarantine tank, test the water temperature, salinity, and pH, both in the shipping container and in the tank, and adjust the tank conditions accordingly. Dim the light over the aquarium during specimen introduction to minimize shock.

As a general rule, all new marine fishes should be isolated in quarantine for at least twenty-one days. The older recommendation of ten to fourteen days has been shown to be inadequate for certain diseases. The twenty-one-day period is based on the time required for most piscine parasites to complete their life cycles. During this time, careful attention must be paid to general overall conditions and feeding behavior. All fishes must be quarantined, without exceptions, if one is to avoid the possibility of disease agent introduction.

Medication during quarantine: During the quarantine period it often will be necessary to administer chemical treatments to control common parasites as well as any existing bacterial or fungal infections. The medications selected will depend upon the specific disease agent to be eradicated, the species of fish, and other factors. The chemicals selected must be labeled specifically for aquatic system use.

Chemicals and drugs which have a long history of usefulness include acriflavine, formalin, malachite green, copper compounds, trichlorfon, and nitrofurazone.

Caution should be exercised with any new chemical treatment, especially those which are relatively new for use in treating marine fishes. Never expose large numbers of fish to new chemicals without prior testing of chemicals with a small group of fish, as some fish species may be highly sensitive to particular chemical treatments.

Standard preventative procedures are recommended for use on the most common marine fish parasites. New marine fishes should receive a minimum of a twenty-one-day treatment with copper or other appropriate medications to eradicate external parasites, including *Cryptocaryon* and *Amyloodinium.* In addition, they also should be treated with other parasiticides, such as formalin for eradication of flukes and copepods.

Antibacterials can also be used to treat fish showing signs of secondary bacterial infections. Antibacterial medications should be selected carefully, as some commercially available ones such as tetracycline preparations are not suitable for use in marine systems.

The most common method for treatment of aquarium fishes is the addition of chemicals directly to the water. Less frequently, medications may be added to food or injected.

The administration of drugs to water is often referred to as the immersion, or bath, method. Fish may be immersed in short-term baths or dips using drugs at fairly high concentrations for thirty seconds to several minutes. Or they may be subjected to long-term baths, immersion treatments in which the treated fish are exposed to a reduced concentration of the drug for hours or indefinitely.

Disinfection: As a final point, it is worth noting that disease agents can spread from one aquarium to another through contaminated equipment such as nets, unwashed aquarium rock, reused plastic bags, or unwashed hands. Proper disinfectants should be used to destroy potential disease-causing organisms. Those that commonly have been used are formalin, chlorine compounds such as bleach, potassium permanganate, and benzalkonium chloride solutions.

Benzalkonium chloride solutions are highly

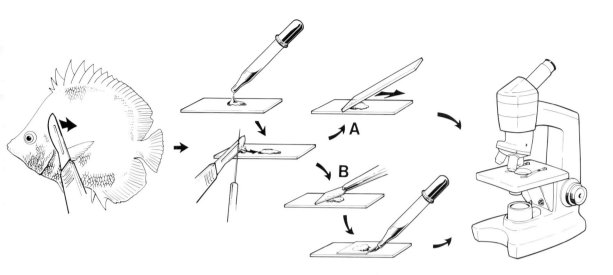

Procedure for making a skin smear. Place a drop of salt water on a microscope slide. Add sample taken from fish. A. For a dry-mount preparation, spread material on slide and allow to dry in air. B. For a wet-mount preparation, place a coverslip on the slide and add additional water if necessary.

recommended. These compounds are colorless, tend to be odorless, and have a marked antimicrobial activity. They are sold under various trade names and have been used widely on poultry farms, in laboratories, zoos, public aquaria, and veterinary hospitals. For disinfecting nets, benzalkonium chloride is generally used at 10 to 12 ppm.

Fundamentals of Disease Identification

One must become somewhat proficient in the diagnosis of marine fish diseases in order to treat them effectively and control them properly. Disease diagnosis becomes easier if one is already a good observer with some prior familiarity with common fish diseases.

Although many disease-causing agents are visible with the naked eye, a light microscope is an important tool for the definitive diagnosis of diseases, particularly parasitic ones. For this you will also need glass microscope slides and coverslips.

To ensure that poor water quality is not the basic cause of the poor state of health of the fish, water tests must be made. Water-quality testing is always the first step in ascertaining the cause of a disease problem. If the test results are within acceptable parameters, then one can proceed to attempt to identify a biological agent responsible for the disease.

Each disease or condition, whether it be related to water quality or to a biological agent, has its own associated clinical signs. Some signs readily pinpoint a particular cause of the condition. Many others are nonspecific. In order to be interpreted accurately, such nonspecific signs require additional information.

When a fish is suspected of being diseased, begin by making careful notes of its general behavioral patterns and any external abnormal body characteristics. Abnormal actions such as scratching on the bottom of the aquarium, heavy respiratory rates, or lack of appetite are important to consider. Abnormal signs such as ulcers, protrusions, fin ray atrophy, exophthalmia, raised scales, body lumps, or reddened areas must also be noted. Do not overlook historical data or the background information. "When did the problem start?", "How long has it been going on?", and "When were new fish added?" are questions, among others, that should be asked.

Next, obtain a fish that has just died or some of those that are ready to do so. It is best to remove as many diseased fish as possible in order to make a series of multiple skin smears. Fish which have been dead for several hours generally are useless for disease identification, particularly if attempting to identify certain protozoans.

Amyloodinium on the clownfish (*Amphiprion percula*). Infested fish have an increased respiratory rate and look as though fine powder were sprinkled on their body. *Source:* Tetra Archives.

Net a fish from the aquarium and place it on a flat surface. Moving from the head region just behind the gill cover (operculum) and toward the tail, use a scalpel or coverslip to make an even and rapid scrape on the skin surface. The pressure should be even and uniform, but not so hard as to remove scales. If scales are found in the smear, undoubtedly too much pressure was applied to the body surface. If performed properly, mucus will be apparent on the scalpel. Place this material on a slide. Add a drop of salt water, then a coverslip. Blot away excess water on the slide or add additional salt water, if necessary. Examine the slide immediately under the microscope. A dry mount is made in a similar manner, except that it is air-dried prior to examination.

After preparation of skin scrapings, a more detailed overall examination of the fish should be made to note any lumps, discolored areas, frayed fins, embedded parasites, or other abnormal conditions. Then the operculum should be removed. Note the condition of the gills and then remove a portion of the gill. Place this on a slide with a coverslip and examine it under the microscope, noting any abnormalities or parasites.

For an internal examination, lay the fish flat on a surface. Open it from just midway between the pectoral fins toward the anus. Then carefully cut upward in a semicircle toward the dorsal fin, making sure not to cut the intestinal tract. Continue to make a semicircle as you move forward, finally meeting just behind the operculum and then down to the point of the original cut. The flap can then be removed easily, exposing the organs.

Gross examination of the internal organs should be made, looking for any abnormal growths, discoloration, and encysted parasites such as nematodes, as well as mycobacterial granulomas or other abnormalities.

Once all information has been gathered, it is possible to make a diagnosis. An initial hunch is known as a tentative diagnosis or a best guess. It must include all relevant information that has been gathered, for this will aid in making the definitive diagnosis.

Arriving at a proper definitive diagnosis may not be an easy matter. Many diseases have non-specific clinical signs. For this reason, simplified keys for diseases sometimes may be useless, misleading, and/or confusing. An accurate diagnosis of a disease sometimes requires years of experience of working with the diseases of aquatic animals.

Infectious Diseases of Marine Fishes

Infectious diseases of marine fishes are certainly the most serious maladies one encounters, since they can be transmitted easily from one fish to another. (This is in contrast to noninfectious diseases, which are not transmissible.) Diseases that normally are not a problem in the natural habitat can quickly cause extensive mortalities in captive closed systems. The crowding of fish in aquatic systems aids in the rapid transmission of disease agents. Prevention is far easier to implement than chemotherapy, particularly in the case of parasitic diseases.

Parasites are the most common disease-causing agents in marine aquaria. This broad group includes the protozoa, platyhelminths, crustacea, and other metazoans. Various abiotic and biotic factors in the aquarium affect their development, life cycle, and transmission, including temperature, salinity, crowding, availability of intermediate hosts, and deterioration of water quality.

Protozoa

By far the most serious parasites are the protozoa, which account for extensive and often rapid mortalities of marine fishes. Most protozoa are microscopic, although some are visible to the naked eye, and undergo simple or complex life cycles. Protozoan species affecting marine fishes include both obligate parasites requiring a host for their development and facultative parasites, which will attack marine fishes only under certain circumstances. Facultative parasites do not require a host to reproduce.

Amyloodinium ocellatum (common names: saltwater velvet, coral reef disease)

Amyloodinium ocellatum, often referred to as *Oodinium,* was the first marine protozoan known to be responsible for massive mortalities of marine fishes in aquaria. It was reported in 1931 by Eleanor Brown from an epizootic at the Zoological Society of London Aquarium. In the United States, epizootics were reported from the New York Aquarium by Nigrelli in 1936 and by Dempster from Steinhart Aquarium after 1951.

Clinical signs: *Amyloodinium* primarily parasitizes the gills, but will attack other portions of the body, including the fins, causing moderate to severe infestations. Although rare, it has been reported to parasitize the internal organs of marine fish. In one report, trophonts were found in the pharynx and kidney of the pork fish, *Anisotremus virginicus.*

The parasites are visible with the naked eye and appear on the body as a fine powder with a velvety sheen, prompting the name "velvet" for the disease. The parasites are most readily seen on the transparent portions of the fins or on dark-pigmented portions of the body. The greatest concentrations of parasites occur on the gill epithelium. Ulceration and hypersecretion of mucus are also evident. Hemorrhage, inflammation, and cellular necrosis are common pathological consequences of this infestation. Other signs include pallid color, respiratory distress, lethargy, irregular opercular beat, and frequent scratching (flashing) on the aquarium bottom or on objects such as coral. Parasitized fish frequent areas of high oxygen content such as near airstones or near surface turbulence.

Epizootiology: *Amyloodinium* is infectious for all tropical and temperate teleost (bony) fishes, although elasmobranchs (sharks and rays) appear to be immune. The disease spreads rapidly, particularly in overcrowded aquatic systems.

A parasitic dinoflagellate in the family Blasto-

diniidae, *Amyloodinium ocellatum* has a life cycle with three stages: the nonmotile parasitic trophont stage, the encysted or palmella stage, and the dinospore stage. The dinospores are free-swimming, flagellated, and capable of infecting new hosts. In general, they must find a host within twenty-four to thirty-six hours or they perish. The dinospores attach to the host, lose their flagella, and are then transformed into the feeding trophont stage. After a period of growth and maturation, they drop off the host and fall to the substrate, where they undergo vegetative divisions. The de-

Close-up views of *Amyloodinium.* Top: Tomont with developing dinospores. Bottom: Dinospores. *Source:* Tetra Archives.

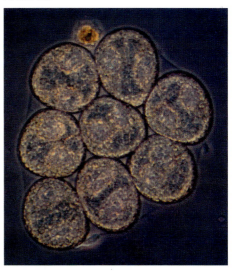

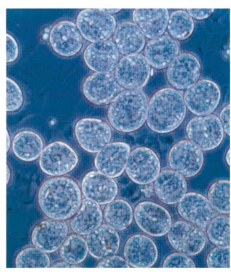

velopment of the cysts is influenced by various factors, including temperature and salinity. Above 25 degrees C (77 degrees F), development of the cysts and release of the dinospores is usually accomplished within three days. In temperatures from 10 to 20 degrees C (50 to 68 degrees F), development is reduced. Below 10 degrees C (50 degrees F), development is inhibited.

Pathogenesis: Parasitization of the gills causes tissue ulceration and hypersecretion of mucus. The mucous cells of the gill epithelium may be partially or completely destroyed in severe infestations. Hemorrhage, inflammation, and cellular necrosis are common pathological consequences. Hyperplasia and filament adhesions are not uncommon.

The parasite attachment causes severe cellular damage, for it derives all its nutrients form the host by a specialized attachment organ comprised of numerous rootlike processes which penetrate host cells and absorb tissue fluids.

Diagnosis: A presumptive diagnosis is based on observation of clinical signs associated with the disease, including the presence of diffusely distributed spots with a golden, yellow-brown cast. Skin and gill scrapings must be made and examined. Live fish can be examined after anesthetizing them with a suitable anesthetic such as tricaine methanesulfonate or quinaldine sulfate.

Under the microscope, the parasite appears oval to pyriform, with a large vesicular nucleus. The cytoplasm is filled with numerous starch granules. A conspicuous eyespot (stigma) is also present. The attached parasitic stage varies in size from 20 to 120 microns or more.

The free-swimming dinospores are highly motile, and have flagella, an eyespot, and a visible constriction called an annular furrow extending across the body. Dinospores measure approximately 12 microns in length when mature.

Prevention and treatment: Epizootics can be prevented by use of quarantine procedures. The treatment of choice for *Amyloodinium* infestations is use of copper-based medications. Other chemotherapeutics, including quinine compounds, have had a mixed history of success.

Copper-ion medications should be maintained at a concentration of 0.115 to 0.18 ppm for not less than ten days but preferably fourteen days. Higher dosages of free-ion copper are unnecessary and can be harmful to copper-sensitive fishes such as *Amphiprion*. Caution must also be exercised when adding copper to tanks with juvenile fishes, which can be sensitive. Severe pathological damage can result if fish are maintained in higher-than-recommended copper concentrations. Sublethal effects of copper include a disruption of osmotic and ionic homeostasis and accumulation of copper in the internal organs.

Chelated coppers, that is, those complexed with chelating agents such as EDTA, can also be used, but generally must be used at substantially higher concentrations than ionic copper. Dosages of chelated copper formulations used in chemotherapy often exceed 2.0 ppm. Due to their inherent stability, chelated copper formulations have the advantage of remaining in solution for longer period than ionic copper solutions.

A copper-ion test kit is necessary to monitor the proper ionic copper concentration. In new systems, an initial dose of copper will decrease rapidly, and booster doses will be required shortly after the first dosage. Copper ions will be removed from water by various factors, including precipitation, binding to organics, binding to carbons, and adsorption to substrates. Studies have recently demonstrated that adsorption by coral, dolomite, or oyster shell is the primary route by which copper ion is removed from circulating aquarium water. Tests should be done daily, and additional copper- ion solution added to the tank if necessary.

Since copper ion is extremely toxic to invertebrates, they must be removed from the tank before commencing the treatment. Upon termination of the treatment period, invertebrates must not be returned until the concentration drops below 0.03 ppm.

Brooklynella hostilis (common name: anemonefish disease)

Brooklynella hostilis was first reported in the scientific literature in 1970 as a causative agent responsible for mortalities of aquarium fishes at the New York Aquarium. The first popular account of the problems caused by the parasite appeared in 1980. Less well known than other parasitic diseases of marine fishes, *Brooklynella* is capable of causing rapid mortalities of marine fishes.

Clinical signs: *Brooklynella hostilis* parasitizes both the skin and gills of fish. Clinical signs of affected fish include lethargy, lack of appetite, hypersecretion of mucus, and respiratory distress. Body lesions originate as small, diffuse, discolored foci which involve larger portions of

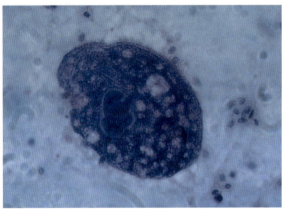

Brooklynella infestation. Top: Appearance on a seahorse (*Hippocampus kuda*). Note abnormal body coloration and sloughing of epithelium. Above: Dried and stained smear.

the fish's body. In advanced stages, the epithelium sloughs off the fish's body. The characteristic sloughing is an important diagnostic sign associated with *Brooklynella* infestations.

Epizootiology: *Brooklynella* is infectious for all tropical teleost fishes and can affect temperate species as well (Blasiola, unpublished). Currently, no parasitism of elasmobranchs has been reported. *Brooklynella* is a "debility parasite," affecting fish that have been severely stressed and maintained in crowded conditions. Clownfish appear to be particularly susceptible, as do seahorses (*Hippocampus*). Affected seahorses exhibit similar clinical signs, including the characteristic

epithelial sloughing.

A ciliated parasite in the family Dysteriidae, *Brooklynella hostilis* is an obligate parasite of fishes. The life cycle of *Brooklynella* is similar to that of its freshwater counterpart, *Chilodonella*. Reproduction occurs by simple cell division with transmission of the parasites directly to other hosts.

Pathogenesis: Severe damage to the host results from the presence of large numbers of parasites and their associated feeding and locomotor activities. The most serious area of damage is the gill epithelium, which is often extensively destroyed. *Brooklynella* feeds on epithelial and blood cells of the host. Death is primarily attributed to loss of epithelium and the subsequent impaired osmoregulatory capabilities of the host.

Diagnosis: A presumptive diagnosis is based on observation of clinical signs and epithelial sloughing. The parasite is not visible with the naked eye. Skin and gill smears from moribund fish examined microscopically can confirm the presence of the parasite. Only live fish are suitable for examination. (Frozen fish are useless for diagnostic work.) *Brooklynella* is highly ciliated and mobile. The parasites occur in large numbers and are easily found on the body and on gills. They range in size from 58 to 80 by 40 to 48 microns. Living parasites are heart-shaped or kidney-shaped, with an oval macronucleus, several micronuclei, and numerous food vacuoles. Notable diagnostic structures include the posterior-ventral adhesion organ used for attachment to the host and the basketlike cytopharyngeal tube.

Prevention and treatment: A combination of formalin and malachite green solutions is recommended for rapid eradication of *Brooklynella*. Combination liquids of formalin and malachite green are readily available commercially. Enough of the solution should be added to produce 15 to 25 ppm of formalin and 0.05 ppm of malachite green. Usually the treatment must be repeated every other day for a minimum of three treatments. Partial water changes should be made between treatments. Freshwater dips are also useful, but should be followed by the malachite green treatment of 0.10 ppm or with the formalin and malachite green combination. Formalin dips must be avoided in cases where fish have sustained severe skin damage.

Brooklynella is resistant to copper treatments and will reproduce in systems treated with cop-

Uronema marinum infestation. Top: Ulceration, hemorrhage, and skin pitting are evident on this maroon clownfish (*Premnas biaculeatus*). Above: Isolated organism.

per. In many cases, the control of parasites must be followed with antibacterial treatments to control topical or systemic bacterial infections that may have developed during parasitization of the host.

Uronema marinum (common name: uronema)

Normally a free-living ciliate, *Uronema marinum* is known to parasitize and cause extensive damage to captive marine fishes. The parasite was first reported in 1980 from fishes in the New York Aquarium. The freshwater counterpart of *Uronema* is *Tetrahymena,* often responsible for the dreaded "guppy killer" disease.

Clinical signs: *Uronema marinum* initially does not produce readily diagnostic lesions. Small discolored areas eventually spread, resulting in ulcerations. In advanced stages, lesions can easily be misdiagnosed as a topical bacterial infection. Sloughing of the epidermis is similar to that of fish parasitized with *Brooklynella.* However, a pro-

nounced pitting of the skin is often evident. Not always limited to the skin, the protozoans can also be found in the internal organs. Some species of parasitized fishes, such as seahorses, may not exhibit external lesions.

Parasitized fish are generally listless, anorexic, and demonstrate abnormal respiratory distress. They can appear pale in color, and secondary bacterial infection is quite common.

Epizootiology: *Uronema marinum* rapidly kills tropical marine teleost fishes, but has not been reported from elasmobranch fishes. A ciliate in the family Uronematidae, it normally occurs as a free-living species but can become parasitic on fishes under certain conditions, often accompanying episodes of trauma. It is usually found on the skin and gills but can become invasive in the internal organs.

The life cycle is uncomplicated, with the parasite reproducing by simple binary fission. The ciliates reproduce rapidly, and large numbers are often found on infested fishes.

Pathogenesis: Parasitization of the gills and epithelium of the body causes ulceration. The musculature is also involved and can be hemorrhagic. Cellular necrosis is evident. *Uronema* can invade internal organs, including the kidney and urinary bladder. Ciliates can be found in capillaries of the gill lamellae, obstructing normal blood flow to the distal portions of the lamellae.

The parasite causes extensive damage to the fish tissue by its feeding activity. Secondary infection almost always accompanies infestation by *Uronema.* Impairment of normal osmoregulatory processes are suspected to contribute to death of the host.

Diagnosis: A presumptive diagnosis is based on observation of clinical signs, including ulcerations, hemorrhage, and sloughing of skin. Skin and gill scrapings should be made and a muscle biopsy obtained to examine for ciliate invasion. Smears can be made from the skin and gills. Only live fish should be used for diagnostic work.

Under the microscope, the ciliates appear teardrop-shaped, with a pointed anterior and rounded posterior. Ciliates measure approximately 32 to 38 by 13 to 20 microns. A single oval macronucleus is present, as well as a single micronucleus. The parasite is highly motile.

Prevention and treatment: *Uronema* can be controlled with use of parasiticides in combination with freshwater dips. Prepare a freshwater

Saltwater ich (*Cryptocaryon irritans*) is readily apparent on this lionfish (*Pterois volitans*). *Source:* Tetra Archives.

dip with a pH equal to the pH of the water into which fish will be transferred after treatment. Dip new fish for three to fifteen minutes, depending on species. Then twenty-four to thirty-six hours afterward, treat the fish either with formaldehyde at 15 to 25 ppm or with a formalin/malachite green combination. Commercial solutions of formalin/malachite green are available that produce a final concentration in the water of 15 to 25 ppm formalin and 0.05 to 0.10 ppm of malachite green. A minimum of three treatments is required. Additional treatments can be required, particularly if the disease is in the advanced stage and the parasite has burrowed under the skin. *Uronema* tends to be more difficult to eradicate than *Brooklynella hostilis*, due to the invasive nature of the former.

Additional adjunct treatments to control topical secondary bacterial infections are required with fish that have already contracted the disease.

Cryptocaryon irritans (common names: saltwater ich, white spot disease)

As with *Amyloodinium*, *Cryptocaryon irritans* has been responsible for mass mortalities in marine aquaria and oceanaria. The incidence of *Cryptocaryon* infestations has become more of a prob-

lem over the past decade than *Amyloodinium*. Outbreaks of cryptocaryoniasis are correlated with adverse conditions, including overcrowding, extremes of water temperature, and induced stress during transport.

Cryptocaryon was first named by Brown at the Zoological Society of London in 1951. However, the disease and the parasite were first reported from infested fishes by Sikama in Japan in 1938. He described the parasite in 1961, naming it *Ichthyophthirius marinus,* unaware that the parasite had already been described by Brown.

Clinical signs: *Cryptocaryon irritans* produces white opaque to grayish papules on the eyes, gills, and skin of the host. The ciliates are found within the papules. The lesions produced are characteristic of the disease and similar to those caused by its freshwater counterpart, *Ichthyophthirius multifiliis.* The lesions are considerably larger than the fine dustlike spots observed on fish infected with *Amyloodinium ocellatum.* Macroscopically, the papules are readily seen on transparent portions of the fins on darkly pigmented areas of the body. In addition, the fins may appear to be torn and ragged. In moderate to severe infestations, the papules are often clustered and

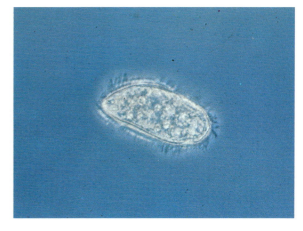

Close-up views of *Crytocaryon*. Top left: Trophont. Below left: Tomont. Above: Tomite (the infective stage). *Source:* Tetra Archives.

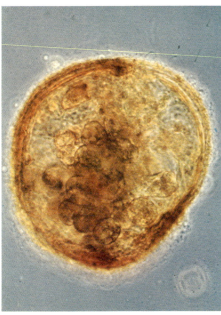

without immediate treatment.

Epizootiology: All tropical and temperate teleost fishes are susceptible to *Cryptocaryon irritans.* Elasmobranchs tend to be resistant to infestations. *Cryptocaryon* can spread rapidly in crowded systems.

Cryptocaryon irritans is a holotrichous ciliate of the family Ichthyophthiriidae in the order Hymenostomatida. Its life cycle and morphological characteristics are similar to the freshwater ciliate *Ichthyophthirius multifiliis,* but it differs in cytological characteristics and host specificity.

The life cycle of *Cryptocaryon irritans* involves three stages: The tomite or infective stage, the trophont or feeding stage, and the tomont or encysted stage. Free-swimming tomites locate a suitable host and burrow into the epithelium of the gills or into the epidermis, after which they transform into the trophont stage. Trophonts are active feeders subsisting on the host's cellular debris and tissue fluids. After a period of growth and maturation, the trophonts fall to the substrate and encyst, becoming tomonts. After a series of multiple divisions and maturation, the free-swimming tomites are released and seek new hosts. Developmental time of the tomont is strongly dependent on temperature and salinity. Above 37 degrees C (98.6 degrees F) and below 7 degrees C (44.6 degrees F), the parasite cannot encyst.

Pathogenesis: *Cryptocaryon irritans* causes severe tissue irritation, resulting in epithelial hyperplasia and hypersecretion of mucus by the fish. In

can coalesce. Epithelial tissue can be observed to fall off in stringlike masses.

Parasitized fish are restless, dart suddenly, and exhibit marked respiratory distress. In the early stages of the infestation, the fish occasionally scratch on the substrate or on objects such as coral or rock. As the disease progresses, the scratching becomes more frequent and normal body coloration is lost, with turbid skin often appearing. Death ensues rapidly

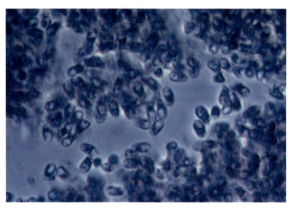

Glugea heraldi. Top: cysts on the seahorse
(*Hippocampus erectus*). Above: spores as they
appear under phase microscope.

advanced cases of the disease, the epithelial
tissue becomes inflamed and hemorrhagic. The
ciliate's presence is accompanied by hypersecretion of mucus, cellular hyperplasia, petechiae,
and lamellar tissue erosion. Parasites frequently
are known to invade the corneal epithelium, causing opacity of the eyes, and on occasion, permanent blindness.

Diagnosis: A presumptive diagnosis is based on
the observation of diffusely distributed white
papules on the gills and skin. Skin scrapings
should be made and examined under a microscope to confirm the disease. The diagnostic
features of the parasite include a large four-lobed
macronucleus and several micronuclei. Both the
macronucleus and micronuclei are readily observed in the tomite, but tend to be obscured by
vacuoles in the trophont. Trophonts are oval to
spherical, and move by means of short, uniformly
distributed cilia. Close observation discloses a

buccal cavity and well-developed feeding appa-
ratus.The cytoplasm contains food vacuoles and
many dark granules. Trophonts vary in size from
160 to 454 microns.

Tomites are pear-shaped and have longer cilia
than do trophonts. They are highly motile compared with the slower-moving trophont. Numerous vacuoles, dark granules, and ingested food
materials are observable in the cytoplasm.
Tomites measure approximately 30 to 50 microns
along the major axis.

Prevention and treatment: The treatment of
choice for eradication of *Cryptocaryon* involves
copper compounds. Other chemicals such as
quinine compounds may also be used, but may
not be as consistently effective as copper. Qui-
nacrine hydrochloride has shown promise as an
alternative to copper, and can be used directly in
a tank. A combination of quinine HCl (2.64 milligrams per liter) and chloroquine (10.6 milligrams
per liter), used in conjunction with hypersaline (45
ppm) treatment for twenty minutes prior to treatment, has proven to be successful.

Copper should be used in the same manner as
outlined for the treatment of *Amyloodinium ocellatum.* Extended treatments, perhaps for up to
four weeks, are sometimes necessary. Recent
studies have indicated that a ten- to fourteen-day
treatment period may not be long enough to fully
eradicate the parasite. *Cryptocaryon* tends to be
more difficult to eradicate than *Amyloodinium.*
Chelated compounds are not recommended for
treatment of fishes parasitized with *Cryptocaryon*
due to their relative ineffectiveness compared
with ionic copper medications.

Microsporea and Myxosporea

Once grouped in the Sporozoa with other microorganisms, these microbes are all obligate parasites. All species in these groups produce spores,
and many have complex life cycles. Numerous
species of both orders parasitize fishes. Only a
few representative species will be discussed in
the following sections. In general, these parasites
are secondary in importance to the protozoans
previously discussed.

Microsporea (common name: boil disease)
The Microsporea are comprised of some of the
smallest and most widely distributed parasites
infecting fishes. Many are no larger than a bacterial cell. They are intracellular parasites which

cause marked host-cell hypertrophy and the formation of cysts. *Glugea* and *Pleistophora* are two of the most important genera parasitizing marine fishes.

Clinical signs: Lesions generally appear as small, pale opaque or white swellings, found externally or internally. They can be found on the gills, body, connective tissue, liver, and musculature.

Behavior signs of the host can vary from little alteration in behavior to pronounced behavior changes. When the seahorse (*Hippocampus erectus*) is infested with the microsporidan *Glugea heraldi,* it becomes lethargic, anorexic, and emaciated as the disease progresses. Normal locomotor ability becomes impaired in later stages of the infestation as the parasite destroys cells while encysting in the connective tissue.

Epizootiology: The Microsporea are infectious, although the exact mode of transmission of these parasites is not known in fishes.

A generalized life cycle of the Microsporea involves the release of spores from a dead and decaying host. The spores are taken up by a host, either directly or possibly indirectly through an intermediate host. In the intestinal tract, they attach to the gut epithelium via the polar filament. At this time, the sporoplasm emerges from each spore and migrates to the infection site. Once the sporoplasm reaches the site of infection, the sporoplasm (now called trophozoite) enters a host cell and undergoes multiple cellular divisions. This process is followed by the formation of spores (sporogony). During sporogony, a maturation of young spores or sporoblasts results in development of mature spores. Autoinfection by the vegetative stages developing during the multiple cellular division stage can also occur. During the development stages swellings occur, the result of the enlargement of single parasitized cells. With species such as *Glugea,* the "cyst" which forms in response to the increasing number of parasites and the cellular response is referred to as a xenoma.

Pathogenesis: Parasitism by Microsporea has various pathological consequences. During initial infestation, the cysts will increase in size, involving larger areas of the host's body. Cellular responses include the infiltration and/or proliferation of migratory cells and formation of multinucleate giant cells. Connective tissue encapsulations are readily evident in many infestations. With some microsporean species, only slight cellular response is evident.

Infestation of host musculature causes destruction of the muscular fibers, with accompanying congestion, hyalinization, and paralysis. Infestation of the ovaries interferes with egg development. Invasion of the host's gills by Microsporea results in epithelial hyperplasia and lamellar fusion. Parasitization of other organs can cause metabolic dysfunctions.

Diagnosis: A presumptive diagnosis is based on the appearance of small cysts or swellings which gradually enlarge and proliferate. This can be evident on skin, gills, or internally in the musculature during necropsy. Possible infected fishes should be anesthetized, the cysts examined and lanced, and the material placed on a microscope slide for examination. The use of phase microscopy is recommended for detection of microsporidean spores. Additional tissues should be fixed for routine histological sectioning.

Mature spores are identifiable primarily on the basis of their morphology. The spores vary in shape and can be oval, tubular, spherical, or pyriform. The oval form is the most commonly observed. Spores can vary in length from 1.5 to over 10 microns. At high magnification, clear areas will be observable at the ends of the spore. The spores are surrounded by a limiting membrane which tends to be refractive and usually can be observed in fresh wet mounts.

In cases where mature spores are absent, immature stages of the parasites can be observed, but classification of the parasite is not possible without the presence of mature spores.

Prevention and treatment: No known chemotherapeutic control is available to eradicate Microsporea from fishes. Thus one must isolate the parasitized fish or destroy it to avoid infecting other fishes. The use of ultraviolet light at 35,000 microwatts per square centimeter on a continual basis has had some success in destruction of spores in contaminated water systems. Because of the infectious nature of many microsporidians, all equipment that comes in contact with the infected aquatic system or with the infected fishes must be thoroughly disinfected with sodium hypochlorite or other disinfectant agents.

Myxosporea

As protozoan parasites of lower vertebrates, the myxosporeans consist of numerous coelozoic (living in the body cavity) and histozoic (living in tissues) species. Like the microsporidans, the myxosporeans are very small parasites. The mature spore is very distinctive and easily identified as a myxosporean. Various species of a number of genera, including *Kudoa, Myxobolus, Henneguya, Myxosoma,* and others, parasitize marine fishes.

Clinical signs: These parasites may live in tissues or in the body cavity. Histozoic myxosporean parasites affect various fish tissues and organs, including gills, cartilage, and musculature. Coelozoic species are found primarily in the gallbladder. Gross lesions appear as cysts or swellings visible in tissues and organs of the host. Cysts can be found on the fins, skin, musculature, or in internal organs.

Fish infested with myxosporeans may demonstrate a multitude of abnormal behavior signs, including lethargy, emaciation, dropsy, whirling behavior, and increased respiration rate.

Epizootiology: Like the Microsporea, Myxosporea are infectious, but their mode of transmission has not been established. The life cycles of many of the myxosporeans are virtually unknown.

A generalized life cycle begins with the release of spores into the water after the decay of an infested host. External cysts in the gills or body can also rupture while the host is alive, thereby releasing spores. The spores may be ingested directly or via an intermediate host. In the digestive tract, gastric secretions cause the spores to extrude their polar filaments, anchoring the spore in the host's gut. The sporoplasm emerges, migrates to the infection site, and transforms into a feeding trophozoite, which either subsists on the absorption of the host's body fluids or is saprozoic. After undergoing shizogony, sporonts are formed in which distinct cell types appear and which differentiate into specific parts of the spore.

Pathogenesis: Parasitization of the host by histozoic myxosporeans has serious consequences for the host. Musculature invasion generally causes degeneration and liquification of the muscle fibers. The liquification is believed to be caused by enzymes secreted by the parasites.

A new myxosporean was recently described from the collared butterfly fish (*Chaetodon collare*). The fish were in captivity for two months. No ulcerations or any other external signs were apparent. However, a marked atrophy of the dorsal musculature was noticed. On examination, the musculature was soft and mushy. Smears made from the tissue showed numbers of cysts in the muscle fibers. The parasite has been described as *Pentacapsula muscularis,* a species which is characterized by the presence of five polar capsules.

Parasitism of the gallbladder results in organ inflammation and enlargement. Parasitism of the gills is very serious, interfering with normal respiration. The lamellae can thicken and fuse as cysts of the parasites develop. Normal blood circulation through the capillaries can be obstructed, causing necrosis.

Diagnosis: A presumptive diagnosis is based on the appearance of cysts, swellings, and ulcerated or light-colored areas of the body. The light-colored areas tend to be soft to the touch. Cysts should be lanced and the exudate examined microscopically.

Examination of wet mounts confirms the presence of Myxosporea. Spores will contain characteristic polar capsules grouped at one end or at opposite ends of the spore. Phase microscopy, if available, is useful in distinguishing these, especially if slides can be stained with Giemsa or Trichrome. Stained spores will show distinct stained dark polar capsules. The sporoplasm can be seen in the proximity of the polar capsules. In immature spores, sporoplasm nuclei may be distinguishable.

Tissues sampled during necropsy should be fixed in standard 10 percent buffered formalin fixative solutions for histological sectioning.

Myxosporean spores are considerably larger than those of Microsporea. Depending on species, their size varies from as little as 5 to over 40 microns. The shape of the spores will vary and can include oval, fusiform, spherical, and stellate forms. Some species such as *Henneguya* possess long characteristic tail-like spore extensions.

Prevention and treatment: Currently no known chemotherapeutic agent will control Myxosporea, although furazolidone has been claimed to be moderately successful in controlling some species. Infested fish must be isolated or destroyed to prevent possible spread of the parasite. Ultraviolet disinfection of water is useful in destroying spores.

Platyhelminthes

The phylum Platyhelminthes includes both free-living and parasitic species. The majority of these flatworms are parasitic, and a large number have complex life cycles which require intermediate hosts. The group is comprised of three classes: the Turbellaria (free-living flatworms), Trematoda

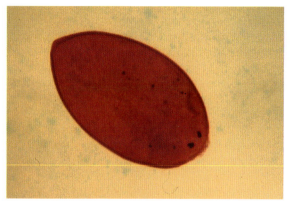

Turbellarians which give rise to the condition sometimes called "black ich;" top: on the skin of a yellow tang (*Zebrasoma flavescens*); above: removed from infested tang and stained. Note prominent eyespots.

(flukes), and Cestoda (tapeworms).

The turbellarians are largely a free-living class of worms. However, a few notable exceptions parasitize fish under certain conditions. The most common is a small turbellarian infesting species of Acanthuridae, Chaetodontidae, and Labridae but not restricted to those families.

The class Trematoda is divided into three main orders. Two of these, the Monogenea or monogenetic trematodes, and the Digenea or digenetic trematodes, contain numerous species of parasites affecting marine fishes.

Members of the Cestoda, the most specialized class of the Platyhelminthes, are segmented, covered by a nonliving cuticle, and lack a digestive system. Deriving their nourishment directly from their host, they attach by means of a specialized organ called a scolex. Cestodes are not generally a serious problem for ornamental marine fishes.

Most cestode species require one or more intermediate hosts to complete their life cycle.

Ichthyophaga (common names: tang turbellarian, black ich)

At the writing of this chapter, the taxonomic position of the tang turbellarian is questionable but under study. In 1976, this author first reported the occurrence of the turbellarian from the yellow tang (*Zebrasoma flavescens*), sailfin tang (*Z. veliferum),* imperator angelfish *(Holacanthus imperator*), and the lemon peel angelfish (*Centropyge flavissimus*). Condé independently reported a small turbellarian parasitizing two species of Caribbean wrasses, *Halichoeres bivittatus* and *Thalassoma bifasciatum*, and a species of scarid, *Scarus croicensis.* Both infestations undoubtedly were caused by the same turbellarian species.

Clinical signs: The turbellarian parasitizes the skin and gills of fishes. The worms appear externally as minute black spots randomly distributed on the host's body, but mainly on the body proper and rarely on the fins. In moderate to severe infestations, inflammation of the skin is readily apparent.

Behavioral signs include frequent scratching on the aquarium bottom and on objects, cessation of normal feeding patterns, general listlessness, and pallid body coloration.

Epizootiology: The tang turbellarian is infectious to teleost fishes. It is not known to parasitize elasmobranch fishes. The life cycle is direct, with the young worms developing within the adults. The worms are believed to be parthenogenic. After approximately six days on the host, the worms drop off. On the substrate, the juvenile worms continue to mature and then are released by rupture of the body wall. As many as 160 juvenile worms per adult are released. The free-swimming larvae seek other hosts, where they attach and mature into adults.

Pathogenesis: Infestation is primarily on the body surface, although worms can be detected in the opercular cavity and on the gill filaments. Lesions and diffuse dermal hemorrhaging are caused by the parasites' movement and the feeding of the worms on the cellular debris of the skin. Untreated fishes become emaciated and die with heavy infestations.

Diagnosis: A presumptive diagnosis is based on the appearance of small black spots on the fish, with accompanying listlessness. Fish should be

The eye fluke (*Neobenedenia*). Note oval attachment organ, opisthohaptor, with anchors, and oral sucker.

anesthetized and examined under a microscope. The worms are small and confirmed as those which measure approximately 110 to 115 microns in length and 70 to 78 microns in width. The worms appear oval or leaflike, with two prominent eyespots and numerous cilia. Developing young can be observed within the body of mature turbellarians.

Prevention and treatment: Infestations can be controlled by the use of organophosphates, formalin dips, or freshwater dips. Formalin is effective when used at 1.0 milliliter per gallon (3.8 liters) for a twenty- to thirty-minute bath. Several treatments may be required. However, this method is not the most suitable one for established aquaria, as formalin is toxic to nitrifying bacteria and to invertebrates. In addition, the entire volume of the aquarium has to be changed after treatment. Alternative treatments are therefore recommended for eradication of turbellarians.

Organophosphates (for example, Masoten^{TM}, trichlorfon) are effective when used at the rate of 0.80 to 1.0 milligram (active) per liter of water. They must not be used in aquaria with crustaceans, because organophosphates are quite toxic to shrimp, lobsters, and crabs.

Freshwater dips are effective if used when fish are lightly infested. Secondary infection by bacteria can occur and will require adjunct chemotherapy with appropriate antimicrobial drugs.

Monogenea (common name: flukes)

The Monogenea are by far the most serious of the trematode parasites affecting fish. They can account for large numbers of aquarium mortalities and are often small enough to go unnoticed. Flukes are ectoparasitic and only require one host to complete their life cycle. Almost all fishes harbor flukes. The worms usually vary in size from 0.4 to 1.0 millimeter in length. Although some species exceed 2.0 millimeters in length, most of the common species are too minute to be seen with the naked eye.

Clinical signs: Monogenetic trematodes are parasites of the skin and gills. Unless the worm is a large species like *Neobenedenia* (the eye fluke) or *Microcotyle,* common on the gills of butterfly fishes and angelfishes, they are not easily detected. Behavioral signs include frequent scratching on objects, pale body color, and respiratory distress. In moderate to severe infestations, mechanical damage and ulceration will be evident. This is most often accompanied by a secondary bacterial infection.

Epizootiology: Monogenetic trematodes are parasites of both teleost and elasmobranch fishes. The genus *Dermophthirius* is represented by several species parasitic on sharks, including the lemon shark (*Negaprion brevirostris*) and the dusky shark (*Carcharhinus obscurus*).

The life cycle is direct, with the parasites laying eggs that develop into larvae which reinfect the host or infest other susceptible fishes. Members in the Gyrodactylidae bear their young alive, some with two generations developing within the uterus of the worm.

Pathogenesis: Parasitism of the gills and skin causes serious tissue and cellular damage to the host. The movements of the parasite cause damage by a special attachment organ, the opisthohaptor, which consists of either anchors, clamps, or hooklets. Trematodes feed directly on the blood, mucus, and tissue fluids of the host. This damage opens the way for secondary infections which can develop into systemic infection when not treated promptly. In freshwater fish, flukes can act as vectors for bacteria. Microcolonies of bacteria have been found on parasites and on the site of opisthohaptor attachment. It is plausible that the same situation could exist with marine fish flukes, particularly with regard to the bacterium *Vibrio.*

Diagnosis: A presumptive diagnosis is made from observation of clinical behavioral signs and appearance of worms and ulcerations or reddened areas on the skin. Confirmation of disease requires observation of the worms in smears from the skin and gills of the fish.

Monogenetic trematodes are generally either elongate or oval flatworms which lack a ciliated epidermis. (The young do, however, have a ciliated epidermis.) A characteristic attachment apparatus will be observed on the posterior portion of the body. This organ is often elaborate and composed of suckers, anchors, clamps, and hooks. Anterior attachment suckers will also be evident.

Prevention and treatment: Freshwater dips, formalin dips, or organophosphate compounds are effective in control of monogenetic trematodes.

New fish can be treated with a standard freshwater dip for five to fifteen minutes, depending on species. Generally, however, freshwater dips are not sufficient to eradicate trematodes completely, and should be followed by either formalin dips or organophosphate treatments within thirty-six to forty-eight hours.

Organophosphates are recommended for eradication of flukes. The dosage is dependent on the pH and temperature. Recommended concentrations range between 0.75 and 1.0 ppm. Severe infestations require more than one treatment. A series of three treatments, spaced a week apart, is a suggested regime. Apparent resistance developed by flukes to organophosphates is not a problem with marine fish species as compared with freshwater species. However, repetitive treatments of marine fish with organophosphates, such as found in public aquaria conditions, could possibly induce resistance.

Treatment with a combination of mebendazole (0.2 milligram per liter) and trichlorfon (0.9 milligram per liter) for twenty-four hours has been shown to be successful in controlling freshwater *Gyrodactylus.* The use of this combination could also be useful in controlling *Gyrodactylus* in marine environments.

Formalin is also an appropriate treatment. However, the nature of the chemical makes it hazardous to use and caution must be exercised. Formalin must never be used on fish that have just been received or handled, or when ulcers are evident on the fish. Traumatized fish are very sensitive to formalin treatments, and not all species can withstand treatment episodes. Bath treatments for twenty to thirty minutes are recommended for most fishes. However, the treatment must be terminated at any point at which the fish begin to appear unduly stressed.

Formalin also is known to reduce dissolved oxygen levels in water. Supplementary aeration should always be provided during treatments.

Digenea (common name: digenetic trematodes)
The Digenea require one or more intermediate hosts in order to complete their life cycle, with a mollusk being one of the intermediate hosts. The final host can be a fish, bird, or carnivorous mammal. Unlike the monogenetic trematodes, all digenetic trematodes are endoparasitic. Their attachment organs are simple disks without hooks or anchors. The digenetic trematodes are less serious parasites of marine fishes than are the monogenetic trematodes, and are of secondary importance as causes of captive fish mortalities.

Clinical signs: Digenetic trematodes can be found on marine fishes either as adults or as the larval forms, called metacercariae. The adults are easily seen and can be found in the intestine, esophagus, stomach, circulatory system, or internally in other areas of the fish's body. Metacercariae can be found in the skin, eyes, and muscles. Often, metacercariae are encysted and appear as spherical melanin-pigmented cysts. Nonmelanized cysts are white and will be present on internal organs. Virtually no unusual behavioral signs will be observed in fishes parasitized with digenetic trematodes.

Epizootiology: Digenetic trematodes are fairly species-specific. Life cycles differ accordingly. A typical life cycle is that of *Sanguinicola,* a blood fluke that parasitizes the gill arches of various fish species. Eggs develop in the capillaries, and small larvae called miracidia break through the gills. Miracidia then invade an intermediate host, in this case a snail of the genus *Oxytrema.* In the snail, the miracidia metamorphose through various other larval stages, and emerge as cercariae. The cercariae parasitize a fish and develop into adults to complete their life cycle.

In another common life cycle, metacercariae encyst and remain in the host until the host is consumed by another animal. Within the next host, the parasites may continue their life cycle or the metacercariae may remain encysted. In general, this cycle involves the same larval stages. When cercariae leave the snail, they infect fish, where the larvae encyst.

Pathogenesis: Damage to the host fish occurs when large numbers of larvae leave the gills, causing extensive hemorrhagic and tissue damage. Eggs of trematodes can also interfere with normal circulation in the capillaries of the gills, liver, kidneys, and other organs. Metacercariae encysted in the eye will cause extensive pathology and permanent blindness.

Diagnosis: A diagnosis is based on the finding of adult worms or metacercariae in the fish. Adults will be found anywhere in the body internally. The worms vary in size, depending on species, but are visible with the naked eye. Their attachment organs are simple disks without accessory hooks or anchors. The oral sucker is located anteriorly and an acetabulus (abdominal sucker) is located at the posterior position of the parasite or near the center of the body. When metacercariae are found on the body, they appear as small to large gray to black eruptions.

Prevention and treatment: Treatment for digenetic trematodes is more difficult than for monogenetic trematodes. A few metacercariae on fish have little effect on the health of the fish. No known chemotherapy for treatment of metacercariae has been found, and it is best to leave affected fish alone.

Di-N-tin-butyl oxide was used in the past to eradicate digenetic trematodes. However, since the parasites do not cause significant mortalities in marine fishes, such treatments are unnecessary. Under aquarium conditions, the life cycles of digenetic trematodes cannot be completed due to absence of other required intermediate hosts.

Cestoda (common name: tapeworms)

Cestodes can appear in marine fishes in either an adult or a larval form. Adults inhabit the intestine or pyloric cecae. Larval forms (plerocercoids) are typically found encysted or free in the liver, muscle, and body cavity.

Clinical signs: Parasitized fish generally demonstrate no abnormal behavioral or physical signs except in cases of severe infestation. Severely parasitized fish tend to be lethargic, and can show abdominal enlargement due to the presence of adult or larval forms in the abdominal cavity.

Epizootiology: The life cycles of cestodes vary, depending on the species. A typical life cycle is illustrated by a trypanorhynch cestode, *Grillotia erinaceus,* whose definitive hosts are elasmobranch fishes. The adult cestodes shed eggs which pass out of the host via the feces. An intermediate host becomes infested, in this case a copepod. Within the copepod, the parasite de-

velops into a procercoid form. When the copepod is eaten by a bony fish, the second intermediate host, the procercoid develops into a plerocercoid. These larval forms inhabit the pyloric cecae, intestine, and stomach. The cycle is complete when the bony fish is eaten by the definitive host, in this case a ray.

Pathogenesis: Damage to the host occurs by the presence of the adults and the larval forms. Migrating forms especially can cause extensive damage to the host's body organs by compression of the organs, adhesions, and a proliferation of fibrous connective tissue. Damage to the reproductive organs is quite common and impairs normal spawning.

Adult cestodes tend to live in the intestine and pyloric cecae, causing damage to the intestinal walls by their attachment and by direct absorption of nutrients. Severe infestations are accompanied by anemia and peritonitis. When parasites are present in large numbers, obstructions of the intestinal tract can cause death of the host.

Diagnosis: A diagnosis is based on the confirmation of adult cestodes or larval forms. Adults are segmented, ribbonlike, and attach by means of a scolex to the host. Plerocercoids tend to be white or cream-colored, with a superficial fine segmentation. They are visible to the naked eye.

Prevention and treatment: The treatment of cestodes in marine fishes is very difficult. For all practical purposes, the condition is not treatable. However, it is unlikely that treatment of marine fishes will ever be necessary. Some success has been shown in the administration of various anthelmintics such as Yomesan®. A recommended starter dose is 1.0 milligram per 90 grams (0.2 pounds) of fish weight. Generally only one dose is required. Usually adult cestodes are shed within twenty-four hours. Caution must be used, as fish are sensitive to this drug.

A new anthelmintic, praziquantel, has been shown to be effective in controlling freshwater cestodes in immersion treatments. It is likely that it could also be used for treatment of marine fish.

Nematoda

The nematodes, or roundworms, comprise a large group of both free-living and parasitic forms. Nematodes are elongated, cylindrical worms tending to taper toward the body ends. They frequently are red, reddish-orange, or white and opaque. It is quite common to find numerous free-living nematodes in aquarium gravel filter beds. They are generally harmless. Parasitic nematodes are encountered from time to time in marine fishes. However, they are insignificant as a cause of diseases in marine fishes. When found, they tend to parasitize the intestine, internal organs, eyes, mesenteries, and other areas. Immature forms are found in mesenteries and internal organs, with adults primarily in the digestive tract. One or two intermediate hosts are required before development in the definitive hosts. Nematodes are not considered serious parasites of marine fishes in aquaria. Most parasites come in via new fishes and cannot complete their life cycle, as they usually require an intermediate host.

Crustacea

The class Crustacea is a large one which includes parasitic and free-living species. Three major groups having species parasitizing fishes are the Branchiura, Copepoda, and Isopoda. The first two groups include the most serious crustacean parasites of fish in captivity. Isopods are less frequently encountered.

The crustaceans affect their hosts by causing pressure atrophy to the soft tissues of the host, by damage caused by their attachment, and by damage inflicted by their feeding on the host.

Branchiura

The Branchiura include various species exclusively parasitic on fishes. *Argulus* is the major genus in the group and the only genus that has

The copepod (*Serpentisaccus magnificae*) on the firefish (*Nemateleotris magnifica*). Trailing yellow egg strings are visible just above the pelvic fins.

marine representatives. As an obligate parasite, it cannot survive without its host.

Clinical signs: *Argulus* is an external parasite found on the body surfaces of fish. Affected fish tend to scratch repeatedly on the aquarium bottom and on other objects. Inflammation and congestions are evident on the skin of parasitized fishes. Fish can be observed to dart, causing abrasions that can develop secondary infections.

Epizootiology: *Argulus* is easily transmitted due to its mobility and its ability to move from one fish to another. It can reproduce rapidly in closed systems. On submerged objects, the females deposit eggs which develop into larvae that reinfect the hosts or new hosts. No intermediate host is involved. A well-known Atlantic species is *Argulus bicolor*, which parasitizes the redfin needlefish (*Strongylura notata*) and the barracuda (*Sphyraena barracuda*).

Pathogenesis: Parasitization of the skin or gills causes epidermal inflammation and subsequent ulceration. Secondary infection accompanies this damage. The parasites pierce the body of the host with their stylet, release a toxin, and feed on hemolymph and tissue fluids. Digestive secretions are used to aid in ingestion of blood. Inflamed lesions are inevitable on the fish during prolonged attachment of the parasites.

Diagnosis: Live fish must be examined to locate small, dorsoventrally flattened parasites on the skin. The parasites are equipped with a feeding apparatus consisting of a proboscislike mouth, suckers, and a piercing stylet. The shieldlike carapaces of various species of *Argulus* tend to be pigmented and appear as dark areas on the body of the parasitized fish.

Prevention and treatment: All new fish should be quarantined prior to introduction into the aquarium system. The parasite is very susceptible to organophosphate compounds. Formalin treatments are also effective.

Copepoda

The copepods are by far the largest group of crustacean parasites affecting marine fishes. Copepod crustaceans have evolved free-living and parasitic forms with accompanying bizarre morphology to adapt to their diverse ecological niches. Of the various taxonomic orders in the Copepoda, the largest number of species that are parasitic on fishes are in the orders Caligoida and Cyclopoida.

Clinical signs: In many cases, very few behavioral or physical signs are evident on parasitized fish. Only in severe cases of parasitism do ulcerated areas appear, accompanied by secondary infection.

Parasites are seen on the body or gills. The easiest diagnostic sign is the presence of trailing egg strings. These may be straight, coiled, or serpentine. The copepod's cephalothorax is embedded into the fish's body, and only the trunk and egg string of the parasites are usually seen.

Epizootiology: Species of copepods affect virtually every species of marine fish, including bony fishes and elasmobranchs. Many are host-specific. Others involve intermediate hosts to complete the life cycle. Only the females attach to the host. Attachment of some copepods is superficial. Other species burrow quite deeply into the host. After maturing on the host, the females produce eggs which subsequently develop with the release of larvae.

Pathogenesis: Copepods are capable of severe damage to the host tissues, integument, gills, eyes, muscles, and internal organs. Those on the surface cause erosion of the epithelium and hyperplasia. The site of attachment is almost always ulcerated. Attachment to the gills by copepods can cause hypertrophy of both the epithelial and connective tissues of the lamellae, impairing normal blood circulation and respiration. Species which burrow deeply in the body can cause extensive damage. For example, *Cardiodectes* burrows in to attach its holdfast to the heart of the host fish. The area of attachment appears as a reddened depression.

Diagnosis: The diagnosis is based on external examination of the fish for attached parasites, which are recognizable by a body which is either dorsoventrally flattened or laterally compressed, jointed appendages, a cephalothorax, and egg strings. Some species move freely on the body. Others are permanently fixed by their attachment processes. The attachment area has a raised ulcerated ring, and is hemorrhagic and inflamed.

Prevention and treatment: The free-moving forms are more easily controlled than are attached forms. Treatment is aimed at controlling any further attachment by larvae. Organophosphates or formalin are useful for treatment. Repeated treatments are necessary. When using organophosphates, the concentration must be at least 0.60 milligrams per liter. The chemical can be added to an aquatic system once a week for

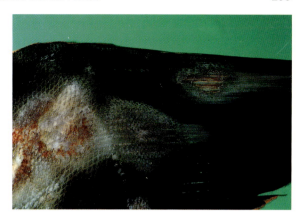

Large lesions caused by *Vibrio* on the batfish (*Platax*).

a period of at least three weeks.

Bacterial Diseases

Bacteria are ubiquitous in the marine environment and tend to cause disease only under conditions favoring their development and invasion of a stressed host. Fishes are subject to stress brought on by a variety of abnormal environmental conditions, including low dissolved oxygen, high carbon dioxide, elevated temperatures, and high concentrations of ammonia.

The majority of bacterial infections are initiated by stress factors such as are caused by parasitic infestations or deterioration in water quality. Bacteria encountered in infections of marine fish include species of *Vibrio, Mycobacterium,* and *Pseudomonas.*

Vibrio

Vibrio is implicated in many infections, primarily in marine fishes but also in brackish-water species. It is a significant cause of bacterial diseases of ornamental species. Known species include *V. anguillarum, V. damsela,* and *V. carchariae,* the latter species virulent to carcharhinid sharks.

Clinical signs: Affected fish are listless and have body ulcerations and inflammation of the skin and fins. Petechiae are visible on the mouth, opercula, and ventral body surfaces. Hyperemia of skin and fins occurs, with congestions of the median and paired fins. Hemorrhagic lesions are notable, and exophthalmia may be exhibited. Lesions on fins cause necrosis and exposure of spines and rays.

Epizootiology: *Vibrio* is infectious for all marine teleost and elasmobranch fishes by contact. It also has been postulated the infection can occur

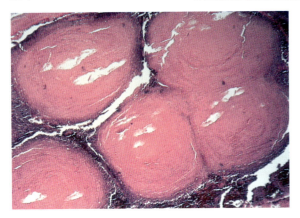

Granulomas in the liver of the triggerfish
(*Balistoides*) caused by *Mycobacterium
marinum*.

when fish are fed previously contaminated foods.

Pathogenesis: It is assumed that *Vibrio* releases an endotoxin responsible for the observed pathology. Transmission appears to be by direct contact in environmental conditions favoring its development. Elevated water temperatures are thought to favor the initiation of *Vibrio* infections.

Diagnosis: One can obtain preliminary evidence from external clinical signs. A definitive identification of the organism is best accomplished by using a sterile inoculating loop to obtain a sample from the desired organ. Only moribund fish should be selected for examination. Dead fish should never be used due to rapid postmortem changes and invasion by other bacteria. A sampling of these fish could give an inaccurate picture of the flora that caused the condition. The kidney, liver and heart are the recommended choices, although any other organs can be selected for sampling. First, sterilize the desired organ with a heated scalpel, then insert the loop into the organ, and streak the inoculum on a culture plate. The inoculum should be cultured on TSA agar supplemented with blood. Generally, finding a gram-negative, polar-flagellated carbohydrate fermenter indicates a species of *Vibrio*.

Prevention and treatment: Prompt treatment is necessary. *Vibrio* is sensitive to various nitrofurans such as nitrofurazone and other broad-spectrum antibacterial drugs. Nitrofurazone can be used at 3 to 9 milligrams per liter (active). Treatment with potentiated sulfonamides is also very useful in control of *Vibrio*. Nifurpirinol has proven very effective in controlling infections in fishes. When used in a bath, therapeutic blood

levels have been attained within one hour. The absorption route is primarily through the gills. Preventative measures must also include avoidance of crowding in holding tanks and aquaria, and maintenance of good water quality.

Mycobacterium marinum (common names: mycobacteriosis, piscine tuberculosis)

Mycobacteriosis, one of the most well known systemic diseases of marine fish, is caused by an acid-fast bacterium, *M. marinum.* The disease is also referred to as piscine tuberculosis. However, due to the differences in pathology between tuberculosis of other animals and of fish, the term is not technically correct and should be avoided. The infection is classed, in most cases, as a chronic disease.

Clinical signs: Affected fish swell and may become dark. Other signs are variable, depending on the stage of the disease. Fish can become emaciated, demonstrate exophthalmia, have cloudy eyes, and exhibit degeneration of the fins. In advanced stages, hemorrhage and formation of ulcers can appear.

Epizootiology: Mycobacteriosis is infectious for all marine fishes. The disease can be acquired by direct ingestion of the bacteria, such as in feed that contains animal matter. In the aquarium, it can be acquired by fish picking on dead fish that have had the disease.

Pathogenesis: Mycobacteria produce necrotic lesions in the internal organs of the affected fish, causing abnormal function of the organs. Over time, the disease causes mortalities, which tend to be sporadic. Tubercules can be found in virtually any internal organ, but usually occur in the

Lymphocystis on the rockfish (*Sebastes*). Nodules can be seen on the pectoral fin.

kidney, spleen, or liver.

Diagnosis: Live fish should be used for identification. Squash preparations should be made from the intestine, liver, spleen, heart, or other organs and examined under 100x to 400x magnification. The Ziehl-Nielsen method is necessary for staining and identifying acid-fast bacteria. With this procedure, acid-fast bacteria stain red. Other bacteria and cellular debris stain blue. Bacteria tend to be straight or curved bacilli found in nests. The bacteria are usually nonmotile rods.

Prevention and treatment: Although kanamycin has shown promise in controlling the disease, no practical treatments are currently available. Claims that isoniazid is effective as a cure are still unsubstantiated. Prevention is the only method of curtailing the spread of the disease. Good sanitation in holding aquaria is important. Presence of this disease in aquaria can indicate poor environmental conditions.

Viral Diseases

Viral infections are caused by organisms smaller than bacterial cells that are essentially parasitic on living cells. Few marine viruses have been identified. This is not to imply that there are only a few marine viruses, only that current research has not been oriented toward marine ornamental fish but rather to more commercially important species.

Lymphocystis (common name: lymphocystis disease

Lymphocystis is without a doubt the most well known of fish viruses. It is also the oldest known, dating back to when it was first described from a flatfish in 1874. The virus affects not only marine fish but also freshwater fish species.

Clinical signs: The virus produces chronic skin lesions, but seldom is the cause of death. Normal fish behavior is not affected in most cases. The lesions are white to pink in appearance, nodular, and may form a mulberrylike growth. They commonly are found on distal ends of fins and on the body. The nodules occur singly or in groups. Enlarged cells average 100 microns in diameter.

Epizootiology: The virus is infectious for all teleost fishes, but infection of elasmobranchs is unknown. The virus infects cells and makes them produce additional viruses by combining with their nuclear component. The transmission of the virus is direct. Sloughing or rupture of the infected

Section through the muscle of a marine fish infected with *Exophiala*. Numerous darkly stained fungal hyphae can be seen throughout the muscle.

cells releases the virus into the water. Upon death of the host, there is also a release of viruses. It has been suggested that damaged skin can predispose a fish to infection by lymphocystis disease. In one study it was observed that the blennioid fishes *Hypsoblennius jenkinsi* and *H. gentilis* developed an infection at damage sites after territorial disputes during the breeding season.

Pathogenesis: Infection of the skin and fins causes appearance of nodules with a hyaline capsule. The disease is benign and seldom causes death of the host.

Diagnosis: The disease is diagnosed grossly by the appearance of nodular, hard, mulberrylike growths on body, fins, or lips. Confirmatory diagnosis must be from histological sections and ultrastructure studies.

Prevention and treatment: No effective treatment is known for lymphocystis. Sometimes the lesions will slough off and not reappear. Surgical removal is sometimes effective. Care must be used to avoid rupture of infected cells around the lesion that could reinfect the site. Fish that have undergone this surgical procedure must be treated with an antimicrobial drug for three to five days to prevent secondary infection. Care should be taken in disinfecting all equipment used near infected areas. *Lymphocystis* virions will survive drying and retain their infectivity for long periods. In one study, dried viruses retained infectivity for fifteen years. The reintroduction of the virions into the aquarium can cause lymphocystis infection.

Recently a nonlymphocystis virus was suggested during studies of lesions from a flounder,

Starvation is not uncommon in marine fish. Note the sunken and apparently enlarged head of this clownfish.

Pseudopleuronectes americanus. The fish showed characteristic papilloma lesions on its dorsal surfaces. There were irregular swellings with a blister-like appearance similar to lymphocystis. Further examination showed the presence of viral particles.

Fungal Diseases

Fungal diseases are quite uncommon in marine fishes, despite accounts in various popular texts of *Saprolegnia* fungal infections of marine fishes, complete with pictures. While *Saprolegnia*-type infections are common in freshwater fishes, there is no such counterpart in marine fishes. Popular accounts of *Saprolegnia* infections of marine fishes should for the most part

Erosion of the head region in this sailfin tang can be attributed to a dietary imbalance. *Source:* Tetra Archives.

be considered erroneous.

Another commonly mentioned and supposedly common fungal infection is that caused by *Ichthyophonus.* In older texts on fish diseases, the accounts of this fungus are pages in length. The organism is uncommon as an infection of ornamental fish in marine aquaria, but has affected clupeid fishes in the wild, causing extensive epizootics. Many of the descriptions of the fungus occurring in ornamental marine fishes are probably due to misdiagnosis.

One fungus, *Exophiala,* is an occasional parasite of ornamental marine fishes. This fungus is pigmented and appears as a black tuft on the body, often in an area which has sustained damage. The fungus is invasive, affecting the musculature and the internal organs.

In the rare instances where fungi such as *Exophiala* are present, standard treatments with formalin or malachite green prove useful for control.

Noninfectious Diseases

In addition to diseases which are infectious, maladies and problems which occur in marine aquaria may be directly linked to a group of noninfectious diseases. These problems are often caused by a multitude of factors, such as poor nutrition, toxic water conditions, tumors, and genetic anomalies. Discussion of a few of the most common noninfectious diseases follows.

Nutritional Diseases

Three major problems can occur in this category in marine aquaria: starvation, imbalance of nutrients, and an excessive intake of lipids or carbohydrates.

Starvation is a serious problem with captive marine fishes if prolonged. While it is common for some fish to refuse food during trauma, usually they should begin to eat within four to six days after being moved to an aquarium. After this period, the longer the animal refuses food, the poorer its chances of recovery. Starvation can be related to various factors. A major factor with some species such as some butterfly fish and angelfish is their stringent requirements for a specific type of food. Obviously, such species should not be maintained in aquaria unless their food requirements can be met. Other causes for starvation can include anorexia, parasitism, infection, incompatibility with other fishes in the aquarium, and other factors.

Fishes require proper intake of protein, carbohydrates, vitamins, and minerals. Low protein or incomplete protein levels affect normal growth, tissue repair, and disease resistance. Excess lipids in the diet cause abnormal buildup of them in internal organs, resulting in severe pathological consequences, such as fatty infiltration of the liver and kidney. Excess carbohydrates can cause liver glycogen deposition and liver degeneration.

Vitamins, the catalysts for biochemical transformation of other nutrients, are essential in all diets. A deficiency of any of the fat-soluble or water-soluble vitamins can cause weight loss, slow growth, exophthalmia, anemia, scoliosis, and other conditions. Vitamin C, for example, is required for normal tissue repair and maintenance of disease resistance. It is also required for the production of collagen, a component of connective tissue. A deficiency in vitamin C can manifest itself in spinal abnormalities such as scoliosis or lordosis, abnormal cartilage production, and hemorrhage of the skin, liver, intestine, muscle, and kidney.

Mineral deficiencies are unknown in marine fishes. However, iodine deficiency can result when fish are fed a poor diet or when water quality has deteriorated. The development of hyperplasia, or enlargement of the thyroid, has been reported in marine fishes.

Providing a variety of foods ensures that a proper supply of nutrients is available. Use of dry foods and frozen foods, supplemented with brine shrimp, algae, clams, and fish, is a safeguard to increase resistance to disease. Reliance on dry prepared foods alone is not recommended. If at all possible, the types and variety of foods should be matched closely with the natural diet and feeding habits of the fish species in the wild.

Diseases Caused by Toxic Environmental Conditions

High ammonia concentrations, low oxygen, low pH, and presence of toxic metals such as zinc or mercury can all affect fish health. Municipal water supplies are often treated with chlorine and recently with chloramines. Such water can also contain toxic quantities of copper, aluminum, or fluoride, which can cause fish mortalities.

Ammonia: This is the most toxic of the nitrogen

Gas-bubble disease. Top: Note the air in the gills. Above: Involvement of the eye of a squirrelfish (*Holocentris*).

compounds found in aquaria. Ammonia actually exists in two forms in water, one which is ionized (NH_4^+) (ammonium) and one which is not (NH_3). The latter is the toxic form. Its toxicity is related to an increase of ammonia in the blood and tissues. As ammonia concentration increases, normal excretion rates are reduced. It also affects the osmoregulatory mechanisms and the normal transport of oxygen to the tissues due to damage of the gills and red blood cells.

Ammonia accumulation in a system initially occurs during the conditioning of an aquarium, when it is caused by excretion by the animals and by decaying foods. The toxicity of ammonia depends on various factors, primarily pH and temperature. Generally, there should be less than 0.01 milligram of NH_3 per liter in marine aquaria. Ammonia concentrations can be monitored in aquaria by use of commercially available test kits.

Nitrite: Though less deadly than ammonia, ni-

Malignant tumor of the thyroid which has
spread to the gills, causing large nodules.

trite is still toxic to marine fishes. High concentrations of nitrite are common in new tanks. Affected fish show respiratory distress. The physiological response of the fish to nitrite concentration is methemoglobinemia. This condition occurs when nitrite chemically binds with oxygen and prevents hemoglobin from taking up oxygen. Experiments on the effects of nitrite with the sea bass (*Dicentrachus*) have demonstrated that at high concentrations of nitrite, methemoglobinemia begins at once. After twenty-four hours, hemoglobin concentration declined. Fish began dying after sixty hours, at which time the hemoglobin level dropped to 50 percent of the control values. The experiments were done at 27 degrees C (80.6 degrees F) and 36 percent salinity. Nitrite levels in aquaria should never exceed 9.1 milligrams per liter as nitrite ion (NO_2).

Nitrate: Nitrate, the least toxic of the three nitrogen compounds found in water, accumulates continuously. It can have a profound effect on proper growth and survival of juvenile marine fish. Experiments with clownfish (*Amphiprion*) showed a reduction in larval growth, metamorphosis, and survival when they were maintained in 100 milligrams of NO_3-N per liter. The presence of green algae in the aquarium plays an important role in reducing the level of nitrates in recirculating aquatic systems. It is generally accepted that nitrate should be less than 20 milligrams per liter as nitrate ion in aquaria.

Chlorine/chloramine: Municipal water supplies have traditionally treated water using the chlorination process for purification. Chlorine removers, mostly based on sodium thiosulfate

and water conditioners, have been used to condition water prior to introduction of fish, for chlorine and related compounds are extremely toxic to aquatic life.

Recently, chloramines have been introduced as an alternative for water purification. Chloramines are basically a combination of ammonia and chlorine. Chloramines are also very toxic to aquatic life. As little as 0.05 milligrams per liter can kill fish. Chloramines differ from chlorines in that: 1) they are not as easily dispersed from water; 2) their decomposition yields ammonia, also a toxic product; 3) the molecule is more stable; and 4) chloramines readily pass through gills.

Chloramines are now being used worldwide, particularly in the United States, Canada, and Australia. To render chloramines nontoxic, specific water conditioners can be used. However, it may be necessary to remove the ammonia using a specific ammonia remover or activated carbon.

Gas-bubble disease: The so-called gas-bubble disease can be initiated by a variety of causes. These might include a leak in a hose, causing supersaturation of gas in the aquarium, an imbalance in the enzyme system of the fish, or inadequate decompression of fish when captured. The appearance of a swollen eye or eyes, referred to as exophthalmia, is a common sign of gas-bubble disease. When caused by supersaturation of gases, gas-bubble disease causes skin lesions, which can develop secondary bacterial infections. Upon close observation, gas bubbles can be found in the skin and gills. They are most readily seen in capillaries of the gills, where the gills take on a silvery appearance.

Neoplasia: Tumors can be external or internal, benign or malignant. Benign tumors tend to develop slowly. Malignant tumors or cancers proliferate rapidly and are invasive, involving other organs. The appearance of tumors on marine fishes can be caused by other factors, including viruses, pollutants, imbalance of nutrients, and hormonal imbalances. Thyroid tumors are relatively well known and can be caused by inadequate intake of iodine. They are rare in aquaria when fish are being fed well-balanced diets. Tumors which appear on fins or other parts of the body can be removed in cases where they are determined to be benign.

Genetic and induced anomalies: Most aquarists will not encounter fish that have anomalies, as fish have already been sorted and selected during capture and before being sent to stores. Genetic anomalies such as deformed bodies or fins are uncommon. However, fish acquired when in the juvenile stage may develop anomalies as a result of poor nutrition or exposure to chemicals. Care must be exercised when raising young fish to make sure they are not exposed to chemicals which are known to cause anomalies. Such chemicals as trichlorfon can result in permanent nervous disorders if used at high concentrations with juvenile fish.

Selected References

Blasiola, G. C. 1976. Ectoparasitic turbellaria. *Marine Aquarist* 7(2): 53–58.

———. 1979. *Glugea heraldi*, a new species of microsporida from the seahorse, *Hippocampus erectus* Perry. *J. Fish Dis*. 2(6): 493–500.

———. 1980. *Brooklynella hostilis,* a protozoan parasite of marine fishes. *Freshwater and Marine Aquarium* 3(3): 18–19, 82–83.

———. 1984. Protecting aquarium and pond fish from the dangers of chloramines. *Freshwater and Marine Aquarium* 7(4): 10–12, 78–80, 82–83.

Blazer, V. S., and Wolke, R. E. 1979. An *Exophiala*-like fungus as the cause of a systemic mycosis of marine fish. *J. Fish Dis*. 2: 145–52.

Cheung, P.; Nigrelli, R. F.; and Ruggieri, G. D. 1980. Studies on the morphology of *Uronema marinum* Dujardin (Ciliata: Uronematidae) with a description of the histopathology of the infection in marine fishes. *J. Fish Dis*. 3: 295–303.

———. 1981. *Oodinium ocellatum* (Brown, 1931) (Dinoflagellata) in the kidney and other internal tissues of pork fish, *Anisotrema virginicus* (L.). *J. Fish Dis*. 4: 523–25.

———. 1983. *Pentacapsula muscularis* sp. nov. (Myxosporea: Pentacapsulidae): a histozoic parasite of butterflyfish. *Chaetodon collare* Bloch. *J. Fish Dis*. 6: 393–95.

Cheung, P. J., and Ruggieri, G. D. 1983. *Dermophthirius nibrelli* n. sp. (Monogenea: Microbothriidae), an ectoparasite from the skin of the lemon shark, *Negaprion brevirostris. Trans. Am. Microscop. Soc*. 102(2): 129–34.

Colornia, A. 1985. Aspects of the biology of *Cryptocaryon irritans,* and hyposalinity as a control measure in cultured gilt-head sea bream *Sparus aurata. Dis. Aquat. Org*. 1: 19–22.

Condé, B. 1976. Parasitisme de Labrides de la region Caraibes par une Planaire. *Aquariol. Herpetol*. 3: 23–24.

Cusak, R., and Cone, D. K. 1985. A report of bacterial microcolonies on the surface of *Gyrodactylus* (Monogenea). *J. Fish Dis. 8: 125–27.*

Emerson, C. J.; Payne, J. F.; and Bal, A. K. 1985. Evidence for the presence of a viral non-lymphocystis type disease in winter flounder, *Pseudopleuronectes americanus* (Walbaum), from the north-west Atlantic. *J. Fish Dis*. 8: 91–102.

Frakes, T., and Hoff, F. H., Jr. 1982. Effect of high nitrate on the growth and survival of juvenile and larval anemonefish, *Amphiprion ocellaris. Aquaculture* 29: 155–58.

Goven, B. A., and Amend, D. F. 1982. Mebendazole/trichlorfon combinations: a new anthelmintic for removing monogenetic trematodes from fish. *J. Fish Biol*. 20: 373–78.

Goven, B. A.; Gilbert, J. P.; and Gratzek, J.B. 1980. Apparent drug resistance to the organophosphate dimethyl (2,2,2,-trichloro-1-hydroxyethyl) phosphonate by monogenetic trematodes. *J. Wildl. Dis.* 16(3): 343–46.

Gratzek, J. B., and Reinert, R. 1981. Physiological responses of experimental fish to stressful conditions. *Symposium on the Use of Small Fish Species in Carcinogenicity Testing.* Natl. Institutes of Health, Bethesda, Md.

Grimes, D. J.; Gruber, S. H.; and May, E. B. 1985. Experimental infection of lemon sharks, *Negaprion brevirostris* (Poey) with *Vibrio* species. *J. Fish Dis*. 8: 173–80.

Huff, J. A., and Burns, C. D. 1981. Hypersaline and chemical control of *Cryptocaryon irritans* in red snapper, *Lutjanus campechanus,* monoculture. *Aquaculture* 22: 181–84.

Kabata, Z. 1970. *Crustacea as Enemies of Fishes.* Neptune City, N.J.: T.F.H. Publications.

Keith, R. E. 1980. Disease prevention and control. *Freshwater and Marine Aquarium* 3(1): 20–23, 74.

Kent, M. 1981. The life cycle and treatment of a turbellarian disease of marine fishes. *Freshwater and Marine Aquarium* 4(11): 11–13.

Lawler, A. R. 1977. The parasitic dinoflagellate *Amyloodinium ocellatum* in marine aquaria. *Drum & Croaker* 17(2): 17–20.

Lom, J., and Nigrelli, R. F. 1970. *Brooklynella hostilis* n.g., n. sp., a pathogenic cyrtophorine ciliate in marine fishes. *J. Protozool*. 17(2): 224–32.

Love, M.; Teebken-Fisher, D.; Hose, J. E.; et al. 1981. *Vibrio damsela,* a marine bacterium, causes skin ulcers on the damselfish, *Chromis punctipinnis. Science* 214: 1139–40.

McCosker, J. E. 1969. A behavioral correlate for the passage of lymphocystis disease in three blennioid fishes. *Copeia* 3: 636–37.

Nigrelli, R. F., and Ruggieri, G. D. 1966. Enzootics in the New York Aquarium caused by *Cryptocaryon irritans* Brown, 1951 (=*Ichthyophthirius marinus* Sikama, 1961), a histophagous ciliate in the skin, eyes and gills of marine fishes. *Zoologica* 51: 97–102.

Paperna, I. 1980. *Amyloodinium ocellatum* (Brown, 1931) (Dinoflagellida) infestations in cultured marine fish at Eilat, Red Sea: epizootiology and pathology. *J. Fish Dis.* 3: 363–72.

———. 1984. Chemical control of *Amyloodinium ocellatum* (Brown, 1931) (Dinoflagellida) infections: in vitro tests and treatment with infected fishes. *Aquaculture* 38: 1–18.

Pearse, L.; Pullin, R.S.V.; Conroy, D. A.; et al. 1974. Observations on the use of Furanace for the control of *Vibrio* disease in marine flatfish. *Aquaculture* 3: 295–302.

Scarano, G.; Saroglia, M. G.; Gray, R. H.; et al. 1984. Hematological responses of sea bass, *Dicentrarchus labrax,* to sublethal nitrite exposures. *Trans. Am. Fish. Soc.* 113: 360–64.

Shotts, E. B. 1981. Bacterial disease of fish. Proceedings, Republic of China – U.S. Cooperative Science Seminar on Fish Diseases. *NSC Symp.* Series no. 3: 7–9.

Sindermann, C. J. 1966. *Diseases of Marine Fishes.* Neptune City, N.J.: T.F.H. Publications.

Sniesko, S. 1974. The effects of environmental stress on outbreaks of infectious diseases of fishes. *J. Fish Biol.* 6: 197–208.

Stagg, R. M., and Shuttleworth, T. J. 1982. The accumulation of copper in *Platichthys flesus* L. and its effects on plasma electrolyte concentrations. *J. Fish Biol.* 20: 491–500.

Wilkie, D. W., and Gordon, H. 1969. Outbreak of cryptocaryoniasis in marine aquaria at Scripps Institute of Oceanography. *Calif. Fish and Game 55(3):* 227–36.

Wolf, K. E.; Quimby, M. C.; Carlson, C. P.; et al. 1979. Lymphocystis virus: infectivity of lesion preparations stored after lyophilization or simple desiccation. *J. Fish Dis.* 2: 259–60.

Checklists, Quarantine Procedures, and Calculations of Particular Use in Fish Health Management

John B. Gratzek and George C. Blasiola

Where does one begin when faced with a sick fish? How does one begin to determine the causes of the illness? How does one decide what to do first? Where—even in this book—does one begin in the search for information relevant to a problem?

It was in response to such questions that this appendix was developed. It is intended as a brief, nonexhaustive, but hopefully helpful, guide to some types of information of particular use in fish health management. Here the reader will find a diagnostic guide to help the aquarist determine the cause of the fish problems he or she is facing, an explanation (with examples) of the calculation of various medicinal dosages, and a guide to the quarantine procedures which are essential to preventing fish disease from spreading.

A Brief Guide to Diagnosing Fish Health Problems

When one or more fish in a tank are dying or dead, panic is understandable. Before immediately deciding that the problem must be an infectious disease or parasite, it is worthwhile to consider the possibility of noninfectious causes. Refer to the index to locate further information about possible noninfectious causes of problems outlined below.

Is the problem related to the aquarium water?

A. *Check temperature.* It should be 75 to 85 degrees F (about 24 to 29.5 degrees C) for most tropical fish. Goldfish and other cold-water species tolerate lower temperatures and can easily overwinter in frigid water.

B. *Check for ammonia and nitrites.* Test results should be negative in a well-established aquarium.

C. *Check pH.* The optimum for freshwater fish is close to neutrality (pH 7.0); the acceptable range is between 6.8 and 7.8. For marine systems, a pH of 7.8 to 8.3 is acceptable.

D. *Check for presence of toxins.*
   1. Was water dechlorinated properly?
   2. Have medicaments such as copper been added? Accidental spills? Any unusual items added to aquarium?
   3. Source of water? Municipal water may have chloramines. Shallow wells can be contaminated with bacteria. Water taken directly

from rivers or lakes could introduce parasites or contain pesticides.

E. Check hardness of water. About 100 ppm minerals is desirable. Avoid excessively soft (less than 57 ppm minerals) or distilled water. Extremely hard water may create excessively high pH.

Is the problem related to basic aquarium setup and management?

A. Is aquarium size adequate for the number and size of the fish?

B. Is there adequate filtration and aeration?
1. Are filters periodically rinsed or replaced?
2. Is detritus removed from gravel periodically?

C. Is aquarium covered to prevent jumping?

D. Have adequate shade and escape room been provided?

E. Is water changed periodically? How frequently? Amount?

F. Have plants been disinfected prior to introduction?

Is the problem related to choice of fish?

A. Are the fish species compatible?

B. Is stocking density appropriate for the species?

C. What is the age of the fish? Might they be at the end of their expected life-span?

D. Were the fish quarantined and treated prior to addition to aquarium? If so, for how long? Which medicaments were used, if any?

E. Were fish treated previously for problems? How? Was the treatment method effective?

Is the problem related to food or nutrition?

A. Is the food choice nutritionally balanced?

B. Is the food fresh? How long in storage?

C. Is the feeding frequency appropriate?

D. Are sinking pellets being fed to bottom feeders?

E. Are live foods fed? What is their source?

F. Is food medicated? If so, with what?

After noninfectious causes have been ruled out, one can begin the search for other possible reasons for illness. Careful examination of the death pattern, fish behavior, and external and internal lesions (such as spots, blemishes, etc.) will provide valuable clues. Check each of these

in turn. Refer to the index in this volume to locate further information about the problems outlined below.

How many fish have died? Over what time period?

A. Majority of fish died within a very short period of time:
1. Toxic problem. Check water quality.
2. *Ichthyophthirius multifiliis.*
3. Overcrowding, with lack of oxygen.

B. Gradual death rate over long period:
1. Old age, perhaps complicated by *Mycobacterium* or tumors.
2. Poor food quality.
3. Low-level toxicity.
4. Immunological failure associated with poor water or poor food quality, leading to bacterial diseases.

C. Approximately 20 to 60 percent of fish sick or dying:
1. Acute parasitic infection following shipment or addition of disease-carrying fish to aquarium. (See *Ichthyophthirius; Chilodonella; Ichthyobodo; Tetrahymena.*)
2. Acute bacterial infection. Check water quality.

Do dying fish show unusual swimming patterns?

A. Fish at surface near water outlet:
1. Low oxygen.
2. Gill parasites.
3. Gill damage.

B. Sluggish movements, fish at bottom:
1. Parasites.
2. Bacteria such as *Cytophaga.*
3. Poor water conditions.

C. Circling, twirling, or erratic motion:
Chronic bacterial problem. (See *Streptococcus; Edwardsiella; Eubacterium.*)

D. Flashing, scratching:
Skin irritation; check water, parasites on body or gills.

Do fish show external clinical signs of disease?

A. White spots on body and fins.
1. Spots less than 2 millimeters (0.08 inches) in diameter. Parasites. See *Ichthyophthirius* (freshwater fish) or *Cryptocaryon* (saltwater fish).
2. Small, white, focalized areas. Cysts of vari-

ous sizes may be elevated to form small nodules. Fish do not appear to be clinically sick. (See Sporozoans.)

3. White tufts resembling cotton balls. May be seen on mouth, eye, or body. Can be up to 10 millimeters (0.4 inches) in size. Common on fish eggs. Fungal infection (frequently following an injury) or bacterial infection.

4. Small white tufts. Smaller than fungal growths. Frequently are colonies of *Heteropolaria,* a stalked protozoan.

5. "Saddleback"— whitened area on fish's back. (See F, below.)

B. *Fine, dusty golden or "velvet" appearance.* Best seen with incident light from above. Cysts of *Oodinium,* a parasitic dinoflagellate for both freshwater fish and marine species.

C. *Tumorlike cellular masses. Lymphocystis* virus causes enlarged cells on surface of skin, tumor-like masses on lips or eyes, and masses of cells resembling grape clusters on tips of fins.

D. *Large (3 to 4 millimeters, or 0.1 to 0.15 inches) white, yellow, or (rarely) black lumps on skin.* These are usually metacercariae of digenetic trematodes.

E. *Excess slime on skin.* Best seen with incident light from above.

1. Check pH.
2. Can be caused by excessive medication.
3. Frequently associated with heavy parasitic infestations from *Ichthyophthirius, Chilodonella, Ichthyobodo,* or monogenetic trematodes.

F. *Fin and body rot.* Fins may appear white, incomplete, or frayed. Eyes may be cloudy, and mouthparts may be affected. Lesions on body may appear as whitened areas over dorsal part of body, referred to as "saddleback" disease. (See *Cytophaga; Flavobacterium; Aeromonas;* and other species of bacteria.)

Are parasites themselves visible on fish?

A. *Elongated white parasites attached to skin.* May protrude as much as 1 centimeter (0.4 inches), depending on maturity. Anchor worms. (See *Lernaea, Ergasilus;* a closely related species parasitizes gills.)

B. *Disc-shaped parasites that move freely about the surface of fish.* Their size, up to 1 centimeter (0.4 inches), allows them to be seen easily. Fish lice (see *Argulus*).

C. *Elongated isopods up to 1 centimeter (0.4 inches) in length.* They are freely mobile and frequently burrow a hole in the fish, where they reside. (See *Livoneca.*)

D. *Oval "worms" whose bodies can elongate up to 2 centimeters (0.8 inches) in length upon being disturbed.* In addition to being seen on fish, they may be found on plants or on the surface of gravel. (See Leeches.)

E. *Small white worms 2 to 3 millimeters (0.08 to 0.1 inches) long.* May also be found on glass. (See Turbellarians.)

F. *Intestinal worms protruding from anal opening.* (See Nematodes; Tapeworms.)

Are bloody or reddened areas visible?

A. *"Injected" blood vessels.* Handling fish will result in a reddening of fins, caused by the dilation of blood vessels. "Injected" vessels can also frequently be seen during the initial phases of a systemic bacterial disease or severe stress.

B. *Hemorrhage.* Bloody areas of the skin can be pinpoint to brushlike in character.

1. Usually associated with parasitic bacterial or viral infections. (See *Tetrahymena; Uronema; Aeromonas.*)

2. Subcutaneous hemorrhaging about the mouth, throat, and base of fins. Enteric red mouth disease. (See *Yersinia.*)

3. Red necrotic lesions on skin, mouth, vent, base of fins, coupled with bloat. (See *Vibrio; Pseudomonas; Mycobacterium; Aeromonas.*)

C. *Ulcerations.*

1. Deep ulcers with circumscribed hemorrhagic areas are commonly associated with bacterial infections.

2. May be seen as a result of *Tetrahymena; Uronema; Pseudomonas.*

3. Ulcer disease, common in goldfish and koi. (See *Aeromonas salmonicida.*)

4. "Hole-in-the-head" disease, lateral line erosion. Shallow ulcerations seen over lateral line area, extending to head. May note small white blebs prior to onset of necrosis. Long strands of exudate may resemble worms. Etiology unknown. (See *Hexamita; Edwardsiella.*)

Are there problems in the musculature and/or deep skin areas?

A. *Deep ulcerations.* (See Bacteria.)

B. *Diffuse whitening of muscles.* (See Sporozoans.)

C. *White foci in musculature.* (See Sporozoans; Digenetic Trematodes; encysted Nematodes.)

D. Lumpy, uneven musculature. (See *Pleistophora.*)

Are the fish's eyes affected?

A. *Exophthalmia, or "popeye."* May occur in one or both eyes. Can be caused by tumors, bacterial diseases, or gas-bubble disease. May follow handling of fish.
B. *Cloudy eye.* May involve one or both eyes. Can be initiated by attacks from other fish. (See *Myxobacterium;* columnaris disease.)
C. *Opacity of lens.* (See Digenetic Trematodes; nutritional deficiencies.)
D. *Area surrounding eye is white.* (See *Tetrahymena*; *Heteropolaria*; *Lymphocystis* virus.)
E. *Missing eye.* Result of injury, infectious disease, or tumor.

Are there abdominal problems?

A. *Abdominal distention (bloat, dropsy).*
1. Internal tumors.
2. Parasitic infestations of kidneys. (See *Mitraspora.*)
3. African/Malawi bloat. (See *Aeromonas; Clostridium.*)
4 Cystic kidneys. Possibly inherited or due to toxic metals.
5. Mycobacterial infections. (See *Mycobacterium.*)
6. Tapeworms. May protrude from anal opening.
7. Pseudokidney disease. (See *Lactobacillus.*)
B. *Emaciation/wasting, "hollow belly."*
1. Nutritional problem.
2. Mycobacterial infection.
3. Chronic parasitism. Intestinal parasites, *Hexamita,* migrating nematodes within abdominal cavity.
4. Internal tumors.

Quarantine and Treatment of Freshwater Ornamental Fish

To quarantine an animal means to isolate it from healthy animals for a period of time. Historically, the word "quarantine" meant a forty-day isolation period. The basic concept of quarantining fish for a period of time is to ensure that the fish will not introduce disease organisms into an aquarium full of healthy fish. During the holding period, a carrier fish may in fact develop a disease and die. Alter-natively, a carrier fish may shed a particular parasite during the quarantine period. Routine treatment should be instituted during the quarantine period to rid the fish of any parasites.

Aquarists with large investments in fish realize that the introduction of new fish into a breeding colony without quarantine leads to problems. Parasites such as *Ichthyophthirius, Ichthyobodo, Chilodonella, Oodinium, Hexamita,* and monogenetic trematodes can be introduced into aquaria by carrier fish which appear to be healthy. Routine quarantining of fish prevents many common and highly dangerous diseases from being introduced into an aquatic system. However, one must note that there are groups of parasites and bacteria which may not be affected. For example, sporozoan parasites or mycobacterial infections are not treatable and may be introduced even though a fish is treated during the quarantine period.

How to quarantine fish: Fish must be held in an aquarium which is supplied with good water

Generalized Quarantine Procedure for Fish.

Prepare quarantine facilities. Make necessary temperature, salinity, and pH adjustments of water.

⇓

Add fish to quarantine holding facilities. Allow fish to acclimate twenty-four to forty-eight hours before treatment.

⇓

Assess the fish's condition. Note any serious problems requiring immediate attention.

⇓

Perform required water tests throughout the quarantine period.

⇓

Conduct frequent inspections of quarantine facility. Remove dead fish promptly.

⇓

Administer recommended chemical treatments to control common disease agents.

⇓

After fourteen to twenty-one days, transfer fish to permanent display aquarium.

Source: G. C. Blasiola.

Quarantine and Treatment Record

Date: _____

Fish Quarantined:

Scientific Name: _____

Common Name: _____

Quarantine

Aquarium No(s): _____ Purchased from: _____

Date of Arrival: _____ DDAs: _____

Required Quarantine Dates:

From: _____ To: _____

Clinical Signs upon Arrival:

_____

_____

Preliminary Diagnosis: _____

_____

Treatments

Dates: From: _____ To: _____

Chemicals Used: _____

Dosages: _____ Duration of Treatment_____

Administration Method: ( ) Dip ( ) Bath ( ) Oral ( ) Injection

Results of Treatment: _____

_____

Remarks:_____

_____

Example of a quarantine and treatment record form.
Source: G. C. Blasiola.

and/or where the filtration system maintains good water quality with respect to pH, ammonia, and nitrites. This can be done in various ways, and a genralized procedure is given in the flow chart on the previous page. It is important to maintain records on any quarantined fish; the sample form above is used for keeping track of quarantine and treatment.

A flow-through system can be installed where fresh, dechlorinated water is dripped slowly into an aquarium, with provision for overflow. However, in this situation, water must be heated and dechlorinated, and this can involve complex water-handling systems. If a flow-through system is not practical, one can quarantine fish in a suitable aquarium (10 to 30 gallons, or 38 to 114 liters, depending on size and number of fish to be quarantined) in which aquarium water is maintained at about 75 to 80 degrees F (24 to 27 degrees C) and pH is adjusted to 6.8 to 7.2. Place plastic pots and/or plants in the aquarium to provide shelter and hiding areas. Provide conditioned filter substrate (such as gravel) within a filter. Conditioned gravel can be placed in mesh bags for this purpose. Also, conditioned foam filters can be used in a quarantine tank. Periodically test water for ammonia, nitrites, pH, and temperature in order to gauge when water changes should be made.

Quarantining fish in an aquarium with an unconditioned filter is possible if water is changed regularly to avoid ammonia and nitrite buildup. Water should be tested periodically for pH, ammonia, and nitrites. Ammonia toxicity can be reduced by using ammonia-adsorbing clays in filters, by maintaining a neutral pH, and by water changes. When changing water, it is important to avoid stress upon the fish by making sure that the water temperature does not fluctuate by more than a few degrees. A water temperature between 75 and 80 degrees F (about 24 to 27 degrees C) is adequate. Chlorine can be removed by addition of sodium thiosulfate (2 drops per gallon or per 3.8 liters of a 13 percent solution), and pH should be kept at approximately 7.0 by use of commercially available buffers. If nitrites are detected (a situation which usually occurs after three to seven days in an unconditioned aquarium), water should be changed. Addition of 1 teaspoon of salt per gallon (3.8 liters) will interfere with nitrite-ion uptake in some nitrite-sensitive fish. Combine the addition of salt with water changes if nitrites are a problem.

The longer the quarantine period, the greater the chance that fish will have shed any parasites or recovered from other infections. For absolute safety, a period of thirty days is recommended. A fourteen-day period is minimum. During this period, water changes alone may serve to rid the fish of parasites by diluting their numbers and minimizing reinfection, as in the case of *Ichthyophthirius multifiliis.* In some cases, fish may die of known or unknown causes. Unfortunately, clients may lay the blame for fish deaths on the quarantine procedure; this emphasizes the importance of maintaining and testing for good water quality. Treatment of fish during the quarantine period is essential since, in most cases, the resident population of parasites cannot be determined and many will remain on or in the fish. In cases where many fish are to be quarantined and a few can be spared, the results of a routine necropsy examination may uncover parasites toward which specific therapies can be directed. Although quarantine could be done without any routine administration of parasiticides, the incidence of parasitism in ornamental fish is enough reason to routinely medicate fish during quarantine.

How to medicate quarantined freshwater fish safely: Not all parasitic conditions are readily treatable, and even with the best of available medications, some parasites may kill the fish during quarantine or survive quarantine altogether. However, from a clinical approach, one can attempt to rid fish of known highly infectious problems which are readily treatable and which are the primary agents of disease.

Medicaments which aquarists have traditionally used include salt, methylene blue, and acriflavine. The following suggestions for an increased drug arsenal (see accompanying table) are based on: 1) the availability of the drug, 2) the efficacy of the drug for a broad spectrum of parasites, and 3) the safety of the drug.

A summary of the indications and use of the most efficacious drugs for routine antiparasite treatment of freshwater fish during quarantine.

Formaldehyde or formaldehyde–malachite green mixtures	
Use indications	External protozoans, monogenetic trematodes.
Dose	1 milliliter of formaldehyde (25 ppm) or 1 milliliter of formaldehyde–malachite green mixture, for no longer than twelve hours.
Precautions	Preparations of formaldehyde will kill severely sick fish. If fish are of a species judged to be sensitive to either formaldehyde or malachite green (scaleless fish, neon tetras), terminate treatment after one to two hours by water changes or by removal of fish to nonmedicated water.
Metronidazole	
Use indications	Effective against flagellated protozoans such as *Hexamita* and *Spironucleus*. May be effective against *Ichthyobodo necatrix* and species of *Oodinium*. Presently used against internal flagellates.
Dose	250 milligrams per 10 gallons (38 liters) (6ppm) for twenty-four hours. In food , at a concentration of 0.25 percent.
Precautions	This medicament does not appear to be toxic to fish at the levels used. Terminate medication at twenty-four hours.
Praziquantel	
Use indications	Effective against monogenetic trematodes and tapeworms. May kill digenetic trematode metacercariae and larval tapeworms. Its efficacy against adult tapeworms in fish has been demonstrated when drug is administered via water.
Dose	The drug has been shown to remove external trematodes at 2 ppm after twenty-four hours and will remove intestinal tapeworms within an hour.
Precautions	Toxicity problems have not been encountered at 2 ppm.
Ivermectin	
Use Indications	Nematodes in fish (highly toxic).

(continued)

Dose	Used as an injectable solution in mammals, but addition of the drug to water will remove nematodes. A common stock solution is available to veterinarians as a 1 percent injectable solution. One part of this solution diluted with 19 parts of water will yield a stock solution. Add 0.7 milliliters of the stock solution per 76 liters (20 gallons) of water, and give as a split dose over a four-day period (0.2 milliliters on days 1 and 2, and 0.3 milliliters on day 3). Change water on day 4.
Precautions	Ivermectin is a very effective drug for nematodes, but should only be used on an experimental basis because of its toxicity.

Panacur™

Use indications	Nematodes. Possibly the broadest spectrum nematocide for fish.
Dose	In food, at a concentration of 0.25 percent.

Sodium chloride

Use indications	Sodium chloride has been used for many years, most often as a "tonic" for fish. While not mandatory for raising fish (as some aquarists believe), it is advantageous under certain circumstances. Obviously sick or stressed fish may benefit from added salt by the replacement of sodium or chloride ions that are lost to the water. Salt has been shown to be antiparasitic. Low levels of salt (10 ppm) will block the uptake of nitrites in some fish.
Dose	For use as a parasiticide, a solution of 2.5 percent salt has been used as a dip. Fish are placed in a well-aerated solution until balance cannot be maintained. Many parasites of freshwater fish will be killed by placing the latter into water suitable for marine fish (specific gravity from 1.017 to 1.023) for a period of ten to fifteen minutes. Fish should be removed at the first signs of stress, regardless of time. Many aquarists believe that routine use of added salt is beneficial to live-bearing fish and some cichlids. All agree that salt is not tolerated by some catfish such as *Corydoras*. On an experimental basis, we have successfully used as much as 0.3 percent salt (115 grams [4 ounces] per 10 gallons or 38 liters of water) in aquaria.
Precautions	If using salt as a parasiticide, remove fish as soon as they show signs of stress. Some species may be sensitive to salt. Some aquarium plants may not tolerate salt if higher concentrations (0.3 percent) are used.

Acriflavine

Use indications	Acriflavine, a yellow dye, has both antibacterial and antiprotozoan activities. It has been used to treat fish with external protozoan parasites and has been used for surface bacterial infections of fish. Acriflavine is not as effective as formaldehyde as a general parasiticide and has been largely replaced by antibiotics for treatment of bacterial infections.
Dose	2 to 3 ppm.
Precautions	This medicament will turn water yellow and can be toxic to fish. Other antiparasiticides and antibiotics have been shown to be more effective without affecting the color of the water.

Methylene blue

Use indications	Methylene blue was one of the first aquarium medications used primarily for treatment of external parasites. Other parasiticides have been shown to be more effective. This drug is relatively nontoxic to fish and has been used to treat weak fish soon after arrival. The use of methylene blue with 0.1 to 0.3 percent salt represents a mild treatment for recently transported fish which are under severe stress.
Dose	5 ppm.
Precautions	Methylene blue has been shown to inactivate nitrifying bacteria. The drug should not be allowed to permeate gravel beds. It is possibly best used in circumstances where biological filters are not present.

Potassium permanganate

Use indications	Potassium permanganate is an oxidizing agent. It is used primarily in aquaculture for algae control and as a clarifying agent. It also will kill external parasites and possibly externally located bacteria. At this writing, it is one of the most frequently used parasiticides in ponds, although it is not approved for food fish. For aquarium use, it has been used as a clarifier and as a parasiticide. However, other parasiticides and antibacterial drugs have been shown to be more effective.
Dose	1 to 3 ppm in ponds, depending on the organic load.

(continued)

| Precautions | Potassium permanganate can oxidize and burn tissues of fish. If water is exceptionally clear, a dose of 3 ppm could damage gills, resulting in deaths. If water contains high plankton levels, a dose of 2 ppm may not be enough to kill parasites. Tests for effectiveness and proper dosage should be done in vats prior to treating entire ponds. The drug initially turns water red and will oxidize any living materials. If used on already stressed or severely parasitized fish, expect deaths from the added stress of the treatment. |

Copper sulfate	
Use indications	Copper sulfate is frequently used for weed and algae control in ponds. It is also an effective parasiticide when properly administered.
Dose	0.1 to 0.2 ppm of copper ion (hydrated copper sulfate, $CuSo_4 \cdot 5H_2O$ is 25 percent copper ion).
Precautions	The proper dosing of copper sulfate is complicated by the chelation of the copper ion by carbonates and other anions in water. In freshwater systems, the amount of copper sulfate to be added will depend on the hardness level. It is always best to determine the effect of hardness on the amount of free copper ion prior to addition of copper sulfate to an aquarium or fish culture system. Accurate measurements of copper ion may be obtained with a copper test kit. Copper can be very toxic to fish and plants. Its use in freshwater systems is dangerous. Chelated copper forms are safer than using copper ion, but also less effective. Most copper test kits will detect chelated copper, leading the aquarist to the erroneous conclusion that the copper is biologically active.

In fish therapy, a wise adage states, "Know your fish, the chemical, and the water." First, some fish are more sensitive to a medication than others. For example, some species of ornamental catfish such as *Corydoras* do not tolerate salt. Second, the nature of the water may affect medication. For example, the effective therapeutic dose of a drug may differ with the ionization and pH of water. Organophosphates degrade more quickly at higher water pH levels. Organic substances in water may bind medicaments and reduce their efficacy. Unfortunately, these idiosyncrasies have not been cataloged, especially with the appearance of new parasiticides. Third, the route of medication must be tailored to the situation. When medicating fish, it is often impractical to add medicaments to feed since sick fish will not eat. One might add the medicament to the water in the hope that sufficient adsorption will result in a clinical effect. However, while saltwater fish drink copious amounts of water for osmoregulatory purposes, freshwater fish drink little or none. Obviously this behavior alone could influence dosage, toxicity, and efficacy. At this writing, there is very little hard information on such questions. Presumably, many medications added to fresh water are adsorbed via gills.

Safety can be maximized by using correct dosages and by limiting the time of treatment to minimize toxicity. In all medication schemes, aeration should be maintained by agitation of water (filters, air bubblers), but activated carbon must be removed since it will remove medicaments. Air-stems should be removed from lift stacks of undergravel filters to avoid pulling the medicament through the gravel substrate while providing aeration. Termination of the treatment is best done by water changes, or in the case of saltwater systems, by filtration through activated carbon.

Suggested treatment for external trematodes and/or protozoans: Formaldehyde at 25 ppm (1 milliliter [20 drops] per 10 gallons, or 38 liters, of water) is considered a long-term treatment for parasites such as *Ichthyophthirius, Chilodonella, Ichthyobodo,* and monogenetic trematodes. At this dosage, formaldehyde is considered to be an indefinite treatment and could be left in the aquarium to dissipate gradually. Since most parasites will be killed within minutes or hours, we suggest treatment in the morning, followed by a 70 to 90 percent water change after six to eight hours of exposure. Maintain aeration, remove activated carbon from filters, and remove air-stems from undergravel filters, if used. This general treatment can be repeated at three-day intervals if infections of ich are suspected.

In some cases, increased levels of formaldehyde can be administered for shorter periods of time. Thus, at a 75 ppm level, treatment time may be reduced to not more than eight hours or until fish begin to show signs of stress. Such treatments are best done as baths in special treatment aquaria. If this approach is used, the display aquarium should be treated with a lower dose (25 ppm) for a few hours, followed by a complete water change. Failure to do this may result in reinfection of the fish when returned to the aquarium. Short baths (ten to fifteen minutes) in 250 ppm formaldehyde have also been used in treatment aquaria, but this may represent too severe a stress for sensitive species of ornamental fish.

Mixtures of formaldehyde and malachite green have been shown to be superior to the independent use of either medicament. Our experience suggests that formaldehyde has a wider efficacy than malachite green when either chemical is used alone. A stock solution can be made by adding 1.4 grams of zinc-free malachite green to 380 milliliters of formaldehyde solution (0.49 ounces in a gallon of solution). The dose per 10 gallons (38 liters) of water is 1 milliliter (20 drops), resulting in approximately 25 ppm of formaldehyde and 0.01 ppm of malachite green. This formulation should not be used on food fish since malachite green has been shown to be carcinogenic. Treatments can be as short as five hours and can extend to twelve hours. Water changes to avoid toxicity to fish are suggested at the termination of the treatment.

Organophosphates at 0.25 ppm have been used to remove monogenetic trematodes from ornamental fish, but these drugs appear to yield no better results than formaldehyde. Furthermore, their repeated usage for removal of trematodes from goldfish has resulted in the emergence of organophosphate-resistant forms. Organophosphates have no effect on external protozoan parasites, but are particularly effective for the control of parasitic copepods, *Argulus,* and leeches.

Results from our laboratory suggest that praziquantel (Droncit™) added to water at 2 ppm will remove monogenetic trematodes from both gills and skin of infested goldfish. This drug has been used on a variety of freshwater and marine ornamental fish without problem, and is effective in removal of tapeworms and may kill larval forms of digenetic trematodes. We suggest adding this drug during the final two or three days of quarantine. Our results suggest that trematodes will be gone twenty-four hours after treatment. At 2 ppm there appears to be no effect on the biological filter and no toxicity to fish. The drug is quite expensive, but may be the drug of choice for removing external trematodes and larval forms of digenea and tapeworms.

Suggested treatments for internal parasites: To treat fish for *Hexamita,* add metronidazole at 6 ppm directly to the water. Our experience suggests that a single treatment is adequate to rid fish of parasites. The drug is apparently adsorbed via skin or gills and appears to be nontoxic even

at 20 ppm. We have noted no effect on biological filters, but as a precaution one should avoid pulling medicament through filters. Metronidazole can also be added to food at 0.25%.

Nematode removal can be approached by incorporating drugs such as fenbendazol (Panacur™) or piperazine in food at a level of 0.25 percent. Ivermectin has been used at 0.7 milliliters (14 drops) of an injectable formulation (0.05 percent active compound) per 76 liters (20 gallons) to give a calculated dosage of approximately 0.005 ppm. The total dose was given over a period of four days (0.1 milliliter [2 drops] on the first day, then 0.2 milliliter [4 drops] on each of the following three days). Products such as Ivomec™, which are supplied as sterile 1 percent solutions, would have to be diluted 1 part to 19 parts of water to obtain a solution containing 0.05 percent active compound. This drug must be protected from light. As the drug is very toxic to fish, its use should be preceded by ample biological testing. **Using combinations of drugs during quarantine:** In quarantine situations, it is best not to administer any drugs until the fish have adapted to the quarantine tank and are feeding. This may take three to four days. We have used formaldehyde (25 ppm), metronidazole (6 ppm), and praziquantel (2 ppm) in combination for twelve- hour treatments without harm to the fish. In practice, the use of formaldehyde and metronidazole toward the beginning of the quarantine period, followed by praziquantel toward the end of it, would represent a more conservative and possibly safer use of these drugs. In all cases, we suggest that medicaments be removed from water after treatment to avoid a possible toxic effect on the fish. This removal can be done by water changes or by filtration using activated carbon.

Quarantine and Treatment of Saltwater Fish

Because of the higher cost of saltwater fish and the cost of synthetic sea salts for water preparation, the marine aquarist is more likely than the freshwater aquarist to quarantine fish, especially if he or she has had disease problems in the past. Traditionally, treatment during quarantine has been directed toward removing external parasites (see accompanying table). Purchasing saltwater fish from dealers who are aware of disease prob-

---

A Method for Ridding Saltwater Fish of External Protozoans and Trematodes During the Quarantine Period

1. Make a 0.75 percent solution of copper sulfate-penthydrate ($CuSO_4 \cdot 5H_2O$). Use 5 milliliters (0.17 fluid ounces) of this mixture per 38 liters (10 gallons) of water to give a copper sulfate dose of approximately 0.25 ppm. The objective of the treatment is to keep the copper-ion level at 0.1 to 0.2 ppm for ten days. Because the initial dose will tend to be chelated, readings on a copper test kit will be lower than expected. Test water daily. In some cases, no copper ion will be detected and it may be necessary to add an additional half-dose on the first day. If the copper-ion reading is below 0.1 ppm, add a half-dose and retest. Eventually, the level of copper ion will stabilize, and no additional doses may be needed.

2. On the next-to-last day of the quarantine period, add 2 ppm of praziquantel to remove trematodes and kill larval forms.

3. On the last day of quarantine, bathe fish in pH 8.3 fresh water for fifteen to thirty minutes or until fish begin to appear stressed. Formaldehyde can be added at the rate of 100 ppm (4 milliliters per 10 gallons or 38 liters of water). Maintain vigorous aeration during this bath treatment.

---

lems is important. Such dealers may have initiated their own quarantine systems and may have central filtration systems where copper levels are maintained at between 0.1 and 0.2 ppm. Many knowledgeable retailers routinely expose saltwater fish to a half-hour dip in fresh water at pH 8.3 to remove external trematodes and other protozoans. Many people purchase a fish and keep it under observation within the retailer's aquarium for a period of time. In effect, this serves as an ersatz quarantine period which, in relation to a strict quarantine, may be likened to playing Russian roulette.

It should be noted that maintaining copper-ion levels at 0.1 to 0.2 ppm will control *Cryptocaryon* and *Oodinium,* but may not "cure" carrier fish if they are sold prior to the time when all trophonts have left the fish and the fish has developed some degree of immunity. Our experience suggests that fish from some such systems may still carry monogenetic trematodes, and if they have not been kept under copper treatment for a sufficient time period, they may still carry the two previously mentioned protozoan parasites.

Method: Depending on the size and number of fish to be quarantined, set up a 10- to 50-gallon

(38- to 190-liter) aquarium with sufficient conditioned gravel in a filter to oxidize ammonia and nitrites. Use commercially available salts with a pH from 7.8 to 8.3 and specific gravity from 1.017 to 1.023, and maintain a temperature of approximately 73 to 77 degrees F (about 23 to 25 degrees C). Provide plenty of aeration using bubbling stones and/or outflow from a filter. Provide hiding areas for fish using plastic pots, pipes, or coral. While fish are in quarantine, continue to feed them whatever they were eating in the store (frozen brine shrimp, flakes, etc.). To prevent ammonia accumulation, do not overfeed, and periodically remove any uneaten food from the aquarium. Throughout the quarantine period, pH, ammonia, and nitrite levels must be monitored daily or every other day, and water changes must be made if ammonia and/or nitrite levels go over 0.1 to 0.2 ppm.

Treatment during quarantine should be directed toward ridding fish of external protozoans and trematodes. As with freshwater fish, internal parasites (nematodes, larval forms) may be a problem. In experiments at the University of Georgia, we have maintained fish at a 0.1 to 0.2 ppm copper-ion concentration for at least ten days, then treated them with 2 ppm of praziquantel toward the end of the fourteen-day quarantine period. Before placing fish in the display aquarium, they have been given a freshwater dip (with or without formaldehyde) as a final insurance measure for trematode removal.

When reintroducing fish into the main display tank after quarantine, rearrange coral or other landmarks in conjunction with a routine water change and cleaning. This will serve to disorient older inhabitants from territorial behavior and tend to spare the newcomer(s). Introducing new fish at night may also reduce fighting. In some cases, dominant fish may have to be removed to avoid deaths from biting.

Disinfection to Prevent Disease Spread

In any wholesale, retail, research, or home facility where multiple tanks are used, sharing of nets, hoses, or other objects between aquaria may spread pathogenic organisms such as parasites, bacteria, and viruses.

How to disinfect nets and solid objects: Many

disinfectants have been used. All should be changed at least once weekly. It is very important to rinse items in clear water after disinfection, since there can be a carryover problem resulting in death of sensitive fish. This is especially true in small aquaria.

A. Air drying: Drying eventually will kill parasites and other organisms, but this process is not strictly disinfection. Spores and cyst forms of such parasites as *Ichthyobodo necatrix* can withstand drying. In establishments with multiple tanks, air drying would necessitate the use of many nets.

B. Chlorine: Chlorine is an excellent disinfectant, but will destroy nets. Chlorine is best used for disinfection of solid objects such as aquaria or hoses. Since organic films will protect bacteria from the effects of chlorine, the surfaces of the objects being cleaned should be scrubbed prior to addition of chlorine. Follow instructions on the bottle for normal disinfection purposes. If scrubbing is not feasible, as in the inside of aquarium piping, 300 ppm of active chlorine may be required.

C. Quaternary ammonia compounds: Various surfactants for general disinfection purposes are available under a variety of trade names, such as Roccal™. These disinfectants are particularly useful as net dips. Follow dilution instructions given on the bottle. Depending on use, the solution may have to be changed two or three times a week. It is important to rinse nets in clear water after disinfection, since carryover of disinfectant may kill small fish.

D. Formaldehyde: Used at 75 to 100 ppm (3 to 4 milliliters, or 0.1 to 0.14 fluid ounces per 10 gallons or 3.8 liters of water), formaldehyde is a good parasiticide. However, it is not recommended due to generation of formaldehyde fumes.

E. Potassium permanganate: Although effective at 50 ppm, since it is an oxidizer and will stain hands, its use is not recommended.

F. Salt: At 3 percent, salt works as a disinfectant for parasites, but in a multiuse situation surfactants have been shown to be more effective.

How to Calculate Water Volume and Medicinal Dosage

When it becomes necessary to medicate fish for health problems, some mathematical figuring becomes essential if the matter is to be done properly and safely. As the following examples illustrate, the calculations involved are much simpler when one uses the metric system. However, in many cases the English system will be included because of its familiarity to North American aquarists.

Safety considerations, both for the fish and for the aquarist, require special mention any time medication is involved. All drugs should be kept under lock and key. They should be handled carefully to avoid skin contact or inhalation contact. If liquid formulations are to be dispensed, never perform mouth pipetting. Inexpensive pipettors are available, or syringes can be attached to the end of a pipette using a small piece of rubber tubing.

Safety of drugs for fish also is a matter of serious concern. Dosages of drugs must be very accurate to avoid poisoning of fish. For example, both formalin (at 25 ppm) and malachite green (at 0.1 ppm) can be toxic to selected species of fish. Smaller fish of any species will be more sensitive to these drugs. Fish with fine scales or scaleless fish will be more sensitive than their larger-scaled relatives. These more sensitive species include eels, loaches, knife fish, and catfish such as *Pimelodella* species and shovel-nose catfish. These species should be treated conservatively by using alternative treatments covered in the text.

Biotesting refers to the trial treatment of a few fish to determine safety and effectiveness of a specific dose of a drug. It is always an advisable procedure before treating large quantities of fish, and is particularly essential if using a treatment which is relatively untested.

Dosages of Common Medicines Used in Water.[1]		
Drug	**Use**	**Dose (ppm)**
Formalin	External parasites	25 to 100
Copper sulfate	External parasites in marine systems	0.1 to 0.2
Metronidazole	Hexamitiasis	3 to 6
Praziquantel	Tapeworms, external trematodes	1 to 3
Antibiotics	Bacterial infections	0.1 to 12[1]

[1] See text for suggested treatment schemes.

A number of common fish medicaments are given in water (see acccompanying table). To provide an accurate dosage when medicine is added to water, one must carefully calculate both the volume of water to be treated and the amount of active drug required (which often differs from the amount of formulated compound to be used).

How to measure the volume of a rectangular aquarium: This seemingly simple procedure is the key to all water-based fish treatments.

A. English system. Measure the inside dimensions of the tank in inches. For height, measure from the middle of gravel, if present, to the top of the water. Multiply the length x width x height in inches. Divide product by 231 = U.S. gallons.

Example: Aquarium is 30 inches long, 14 inches from front to back, and measures 18 inches from middle of gravel to top of water. 30 x 14 x 18 = 7,560 cubic inches. 7,560/231 = 32.7 gallons of water.

B. Metric system. Measure the inside dimensions of the tank as above, but in centimeters. Multiply length x width x depth. Divide product by 1,000 = liters.

Example: Aquarium is 75 centimeters long, 35 centimeters from front to back, and depth of water from middle of gravel to top of water is 45 centimeters. 75 x 35 x 45 = 118,125 cubic centimeters. 118,125/1,000 = 118.1 liters of water.

How to measure the volume of a cylindrical tank or vat: Fall back upon your knowledge of the volume of a cylinder to determine the water it contains.

A. English system. Measure diameter of base and height of water column in inches. Divide diameter by 2 to obtain radius. Square this number, and multiply by 3.14 and by water column height. Divide by 231 to obtain U.S. gallons.

Example: What is the volume of a cylindrical tank with a 24-inch diameter base and a water height of 36 inches?

Solution: 24/2 = 12-inch radius. Applying the formula, 3.14 x (12 x 12) x 36 = 16,277.7 cubic inches and 16,277.7/231 = 70.5 U.S. gallons of water.

B. Metric system. Measure diameter of base and height of water column in centimeters. Divide diameter by 2 to obtain radius. Square this number, and multiply by 3.14 and by water column

height. Divide by 1,000 to obtain liters.

Example: What is the volume of a cylindrical tank with a 30-centimeter base and a water height of 35 centimeter?

Solution: 30/2 = 15 centimeter radius. 3.14 x (15 x 15) x 35 = 24,727.5 cubic centimeters. 24,727.5/1000 = 24.7 liters.

How to calculate how much drug to add to water to obtain a specific dosage: Dosages are most easily calculated in parts per million (ppm). A part per million equals 1 milligram of chemical in 1,000 milliliters of water. It also equals 3.8 milligrams in one U.S. gallon of water, so 0.0038 is the conversion factor to change from metric units to gallons, since 38 milligrams per gallon results in 1 ppm.

One cannot assume that a drug is 100 percent pure. In many cases, especially in working with bulk powders, the drug may be mixed with various "carrier" substances. This will be indicated on the drug label. One compensates for this lack of purity by adding an increased amount of chemical. To determine how much of an increase, a "purity factor" term is added into the formula for calculating dosage.

A. English system. Dose in grams = U.S. gallons x desired dosage in ppm x 0.0038 x "purity factor."

Example: You are asked to treat a goldfish pond with Masoten™ (an organophosphate used to treat monogenetic trematodes, anchor worms, and fish lice). The label states that the drug is 80 percent pure. The owner has calculated the volume of water in the pond to be 1,500 gallons. You want to obtain a dosage of 0.25 ppm.

Solution: You note that in the formula, dose is in grams, and recall that 1.0 gram = 1,000 milligrams, 0.1 gram = 100 milligrams, and 0.01 gram = 10 milligrams. Because the drug has inactive ingredients in it, you will need to use more of the chemical than if it were fully active. Convert 80 percent to 100/80 (the "purity factor") to figure out how much more. Now, use the formula. Compound needed for a 0.25 ppm dosage of the drug = 1,500 gallons x 0.25 ppm x 0.0038 x 100/80 = 1.78 grams.

B. Metric system. Follow the same basic procedure as above, but no conversion factor is needed. Dose in grams = liters of water x desired dosage in ppm x "purity factor."

How to calculate dosage when a medication is available in a specified formulation for some

other use: Occasionally, useful medications for fish are available in existing formulations for non-aquatic species. For example, many liquid formulations of organophosphates used to control grubs and lice on pigs and cattle are suitable for treatment of parasitic copepods such as anchor worms, fish lice, and monogenetic trematodes. While their use for food fish is prohibited, such drugs may be used for aquarium species. Of course, prior to using any such drug, preliminary testing should always be done to establish safety.

Example: You have a commercial preparation of a stabilized organophosphate solution containing 8 percent active drug, and you wish to treat goldfish in a 100-gallon vat for *Argulus* using 0.5 ppm of organophosphate.

Solution: Quantity of preparation to use in order to have 0.5 ppm of active drug = 100 gallons x 0.0038 x 0.5 ppm x 100/8 = 2.38 milliliters.

How to calculate dosage when using preweighed tablets or capsules: Many commercial medications are provided with full instructions for use. Other useful medications such as antibiotics, Flagyl™, praziquantel, and nematocides are supplied as preweighed tablets or capsules. When the following amounts of any active drug are added to 10 gallons of water, the following dosages are obtained:

50 milligrams = 1.3 ppm; 100 milligrams = 2.6 ppm; 150 milligrams = 3.9 ppm; 200 milligrams = 5.2 ppm; 250 milligrams = 6.5 ppm.

How to calculate the dosage of specific commonly used chemicals: Because they are in such common use, calculation of dosages for formaldehyde, copper sulfate, and sodium chloride are outlined below.

A. Formaldehyde: When added to 10 gallons (38 liters) of water, the following quantities of formalin (37 percent formaldehyde) will result in the following concentrations: 1 milliliter = 25 ppm; 2 milliliters = 50 ppm; 3 milliliters = 75 ppm; 4 milliliters = 100 ppm.

Always keep formalin in a dark bottle. Formalin with a white precipitate at the bottom of the bottle should not be used.

B. Copper sulfate: Copper is available as powdered copper sulfate with 5 waters of hydration ($CuSO_4 \cdot 5 H_2O$). The formula weight of the copper sulfate molecule is 249.5 and the atomic weight of copper is 63.5. Therefore, every gram of copper sulfate with 5 waters of hydration contains just

over 25 percent copper. The "purity factor" is 100/25, or 4.

Example: You have a 10,000-gallon central salt-water system in which you would like to maintain a copper level of 0.2 ppm. You have purchased powdered copper sulfate with 5 waters of hydration.

Quantity of copper sulfate needed to achieve a 0.2 ppm copper level = 10,000 gallons x 0.0038 x 0.2 ppm x 100/25 = 30.4 grams.

Note: Copper sulfate will chelate with hard water. Daily testing of copper-ion levels will determine the need for addition of more copper. Eventually, the dose will stablize, depending on the hardness of the water. As with any solid chemical, copper should be dissolved prior to addition to a water system. Invertebrates are highly sensitive to copper.

C. Sodium chloride (salt): Common noniodized kitchen salt is frequently used as an aquarium treatment. A level kitchen tablespoon measure holds about 15 grams of salt.

Salt is known to inhibit *Chilodonella* at concentrations between 0.1 to 0.2 percent (1,000 to 2,000 ppm). Adding 38 grams (about 2 tablespoons) to 10 gallons (38 liters) of water will establish a dose of 1,000 ppm, or 0.1 percent. Maintaining salt concentrations is best done by use of a refractometer.

Salt has been used to compete with the uptake of nitrites, and may provide replacement of sodium and chloride ions in stressed or injured fish. Baths using 2.5 percent salt can be established by adding 95 grams (6 to 7 tablespoons) of salt to a gallon (3.8 liters) of water. Fish should be immersed for fifteen to thirty minutes or until they appear stressed.

How to establish small dosages when your scale weighs only grams: If it is necessary to establish small dosages of a powdered drug without the benefit of an analytical balance, one can make up a greater quantity of solution than would otherwise be used, then subdivide this solution to obtain the necessary dosage. Check the solution's stability in liquid form or in a frozen state if unused portions are to be stored.

Example: You wish to add 20 milligrams of an active drug to a food preparation, but the smallest your scale will weigh is 1 gram. The drug is available in a formulation which, according to its label, has an activity of 10 percent.

Solution: Weigh out a gram of the material to

be used. Add this gram (1,000 milligrams) to 100 milliliters of water. Now, because 100 milliliters of water contain 1 gram, 1 milliliter of water contains 10 milligrams of chemical, which includes both active drugs and inactive drug carriers. If the activity is 10 percent, then this 1-milliliter solution contains 9 milligrams of inactive substances and only 1 milligram of active drugs. Thus 20 milliliters of the solution is needed to provide 20 milligrams of active drug. Similar procedures can be followed using the English system of measurement.

How to Incorporate Drugs in Fish Food

For treatment of some internal parasites and for the prevention of bacterial diseases after a stress situation such as shipping, some fish breeders find it easier and more economical to medicate food rather than water. Drugs can be incorporated into commercially available foods by binding the drug to the food with oils, albumin, or gelatin. Some suggested drugs, the rationale for their use, and dosages in foods are given in the accompanying table. Medicated feeds should not be given to apparently healthy fish. The following steps show how to prepare a fish diet which can be used for incorporation of medicaments.

A. *Combine these ingredients:*
   35 grams canned sardines, salmon, or tuna
   30 grams finely ground vegetables, fresh or canned (choice of peas, squash, spinach, or carrots finely ground; baby-food preparations work well)
   30 grams cooked oatmeal or other grain
   5 milliliters cod-liver oil, unflavored, food grade
   500 milligrams B-complex vitamins or 2 to 3 grams brewer's yeast
   250 milligrams vitamin C
   50 units vitamin E
   5 to 10 grams gelatin as a binder

B. *Add warm water and blend to make a slurry which is just pourable.*

C. *Add medicaments as appropriate.* Drugs should be predissolved in warm water before they are added to the food slurry.

D. *Dissolve the gelatin in one or two cups (about 100 milliliters) of boiling water.* Allow it to cool for a few minutes, then mix it into the food slurry.

E. *Pour medicated feed mixture into plastic bags and close.* Refrigerate until firm, then freeze.

F. *To feed fish, shave off a portion of the frozen block with a food grater, vegetable peeler, or knife.*

How to Determine Dosages When Treating Fish by Injection

When fish are large and have obvious signs of a systemic bacterial disease such as ulcers or hemorrhages, injection of antibiotics by the intraperitoneal route is indicated. Fish can be restrained in a net and injected through the netting material.

The following dosages (in milliliters) have been calculated to deliver an amount of drug proportional to the normal dose used for small animals in veterinary medicine. Repeated injections may be required, depending on the clinical response of the fish.

Chloramphenicol sodium succinate: Reconstitute each gram of antibiotic with 10 milliliters of sterile water. The resulting stock solution, 100 milligrams per milliliter, will be stable for thirty days at room temperature. For use in smaller fish, add 1 milliliter of the solution to 200 milliliters of sterile water or sterile saline solution. This second dilution will result in a solution of 0.5 milligrams per milliliter. Inject 0.5 milliliters (1 cubic cen-

Useful Medicaments Added To Food			
Drug[1]	Use Indication	Dose in food (percent)	Feeding time (days)
Metronidazole	*Hexamita Spironucleus*	0.25	3 – 7
Praziquantel	Tapeworms	0.25	3
Panacur[TM]	Nematodes	0.25	3 – 7
Antibiotics[2]	Bacterial infections Preshipment conditioning	0.25	7 – 10

[1] Dosages with the listed drugs have been shown to be effective under controlled conditions.

[2] Refer to section on antibiotics for choice of antibiotics.

timeter [cc] is identical to 1 milliliter) for every 10 grams of fish. For larger fish, dilute 1 milliliter of stock in 100 milliliters of water and use 0.05 milliliters per 10 grams of fish. Thus, for a 500-gram fish use 2.5 milliliters of diluted antibiotic.

Gentamycin sulfate: Dilute 50 milligrams (1 milliliter) of liquid drug in 1,000 milliliters of sterile distilled water or sterile saline solution to make a stock solution of 50 milligrams per milliliter.

For smaller specimens, inject 0.5 milliliters per 10 grams of fish. For larger fish, make a more concentrated stock solution (50 milligrams to 100 milliliters of a diluting agent) and inject 0.05 milliliters per 10 grams of fish body weight. Thus, a 500-gram fish would be injected with 2.5 milliliters of the diluted antibiotic.

Contributors

RICHARD E. WOLKE received his Doctor of Veterinary Medicine from Cornell University and his Ph.D. in pathology from the University of Connecticut. He has been employed as a diagnostic and research pathologist at the Comparative Aquatic Pathology Laboratory, University of Rhode Island, for twenty years. Dr. Wolke's experience with fish has included freshwater and marine species, and both cultured and wild populations. Most recently, his work has centered upon environmental biomarkers and diseases in winter flounder. Dr. Wolke has written on fungal, nutritional, bacterial, and neoplastic diseases found in public aquaria, commercial hatcheries, and hobbyists' tanks.

JOHN B. GRATZEK received a bachelor of science degree in biology and chemistry at St. Mary's College in Minnesota, where he studied the parasites of muskrats. Pursuing his interests in animal disease, he was awarded the Doctor of Veterinary Medicine degree from the University of Minnesota in 1956 and a Ph.D. in the study of animal virology from the University of Wisconsin in 1961. Dr. Gratzek presently heads the Department of Medical Microbiology in the College of Veterinary Medicine at the University of Georgia. He is past president of the American College of Veterinary Microbiologists and the International Association for Aquatic Animal Medicine, and serves on the aquaculture committee of the American Association of Animal Health.

EMMETT B. SHOTTS, JR., received a bachelor of science degree from the University of Alabama and master of science and Ph.D. degrees from the University of Georgia. For five years , Dr. Shotts was a member of the Epidemic Intelligence Service, a highly specialized group of "disease troubleshooters" at the Centers for Disease Control in Atlanta, Georgia. Dr. Shotts currently is a professor in the Department of Medical Microbiology at the University of Georgia College of Veterinary Medicine. He has written over 200 scientific articles and numerous book chapters on bacterial diseases of both aquarium and food fishes, and presently is researching the pathogenic mechanisms of fish disease bacteria at a molecular level.

DONALD L. DAWE received a bachelor of science degree in animal science from the University of Wisconsin, a Doctor of Veterinary Medicine from Iowa State University of Science and Technology, and a master of science and Ph.D. degrees from the University of Illinois. A professor at the University of Georgia College of Veterinary Medicine, Dr. Dawe's research interests are in immunity and disease resistance in animals as varied as chickens, swine, and channel catfish, work which has included studies of fish resistance to and immunization against *Ichthyophthirius* (ich). Dr. Dawe is the author or coauthor of sixty-six research publications, nineteen of which relate to fish immunology.

GEORGE C. BLASIOLA received a bachelor of science degree in biology from the University of Miami, Coral Gables, and a master's degree in marine biology from San Francisco State University. From 1973 to 1980, he managed the Water Analysis and Pathology Laboratory at the California Academy of Sciences' Steinhart Aquarium. From then to 1987, he was a research biologist and the AquaVet division manager for Novalek Inc., and from 1987 to 1991 he was the director of research and development for The Wardley Corporation. Mr. Blasiola is a well-known specialist in the diseases of ornamental marine fishes. His articles on fish biology, health, and disease control have appeared in journals and magazines in the United States and internationally.

Index of Scientific Names

Subject Index